KU-205-951

Greek Literature and the Roman Empire

Greek Literature and the Roman Empire

The Politics of Imitation

TIM WHITMARSH

This book has been printed digitally and produced in a standard specification in order to ensure its continuing availability

OXFORD
UNIVERSITY PRESS

Great Clarendon Street, Oxford OX2 6DP

Oxford University Press is a department of the University of Oxford.
It furthers the University's objective of excellence in research, scholarship, and education by publishing worldwide in

Oxford New York

Auckland Bangkok Buenos Aires Cape Town Chennai
Dar es Salaam Delhi Hong Kong Istanbul Karachi Kolkata
Kuala Lumpur Madrid Melbourne Mexico City Mumbai Nairobi
São Paulo Shanghai Taipei Tokyo Toronto

Oxford is a registered trade mark of Oxford University Press in the UK and in certain other countries

Published in the United States by Oxford University Press Inc., New York

© Tim Whitmarsh 2001

The moral rights of the author have been asserted

Database right Oxford University Press (maker)

Reprinted 2004

All rights reserved. No part of this publication may be reproduced, stored in a retrieval system, or transmitted, in any form or by any means, without the prior permission in writing of Oxford University Press, or as expressly permitted by law, or under terms agreed with the appropriate reprographics rights organization. Enquiries concerning reproduction outside the scope of the above should be sent to the Rights Department, Oxford University Press, at the address above

You must not circulate this book in any other binding or cover And you must impose this same condition on any acquirer

ISBN 0-19-924035-3

Cover illustration: A reproduction of a photograph (by Nigel Cassidy), of a cast of the Farnese Hercules, Roman copy of Greek original. The permission of the Museum of Classical Archaeology, Cambridge is gratefully acknowledged.

Short Loan Collection

UNIVERSITY OF GLASGOW LIBRARY

WITHDRAWN

For Julie
to India and beyond...

Preface

WHEN, in the early 1990s, I first turned my attention to the literature of Roman Greece, most publications on the subject seemed to begin with an apology for a deviation from the traditional path of Classical scholarship (which also functioned as an advertisement for the author's ground-breaking foray). Now it is almost as though one needs to apologize for adding to the quantity of works on the subject, many of which are extremely erudite and thought-provoking. There remains, however, a need for a book that supplements the now familiar, historiographical emphasis upon Greek identity (in relation to the Greek past and in relation to Rome), with an awareness of the subtlety and literary panache of much Roman Greek writing. It is the central contention of this book that these two approaches are mutually dependent: it is impossible to consider Greek identity without understanding the ingenuity of the authors, and it is undesirable to consider literary aesthetics in isolation from the circuits of 'power' (however we choose to define that shibboleth of contemporary academia).

All dates are CE unless otherwise stated (and I have preferred BCE/CE to BC/AD). English titles for Greek and Latin works are given in the main text, but the conventional Latin abbreviations (as employed in Liddell and Scott's *Greek–English Lexicon*) are used for footnotes and references. I have retained the familiar Latin spellings of Greek names, rather than attempting to transliterate Greek. Words like 'Akhilleus' and 'Loukianos' are difficult on the eye, and (worse) the practice represents a spurious attempt at authenticity. In a book that often deals with ideological debates concerning links between past and present, any attempted solution to the ongoing problem of representing ancient Greek nomenclature in English risks the charge of disingenuity; but (a sophistic concession) I would rather be open in my disingenuity.

The debts I have incurred during the gestation of this book are many. Let me here acknowledge only those of an intellectual cast. I have benefited immensely from conversations with Rebecca

Langlands, Denise McCoskey, Jon Hesk, Geoff Horrocks, Jason König, and Richard Miles—often, like a parasite, drawing sustenance unbeknown to my hosts. Froma Zeitlin has been ever generous with her penetrating ideas and thoughtful responses. John Kerrigan, Lucy Grig, Jeff Rusten, and Malcolm Schofield gave me invaluable help with specific issues. I owe most to those who read part or all of this work at various stages: to Teresa Morgan, Julie Lewis, Pat Easterling, Ewen Bowie, Christopher Kelly, Jaś Elsner, the anonymous readers for the Press; and, in particular, to Simon Goldhill, Richard Hunter, and John Henderson, who read the entire manuscript. The book, such as it is (notwithstanding the traditional pieties about errors remaining), would have been inconceivable without this help.

Hilary O'Shea and the staff at Oxford University Press (not to mention their excellent copy-editors) have been extremely supportive throughout the gestation of this work. I must also thank the Faculty of Classics at Cambridge, as much the epicentre of Classical learning as I am its least deserving beneficiary; and, most of all, St John's College, a most supportive and stimulating environment in which to think and write. I am immensely grateful to the Master and Fellows for the faith they have shown in me.

T.J.G.W.

St John's College Cambridge
September 2000

Acknowledgements

MUCH of Chapter 3 is reworked from Whitmarsh (2001). Certain sections of Chapter 4 also previously appeared in Whitmarsh (1998*a*). My sincere thanks to Cambridge University Press for their kind permission to reuse this material.

Chapter 3 also contains passages first published in *JHS* 119 (1999) (Whitmarsh 1999a). I am grateful to the Hellenic Society for their co-operation in republication.

Contents

Abbreviations xiii

Introduction 1

Greek Literature and the Roman Empire 1
Literature, Power, and Culture 17
A Geography of the Imagination 20
Imitation and Identity 26
The Politics of Imitation 29

PART ONE: THE POLITICS OF IMITATION

1. Repetition: The Crisis of Posterity 41

A Secondary Society 41
Repetition and *Mimēsis* 46
Rescuing *Mimēsis* 47
Sublime *Mimēsis* 57
Art and Artifice 71
Conclusion: From 'Past and Present' to 'Prior and Posterior' 88

2. Education: Strategies of Self-Making 90

Strategies of Self-Making 91
Paideia and Social Status 96
Paideia and Gender 109
Paideia and Hellenism 116
Pedagogy, Identity, Power 129

PART TWO: GREECE AND ROME

3. Rome Uncivilized: Exile and the Kingdom 133

Exile and the Kingdom 134
Musonius Rufus, the 'Roman' 'Socrates' 141
Dio Chrysostom: Exile and Sophistry 156

Favorinus: Exile and Literary Alienation 167
Conclusion 178

4. Civilizing Rome: Greek Pedagogy and the Roman Emperor 181
Staging Philosophy: The Dionic Man 183
The *Kingship orations*: Performance and/of Power 186
Staging the Self: Sophistry in Motion 190
Greek Pedagogy and Roman Rule 200
Marcus Aurelius: Internalized Pedagogy 216
Dio and Philostratus 225
Conclusion: On Kingship 244

5. Satirizing Rome: Lucian 247
Satire and Satirical Identity 248
Rome, City of Spectacles 254
The Satirical Show 257
Nigrinus: Yearning for Philosophy 265
The Wrongs of Passage: *On salaried posts* 279
Conclusion 293

Conclusion 295

Appendices:
1. Translation of Favorinus, On Exile *(*P.Vat. *11)* 302
2. *The Performative Context of Dio's* Kingship orations 325
References 328
Index Locorum 365
Index of Greek Words 370
General Index 371

Abbreviations

In footnotes and references, Greek and Latin authors and works are cited conventionally.

CAH[3]	I. E. S. Edwards *et al.*, *The Cambridge ancient history*, 3rd edn. (Cambridge, 1970–)
CHCL	P. E. Easterling *et al.*, *The Cambridge history of classical literature*, vol. 1: *Greek literature* (Cambridge, 1985)
CIL	T. Mommsen *et al.*, eds., *Corpus inscriptionum Latinarum* (Berlin, 1863–)
DK	H. Diels and W. Kranz, *Die Fragmente der Vorsokratiker*, 6th edn. (Berlin, 1951–2)
EG	G. Kaibel, ed., *Epigrammata Graeca ex lapidibus conlecta* (Berlin, 1878)
FGE	D. L. Page, ed., *Further Greek epigrams: epigrams before A.D. 50 from the Greek anthology and other sources, not included in Hellenistic epigrams or The garland of Philip*, revised and prepared for publication by R. D. Dawe and J. Diggle (Cambridge, 1981)
FGH	F. Jacoby *et al.*, eds., *Die Fragmente der griechischen Historiker* (Berlin, 1923–)
FHE	*Fondation Hardt pour l'étude de l'antiquité classique: entretiens* (Geneva)
FPL	J. Blänsdorf, ed., *Fragmenta poetarum Latinorum epicorum et lyricorum praeter Ennium et Lucilium* (Leipzig, 1995)
IG[2]	F. H. de Gaertingen *et al.*, eds., *Inscriptiones Graecae*, 2nd edn. (Berlin, 1924–)
KA	R. Kassel and C. Austin, eds., *Poetae comici Graeci* (Berlin, 1983–)
KRS	G. S. Kirk, J. Raven, and M. Schofield, *The presocratic philosophers: a critical history with a selection of texts*, 2nd edn. (Cambridge, 1983)

LS	A. A. Long and D. N. Sedley, *The Hellenistic philosophers* (Cambridge, 1987)
LSJ	H. G. Liddell, R. Scott, *et al.*, *A Greek–English lexicon*, 9th edn. (Oxford, 1996)
N^2	A. Nauck, ed., *Tragicorum graecorum fragmenta*, 2nd edn. (Leipzig, 1889)
OGIS	W. Dittenberger, ed., *Orientis Graeci inscriptiones selectae: supplementum sylloges inscriptionum Graecarum* (Leipzig, 1903–5)
OLD	P. G. W. Glare, ed., *Oxford Latin dictionary* (Oxford, 1982)
P.Vat.	*Vatican papyrus*
PLG	T. Bergk, ed., *Poetae lyrici Graeci*, 4th edn. (Leipzig, 1878–82)
RAC	T. Klauser *et al.*, eds., *Reallexicon für Antike und Christentum* (Stuttgart, 1950–)
RE	G. Wissowa *et al.*, *Paulys Realencyclopädie der classischen Altertumswissenschaft* (Munich, 1903–78)
RG	L. Spengel, ed., *Rhetores Graeci* (Leipzig, 1853–6)
SH	H. Lloyd-Jones and P. Parsons, eds., *Supplementum Hellenisticum* (Berlin, 1983)
SIG	W. Dittenberger, ed., *Sylloge inscriptionum graecarum* (Leipzig, 1883)
SVF	H. von Arnim, ed., *Stoicorum veterum fragmenta* (Leipzig, 1923–4)
TGF	B. Snell *et al.*, eds., *Tragicorum graecorum fragmenta* (Göttingen, 1971–)

Introduction

GREEK LITERATURE AND THE ROMAN EMPIRE

This is a book about the Greek literary culture of the period from the mid-first to the early third century of the common era (CE), the revival of Classicizing ideals that modern scholars often call the 'Second Sophistic'.[1] It seeks to analyse the various associations between 'Greek literature' and 'the Roman empire'. Although my title echoes that of Bowersock's influential *Greek sophists in the Roman empire*,[2] I have forgone any preposition marking the relationship between the two. Greek literature was not, in my view, 'in' or 'under' (i.e. contained by, subsumed by) Rome; nor, for that matter, was it 'above' or 'beyond'. Rather, it is the dynamic and mutually productive (and at times destructive) relationship between the two phenomena that forms my central area of interest. 'And', which equivocates between conjunction ('man and wife') and disjunction ('chalk and cheese') seems the most appropriate marker of that complex reciprocity.

The book is an exploration into the cultural and political values of literature. It is not centrally concerned with the material realities of literature, the circulation, ownership, performance, and reading of texts (though these are in fact important and recurrent issues over the course of the argument). Nor is it fundamentally about the politics of literary language, the intense debates over 'Atticist' morphology and style in the period (though again, that is a crucial matter that will resurface frequently). Nor is it a complete survey of all the many Greek texts that bear upon Rome. Instead, it focuses upon a central question: how literary experience is constructed and thematized in the texts of this period, and how 'the

[1] On the history of this term, see Ch. 1, 'A Secondary Society'. On the phenomenon, see esp. Kaibel (1885); E. Rohde (1886; 1914); Schmid (1887–96); Palm (1959); Bowersock (1969); Bowie (1974; 1982); G. Anderson (1990; 1993); Woolf (1994); Brunt (1994), Swain (1996); Schmitz (1997); Korenjak (2000).

[2] Bowersock (1969).

literary' is employed to construct Greek identity in relationship to the Greek past and the Roman present. The central argument of this book rests on the proposition (hardly contentious now) that literary writing was in this period inherently bound up with the process of negotiation of an identity discrete from Rome. Literary writing was the central (albeit not the only)[3] means of affirming Greekness. Where this book seeks to innovate is in advancing the proposition that authors do not write because they are Greek; they *are Greek because they write*. Literature is an ever incomplete, ever unstable *process* of self-making. Practically all the Greek texts that survive from this period were written by Roman citizens,[4] men whose identity was (I argue) radically fissured. They could not afford to take the word 'and' for granted. Thus it makes no sense to write of 'Rome and the Romans as the Greeks saw them' (to cite the title of a book from the early 1970s):[5] not only was the relationship between 'Greece' and 'Rome' (these terms conceived of as 'imaginary' rather than geopolitical entities) fluid and oscillatory, but also the very concepts of 'Greek' and 'Roman' were under constant definition, scrutiny, review, and redefinition. So far from being self-evident 'givens' that can be assumed to lie anterior to the texts, these notions are effects—and contested effects at that—of literary writing. If the question is 'why the resurgence of interest in Greek literature in this period?', then 'Greek identity' is not the answer but itself part of the problem.

Bowersock's *Greek sophists in the Roman empire* begins with the suggestion that literature has two options, 'acquiescence or dissent', before proceeding to suggest that the Greek sophists took the former path in their relations to Rome.[6] In Bowersock's view, the history of Greek literature in the first three centuries CE shows a progressive subsumption of Greek values into Roman.[7] There are certainly numerous ways in which this proposition might be refined, nuanced, or even opposed in the reading of literary texts: subsequent scholarship has found much more oppositionalism in the texts of Roman Greece.[8] The polarity of acquiescence and

[3] See below, n. 158.

[4] Below, p. 18.

[5] Forte (1972).

[6] Bowersock (1969), 1. Cf. his other work on 'resistance' to Roman rule: (1965), 101–11; (1986).

[7] Bowersock (1994), 29, cf. C. P. Jones (1986), 89.

[8] Bowie has argued that Roman Greek literature represented an attempt to

dissent, however, is reductive and unhelpful. Simon Swain's *Hellenism and empire* has recently challenged this received wisdom with the valuable observation that loyalties can be tangled and at times contradictory: 'only the crude discourse of nationalism' in modern scholarship leads to the assumption that 'the Greek elite must have been pro-Roman in all respects, since they could not otherwise have supported Rome at all'.[9] For Swain, however, these contradictions can be resolved by stratifying levels of intensity: allegiances to Rome may be superficial, whilst what really count are 'the real attitudes of people under foreign rule'.[10] Swain argues that the authors he studies have a primarily Greek 'cultural-cognitive' identity, and objectify Rome as an alien (and at times oppressive) presence. Thus, while he (rightly) refuses to mark any individual in absolutist terms as 'pro-Roman' or 'anti-Roman', Swain can happily separate public (Roman) careers from private (Greek) feelings, and identify the degree of warmth that individuals experienced towards their political masters.

The problem with this strategy is that literary texts are not themselves necessarily univocal. Literature can be sophisticated, ludic, self-ironizing, and/or irresponsible: it can provoke and tease its readership with ambivalences, contradictions, and gaps. To identify an author's views on Rome from a text risks an arbitrary foreclosure of meaning. In Kennedy's words, '[t]he degree to which a voice is heard as conflicting or supportive is a function of the audience's—or critic's—ideology, a function, therefore, of *reception*'.[11] The very fact that critics disagree about the degree to which 'Greekness' can be isolated as an identity discrete from (and occasionally opposed to) 'Romanness' shows the extent of the problem: we cannot 'know' how a 'Greek' 'felt' about 'Rome' without engaging in an interpretative exercise that occludes the violence of its own imposition. How can we identify the author's 'true' feelings? What does it mean to emphasize one area of communication as more intense, meaningful, or sincere than another? Indeed, it is precisely when an author insists that he or she is being

escape the political subordination of the present by recalling the past glories of a free Greece (1974; cf. 1982); Swain (1996) maps out statements of both acquiescence and dissent.

[9] Swain (1996), 70.

[10] Swain (1996), 412; cf. 71

[11] D. F. Kennedy (1992), 41.

sincere (as in the case, for example, of encomia), that the knowing reader tends to be the most suspicious . . .

But this is to move too quickly: the terms of analysis require substantial refinement. The category of the 'literary' (conceived of as a site of emotional and aesthetic intensity spontaneously and sincerely expressed from the heart of a great writer) began to emerge only in the late eighteenth century.[12] This is not the place for a detailed review of all the many recent 'genealogies' of literature that seek to question this category by exposing its grounding in Romanticism, the consolidation of national identity, the construction of barriers of class and gender, the teaching of literacy and social order amongst the working classes, the negotiation of an emergent middle class, and the institutional politics of academies.[13] Suffice it to say that there is no ancient Greek term that maps precisely onto 'literature', and certainly no equivalence between the cultural and political conditions of the post-industrial West and Roman Greece. 'Literature' alludes to an experience (and tightly ravelled skein of issues) alien to the texts studied in this book. This does not invalidate it as a term (what is Classical scholarship but the knowing traffic of ideas between ancient and modern categories of analysis?), but it does mean that we shall have to be very clear about what precisely we are investigating.

What in particular I take from recent analyses of the concept of literature is its role in the contests for the definition of social superiority. 'Literature' never exists in a denationalized form: it is always (whether implicitly or explicitly) qualified as 'French', 'Yoruba', 'American', and so forth. It is, moreover, inevitably elitist: 'literature' is inherently bound up with issues of cultural 'value' and distinction. Whatever criteria (formalist, aesthetic,

[12] Although etymologically, of course, the term comes from the Latin *litteratura*: see Quint. *Inst. or.* 2.1.4; 2.14.3, where it refers to linguistic training.

[13] For a concise and lucid account of the issues, at least as they relate to English literature, see Eagleton (1983), 17–53. For other excellent accounts, see Doyle (1989), a brief but sophisticated account of the various academic and national debates and the ideologies that underlay them; Court (1992) on the institutional politics of English literature within the academy; Crawford (1992), focusing particularly upon the Scottish context (see also the essays in Crawford ed. 1988, esp. Duncan 1988). See also J. Dubois (1978) on French literature as a social institution (largely synchronic rather than diachronic, but see pp. 37–8); Graff (1987) on the institutional politics of literature in America (see esp. pp. 209–25 on the relative failure of 'American literature'); Lambropoulos (1988), 23–43 for a 'genealogy' of modern Greek literature.

sociocultural) we use to demarcate the limits of the literary, it is always a matter of the definition of a collective group. In Roman Greece, elite Greeks defined their superiority in terms of education; or, rather, in terms of *paideia*, the Greek word that also connotes civilization and culture.[14] They were the *pepaideumenoi*, the 'educated', as opposed to both the *idiōtai* (i.e. the sub-elite) within Greek culture and the *barbaroi* ('barbarians') without.[15]

The precise nature of the ideal 'education' was a subject of ongoing debate. *Paideia* was not a single, doctrinally coherent system, but the locus for a series of competitions and debates concerning the proper way in which life should be lived. One of the primary differences between modern 'literature' and the texts studied in this book lies in the generic multiplicity of the latter: they include philosophy, rhetoric, history, satire, and biography. All of these genres were subject to internal dissensions and rivalries: rhetoricians argued about style, historians and biographers argued about subject-matter, and philosophers were the most argumentative of the lot. In the first three centuries of the Roman principate there were numerous rival philosophies: there were Pythagoreans, Academics, Peripatetics, Epicureans, Stoics, Cynics, and Sceptics (even leaving out religious cults: Judaism, Christianity, Mithraism, and the cults of Isis and the Magna Mater).[16] The second-century satirist Lucian (echoing Socrates' frustration with contemporary philosophers in Plato's *Apology*) writes of his visit to a number of different philosophers that they all sought to persuade him of their own opinions, 'though none of their pronouncements chimed with those of anyone else, rather they were all conflicting and contradictory' (μηδὲν ἅτερος θατέρωι λέγοντες ἀκόλουθον ἀλλὰ μαχόμενα πάντα καὶ ὑπεναντία, Luc. *Icar.* 5).[17] In addition, philosophers were competing for paideutic primacy with rhetoricians, sophists, and the many occupants of grey areas between the various manifestations of philosophy and

[14] See esp. Reardon (1971), 3–11; Bowie (1974); G. Anderson (1993), 8–11; Gleason (1995), xxi-xxiv; Swain (1996), 18–64; Schmitz (1997), *passim*, esp. 39–66; Whitmarsh (1998*a*). On education as social practice, see Kaster (1988); T. Morgan (1998).

[15] See Ch. 2, '*Paideia* and Social Status' on the strategies of social exclusion operated by *paideia*.

[16] On the philosophical schools, see André (1987); Whittaker (1987).

[17] For this theme, see also *Men.* 4; *Symp.*, *passim*. For the Platonic model, see *Apol.* 20b–d. On Lucian's representation of philosophers, see Alexiou (1990) and below, Ch. 5.

sophistry (sometimes referred to as *Halbphilosophen*).[18] Though this book focuses on intellectual practice, it should moreover be borne in mind that music and athletics were also constitutive of *paideia*.[19] In the highly competitive world of elite ambition (or *philotimia*),[20] differences between factions in paideutic methods and ideals mapped out the struggles within the elite for prestige and status.[21]

Across the multiplicity of forms and modes of Roman Greek education, one feature remained common: the attempt to root all forms of status and identity in the prestigious past.[22] Although all cultures at all times evoke a sense of the past, the extraordinary nature of this specific phenomenon should not be underestimated. In the period under study, to be 'educated' generally meant to be able to write and declaim fluently in a form of Greek that had passed from popular currency some five centuries earlier. 'Attic' Greek, the dialect written by the canonical authors (primarily Thucydides, Plato, Xenophon, Demosthenes) in the fifth and fourth centuries BCE, may have been barely intelligible (and was certainly bizarre) to most contemporary demotic speakers.[23] The satirist Lucian mocks the linguistic excesses of a certain Lexiphanes ('word-flaunter'):

Can't you hear how he talks? Abandoning us, who converse with him now, he talks to us from a thousand years ago, twisting his tongue, combining these alien elements (*allokota*), and taking himself very seriously in the matter, as if it were a great thing for him to speak a foreign language (*xenizoi*) and debase the established currency of speech.

[18] Von Arnim (1898), 4–114; Stanton (1973); Hahn (1989), 46–53; G. Anderson (1993), 133–43; Schmitz (1997), 86. On the exterior semiotic distinctions between philosophers and rhetoricians, see Hahn (1989), 33–6; Schmitz (1997), 86. On the topos of 'conversion' from one discipline to the other, see G. Anderson (1993), 134, and esp. the interesting discussion of Sidebottom (1990), 1–31.

[19] See esp. van Nijf (1999) and König (2000) on athletics and Graeco-Roman identity.

[20] Brown (1978), 27–53. On the endemic competitiveness of the Greek world in this period, see also Gleason (1995), xxiii, 9; and esp. Schmitz (1997), 97–135.

[21] Although Epictetus was from a less privileged, indeed servile background, this fact was itself no doubt primarily a sign of 'authenticity' within elite culture. certainly, Epictetus' students (such as Arrian) seem to have been dignitaries. Against the overstated case for lower-class rhetoricians, see Bowie (1982), 54–5.

[22] On uses of the past, see esp. Bowie (1974); Swain (1996), 65–100.

[23] On the technical aspects of Atticism (and its difference from Greek koine), see Swain (1996), 27–33, Schmitz (1997), 67–83, and esp. Horrocks (1997), 78–86.

οὐκ ἀκούεις οἷα φθέγγεται; καὶ ἡμᾶς τοὺς νῦν προσομιλοῦντας καταλιπὼν πρὸ χιλίων ἐτῶν ἡμῖν διαλέγεται διαστρέφων τὴν γλῶτταν καὶ ταυτὶ τὰ ἀλλόκοτα συντιθεὶς καὶ σπουδὴν ποιούμενος ἐπ' αὐτοῖς, ὡς δή τι μέγα ὄν, εἴ τι ξενίζοι καὶ τὸ καθεστηκὸς νόμισμα τῆς φωνῆς παρακόπτοι. (*Lex.* 20)

The speaker under attack here is representing as 'speaking a foreign language' (*xenizein*) in relation to the norms of speech, as though the Attic dialect were a different language altogether. The great irony here is that the dialect used by Lucian here is itself conspicuously Attic.[24] Although what he teases is Lexiphanes' *excess*, his own writing is similarly archaic, 'foreign', and complicit in the very process that he mocks (a characteristically Lucianic self-ironization).[25] The difference between Lucian's Atticism and that of Lexiphanes is one of degree, but such relative judgements only serve to expose the arbitrariness of any fixed point of division between the acceptable and the ludicrous.

The primary focus of this book is upon the role of *paideia* in defining the 'cultural' category, 'Greekness' (or, to use a more properly Greek term, 'Hellenism'). Since the fifth century BCE, education had played a centrally constitutive role in defining what it is to be Greek. Thucydides presents Pericles as publicly praising Athens as an 'education (*paideusis*) for Greece' (*τῆς Ἑλλάδος παίδευσιν*, Thuc. 2.41.1).[26] In the context of this stage of Greek history, in which various Greek city-states were vying for supremacy, Pericles' words here represent an attempt to render the democratic civic ideology of Athens paradigmatic of Greek identity as a whole. Pericles aims to achieve this, significantly, through the language of education (*paideusis*, cognate with *paideia*). Athenianism is (to be conceived of as) exactly commensurate with Hellenism.[27] Athens's self-representation as a cultural

[24] In this passage, he uses the double tau (*γλῶτταν*: on this distinctively Attic formation see *Iud. uoc.* 7, with Swain 1996: 48–9), the 'deictic' iota (*ταυτὶ*), and the optative (*ξενίζοι, παρακόπτοι*).

[25] Below, pp. 263–4; 278; 292.

[26] Thucydides does not, however, silence the alternative, and less flattering, descriptions of Athenian hegemony as a 'tyranny' or an 'enslavement': see e.g. Thuc. 2.8.4; 2.63.2 (where Pericles himself describes the empire as a 'tyranny'); see further de Ste Croix (1954–5). The role of Athens as educator of Greece is clearly expressed in other funeral speeches: see Lys. 2.69; Dem. 60.16; Hyp. 6.8; Ober (1989), 157. Athens was also the context in which literate, musical, and athletic education first took on the form that would later become canonical: see Marrou (1956), 36–78; T. Morgan (1999).

[27] On the uneasy relationship between Panhellenism and Athenian ideology, see E. Hall (1989), 16–17.

super-state paved the way for a subsequent more all-encompassing presentation of Hellenism as *paideia*. In a famous passage in his panegyric to Athens, the fourth-century orator Isocrates writes (echoing Pericles' words) that

Athens has so surpassed other men in thought and speech that its pupils have become teachers of others, and it has made it seem that the name of Greeks belongs more to cast of mind than to descent, and that it is those who share our education (*paideuseōs*) who are called Greeks rather than those who share our common nature.

τοσοῦτον δ' ἀπολέλοιπεν ἡ πόλις ἡμῶν περὶ τὸ φρονεῖν καὶ λέγειν τοὺς ἄλλους ἀνθρώπους, ὥσθ' οἱ ταύτης μαθηταὶ τῶν ἄλλων διδάσκαλοι γεγόνασιν, καὶ τὸ τῶν Ἑλλήνων ὄνομα πεποίηκεν μηκέτι τοῦ γένους, ἀλλὰ τῆς διανοίας δοκεῖν εἶναι, καὶ μᾶλλον Ἕλληνας καλεῖσθαι τοὺς τῆς παιδεύσεως τῆς ἡμετέρας ἢ τοὺς τῆς κοινῆς φύσεως μετέχοντας. (*Panegyr*. 50)[28]

Education here becomes a rallying-cry for a proposed Panhellenic conquest and 'civilization' of the East. Later, Hellenistic Alexandrians, like their Athenian precursors, presented themselves as educators, but now as 'the educators of all the world, of both Greeks and barbarians' (*οἱ παιδευσάντες πάντας τοὺς Ἕλληνας καὶ τοὺς βαρβάρους*, *FGH* 246 F 1 Andron = Athen. *Deipn*. 184b).[29] The knowing literary allusion to both Pericles' famous words and Isocrates' transformation of them is both medium and message: Alexandria is now the true centre of Greek learning. The famous library and Museum ('temple of the Muses') in Alexandria, containing 'all the books in the world' (*ἅπαντα τὰ κατὰ τὴν οἰκουμένην βιβλία*, Aristeas, *Ep*. 9 = Euseb. *Praep. eu*. 8.2.2),[30] represented an attempt to construct prestigious cultural links back to the old Greek world;[31] and, at the same time, the importance of royal patronage to these institutions pointed to the sociological trans-

[28] On this passage, see Trédé (1991); Usher (1993); Livingstone (1998), 274–5. Isocrates also alludes to Pericles' words at *Antid*. 293–5.

[29] Cf. 270 F 9 Menecles; and see further Pfeiffer (1968), 252–3; Fraser (1972), 2.745–6.

[30] On the identification of the founder with Ptolemy II (Philadelphus), see Pfeiffer (1968), 100. The title of Callimachus' index of the works in the Library was *Tables of all those who were eminent in every kind of education (paideia) and of their writings, in 120 books* (*πίνακες τῶν ἐν πάσῃ παιδείαι διαλαμψάντων καὶ ὧν συνέγραψαν, ἐν βιβλίοις κ' καὶ ρ'*): see *Suda* s.v. *Καλλίμαχος* (= Call. test. 1 Pfeiffer). On this work, see esp. Blum (1991), 182–8. On the rhetoric of globalization in Hellenistic Alexandria, see Too (1998), 124–5.

[31] On the library and Museum, see Pfeiffer (1968), 98–104; Fraser (1972), 1.312–35; Too (1998), 117–26.

formation of the role of learning in Ptolemaic Egypt.[32] It was in Hellenistic Egypt that *paideia* first began to assume the task of creating cultural continuity (especially in situations where that continuity could not be taken for granted) that we see so visibly marked in Roman Greece.[33]

The conquest of the Greek world by Rome (beginning in the second century BCE), however, added a new layer of complexity to the representation of education as constitutive of Greekness, for Greek *paideia* also played a fundamental role in Rome's own narrative of self-definition. The conventionalized account ran that early Rome was idyllic but barely civilized: Hellenization brought more sophistication, but also risks of luxury and decadence.[34] A poetic fragment of Porcius Licinus (late second century BCE) states that 'in the second Punic war, the Muse with winged step entered among the savage (*feram*) people of Rome in a warlike state (*bellicosam*)' (*Poenico bello secundo Musa pinnato gradu | intulit se bellicosam in Romuli gentem feram*, fr. 1 *FPL*): Rome is 'savage' (*feram*), but does the arrival of the Muse bring peace and civilization or discord? This ambivalence is signalled by a syntactical ambiguity, whereby it is unclear whether it is the Muse or the Roman people that is *bellicosam* ('in a warlike state').[35] This clever, punchy couplet (itself indebted, of course, to Hellenistic Greek models for its ingenuity) neatly instantiates the double bind of Romano-Greek cultural relations.

The narrative of Hellenization as civilization/luxurious decline was reinvoked with particular intensity during Augustus' foundation of the principate subsequent to his victory at the battle of Actium (31 BCE).[36] Alongside their leader's championing of supposedly indigenous religion (the Arval Brethren, the Sodales

[32] On the influence of the Ptolemies on Alexandrian intellectual development, see esp. Pfeiffer (1968), 96–102; Fraser (1972), 1.305–12; Weber (1991).

[33] T. Morgan (1998), 22–3.

[34] Gruen (1992), *passim*, esp. 223–71.

[35] See Skutsch (1970), 120–1 on this debate (arguing for *Musam*: this, he argues, identifies the poem in question as Naevius' martial epic, the *Punic war*). Mattingley (1993) discusses the historical context of the fragment. Discussion of this fragment is oddly omitted from Hinds's otherwise excellent discussion of 'importing the Muse' at (1998) 52–63.

[36] See e.g. Virg. *Aen.* 8.97–368; Tib. 2.5.23–38; Prop. 4.1.1–38; 4.4.1–14; 4.9; Ov. *Ars am.* 1.103–8; for the uncouth inhabitants of early Rome, see e.g. Liv. 1.8.5–6; Dion. Hal. *Ant. Rom.* 1.79.11. On these Augustan topoi, see White (1993), 182–90; C. Edwards (1996), 30–42.

Titii, the Vestal Virgins),[37] contemporary Roman writers enacted a narrative return to Rome's origins, a literary-mythical refoundation of Rome that sought to obliterate both the trauma of the recent civil war and the deleterious effects of Hellenism.[38] Paradoxically, of course, these writers simultaneously celebrate the sophistication of the Greek literary culture that enables their own composition: Hellenism is both a resource and a threat. Not for nothing is it a Greek, Evander, who in Virgil's *Aeneid* shows Aeneas around the rustic site, 'shaggy with woodland copses' (*siluestribus horrida dumis*), that one day will become the Capitol (8.347–8).

Reactions to this process of Hellenization continued to be ambivalent. While philosophers and poets turned to Greece and bewailed the poverty of Latin learning,[39] and the early Roman lawgiver Numa was held in some quarters to have been inspired by Pythagoras,[40] Greeks were also blamed by moralists and satirists (from Cato in the second century BCE to Juvenal in the second CE) for Rome's perceived descent into luxury and effeminacy.[41] Although this narrative of Rome's origins is a *post euentum* construction, heavily steered particularly (but not exclusively) by Augustus' preoccupation with restoration, there was nothing new about the practice of suspecting Greeks of importing luxury and impropriety: in the second century BCE, for example, Greek philosophers were periodically exiled from Rome.[42]

Much work has been done in recent times upon Rome's ambivalent and selective response to Greek culture.[43] As Woolf puts it,

[37] See August. *Res gest.* 7.3, with Brunt and Moore eds. (1967), 49–50.

[38] For this interpretation of Virgil's *Aeneid*, see Quint (1989); of Livy, see Kraus (1994); Jaeger (1997), 10–12.

[39] See e.g. Lucr. *De rer. nat.* 1.136–9: 'my mind is not deceived as to the difficulty of illuminating the obscure discoveries of the Greeks in Latin verses, especially when I must introduce many aspects with new coinages, thanks to the poverty of the language and the novelty of the subject' (*nec me animi fallit Graiorum obscura reperta difficile inlustrare Latinis uersibus esse, multa nouis uerbis praesertim cum sit agendum propter egestatem linguae et rerum nouitatem*). On the contrast between 'illumination' and 'obscurity' (used elsewhere by Lucretius in a more conventional sense: see e.g. 1.144–5), see below, n. 48.

[40] Gruen (1990), 158–70.

[41] Juv. *Sat.* 3, *passim*, esp. 60–1: see further Petrochilos (1974), 69–87; C. Edwards (1996), 126–7.

[42] Gruen (1990), 173–9.

[43] See esp. the lucid account of Beard and Crawford (1985), 12–24; also Ferrary (1988), 505–26 on the rebranding of Hellenism as 'universal' (read: Roman) *humanitas*. On the selectivity of Roman *paideia*, see Rawson (1985), 84–99

Roman responses to Hellenism consisted of a complex and partly incoherent mixture of adoption, adaptation, imitation, rejection and prohibition, while the rhetorical poses repeatedly struck included assertions of admiration, of condemnation and of reconciliation.[44]

The phrase usually cited to exemplify Rome's uneasy relationship with Greek culture comes in Horace's *Letter to Augustus* (composed some time soon after 17 BCE), where the poet writes that 'captive Greece has captured its feral captor, and brought into (*inferre*) Latium its arts' (*Graecia capta ferum uictorem cepit et artis | intulit agresti Latio*, *Epist*. 2.1.156–7). Although its epigrammatic acuity invites excerption, this passage bears some further consideration in its context. As Charles Brink observes, this statement is a deliberate echo of 'one of the bellicose slogans of anti-Hellenism', a familiar vaunt of triumphalism;[45] at the same time, however (as Brink also observes), it represents a more complex response to Greek culture. In this narrativization of Rome's present, captive Greece is, via a deliberate paradox, imaged as a conquering force: the expected object of *inferre* ('bring into') is not *artis* ('arts'), but *signa* ('military standards') or *arma* ('arms').[46] The debilitation caused by the advent of the arts, of course, is the dilution of Rome's feral qualities with what the poet calls (in a fine oxymoron) 'the grave poison of elegance' (*graue uirus munditiae*,

(somewhat uncritical, but see Wallace-Hadrill 1988: 230–3). Erich Gruen has argued against the idea of an 'ambivalent' Roman response to Greek culture, suggesting that it was in fact 'consistent, sophisticated and purposeful' (Gruen 1992. 235): see (1990), 158–92; (1992), *passim*, esp. 223–71. His argument is that Hellenism was never viewed by Romans as intrinsically bad (and, indeed, was often appreciated); on the occasions when it was excoriated, the aim was more to distinguish and promote Roman identity than to criticize Greek (1992, *passim*, esp. 68; 94–103; 123–9). This latter distinction, however, is specious (why not both at once?); and, conversely, 'admiration' can be double-edged, condescending and exploitative, not simply benevolent (as is exemplified by certain British right-wingers' 'admiration' for India). See more recently (and with more nuance) Habinek (1998), 34–9.

44 Woolf (1994), 120.

45 Brink (1982), 200–1. Cf. Cic. *Brut*. 254: 'For the one matter in which conquered Greece remained our conqueror, we have now wrested from her; or, at any rate, we now share with her' (*quo enim uno uincebamur a uicta Graecia, id aut ereptum illis est aut certe nobis cum Graecis communicatum*); Liv. 34.4.3: '. . . lest those things [Greek and Asian luxuries] capture us more than we have captured them' (*ne illae magis res nos ceperint quam nos illas*).

46 *OLD* s.v. *infero* 2a. If Horace *had* written *arma*, the sentence would have constituted an example of *hysteron proteron*, the capturing coming syntactically before the invasion.

Epist. 2.1.158–9), a sentiment that would have been approved by the emperor who sought to return Rome to its moral roots.

In Horace's formulation, however, Greece's 'victory' over Rome is not complete: he proceeds to state that 'traces of the rustic remained for a long period, and remain today' (*in longum . . . aeuum manserunt hodieque manent uestigia ruris*, *Epist.* 2.1.159–60). Unlike the absolute Roman (military and political) conquest of Greece, the Greek (artistic) conquest of Rome remains partial and ambiguous. The advent of Greek arts, however, is also ambiguous in a more fundamental way. The Greek arts brought, as well as luxury and decadence, the preconditions for Horace's own writing. Without Greece there would be no civilized, modern Rome: in this respect, Horace advertises a certain respect for Greek culture. Indeed, Rome's very imperialist myth of itself as a civilizer of the world was premised upon the notion that Romans had internalized Greek ideals of culture and civilization.[47]

Roman self-definition was articulated temporally, in terms of a relationship between civilized present and savage past; and Rome's conquest of Greece marked a decisive point in that ideologically constructed narrative. A generation earlier, Cicero had positioned himself even more subtly in this complex negotiation of the twin poles of political supremacy and cultural dependency. At the beginning of his *Tusculan disputations*, he explains his decision to 'illuminate' (*illustrare*)[48] philosophy in Latin: not that philosophy cannot be grasped through Greek writings, but because 'our thinkers have always either discovered theories for themselves in a wiser way than the Greeks, or improved upon the things they have taken over (*accipere*)' (*omnia nostros aut inuenisse per se sapientius quam Graecos aut accepta ab illis fecisse meliora*, 1.1). To 'take over' or 'appropriate' (*accipere*; also *accepimus* and *recepti* at 1.3) appears to be a euphemistic reference to the processes of conquest whereby Greek material becomes Roman property: as ever, Rome's status as imperial conqueror is not far in the background. This is further emphasized in the following passage, where Cicero proceeds to list the ways in which Roman culture is better, focusing on ethics (*mores*) and warfare (1.2). The superiority of Greece is marked in

[47] Woolf (1994), 118–25.

[48] *Tusc. disp.* 1.1. Imagery of 'enlightenment' through translation from Greek to Latin recurs later on in the passage (philosophy lacks the 'light of Latin letters': *lumen litterarum Latinarum*, 1.5; it must therefore be 'illuminated': *illustranda*, 1.5), and in Lucretius' *On the nature of the universe* (see above, n. 39).

terms of nature and culture: the qualities of Roman warriors sprang from 'nature' (*natura*), not from 'books' (*litteris*, 1.2). The subtext here is that Greeks' preoccupation with learning led to their conquest at the hands of the more bellicose Romans.[49]

As Horace also does, Cicero provides a temporal narrative describing the advent of Greek culture. 'Greece used to defeat us (*superare*) in learning and every literary genre, in a situtation in which victory (*uincere*) was easy against men who were not fighting back (*repugnantes*)' (*doctrina Graecia nos et omni litterarum genere superabat, in quo erat facile uincere non repugnantes*, 1.3). Again the language of conquest (*superare*, *uincere*, *repugnantes*) is paradoxically applied to those who had been, by Cicero's day, long marked out as the losers in the military campaign (even if Cicero makes a particular point of observing that this 'victory' was only possible because the Romans did not fight back); and again the emphasis upon the 'late' (*serius*; *sero*, 1.3) arrival of literary culture at Rome. Once more, we see that the Roman conquest of Greece is intimately linked with the narrativization of Rome's progress from its origins to the here and now, from primitivism to (a morally equivocal) hyper-sophistication.

At the conclusion of his preface, however, Cicero makes an abrupt and intriguing volte-face, appearing now as the champion of Greek learning at Rome. Philosophy has been neglected 'up until this time' (*usque ad hanc aetatem*, 1.5), he writes, with a typically Ciceronian reticence as to the importance of his own role. Many Latin works on the subject of philosophy, he says, have already been written, but they have been written 'carelessly' (*inconsiderate*), by men who are 'excellent . . . but insufficiently educated' (*optimis . . . sed non satis eruditis*, 1.6). Unlike his Roman competitors, Cicero can articulate these matters 'in a polished way' (*polite*, 1.6). Implicitly, Cicero casts himself as the man for the job precisely because his learning (that is to say, his familiarity with the Greek canon) exceeds that of most Romans. In the context of the intense competition for status in Rome, *paideia* singles out its possessor as a man of prestigious position. Cicero is clear, however, that Greek culture is useful and acceptable only when it is

[49] This further explains the rhetorical question 'why should I speak on military matters?' (*quid loquar de re militari?* 1.2), which is more than a simple *praeteritio*: *de re militari* sounds like the title of a technical work on military tactics, a work that would be unnecessary for the 'naturally' adept Roman.

dominated by Roman power, not vice versa: hence the necessity of a lengthy preamble that celebrates the superiority of Roman achievements, prior to any statement of allegiance to Hellenic values. Between Romans, Greek *paideia* must always appear the object of socio-economic exploitation, not (solely) of veneration: it only has value (in both the mercantile and the aesthetic senses) when it is taken over from its native context and resited in Rome's agonistic market of elite *ambitio*.[50] Cicero's (ab)use of *paideia* sits on the prima-facie more acceptable end of a continuum of Roman practices that stretches from tourism in Greece,[51] through depredations of art (most notoriously by Marcellus, Mummius, and Sulla)[52] and books,[53] to, at least in the third and second centuries BCE, the enslavement of educated Greeks (such as the man who became Livius Andronicus, traditionally the earliest poet who wrote in Latin) for the instruction of the Roman young.[54]

There was, then, a twofold ambivalence towards Greek *paideia* in Roman society.[55] On the one hand, in terms of cultural definition, Rome used the advent of Greek *paideia* as a narrative stage in Roman history, marking the transition from origins to civilization: this could be presented as either a civilizing or a luxurifying process. On the other hand, in terms of competitive ambition within the Roman hierarchy, the possession of Greek education ('possession' implying imperialist dominance in addition to ownership) could be used as a counter in the game of elite self-positioning (and, conversely, the accusation of excessive devotion to Greek arts could be used rhetorically to impugn an enemy, as Cicero's opponent Verres found).[56] At all times, however, Romans

[50] Cf. Habinek (1998), 34. 'For the Romans, Greek culture, like the Greek population and Greek material wealth, was a colonial resource to be exploited and expropriated; to the extent that Greek culture was admired, it was as much for its potential to augment Roman power as for any immanent qualities or characteristics.'

[51] Swain (1996), 66–7.

[52] Marcellus: Polyb. 9.10.1–13; Liv. 25.40.1–3; Plut. *Marc.* 21 (with Pelling 1989: 199–203). Mummius: Vell. Pat. 1.13.4; Plin. *NH* 35.24; Paus. 7.16.8. Sulla: Plut. *Sull.* 12; Paus. 9.7.5; 9.33.6. See further Gruen (1992), 94–103, 123–9; Arafat (1996), 92–7, 102–4.

[53] See e.g. Diod. Sic. 1.4.2–3; Plut. *Aem. Paul.* 28; Athen. *Deipn.* 2b–3d. See further Fantham (1996), 34–6.

[54] Marrou (1956), 246–7.

[55] See further Woolf (1994), 120.

[56] See e.g. Cic. *In Verr.* 2.1.49–61; Petrochilos (1974), 76–80, noting Cicero's inconsistency given the desire to collect Greek artworks expressed in a letter to Atticus (1.8.2).

were expected to keep in view the military and economic subordination of Greece to Rome. Rome invented the equation of Hellenism exclusively with 'culture': in this Roman market-place, Greek learning was a commodity that could be bought and sold, displayed or excoriated for its decadence.

The suggestion that Greeks were definitively characterized by paideutic activity, then, is produced not only 'internally' by Greeks seeking to construct cultural continuity with the past, but also 'externally' by Romans seeking to articulate their own collective relationship with the past and individual statuses within the ambition-led hierarchy at Rome. In a famous passage (6.847–53) in Virgil's monumental testament to Augustan Rome, the *Aeneid*, Anchises, explaining to Aeneas the panorama of past Romans he sees before himself, constructs a programmatic distinction between two types of people: 'others' (*alii*)—usually, and most obviously, taken to refer to Greeks—may perfect the arts of sculpture, oratory, and astronomy, but (here he apostrophizes 'the Roman'), 'make sure you remember to rule people with empire (*imperium*): these qualities will be *your* arts (*artes*)' (*tu regere imperio populos . . . memento (hae tibi erunt artes)*, 851–2).[57] Whereas Horace ironically applies the language of power and conquest to Greek culture, Virgil's Anchises, with equal boldness, refers to Roman imperialism as an 'art'.[58] In such cases of surprising terminological interchange, the exceptions as it were proving the rule, it becomes clear that in the Roman imaginary, Greece's status as 'educator' was intrinsically linked with Rome's as conqueror.

In the second century CE (the setting for most of the literature in this book), the Roman association of Greekness with *paideia* acquired a new intensity. Although the process was cumulative over a long period, the decisive break came with the passing of the hated emperor Domitian (in 97 CE). Trajan, who in 98 CE acceded after the short-lived reign of Nerva, began to promote his own rule as the inverse of Domitian's, and thereafter a primary means for

[57] For other examples of this distribution between Greek and Roman, see Petrochilos (1974), 58–62.

[58] Ovid, typically, provides a parodically overwrought version of this sentiment, referring to the time before the Hellenization of Rome: 'a good fighter understood the art (*ars*) of Rome; a hurler of javelins was eloquent (*disertus*)' (*qui bene pugnabat, Romanam nouerat artem; mittere qui poterat pila, disertus erat*, *Fast*. 3.103–4). But Virgil may be alluding more precisely to Hellenistic kingship theory, which presented ruling as a philosophical art (see below, pp. 181–2).

an emperor to project an anti-tyrannical (i.e. non-Domitianic) persona was publicly to embrace and submit to Greek 'culture'.[59] Thus, whereas Domitian had exiled philosophers, Trajan and Hadrian cultivated and promoted Greek intellectuals,[60] a practice also followed by the Antonine emperors; from Trajan's time, imperial building in Athens (dormant since the time of Augustus) was revived, particularly in the form of libraries and performance halls;[61] iconography represented emperors from Hadrian onwards bearded in the style of Greek intellectuals;[62] Marcus Aurelius wrote Greek philosophy and founded highly paid chairs of rhetoric and philosophy in Athens;[63] emperors from Hadrian onwards reinvoked and reinforced the system of tax breaks for philosophers and teachers.[64] The intensified Hellenization of imperial self-representation in this period follows within a long (and contested) tradition of Roman appropriations of Greek *paideia*.

Paideia, then, was not simply a form of social practice (though, of course, it was that too): at a more abstract level, it was also a means of constructing and reifying idealized identities for Greek and Roman, a privileged space of complex cultural interaction (or 'contact zone')[65] between Roman ideology and Greek identity, a foundation upon which both peoples constructed their own sense of their place in the world. This book is a work not of social but of 'cultural' history. The term 'cultural' is problematic, and I shall have more to say about it presently; for now, I use it to mark an intellectual methodology, a means of exploring the multiple relationships between 'social' issues of power and identity, on the one hand, and the world of artistic and literary ideas on the other.[66] As I hope to show, Greek literature in this period is not simply

[59] Below, pp. 165–6; 183–4.

[60] Fein (1994).

[61] Shear (1981), 368–77; generally on building in Athens in the period, see Alcock (1993), 93–128, emphasizing the changed relationship between Athens and the countryside.

[62] Zanker (1995), 217–33.

[63] On Marcus' *Meditations*, see below, pp. 216–25; on the chairs of philosophy and rhetoric, see Marrou (1956), 303. Vespasian had already established chairs of Greek and Latin rhetoric at Rome: see Marrou, ibid.

[64] Marrou (1956); Fein (1994), 291–6; Schmitz (1997), 22–3 rightly cautions against too much credulity as to the degree to which such tax breaks were enacted in practice.

[65] Pratt (1992) for this term.

[66] See e.g. Burke (1997). I am not sure whether any meaningful distinction can be drawn between 'cultural history' and 'new historicism' (for which see e.g. Veeser ed. 1989): both terms are provisional and imprecise.

'evidence' for the role of *paideia* in constructing Greek identity and exploring Roman power; it is also an active participant in this very process, to the extent that understanding Greekness in this period (or, at least, the form of Greekness espoused by the literary texts under consideration) is inseparable from processes of sophisticated literary interpretation.

LITERATURE, POWER, AND CULTURE

How are we to conceptualize this abstract distinction in terms of *paideia* (particularly marked in the second and third centuries CE) between Greek and Roman? The period, or rather the literary tradition that emerged within it (the so-called 'Second Sophistic'), has commonly been characterized as a 'cultural phenomenon',[67] a compensatory response to Roman 'power': the overwhelming focus in this period upon the cultural heritage of Greece was thus (we are told) a means of defraying the loss of political power in the present.[68] On the one side stood 'power', collocated with politics, Rome, the imperial household; on the other, 'culture', with literature and Hellenic identity. The two were conceived of as 'autonomous terrains',[69] opposed yet complementary. According to such commentators, this culture–power polarity is a sign of Greek submission to Roman dominance.

Such an opposition between 'power' and 'culture', however, is extremely problematic. What do we mean by 'culture' in this context? The word has a broad semantic range (according to Raymond Williams, it is 'one of the two or three most complicated words in the English language'),[70] and I shall argue presently that it has a certain utility in a different sense;[71] in the sense evoked in the previous paragraph, however, it is inappropriate when used in relation to the ancient world.[72] In the nineteenth century, when the notion first emerged under the influence of Romanticism, the

[67] G. Anderson (1993), title.

[68] Bowie (1974), rich and still fundamental; approved with some modifications by G. Anderson (1990), 101–3.

[69] Flinterman (1995), 45; cf. Dubuisson (1984–6), 189.

[70] R. Williams (1976), s.v. 'Culture'. The classic account of the emergence of the notion of 'culture', still fundamental, is R. Williams (1958); see id. (1986); Hunt (1989), and Greenblatt (1990) on the recent emergence of 'culture' as a critical term. For further bibliography, see Wallace-Hadrill (1997), 6–7.

[71] Below, pp. 35–6.

[72] On the problems of applying the notion of 'culture' to the ancient world, see Habinek and Schiesaro (1997); Wallace-Hadrill (1997), 6–11.

word suggested a commendable disimplication from the banausic banalities of practical life.[73] When Greek 'culture' is represented as a disengaged activity opposed to 'power', the formulation conveys a strong whiff of Arnoldian aesthetics. Conversely, the idea that Greeks engaged in 'cultural' activity had no 'power' has little foundation, for two primary reasons. First, as has already been mentioned, certain forms of 'cultural' activity (principally sophistic declamation and sporting competition) were fundamental means of vying for elite status within the city-states of the Greek East:[74] to this extent, '[t]he star performers who attracted large audiences valorized *paideia* by making it appear to be the prize of a bruising competition for status dominance'.[75] Secondly, even in terms of specifically Roman power, Greek *pepaideumenoi* were amongst the *most* empowered of provincials. Almost all of the authors discussed in this book are known to have been Roman citizens (and none are known not to have been), some (notably Plutarch, Arrian, and Philostratus) figures of some considerable influence at Rome.[76] Greeks of the highest socio-economic ranks were, during this period, increasingly implicated in structures of Roman power: ever larger numbers of elite Greeks acted as intermediaries between their cities and Rome,[77] were awarded Roman citizenship, found their way into the Roman senate, and attained important offices.[78]

Over the last twenty or so years, the scope of 'power' has been interpreted with an increased latitude. The works of Michel Foucault have been instrumental in this process, arguing that power is (in the modern world, at any rate) not simply held and exercised by one individual or group over another. In Simon Price's words, 'the notion of power as a possession of political leaders is . . . highly questionable'.[79] 'Power' is, instead, to be

[73] R. Williams (1958).

[74] See esp. Schmitz (1997), 97–135.

[75] Gleason (1995), xxi.

[76] On increased Roman citizenship and enfranchisement in this period, see n. 78.

[77] On embassies, see Bowersock (1969), 43–6; Millar (1977), index s.v. 'embassies', and esp. 110–12; Gruen (1984), index s.v. 'embassies'.

[78] On the extension of Roman citizenship to Greeks, see Millar (1977), 477–90, esp. 479–81. On Greeks in positions of political influence, see Millar (1964), 182–8; Bowersock (1965), 30–41, and (1969), 43–58; Halfmann (1979); Lewis (1981); Bowie (1982), 39–53; Salmeri (1982), 5–9; Syme (1982); de Blois (1984), 360; Sirago (1989), 58–9; Fein (1994); Schmitz (1997), 50–63.

[79] Price (1984), 241.

viewed as a complex matrix of relations disseminated, and indeed contested, through linguistic and symbolic relationships: 'discourse transmits and produces power; it reinforces it, but also undermines and exposes it, renders it fragile and makes it possible to thwart it'.[80] Cultural anthropology has provided yet another challenge to the culture–power polarity: Clifford Geertz's celebrated analysis of a Balinese cockfight, for example, shows how a site of 'play' is used to articulate structures of power within the community.[81] From this perspective, 'cultural' activity can be analysed as a primary locus for the distribution, enforcement, and contestation of 'power'.

Following these conceptual reorientations, certain commentators on Roman Greece have sought to transcend the association of Greece with 'culture' and Rome with political 'power'. Simon Swain argues against styling the literary culture of Roman Greece a 'cultural phenomenon', on the grounds that ' "cultural" is far too innocent and passive a word'; instead, he proposes interpreting 'in political-ideological terms, too, while shying away from connotations of "political" that are too active'.[82] In this formulation, which in point of fact maintains the culture–politics polarity, there is a crucial grey area between the two, an area that is both 'cultural' and 'political-ideological'. Thomas Schmitz, meanwhile, has employed cultural anthropology to explore the politics of *paideia*. Using the terminology of Pierre Bourdieu, he marks sophistic *paideia* as a 'habitus' within which the elite vied for social status and exchanged 'symbolic capital'.[83] In this sense, *paideia* played a vital political role: it provided the central forum for the competition between the elite that was so central to the hierarchical structure of the cities in the Greek East.[84] The contributions of Swain and Schmitz represent important advances in our understanding of the period, serving to move the debate on from the times when scholars debated whether the 'Second Sophistic' had more importance in the discipline of Roman history or that of Greek literature.[85] The problem with dilemmas of the latter kind lies with the institutional parameters of the modern academy, not with the

[80] Foucault (1981), 101.
[81] Geertz (1973), 449–51.
[82] Swain (1996), 88; see further ibid. 6.
[83] Schmitz (1997), esp. 26–31; see also Gleason (1995), xx-xxi.
[84] Schmitz (1997), 97–135.
[85] Bowie (1982), esp. 53–4, (wittily) contra Bowersock (1969), 28, 58.

'Second Sophistic' itself (needless to say, no contemporary would have framed the question in such terms); and it is helpful to consider the ways in which literary 'culture' embodies, refracts, and contests different forms of social power.

Yet there are also certain problems raised by questioning the culture–power polarity. In particular, there is a risk of losing sight of the specific ways in which Greek identity *was* conceived of in a paideutic dyad alongside Roman power: the paradigmatically idealized relationship between Greek and Roman, as we have seen, is presented by ancient authors in terms of education.[86] The Greeks and the Romans themselves were the authors of the culture–power polarity (notwithstanding the inappropriately impertinent use of modern terms). It may be that this particular construction of the relationship does not satisfy the requirements of modern historical or anthropological analysis of the 'reality' of the situation, but this is not necessarily the point: Greek identity in the period in question was constructed by means of ideations that were abstracted from what modern scholars may style 'historical reality'. I am not, of course, proposing a reversion to the time when the culture–power polarity was accepted as a framework of *academic methodology* whereby to approach Graeco-Roman relations; rather, I aim to explore the ways in which the ancients themselves constructed the relationship. That is to say, whilst it is important to retain the focus of much current scholarship upon the urgent questions surrounding 'power', 'politics', and 'cultural identity' in Greek literary representation in the period, it is equally important to consider why Greeks were so keen to represent themselves as lacking in power but compensating for it with *paideia*.

A GEOGRAPHY OF THE IMAGINATION

'Cultural' activity—and in particular writing 'literature'—was a fundamental means of constructing a Greek identity discrete from Rome. 'Greek' and 'Roman', in this book, will be interpreted as constructed subject-positions, idealized reifications rather than self-evident subjectivities. (For the sake of the reader's comfort, I do not apostrophize 'Greek' and 'Roman' throughout; but I wish

[86] 'Die Hellenen sahen es als ihre Aufgabe an, als politisch-ethische Ratgeber zu sein' (Palm 1959: 80); see also Rawson (1989) on stories of Greeks advising Romans.

it to be understood that these terms are sites of continual contestation and reassessment.) In a strict, geopolitical sense, *Hellas* (to use the Greek word that came to denote 'Greece' at some point in the period after the composition of the Homeric poems)[87] had ceased to exist during the time of Augustus, when the province of Achaea was formed.[88] Yet in another sense, of course, there was, always had been, and always would be *Hellas*, even though the precise significance of the word was ever debated. Identity was not compromised or diluted by Roman conquest: it was, rather, shifted into the realm of the imaginary, where it had always partially resided. 'Greekness' (*Hellēnismos*) was constituted by an aggregation of civilized and intellectual values: *praiotēs* ('gentleness'), *sōphrosynē* ('self-control'), *epieikeia* ('decency'), *philanthrōpia* ('benevolence'), and—most importantly—*paideia*.[89] In this respect, every civilized person had the capacity to be a Hellene (even though in practice, of course, few if any barbarians could 'Hellenize' with conviction).[90] The name of Rome was similarly overdetermined: by a nice (and etymologically insignificant) quirk of fate, the Greek word *rhōmē* means both 'Rome' and 'physical power' (and the lack of capitalization in ancient orthography reinforces the ambiguity).[91]

The imaginary status of these hypostatizations of 'Greece' and 'Rome' is crucial because in practice, of course, the distinction between Greek and Roman in 'reality' was much more fluid. The prolific writer Arrian was in literary terms a 'Greek'—but he was also Lucianus Flavius Arrianus, a Roman suffect consul and governor of Cappadocia.[92] What of Claudius Aelianus (Aelian), the author of the learned Greek texts *On the nature of animals* and the *Miscellaneous history*, whose pride at never having left Italy is recorded by Philostratus?[93] Or even of Marcus Aurelius, the bearded emperor and writer of Greek philosophy?[94] In a world

[87] Lévy (1991). I use the Latinized terms 'Greek' and 'Greece' throughout this book, not only for ease of reading but also because our experience of Roman Greece is necessarily mediated through Rome: to attempt to correct the English language would constitute a spurious attempt at authenticity.

[88] Alcock (1993), 8–24.

[89] Ferrary (1988), 494.

[90] Ch. 2, '*Paideia* and Hellenism'.

[91] For this pun, see Plut. *Rom.* 1.1; Ael. Ar. *Ad Rom.* 8; Erskine (1995).

[92] See also n. 120.

[93] Philostr. *VS* 625: see below, p. 108.

[94] Ch. 4, 'Marcus Aurelius: Internalized Pedagogy'.

before 'nationality' and passports, cultural miscegenation was easier, and it was possible to be (for example) a Roman Greek Alexandrian Jew. Different aspects of identity, however, could be articulated strategically at different points. We would not know of Plutarch's Roman citizenship if we only had his texts, where he adopts an unwaveringly Greek perspective; but the discovery of a statue-base has revealed that, in a civic context, he was happy to proclaim his name to be Lucius Mestrius Plutarchus.[95] It will not do to explain away such statements of Roman identity as mere public posturing, and to assert that '[c]ognitively and spiritually' the authors in question 'were avowedly Greek'.[96] There is, in point of fact, no reason to suppose that Plutarch would have felt anything other than pride at the mark of social distinction conferred by Roman citizenship, in the civic context for which it was intended. Conversely, literary texts do not provide a clear window into the souls of their authors. They too are public documents: they *perform* a certain aspect of the identity of the author. The Hellenism of the Greek literature of the period is neither natural nor self-evident: it is, rather, artfully *created*.

Indeed, to an extent, even the very concept of 'Greek' as a meaningful descriptive was circumscribed by Roman domination. Of course, the idea of a collective Greek identity that transcended membership of an individual *polis* had been current since the earliest days of Panhellenism, roughly the eighth century BCE. From the time of the Persian Wars in the fifth century, the definition of Greece attained a particular concision and sharpness by virtue of its opposition to Persia and Egypt, the barbarian 'others';[97] and much of the writing of the fifth and fourth centuries bears upon this polar opposition between Greek and non-Greek.[98] In the Hellenistic period, the 'Hellenizing' of the East entailed a certain (strategic) projection of Greek unity; and in the 'old world', successions of leagues and confederacies tested the possibilities of a unionist Greece. However, the notion that all of

[95] *SIG*³ 829a.

[96] Swain (1996), 412, 71, on the inscriptional record; quotation from p. 70.

[97] E. Hall (1989), esp. 56–69.

[98] See Hartog (1988) on Herodotus; E. Hall (1989) on tragedy; and, generally, Cartledge (1993), 36–62. According to Herotodus (8.144.2), Greekness (τὸ Ἑλληνικόν) is defined by common blood, shared cult practices, and common customs. As J. M. Hall (1995), 92 observes, however, this definition underplays the great variety in Greek religious and linguistic practice.

mainland Greece could or should be united into a single administrative unit—that is, that 'Greece' should be a more significant political unit than the individual city-states—came only with Roman conquest.[99] When Augustus created the province of *Achaea* (after the battle of Actium in 31 BCE), it was the first time that these city-states had been ruled by a single, centralized administration. Moreover, as Elsner observes, the mythicizing of the free Greece of the past is necessarily dependent upon Roman conquest.[100] Indeed, the Roman empire controlled Greekness in a still more direct way. When Hadrian created the Panhellenion,[101] an institution centred in Athens that determined which cities were to be named 'Greek' (and thereby receive the associated tax breaks), it was the first time that the notoriously slippery notion of 'Greekness' had ever been subjected to authoritatively definitive criteria (or, at least, what presented themselves as such). In all these ways, Romanness circumscribed Greekness.

Being Greek, then, was not a self-evident activity. The representation of Greeks as educators served to foreground the Greek personae of those most compromised by Romanness: it enacted a spurious clarification on behalf of those whose identities were most discombobulated. Greg Woolf has discussed the process of 'becoming Roman, staying Greek',[102] but in fact Greekness was not a natural, inherited state: 'becoming Greek' (in the sense of constructing an identity as a *pepaideumenos*) was as arduous and time-consuming a process as 'becoming Roman'. This book argues that the Hellenism embodied in paideutic culture was not a reflex reaction to the oppression of an indigenous group by a foreign oppressor, but was a shifting terrain over which identities were created, contested, denied, impugned, crushed, reaffirmed. Maud Gleason's recent work, drawing on such ideas of manhood as a negotiable commodity, emphasizes that rhetoric in the early principate is a *process* whereby identity is both displayed and

[99] This is not to deny the continuing importance of civic identity: see esp. the excellent discussion Schmitz (1997), 181–93.

[100] 'Greece is "Greece" (one country and not many *poleis*) only because it is a province in an empire whose various cities are united through having lost their freedom . . . "Greece" can exist only when its freedom not to be united is over and the myth of a freedom-in-the-past has begun' (Elsner 1995), 142–3.

[101] On the Panhellenion, see Spawforth and Walker (1985; 1986); Alcock (1993), 153, 166–8; C. P. Jones (1996); Swain (1996), 75–6. See also below, n. 151.

[102] Woolf (1994).

contested;[103] and though her primary focus is sexual identity, her approach is suggestive of how profitably the idea of identity as process might be applied to questions of cultural identity.[104]

Because cultural identity in the ancient world was (unlike 'nationality' in the modern world) not determined by geopolitical boundaries, there was no Greek who could take his Greekness for granted. The satirical works of Lucian and the lexical works of Phrynichus are full of accusations of 'barbarism' that impugn the victim's Hellenism, directed alike at those who are 'ethnically' Greek and those who are not.[105] Conversely, it was possible (through laborious *paideia*) for barbarians to attain a degree of Greekness. Favorinus famously celebrates his own success at this project (*Cor.* 25–7).[106] Similarly, Damis, in Philostratus' *In honour of Apollonius of Tyana*, reveals his aims in following the sage: 'to cease to be an unwise philistine and to seem wise, to cease to be a barbarian, and to seem educated' (*σοφὸς . . . δόξειν ἐξ ἰδιώτου τε καὶ ἀσόφου, πεπαιδευμένος δὲ ἐκ βαρβάρου*), and to 'become Greek' (*Ἕλλην . . . γενόμενος*, 3.43).[107] It is no coincidence that it is here, at the margins, that 'Greekness' is most clearly articulated. Identity is predicated upon difference:[108] it is a relative, not an absolute state. To be Greek—a non-barbarian—requires a continual construction and parading of distinctions. The other is the shadow of the self.

Hadrian's Panhellenion, so far from clarifying the frontiers of Hellenism, muddied them still more. This institution also admitted cities whose claims to be Greek were prima facie questionable. The Panhellenion was centred in Athens, the heart of 'old' Greece, but the member-states included cities that were not familiar Greek settlements but centres of Roman political and economic importance (e.g. Sardis, Cibyra, and Synnada in Asia Minor).[109] These cities established their own right to be called Greek by means of clever genealogies detailing the colonial history

[103] Gleason (1995), xx-xxix.

[104] Gleason (1995), 16–17. See already S. Hall (1990), 225–6: 'Cultural identity . . . is a matter of "becoming" as well as "being" . . . [it is] not an essence but a *positioning*' (author's emphasis).

[105] Swain (1996), 44–63.

[106] Ch. 2, '*Paideia* and Hellenism'.

[107] See further Ch. 4, 'Dio and Philostratus'.

[108] J. Rutherford (1990), 21–2.

[109] Spawforth and Walker (1985), 79–81.

of the state in question. Such aetiological operations, (?re)-enacting narratives of colonization (as Pindar and Callimachus had done in previous ages), pose imaginative challenges to received conceptions of time and space, fusing past and present and linking distant territories. They are, however, self-consciously bold and provocative. The inscription commemorating the admission of Cibyra praises the *paideia* of the genealogist in question, one Publius Antius Antiochus:[110] does this refer to his learnedness or to his ingenuity? Is this a playful admission of the tenuousness of Cibyra's colonial narrative? In practice, it is unlikely that the Hellenism of Cibyra (noted as a non-Greek foundation by Strabo)[111] would have been accepted unconditionally by the 'other' Greek states. The point, however, is not simply that some cities belonging to the Panhellenion were self-evidently *echt* Greek and some not, but that this institution reflected the widespread tension between Greekness as an ethnic marker and as a lingua franca uniting the eastern empire.

Indeed, as a matrix of privileged 'cultural' activity, Hellenism linked together not just the East, but also Rome, Gaul, and Africa. This new-style Hellenism, the pluralist, multicultural, Roman-inspired web that embraced the entire civilized world, contradicted the old-style Hellenism, constructed on the Classical, exclusivist model of binary opposition (Greek versus barbarian).[112] As Aelius Aristides puts it in his oration *To Rome*, the world is no longer divided into Greeks and barbarians, but into Romans and non-Romans.[113] In other words, the forces that unite the empire now transcend those that create distinctions within it. Yet Aristides' very highlighting of the 'replaced' polarity of Greek versus barbarian begs questions: the two, non-complementary polarities have presented themselves to him as exclusive options, and, in privileging Roman versus non-Roman, he has made an active choice. Aristides identifies a widespread tension in the construction of Hellenic identity: a dilemma that offers on the one hand a sophisticated, modern cosmopolitanism drawing a line under the past (and thereby confining the rich paideutic legacy of Greece to mere antiquarian or recreational interest), and on the

[110] Curty (1995), 13–15. On Publius Antius Antiochus, see Philostr. *VS* 568–70; Bowersock and Jones (1974), 36. See further below, p. 36.

[111] Strab. 13.4.17; see further Spawforth and Walker (1985), 81–2.

[112] Ch. 2, '*Paideia* and Hellenism'.

[113] *Ad Rom.* 63, with Pernot (1997), 91 n. 123 on the interpretation.

other an overdependence upon the past, risking serving up a barren, jejune repetition of clichés that have lost their vitality. Although the circumstances are radically different, Kevin Robins's description of post-Kemalist Turkey's relationship to Europe has some interesting points of similarity. As Robins describes it, the 'modernization' (i.e. westernization) of Turkey has offered a choice between an 'illusory, specious modernity' that would destroy traditional foundations without effectively replacing them, and a 'compensating and protective retreat into the closure of tradition', a process that risks a similar cultural desiccation.[114] Like twentieth-century Turkey, the Greek world under the Roman principate faced a conflict between preserving its own deeply entrenched cultural traditions in isolation and adapting to a new, multicultural modernity.

IMITATION AND IDENTITY

This complex relationship between past and present necessitated an intense focus upon the question of tradition, and in particular upon literary tradition. Post-Classical Greek culture was heavily burdened by its own cultural past.[115] In the second century BCE the critic Aristarchus of Samothrace, head of the Museum of Alexandria, referred to poets of his day as 'neoterics' (νεώτεροι) or 'latecomers', an appellation (hinting at insubordination and insurrection) also taken over to apply to Hellenizing Roman poets in the first century BCE.[116] (Homeric scholiasts, with the superciliousness of the pious acolyte, use the term with reference to *any* poet later than Homer.)[117] In his treatise on syntax, Dionysius of Halicarnassus (writing in the late first century BCE) distinguishes between 'writers of old' (οἱ ἀρχαῖοι) and 'latecomers' (μεταγενέστεροι).[118] To engage in literary practice was necessarily to anchor the present in tradition and to reanimate the past. The dominant notion in the literary aesthetic of Roman Greece was *mimēsis*, a complex term that covers both 'artistic representation'

[114] Robins (1996), 62–3.
[115] See esp. Bing (1988); Schmitz (1997), 220–31.
[116] Cic. *Att.* 7.2.1. See further A. N. Cizek (1994), 64–5.
[117] Σ Hom. *Il.* 16.574; 24.257.
[118] Dion. Hal. *De comp. uerb.* 4.14. See further Hidber (1996), 18 n. 98: 'Die . . . Trennung . . . durchzieht das ganze Werk des Dionys.'

and 'imitation' of predecessors.[119] Impersonation of figures from the Classical past was ubiquitous in Greek culture during the period of the Roman principate. At times, the degree of identification between past and present could be embarrassingly (for modern scholarship, at least) close: the best known case is that of Arrian, who styled himself 'the new Xenophon' (or sometimes simply 'Xenophon'),[120] but there are numerous other examples.[121] In literary terms, 'becoming Greek' meant constructing one's own self-representation through and against the canonical past.

This much is well known, but *mimēsis* involves a more complex and contested process than is often acknowledged. *Mimēsis* marks not only the traditional temper of Roman Greek culture, but also its modernity: an 'imitation' of a literary forebear is not simply a xerographic reproduction but also (and this applies even to the extreme case, literal citation) a transformation. Roman Greek literature marks its innovative flavour in numerous ways, but most conspicuously by the near universal adoption of prose ahead of poetry: unsurprising perhaps for the genres of philosophy, rhetoric, and history, but ostentatious in the case of Aelius Aristides' prose hymns.[122] Plutarch even claims that the Delphic oracle has begun to prophesy in prose rather than verse.[123] The

[119] Below, p. 48.

[120] For his self-description as Xenophon (implied at *Cyn.* 16.6) see *Ect. contr. Alan.* 10, 22; for the appellation 'the new Xenophon' (ὁ νέος Ξενοφῶν), see Phot. *Bibl.* cod. 58; *Suda* A 3868. Stadter (1967) argues that 'Xenophon' was Arrian's *cognomen*, unconvincingly I think: see Ameling (1984), whose suggestion that it was an *Ehrentitel* bestowed by Hadrian is, however, equally implausible. I take it as Arrian's own self-styling. On Xenophon's influence on Arrian, see Stadter (1967), 156–7; Oliver (1972); Stadter (1980), *passim*; Tonnet (1988), 1.225–81; Bosworth (1993), 272–5. Oliver (1972) discusses a double bust representing Xenophon and (in his view) Arrian.

[121] Fein (1994), 120–1; Schmitz (1997), 46–7 (with n. 25), 226–7, noting the *Selbstbewußtsein* in respect of tradition implied by this process.

[122] See esp. the programmatic statements at Ael. Ar. *Hymn. Sar.* 4–8 (including a sophistic rebuttal of the claim that poetry is older than prose). The Greek novels also represent a prosification of a verse form, the epic: although the constituent parts of this most intertextual of genres also include prose forms (history, rhetoric, philosophy), the choice of a prose form for 'fictional' events is a striking innovation. Relevant also is Lucian's castigation of those who introduce poetic licence into history, producing a 'poetic prose' (πεζή τις ποιητική) that he compares to an athlete dressed up as a prostitute (*Hist. conscr.* 8). Some poetry was, however, still written in this period: for selected texts, see Heitsch ed. (1963–4); Hopkinson (1994*a*); for discussion, see Bowie (1989; 1990).

[123] Plut. *De pyth. passim.* Particularly significant is Theon's concluding argument (403a–409d), where he asserts that prose is particularly suited to the present times of peace (408b–c), and preferable on the grounds that it allows one 'to learn

manifold shapes that a mimetic relationship to the past can take form the subject of the first part of this book, Chapters 1 and 2, which deal respectively with the mimetic construction of literature and that of the self as a social agent. The relationship between past and present can be construed in different ways by different writers with different agendas, according to the view of Hellenism they wish to activate. From Plato on, substantial dispute surrounded the question of the ontological status of the mimetic artefact. Does it have a natural, self-evident, genetic relationship with the object it imitates? Or is it a spurious fake? These issues raise concomitant queries about the status of Hellenism in Roman Greece: are Roman Greeks the natural inheritors of Classical Greece? Or are they interloping impostors masquerading as the real thing?

These questions are strategic rhetorical effects of an attempt to construct a modernist literary aesthetic: they cannot be answered definitively by modern scholarship. Roman Greek literature is not *essentially* 'secondary', 'parasitic', and 'mimetic'. (Nor, conversely, is it *essentially* 'original' and 'fresh'—but that may be another matter.) Its relationship with Classical literature is mutually constitutive: the 'prior' period is constructed (idealized, reified) by relation to the 'posterior' literature of Greece (whether Hellenistic or Roman). Periodization involves a process of unstable relativism (hence my adoption of the comparatives 'prior' and 'posterior' for the conventional 'past' and 'present'). Hinds's discussion of the Roman poetics of posterity are instructive in this connection. Substitute 'Classical' for 'archaic' in the following quotation:

> An 'archaic period' is always something invented by later poets or critics. Therefore, in studying poets commonly deemed to be 'archaic' it is important not to leave that term uninterrogated. To construct a poet as 'archaic' is necessarily to be complicit with a history of reception.[124]

Conversely, a 'later' writer is only 'later' by virtue of rhetorical effect. Modern scholarship has traditionally invested a considerable amount in the myth of the primacy of Classical Greece, to the extent that all post-Classical ancient societies are viewed (with whatever degree of affection) as secondary, non-original, non-

each thing clearly and easily and without pomp and fiction' (σαφῶς καὶ ῥᾳδίως ἕκαστα καὶ μὴ σὺν ὄγκωι μηδὲ πλάσματι μανθάνειν, 407a).

[124] Hinds (1998), 55.

authentic.[125] German *Altertumswissenschaft* in the late nineteenth and early twentieth centuries reconstructed 'sources' that Roman Greek authors were held to have plagiarized;[126] more recently, Francophone scholars have sought to rescue these texts from disrepute, explaining their derivativeness by imputing to them a doctrine of *imitation créative* that had little place for original thought.[127] But *mimēsis*, as this book seeks to show, was not simply a means of marking a stable relationship between two fixed coordinates, the present and the past; it was a locus of conflict between various groups trying (vainly) to define that relationship in different ways.

For the elite writers who form the subject of this book, the struggle for Greek identity in this period took place largely (though not exclusively) in the realm of the literary imagination. The central points, however, are two: first, that this imaginary 'Greece' was always circumscribed by the Roman empire (and this is the case even when the Roman present seems most explicitly ignored); secondly, that Greekness was not a self-evident essence, but a locus of conflict between multiple, at times exclusive, definitions. The answer to the question 'why is *paideia* used to define Greek identity?', then, will not be unitary: rather, it will identify a core of concerns that are negotiated in different ways by different authors in the period.

THE POLITICS OF IMITATION

This book is subtitled 'The Politics of Imitation':[128] this is intended to signal a departure from the conventional ways of interpreting Greek responses to Roman rule. Traditionally, these texts have been scanned for spoors of the 'beliefs', 'attitudes', or 'opinions' of their readers, as though the psyche of the author were dimly visible through the opaque fug of literature, as though the analytical procedures of modern scholarship were sufficient to

[125] See, most conveniently, the excellent discussion of Feeney (1998), 22–8 and esp. 57–63.

[126] See esp. E. Rohde (1914) on the Greek novel (1st edn. in 1876); Helm (1906) on Lucian.

[127] Bompaire (1958); Reardon (1971).

[128] 'Imitation' translates the Greek word *mimēsis*, albeit inaccurately. 'Representation' is the preferred rendition of most scholars, but that too has its limitations; and 'the politics of representation' inspires misleading reminiscences of US civil rights movements.

reanimate the author as a real person with real political views.[129] This mode of interpretation follows what Belsey calls the 'expressive-realist' school of literary criticism: '[t]he text is seen as a way of arriving at something anterior to it: the convictions of the author, or his or her experience as part of that society at that particular time'.[130] Like all critical systems, expressive-realism is the product of a certain historical moment (roughly the last century and a half); but (as Belsey shows) what is particularly seductive about this interpretative practice is that it conceals its historical contingency under the guise of a universally self-evident and commonsensical approach to literature.

In the last twenty years or so, however, literary theorists, anthropologists, and sociologists have been progressively less keen to interpret literature as though it were fundamentally a means of articulating the inner self. Literary theory has emphasized the degree to which the notion of 'the author' as the owner and godlike creator of a work is a function of bourgeois capitalism.[131] Texts are, correspondingly, viewed not so much as means of expressing a univocal self, but as sites of conflict between different voices (some, for sure, louder than others). Certain anthropologists, meanwhile, have emphasized the extent to which ludic forms—music, art, 'literature'—constitute not secondary reflections upon social practice, but primary means through which social hierarchies are constituted. For Victor Turner, ritual and theatre (the two, in his view, perform analogous functions) are fundamental aspects of social process and collective decision-making.[132] Following Turner, Geertz asserts that the best metaphor for social interaction is literary—a 'poetics of culture'—not mechanical, as functionalists have implied.[133] Indeed, for some anthropologists—the so-called 'performative school'—social interaction is a fundamentally theatrical experience, with actors playing out social roles

[129] The approach implicit in e.g. Palm (1959), Forte (1972), and explicit in Swain (1996) ('views', 'attitudes', 'opinions': see p. 12).

[130] Belsey (1980), 13; see pp. 7–14 *passim* on 'expressive-realism'.

[131] See esp. Barthes's essays 'The death of the author' and 'From work to text', conveniently translated and printed in Barthes (1977), 142–8, 155–64; and in (1986), 49–55, 56–64.

[132] V. Turner (1957; 1974; 1982). The conflation of ritual and theatre is particularly developed by Schechner (1988; 1993). See, however, the astute critique of Goody (1997), 99–152: if theatre is isomorphic with other modes of social activity, why is it so frequently constructed as a unique and idiosyncratic form of activity?

[133] See e.g. Geertz (1979–80).

rather than expressing inner selves.[134] If these tenets are accepted (as they are in this book), then identity is not *expressed through* but *constituted by* social discourse. Or, to use Butler's words,

Where there is an 'I' who utters or speaks and thereby produces an effect in discourse, there is first a discourse which precedes and enables that 'I' and forms in language the constraining trajectory of the will. Thus there is no 'I' who stands *behind* discourse and executes its volition or will *through* discourse. On the contrary, the 'I' only comes into being through being named, called, interpellated . . . and this discursive constitution takes place prior to the 'I'.[135]

The name generally (and loosely) given to the heterogeneous body of scholars associated with 'performative' approaches to the role(s) of literature in society is 'New Historicism'.[136] To the extent that 'New Historicism' has any identifiable or coherent dogma (and this, it must be granted, is a limited extent), it emphasizes simultaneously the grounding of literary texts in political and socio-economic materiality, and simultaneously the constitution of power and identity primarily through 'literary' (or, at least, symbolic) modalities that require thoughtful and attentive unpacking: to quote Montrose's celebrated dictum, 'the historicity of texts and the textuality of history'.[137] Clearly, this preoccupation with performance and self-presentation is largely informed by postmodernist theory and practice: we moderns inhabit a world dominated by simulacra and semiotic images. It is not my intention (in the crude parlance of some criticism) to 'apply' 'theories' to Roman Greece, as though they constituted some transcultural, transhistorical key to cultural praxis. I evoke these approaches primarily to draw attention to the degree to which assumptions about authorial intention and sincerity (for all their apparent simplicity) are grounded in a critical idiom (Romanticism) that is both circumscribed by socio-historical contingencies and intellectually outmoded. This book does not represent a 'new historical' 'approach' to ancient literature, in that I am aware of the degree to which new historical theory is circumscribed by the preoccupations

[134] See esp. Schieffelin (1985; 1998), owing much to Goffman (1969). For a discussion of the relevance of performance theory to Classical Athenian culture, see the essays in Goldhill and Osborne eds. (1999).

[135] Butler (1993), 225.

[136] Veeser ed. (1989) is the closest thing to a manifesto, but even there 'heterogeneity and contention' (p. x) are foregrounded.

[137] Montrose (1989), 23.

of the modern West. Still, it would be disingenuous, as well as methodologically unsound, to deny that many of the concepts employed here are taken over—I hope judiciously, but also eclectically and with allowance for cultural-historical difference—from contemporary criticism. The literature of Roman Greece, as I hope to show in this book, does not simply reflect a set of views on Rome; rather, it engages dynamically with inherited images, tropes, and identities, actively constructing new ways of looking at the world. This is why I write of a 'politics' of imitation: the composition of literature in this period is a fundamentally creative *act* that possesses its own materiality and ideological immediacy; it is not simply the monumentalization of the author's psychic preoccupations. To use Victor Turner's terms, literature has an 'ontological' rather than an 'epiphenomenal' relationship to Graeco-Roman culture: it is not a reflex of a pre-existing Greek identity, but precisely the space in which identity is constructed and disseminated.[138] These concepts are 'anachronistic' (an unfocused and misleading word), but they are designedly so: all interpretative approaches to the ancient world are constrained by contemporary and local exigencies in the modern world, and the important question to ask is how *useful* they are for the job in hand. This book seeks to *interpret plausibly* (i.e. to expropriate into a sociolect comprehensible to modern readers) the literature of Roman Greece, not to replicate the experience of ancient readers (a chimerical task).

It is not, however, intended to be forbiddingly 'theoretical': I have sought to avoid esoteric jargon. Indeed, in certain ways, my critical practice is that of a traditional commentator on an ancient text: I read texts closely, considering problems of interpretation, observing allusions. My aim here, though, is to demonstrate the degree to which close-reading is a political exercise: the texts I study strategically invite literary analysis as an identity-forming activity. To read these texts—and I take 'reading' to be a highly intellectual enterprise—is to learn how to become Greek, and also what problems arise in such a process of becoming. Although the texts of Roman Greece were not composed in an exclusively scholarly environment like that of the Museum of Alexandria, there is substantial evidence for detailed and sophisticated reading

[138] V. Turner (1974), 57.

practices. The texts of Homer, in particular, were subjected to minute analysis.[139] Although some authors (such as Lucian) seem to have encountered canonical texts primarily in well-known excerpts,[140] there are examples in others (Plutarch and Philostratus, for example) of independent and highly sophisticated readings.[141] Sophistic performance, too, encouraged an ear attentive to nuance and the possibility of error: 'the audience itself played a critical role, as arbiter of a suspenseful process . . . Spectatorship provided an affective education'.[142] Sophistry was the medium of 'figured speech',[143] language that dissimulates its intentions through allegory and analogy, requiring readers to work at the process of uncovering 'meaning' (the quotation marks are necessary, since different audiences are to take away different ideas of what is the authorized significance of the utterance).

A central foundation of this book's argument is that Greek literary culture in the second and third centuries CE defines itself in terms of such tricksy, hyper-sophisticated, meta-linguistic forms. If we are in search of Greek 'identity', we cannot expect these authors to tell it 'straight': in this highly self-conscious thought-world, even the occasional apparent *cri de cœur* is automatically overdetermined, apostrophized, ironized. Indeed, in many cases, 'Greekness' consists precisely *not* in revealing one's inner intentions, but rather in demonstrating an impressive facility with the manipulation, innovation, and combination of personae, both 'literary' and 'cultural'. This process, of course, works in degrees (Plutarch, for example, is in general less ironical about his own moral authority than Dio Chrysostom or Lucian);[144] but even

[139] Lamberton (1986).

[140] G. Anderson (1976). See Householder (1941) for a detailed breakdown of Lucian's reading, concluding that he had a standard 'grammatical and rhetorical education' without progressing to 'dogmatic philosophy and . . . advanced grammar' (p. 97).

[141] See e.g. Ch. 2, *passim*, on Plutarch's *How to listen to poetry*; Philostratus' *Heroicus* makes comprehensive intertextual use of the Homeric texts. See also Kindstrand (1973), 13–110, although the authors he studies (Dio Chrysostom, Aristides, and Maximus) show a marked leaning towards quotations from *Iliad* 1–2!

[142] Gleason (1995), xxiii.

[143] Ahl (1984); see Whitmarsh (1998*a*) on the relevance of 'figured speech' to the literature of Roman Greece.

[144] But see Duff (1999) on the degree of experimental provocation in Plutarch's moral stance, emphasizing the ways in which 'Plutarch's texts resist simplistic univocal presentations of the past, but are complex, exploratory and challenging' (p. 309).

so, there *is* a consistency across the texts in this period, and this lies in the (various) ways in which the question of what it is to be a Greek is *both* defined through linguistic articulation *and* subjected to a radically ludic uncertainty by means of a range of literary strategies.

This is a period that sees some of the most clever, witty, playful, ambitious, and flamboyant writing of antiquity. The ironical masking that I have identified as one of the central characteristics of the literature of this period is, however, not simply a formal feature: it is also a socio-political force, a response to the exigencies of imperial dominion. In his ground-breaking book *The practice of everyday life*, Michel de Certeau points to the strategic and highly creative 'uses' that consumers make of the ideological images and symbols that are directed at them by the hegemonic agencies that seek to organize quotidian life.[145] In an instructive passage, he compares the creative role of the consumer with the reappropriations practised by native Americans upon the habits imposed by their Spanish colonizers: 'they subverted them from within—not by rejecting them or transforming them (though that occurred as well), but by many different ways of using them in the service of rules, customs, or convictions foreign to the colonization that they could not escape. They metaphorized the dominant order: they made it function in another register.'[146] Analogously, the image of Greeks as disenfranchised purveyors of education was produced by conquering Romans as a technique of control, but re-made by Greeks into a creative force, 'metaphorized' into a set of resources that enabled parasitic irony and esoteric hermeneutics to take over. Literary ingenuity is one primary means of negotiating the imperialism of language and thought.

The image of the cultured Greek and the empowered Roman is not simply a blazon, an emblem synecdochic of Graeco-Roman complementarity as whole: it provides an opportunity for individual writers to exercise their wit and intellectual agility. The second part of this book is focused on paradigmatic models for relations between Greek *paideia* and Roman power. Chapter 3 treats the construction of Greek philosophy as an oppositional voice through the discourse of exile that emerged under Nero and Vespasian, and reached a peak under Domitian. The exile is a

[145] de Certeau (1984). [146] de Certeau (1984), 32.

figure overdetermined by literary tradition, stretching right back to Odysseus: the Roman Greek exile writers manipulate the full range of conventions, knowingly and self-consciously constructing 'fictive' self-representations. The figure of the pedagogical adviser of emperors (the subject of Chapter 4) is similarly freighted with literary tradition and self-awareness, this time proposing a more complementary relationship between Greek *paideia* and Roman power. In each of these chapters, it is a question of discovering not the 'true views' of the authors in question, but their narrative and rhetorical strategies, their subtle and often playful appropriation of literary models to construct a role for themselves in the present. Chapter 5, meanwhile, considers how satire constructs Rome as an 'other' that all right-thinking Greeks should oppose. As I seek to show, however, there are risks (and opportunities) in this polarization, too.

It is precisely because of the ludic and elusive temper of Greek self-representation in this period that I have employed the phrase 'cultural identity'[147] in this book, even despite the problems (alluded to above) clustering around the anachronistic notion of culture. I have preferred 'cultural identity' to 'racial' or 'ethnic' ('national' would be wholly inappropriate)[148] not because of the element of evident anachronism involved in the latter terms[149]—after all, 'culture' is itself an entirely modern notion[150]—but because it implies social aggregation through shared institutions, values, and preoccupations, rather than through lineage. This is not to deny that genealogy was, in certain contexts, an important constitutive feature of Greekness. Myths of shared descent (*syngeneia*) were one means by which Greekness could be articulated in Roman times, especially after the foundation of Hadrian's Panhellenion.[151] Such *syngeneia*, however, was not articulated

[147] An enormous topic: for central contributions to the debate, see Said (1978); B. Anderson (1983); Gellner (1987); Spivak (1988); Bhabha ed. (1990); S. Hall (1990; 1992); Rutherford ed. (1990); Young (1990); Viswanathan (1990); Bhabha (1994); S. Hall and du Gay eds. (1996). For lucid discussion of the relevance of 'identity' in ancient contexts, see Grahame (1998), 157–60; Miles (1999).

[148] 'Nationality' suggests the processes of modern nation-formation that began in the 18th cent.: see e.g. Hobsbawm (1992).

[149] 'Race' and 'ethnicity', implying genetic descent, evoke the racial theories of the 19th cent.: for good discussion of the relevance of such terms to Classical Greece, see J. M. Hall (1997), 1–33

[150] Above, pp. 17–18.

[151] Above, pp. 23–5 on the Panhellenion. On *syngeneia*, see Spawforth and Walker (1985), 82; Woolf (1994), 129; Curty (1995); Schmitz (1997), 184–5.

through biological science, as it was in the nineteenth century, but through mythical narrative: a prominent example would be the inscription recording Antiochus' 'renovation' (ἀνανε]ώσασθαι) of Aegeae's links with Argos, via an account of the Perseus myth.[152] The construction of the story constitutes the reactivation of the genetic relationship: the genealogy is constituted in a 'cultural' form.

A 'culture' is an associative system defined through pleasure and play: through leisure time in capitalist societies, through art, literature, and the festive in pre-industrial societies, and through the 'deep play' of ritual and festive practice in primitive societies. 'Cultural identity' (as though from a Latin word *identitas*, which would mean 'sameness') denotes any manifestation of communality produced by that system. It will be clear from this way of phrasing the matter that identity is to be conceived of as the *construction*, not the motivational inner force, of cultural praxis. As Miles argues, 'identities are produced, consumed and regulated within culture'.[153] Rather than seeking to establish how 'Greeks' related to 'Romans'—as if either of these two were an unproblematic category anchored in a secure ontology anterior to the texts—this book considers how the categories of 'Greek' and 'Roman' are both constructed (and deconstructed) through literature. Any self-arrogation of 'Greekness' should be seen as a creative, and in a sense 'fictive' move. Stuart Hall's definition of a nation as a 'system of cultural representation' is helpful here:

> The argument we will be considering here is that national identities are not things we are born with, but are formed and transformed within and in relation to *representation*. We only know what it is to be 'English' because of the way 'Englishness' has come to be represented, as a set of meanings, by English national culture. It follows that a nation is not only a political entity but something which produces meanings —a system of cultural representations.[154]

The ancient world, however, stood prior to the processes of nation-forming that sought to homogenize traditions, language, and culture from the eighteenth century onwards. To the extent that there was a *system* of representations of Greekness in the

[152] Curty (1995), 13–15; see also above, n. 110. Narrative had been central to Greek genealogy since the earliest times: see Fowler (1998).

[153] Miles (1999), 8.

[154] S. Hall (1992), 292.

Roman period, the magnetic pull of centripetal unification (most notably evidenced in Atticism and the archaizing tendency) was counterbalanced by centrifugal forces of diversity and contestation, not only in the matter of rivalries between cities (and *stasis*, or factional strife, within them), but also in intellectual disputes over the nature and valency of different aspects of the Greek tradition. All were agreed that there was an entity called Greece, inscribed by tradition; but there was little agreement what that entity was, or by what traditions it was constituted.

As we have seen, Greek *paideia* was intrinsically bound up with structures of power, those of both Roman imperialism and Greek civic politics. 'Culture', as I see it, is the medium that allows for this articulation of power: it is a flexible, dynamic social system, providing the structures that both enable and limit the construction of identity positions, as well as the creative resources which allow the subject to transcend apparent regulations and thus to recompose them as new structures.[155] Literary texts both employ the resources available in the form of the canon and seek to transform one's interpretation of the world by reconfiguring the conceptual frames which underlie prior literary work. Power is thus arrogated and usurped through literary self-representation: the imaginary worlds of literary space are none the less 'real' in terms of the effects they can have upon readers' and audiences' conceptual categories.

This is not to suggest that literature is the sole medium for the articulation of cultural identity: landscape,[156] art,[157] civic life (as traced through inscriptional records),[158] and architecture[159] were all crucial media, and a full account of identity politics in the period (if such a thing could exist) would have to take into account all of these, and no doubt more. This book has a more restricted aim: to explore, using selected examples, the modalities of

[155] This formulation owes much to Greenblatt (1990).

[156] Alcock (1993); the essays in Alcock ed. (1997), esp. Woolf and Rizakis; Petts (1998).

[157] Elsner (1995), 125–55; for the more extreme argument that art was a form of 'resistance' to Roman imperialism, see id. (1997*a*). See also Stewart (1999) on statuary and identity.

[158] I mention here only recent work dealing directly with the theme of identity: Rogers (1991), on processional culture at Ephesus; van Nijf (1997), primarily on civic identity; (1999) on athletic inscriptions and Hellenism; Hope (1998) on gladiatorial inscriptions.

[159] See esp. the essays in Walker and Cameron eds. (1989).

identity-construction that are specific to literary representation. I have sought to avoid generalizing in this matter: the types of identity-construction that occur in literature written in Greek are not necessarily the same as those that occur in other contexts. Nevertheless, a case can be made for the particularly central importance of literature as a means of constructing Greekness in the period: although *paideia* could comprehend musical, artistic, and athletic excellence, it was literature that occupied the primary focus of Roman Greek *pepaideumenoi*. And, as we shall see, it was through writing literature (and writing about writing literature, and rewriting literature intertextually) that Greek cultural identity was most richly and intensively explored.

Part One
The Politics of Imitation

1

Repetition: The Crisis of Posterity

'[T]he central problem for the latecomer necessarily is repetition' Harold Bloom[1]

'[T]he three Rs: repetition, repetition, repetition' Mark E. Smith, 'Repetition'

A SECONDARY SOCIETY

In 1964 Bernard van Groningen responded to an invitation to speak on the subject of 'General literary tendencies of the second century AD' at the fourth International Congress of Classical Studies in Philadelphia. His oration, subsequently published,[2] is one of the most hostile of the many attacks upon Greek literary culture under Roman rule, a blunt, historically insensitive, and occasionally incoherent diatribe against what he sees as 'an essentially weak literature'.[3] 'Reading the bulk of second-century literature,' he argues, '. . . one is not transported into a real world, but into [*sic*] a sham one, in a museum of fossils.'[4] The reason he suggests for this decadence is a 'weakening of the will',[5] caused by the supplanting of rationality by religion, and particularly by Roman conquest:

> Real art, real literature as well, cannot thrive unless in freedom. It is the achievement of independent, responsible minds . . . The Greek literature of the second century is the work of a powerless community . . . It [*?the literature?*] is a neglected one in a neglected century, and, generally speaking, it deserves this neglect.[6]

The idea that only a politically dominant community can produce worthwhile cultural products runs through this article: the only writer of Greek fully exonerated is Marcus Aurelius, a Roman emperor . . . Despite the imperialist presumptions and

[1] Bloom (1997), 80.
[2] Van Groningen (1965).
[3] Van Groningen (1965), 51.
[4] Van Groningen (1965), 52.
[5] Van Groningen (1965), 54.
[6] Van Groningen (1965), 55–6.

argumentative lapses of this article, however, it played an influential role in determining the course of studies of second-century Greek literature for a generation. In his highly influential monograph *Greek sophists in the Roman empire*, Glen Bowersock points the reader to the published form of van Groningen's address in his very first footnote in order to substantiate his claim that the 'literary quality' of the texts with which he is dealing is not worthy of consideration.[7] In recent years, of course, the tide of scholarly opinion has turned, and the texts are better appreciated as products of literary ingenuity and sophistication:[8] van Groningen's vitriol is seen as motivated by the misplaced high-handedness of an earlier period.[9]

This sea change in opinion has focused particularly upon a reassessment of Roman Greek literature's preoccupation with secondariness, mimeticism, and repetition in relation to earlier literature.[10] For van Groningen, the fact that 'this rhetorical literature . . . tends towards a repetition of former times' was one of the clearest indices of its fundamental 'weakness'.[11] The reassessment in recent times can be mapped out in terms of the changing responses to the phrase 'the Second Sophistic' (ἡ δευτέρη σοφιστική), often used (somewhat inappropriately, as we shall see) to identify the period of the first to third centuries CE or its literary culture. The phrase is first found in an early passage of Philostratus' third-century *Lives of the sophists* (481; see also 507), where the biographer applies it to a style of rhetorical performance in the persona[12] of historical figures founded by Aeschines (the Athenian orator of the fourth century BCE). Although Philostratus does concentrate upon Roman Greece (after Aeschines, the next figure chronologically is Nicetes of Smyrna, in the time of Nero: *VS* 511), it is clear that for him the phrase denotes a literary style cultivated particularly (but not exclusively) in the Roman period, not the Roman period itself.

[7] Bowersock (1969), 1 n. 1.

[8] e.g. esp. R. Hunter (1983); Branham (1989); Zeitlin (1990*a*); Goldhill (1995).

[9] e.g. Gleason (1995), xviii–xix.

[10] In this respect, scholarly treatment of the literature of Roman Greece is merely an intensified case of the general pattern whereby pre-4th-cent. Greece is viewed as 'primary' and everything later 'secondary': see e.g. Feeney (1998), 57–60.

[11] e.g. van Groningen (1965), 49.

[12] I interpret τὰς ἐς ὄνομα ὑποθέσεις (Philostr. *VS* 488) as meaning 'performances *in persona*', not 'definite and special themes' (Wright 1921: ad loc.): for εἰς ὄνομα meaning 'in the name of', see LSJ suppl. s.v. ὄνομα.

Modern scholarship, however, has appropriated the phrase as a periodization. When Erwin Rohde, in the nineteenth century, inaugurated the modern interest in the *zweite Sophistik*, he employed the label to refer to a putative rise in 'Asianic' rhetoric until the middle of the second century, when (he argued) Atticism took over.[13] The great debate among nineteenth-century German *doctissimi* focused primarily upon the question of whether the rise in display oratory in the first and second centuries was an Asianizing or Atticizing phenomenon;[14] and the debate was foreclosed by Wilamowitz's assertion that there was no such thing in reality as a *zweite Sophistik*.[15] More recently, however, the term has been applied even more loosely, with reference to the entire literary culture of that period of Greek history. The modern use of the phrase 'the Second Sophistic' is, thus, not consonant with Philostratus' use. There is nothing inherently wrong with this, but we should at least be aware that 'the Second Sophistic' is a construction of modern scholarship, formed under the disciplinary influences of the modern academy, and in no sense simply a translucent window onto the 'real' practices of the ancient world. Such heuristic fictions are both enabling devices, indispensable to historical research, and constraints, closing off avenues of research and occluding important questions: it is crucial to interrogate their validity.[16]

The notion of the 'Second Sophistic' has defined the scope of research into the Greek East under imperial occupation in a number of ways.[17] First, the application of a literary-generic term to a historical period has facilitated the association of Greeks with 'culture' in opposition to Roman 'power', discussed in my Introduction. (No one would consider naming the 'Augustan age' the 'elegiac period'.) Secondly, and more significantly for current

[13] E. Rohde (1914), 310–87 (1st edn. pub. in 1876). The problem Rohde set himself was how to reconcile Philostratus' account in the *Lives of the sophists* with Dionysius' account of the recent victory of Atticism over Asianism (*De uet. or.* 1).

[14] Kaibel (1885); E. Rohde (1886); Schmid (1887–96); Norden (1898), 351–4; Wilamowitz (1900); (1925), 126–7.

[15] Wilamowitz (1925), followed by Brunt (1994), rejects the notion of a 'Second Sophistic', arguing that the evidence for a rise in declamatory sophistry in the period is insubstantial. That is as may be, but sophistry was certainly valorized with a new intensity.

[16] Morris (1996), 96–7.

[17] For further discussions of aspects of the reception of the 'Second Sophistic', see C. P. Jones (1986), 1–5; Holzberg (1988); Gleason (1995), xvii-xx.

purposes, the terms 'second' and 'sophistic' often convey a distaste for a literature, and indeed an entire society, that is supposedly unoriginal and trivial. This has been the case since the rebirth of the phrase in the nineteenth century,[18] and has persisted in some quarters. It can be a short step from the 'Second Sophistic' to van Groningen's shrill jeremiad denouncing the 'sham', 'weak' 'repetition' of Roman Greek literary culture (though, in fact, he does not use the phrase 'Second Sophistic').

More recently, however, certain critics have sought vigorously to rescue the notion of 'secondary sophistry' by allying it more or less explicitly to a textualist poetics, whereby 'lateness' comports a laudably self-conscious appreciation of the literariness and intertextuality of writing. The 'Second Sophistic' is sometimes reaffirmed as a period of literary growth, where 'sophistic' denotes sophistication and 'second' a deoriginated, deauthorized form of literary *jouissance*. Froma Zeitlin, in her (brilliant) analysis of *Daphnis and Chloë*, having sited the text explicitly in the 'Second Sophistic',[19] writes that 'belatedness is the factor that not only allows a far-ranging surveillance over the whole domain [of Greek literary tradition] but encourages (and promotes) a self-conscious stance toward what it sees and knows.'[20] 'Belatedness', however, is a relative rather than an absolute marker. The literary trope of epigonality is prominent in Hellenistic poetics, but is found in the Classical period too (and, arguably, even in Homer).[21] In this refined sense of the word, *Daphnis and Chloë* is not necessarily 'later' (i.e. more conscious of its epigonality) than Callimachus' *Aetia*, or for that matter Aeschylus' *Oresteia*. But Zeitlin seems to imply that self-consciousness follows from *historical* posterity. The suggestion that *Daphnis and Chloë* is self-conscious because written at a late date underplays the rhetoric of 'coming after', which is not a historical marker but a means of negotiating a place in literary tradition. More pertinently to my present argument, it

[18] e.g. E. Rohde (1914), 323. Some representatives of German *Altertumswissenschaft* were so keen to deny originality to the literature of Roman Greece that they invented lost sources from which later writers were supposed to have plagiarized (e.g. Helm 1906: see C. P. Jones 1986, 3–4).

[19] Zeitlin (1990*a*), 417.

[20] Zeitlin (1990*a*), 420.

[21] On 'belatedness' in Hellenistic poetics, see esp. Bing (1988); Goldhill (1991), 284–6; R. Hunter (1993), esp. 101–29, and (1996), *passim*, esp. 1–13. For the 'belated' topos in the Classical period, see esp. Choerilus at *SH* 317 and Astydamas at *FGE* 33–4. On 'belatedness' in Homer, see Ford (1992), *passim*, esp. 138–68.

also 'naturalizes' the view that Roman Greece was an 'unoriginal', second-order culture, even if it is combined with a more positive (and, indeed, subtle) interpretation of this secondariness.

Broadly, this positive reassessment of the term 'Second Sophistic' reflects the change in critical priorities that has emerged in the last one hundred or so years. Whereas the dominant critical voice before the 1960s was still largely conditioned by Romanticism's preoccupation with the sincerity and sublimity of the 'original', the rise of postmodernism has entailed a new appreciation of icons, simulacra, and copies. As Johnston expresses it, postmodernism (in contrast to Platonism's idea of the copy as an inferior shadow of the original) 'implies a series without a founding original or true version . . . since there is no original, the model for the copy is itself a copy, and the copy is the copy of a copy'.[22] The new-found appreciation of a supposedly 'textualist' culture, advertising a self-consciously secondary relationship with the literature of an early period, is clearly inspired by the changed priorities of literary criticism. (Indeed, it is interesting to note a postmodern theorist proclaiming the contemporary advent of the 'third sophistic'!)[23]

When presented in such stark terms (and I have not done justice to the keen sensitivity of some of the literary critics I have cited), the inappropriateness of anachronistic responses to 'secondariness' becomes clearly visible. It is not possible for scholarship to transcend the priorities of the time and milieu in which it is undertaken, but it is possible to provide a more nuanced and detailed analysis of a phenomenon that has in general been treated in too monolithic a manner. The central problem with the notion of the 'Second Sophistic' lies in its posited unitariness, and the concomitant implication that there was a single, uncontested way of constructing the relationship between past and present. In fact, Roman Greek literary culture neither uniformly aimed to repeat the past, nor always sought to transform it. In fact, as we shall see, there was a range of responses to the traditional canon, and these mapped out a variety of different conceptions of Greek identity, from exclusivist, traditional autochthonism to a more inclusive modernism.

[22] Johnston (1990), 21. [23] Vitanza (1997).

REPETITION AND *MIMĒSIS*

This chapter explores the role of literary repetition and imitation in the (plural) constructions of Greek cultural identity in Roman Greece. In literary theory, such ideas cluster around the concept of *mimēsis* ('imitation'), a notion that is absolutely central to the Greek literature of the principate.[24] Because of the centrality of imitation to post-Classical ancient writing, scholars have been alert to the need for aesthetic relativism when dealing with literature from this period. DuQuesnay writes of Virgil's *Eclogues* that

> To call these poems imitations is not to deny Virgil originality . . . All our post-Romantic notions and ways of thinking about the relationship between a Roman writer and his model must be discarded . . . Literature is what literature is agreed to be at any time in any culture and if we wish to read any literature but our own we must learn the appropriate conventions . . .[25]

It is undeniable that a post-Romantic excoriation of Virgil's lack of 'originality' in the *Eclogues* would be misplaced. It does not follow, however, that imitation was naturalized and formalized into a set of clearly defined 'appropriate conventions'. Ever since the time of Plato, the nature and value of artistic *mimēsis* was subject to ongoing dispute.[26] In particular, *mimēsis* raises profound questions about the nature of reality, and about the degree to which an imitation partakes thereof.[27] For Plato's Socrates, *mimēsis* is a deceptive, artificial phenomenon;[28] for Aristotle, replying to Plato, it is a 'natural' feature of human development.[29] 'Art' is thus (for Aristotle) not opposed to nature, but an extension

[24] Bompaire (1958), 21–32; Reardon (1971), 7–11; Flashar (1978), Russell (1979); G. Kennedy (1994), 231; T. Morgan (1998), 241–2. See also A. N. Cizek (1994), esp. 1–116, although the synchronic approach makes for a relative lack of focus.

[25] DuQuesnay (1979), 37; cf. Bompaire (1958), 8.

[26] Prendergast (1986), 1–82.

[27] A. N. Cizek (1994), 69–71 (though somewhat superficial).

[28] According to Socrates, the particulars in the world around us are merely mimetic versions of the 'ideas' (or 'forms'); while literary and artistic representations, being imitations of imitations, are one further step away from 'reality', and appeal to the emotions rather than to truth-seeking reason. See Pl. *Resp.* 602d–603c; 605a–c.

[29] Aristotle claims that *mimēsis* is a 'natural' part of human development from earliest youth (*Poet.* 1448[b]), and that the pleasure inspired by mimetic art is valid and intelligent (*Rhet.* 1370[a]). See below, pp. 51–2.

thereof.[30] In an aesthetic system predicated upon the idea of imitating canonical models, such philosophical questions have more than mere interest value: they raise questions about the entire culture-defining role of literary *mimēsis*. Does mimetic writing join the contemporary Greek world seamlessly, 'naturally', to its past by means of the agglutinative continuity of traditions? But imitation necessarily enforces an awareness of *difference* and discontinuity: citation is an act of reframing, and thus also of remaking, meaning.[31] How different—indeed, in a sense, how 'fake'—are Roman Greece's attempts to revitalize the past? The point is not simply that Roman Greek authors are divided (which they are) on the question of whether the literature of the present can match that of the past for quality.[32] There is a more deep-seated problematization: any imitation of a paradigm necessarily marks the difference between past and present at the same time as it proclaims the sameness. Or, to put the matter in a way that brings out more strongly the relevance to cultural identity: the *assertion* of continuity with the past indicates (by simultaneously asserting the *need* to assert) the presence of discontinuity.

RESCUING *MIMĒSIS*

Let us turn to one of the most powerful and influential theorizations of *mimēsis*. Plato's critique of mimetic art in the tenth book of the *Republic* represents, potentially, a devastating indictment of Roman Greek literary culture.[33] If the experiential world is at one

[30] The presence of this doctrine in ps.-Longinus *On the sublime* is argued for by Segal (1959), 122–3 and Walsh (1988), 264 n. 47.

[31] This point is nicely made by Derrida (1982), 320–1: thanks to citation, a linguistic sign 'can break with every given context, and engender infinitely new contexts in an absolutely nonsaturable fashion'.

[32] e.g. Arrian presents his *On hunting with dogs* as a more sophisticated updating of Xenophon's (if in fact it is Xenophon's) original: see Stadter (1980), 59; and compare Herodes Atticus' claim to superiority over Antiphon at Philostr. *VS* 564. Sometimes, however, the literature of the past is presented as insurpassably superior to that of the present: the unnamed philosopher at ps.-Long. *De subl.* 44, for example, blames the supposed decline of literature on changes in political structure; on this passage, see below, pp. 66–8. Generally on the ambivalent relationship between past and present, see the excellent account of Schmitz (1997), 220–31. Laments of declining literary standards are equally intense in the Roman literature of the principate, equally troubled by the sense of imitative posterity: see Vell. Pat. 1.17.6–7; Sen. *Controu.* 1.6–10; Tac. *Dial.* 1.

[33] Pl. *Resp.* 602d–603e; 605a–c. For Aristotle's reply, see *Poet.* 1448[b]; *Rhet.* 1370[a] and below, pp 51–2. On Platonic and Aristotelian *mimēsis*, see esp. Vernant,

remove from the reality of the forms, then art is at two removes, and art that imitates art is at three removes. It is this Platonic notion of a mimetic 'chain' that motivates van Groningen's criticisms of second-century literature as 'sham'. Although this latter view can be challenged easily enough (the unstated assumption being that Classical literature simply imitates 'reality': this neglects the pronounced intertextual relationship of, for example, tragedy with the Homeric texts), the original-copy model still presents a fundamental challenge to a literary culture based around this idea of repetition.

It has sometimes been held that the Platonic, ontological conception of *mimēsis* has little to do with its later sense as 'imitation of literary models'.[34] On this interpretation, the *imitation créative* practised by Roman Greek writers would carry no connotations of ontological anxiety, of a crisis concerning the nature and status of 'the real'. As Russell observes, however, such a nice distinction between two meanings of the term *mimēsis* is unlikely to have obtained in practice: 'once these terms [i.e. *mimēsis* and its cognates] had been used [by philosophers] in an attempt to explain what in general poetry does and is, their later literary usage could not fail to be affected by the associations they had thus acquired'.[35] Indeed, as we shall see in the course of this chapter, Plato's canonical account is answered by 'philosophical' and 'rhetorical' writers alike, each group equally concerned to explore the claim that the 'secondary' literary culture of Roman Greece can stake to 'reality'.

The most vigorous response to Plato was provided by Plutarch of Chaironeia, one of the most important and influential Greek writers of the early empire.[36] Plutarch's life spanned the period from the early 40s to just after 120, and most of his writings seem to have been composed under the emperors Trajan (98–117)

'The birth of images', in Vernant (1991), 164–85; Ferrari (1989), 108–41; Halliwell (1989), 151–64; also Sörbom (1966) for a speculative archaeology of the term.

[34] Some scholars (e.g. Bompaire 1958; Reardon 1971; following Stemplinger 1913) insist upon a distinction between 'philosophical' and 'rhetorical' theories of *mimēsis*, between what Germans call *Darstellung* (representation) and *Nachahmung* (literary imitation). 'Philosophical' *mimēsis* is the 'imitation' of reality, as discussed by Plato; 'rhetorical' *mimēsis* is the imitation of literary paradigms.

[35] Russell (1979), 4.

[36] On Plutarch's influence on subsequent literature, see Hirzel (1912), 74–206; Russell (1972), 143–58; Boulogne (1994), 17–22.

and Hadrian (117–38).[37] He was a Roman citizen (L. Mestrius Plutarchus),[38] familiar with many Romans (some of whom are addressees of his works),[39] and even perhaps an acquaintance of emperors.[40] Plutarch's moral essays (grouped together in the medieval period under the Latin title *Moralia*, or *Moral essays*) are of central interest to any discussion of *paideia* under the early principate; and of particular importance are his three explicitly educative essays, *On the education of children* (henceforth *Education*), which is not usually attributed to Plutarch himself,[41] *On listening to lectures*,[42] and *How a young man should listen to poetry* (henceforth *Poetry*). It is the last of these three essays that provides the most thoroughgoing revision of the Platonic position.

Plutarch's primary interest lies in ethics:[43] debates concerning the validity of *mimēsis* are fought out over the terrain of the soul. *Poetry* is addressed by Plutarch to a specific individual (a certain Marcus Sedatus, in respect of whose son Cleander, a coeval of Plutarch's son Soclarus, the essay is presented). It deals with the lures of poetry, which the author defines as a 'mimetic art and power' (μιμητικὴ τέχνη καὶ δύναμις, *Poetry* 17f), and the potential threats posed by poetry to the education of Cleander and Soclarus. Although the discussion is characteristically ethical (and constructed as a private missive from one man to his friend), Plutarch's discussion is inspired by and deeply concerned with larger questions of social propriety and cultural definition. In

37 For biographical information on Plutarch, see Ziegler (1949), 4–60; C. P. Jones (1971), 3–38; Russell (1972), 1–17; Swain (1996), 134–7. On the chronology of his works, see C. P. Jones (1966).

38 *SIG* 829a.

39 For a prosopography of Plutarch's Roman friends, see Puech (1992), building on Ziegler (1949), 30–60.

40 On the vexed issue of Plutarch's acquaintance with Hadrian, see most recently Bowie (1997). The late notice that Plutarch received from Trajan the highest imperial award available to non-senators, the *ornamenta consularia,* as well as an honorific procuratorship of Achaea (*Suda, Π* 1793) results no doubt from later antiquity's embellishment of the tradition of Trajan's 'philhellenism', but also shows that ancient writers at any rate considered Plutarch to have combined Greek *paideia* with shrewd interaction with Roman potentates. C. P. Jones (1971), 29 accepts this information, but see the important objections of Babut (1975), 207 and the caution of Swain (1996), 171–2. I revoke the slender credence granted to the *Suda*'s account at Whitmarsh (1998*a*), 202.

41 See e.g. Berry (1958), 387–8; Ziegler (1949), 174–5. For a history of the debate, see Albini (1997), 69 n. 2. The question of the authorship of this essay is not of great importance to the current discussion.

42 For commentary, see Hillyard (1981).

43 See Swain (1999); Duff (1999), 53–71, with further references.

attacking Plato's *Republic* directly,[44] Plutarch (whose works in general manifest an enduring engagement with those of Plato)[45] raises and explores the question of the ideal city. In the *Republic*, Socrates 'expels' (ἀπεστέλλομεν, *Resp.* 607b; cf. ἀποπέμποιμεν, 398a) all mimetic art from his *polis*, on the grounds that it is ontologically inaccurate and thus a corrupting influence (*Resp.* 602d–603e; 605a–c); Plutarch counters that we should not 'drive out' (παρεξελαύνειν) poetry, but instil in the young a 'faculty of discernment' (κρίσις)[46] that will allow them to realize for themselves its ontological limitations (*Poetry* 15d). That the essay presents itself as an inversion of the *Republic* is most clearly indicated by a powerful image near the end: if used correctly, he argues, poetry is a form of *propaideia* ('primary education')[47] in philosophy (*Poetry* 37b; cf. 15f) that allows its subjects to familiarize themselves with a 'bastard light' before confronting the dazzling sun of philosophy (36e). This image clearly evokes Plato's celebrated cave simile in the *Republic* (515e), with the important modification that, according to Plutarch, mimetic art aids the subject to see the light rather than being intrinsically connected with the deception reflections inside the cave. For all such reasons, Plutarch implies, Plato was wrong to see *mimēsis* as detrimental to the well-being of the ideal city. The crucial point for the present argument, however, is that the ethical exploration of the effects of poetry upon the soul is inseparable from the social question of whether it is right or wrong for a society to practise *mimēsis*.

Plutarch's more favourable (relative to Plato) view of *mimēsis* is partly the result of his philosophical conviction that the soul is

[44] Though Plutarch may also attack Stoic targets, among them Chrysippus, who also wrote an essay (now lost) on *How a young man should listen to poetry* (known from Diog. Laert. 7.200). See Ziegler (1949), 170.

[45] On the subject of Plutarch's Platonism, R. M. Jones (1916) and Dörrie (1971) focus primarily upon metaphysics; the best general account is Dillon (1977), 184–230. He was not simply a Platonist, however: on his eclecticism, see Russell (1972), 63–83; and on his Stoicism, Babut (1969).

[46] On κρίσις ('discernment', 'discrimination') in ancient literary criticism (though not in *Poetry*) see Too (1998), e.g. pp. 9–10, 131, 206 (though overplaying the universality of the social/ideological slant of the term).

[47] Recalling Plato's assertion that arithmetic and geometry are a *propaideia* to dialectic in the education of philosopher-kings (*Resp.* 536d). Longus may echo Plutarch's formulation of the role of poetry when he offers *Daphnis and Chloë* as a *propaideia* for those inexperienced in love (*D&C praef.* 3; retaining προπαιδεύσει, as in the Budé and Teubner editions, against the less attractive παιδεύσει printed in the Loeb).

'naturally' (φύσει) dual, that emotion and the irrational are as inherent as reason and logic and thus cannot be expunged.[48] Accordingly, mimetic poetry, as an 'emotional' literary experience, should not (or could not) be banned, only controlled so as to serve the higher end of rationality. *Paideia* necessarily proceeds via the emotions, as Plutarch writes elsewhere (*On moral virtue* 452c–d), and the case of poetry shows that it is possible to find 'utility in what gives pleasure' (ἐν τῶι τέρποντι τὸ χρήσιμον, *Poetry* 15f).[49] Poetic pleasure is thus an intrinsic part of human experience, and although it can be dangerous if given free rein (*Poetry* 16d, 31c), proper instruction can render it harmless (28d). This 'naturalizing' of poetry, *mimēsis*, and the irrational is central to Plutarch's thought, as we shall see.

Plato's criticism of poetry is that it aims at emotional gratification through *mimēsis* of the untrue, rather than at philosophical truth. In order to counter this charge, Plutarch seeks to show that a full pedagogy should teach the student to discern for himself what is advantageous and what deleterious in poetry (*Poetry* 15d). This involves teaching a number of skills. First, the student must recognize that poetry is a mimetic art (17f), and that its power comes from its ability to replicate what it imitates. Thus good art can imitate bad things: its excellence lies in its *homoiotēs* ('likeness', 18a), not in what it represents (18a–d). This position owes much to Aristotle, who writes in the *Rhetoric* that the pleasure that derives from viewing mimetic art derives not from the object itself but from the cognitive process of 'comparison' (συλλογισμός) of original to copy (*Rhet.* 1370ᵃ); thus, as he writes in the *Poetics*, we can take pleasure from beholding representations of ugly things, for when we observe pictures of low animals and corpses, we can 'learn by comparison' (μανθάνειν καὶ συλλογίζεσθαι) what each thing is (*Poet.* 1448ᵇ). A mimetic representation of something bad, for Aristotle, does not necessarily encourage the individual to imitate that thing mechanically: we learn through *mimēsis*. Indeed, it is through *mimēsis* that we achieve our first understandings (μαθήσεις) of the world, and it is humans' exceptionally advanced mimetic

[48] *De uirt. mor.* 441d; 443b–c.

[49] Plutarch here evokes a polarity fundamental to ancient literary criticism, that of pleasure and profit. The opposition goes back to Thucydides (1.22.4), but is particularly developed in Hellenistic poetics: see Philodem. *Poet.* 5.3.23–7.16; 5.13.4–28, criticizing Neoptolemus of Parium; Strab. 1.2.3–9; Hor. *Ars poet.* 334, 343.

ability that distinguishes them from animals (*Poet.* 1448[b]). Aristotle's emphasis upon the naturalness of human *mimēsis*[50] and upon its educational utility provides Plutarch with an authoritative precedent in resisting the Platonic argument that *mimēsis* should be banned from the city.

The argument that mimetic poetry can be good even if it represents bad people constitutes an implicit correction of Plato's argument that the ideal *paideia* would involve no stories of moral turpitude (*Resp.* 377d–380c). Plutarch argues that, on the contrary, the student must learn not only what he is to imitate, but also what he is to avoid. Poetry does not present perfect people—it is an 'imitation of characters and lives' (μίμησιν . . . ἠθῶν καὶ βίων, *Poetry* 26a) and thus represents bad as well as good. It is imperative that the student learn that poetry does not represent only exempla for imitation, but a range of 'characters' (ἤθεσι, 18f). Learning to read properly (i.e. ethically), for Plutarch, means learning to read the poet's *emphaseis* ('insinuations') about the ethical quality of the character in question (19a). The word *emphasis* belongs to rhetorical theory, referring to the orator's nudges and winks that, for a knowing audience, 'creates a different meaning than that literally proposed by the words'.[51] *Mimēsis* is only dangerous, Plutarch suggests, in a city that has not learned sophisticated reading habits. The implication is that a highly developed interpretative culture (like that of elite Roman Greece) will not encounter the problems with *mimēsis* that Plato foresaw.[52]

Still more interpretative ingenuity is required in relation to the gods. Plato's critique of Homer focuses primarily (though not exclusively) upon the poet's representation of divine error: the gods, he asserts, should be perfect.[53] Plutarch is no more willing than Plato to tolerate the idea that gods might do wrong; but, once

[50] See also above, n. 33.

[51] *altiorem praebens intellectum quam quem uerba per se ipsa declarant* (Quint. *Inst. or.* 8.3.83); see also 9.2.64; Demetr. *De eloc.* 130; Ahl (1984), 176–9.

[52] Less sophisticated, at least in the eyes of a modern readership, is Plutarch's subsequent argument that ethically incorrect statements should always be 'balanced' (ἀνταναφέρειν, 20c) with ethically correct statements expressed elsewhere by the same writer, or, if necessary, by another (20c–22a). Plutarch's technique of 'balancing' poetic utterances, however, was influential upon Proclus' allegorical technique: see Lamberton (1986), 184–5.

[53] Pl. *Resp.* 377e–378a, an influential criticism of Homer: see e.g. Heraclit. *Quaest. Hom.* 1 ('If he composed none of it allegorically, then he was thoroughly irreligious': πάντα . . . ἠσέβησεν εἰ μηδὲν ἠλληγόρησεν); ps.-Long. *De subl.* 9.7–8. See further Lamberton (1986), 16–19.

again, sophisticated reading practices come to his rescue. The gods' names, he argues, do not always refer to the divine beings themselves, since at times they refer metaphorically to abstractions (23a–24c).[54] Thus 'Zeus' sometimes refers to the god, sometimes to 'fate': glossing Homer's sentence 'the will of Zeus was completed' (*Διὸς δ' ἐτελείετο βουλή*, *Il.* 1.5), Plutarch argues that it was not the god who contrived such sufferings as the Trojan war brought, but 'the necessary course of affairs' (*τὴν τῶν πραγμάτων ἀνάγκην*, 23d). To an unsympathetic eye, Plutarch's ethical priorities have led him to a circular argument: if Zeus acts morally, then he is Zeus, but if he acts immorally, then he is fate. Yet Plutarch is at pains to stress that such interpretation is born not of the will of the reader, but of her or his sensitivity to Homer's use of 'words' (*ὀνόματα*, 24c, 24f). The semantic meaning of words also changes over time, another aspect likely to trip up the naïve reader (24d).[55] In other words, Plutarch strives to show (as always, against Plato) that *mimēsis* can be rescued as a socially useful practice, so long as that society inculcates sophisticated interpretative strategies.

In what follows, Plutarch further underscores the message that reading practice is all. 'We must pay careful attention to the other words, too' (*σφόδρα . . . δεῖ καὶ τοῖς ἄλλοις ὀνόμασι προσέχειν*, 24c). Terms such as 'virtue' (*ἀρέτη*) and 'vice' (*κακία*) are used in all sorts of extended senses by the poets (24c); if one does not recognize 'the metaphorical and catachrestic uses of words' (*ταῖς μεταφόροις καὶ καταχρήσεσι τῶν ὀνομάτων*, 25b), one is likely to be deeply confused. Indeed, even textual emendation, as (supposedly) practised by Cleanthes and Zeno (33b–d),[56] is proposed as a corrective to insalubrious moral implications in literature. Given this, it may be surprising to learn that Plutarch considers there to be any limits to the interpretative ingenuity one might apply to maintain the ethical status of texts. 'Allegorical' exegetes, however, are said to be guilty of 'violent distortion' (*παραβιαζόμενοι*) and 'twisting' (*διαστρέφοντες*) the meaning of texts (19e–f),[57] and

[54] Elemental interpretations of the gods begin with Empedocles (see KRS 286), and reach their peak with the complex theories of Proclus: see Lamberton (1986), 218 with n. 226.

[55] Russell (1989), 303 notes the particular sophistication of this point.

[56] So far as it is possible to judge, it seems that Plutarch is right about the moral tenor of Hellenistic scholarship: see Too (1998), 145–8.

[57] In decrying allegorical interpretation, Plutarch follows the lead of Plato's Socrates: see Pl. *Resp.* 378d–e, with Too (1998), 140–3.

Cleanthes of 'forcing' (παραβιαζόμενος) interpretations of the text (31e).

Although *Poetry* is, at the explicit level at any rate, a primarily ethical tract orientated towards the souls of Cleander and Soclarus, it also sends out a powerful message about the social role of *mimēsis* and the cultural positioning of Roman Greece. In rejecting Plato's view that mimetic art should be 'expelled' from the city, Plutarch asserts that it plays a creative and positive role in society, so long as that society has deep resources of literary exegesis. Imitation is safe if sophisticated hermeneutic techniques can recoup its moral function. Implicitly, Plutarch constructs an imaginary, idealized pedagogical community possessed of such interpretative skills in the Roman Greek present.

Indeed, the theory that *mimēsis* might be of positive benefit to the state is enacted in Plutarch's biographical works. The *Parallel lives* (paired biographies of famous Greeks and Romans), like the *Moral essays*, take a primarily ethical approach to their subject-matter.[58] In a famous passage, Plutarch comments that 'I am not writing *Histories* but *Lives*',[59] proceeding to gloss the distinction with the comment that battles, sieges, and so forth do not provide such an 'impression of the character (*ēthos*)' as a brief event, a bon mot, or a joke.[60] History is about politics and warfare, but 'Lives' are about ethics.[61] Plutarch's interest is thus not so much in referential description as in the construction of an ethical subjectivity that is designed to improve and educate the reader.[62] This

[58] See e.g. Pelling (1990) on Plutarch's readiness to sacrifice historical accuracy for the sake of ethical point.

[59] οὔτε ἱστορίας γράφομεν ἀλλὰ βίους (Plut. *Alex.* 1.2).

[60] ἔμφασιν ἤθους (*Alex.* 1.2). On this passage, see esp. Desideri (1995*a*); Duff (1999), 14–22, against the 'formula biografica' reading; cf. also *De fort. Alex.* 330e; *Lyc.* 20.10; *Pomp.* 8.7; *Dem.* 11.7. Plutarch's words modify the language of theories of encomium: Men. Rhet. 372.5 Russell and Wilson writes that panegyric should produce an 'impression of the character' (ἤθους ἔμφασιν); while Julian, in an encomium of Constantius, writes of 'deeds' (πράξεις) as 'tokens of the virtues of the soul' (γνωρίσματα τῶν τῆς ψυχῆς ἀρετῶν, *Or.* 1.4d), just as Plutarch writes of the events he describes as 'signs of the soul' (τὰ τῆς ψυχῆς σημεῖα, *Alex.* 1.3). The theme of 'character' in the *Lives* has received considerable attention in recent years: see esp. Russell (1966), 144–7; Brenk (1977), 176–83; Gill (1983); Pelling (1988); Swain (1989*a*).

[61] On the development of the genre of the *bios*, see esp. Momigliano (1993), against the 'Peripatetic theory' of Leo (1901) and Dihle (1956).

[62] On the *Lives* as ethical paradigms for the reader, see also *Per.* 1–2; *Demetr.* 1; Frazier (1992), 4489–91. See also *Quomodo quis suos in virt.* 84d–e. The paradigmatic status of the subject is a fundamental issue for all historiography (Stierle

theme is most clearly articulated in the preface to the *Life* of Aemilius Paulus.[63] Plutarch's role here oscillates between that of writer and that of reader: his texts, we read, have enabled him to improve himself by 'selecting from the subject's deeds which are the most impressive and noble to know . . . What could be a more vigorous corrective of characters (*ētheōn*)?' (τὰ κυριώτατα καὶ κάλλιστα πρὸς γνῶσιν ἀπὸ τῶν πράξεων λαμβάνοντες . . . τί . . . πρὸς ἐπανόρθωσιν ἠθῶν ἐνεργότερον; *Aem. Paul.* 1.2–4). The notion of 'selecting' is important, for it implies an active, discriminatory role for the reader in relation to the subject-matter, a feature shared with *Poetry*:[64] the precondition for ethical improvement is the interaction of edifying material and a keen, critical intelligence. As in the essay on listening to poets, he sees the primary pedagogical virtue of mimetic characterization as lying in the inculcation of the ability to discern between the representation of good and that of bad:

Thanks to the study of history, and the familiarity with it which my writing produces, I make myself capable of receiving in my soul the memories of the very best and most estimable men, and of driving away and pushing aside anything base, malicious or ignoble enforced upon me by my associations with those who meet me, turning my thoughts calmly and gently to the most noble paradigms.

ἡμεῖς δὲ τῆι περὶ τὴν ἱστορίαν διατριβῆι καὶ τῆς γραφῆς τῆι συνηθείαι παρασκευάζομεν ἑαυτούς, τὰς τῶν ἀρίστων καὶ δοκιμωτάτων μνήμας ὑποδεχομένους ἀεὶ ταῖς ψυχαῖς, εἴ τι φαῦλον ἢ κακόηθες ἢ ἀγεννὲς αἱ τῶν συνόντων ἐξ ἀνάγκης ὁμιλίαι προσβάλλουσιν, ἐκκρούειν καὶ διωθεῖσθαι, πρὸς τὰ κάλλιστα τῶν παραδειγμάτων ἵλεω καὶ πραεῖαν ἀποστρέφοντες τὴν διάνοιαν. (*Aem. Paul.* 1.2).

This passage is subtle in its celebration of *mimēsis*. Life and literature are thoroughly interpermeated, and the subjects of his narratives are discussed as though they had an actual physical presence: he 'receives' (ὑποδεχομένους) good exemplars into his soul, and rejects anything bad 'enforced upon me by my associa-

1972), and issues concerning exemplarity are raised in literature throughout the Middle Ages and Renaissance (Delcorno 1989, who, however, neglects the important Classical heritage of such ideas). On the paradigmatic tradition in general, see the stimulating remarks of Goldhill (1994).

[63] I follow the MSS and Ziegler in attributing this preface to the *Aemilius*, not the *Timoleon*. For fuller discussion of this passage, see Desideri (1989), 212–13 (though somewhat blinkered by his argument about Plutarch's demonology); Duff (1999), 30–4.

[64] Desideri (1989), 202.

tions with those who meet me' (αἱ τῶν συνόντων ἐξ ἀνάγκης ὁμιλίαι). Plutarch seems to stray dangerously (from a Platonic perspective) close to confusing mimetic representation with reality. Earlier, Plutarch has written of himself and his subjects as resembling 'spending time together and living together (*symbiōsei*)' (συνδιαιτήσει καὶ συμβιώσει, *Aem. Paul.* 1.1). The use of the word *symbiōsis* ('living together') is significant, because it activates the pun upon the dual meaning of the Greek word *bios*: both 'life' and the *Life* that Plutarch composes.[65] 'I first began writing my *Lives* (*bioi*) for the sake of others' (ἐμοὶ τῆς τῶν βίων ἅψασθαι μὲν γραφῆς συνέβη δι' ἑτέρους, *Aem. Paul.* 1.1), he writes, but he soon found that he persisted for his own sake, too: 'I strove, as it were, to adorn my life (*bion*) with and assimilate it to the virtues of my subjects, as though in a mirror' (ὥσπερ ἐν ἐσόπτρωι τῆι ἱστορίαι πειρώμενον ἁμῶς γέ πως κοσμεῖν καὶ ἀφομοιοῦν πρὸς τὰς ἐκείνων ἀρετὰς τὸν βίον, *Aem. Paul.* 1.2). Plutarch's writing constitutes a hinge connecting signifier to signified, *mimēsis* to subject, *Life* to life. No sense here that textual imitation is a pale shadow of reality: 'literature', for Plutarch, is as animate as 'life'. As ever with Plutarch, however, the critical role of the reader is paramount: he needed to 'strive' (πειρώμενον) in order to effect this harmonious union of textuality and reality. In this connection, the mirror is an ingenious metaphor. Not only does a mirror passively reflect 'reality' (and so Plutarch claims mimetic fidelity for his own work),[66] but also it actively confronts the viewer with an image of her- or himself, providing a stimulus for self-correction.[67] Plutarch's *Lives* demand an engaged, discriminatory, critical response. As recent commentators have stressed, his biographical works present not so much a rule-book for behaviour as a crucible in which moral complexities might be explored, leaving the final assessment to us.[68] Plutarchan *mimēsis* presupposes an

[65] Duff (1999), 33, with n. 58 for similar ambiguities at *Demetr.* 1.5–7 and *Tim.* 15.11.

[66] Duff (1999), 33–4, with references to other 'mirror' imagery signalling accurate *mimēsis* (add Arist. *Rhet.* 1406^{b} for Alcidamas' description of the *Odyssey* as 'a fine mirror of human life', καλὸν ἀνθρωπίνου βίου κάτοπτρον).

[67] A similar specular image is used in the *Education* of a father providing a paradigm for imitation to his son (14a); cf. *Quomodo quis suos in uirt.* 85a–b.

[68] Pelling (1995) distinguishes between Plutarch's 'protreptic moralism', i.e. moralism that seeks to guide the reader in a certain direction, and his 'descriptive moralism', which explores moral complexities in practice. Duff (1999) generalizes the model of 'descriptive moralism': see esp. p. 69.

intelligent reader capable of making informed and independent judgements.

Plutarch's repudiation of Platonic views of *mimēsis*, then, is founded upon his confidence in the acuity and sophistication of contemporary reading practice. The readmission of mimetic art to the ideal society is premised upon a sense of satisfaction with cultural activity in the here and now. In rescuing *mimēsis* as an ethically beneficial phenomenon, Plutarch affirms the positive benefits of life in a 'secondary' society, a world in which literary posterity inspires a sense of mature reflection upon and profound comprehension of literary artistry and technique.

SUBLIME *MIMĒSIS*

I turn now to perhaps the most celebrated and tantalizing pedagogical text of the Roman period, the tract *On the sublime* (*De subl.*), attributed in the archetypal manuscripts both to 'Dionysius "Longinus"' and to 'Dionysius or "Longinus"'—but usually held to have been the work of an unknown writer of some distinction in the first century CE.[69] This text, profoundly influential on later aesthetics (and in particular upon the anti-materialist Romanticism of the eighteenth century),[70] has in recent years been reconsidered as an important document of Greek ideology and cultural history.[71] Given the radical uncertainty about dating, there are great potential pitfalls in such an approach; nevertheless, the text is evidently a product of Roman Greece (the addressee is a Roman), and the text can be seen to intersect nicely with the concerns we have traced thus far in the literature of the early principate with authenticity, *mimēsis*, and cultural continuity.

For 'Longinus', *mimēsis* of the great writers of the past achieves a similar effect to the intoxicating transport enacted by the sacred exhalations at Delphi:

[69] On the ascription, see Russell (1964), xxii–xxx and Russell (1981), 64–6; on the dating see Häusler (1995); and esp. Heath (1999), who shows how fragile is the case for rejecting Longinian authorship (without, however, convincingly demonstrating the converse). The author will henceforth be referred to as 'Longinus', notwithstanding doubts over authorship (which do not substantially affect the argument here).

[70] See esp. Hertz (1983). For further bibliography on the influence of 'Longinus', see Ashfield and de Bolla, eds. (1996), 307.

[71] See esp. Too (1998), 188–207.

Plato, if we are willing to pay attention, manifests yet another path to sublimity, besides those discussed. What is this? The way of imitation (*mimēsis*) and emulation (*zēlōsis*) of great writers of the past. Here too, my friend, is an aim to which we must hold fast. Many are possessed by a spirit not their own, just as (so we are told) the Pythia is: she draws close to the tripod near the chasm in the ground, from which (so they say) a divine vapour is exhaled, and she is thereby made pregnant by the divine power and prophesies, inspired. Similarly, effluences are emitted into the souls of emulators from the genius of the ancients, as though from a sacred cleft.

ἐνδείκνυται δ' ἡμῖν οὗτος ἀνήρ, εἰ βουλοίμεθα μὴ κατολιγωρεῖν, ὡς καὶ ἄλλη τις παρὰ τὰ εἰρημένα ὁδὸς ἐπὶ τὰ ὑψηλὰ τείνει. ποία δὲ καὶ τίς αὕτη; ⟨ἡ⟩ τῶν ἔμπροσθεν μεγάλων συγγραφέων καὶ ποιητῶν μίμησίς τε καὶ ζήλωσις. καί γε τούτου, φίλτατε, ἀπρὶξ ἐχώμεθα τοῦ σκόπου. πολλοὶ γὰρ ἀλλοτρίῳ θεοφοροῦνται πνεύματι τὸν αὐτὸν τρόπον ὃν καὶ τὴν Πυθίαν λόγος ἔχει τρίποδι πλησιάζουσαν, ἔνθα ῥῆγμά ἐστι γῆς ἀναπνέον, ὥς φασιν, ἀτμὸν ἔνθεον, αὐτόθεν ἐγκύμονα τῆς δαιμονίου καθισταμένην δυνάμεως παραυτίκα χρησμῳδεῖν κατ' ἐπίπνοιαν. οὕτως ἀπὸ τῆς τῶν ἀρχαίων μεγαλοφυΐας εἰς τὰς τῶν ζηλούντων ἐκείνους ψυχὰς ὡς ἀπὸ ἱερῶν στομίων ἀπόρροιαί τινες φέρονται. (13.2)

Although 'Longinus' is referring to the imitation of Homer by *Classical* authors (Plato, Herodotus, Stesichorus, Archilochus), his analysis of the effects of *mimēsis*[72] have important ramifications for the cultural positioning of Roman Greece, too. Indeed, at the beginning of the following section, the author explicitly points to the moral: 'therefore we too' (οὐκοῦν καὶ ἡμᾶς) should imitate not only Homer, but also Plato, Demosthenes, and Thucydides. In Too's words, '[t]he Longinian sublime presents imitation (*mimēsis*) as a strategy . . . for the reclamation of past authors and the literary tradition that make the sublime possible'.[73] The metaphors used in the passage cited above indicate that imitation is an organic, indeed mystical, means of maintaining the vitality of the past in the present. Although (as Russell observes) the metaphor of literary composition as 'inspired' is widespread,[74] it plays a crucial role here, and for two reasons. First, in a Platonic context, it is appropriate to employ Platonic imagery: Plato is the canonical instigator of such an association between inspiration and composition, and moreover the use of the word 'divine' (δαιμονίου) reminds

[72] Here used in conjunction with, but not obviously differentiated from, *zēlōsis* ('emulation'): see Russell (1964), 113 on the conventional distinction.

[73] Too (1998), 210.

[74] Russell (1964), 115.

the reader of Socrates' inspiration by 'the divine' (τὸ δαιμόνιον).[75] Secondly, and perhaps more importantly, this constitutes an important intervention in the identity-defining debates this chapter is tracing concerning the relationship between Roman Greek society and its literary and cultural past. By imaging the relationship in terms of the Pythia and 'divine power', 'Longinus' is indicating the passive dependence of the one upon the other.

Indeed, we can go further: the reference to the 'impregnation' of the Pythia, linking literary with biological fecundity (albeit indirectly),[76] implies a 'natural' relationship of submission to paternal authority. The text to be imitated is a 'father-text', imbued with generative potency (as Harold Bloom emphasizes, 'modernity' has since the Hellenistic period been expressed in terms of an epigonal relationship with Homer).[77] Despite the genealogical imagery, however, *mimēsis* does not construct a simple, self-evidently genetic relationship with the past. 'Longinus' presents it as an eccentric aberration from rationality, a divine possession: it involves being consumed by a spirit that is 'not one's own', 'other' (ἀλλοτρίωι). The paternal text dominates the imitator, inseminating him or her with an alien presence.

So the literary filiation engendered by *mimēsis* is, according to *On the sublime*, complex: the relationship between imitator and

[75] 'So far as Hellenistic and Roman writers are concerned, the chief sources of the doctrine [*sic*] are Plato . . . and Democritus' (Russell 1964: 114). For Plato on literature and divine inspiration, see *Phaedr.* 245a, c; *Ion* 533c–d; *Men.* 99c–d; for Socrates' possession by 'the divine' (τὸ δαιμόνιον) see *Euthyphr.* 3b; *Apol.* 31c; *Euthyd.* 272e; *Phaedr.* 242b; cf. voices in the head at *Cr.* 53d; also Xen. *Apol.* 10–14. Plato never uses τὸ δαιμόνιον as a noun, only as a substantivized adjective (see Burnet 1924: 96–7; with p. 245 on *Cr.* 40a, probably an interpolation); by Roman times, however, δαιμόνιον is a neuter noun and associated with Socrates' inner voice (see e.g. Plutarch's essay περὶ τοῦ Σωκράτους δαιμονίου). 'Longinus', though, uses the word in the Classical form as an adjective (though as a two-termination form, a largely unclassical morphology): see 9.5; 9.8; 33.5 for the 'Platonic', substantivized usage; and 35.2; 43.1 for the adjectival usage.

[76] The metaphorical language of procreation runs throughout *On the sublime*: see 6; 7.2; 7.4; 8.1; 9.1; 13.2; 13.4; 14.3; 31.1; 44.3; and further, Walsh (1988), 266.

[77] Bloom (1975), 33–4: 'everyone who now reads and writes in the West, of whatever racial background, sex or ideological camp, is still a son or daughter of Homer . . . We are Alexandrians still.' For 'father Homer', see Nonn. *Dion.* 25.265 (πατρὸς Ὁμήρου), and the strategic use of the motif of the 'bastard' (νόθος) throughout his text (see Hopkinson 1994*a*: 127; 1994*b*: esp. 9–14). The theme is, however, no doubt much older: as noted by Hopkinson (1994*b*), 35 n. 37, the notion of Homer as a 'father' is already implicit in the name Ὁμηρίδαι or 'children of Homer' given to rhapsodes. On the theme of the 'anxiety of influence' in Roman Greece, see further Schmitz (1997), 224–5.

imitatee is divine and irrational, but natural and organic. It is, however, clearly the case that the author (qua vehicle) must submit to the 'parent' text. But even this relationship is immediately subverted, as 'Longinus' proceeds to praise a more active, agonistic relationship with literary authority.[78] Plato is presented as an example of an author who would not have achieved such success

> had he not fought with all his spirit for the first prize—by Zeus!—with Homer, like a young rival against one already marvelled at. Perhaps he did this too competitively and (as it were) breaking his spear, but nevertheless his endeavours were not useless: for (in Hesiod's words) 'this strife is good for mortals' (*Op.* 24). And indeed this is a fine contest and garland of fame, and most worthy of winning; even defeat by one's ancestors is not without glory.
>
> . . . *εἰ μὴ περὶ πρωτείων νὴ Δία παντὶ θυμῶι πρὸς Ὅμηρον, ὡς ἀνταγωνιστὴς νέος πρὸς ἤδη τεθαυμασμένον, ἴσως μὲν φιλονικότερον*[79] *καὶ οἱονεὶ διαδορατιζόμενος, οὐκ ἀνωφελῶς δ' ὅμως διηριστεύετο· "ἀγαθὴ" γὰρ κατὰ τὸν Ἡσίοδον "ἔρις ἥδε βροτοῖσι." καὶ τῶι ὄντι καλὸς οὗτος καὶ ἀξιονικότατος εὐκλείας ἀγών τε καὶ στέφανος, ἐν ὧι καὶ τὸ ἡττᾶσθαι τῶν προγενεστέρων οὐκ ἄδοξον.* (13.4)

Here, 'Longinus' adopts suitably military metaphors in relation to a poet of war, evoking the Homeric discourse of glory through warfare (*πρωτείων, ἀνταγωνιστὴς, φιλονικότερον, διαδορατιζόμενος, διηριστεύετο, ἔρις, ἀξιονικότατος, εὐκλείας, ἀγών, ἡττᾶσθαι, ἄδοξον*).[80] The 'Platonic' repertoire of imagery in the earlier passage is now supplanted by the 'Homeric' language of war. In a concomitant process, the style is also transformed: gone is the hazy mythicism of the earlier passage,[81] replaced now with a strident assertiveness (particularly in the conditional, 'he would not have . . . had he not', and in the sententious citation from Hesiod). It is as if 'Longinus', while discussing the theoretical issues of imitation, dramatizes in

[78] Walsh (1988), 266.

[79] This is Russell's emendation for MS *φιλονεικότερον*, but the choice between *φιλόνεικος* and *φιλόνικος* (which were phonetically indistinguishable at this time) is problematic and pretty much intractable for all literature of the period: see Duff (1999), 83 with n. 38 for a brief summary of the issues.

[80] The violent language continues in the following sections: vivid description 'enslaves' (*δουλοῦται*) the hearer (15.9); figures 'are allies of' (*ἀντισυμμαχεῖται*) the sublime (17.1).

[81] 'So they say' (*ὥς φασιν*, 13.2) marks the folkloric quality (*pace* Russell 1964: 114, who seems to take it to imply a 'philosophical hypothesis'); also, the simile ('like . . .', *ὡς*, 13.2) and the metaphor of pregnancy add to the air of disorientated other-worldliness.

his own practice the difficulty of maintaining one's own literary identity. This interlacing of theme and style is consistent with his advice elsewhere that 'the meaning of a text and its expression are usually interwoven with each other' (*ἡ τοῦ λόγου νόησις ἥ τε φράσις τὰ πλείω δι' ἑκατέρου διέπτυκται*, 30.1).

Concomitant with these stylistic variations comes an apparent conceptual clash. If the passage cited previously represented later literature as filial, this passage articulates an Oedipal relationship of strife between 'the young' (*νέοι*) and their 'ancestors' (*προγενέστεροι*). *Mimēsis* is here a far from passive activity: it is, rather, a direct and combative engagement with the 'father-text'. This contest for cultural authority implies a more discriminatory approach to the literature of the past.[82] Yet the dissonance between the two characterizations of literary *mimēsis* is not simply an error or a confusion. Sublime writing (and 'Longinus' is insistent that his own work should partake of the sublime)[83] is fractured and transgressive, in Too's terms 'dislocated';[84] it admits of errors and inconsistencies of expression, since a great writer 'often buys off all his slips with a single instance of sublimity that sets it all aright' (*ἅπαντα τὰ σφάλματα ἑνὶ ἐξωνεῖται πολλάκις ὕψει καὶ κατορθώματι*, 36.2).[85] Uniformity is for *skholastikoi* ('academic pedants') (2.4; *skholikos* at 10.7, cf. 3.5);[86] 'accuracy in every detail runs the risk of petty-mindedness' (⟨*τὸ*⟩ . . . *ἐν παντὶ ἀκριβὲς κίνδυνος μικρότητος*, 33.2). Instantiating these principles, 'Longinus'' own writing 'tends to drift', a process he nevertheless 'resists . . . by correcting

[82] For criticism of ancient writers, see e.g. *De subl.* 4.4 (Plato and Xenophon); 15.3 (Euripides); 32.7 (Plato); and further Segal (1959), 125.

[83] Implied in the criticism of Caecilius' handbook as 'too humble for its subject-matter' (*ταπεινότερον τῆς ὑποθέσεως*, *De subl.* 1.1). See 33.2 on writers with 'humble natures', with Innes (1995) on the thematic importance of the word *ταπεινός*. This Caecilius is probably the famous critic Caecilius of Caleacte (on whom see Swain 1996: 23–4), of whose works numerous fragments are extant: see Russell (1964), 58–9.

[84] Too (1998), 188–207. Recent scholarship has tended to overstate the transgressive elements in *On the sublime* (see below on transgression as a form of conservatism): cf. the interesting arguments of Salamone (1993), who argues that the Longinian sublime is paradoxical because it aims to imitate not reality but a super-idealized crystallization of cultural tradition. Guerlac (1985) points to 'Longinus'' disruption of 'fundamental category oppositions' (276), but her argument seems to me overly focused upon the 'Western philosophical tradition' (which she reifies), and insensitive to rhetorical and literary theoretical currents in the ancient world.

[85] For 'Longinus'' views on error, see 33–6 *passim*, with Walsh (1988), 254–7.

[86] The *skholastikos* was a standard butt of jokes: see Plut. *Cic.* 5.2; Arr. *Diss. Epict.* 1.11.39; and further, Winkler (1985), 160–5.

himself, constantly changing direction in an effort to find his target'.[87] 'Longinus' ceaselessly reworks and reconfigures the terminology he uses, making it impossible to reduce his complex, plural prose into a schematic system. This principle, as we have seen, underlies 'Longinus'' knowingly oscillatory presentation of *mimēsis* as both a 'natural' relationship of filiation and a confrontational struggle. In its subtle self-contradictions, *On the sublime* enacts the manifold complexities of the imitative process. The act of allusion to the literature of the past simultaneously exalts it and seeks to neutralize its superiority.

In a move that further compounds the air of unevenness and sublime disorientation, 'Longinus' presently proceeds to use *mimēsis* in the so-called 'philosophical' sense (that is, to mark the imitation of nature, *physis*, by art, *tekhnē*: 22.1). As has already been argued, however, the 'philosophical' and the 'rhetorical' senses cannot simply be securely separated, as though the connotations of one never infected the other.[88] In a discussion of the figure of hyperbaton (syntactical dislocation), 'Longinus' writes that

> Those who in real life (*tōi onti*) feel anger or fear or disquiet because of jealousy or some other cause . . . vary their word-order in all sorts of ways using myriad tropes; thus, among the best writers, thanks to hyperbaton *mimēsis* approaches the effects of nature (*physeōs*). For art (*tekhnē*) is perfect when it resembles nature (*physis*), whereas nature (*physis*) is successful whenever it encompasses concealed art (*tekhnēn*).
>
> *οἱ τῶι ὄντι ὀργιζόμενοι ἢ φοβούμενοι ἢ ἀγανακτοῦντες ἢ ὑπὸ ζηλοτυπίας ἢ ὑπὸ ἄλλου τινὸς . . . παντοίως πρὸς μυρίας τροπὰς ἐναλλάττουσι τάξιν, οὕτως παρὰ τοῖς ἀρίστοις συγγραφεῦσι διὰ τῶν ὑπερβατῶν ἡ μίμησις ἐπὶ τὰ τῆς φύσεως ἔργα φέρεται. τότε γὰρ ἡ τέχνη τέλειος ἡνίκ' ἂν φύσις εἶναι δοκῆι, ἡ δ' αὖ φύσις ἐπιτυχὴς ὅταν λανθάνουσαν περιέχηι τὴν τέχνην.* (22.1)

This important passage, with its vigorous assertion of the principle that *ars . . . latet arte sua* ('art is hidden by art'), marks the unnaturalness of *mimēsis*, its implication with literary artifice. In a text that marks itself explicitly as a 'technical tract' (*τεχνολογία*, 1.1), and indeed in a literary culture that is self-consciously mired in artificial and knowing literary techniques, 'Longinus' here (in contrast to the earlier, 'naturalizing' explana-

[87] Walsh (1988), 253.

[88] Contra e.g. Russell (1964), 138: 'the mimesis here meant is the imitation of things, not that of literary models'. See further above, p. 48.

tion of literary 'pregnancy') presents *mimēsis* as a dissimulative device that engenders resemblance and concealment. In this respect, the 'secondary' culture that 'Longinus' inhabits is implicitly linked with artful repetition. At the same time, however, 'secondary' elaboration is praised as a means of improving upon nature, 'encompass[ing] concealed art'.

Indeed, this complex intertwining of 'nature' (*physis*) and 'artifice' (*tekhnē*) permeates the entirety of *On the sublime*.[89] In the second paragraph of the text, 'Longinus' raises the question of whether there is an 'art' (*tekhnē*) of sublime writing (2.1),[90] in response to those who hold that 'artificial precepts' (*tekhnika parangelmata*, 2.1) cannot teach composition, that *physis* alone teaches great writing, and that *tekhnē* can only spoil such a naturally good writer (2.1). 'Longinus' counters with three points. First, he tells us, nature (*physis*) does not operate 'at random and without any method (*amethodos*) altogether' (*οὐκ εἰκαῖόν τι κἀκ παντὸς ἀμέθοδον*, 2.2); secondly, although nature is primary, it is only method (*methodos*) that can teach 'the correct quantities and the timing (*kairos*) for each thing and the least erroneous preparation and use' (*τὰς . . . ποσότητας καὶ τὸν ἐφ' ἕκαστου καιρὸν ἔτι δὲ τὴν ἀπλανεστάτην ἄσκησίν τε καὶ χρῆσιν*, 2.2); and, thirdly, 'greatness' (*τὰ μεγάλα*)[91] is very dangerous when

left alone without learning, unsupported and unmoored, abandoned to instinct alone and untaught audacity—for it often needs the bit as well as the spur.

αὐτὰ ἐφ' αὐτῶν δίχα ἐπιστήμης ἀστήρικτα καὶ ἀνερμάτιστα ἐαθέντα . . . ἐπὶ μόνηι τῆι φορᾶι καὶ ἀμαθεῖ τόλμηι λειπόμενα· δεῖ γὰρ αὐτοῖς ὡς κέντρου πολλάκις οὕτω δὲ καὶ χαλινοῦ. (2.2)

There is (as so frequently in *On the sublime*) a conceptual catachresis at work here (in the first defence, 'Longinus' evokes the Stoic view of nature as fundamentally rational and 'methodical', whereas in the second and third cases he presents it as lacking in the method that human intelligence can give it). With a

[89] See Segal (1959), 122–3; Walsh (1988), 253

[90] 'Longinus' recalls Socrates' discussion of the *tekhnē* of rhetoric in Plato's *Gorgias* (459a and following). Nesselrath (1985), 155–6 sites the passage from 'Longinus' in the context of ancient traditions of *tekhnē*-writing.

[91] Evoking Pl. *Resp.* 491d–492a, the so-called 'theory of great natures' (i.e. individual natures that are most prone to either outstanding or deleterious effects). See Duff (1999), 47–9, 60–5 on Plutarch's use of this passage, and his p. 48 n. 103 for other instances of reference to it.

characteristic self-referentiality, however, this catachresis serves only to exemplify the point that 'Longinus' is making: sublime writers strain the limits of regular linguistic usage. Indeed, in the third argument, a great 'nature' is implicitly compared to a beast, requiring the control of the 'bit' and the 'spur' to prevent it from rampaging.[92] Sublimity, then does not simply proceed unilaterally from nature,[93] but from the dialectic of control and chaos. In another sense, the sublime can be said to be a form of violence to nature. A rhetorical 'figure' (*skhēma*) is represented as precisely the opposite of 'natural usage' (ἡ κατὰ φύσιν χρῆσις, 16.2).[94] In his discussion of hyperbaton, already alluded to above, he describes this rhetorical figure as 'word-order (*taxis*) that deviates from the natural sequence' (τὴν ἐκ τοῦ κατὰ φύσιν εἱρμοῦ . . . τάξιν, 22.1).[95] The word *taxis*, from the verb *tattein* ('order', 'structure', 'arrange', 'command') implies a proper arrangement sanctioned by authority. Hyperbaton is an act of insubordination against nature, implying transgression in its very name (*hyperbainein* is 'to cross over'; *transgressio* is the Latin equivalent).[96] In the course of his examples drawn from Herodotus and Thucydides, 'Longinus' refers to the former as having 'twisted askew the order (*taxis*) of thoughts' (τὴν τῶν νοημάτων ἀπέστρεψε τάξιν, 22.2), and to the latter as 'even (*kai*) taking elements that have been absolutely united by nature and indivisible and nevertheless (*homōs*) separating them from each other with his hyperbata' (καὶ τὰ φύσει πάντως ἡνωμένα καὶ ἀδιανέμητα ὅμως ταῖς ὑπερβάσεσιν ἀπ' ἀλλήλων ἄγειν, 22.3). This last sentence, with its emphatically concessive 'even (*kai*) . . . nevertheless (*homōs*)' structure, vividly asserts the transgressive boldness of Thucydides' syntax.

Transgressiveness, though, is a technique for institutionalizing

[92] Russell (1964), 65 asserts that this metaphor is 'much used by educators', citing Cic. *Brut.* 204 (Isocrates on Ephorus and Theopompus); Diog. Laert. 4.6 (Plato on Aristotle and Xenocrates); 5.39 (Aristotle on Callisthenes and Theopompus). There are, however, further implications here, particularly of tyrannical behaviour: see Villari (1988).

[93] And as argued by Segal (1959), 122–3.

[94] Caecilius defined a *skhēma* as a 'trope/turning towards the unnatural in thought and expression' (τροπὴ εἰς τὸ μὴ κατὰ φύσιν τῆς διανοίας καὶ λέξεως, fr. 50 Ofenloch). Russell (1964), 127 notes the naïveté of a belief in a fundamentally 'natural' form of expression; see, however, Plutarch, *Quomodo adulesc.* 23a for an example in Classical criticism of a more sophisticated awareness of lexis.

[95] See further Too (1998), 198–9 on the disruptive effects of Longinian hyperbaton.

[96] *Rhet. ad Her.* 4.32.44; Quint. *Inst. or.* 8.6.62.

a different set of values: crossing boundaries necessitates the erection of new ones. 'Longinus' is not simply a nihilist revelling in subversion and disorder, but a committed writer with deeply rooted, indeed at times conservative, ethical priorities.[97] He writes of the need to compose 'with symmetry' (*συμμέτρως*, 29.1),[98] and the word *kairos* ('timing' or 'measure') recurs (12.5; 18.2; 27.2; 32.1), often emphasized as an important oratorical quality (2.1; 16.3; 42; cf. 22.4; 29.1; 32.4). Elements in a sentence need to be 'built up together' (*συνοικοδομούμενα*, 10.7).[99] In certain places, 'Longinus' recalls Aristotle's theory of the mean in his emphasis upon the importance of the avoidance of excessively polarized states.[100] The author's oscillation between subversion and regulated order can also be seen in his style: for example, in his discussion of hyperbaton, he follows an inordinately complex, hyperbatic sentence of 101 words with a terse expression of self-restraint (eight words in the original): 'But I must be sparing in my use of examples, because of the number of them' (*φειδὼ δὲ τῶν παραδειγμάτων ἔστω διὰ τὸ πλῆθος*, 22.4).[101] After the explosion of excess comes self-regulating parsimony. These two trajectories, centrifugal and centripetal, define and offset one another throughout the essay *On the sublime*.

The concepts of 'order' and 'transgression', and the dialogic relationship between the two, are thus central concepts to *On the sublime*. As political metaphors, however, they raise an interesting set of questions concerning the relationship between literature and the socio-political climate of the time. This, indeed, is one of the most tantalizing features of *On the sublime*, a text that teases its readers by *almost* explicitly articulating a cultural-political agenda. For a start, it self-consciously trades upon the relationship between past and present that was so central to Greek self-definition during

[97] At *De subl.* 5.1, 'the urge for innovation' (*τὸ καινόσπουδον*) is decried.

[98] The MS reading; Russell reads *σὺν μέτρωι* with Morus, so as to account convincingly for the subsequent *τινί* ('with a certain moderation'). The emendation does not affect the point made here.

[99] A textually difficult sentence: *συνοικοδομούμενα* is Manutius' emendation for MS *συνοικονομούμενα* (Russell 1964: 106 compares 39.3: *τῆι . . . τῶν λέξεων ἐποικοδομήσει τὰ μεγέθη συναρμόζουσαν*). Again, emendation does not effect the point.

[100] Coulter (1964). Laurenti (1987), 25–6 argues unconvincingly for a Stoic source for these ideas.

[101] That the previous sentence exemplifies the principles it describes is noted by Russell (1964), 139; cf. 134.

the period. As we have seen, *mimēsis* of writings of the past has a thrilling effect, inspiring the contemporary author 'like the emanations from sacred clefts' (ὡς ἀπὸ ἱερῶν στομίων ἀπόρροιαί τινες, 13.2). As Too has shown, 'Longinus' employs a series of metaphors of spatial dislocation to reinforce the concept of Apollonian 'transport', suggesting that literature can lead one away from the present into the past.[102] The sublime is a means of transcending the present: great art is not tied to the present but aims at the universal (αἰών);[103] its grandeur exceeds the human sphere, making it divine and cosmic.[104] Just as sublime style flits between order and chaos, so it probes the barriers of time and culture. At the same time as he recognizes a substantive difference between the ancients and 'us' (ἡμεῖς, 14.1), 'Longinus' presents sublime writing as an effacement of that difference, a form of communion with the greats. Even as he asserts the 'agonistic' aspects of the mimetic relationship, 'Longinus' nevertheless attempts to construct an imagined community of universal Hellenism, a Hellenism that is strong enough to incorporate references to Jewish (9.9, on Genesis 1: 3–9)[105] and Latin literature (12.3–5; but see below on this passage) without spending its vigour.

Yet 'Longinus' is also aware of the immense gulf that lies between the Classical past and the Roman present. Indeed, in the famous closing[106] chapter (44) of the work (as we have it, any rate), he reports a debate between himself (or, at least, the persona he adopts here) and 'one of the philosophers' (τις τῶν φιλοσόφων, 44.1), who attributes apparent literary decadence to the advent of that 'just slavery' (δουλείας δικαίας, 44.3). Though this phrase has been taken as a reference to the transition in Roman politics from republic to principate,[107] it has recently (and no doubt rightly)

[102] Too (1998), 196–202.

[103] *De subl.* 1 3, 4.7; 9.3; 14.3, 36 2, 44.1; 44.9; Segal (1959), 122–3.

[104] *De subl.* 35.3; Segal (1959), 135. I am not convinced by West (1995) as to the Near Eastern origin of such ideas of cosmic grandeur: cf. e.g. Lucr. 1.72–4 for a Classical parallel.

[105] See Russell (1964), 92–4, rightly arguing against the suggestion of interpolation.

[106] The essay breaks off midway through a quotation from Euripides. It is sometimes argued either that a substantial portion is missing at the end or that ch. 44 is misplaced: see contra most recently Mazzuchi (1990), though the interpretation of the text as fundamentally 'about' the social benefits of literature is reductive.

[107] Russell (1964), 185–7. The argument for this interpretation rests upon analogies from Latin literature, which link literary decline to the advent of the principate (esp. Vell. Pat. 1.6.16–17; Sen. *Controu.* 1 *praef.* 6; Tac. *Dial.* 36–40); but recent

been claimed that the primary reference is to Macedonian and then Roman domination of Greece.[108] The philosopher claims that great literature has died with the passing of democracy and the advent of slavery (44.1–5), while 'Longinus' replies that it is not Rome that has enslaved men, but their own appetites (44.6–12). It is significant that the proponent of the first belief is a philosopher, for philosophers are commonly associated in this period with defiant and principled stances, and with free speech (*parrhēsia*).[109] 'Longinus' introduces the figure of the unknown philosopher in order to experiment with the bold proposition that Greek literature in the past was great because of Greek freedom; and, by implication, that cultural continuity can only be constructed if Greece is liberated from Roman domination.

'Longinus' professes, of course, to reject this interpretation. This text appears deliberately to depoliticize itself: it offers up the possibility of an ideological interpretation, the sublime proposed as a form of resistance to Roman domination, only to withdraw it. In this respect, Segal (who argues for an apolitical reading) is right to point to 'Longinus'' anti-materialist 'idealism'.[110] Yet it would be naïve to conclude that the political is simply marginal to the author's interests. Why, in that case, would he bother including the figure of the philosopher at all? It is preferable to explore the rhetorical effects of this paraliptical disavowal. (Comparable is Tacitus' use of vulgar rumours, which he decries for their ignorance and sensationalism . . . but nevertheless incorporates into his imperial portraits.)[111] To an extent, Segal already allows for the 'repoliticization' of *On the sublime*, by arguing that the

scholarship has been less inclined to view Greek and Roman literature as homogeneous, and has been more sensitive to the differing cultural priorities.

[108] Heath (1999), 53–4, esp. p. 54: 'it would only make sense to say that the end of the Roman republic explained the lack of sublimity in Greek literature if one were willing to assert that Hellenistic authors had achieved it—not an opinion we can attribute to ['Longinus']' For a comparable interpretation of the ebbs and fluxes of Greek literary prowess in terms of political change, cf. Dion. Hal. *De uet. or.* 1.2, who blames literary decadence on the conquest of Greece by Alexander, but points to a recent resurgence (see *Ant. Rom.* 1.2.3 for a similar comment on the decline of post-Alexandrian Greece). Philostr. *VS* 511 does not provide an explicitly political explanation, but there is a strong implication of a peak in the Classical period and subsequent decadence until the resurgence in the 2nd cent. CE: see e.g. G. Anderson (1986), 12–13; Rothe (1989), 7–8

[109] e.g. Dio Chr. 3.12–25; Luc. *Peregr.* 18; Glad (1996); Konstan (1997), 108–13.

[110] Segal (1959), 139–40.

[111] Shatzman (1974).

debate in chapter 44 may represent 'a struggle within the mind of 'Longinus' himself.'[112] Not wishing to put the matter in such 'expressive-realist'[113] terms, we might rephrase this idea: the conclusion of *On the sublime* enacts a movement away from the political, but suggests the possibility of an alternative, 'philosophical' interpretation; and this duality seeks to engender an uncertain ambivalence in the *reader*'s mind as to the relationship between politics and literature.

If this interpretation is right, then the next question is: *why* has 'Longinus' concealed his motives for advancing the political interpretation? The answer has to do with the addressee of the essay, the otherwise unknown Terentianus, who is explicitly advertised as a Roman.[114] Terentianus may be addressed as 'my best friend' (*philtate*, 1.1; 1.3; 7.1; 12.4; 17.1; 29.2; 44.1), but the cultural difference between the two is an important element: in his comparison between Cicero and Demosthenes (12.4–5), 'Longinus' underlines the distance between 'you [Romans]' (ὑμεῖς) and 'we Greeks' (ἡμῖν . . . Ἕλλησιν). In the first place, he apologizes for discussing Cicero with the words 'insofar as it is permissible for us, Greeks as we are, to know anything [sc. about Latin authors]' (⟨εἰ⟩ καὶ ἡμῖν ὡς Ἕλλησιν ἐφεῖταί τι γινώσκειν, 12.4). Cicero is contrasted with 'our man' (ὁ . . . ἡμετέρος, 12.4) Demosthenes. In concluding his discussion of Cicero, he writes 'but you people would be better judges of such matters' (ἀλλὰ ταῦτα . . . ὑμεῖς ἂν ἄμεινον ἐπικρίνοιτε, 12.5). The Roman Terentianus plays the role of empowered recipient, perhaps even patron: he has 'ordered' 'Longinus' to write, and will 'judge' the product (ἐνεκελεύσω . . . συνεπικρινεῖς, 1.2).

This assertion of difference between Greek and Roman is meaningful and deliberate. 'Longinus' (who clearly reads Latin, and may well have been in actuality a Roman citizen) could have emphasized his close cultural bonds with Terentianus (who is sufficiently Hellenized to understand a text written in sophisticated, and sometimes recondite, prose).[115] 'Longinus' could pre-

112 Segal (1959), 140.

113 See Introd., 'The Politics of Imitation'.

114 The political importance of the addressee is noted by Guerlac (1985), 279–80. For some guesses as to the 'real' identity of Terentianus, see Laurenti (1987), 18.

115 Plutarch, for example, nowhere tells us whether Q. Sosius Senecio, the addressee of the *Parallel lives*, *On progress in virtue*, and *Table-talk*, is an Easterner who has acquired Roman citizenship or a Hellenized Roman. He was probably the

sumably have written of Romans as 'we', just as Lucian famously does on occasion.[116] This schematic polarity between 'we' and 'you', then, is not so much an articulation of a self-evident fact as an artful structuring device, designed to create a dilemma for the reader: which side are you on? Are you with 'us' or 'them'? And, a further ramification, given the ambivalences we have noted in the final chapter: which way will you read this text? Will you accept its superficial rejection of Greek subjection as an explanation for literary decline, or will you probe deeper, recovering the 'philosophical' interpretation?

Indeed, during the course of the discussion, 'Longinus' explicitly discusses the importance of using 'figured' speech, language that conceals its own intentions, in situations where there is a differential of power. In such instances, we read, the person in question is driven to suspect an insidious attack:

It is a property of devious figuring that it should be suspicious, and provoke thoughts of an ambush, conspiracy or hoodwinking, particularly whenever one addresses an important judge, and especially tyrants, kings or consuls—anyone in power over you.

ὕποπτόν ἐστιν ἰδίως τὸ διὰ σχημάτων πανουργεῖν καὶ προσβάλλον ὑπόνοιαν ἐνέδρας ἐπιβουλῆς παραλογισμοῦ, †καὶ ταῦ'† ὅταν ᾖι πρὸς κριτὴν κύριον ὁ λόγος, μάλιστα δὲ πρὸς τυράννους βασιλέας ἡγενόνας ⟨πάντας τοὺς⟩ ἐν ὑπεροχαῖς. (17.1)

Language is imaged here as a form of military power—an 'ambush' (*ἐνέδρα*)[117]—that competes with political power. It also can raise very serious dangers: the potentate in question 'sometimes goes completely wild (*apothērioutai*, 17.1)', recalling the theriomorphism of Plato's tyrant in the *Republic*;[118] while 'even if he masters his anger, he is altogether hostile to persuasion'

latter (see Swain 1996: 426–7, against C. P. Jones 1970); but the very fact that we do not know points to Plutarch's desire to conceal cultural differences between himself and his addressee.

[116] Luc. *Alex.* 48; *Hist. conscr.* 5, 17, 29, 31; Palm (1959), 54. See, however, Ch. 5 n. 11.

[117] Figured speech is also said to 'fight as an ally' (*ἀντισυμμαχεῖται*) with the speaker (17.1).

[118] One who becomes a tyrant turns 'from a man into a wolf' (*λύκωι ἐξ ἀνθρώπου*, *Resp.* 566a; cf. 565d–566a), and 'bestiality and savagery' (*τὸ . . . θηριῶδές τε καὶ ἄγριον*) dominate his soul (*Resp.* 571c). As is pointed out by Bushnell (1990), 16, Thrasymachus, Socrates' violent interlocutor, is repeatedly imaged in bestial terms (336b, 341c, 358b), and thus assimilated to the tyrant (see also the interesting comments of Farenga 1981).

(*κἂν ἐπικρατήσῃι δὲ τοῦ θυμοῦ, πρὸς τὴν πειθὼ τῶν λόγων πάντως ἀντιδιατίθεται*, 17.1). Speaking to the empowered is a highly risky business, and the hegemonic differential necessarily 'politicizes' everything one says. 'Longinus' now proceeds to show how to conceal 'the art of deviousness' (*ἡ τοῦ πανουργεῖν τέχνη*, 17.2). by using sublime, emotive language as a 'palliative and amazing protection against the suspicion that one is using figures' (*τῆς ἐπὶ τῶι σχηματίζειν ὑπονοίας ἀλέξημα καὶ θαυμαστή τις ἐπικουρία*, 17.2). Figured speech *is* a kind of power-play, but it depends for its success upon disguising that fact: 'a figure works the best when it conceals the very fact that it is a figure' (*τότε ἄριστον δοκεῖ τὸ σχῆμα, ὅταν αὐτὸ τοῦτο διαλανθάνηι, ὅτι σχῆμά ἐστι*, 17.2).[119] The embattled context wherein one addresses a superior necessitates quasi-theatrical strategies of disguise and deception.

This discussion of figured speech can be read as a cue to a more disruptive reading of *On the sublime* itself. Is this not a text addressed by a clever Greek to a Roman? Is it not a text that cleverly insinuates subversive readings whilst maintaining a superficially compliant attitude towards Roman domination? When we construct mimetic links back to autonomous Greece, are we simply making an aesthetic point, or do we also engender a concomitant challenge to Roman hegemony? Is 'Longinus' simply exemplifying linguistic points when he cites Plato's jingoistic assertion that 'we are not half-barbarians who live here, but *Greeks*' (*αὐτοὶ Ἕλληνες οὐ μιξοβάρβαροι οἰκοῦμεν*, 23.4)? Similarly provocative is his citation of Demosthenes' excoriation of

> Vile men, flatterers who have each amputated your own fatherlands, drinking away your freedom first to Philip, now to Alexander, measuring your happiness by your bellies and the most shameful practices, overturning freedom and autonomy, which the Greeks of old thought of as the definitions and yardsticks of good men.
>
> *ἄνθρωποι . . . μιαροὶ καὶ κόλακες, ἠκρωτηριασμένοι τὰς ἑαυτῶν ἕκαστοι πατρίδας, τὴν ἐλευθερίαν προπεπωκότες πρότερον Φιλίππωι, νυνὶ δὲ Ἀλεξάνδρωι, τῆι γαστρὶ μετροῦντες καὶ τοῖς αἰσχίστοις τὴν εὐδαιμονίαν, τὴν δ' ἐλευθερίαν καὶ τὸ μηδένα ἔχειν δεσπότην, ἃ τοῖς πρότερον Ἕλλησιν ὅροι τῶν ἀγαθῶν ἦσαν καὶ κανόνες, ἀνατετροφότες.* (32.2)

Is this Demosthenes addressing the Athenians or 'Longinus' addressing his readers, *mutatis mutandis*? Is it possible to quote

[119] On concealment as a strategy in Greek rhetorical theory, see Cronje (1993).

the formal properties alone of such inflammatory utterances, especially in the context of a text that itself urges an analogous instauration of the values of 'the Greeks of old' (*οἱ πρότερον Ἕλληνες*)? If we emphasize such hints and uncertainties as these, then we conclude that the depoliticization that the text dramatizes at the conclusion is a *strategic* effect, designed to draw attention to the very movement that it traces: as in a palimpsest, the process of overwriting is not sufficiently complete to conceal the words beneath. *On the sublime* is, thus, politically ambivalent. As we saw earlier, it describes a continual tension in sublime writing between order and disorder. These principles can also be understood in political terms: Longinus at once proposes and rejects the 'subversive' explanation of the philosopher, thereby both consolidating the *Pax Romana* and, implicitly, challenging it; or, better, forcing the reader to bring his or her own interpretative judgement to bear upon the issue.

On the sublime is a highly complex and wilfully inconsistent text. Like Plutarch, 'Longinus' is ever aware that he is writing in and for a culture that bears a secondary, 'mimetic' relationship to the privileged, canonical past. Whereas Plutarch seeks to construct cultural continuity (presenting *mimēsis* as a 'natural' outgrowth of the past), however, this author dramatizes a much more problematic, embattled terrain. At times, *mimēsis* is a form of inspired possession, at other times it is an agonistic contest; at times it interweaves harmoniously with nature, at other times it violently disrupts it. In the political sphere, too, 'Longinus' presents a complex problem: does reactivating the Greek past (and the concomitant language of freedom and anti-barbarism) represent a challenge to Roman dominion? Such ambivalences and 'figurings' form part of the power of this text, a text that mimics the ability of the sublime both to consolidate order and to disrupt it.

ART AND ARTIFICE

Plutarch and 'Longinus', in their very different ways, present *mimēsis* as a means of constructing cultural continuity with the past. This, however, is not the only way of interpreting the 'secondariness' of Roman Greek literature. In order to introduce the interpretation of *mimēsis* as an 'artificial' concoction, I wish now to consider Dionysius' *On mimēsis* (now extant only in fragments).[120] Although Dionysius (a native of Halicarnassus on the southern coast of Asia Minor, who moved to Rome in around 30 BCE)[121] is substantially earlier than the majority of writers treated in this book (writing when both the Roman principate and the Greek 'Atticist' movement were in their infancies), it will become clear that the themes he raises are thoroughly germane to the literature of second- and third-century Greece.

Like Plutarch, Dionysius stresses the educative advantages of *mimēsis* in the creation of proper subjects, but his primary interest is in the formation not of philosophers but of rhetoricians. Again like the later writer, Dionysius is keen to 'rescue' *mimēsis* from Platonic opprobrium, but he proceeds in a very different manner. For Dionysius, literary *mimēsis* is a process of artful creation unlike, indeed conceptually opposed to, nature's own acts of creation: according to this writer, artificiality is a mark of superiority, of man's ability to transcend the crudity of nature. This celebration of nature's limited rôle in the education of the rhetorician can be discerned in the very project of *On mimēsis*. An 'able nature (*physis*)', Dionysius tells us, is among the requirements for rhetoric, but so are 'careful learning' and 'assiduous practice' (φύσις δεξιά, μάθησις ἀκριβής, ἄσκησις ἐπίπονος, *De imit*. fr. 2 Usener–Radermacher)—and it is upon the latter two, that is to say upon the acculturating process, that Dionysius focuses.[122] The sixth (and longest extant) fragment discusses the process whereby 'the soul of the reader draws into itself an assimilation (*homoiotēta*) of style [i.e. that of the original author], thanks to continual vigilance' (ἡ γὰρ ψυχὴ τοῦ ἀναγινώσκοντος ὑπὸ τῆς συνεχοῦς

[120] Partly summarized in Dionysius' own *Letter to Pompeius Geminus*.

[121] On Dionysius' life and dating, see G. Kennedy (1994), 161–6; Hidber (1996), 1–8.

[122] A similar thought at ps.-Plut. *De lib*. 2d: 'by labour (*ponos*), that which is contrary to nature (*physis*) becomes stronger than that which is in accordance with it' (τὸ παρὰ φύσιν τῶι πόνωι τοῦ κατὰ φύσιν ἐγένετο κρεῖττον, 2d). This emphasis upon the unnaturalness of education is one of the features that identifies this text as non-Plutarchan. I am not convinced by the argument of Berry (1958), 392–3 that this focus upon *ponos* has a conspicuously Xenophontic ring to it. Plutarch himself does, however, refer to the 'labour' (πόνος) involved in *paideia*, comparing agricultural toil (*De rect*. 38c): see T. Morgan (1998), 255–8 on this simile, widespread in educational writings. The question of whether good oratory owes more to 'nature' or to 'art' seems to have been a subject of controversy in Cicero's time (*Brut*. 25). Dionysius also refers to *mimēsis* as a product of *tekhnē*, not *physis* at *Is*. 16.1 (cf. *De imit*. fr. 10 Usener–Radermacher); *De comp. uerb*. 20.15.

παρατηρήσεως τὴν ὁμοιότητα τοῦ χαρακτῆρος ἐφέλκεται, *De imit.* fr. 6.1 Usener–Radermacher). The use of the word *homoiotēs* ('assimilation', 'likeness') is significant: by using a term that often refers to accuracy of verbal or artistic portrayal,[123] Dionysius implicitly links the formation of the subject with the creation of a skilful mimetic work. For Dionysius, the self (or, at least, the elaborated, sophisticated, rhetorical self) is itself a product of art.

In order to exemplify the artificiality of education through literary *mimēsis*, Dionysius introduces two extraordinary and famous parables. In the first, he tells the story of a rustic couple who wanted children, but were worried about the outcome, since the husband was ugly. Accordingly, he set up a series of paintings (*eikones*), and habituated his wife to look at them; then, 'he had sex with his wife, and was blessed with the beauty of the paintings' (συγγενόμενος αὐτῆι τὸ κάλλος εὐτύχησε τῶν εἰκόνων, *De imit.* fr. 6.1 Usener–Radermacher).[124] Procreation is normally a paradigmatically 'natural' process (as opposed to the definitively 'cultural' practice of homosexual sex),[125] but on this occasion, the farmer artfully improvises: 'this fear taught him an artifice (*tekhnēn*) whereby to have good children' (ὁ φόβος δὲ αὐτὸν οὗτος εὐπαιδίας ἐδίδαξε τέχνην (*De imit.* fr. 6.1 Usener–Radermacher). Thanks to human ingenuity, the weaknesses of nature may be transcended. Here lies the parallel between unnatural birth and rhetorical training: 'thus is assimilation (*homoiotēs*) born (*tiktetai*) also from imitations (*mimēsesin*) of language' (οὕτω καὶ λόγων μιμήσεσιν ὁμοιότης τίκτεται, *De imit.* fr. 6.1 Usener–Radermacher). The use of the language of birth (*tiktetai*) in this passage invites the reader to map the one narrative of 'conception' onto the other, and to compare the deviations from 'natural' processes that occur in either case. In this striking anecdote, then, rhetorical *mimēsis* is presented not as an organic process but as an artificial elaboration upon nature.

The second parable is well known from other sources.[126] The painter Zeuxis, wanting to portray Helen naked, paraded a series

[123] Plut. *De aud. poet.* 18a; see above, p. 51.

[124] The idea of 'maternal impression' is found elsewhere in the literature of antiquity, and indeed in later traditions too: see M. D. Reeve (1989).

[125] See esp. Goldhill (1995), 62–4.

[126] Cic. *De inu.* 2.1; Plin. *NH* 35.64; see Rouveret (1989), 36. This story also seems to be evoked and inverted in Lucian's *Imagines*, where Panthea (the mistress of Lucius Verus) is described by reference to a series of parts of statues: see Korus (1981), 53; Maffei (1986), 155–6. The story may have originated with Douris of Samos, as claimed by Aujac (1992), 149.

of young girls before him: 'the feature in each one of them that was worthy of being painted was then selected and drawn together into one picture of a body, and art (*tekhnē*) created a single, perfect form out of the collocation of parts' (*ὅ δ' ἦν ἄξιον παρ' ἑκάστηι γραφῆς, ἐς μίαν ἠθροίσθη σώματος εἰκόνα, κἀκ πολλῶν μερῶν συλλογῆς ἕν τι συνέθηκεν ἡ τέχνη τέλειον εἶδος*, *De imit.* fr. 6.1 Usener–Radermacher). This anecdote is extremely revealing, not only for the disturbingly 'fetishistic' reduction of female representation to an aggregate of beautiful body-parts,[127] but also for the implications of the anecdote for the identity-construction of the educated orator. What sort of Frankenstinian self is forged from a collection of limbs? Ancient literary terminology routinely associated bodily limbs and organs with parts of literary discourse,[128] but praise is usually reserved for the 'organic' whole: 'the whole of the speech must cohere, like an animal', as Plato puts it (*δεῖν πάντα λόγον ὥσπερ ζῶιον συνεστάναι*, *Phaedr.* 264c).[129] In Dionysius' anecdote, however, art (*tekhnē*) creates something unnatural and hybrid.[130] *Mimēsis* is presented as a deviation from the normal organic unity of a natural being. Paradoxically, this is closer to Plato's attacks upon imitation than to Aristotle's more accommodating theory. Dionysius' 'rescue' of *mimēsis*, however, is premised upon the notion that the artful, artificial, and secondary is, in fact, superior to the natural; or, rather, nature is best represented through non-natural combinations.

For Dionysius, the *paideia* bestowed upon the individual by careful and selective reading and imitation is not simply a continuation of natural processes. On the contrary, *tekhnē* marks a

[127] See e.g. Barthes (1990), 112: 'the subject . . . knows the female body only as a division and dissemination of partial objects: leg, breast, shoulder, neck, hands. Fragmented woman is the object offered to Sarrasine's love. Divided, anatomized, she is merely a kind of dictionary of fetish objects. This sundered, dissected body . . . is reassembled by the artist (and this is the meaning of his vocation) into a whole body, the body of love descended from the heaven of art, in which fetishism is abolished . . .'. This process, according to one definitional criterion proposed by Andrea Dworkin and Catharine MacKinnon, is precisely pornographic: 'women's body parts . . . are exhibited, such that women are reduced to those parts' (cited and glossed at Parker 1992: 99).

[128] Ar. *Ran.* 862; Pl. *Phaedr.* 264c; Arist. *Poet.* 1451[a]; 1459[a]. Good discussion of this topos at Most (1992), 407, with 418 n. 116.

[129] Echoed by 'Longinus': see *De subl.* 10.1, and esp. 40.1

[130] At *Ars poet.* 1–23, Horace compares an unbalanced composition to a centaur; but this example, roughly contemporary with Dionysius, instead constructs the norm as a paradigm of organic unity.

crucial phase of disjunction between the natural and the developed self. At a later point in the sixth fragment of *On imitation*, Dionysius explains why he has gone to the bother of cataloguing the various types of style (*ideai*) of the orators. Careful reading of the ancients is fundamental for those who wish to excel in oratory, he argues: 'in the case of things that give pleasure naturally (*physei*), if they are mixed together through art (*tekhnēs*) into the shape of a single, reasoning body, the style becomes better as a result of the mixture' (ἃ καὶ αὐτὰ μὲν οἰκείαι φύσει τέρπει, εἰ δὲ καὶ κερασθείη διὰ τῆς τέχνης εἰς ἑνὸς τύπον λογικοῦ σώματος, βέλτιων ἡ φράσις τῆι μίξει γίνεται, *De imit.* fr. 6.5 Usener–Radermacher).[131] Once again the somatic metaphor, and once again the appropriation of the somatic to describe the province of art and culture. Nature is not by itself particularly impressive: true excellence comes from *mimēsis*, which is not (as it is in Plutarch) a natural process, but begins at precisely the point where nature stops.

Although Dionysius focuses here upon the education of the individual, and does not treat of larger cultural forces, his discussions of the relative merits of nature and culture have important ramifications for the historical positioning of a post-Classical, 'secondary' Greek world. Dionysius' writings are all directed towards students expected to use the canonical texts of the past critically, and it is precisely this set of critical activities that he aims to inculcate.[132] The entire *raison d'être* of his literary-critical works is to provide students with the resources that will allow them to use their historical posterity effectively. The emphasis upon the role of *tekhnē* ('art', 'artifice') in his mimetic process points to an interpretation of 'secondariness' as indicative of the non-natural, contrived, but most of all hyper-sophisticated tenor of Roman Greek literary culture.

Indeed, certain generically innovative literary products of Roman Greece celebrate precisely these 'artificial' qualities. The prime example is the satirical dialogue invented by Lucian.[133] This form is self-consciously presented as a confection of other literary genres, in particular philosophical dialogue and Old Comedy.[134]

[131] A similar idea is found in 'Longinus' (*De subl.* 22.1): see above, p. 62. Cf. also Philostr. *Dialexis* II, p. 260.3 Kayser.

[132] See the full discussion of Hidber (1996), 56–75, esp. 67–72.

[133] For more on Lucian, see Ch. 2, '*Paideia* and Hellenism'; Ch. 5.

[134] See J. Hall (1981), 13–14, 29–33. Excellent discussion of these themes at Branham (1989), 38–43; Romm (1990), 83–90; see also Dubel (1994), 21.

In *Twice accused*, a personification of Dialogue accuses Lucian (or, rather, his intratextual surrogate persona, 'the Syrian') of making him 'all but laughable' (μικροῦ δεῖν γελοῖον), because he locked him up with 'mockery, iambus, cynicism, Eupolis, and Aristophanes' (τὸ σκῶμμα καὶ τὸν ἴαμβον καὶ κυνισμὸν καὶ τὸν Εὔπολιν καὶ τὸν Ἀριστοφάνη, *Bis acc.* 33; cf. *Pisc.* 25). Dialogue concludes his accusation by representing this generic fusion, in strikingly Dionysian terms, as a bizarre aberration from nature:

How can this not be a terrible affront that I have suffered? I am no longer in my familiar (*oikeiou*) state, but joking and poking fun and acting alien (*allokotous*) plots for him! What is strangest (*atopōtaton*) of all, I am mixed in a paradoxical mixture, neither going on foot [i.e. in prose] nor mounted on metre, but I seem like a composite (*syntheton*) and foreign (*xenon*) apparition, rather like a hippocentaur.

πῶς οὖν οὐ δεινὰ ὕβρισμαι μηκέτ' ἐπὶ τοῦ οἰκείου διακείμενος, ἀλλὰ κωμῳδῶν καὶ γελωτοποιῶν καὶ ὑποθέσεις ἀλλοκότους ὑποκρινόμενος αὐτῷ; τὸ γὰρ πάντων ἀτοπώτατον, κρᾶσίν τινα παράδοξον κέκραμαι καὶ οὔτε πεζός εἰμι οὔτε ἐπὶ τῶν μέτρων βέβηκα, ἀλλὰ ἱπποκενταύρου δίκην σύνθετόν τι καὶ ξένον φάσμα τοῖς ἀκούουσιν δοκῶ. (*Bis acc.* 33)

The references to the 'foreignness' (*allokotous*, *xenon*, even *atopōtaton*: literally 'most out-of-place') of the literary form pick up upon Lucian's self-representation in this dialogue and elsewhere as a Hellenized barbarian (a theme that will be discussed further in the following chapter).[135] The particular relevance of this passage to the present discussion lies in the metaphorical relationship between literary admixture and deviations from nature: Dialogue has now become a *syntheton* ('composite'/'synthetic') apparition, rather like a hippocentaur.[136] The late writer's innovation is represented as a form of artificial warping of the 'natural', organic state of earlier literature. Although the confection of such grotesqueries is presented by Dialogue as a charge against the author and his persona, 'the Syrian' does not countermand this accusation (focusing instead upon the positive benefits that accrue from the livening up of grumpy Dialogue). Lucian subtly reappropriates a potential accusation of literary impropriety as a marker of innovation.

The paradoxical mixture to which Dialogue refers is specifically

[135] Ch. 2, '*Paideia* and Hellenism'.

[136] For similar images, cf. Hor. *Ars poet.* 1–23 (centaur); Hld. *Aeth.* 10.29.1 (hippotaur), with Whitmarsh (1998*b*), 118.

the prosimetric form that Lucian sometimes adopts (e.g. in *Zeus rants*), which makes for a subtle pun: centaurs both travel 'on foot' (i.e. in prose) and ride (i.e. adopt the more 'elevated' form of poetry). Elsewhere, however, the charge of syntheticism and hippocentaurism relates to his generic mixtures, and thus to his works in general. This is particularly the case in his proemial speeches (or *prolaliai*).[137] In the ironically self-critical *You are a Prometheus in words*, he deprecates his own technique by comparing it to Ptolemy Lagos' exotic (*καινά*) imports into Egypt, a completely black Bactrian camel and a piebald man (4). When he led these into the theatre, the effect was not wonder but, respectively, fear and laughter. Similarly, Lucian writes, his own work may be something of a camel in Egypt, for 'the fact that it involves combining even the two finest forms, dialogue and comedy, is not enough to produce beauty if the mixture is not harmonious and in due proportion' (*τὸ ἐκ δυοῖν τοῖν καλλίστοιν ξυγκεῖσθαι, διαλόγου καὶ κωμωιδίας, οὐδὲ τοῦτο ἀπόχρη εἰς εὐμορφίαν, εἰ μὴ καὶ ἡ μίξις ἐναρμόνιος καὶ κατὰ τὸ σύμμετρον γίγνοιτο*, 5). He then proceeds to compare his work to a hippocentaur, 'the most outrageous' (*ὑβριστότατον*) of beasts. Lucian ironically figures his work as a form of affront (*ὕβρις*) to literary tradition, and in particular to the parochial Hellenocentrism of Greek culture: the theme of cultural alienation is marked in this text. Lucian's synthetic technique is set up as an offence to literary propriety; but it is the reader who is really challenged, for her or his overinvestment in received categories and cultural values.

In *Zeuxis*, however, the hippocentaur returns as a positive image. An audience that recently praised the 'foreign' (*ξένην*) temper of his writing, his 'novelty' (*νεωτερισμόν*),[138] his 'innovation' (*καινότητος*), and 'paradoxical language' (*παραδοξολογίας*, 1) is gently chastised for not noticing the other, more traditional features of Lucian's writing: the use of fine words according with 'the ancient canon' (*πρὸς τὸν ἀρχαῖον κανόνα*), and the 'Attic grace' (*χάριτος Ἀττικῆς*) and 'harmony' (*ἁρμονίας*, 2). He proceeds to compare his own compositions to a painting of a hippocentaur by

[137] On *prolaliai* (the word is first attested in the medieval manuscripts of Lucian, but the genre seems to have been established in antiquity) see Mras (1949); Russell (1983), 77–9; Branham (1985), specifically on Lucian (recapped at Branham 1989: 38–46); Nesselrath (1990).

[138] A word that is also suggestive of political revolution: the implication is that innovative art actually threatens social hierarchies.

Zeuxis, a painter who 'was always trying to innovate' (ἀεὶ . . . καινοποιεῖν ἐπειρᾶτο), conceiving of 'something alien and foreign' (ἀλλόκοτον . . . καὶ ξένον, 3). The hippocentaur is a paradigm of 'fusion' (μίξις) and 'harmonizing' (ἁρμογή), and Lucian extols the technique 'whereby the equine part was linked and bound to the female part' (καθ' ὃ συνάπτεται καὶ συνδεῖται τῶι γυναικείωι τὸ ἱππικόν, 6). Zeuxis' audience, like Lucian's own, failed to recognize the 'skill' (τέχνη) of the portrait, emphasizing only its innovations (7). In the closing lines of the speech, the hippocentaur is referred to as *terastios* ('prodigious', *Zeux.* 12). A *teras* ('prodigy') is a deviation from nature, an affront to traditional, Aristotelian taxonomy,[139] an image brilliantly evocative of Lucian's self-construction as a writer both threatening and thrilling.

Lucian's works, then, articulate their artful innovations in Dionysian terms, as a new, non-natural form created by means of artful *mimēsis*; at the same time, however, Lucian is capable of subtle variation in his treatment of this theme, now appearing to celebrate novelty, and now foregrounding the elements of his texts that cohere to traditional, archaizing canons. This oscillation, however, does not disguise his characteristic awareness of the 'strange', 'alien', 'out-of-place' qualities of his own writing. Unlike Plutarch, who constructs his texts as a 'natural' extension of reality, a medium that allows him to 'meet with' and 'live with' long-dead men, Lucian establishes the power of artifice as an aesthetic force.

The other major literary form that marks itself as artificial is the sophistic novel.[140] Although traces of Greek novelistic or novelizing writing can be found as far back as the early first century BCE (to which period the fragmentary *Ninus* is dated),[141] the novel in its received form is very much a product of the period of the Roman principate; and, like Lucianic dialogue, it marks itself generically as innovative and modernist. In particular, the three 'sophistic' novels (Longus' *Daphnis and Chloë*, Achilles Tatius' *Leucippe and Clitophon*, Heliodorus' *Aethiopica*) betray a sense of generic cohesion through their thoroughly self-conscious modernity. All three display a recurrent interest in paradoxes,

[139] Arist. *De gen. an.* 767^{a}36–^{b}7, with Whitmarsh (1998*b*), 116–17.

[140] For recent bibliographies, see Schmeling ed. (1996), 815–64; Swain ed. (1999), 382–412; and, for guidance, Bowie and Harrison (1993).

[141] Stephens and Winkler (1995), 23

innovative 'set-piece' scenes, and the intermingling of nature and culture. In this respect, they demand contextualizing against the background of Roman Greece's preoccupation with the dialectical relationship between tradition and innovation; or, to put it another way, the novelistic genre is predisposed to take a provocative stance vis-à-vis the current debates concerning the ways in which literature 'should' construct its relationship with the past.

Writing in the second century CE,[142] Achilles Tatius (or, rather, his narrator) frequently employs the terms *paradoxos* and *paralogos* ('paradoxical', 'extraordinary') and *kainos* of his descriptions of events.[143] As we have seen, these terms have almost the status of technical terms in Lucian, marking literature that is (or is perceived to be) radically new and untraditional. Let us take only one example. In the fourth book, the piratical 'Herdsmen' spring a trap upon the Egyptians, flooding the causeway along which they are walking. Achilles' description revels in the fusion of land and sea:

> It was impossible to tell what was lake and what was ground . . . A novel (*kaina*) kind of ill-fortune, this: such a terrible shipwreck, with not a ship in sight. Two extraordinary departures from convention (*kaina kai paraloga*): an aquatic infantry-battle and a shipwreck on land!
>
> διακρῖναι δὲ οὐκ ἦν, τί λίμνη καὶ τί πεδίον . . . καὶ ἦν καινὰ ἀτυχήματα, καὶ ναυάγια τοσαῦτα, καὶ ναῦς οὐδαμοῦ. ἀμφότερα δὲ καινὰ καὶ παράλογα, ἐν ὕδατι πεζομαχία, καὶ ἐν τῆι γῆι ναυάγια. (Ach. Tat. *L&C* 4.14.7–8)

This description is conspicuously rhetorical, evoking the sophistic *epideixeis* that compete for ever greater innovation and surprise (indeed, this passage is closely parallelled in a speech of Polemo).[144] In set-piece scenes like this, Achilles establishes a synecdochic definition of the novel itself, the genre that crosses boundaries, gobbling up pre-established literary forms,[145] inter-

[142] Papyrological evidence has confirmed that the late 2nd cent. is a *terminus ante quem*, and indeed the overwrought, 'sophistic' style seems most appropriate to that period. See Reardon (1971), 334 nn 55–7, 402 n. 219.

[143] *paradoxos*: 2.18.6; 4.4.1; 6.2.3; *paralogos*: 4.14.5; 4.14.8; 5.1.6; 5.23.5; 6.2.8; 6.4.3; *kainos* (listing only the uses meaning 'of a novel kind'): 1.9.5; 2.14.4; 3.3.3; 3.16.4; 4.4.6; 4.7.15; 4.12.1; 4.14.8 (*bis*); 5.1.6; 5.14.4, 6.7.3; 6.21.2. See further G. Anderson (1993), 163–5, who, however, underplays the extent to which the paradoxical is already a theme in Chariton (1.1.2; 3.2.7; 8.1.2).

[144] Polem. 1.11: γῆι καὶ θαλάσσηι μεμερισμένος ('divided between land and sea'); and esp. 1.36: ναυμαχίαν ἐν γῆι ('sea-battle on land'); cf 2 11 for another paradox (though dead, Callimachus seemed alive).

[145] See esp. Fusillo (1989), 17–109.

permeating high art and low comedy. Fusion and paradoxical hybridity are the defining indices of novelistic discourse,[146] whether in 'set pieces' such as this or (in a more psychological context) in the topos of the mixed emotions of a character.[147] Historically, the novel is an irredeemably modernist invention, a literary oddity that is parasitic upon epic, tragedy, comedy, history, philosophy, declamation, epigram, elegy, and iambic. The novel has to maintain its novelty (a pun that is more fortuitous than inherently significant).[148] Achilles' internal observers usually respond to extraordinary events with awe (ἔκπληξις), thus constructing one possible response to the novel itself.[149] As Lucian reminds us in his declamation *On the hall*, however, mere 'wonder' (θαῦμα) is the response of an unsophisticate (ἰδιώτης, *De dom.* 2). Similarly in *Leucippe and Clitophon*, the reader is taught that the art of novel-reading consists in expecting the unexpected. This is most notably in evidence in the scene in the seventh book in which Clitophon is falsely informed, for the third time in the course of the narrative, that Leucippe has died. The naïve protagonist and narrator immediately laments and seeks suicide, but Clinias (his more experienced, older cousin: see 1.7.1) encourages him:

> Who knows whether or not she has come back to life? Has she not died many times before? Has she not been resurrected many times before? Why this haste to die?
>
> *τίς γὰρ οἶδεν, εἰ ζῆι πάλιν; μὴ γὰρ οὐ πολλάκις τέθνηκε; μὴ γὰρ οὐ πολλάκις ἀνεβίω; τί δὲ προπέτως ἀποθνήισκεις;* (Ach. Tat. *L&C* 7.6.2)

Clinias shows himself not just more worldly-wise, but also more adept at the reading of novelistic conventions (of which, it must be said, the 'false death' or *Scheintod* is one of the most celebrated and hackneyed). By playing off the knowing responses to surprising situations of the more sophisticated Clinias against those of the

146 See Rommel (1923) on the use of paradoxography by Achilles and Heliodorus.

147 Fusillo (1999), stressing the 'polyphonic' quality of this novelistic topos. The model is Hom. *Il.* 6.484, where it is said that Andromache 'laughed and cried' (δακρυόεν γελάσασα). The scholia ad loc. describe this expression as a *syntheton* ('compound'), and it may be that its 'synthetic' quality is what attracts the novelists to it.

148 There is no ancient Greek word for 'novel' (Reardon 1991: 3–14; Bowersock 1994: 1–27); the English word 'novel' comes from the Italian *novella*, i.e. 'news', 'current affairs'.

149 Ach. Tat. *L&C* 3.15.5; 4.14.5; 5.23.5; 6.4.3; 7.8.1.

naïve Clitophon, Achilles implicitly educates his readers in the art of novel-reading: this is a world in which the norm is surprise, innovation should be anticipated. In this respect, the novel embodies, even exhausts, the principles of artificial creation espoused by Dionysius and Lucian.

The theme of nature and culture is treated only briefly by Achilles (in the debate in book 2 over the relative merits of the 'artful' kisses of women and the 'artless' kisses of boys),[150] but receives considerable emphasis in Longus' *Daphnis and Chloë* and Heliodorus' *Aethiopica*. Both novels provide paradigmatic explorations of identity-construction, experimenting with the relative influences of *tekhnē* and *physis* in the formation of the mature adult. All of the Greek novels are accounts of the maturation of a young couple, who (in the three 'sophistic' novels)[151] marry at the end, thus ending their long periods of adolescence with an initiation into adulthood.[152] In Longus and Heliodorus, however, a series of more conspicuously theoretical debates concerning education and identity is adumbrated. Moreover, as we shall discover, the debates over nature and culture have important ramifications for the project of generic self-definition in the novel.

In the first of these texts *Daphnis and Chloë* (probably written in the late second century CE),[153] the playful interlinking of the themes of art, nature, and education is now well understood.[154] It tells the story of a young girl and boy exposed in the countryside. Daphnis and Chloë fall for one another, but do not know how to consummate their desire: 'they wanted something but did not know what they wanted' (ἤθελόν τι, ἠγνόουν ὅ τι θέλουσι, *D&C*

[150] Ach. Tat. *L&C* 2.37.7; 2.38.5.

[151] The exceptions being Chariton's *Chaereas and Callirhoë* and Xenophon's *Ephesian tale*, in which the couples are married at the start.

[152] On initiation into adulthood in the novels, see Burkert (1987), 66–7; Gual (1992); Whitmarsh (1999*b*), 18–20. All the novelistic protagonists whose ages are cited are teenagers: Habrocomes is 16 (Xen. Eph. *Eph.* 1.2.2), Daphnis and Chloë 15 and 13 respectively (Long. *D&C* 1.7.1), Clitophon is 19 (Ach. Tat. *L&C* 1.3.3), Charicleia is 17 (Hld. *Aeth.* 1.3.3). I owe these calculations to J. R. Morgan (1997), 165 n.7.

[153] R. Hunter (1983), 1–15.

[154] See R. Hunter (1983), 45; Zeitlin (1990*a*), 430–44; Teske (1991); J. R. Morgan (1997), 167–72. My discussion here owes much to each of these, and in particular to Zeitlin, who argues (surely rightly) that the themes of art and nature reflect upon the literary status of the text itself. As R. Hunter (1983), 84–98 shows, Longus shows clear affiliation to the style known as *apheleia* ('simplicity'), which rhetorical theorists connect with the art of appearing natural (see most recently I. Rutherford 1998: 64–79).

1.22.4). Consummation is comically deferred, as their naïveté leads them to draw the wrong conclusions from all the signs they see around them. A certain Philetas (whose name suggests the supposed founder of the pastoral genre of poetry)[155] 'educates' (*paideusas*, 2.8.1; cf. *paideutērion*, 2.9.1) them by telling them about *erōs* (2.7); but his knowing advice, that they should cure themselves by means of 'a kiss, an embrace, and lying down next to one another with naked bodies' (*φίλημα καὶ περιβολὴ καὶ συγκατακλιθῆναι γυμνοῖς σώμασι*, *D&C* 2.7.7) is too euphemistic. If this eminently 'cultural' pedagogy fails, then so does Daphnis' attempt to 'imitate' (*μιμούμενος*, 3.14.5) the behaviour of a mating billy-goat. Finally, a certain woman called Lycaenion (who was originally a city-dweller, 3.15.1) presents Daphnis with some 'erotic pedagogy' (*ἐρωτικῆς παιδαγωγίας*, 3.19.1): she 'artfully' (*ἐντέχνως*) positions beneath him the channel he had sought for so long, and 'nature (*physis*) herself taught (*epaideue*) the rest of what had to be done' (*αὐτὴ . . . ἡ φύσις λοιπὸν ἐπαίδευε τὸ πρακτέον*, *D&C* 3.18.4). As Goldhill has shown,[156] the assertion that 'nature did the rest' here is a coy, euphemistic tease to the reader (akin to Ovid's 'who is there who does not know the rest?'),[157] casting a discreet but provocative veil over the final act of consummation. It is, however, also a paradoxical conclusion to the narrative of erotic enculturation, as 'nature' and 'teaching' become fused in the moment of penetration.

As scholars have seen, this entire narrative constitutes a kind of controlled 'experiment' whereby the relative importance of nature and culture in *paideia* may be gauged.[158] Longus is manipulating his readers' awareness of the contemporary debate over the relative roles of nature and culture in the formation of identity. Ultimately, neither art nor nature is granted primacy in the education of Daphnis and Chloë.[159] Although they grow up in the countryside (which, for city-dwellers, represents paradigmatically the absence of culture), their isolation from civic structures is not

[155] Theocr. 7.40; see R. Hunter (1983), 78. Bowie (1985), gallantly speculative, reconstructs the ambit of Philetas' poetry from his *Rezeptionsgeschichte* (including Longus).

[156] Goldhill (1995), 25–6.

[157] *Cetera quis nescit?* (Ov. *Am.* 1.5.25).

[158] See Winkler (1990), 102 for the phrase 'pastoral experiment'; and esp. R. Hunter (1983), 45; Zeitlin (1990*a*), 430; Goldhill (1995), 8–11, 23–7 on *D&C*'s exploration of nature and culture in education.

[159] Teske (1991), 61–72.

absolute:[160] their adoptive parents, for example, know that they are the children of city-dwellers, and so give them a superior education (1.8.1). Moreover, nature is fundamentally ambivalent in *Daphnis and Chloë*, both reassuring and threatening:[161] animals may suckle the two when they are babies at the start (1.2.1; 1.5.2), for example, but wolves (and quasi-wolves) represent a constant menace.[162] Taken as a whole, *Daphnis and Chloë* dramatizes the importance of the principle that the attainment of (erotic) maturity requires a symbiosis of acquired experience and natural instinct. This interfusion of *tekhnē* and *physis* is instantiated at the literary level in the aesthetic intertwining of self-consciousness and 'realism', of intellectualism and stylistic 'simplicity'. Like Achilles, Longus has his set-piece descriptions in which the aesthetics of the novel, as he sees them, are encapsulated: in particular, his luscious descriptions of gardens, natural places in the countryside artificially ornamented for the pleasure of city-folk.[163] In the lyrical description of the *paradeisos* ('Persian garden') that begins the fourth book, Longus tells us that the garden's 'nature seemed the result of art' (ἐδόκει . . . ἡ . . . φύσις εἶναι τέχνης). *Daphnis and Chloë* takes Dionysius' precepts concerning *mimēsis* as an elaboration of the natural, and transmutes them into a tale suffused with both pastoral mythicism and sophistic artifice.

Less well known is the role played by such debates over the roles of nature and artifice in acculturation in Heliodorus' *Aethiopica*. This gargantuan text, probably written in the fourth century CE,[164] is the most complex and narratologically sophisticated of the

[160] Daude (1991), 211–12.

[161] Pandiri (1985), 119–22; Daude (1991), 216. Billault (1996) argues that Longus presents a 'realistic' view of nature, but his realism is more an artful narrative effect than a transparent representation of reality (see Barthes 1986: 141–8 on 'the reality effect' in 19th-cent. fiction).

[162] Aside from the numerous references to threat of wolves (*D&C* 1.12.5; 2.16.2; 2.22.2; 2.26.1; 2.31.1; 3.6.3; 3.23.3; 4.4.3; 4.15.3), we also have Dorcon attempting to rape Chloë whilst wearing a wolfskin (1.20.2), and the predatory initiatrix Lycaenion ('Little-wolf', 3.15.1 etc.). On the 'wolf theme' in *D&C*, see further P. Turner (1960), 120–1; Daude (1991), 217–18; Billault (1996), 514–16.

[163] R. Hunter (1983), 72–3; Pandiri (1985), 118; and esp. the full discussion of Zeitlin (1990*a*), 444–55.

[164] The general consensus favours the late 4th cent. (for a thoroughgoing argument to this effect, see Bargheer 1999: 17–49); some scholars still wish to date the novel to the 3rd cent., though (e.g. Swain 1996: 423–4). My own estimation is that the *Aethiopica* is a 4th-cent. text, given that it seems to echo some of the religious concerns of that period: see below, p. 84.

novels.[165] It tells of a young couple, Charicleia and Theagenes, who meet in Delphi and elope together. It turns out that Charicleia is the daughter of the king and queen of Ethiopia, who was given away by her mother, who feared the charge of adultery when she was born with white skin. Charicleia and Theagenes make their way down the Nile, and, after a number of events, end up in Ethiopia, where they are eventually recognized and allowed to marry and to accept priesthoods.

The extraordinary feature of this tale, without direct parallel in ancient literature, is the mapping of a narrative exploration of black and white skin colour onto what is (in certain respects) a conventional, Odyssean narrative of identity concealed and revealed. By siting the end of the narrative of maturation at the end of the world,[166] Heliodorus brings to the fore the questions surrounding the relationship between acculturation and racial identity.[167] Is Charicleia 'really' an Ethiopian, only superficially playing the role of a Greek? (Indeed, several other figures in the *Aethiopica* seem to feign Greekness.)[168] Or do her white skin, her Greek name, and her Greek education make her definitively Greek? Does the oracle that prophesies 'white garlands on blackening brows' (λευκὸν ἐπὶ κροτάφων στέμμα μελαινομένων, 2.35.5) suggest that, by travelling to and being recognized in Ethiopia, Charicleia and Theagenes 'become' black?[169]

Heliodorus is (as observed above) probably a fourth-century author, and, in his quasi-religious emphasis upon 'escape' to a kingdom of the sun at the edge of the world, seems to show the signs of the extraordinary upheavals of a period that saw a (notionally) empire-wide conversion to Christianity, reversion to paganism, then reconversion. It is possible to make the case that this narrative reflects the mystical worship of the Helios-cult that

[165] On the sophistication of Heliodorus' narrative, see e.g. Winkler (1982); J. R. Morgan (1989*a*; 1989*b*); R. Hunter (1998).

[166] Heliodorus refers to the 'end' of his narrative with the word *peras* (10.14.4), often used of the 'end' of the world: see Whitmarsh (1998*b*), 98.

[167] Whitmarsh (1998*b*; 1999*b*); Perkins (1999). Indeed, this text was celebrated by black intellectuals in the early 20th cent. as a parry to the 'whitening' of the Classical heritage by white-dominated academic culture: Selden (1998).

[168] Calasiris is mistaken for a Greek because of his clothing (2.21.4–6); Theagenes' claim that his race is 'truly Greek' (ἀκριβῶς Ἑλληνικόν, 2.34.1) is treated with irony; and Homer is exposed as an Egyptian (3.14.2–4). On these passages, see Whitmarsh (1998*b*), 100–7.

[169] As suggested by J. R. Morgan (1989*a*), 318.

achieved particular dominance in the time of Julian the Apostate.[170] Such narrowly historical explanations (which, of course, would date the text to within the three years of Julian's reign, i.e. 361–3 CE), however, ignore the text's self-conscious self-positioning within the *longue durée* of the period of novel-writing. The *Aethiopica* also shows signs of generic continuity with the earlier novels of Achilles and Longus; and, although it is (probably) later and (demonstrably) different in orientation, it certainly occupies an important place in an analysis of *mimēsis*, nature, and culture in Roman Greek literature. The politics of periodization in the modern academy demand a break between the 'high principate' and 'late antiquity', but such barriers are (whilst at times heuristically indispensable) fluid and negotiable in practice.

The point of central interest for the present discussion is Heliodorus' use of debates concerning the roles of *mimēsis* and nature in identity-formation.[171] As Charicleia returns towards Ethiopia, the reader is made aware that she is returning to her 'natural' (φύσει) father, in contrast to the two adoptive fathers she has known so far (*Aeth.* 7.14.5–6). Although she has only ever known exile and assumed homelands, she nevertheless retains a strong sense that there is a true parent and origin; and it is towards the revelation of true, 'natural' parentage that this narrative progresses. At one point, Charicleia observes that the recognition tokens she carries cannot constitute absolute proof of her identity: the only undeniable token of parentage is 'maternal nature (*physis*)' (ἡ μητρώια φύσις, *Aeth.* 9.24.8). In one respect, she is right, in that Persinna, her mother, is quick to accept her (10.13.1). But her father Hydaspes requires much more proof, before 'finally he bowed to all-conquering nature (*physeōs*): not only was he convinced that he was a father, but he also betrayed a father's feelings' (τελευτῶν ἡττήθη τῆς τὰ πάντα νικώσης φύσεως καὶ πατὴρ οὐκ εἶναι μόνον ἐπείθετο ἀλλὰ καὶ πάσχειν ὅσα πατὴρ ἠλέγχετο, *Aeth.* 10.16.2).[172]

Offsetting this overwhelming emphasis upon 'natural' identity, however, is the focus upon the role of an artwork in the begetting of Charicleia. We recall that the reason for Charicleia's exposure

170 See most recently Bargheer (1999).

171 See further Whitmarsh (1998*b*), 109–13.

172 Hydaspes makes further reference to his parental *physis* at 10.16.7.

was her having been born white. Her congenital skin-colour was due to her mother's having observed a portrait of Andromeda at the moment of conception (*Aeth.* 4.8.3–5; 10.14.7).[173] This device evokes Dionysius' parable of the ugly farmer's use of pictures to impress beauty upon the foetus, a parable that (as we have seen) is designed to emphasize the crucial role that mimetic artifice can play in creating the self. As a final proof to Hydaspes that Charicleia is his daughter, the priest Sisimithres brings out the painting, and invites the onlookers to compare Charicleia and Andromeda: 'the accuracy of the assimilation (*homoiotētos*) struck them with delighted astonishment; even Hydaspes could hold out no longer in his disbelief, but stood motionless awhile, possessed by a mixture of joy and amazement (*thaumatos*)' (πρὸς τὸ ἀπηκριβωμένον τῆς ὁμοιότητος σὺν περιχαρείαι ἐκπλαγέντων, ὥστε καὶ τὸν Ὑδάσπην οὐκέτι μὲν ἀπιστεῖν ἔχειν, ἐφεστάναι δὲ πολὺν χρόνον ὑφ' ἡδονῆς ἅμα καὶ θαύματος ἐχόμενον, *Aeth.* 10.15.1). 'Assimilation' (*homoiotēs*) is, as we have again seen, an important term in theories of *mimēsis*: it marks the degree of approximation of imitating student to imitated model.[174] Heliodorus is carefully invoking *mimēsis*-theory as an explanation for Charicleia's extraordinary identity. Yet the scene also constitutes a playful reversal of theoretical norms: 'wonder' (*thauma*) is usually occasioned in onlookers by the similarity of a painting to its subject, not the reverse![175] The painting has been refused the role of passive reflector of nature, and takes on an active, creative role in the formation of the human subject, almost as a surrogate parent (and it is worth recalling, in this connection, the emphasis placed in the Greek tradition upon the need for children to show 'likeness', *homoiotēs*, to their parents).[176]

Heliodorus thus presents competing explanations, in terms of

[173] On the representation of Andromeda as white, see Dilke (1980); on the sources for (and subsequent history of) 'maternal impression', see M. D. Reeve (1989).

[174] Above, p. 73.

[175] Cf. ps.-Long. *De subl.* 36.3: 'In the case of art (*tekhnē*), that which is most accurate occasions wonder (*thaumazetai*)' (ἐπὶ . . . τέχνης θαυμάζεται τὸ ἀκριβέστατον). Girls are frequently compared by way of simile to artworks in erotic discourse (Jax 1936: 47–8), which adds another level to Heliodorus' innovation here. Moreover, as is observed by Bartsch (1989), 48, Longus and Achilles open their narratives with descriptions of pictures, and Heliodorus may be cleverly playing upon that convention too.

[176] For the *homoiotēs* of children to parents, see Hes. *Op.* 182, 235; Gow (1952), 2.334.

both nature and culture, for the identity of Charicleia.[177] In this respect, he resembles Longus; and, indeed, the persistence of this topos can be considered an instance of the Greek novel's generically introspective process of self-conscious innovation. Yet what Heliodorus adds is the decisive element of race and cultural identity. It is not simply that this theme is emblematic of a new, late-antique multiculturalism.[178] Rather, Heliodorus' complex play with the categories of the natural and the cultural represents simultaneously an (unresolved) theorematic experiment with current theories of identity-formation *and* a (by now) familiar metaliterary exploration of the novel as the product of 'unnatural', post-Classical *mimēsis*. The intratextual audience's 'wonder' (*θαῦμα*) at the extraordinary phenomenon of 'maternal impression' also prompts the extratextual readership's marvel at the bizarre innovations embodied in this novel.[179] Nor is racial hybridity the only means whereby the *Aethiopica* figures its own bold literary innovation: in the final book, other bizarre distortions of nature are presented, notably the giraffe, a 'marvellous' (*thaumasiou*) hybrid of a camel and a leopard (10.27.1–4), and the 'alien, yoked-together combination, the hippotaur' (*ξένην τινὰ ταύτην ἱπποταύρου ξυνωρίδα ζευξάμενον*) created by Theagenes' simultaneous riding of a bull and a horse (10.29.1).[180] To the alert reader, these bestial cross-breeds (in particular the latter) function metatextually, siting themselves in a direct line with Lucian's hippocentaurs (explicitly marked, as we have seen, as symbols of generic contamination). It is certainly the case that the Greek novels are crucial test-sites for theories of acculturation, education, and identity; but the interwoven discourses of nature and culture are also deployed self-consciously in order to site these texts in a posterior relationship with the Classical world.

[177] I am indebted to conversations with Froma Zeitlin for the formulation of ideas in this paragraph.

[178] See e.g. Bowersock (1994), 53 (of the Greek novels, and in particular of Heliodorus): 'Fiction, and perhaps fiction alone, signals the disappearance of barbarism as a conceptual means of asserting the superiority of Graeco-Roman culture.'

[179] *θαῦμα* and cognates at 9.22.2; 9.22.4; 10.9.1; 10.9.4 (*θάμβος*); 10.12.1, 10.13.2 (*θάμβος*); 10.13.3; 10.15.1; 10.16.6; 10.23.4, 10.30.5; 10.34.2; 10.35.2; 10.39.3; *ἔκπληξις* at 10.15.1; 10.30.7. 'Wonder' is said by Aristotle to be an effect of recognition scenes: see *Poet.* 1454[a] (also 1460[b]), with Cave (1988), 44–5.

[180] On the giraffe as a 'figure du métissage', see Létoublon (1993), 131–2; on its narratological implications, see J. R. Morgan (1994).

CONCLUSION: FROM 'PAST AND PRESENT' TO 'PRIOR AND POSTERIOR'

We began by considering an extreme modern reaction to the repetitive aesthetic of Roman Greek literary culture. Where van Groningen errs is principally in oversimplifying the notion of repetition, which (as we have seen) is not necessarily a process of empty iteration. It may be helpful to invoke Freud's distinction in *Beyond the pleasure principle* between two types of 'repetition compulsion' inspired by a trauma. The first involves neurotically replaying an original trauma, while the second involves enacting a new scenario in which the victim becomes the master.[181] If the 'trauma' for Roman Greeks was the loss of independent sovereignty, then this culture's 'repetition compulsion' was more of the latter kind then the former. Imitative repetition can be (and was for Roman Greeks) a creative, dynamic, articulate *poiēsis* in the present, not simply a neurotic obsession with the past.[182]

Literary *mimēsis*—the imitation of texts written in the Classical past—was a fundamental means of constructing the cultural status of the present. What this chapter has shown is the plurality of possible positions: *mimēsis* was the locus for a series of debates concerning the proper relationship between past and present. The corollary of this assertion is that it was not a pathological symptom of a pre-existent cultural mentality, but an active, dynamic means of creating cultural identity (the precise modalities of which will alter in accordance with the strategies and exigencies of the author). The use of *mimēsis*, moreover, was not simply a nostalgic attempt to ignore the evident disparities between past and present in the hope of creating a deluded, imaginary continuity with the past: the ongoing process of intertextual citation of Classical models draws attention to discontinuity as much as continuity. Just as a quotation on the page of a modern book is cut off from the organic whole of the author's work by quotation marks, visible indices of alien provenance, so mimetic *paideia* necessitated an awareness of the 'otherness' of the literature of the past. In Elsner's words, the mythic values of the past and the exigencies of the present can at times 'intertwine, reinforcing each other like a

[181] Freud's theory as helpfully interpreted by Quint (1989), 118.

[182] The same point made vis-à-vis Virgil's *imitatio* of Theocritus at DuQuesnay (1979), 37.

double helix', but they can also fail to match: '[a]nd so the ideology and identity to which they have given birth are not coherent; they are full of contradiction'.[183]

The texts considered in this chapter explore their mimetic relationship with the canonical past through the semi-technical discourses of nature and culture, allying their literary aesthetics with theoretical explorations of the roles of *physis* and *tekhnē* in identity-formation. Some of these texts (Lucianic dialogue, the novels) have been composed in genres that are new to the period of the Roman principate. Not all literature of the period is equally innovative, and indeed the desire for innovation is sometimes prescriptively excoriated. In the texts considered in this chapter, however, literary innovation is linked to artifice, a movement away from the 'natural' plenitude of the Classical model. The fundamental structures of this aesthetic, namely the privileging of the originary as the site of the 'real', are Platonic; but the terms have been twisted, so that for some writers unnatural, posterior elaboration becomes celebrated over the ontologically prior. In this respect, a strong answer to van Groningen's criticisms of a 'sham' literary culture had already been advanced by the writers of Roman Greece: modernity is defined by secondariness; but this condition may be recouped by a strong writer, transformed from a handicap to an empowering aesthetic.

Literary writing inevitably requires a negotiation of tradition, a sense of the canon. Yet canons are not substantive, self-evident bodies, as even their stoutest defenders aver.[184] Even in the case of those rare figures who are always assumed to be culturally central (Homer, Plato), there is a plurality of possible responses to them. Contest and deviation lie at the heart of the Greek tradition. This, clearly, has implications for cultural definition too: if gaps between literary past and present (perhaps we should say 'prior and posterior') can be interposed or foreclosed strategically, then the question of what it is to be Greek—to be a Greek writer—poses itself with a greater intensity. The paradox is that the only defining constituents of Greek *paideia* are precisely the querulous agonistics that preclude any definitional stability.

[183] Elsner (1995), 150.

[184] Bloom (1994), 37, citing the 'vast complexities and contradictions that constitute the essence of the Canon, which is anything but a unity or stable structure'.

2

Education: Strategies of Self-Making

> Pedagogy cannot but encounter the problem of imitation. What is example? Should one educate by example or by explanation? Should the teacher make an example of himself . . .?
>
> Jacques Derrida, *Of Grammatology*[1]

The previous chapter discussed the multiple ways in which mimetic literature can be used to construct or challenge cultural links with the past. In this chapter, I wish to broaden the focus, so as to encompass the *littérateur* him- or her- (but as a rule him-) self. That is to say, I wish to consider the question of what sort of individual identity accrues to the *pepaideumenos*, the 'educated' man (or woman). Several fine studies already exist dealing with the social implications of the practice of education in this period,[2] and the aim of this chapter is neither to retread familiar ground nor to challenge the general picture that education provided a central means whereby young subjects were implicated into a system of hierarchical difference. Instead, I propose to deal with the intellectual responses to the identity-forming aspects of *paideia* among contemporary Greeks. As we shall see, there is a continuity of concerns between this chapter and the previous one: debates concerning power, cultural continuity, and social stability permeate discussions of the mimetic processes that lead to the formation of both literature and *littérateur*.

The philosopher Iamblichus (fourth century CE) writes, in the context of a discussion of *paideia*, that

> it is thanks to upbringing that humans differ (*diapherein*) from beasts, Greeks from foreigners, free men from household slaves, and philosophers from ordinary people . . .

[1] Derrida (1976), 204.

[2] Kaster (1988); T. Morgan (1998); for Classical education more generally, see the essays in Too and Livingston eds. (1998).

σχεδὸν γὰρ ταῖς ἀγωγαῖς διαφέρειν τοὺς μὲν ἀνθρώπους τῶν θηρίων, τοὺς δὲ Ἕλληνας τῶν βαρβάρων, τοὺς δὲ ἐλευθέρους τῶν οἰκετῶν, τοὺς δὲ φιλοσόφους τῶν τυχόντων . . . (Iambl. *Vit. Pyth.* 44)

Education creates or enforces a difference (note *diapherein*) in social rank, articulated (as so often in the Greek tradition),[3] through polarity. In Iamblichus' formulation, education literally 'identifies' (i.e. makes into an identity) the positive term in a series of highly marked oppositions: human and bestial, Greek and barbarian, free and enslaved, and (appropriately, in the context of a biography of Pythagoras) philosopher and non-philosopher. To these categories, as we shall see presently, are often added elite and sub-elite, and masculine and feminine. One important point may be exemplified by reference to the present tense of the infinitive *diapherein*, marking the effects of *paideia* as ongoing rather than consisting in a single, decisive event (which would be indicated by the aorist tense). As Gleason has recently demonstrated, *paideia* (along with the various social identities it comports) needs to be continually reasserted and revived, so as to counter the threats from others in an aggressively competitive, 'face-to-face' society.[4] Even gender, so often (in ancient times as now) subsumed into a (culturally motivated) matrix of supposedly 'natural' differences, is viewed as a site of turbulence and processual change: education could not make men of women, but it could make both men and women more manly. In the context of such radical uncertainty concerning the self, education seeks to anchor identity in the various polar matrices that are so fundamental to the Greek tradition: to become *pepaideumenos* is to engage in an activity whereby the self may become as much a product of art and ingenuity as the literary work itself.

STRATEGIES OF SELF-MAKING

In the previous chapter it became evident that debates over literary aesthetics are inseparable from theoretical discussions concerning the construction of identity. In Plutarch's essay on *How a*

[3] See Cartledge (1993), 8–17 on 'the ideological habit of polarization that was a hallmark of [Greek] mentality and culture' (p. 11); building on Lloyd (1966), the classic account of the centrality of polarity (and analogy) to early Greek intellectual practice.

[4] Gleason (1995), xxi-xxiv; on *paideia* and competition, see Schmitz (1997), 97–135

young man should listen to poetry and in Dionysius' *On imitation*, as we saw, *mimēsis* is 'rescued' from Platonic opprobrium as a proper part of the process that leads to the formation of the adult male. In Lucian's texts (to which we shall return), the 'composite' literary form underlines Lucian's own 'composite' persona, as a native Syrian Hellenized through education. In the sophistic Greek novels, and in particular in *Daphnis and Chloë* and the *Aethiopica*, the manufacture of the literary status of the novel (an innovative, new, synthetic form) is interlinked with the theorematic exploration of issues concerned with the relative roles of nature and culture in the attainment of adult identity. In all these cases, the status of the literary work as a 'cultural' artefact, a product of *paideia*, is bound up with an examination of the educative and identity-forming aspects of *paideia* itself.

I want to turn now to consider in greater detail the various ways in which *mimēsis* is constructed as a 'strategy of self-making'. In manifold ways, the process of education in Roman Greece is intrinsically connected with the shaping of identity through the repetition of models or paradigms, usually drawn from the literature of the fifth and fourth centuries. The notion of education as *mimēsis* goes back at least to Isocrates,[5] but achieves an increased intensity and urgency in the Greek literature of the principate. Crucially, both literary style and life-style alike are affected by the didactic processes of *mimēsis*, which are thus focused not narrowly upon linguistic etiquette, but on the whole person. Not only do pedagogical texts advise the young on what stylistic, lexical, and morphological 'paradigms' (*paradeigmata*) they are to emulate,[6] but even historical and moralizing texts aimed at adults cast themselves as repertories of virtuous paradigms for the edification of their emulatory readers.[7] This point is exemplified in the writings of Dionysius of Halicarnassus (as we saw in the previous chapter, a formative influence upon later writers). In his stylistic commentaries on the ancient orators, he recurrently provides examples of what should be imitated and what avoided; while in his account of the early history of Rome he follows the precedent of Hellenistic historians by explicitly offering up for emulation examples of

[5] *Evag.* 75; cf. *Ad Nic.* 3; Too (1995), 184–9.

[6] T. Morgan (1998), 251–5.

[7] See e.g. Diod. Sic. 1.1.4; Dion. Hal. *Ep. Gn. Pomp.* 3.18; Plut. *Aem. Paul.* proem 1–3. For discussion, see Stierle (1972); Day (1980), 4–5; Desideri (1995*b*). See also above, p. 54 n. 62.

virtuous behaviour.[8] Both life and literature should be conducted as a mode of eclectic *mimēsis* of the paradigms of the past.

Education constructs identity (in the sense of 'sameness') by editing the models that the student must emulate. Indeed, as Derrida suggests in the epigraph to this chapter, teachers are invariably caught between presenting themselves as paradigms to be replicated and furnishing their students with the means with which to debunk the authority upon which their own paradigmatic status rests. Teaching is both conservative, in that it replicates the social order, and subversive, in that it transforms statuses and redistributes social power. This duality is a widespread motif in ancient texts. In comedy, the pedagogical relationship is likened to a father–son relationship, whereby the son's maturity culminates in his taking on paternity and the role of instructor to another. Roman comedy, as Henderson observes, plays out the 'mythic scene of Roman education', whereby 'Father stands in as teacher of his son and the son will (come to) acknowledge Father as Teacher; they must both learn the *praecepta paterna*, the son-now-Father, the Father-who-is-now-son'.[9] In Heliodorus' *Aethiopica*, the heroine Charicleia, resisting marriage (i.e. becoming a woman/wife, a *gynē*), uses against her supposed father the ethical precepts that he himself has 'taught' (*ἐδιδαξάμην*) her (Hld. *Aeth.* 2.33.5). The father who sought to teach his daughter the means to assume a social role in fact gave her the means to resist it.

The most amusing example of this duality at the heart of conceptualizations of pedagogy comes in the story of the 'Pergamene boy' in Petronius' *Satyricon*, a Latin text (written probably in the middle period of the first century CE)[10] focusing upon the adventures of a series of Greek (would-be) *pepaideumenoi*. At one point (the context is unclear, owing to the lacunose nature of the text), the teacher Eumolpus seduces the boy in his charge. When Eumolpus fails to deliver a gift, the boy proceeds to refuse him his pleasure, with the threat 'Go to sleep, or I shall tell my father at once' (*aut dormi, aut ego iam dicam patri*, 87). The two eventually make up; by now, however, the boy's desire exceeds the tutor's,

[8] Hidber (1996), 56–75, with copious further references.

[9] Henderson (1988), 193.

[10] For a brief summary of the debate, with further literature, see S. J. Harrison (1999), xvi-xvii. This article, a survey of 20th-cent. criticism of the Roman novel, is a useful point of entry into the immense bibliography on Petronius. See further Bowie and Harrison (1993).

and after having been woken up in the night once too often, Eumolpus retorts 'Go to sleep, or I shall tell your father at once' (*aut dormi, aut ego iam dicam patri*, 87). The pedagogue and his student have reversed their positions: the tutee replicates his tutor's habits, pursuer is now the pursued. As commentators have frequently noted, the story of the Pergamene boy parodies the portrait of Socrates in Plato's *Symposium*,[11] where the philosopher is said to have inspired desire in his student Alcibiades (Pl. *Symp.* 219b–c); the difference, of course, is that Socrates' only desire is for philosophical consummation, whereas Eumolpus' intentions are rather less highbrow. The anecdote of the Pergamene boy draws attention to the close relationship between pedagogy and erotics, two spheres in which the subject desires reciprocity.[12]

Pedagogy creates identity, in a dual sense. First, as we have seen, it seeks to engender a 'sameness', replicating the values and preoccupations of the teacher. There is a 'narcissistic desire at the heart of most teaching, a desire upon which the authority of educational institutions depends'.[13] At the same time, however, teaching empowers students by furnishing them with an adult identity, the status of a mature, active, decision-making subject. This is the lesson of Petronius' tale: by teaching the student to be desired, the philosopher also teaches him paradigmatically how *to desire*. This duality of identity-making is captured by the pun that pedagogy is a 'question of impersonation':[14] it both creates the conditions wherein the student can impersonate the teacher and 'im-personates' (i.e. places the 'person' within) the student. Yet this new, 'personal' identity is not simply a state of psychological plenitude: it is also, indeed fundamentally, a social role. Learning involves the enculturation of certain habits, signs, and semiotic modes. In the words of Bourdieu and Passeron, teaching is a mode of 'reproduction':[15] by controlling the routes to empowered, elite, adult identity, it ensures the perpetuation of social hierarchies. Among the several forms of 'repetition' effected by teaching, not least is the replication of inequalities.

[11] Dimundo (1983); R. Hunter (1997), 202. On *Sat.* 65 as a parody of Alcibiades' entry in the *Symposium* (212c), see Cameron (1969).

[12] On pedagogy and erotics, see Simon (1995), 95–100; Schemen (1995), 106; for the sexual possibilities of pedagogy, see e.g. Plat. *Alcib.* 1; [Plut.] *De lib.* 11f; Ach. Tat. *L&C* 8.9.2; Luc. *De merc. cond.* 15.

[13] Amirault (1995), 71.

[14] Gallop ed. (1995), subtitle.

[15] Bourdieu and Passeron (1990).

The role of *paideia* in the making of institutionalized, empowered identity is stressed in the paideutic texts. Let us return to Plutarch, the philosopher of the late first and early second centuries CE, and to his normative texts on education. The most striking feature of Plutarch's approach to education is his multifarious focus upon the numerous forms of power conferred by, and required for, education.[16] In *How a young man should listen to poetry* (*Poetry*), Plutarch's sustained argument for an aural regimen for the young to allow them to deal with poetic pleasurability and deception, the metaphors employed are drawn from battle and violent conflict: preventing boys from listening to poetry will inevitably be unsuccessful, rather like shutting city gates and admitting one of the enemy (*Poetry* 14f); if not properly treated, poetry can 'harm and destroy' (φθείρει καὶ βλάπτει, 15a); it can 'overmaster' (κρατῆται, 16e); one must 'resist' (ἀντερείδων, 28d) and not 'expose one's flanks' (πλάγιον . . . παραδιδοὺς ἑαυτόν, 28d) to it; poetry is a 'power' (δύναμις, 18d; 35f).

In associating mimetic art with power, Plutarch taps into a long tradition that stretches back at least as far as Gorgias in the fifth century BCE.[17] Where Plutarch differs, however, is in his emphasis upon the importance of empowered *resistance* to auditory overload. According to Plutarch, the soul is naturally divided into two primary parts, the 'passions' (*thymos*) or 'irrational part' (*to alogon*) and the *logismos* ('reason'), the latter representing order and the former disorder.[18] Poetry, he argues, appeals at an immediate level to the irrational (it can aim at 'the emotional, the bizarre, the unexpected', (τὸ . . . ἐμπαθὲς καὶ παράλογον καὶ ἀπροσδόκητον) rather than truth: *Poetry* 25d), but the soul can be trained to find 'useful' (ὠφέλιμα καὶ χρήσιμα) things in poetry, like the fruit hidden in a vine (*Poetry* 28e). The Dionysiac image of the vine reinforces the association between poetry and the irrational, the point being that neither the irrational nor poetic pleasure can be extirpated: the vine should not be uprooted but pruned where it is excessive (*Poetry* 15e–f). Crucially, the relationship between the reasoning and the passionate parts of the soul should be one of hierarchical dominance. This is brought out particularly strongly in the essay

[16] For more on the theme of education and power, see T. Morgan (1998), *passim*.

[17] Gorgianic rhetorical theory emphasizes the thrall in which an audience is held by successful oratory: Grg. fr. 11 DK 15; Walsh (1984), 81–4. For an echo of this idea by a (?) contemporary of Plutarch's, see ps.-Long. *De subl.* 15.9.

[18] *De virt. mor.* 441d; 443b–c; Dillon (1977), 202–4.

On moral virtue, where the ideal relation of dominance between the two parts of the soul is repeatedly stressed,[19] and the famous chariot simile of Plato's *Phaedrus* is interpreted to refer to the reining in of the appetite by *logismos*.[20] It is *paideia* that is held by Plutarch to yield the power to rein in any visceral, appetitive responses to poetry, and to replace them with philosophical contemplation. The 'uneducated' (*apaideutoi*) are easily excited by their emotions (*Poetry* 31c), and the indiscriminate reader will find his *krisis* ('judgement') 'enslaved' by literature (*Poetry* 26b). This faculty of *krisis*, along with straight-thinking 'reason' (*logismos*), is what Plutarch seeks to develop in the young reader (*Poetry* 15d). In this way, the young man can remain empowered, and avoid the captivating effects of *mimēsis*.

These metaphors of power are not innocent. In Plutarch's writing, *paideia* is a conservative force, empowering the subject and legitimizing social hierarchies. As we shall see, however, literary education can also be constructed as the means whereby such hierarchies can be transcended and transmuted. Just as literary *mimēsis* can produce 'artificial', synthetic hybrids, so paideutic repetition can empower outsiders and interlopers, allowing for the mimicking of traditional, male, elite, Hellenic identity.

PAIDEIA AND SOCIAL STATUS

Let us consider first of all the interrelationship between *paideia* and high social station, which is of considerable emphasis in the literature of this period.[21] The rewards for *paideia* could be considerable, ranging from patronage and awards of citizenship (at least in the late republican period) right through to political promotion.[22] Plutarch is absolutely and repeatedly clear that his

[19] *De uirt. mor.* 442c; 442e; 445b–c; 450e; 451d.

[20] *De uirt. mor.* 445b–c; cf. Pl. *Phaedr.* 246a–257b. See Trapp (1990) on the popularity of the *Phaedrus* in the Roman period, and Ash (1997), 192–6 on another Plutarchan evocation of this passage.

[21] Above, n. 2.

[22] Bowie (1982) and Lewis (1981) argue against the claims of Bowersock (1969) regarding the political profits that accrued specifically as a result of sophistry, asserting that *paideia* was not the sole or even a primary route to political power within the Roman hierarchy; but see now the convincing discussion of Schmitz (1997), 50–63, a nuanced restatement of Bowersock's position; also Whitmarsh (1998*a*), 196–203. See Cic. *Pro Arch. poet.* 10 for the offer of citizenship to Theophanes, who recorded Pompey's campaigns; and, further, Bowersock (1965), 4; Robert (1969); Millar (1977), 478. Arrian was equally commemorated for *paideia*

educative programme is designed to help men in, or destined for, prominent and elevated positions of power:[23] not for him the Epicurean motto 'live unnoticed'.[24] His philosophy aims at the 'political' or 'practical life', not the 'theoretical' (i.e. contemplative).[25] The socially active programme of *paideia* is also espoused by the earlier Dionysius of Halicarnassus, who defines rhetoric as 'an artful power (*dynamis*) of persuasive speaking in civic affairs, with the aim of good speaking' (δύναμις τεχνικὴ πιθανοῦ λόγου ἐν πράγματι πολιτικῶι τέλος ἔχουσα τὸ εὖ λέγειν, *On imitation* fr. 1 Usener–Radermacher).[26]

Indeed, articulate language itself is held to be the province of the elite.[27] Lucian writes of the differing responses of the *pepaideumenos* and the *idiōtēs* ('sub-elite man') on beholding a beautiful hall: the former pronounces an eloquent oration, seeking 'to respond in speech to the sight' (λόγωι ἀμείψασθαι τὴν θέαν, 2), whereas the latter merely gapes, 'out of fear of not being able to say anything worthy of the things before his eyes' (δέει τοῦ μὴ ἂν δυνηθῆναι ἄξιόν τι τῶν βλεπομένων εἰπεῖν, *On the hall* 2). Education and social status is defined by articulacy, the possession of linguistic resources that will match (note ἀμείψασθαι, 'respond to') the constructed, artificial splendour of the hall. The moral, Lucian asserts, is that 'in all that appeals to the eye, the same law does not hold for ordinary (*idiōtai*) and educated men (*pepaideumenoi*)' (οὐχ

and for politics: see e.g. Luc. *Alex.* 2 ('in the first rank of the Romans and a cohabitant with *paideia* for his entire life', Ῥωμαίων ἐν τοῖς πρώτοις καὶ παιδείαι παρ' ὅλον τὸν βίον συγγενόμενος), and Bosworth (1972), 164–72 on the epigraphic record (for further bibliography, see Whitmarsh 1998*a*: 198 n. 27).

[23] T. Morgan (1998), 262–5.

[24] See *Adu. Col.* 1125c; *An rect. dict.*, *passim*. He also censures the Stoics along similar lines (*Stoic. Resp.* 1033e–f). See further Dillon (1977), 198.

[25] On Plutarch's stress upon the active role of philosophy, see e.g. Aalders (1982*a*), 5–6; id. and de Blois (1992), 3384–6. The opposition between the *bios politikos/praktikos* ('engaged life') and the *bios theōrētikos* ('contemplative life') is a commonplace of Greek philosophy: see Pl. *Resp.* 471c–541b; Arist. *Eth. Nic.* 1095^a; Trapp (1996), 133 for later examples.

[26] Cf. also ps.-Long. 1.2 for the relevance of educated speaking to *politika*. One of the Athenian chairs of oratory was called the 'political (*politikos*) chair' (πολιτικὸς θρόνος). Although the precise meaning of *politikos* in this context is debated by scholars (see E. Rohde 1914: 324; Avotins 1975: 318; Rothe 1989: 23–7), it seems most likely that the chair was awarded to experts in 'political' (i.e. symbouleutic, 'advisory') oratory.

[27] On the general imputation to the masses of silence and inarticulacy, see Schmitz (1997), 91–6; but see also Korenjak (2000), 75–83 on *parasprachlich* communication by the masses.

ὁ αὐτὸς περὶ τὰ θεάματα νόμος ἰδιώταις τε καὶ πεπαιδευμένοις ἀνδρᾶσιν, *De domo* 2).

As we shall discover, however, education does not simply 'naturalize' social hierarchies, it also potentially provides interlopers with the resources wherewith to acquire elite identity. This is particularly visible, in the form of an anxiety, in the pseudo-Plutarchan tract *On the education of children* (*Education*) (the only work in the whole of Greek literature devoted exclusively to the value of education).[28] This text begins with the conception of the child: extolling the importance of *eugeneia* ('good birth'), the author advises his (male) readers to avoid procreating with 'any old woman' (ταῖς τυχούσαις γυναιξί), for children born of low mothers or fathers will carry with them 'indelible disgraces' (ἀνεξάλειπτα . . . ὀνείδη) for the rest of their lives (1b). Like the English 'good birth', *eugeneia* can refer to social station, and the author proceeds to make it clear that this social aspect is at the front of his mind. In what follows, he correlates low birth with poor *physis* ('nature'): the minds of the lowly, we read, 'are by nature' (πέφυκε) given to slipping and being brought down low (1b–c). As ever, the rhetoric of 'nature' is used to consolidate an eminently 'cultural' phenomenon, here social inequality.[29]

Interestingly, however, such disadvantages of nature do not completely disqualify the subject: there are three facets of the ethical being, *physis* ('nature'), learning (λόγος or μάθησις), and practice (ἔθος or ἄσκησις, 2a); and, although absolute perfection cannot be reached if any of these is deficient (2b), 'that which is contrary to nature (*physis*) overmasters that which is in accordance with nature (*physis*) thanks to toil' (τὸ παρὰ φύσιν τῶι πόνωι τοῦ κατὰ φύσιν ἐγένετο κρεῖττον, 2d). According to this argument, natural disadvantages can be surmounted through application, just as natural excellence can be wasted: birth status is, therefore, not a determinant of ethical status. Indeed, we read later on that 'good birth' (εὐγένεια) is 'a fine thing, but the virtue belongs to one's ancestors' (καλὸν μέν, ἀλλὰ προγόνων ἀγαθόν, 5d). In other words, *paideia* is presented as, to a certain extent, a meritocratic principle: it cannot completely efface the institutionalized imbalances of social hierarchies, but it can provide a certain counterbalance. The

[28] Ziegler (1949), 175.

[29] 'For nature read culture', as Winkler puts it apophthegmatically (Winkler 1990: 17).

author of this text considers that the ideal human is created from the union of an excellent (i.e. high-born) nature (*physis*) and an excellent *paideia*, but concedes that, in practice, the impulses of nature and nurture can drag the subject in contradictory directions.[30] This association of *paideia* with the non-natural (that which is παρὰ φύσιν, 'contrary to nature') recurs throughout Roman Greek discussions of the subject, and will be revisited presently. Even so conservative an author as this is drawn into contemplation of the subversion of the social hegemony in his consideration of *paideia*, a complex of ideas that fundamentally rest upon the idea of the transformation of the 'natural' self.

It is not, however, social reform that is uppermost in the author's mind. After cataloguing the various different aspects of tutorial, both mental and physical, that the young man needs (7c–8d), he imagines an objection arising:

> You promised to give advice concerning the upbringing of free-born children, but you are now flagrantly ignoring the upbringing of the poor and the common folk, self-confessedly offering your instructions to the rich alone.
>
> *σὺ δὲ δὴ περὶ τῆς ἐλευθέρων παίδων ἀγωγῆς ὑποσχόμενος παραγγέλματα δώσειν ἔπειτα φαίνηι τῆς τῶν πενήτων καὶ δημοτικῶν παραμελῶν ἀγωγῆς, μόνοις δὲ τοῖς πλουσίοις ὁμολογεῖς τὰς ὑποθήκας διδόναι.* (8e)

To this imaginary objection, the author avers, it is not difficult to respond: ideally, his ideas would be useful to all and sundry; but let anyone who is disqualified by poverty from following his precepts 'blame fortune and not the dispenser of the advice' (*τὴν τύχην αἰτιάσθωσαν, οὐ τὸν ταῦτα συμβουλεύοντα*, 8f). The author finds himself torn in separate directions by conflicting impulses, and ends up equivocating: if education creates a developed, improved identity, then it should be able to allow for the transcendence of social hierarchies; but he is also unwilling to address the consequences of the argument, namely social reform. The author proceeds to close the discussion less than subtly:

> I have overloaded (*parephortisamēn*) my argument with this issue so that I can link together sequentially (*ephexēs*) the other points that lead towards the proper education of the young.

[30] An idea found as early as Euripides' *Electra* (esp. 362–3), behind which is no doubt sophistic relativism (thus e.g. Goldhill 1986: 228).

καὶ ταῦτα μὲν δὴ τῶι λόγωι παρεφορτισάμην, ἵν' ἐφεξῆς καὶ τἄλλα τὰ φέροντα πρὸς τὴν ὀρθὴν τῶν νέων ἀγωγὴν συνάψω. (8f)

Consideration of the socially underprivileged does not 'belong' in a discussion of pedagogy: the extremely rare verb *paraphortizesthai* ('to overload')[31] suggests metaphorically that his account is already complete without any discussion of the lower classes. This reinforces the sense that the author is distancing himself from such views (the point was originally brought up in the voice of not the author himself but an imaginary objector). Yet the argument, in so far as it is constituted by a 'sequentially' (*ephexēs*) structured chain, demands treatment of social class. The author of *Education* finds himself caught between two apparently irreconcilable principles, expressing both the social-consolidatory and the social-transformative roles of pedagogy.

The distinction between elite and non-elite is conventionally articulated in the literature of the period through the polarity of 'the educated' (*pepaideumenoi*) and the 'rustic' (*agroikoi*).[32] This motif is widespread, and often manipulated in surprising ways. The *Letters of rustics* of Alciphron and Aelian (both probably second-century texts)[33] trade upon the irony of constructing a rustic perspective (including the standard excoriations of city-folk)[34] in a context suffused with Atticist sophistication and intertextual reference.[35] Longus' novel *Daphnis and Chloë*,[36] discussed in the previous chapter,[37] revolves around a similarly elaborate

[31] The meaning suggested by Pollux 2.139: '*Parankalisasthai* is when baggage-carriers overload (*paraphortisasthai*) themselves with something' (*παραγκαλίσασθαι δὲ τὸ τοὺς ἀγκαλιδηφόρους αὑτοὺς ἑαυτοῖς τι παραφορτίσασθαι*)

[32] On the ambivalent urban response to the countryside, see Swain (1996), 113–14.

[33] Aelian, writing under Septimius Severus, is known from Philostratus (*VS* 624–5; see further below, '*Paideia* and Hellenism'). The date of Alciphron is much contested: Baldwin (1982) attempts to date him to the reign of Septimius or before, but cf. R. Hunter (1983), 105 n. 55 for deserved scepticism.

[34] e.g. Alciphr. 2.5.1; 2.19.2; Ael. *Ep. rust.* 17.

[35] The letters are dramatically 'set' in the Attica of the democratic period: see e.g. Alciphr. 2.4.3 and esp. 2.19.2 for the democratic context; Ael. *Ep. rust.* 20. Middle Comedy is an evident source: Aelian includes a sequence of letters (13–16) to and from the misanthrope Cnemon, the protagonist of Menander's *Dyscolus* (*Bad-tempered man*).

[36] The question of the putative relationships between Longus, Aelian, and Alciphron is an old one: see Cresci (1999), 218 n. 30 for an abbreviated overview. R. Hunter (1983), 6–15 demonstrates how little can be securely deduced from the various correspondences.

[37] Ch. 1, 'Art and Artifice'. Saïd (1999) establishes the unilaterally urban

irony: written in elegant Attic Greek replete with Theocritean and Sapphic allusions, it centres upon the virginal ignorance of its rustic naïfs.[38] Pastoral invariably constructs a world removed from and defined in opposition to the urban world. It is always 'cited' from outside, a process dramatized by Horace's second *Epode* (in which it only becomes clear in the final four lines that the praise of the countryside is spoken by the moneylender Alfenus, 'always on the point of going rustic').[39] In *Daphnis and Chloë* pastorality is metaphorically interlinked with virginity: both are (for the knowing reader) mythical, lost states that can only be reconstructed through fantasy. Through its ironic interplay between literary awareness and naïve focalization, *Daphnis and Chloë* both underlines the superiority of its readership of *pepaideumenoi* over the ignorant rustics and invokes the nostalgia of the former for a world that, once lost, can never be regained. In his proem, Longus writes that his narrative will 'remind (*anamnēsei*) him who has loved and educate (*propaideusei*) him who has not' (τὸν ἐρασθέντα ἀναμνήσει, τὸν οὐκ ἐρασθέντα προπαιδεύσει, *praef*. 3): those readers who are in the club (and who will confess to not being?), both sexually and culturally, are invited to reconstruct the stages that led to their acquisition of the status of *pepaideumenos*. In reliving the erotic *paideia* of the rustics, the readership also undertakes a paradigmatic cultural journey from the origins of civilization to the hyper-intellectual climate of contemporary Greece.

Yet Longus is not only seeking to inculcate a sense of the superiority of urban Hellenes: the echo in the passage cited above of the Platonic doctrine of *anamnēsis* ('recollection')[40] hints that there is a deeper truth embodied in the novel's presentation of 'nature'. The conclusion of older scholars[41] that this text is a pious hymn to nature is certainly off the mark: in the final words of the book, we learn, just as Chloë is said to have done (cf. ἔμαθεν), that what has happened in the course of the narrative has been just

perspective from which *Daphnis and Chloë* is written, embodying simultaneous revulsion and attraction.

[38] R. Hunter (1983), 59; cf. p. 45, referring to the 'tension between φύσις and τέχνη' as 'reflected in the very artificial form in which the "natural" education of the children is described'. See also Zeitlin (1990*a*), 430–6.

[39] *iam iam futurus rusticus, Epod*. 2.67.

[40] Pl. *Men*. 81a–87b.

[41] G. Rohde (1937); cf. Chalk (1960).

'shepherds' jokes' (ποιμένων παίγνια, 4.40.3).[42] Nevertheless, even though it is not in any sense a straightforward protreptic, the natural upbringing of Daphnis and Chloë does have an emblematic, paradigmatic aspect.[43] Like the narrator who has come to hunt on Lesbos (*praef.* 1),[44] the reader is necessarily cast in the role of outsider looking in on this pastoral, miniature world: 'we' (the implicitly constructed community of knowing, educated readers) could never recapture the (impossible?) ignorance of the protagonists.

Indeed, the urban, cultivated perspective that the novel's readers are required to adopt (notwithstanding that the text is often ironically focalized through the rustic pair) is specifically problematized. The only figure labelled *pepaideumenos* in this text is the urban parasite Gnathon, whose name means 'Jaws': the image indicates (as well as the character's own appetitive nature) the city's voracious relationship with the countryside.[45] His first major contribution to the story is an attempt to use Daphnis for a purpose that strikes the latter as unnatural, in the sense that it is contrary to the practices of beasts (4.12.2). The rustic boy's innocence of the conventions of *paideia* and pederasty may be amusing, but the *pepaideumenos* is also constructed as predatory and aggressive. The bodily integrity of the novel's protagonists serve as metaphors for the self-contained pastoral world (and, of course, vice versa); and any attempt upon their persons constitutes violence done to the serenity of the idyll. Although there are threats from within the rustic world (in the notable cases of Dorcon, whose attempt to rape Chloë fails, 1.20–2, and Lampis, who jealously spoils the beautifully arranged garden that functions metonymically for Chloë, 4.7–8), it remains true that the biggest danger posed to the innocent *Liebespaar* comes from urban outsiders, whose appreciation of the place is predicated upon relations of possession and slavery.[46] The focus upon relations of power and

[42] Echoing the last line of Gorgias' sophistic *Encomium of Helen*, where we learn that the text has been his 'joke' (παίγνιον, fr. 11.21 DK).

[43] Heiserman (1977), 143; Winkler (1990), 102–3; Zeitlin (1990*a*), 422.

[44] Zeitlin (1990*a*), 454.

[45] '. . . educated (*pepaideumenos*) at the symposia of the dissolute' (ἐν τοῖς ἀσώτων συμποσίοις πεπαιδευμένος, 4.17.3). See Winkler (1990), 112–14 for the general point, and Longo (1989) on the prevalence of images of eating and consumption.

[46] R. Hunter (1983), 71; esp. Zeitlin (1990*a*), 443–9. Saïd (1999), 97–107 emphasizes the point that the view of the countryside presented throughout is that of an empowered townsman, but underestimates (I think) the degree to which Longus

exploitation is unsettling, and forcibly reminds the reader of the human cost of urban *paideia* and its disengaged aestheticization of the countryside. Rustic naïveté represents a state exalted above the corruption of the city (as it does elsewhere in the literature of Roman Greece, most notably Dio Chrysostom's *Euboean oration*),[47] even if it is a state inaccessible to Longus' readers.

Daphnis and Chloë, then, implicates the reader's implicit self-construction as *pepaideumenos* into the very narrative, inviting both readerly pleasure (through ironic distance from this enclosed world) and self-awareness as to the exploitative role of the urban rich vis-à-vis the rural poor. Although the text validates a progressivist model of *paideia* as the culmination of a linear process, it also offers an alternative pedagogy, a retracing of the emergence of coercive relations between urban and rural. In this respect, *Daphnis and Chloë* is *both* a validation of the intellectual superiority of urban *pepaideumenoi and* an exposure of the circumstances that allow for it.

This experimental interest in rustic pedagogy is further developed in the dialogue entitled *Heroicus* (or 'heroic tale') by the third-century author Philostratus (who has read Dio's *Euboean oration*).[48] A Phoenician sailor, detained by the weather on the Thracian Chersonese, meets with a rustic vintager. The pastoral setting is repeatedly stressed,[49] and the site (which, it transpires, is a cult-site of the hero Protesileus)[50] is protected from unwary incursion by city-dwellers (the attempt by one of the local

exposes and interrogates that perspective. More explicitly than Saïd, Swain (1996), 116 argues that '[t]o announce that one's text is part of a programme of *paideia* is to situate it precisely within elite society, not to question its validity'. I cannot see why the two possibilities are exclusive.

[47] Dio Chr. 7, with Russell (1992), 9; Swain (1994), 172. See e.g. 7.81 for praise of the life 'according to nature' (κατὰ φύσιν), an idea with Cynic associations (Goulet-Cazé 1986: 57–66). For a prominent example of the extreme naïveté of the rustics, see the misunderstanding of the insult *agroikos* at 7.43, with Russell (1992), 122. Dio's *Euboean oration* may have been one of Longus' sources: see R. Hunter (1983), 66–7. For other rhetorical praises of the countryside, see e.g. Ael. *VH* 3.1; Philostr. *VS* 572; Lib. *Or.* 8.261–7, 349–50 Förster. On the *Euboicus* as a paradigmatic microcosm of Greece, see Trapp (1995), 164–5; and see Moles (1995), 177–80 on implicit anti-Roman feeling.

[48] Philostr. *VS* 487, assuming the two Philostrati are the same. for an argument for their identification, see de Lannoy (1997), 2420–36.

[49] Philostr. *Her.* 2.3; 3.3–4; 4.10; 5.2–4, etc.

[50] My spelling of his name here (usually transcribed as Protesilaus) is intended to reflect Philostratus' own Atticized version. On the location of Protesileus' cult-site on the Chersonese, see Mantero (1966), 106–9.

potentates (*dynatoi*), the suggestively named Xeinias—'Mr Foreign'—to take over this piece of land resulted in his brutal blinding by Protesileus, *Her.* 4.2). In this segregated, rural idyll, the rustic vintager seems oddly sophisticated: not only is his Greek faultless, but also, right from the start he trades Homeric allusions with the Phoenician sailor.[51] To an extent, this is in line with the traditional, unrealistic idealization of peasants,[52] but Philostratus is not unaware of the paradox. In what I take as a sly play upon this tradition of Atticizing peasants, he makes the Phoenician sailor ask: 'How were you educated in speech? You do not seem to me to be uneducated' (τὴν . . . φωνὴν . . . πῶς ἐπαιδεύθης; οὐ γάρ μοι τῶν ἀπαιδεύτων φαίνῃ, 4.5). With this question, Philostratus foregrounds the implausibility of the topos. But the vintager has a plausible reply: he spent the first part of his life 'in the city' (*asty*), 'being taught and philosophizing' (διδασκάλοις χρώμενοι καὶ φιλοσοφοῦντες, 4.6); eventually, his fortunes sank so low that he consulted Protesileus in desperation, who advised him 'change your clothes' (μεταμφιάσαι, 4.9). The vintager presently understood that this was a suggestion to change his life's 'style' (σχῆμα, 4.10: the sartorial pun works in Greek). So the vintager is not a 'real' peasant, but a transvestite (just as Daphnis and Chloë are finally revealed to be the children of wealthy city-dwellers). Interestingly enough, the dialogue opens with an instance of misprision of identity based upon clothing: the vintager asks, basing his assumption upon the sailor's clothing, whether he is Ionian, and the sailor replies that he is in fact Phoenician, but that the Phoenicians have taken over Ionian styles of dress (1.1–2). Appearances can be deceptive—and Philostratus has deliberately misled his readers with his account of the rustic vintager, who claims not even to know what a drachma is (1.7).

Conventionally (for example, in the *Euboean oration* of Dio Chrysostom), peasants are held up to city-dwelling *pepaideumenoi* as paradigms of ethical superiority. In Philostratus' *Heroicus*, on the other hand, the boundaries between the two states are hazier and more permeable: townsfolk like the vintager may convert to the rustic cult of Protesileus, just as the 'sybaritic' (*Her.* 1.1)

[51] Cf. the vintager's reference to Phoenicians as φιλοχρήματοί τε καὶ τρῶκται (1.3; cf. Hom. *Od.* 14.289; 15.416); the Phoenician's reference to Maron's wine (1.4; cf. Hom. *Od.* 9.196–211); the vintager's reference to Cyclopes (1.5).

[52] Dio's peasants speak sophisticated, Atticizing Greek, incorporating some extremely showy words: see e.g. Russell (1992), 121 on δήπουθεν (7.39).

Phoenician sailor does in the course of the discussion.[53] Nor is it the case that the countryside is defined by its lack of *paideia*. The farming undertaken by the vintager is cast as a form of philosophy (2.5–6), and he plucks not only fruit but also *sophia* ('wisdom') from the branches of the trees (4.10), a wisdom that includes the 'true' story of what happened at Troy. There are strong elements of quasi-mystical celebration of nature here,[54] but it would be a mistake to take Philostratus as a religious proselytizer;[55] this dialogue is, rather, a playful experiment with an alternative, non-urban form of paideutic truth. The initial scepticism of the Phoenician (3.1; 7.9; 8.1) represents that of the over-confident, urban *pepaideumenos*, whilst the 'truth' advanced by the vintager (and by Protesileus through him) tests the degree to which the educated reader can suspend his or her disbelief so as to partake of this rustic *sophia*.[56] The dialogue's central (and brilliant) conceit is the 'proof' that, just as conventional education can 'urbanize' rustics, so Philostratus' Protesilean manoeuvres can 'rusticize' his elite readership.

Finally, I want to consider the case of Herodes Atticus' mascot, Agathion, as he is presented by Philostratus in his *Lives of the sophists*.[57] Herodes is the central figure of the *Lives*,[58] the 'king of words' (βασιλεύς τῶν λόγων, 586, 598)[59] and 'tongue of Greece' (Ἑλλήνων γλῶτταν, 598).[60] In his largesse and interactions with prominent Romans, he represents the very pinnacle of sophistic influence, a figure of enormous power and prestige that spreads over the length and breadth of the multicultural empire. Within the biographical narrative of Herodes, however, stands another figure, who offers a competing definition of Hellenism (552–4). Where Herodes is thoroughly modern, his consort Agathion is

[53] The *Heroicus* is a form of 'conversion' dialogue (λόγος προτρεπτικός): see Schäublin (1985) on this genre.

[54] Mantero (1966), 48–51.

[55] On the humour in the text, see G. Anderson (1986), 241–54.

[56] I discuss these concepts further in a forthcoming article, 'Performing heroics: geography, language, and identity in Philostratus' *Heroicus*'.

[57] For more on this text, see Ch. 4, 'Dio and Philostratus'.

[58] G. Anderson (1986), 82–4. On the life of Herodes Atticus, see Graindor (1930); Ameling (1983), vol. 1; Tobin (1997), 13–67. For a comprehensive analysis of the inscriptional evidence, see Ameling (1983), vol. 2.

[59] A common enough phrase (cf. βασιλεὺς ἐν τοῖς λόγοις, Luc. *Rhet. praec.* 11; σοφίης ἡγήτορι, *IG*[2] 3709.11), but not used of anyone else in the *Lives of the sophists*.

[60] Similarly, Marcellus of Side calls him 'the tongue of the Athenians' (*EG* 1046.36–7 = Ameling 1983: 2.153, no. 146).

archaically primitive: some say, Philostratus tells us, that Agathion is 'autochthonous' and born in rural Boeotia. He lives mostly on milk, that most primitive of beverages.[61] He is referred to as Herodes' 'Heracles', dresses in animal skins, and is extremely muscular. To this extent, Philostratus tracks closely the account given by Lucian of a certain philosopher named Sostratus, who seems to be a cover for the historical Agathion:[62] 'the Boeotian Sostratus, whom the Greeks called (and considered truly to be) Heracles' (*τὸν Βοιώτιον Σώστρατον . . . ὃν Ἡρακλέα οἱ Ἕλληνες ἐκάλουν καὶ ᾤοντο εἶναι*, Luc. *Demon.* 1). But there is a characteristically devious twist in Philostratus' account: balancing the 'some' (*οἱ μέν*) who claim that he is Boeotian stands Herodes (*Ἡρώδης δέ*, *VS* 553), who claims that he is the son of Marathon whose statue is at Marathon, a 'farmer hero' (*ἥρως γεωργός*, *VS* 553). In Philostratus'—or Herodes'?—contested rewriting of Agathion's origins, the primitivist icon has been transported from Boeotia, which had a proverbial reputation as a semi-civilized backwater (a slanderous legacy of the 'Medizing' of most of Boeotia during the Persian Wars), to Attica, and to the site of a prestigious episode in Athenian history. Agathion has been Atticized. The consequence of this (conspicuous) shift is a realignment of narrative and cultural dynamics: Agathion becomes not a symbol of 'pure' (Boeotian) primitivism but a means of exploring and contesting the proper form of (Athenian) *paideia*. 'As for your speech,' asks Herodes, 'how were you educated (*epaideuthēs*), and by whom? For you do not seem to me to be uneducated' (*τὴν δὲ δὴ γλῶτταν . . . πῶς ἐπαιδεύθης καὶ ὑπὸ τίνων; οὐ γάρ μοι τῶν ἀπαιδεύτων φαίνῃ*, *VS* 553). The contours of this question follow closely those of the Phoenician's question to the vintager at *Heroicus* 4.5, quoted above: a hint not only at common authorship, but also at the concerns shared by both texts with cultural definition through education. Agathion's reply is highly instructive:

The interior (*mesogeia*) of Attica is a good school for a man who wishes to engage in dialectic (*dialegesthai*). For the Athenians in the city take on for money the youths who come in floods from Thrace and Pontus and the other barbarian tribes, and their own speech deteriorates from the

[61] Hom. *Il.* 13.3–4; *Od.* 4.87–9; 9.246–9; Theocr. 11.34–5; Lovejoy and Boas (1965), 288.

[62] Wright (1921), 153; Ameling (1983), 1.155–8; Swain (1996), 80; Schmitz (1997), 190.

influence of these barbarians to a greater extent than they can contribute to the improvement of the speech of the newcomers. But the interior is untainted by barbarians, and hence its language remains uncorrupted and its dialect sounds the purest strain of Atthis.

ἡ μεσογεία . . . τῆς Ἀττικῆς ἀγαθὸν διδασκαλεῖον ἀνδρὶ βουλομένωι διαλέγεσθαι, οἱ μὲν γὰρ ἐν τῶι ἄστει Ἀθηναῖοι μισθοῦ δεχόμενοι Θράκια καὶ Ποντικὰ μειράκια καὶ ἐξ ἄλλων ἐθνῶν βαρβάρων ξυνερρυηκότα παραφθείρονται παρ' αὐτῶν τὴν φωνὴν μᾶλλον ἢ ξυμβάλλονταί τι αὐτοῖς ἐς εὐγλωττίαν, ἡ μεσογεία δὲ ἄμικτος βαρβάροις οὖσα ὑγιαίνει αὐτοῖς ἡ φωνὴ καὶ ἡ γλῶττα τὴν ἄκραν Ἀτθίδα ἀποψάλλει. (*VS* 553)

Agathion lays claim to *paideia*, albeit a *paideia* of a very different kind to that of Herodes. There are echoes of Socrates here, both in the use of the verb *dialegesthai* ('to hold dialogues', 'to engage in dialectic') and in the rejection of education based upon payment (Socrates famously distinguished himself from sophists by refusing to charge students: Pl. *Apol.* 19d–e). This Socraticism underlines the theme of paideutic agonistics, a competition between sophistic and purist approaches to education. This contrast is further underlined in the opposition between civic space and that of the *mesogeia* ('interior'), elsewhere as here privileged by Philostratus as a place of cultural purity.[63] Unlike the urban *pepaideumenoi*, including (implicitly) Herodes himself, Agathion speaks a language that 'is clean' (*hygiainei*) and pure (similarly, a little later, he detects that some milk is 'unclean' having been prepared by the hand of a woman, *VS* 553).

The point is not simply, however, that Agathion's linguistic purism reinforces the ideals of Herodes.[64] This narrative presents competing, rather than complementary, paradigms of Athenian *paideia*: whereas the former heads inwards towards the centre of Attica, the latter projects outwards towards Rome, the empire, and the world; whereas the former's identity is welded to the rugged, primitive past, the latter represents the progressive cosmopolitanism of the present. Elsewhere in Philostratus, the idea of cultural isolationism such as this is visibly problematized.[65] Like Juvenal's rustics in *Satire* 6.1–10, Agathion is a figure at once of admiration and knowing condescension, representing both the notional ethical superiority of the past and its lack of

[63] *VS* 624 (on which see the following paragraph but one); *Ner.* 1.
[64] Gleason (1995), 145; Swain (1996), 81–2; Schmitz (1997), 191–2.
[65] *VA* 5.33; 6.20; 8.7 (x).

sophistication. Autochthony does not guarantee Hellenic identity in the modern world of Herodes, which instead privileges sophistication and learning.[66]

It is worth contrasting Agathion with the Italian Aelian, who 'could Atticize like those Athenians from the interior (*mesogeiai*)' (ἠττικίζε . . . ὥσπερ οἱ ἐν τῆι μεσογείαι Ἀθηναῖοι, *VS* 624), although he never went to Greece—indeed, he never went on a ship (*VS* 625)! The introverted focus upon the physical space of the *mesogeia* ('interior') of Athens on the part of the autochthonous Agathion appears obsolescent and misplaced when Roman resources can provide the *paideia* to teach perfect Atticism without one's having even to leave the country. Even so, the Aelian passage is not a simple valorization of progressivism over older forms of thought: at the same time as Philostratus extolls the new openness and transferability of Greek culture irrespective of geography, he also humorously emphasizes the bizarreness of the situation of an Atticist who has never been to Attica. Conversely, the rustic, primitivist Agathion is not simply a figure of condescending fun: indeed, Herodes recognizes his 'divine nature' (δαιμονίη φύσις, *VS* 554). There is a marked tension between two different modes of Hellenism: the ancient, ingrained authority of the land of Greece and the modern, pluralist *paideia* accessible to all the Roman elite across the empire. If Philostratus in the *Lives of the sophists* presents the latter mode as necessarily dominant for now, he does not allow it entirely to displace or eclipse the former.

The categories of *pepaideumenos* and *agroikos* ('rustic'), then, are not inert, descriptive labels; rather, they are constantly manipulated in the ongoing, processual debate as to what *paideia* centrally is. Of course, at one level all these texts assume an educated, urbane reader (that is, one who has the time and leisure to read, and who is capable of sophisticated, allusive reading); but rather than reassuringly emphasizing a secure connection between elite status, *paideia*, and virtuous being, they recurrently question and put at risk such links.

[66] Similarly, Favorinus mocks exclusivist cultural definitions founded on autochthony (e.g. Isocr. *Panegyr.* 24; *Panath.* 124; Dem. 60.4) at *De ex.* 10.1 Barigazzi: see also Ch. 3, 'Favorinus: Exile and Literary Alienation'.

PAIDEIA AND GENDER

Discussions of education in antiquity generally assume a male student,[67] and the pseudo-Plutarchan text *On the education of children* is no exception.[68] Although the period of the Roman principate saw an apparent rise in female literacy[69] and a number of high-profile educated women,[70] it remains the case that paideutic theory focuses primarily upon creating a male subject. Outside of such specialized discussions, however, there was considerable interest in the abstract question of whether women should be educated. In the fourth century BCE Plato had asserted the need for a female *paideia* on precisely the same terms as the male (though in different classes and with different teachers).[71] This Platonic precedent inspired a number of variations upon the theme in the early principate. Plutarch himself wrote an essay *That women too should be educated*, of which a few fragments are extant.[72] It is hard to establish what was the tenor of this essay from the few uninformative snippets we possess, but there are other allusions to the topic in the works of Plutarch that allow a coherent pattern to be established.

[67] T. Morgan (1998), 48–9.

[68] Although the texts often write of παῖδες and νέοι (which, whilst grammatically masculine, could theoretically be of common gender), and of τέκνα (neuter, and thus common), the word υἱεῖς ('sons') is at times used, usually in conjunction with πατέρες ('fathers') (*Education* 9d, 9f, 14a, etc.).

[69] Or, at least, in representations of female readers: see Bowie (1994*a*), 437–8, on the Greek novels; Huskinson (1999) on Roman sarcophagi. On the evidence for actual female literacy under the principate, see T. Morgan (1998), 48 n. 149, adding the rather gloomy conclusions of W. V. Harris (1989), 252–3, 262–3, 270–1, 279–80.

[70] See now Hemelrijk (1999). The educated woman with the highest profile was Julia Domna, wife of the emperor Septimius Severus; and it is to the literary 'circle' of this 'devotee and supporter of all rhetorical works' (τοὺς ῥητορικοὺς πάντας λόγους) that Philostratus claims to belong (Philostr. *VA* 1.3; *Ep.* 73 also addresses Julia). For a sceptical account of Julia's circle, see Bowersock (1969), 101–7. Women in the Greek novel are often referred to as possessing *paideia*: see Char. *C&C* 7.6.5; Long. *D&C* 1.8.1; Hld. *Aeth.* 2.33.5; and further Egger (1999), 117–18

[71] Pl. *Resp.* 451d–457b; *Leg.* 804d–805b; 813b. Other Socratics proposed similar theories (Xen. *Symp.* 2.9; Antisthenes reported at Diog. Laert. 6.1.12), as did certain Stoics (*SVF* 3.59, frr. 253–4). See further Clem. *Pedagog.* 1.4 ('That pedagogical reason is possessed equally by men and women'); Hierocles *apud.* Stob. *Flor.* 85.21–4. Aristotle was characteristically unimpressed by such ideas (*Pol.* 1259^{b}; 1260^{a}).

[72] Plut. frr. 128–32 Sandbach = Stob. *Flor.* 18.125–7.

At the conclusion of *Education*, the author (whether he be Plutarch or no) recommends the dedication to her children's education of Eurydice, who, 'though she was an Illyrian and three times a barbarian (*tribarbaros*)' (!), took up *paideia* late in life (14b). In this case, the author is making the moral point that hard work transcends innate disadvantage, and those disadvantages consist in barbarian origin and (implicitly) female sex. Yet despite holding her up as a paradigm for the (male) readership, the author attentively presents Eurydice's motivation as specifically feminine: she took up *paideia* out of maternal protectiveness, 'in the interests of her children's studies' (ἐπὶ τῆι μαθήσει τῶν τέκνων) and out of 'love for her children' (φιλοτεκνίαν, *Education* 14b). While Eurydice's solicitude on her children's behalf is held up as a paradigm for the behaviour of men, it is also presented as circumscribed by her gender.

In the essay *On the virtues of women*, addressed to a certain Clea who is described as 'well-read',[73] he disagrees with the famous dictum of Pericles (as reported by Thucydides) concerning female virtue (*gynaikeia aretē*), namely that great repute comes to a woman who is least talked about by men.[74] On the contrary, Plutarch asserts, it is good for women to be well known, since 'a man's virtue (*aretē*) is one and the same as a woman's' (μίαν . . . καὶ τὴν αὐτὴν ἀνδρὸς καὶ γυναικὸς ἀρετήν, 242f). The notion that Plutarch is here espousing a 'feminist' agenda has been rightly disputed, since the 'female virtues' in question are conspicuously gendered in accordance with the author's patriarchal agenda.[75] Plutarch's undeniable interest in sexual reciprocity and conjugal harmony[76] constitutes not a 'liberation' but an alternative strategy for silencing women. As McNamara writes, Plutarch's seductively egalitarian-seeming approach to women is based upon a 'concept of womanhood whose real happiness lay in finding a man strong enough to master her'.[77]

The most important Plutarchan passage on the subject of women and education comes in the *Advice on marriage*, where he writes of the need for husbands to educate their wives (145d–

[73] βιβλίοις ἐντυχῶσαν (*Mul. uirt.* 243d). Clea is also the addressee of *De Is. et Osir.* On Clea, see further Stadter (1965), 2–3.

[74] Thuc. 2.45.2; Plut. *Mul. uirt.* 242e–f.

[75] Blomqvist (1997), 75 and references.

[76] See esp. the nuanced discussion of Stadter (1999).

[77] McNamara (1999), 160.

146a). It is significant that the woman's access to education is presented as mediated through the husband (as it is in Xenophon's *Oeconomicus* and other prescriptive texts on household-management):[78] the wife's *paideia* is conditioned by her role in the patriarchal household. This point is underlined by two striking images. First, Plutarch writes that, while women cannot conceive without men, they can in certain circumstances create 'disfigured, fleshy foetuses' (ἄμορφα κυήματα καὶ σαρκοειδῆ, *Advice on marriage* 145d) without the presence of males: 'if they do not receive the seed of excellent words and do not unite with their husbands in *paideia*, then all by themselves they gestate many atopic and base thoughts and feelings' (ἂν γὰρ λόγων χρηστῶν σπέρματα μὴ δέχωνται μηδὲ κοινωνῶσι παιδείας τοῖς ἀνδράσιν, αὐταὶ καθ' αὑτὰς ἄτοπα πολλὰ καὶ φαῦλα βουλεύματα καὶ πάθη κυοῦσι, *Advice on marriage* 145d–e). In this extraordinary metaphor, the wife's receipt of *paideia* from her husband is linked to her role as child-bearer in the family: if she does not submit to her husband's instruction, she is prone to unnatural autogenesis. *Paideia* does not 'empower' her, as it does males (a point to be underlined presently), but reinforces her submissive status within the patriarchal *oikos*. Conversely, the husband's paideutic activities are associated with sexual penetration (as we shall see presently, Plutarch is fond of imaging *paideia* as a predominantly phallic quality). In the second image, the wife's education is presented as a form of adornment: she will, Plutarch tells us, be beautified (*kosmoumenē*), in an excellent and dignified manner, with sententious sayings (*apophthegmata*, 145e–146a). Her *paideia* is once again explicitly gendered, and the assumption is that it exists in order to gratify the male spectator rather than to benefit the woman in question.[79] Moreover, the kind of education appropriate to women is apparently limited (though this is not stated explicitly): an ability to reproduce apophthegms is hardly to be equated with the kind of rigorous, philosophical *paideia* that Plutarch espouses for young men. In sum, then, Plutarch is generally in favour of female education, but only in

[78] Xen. *Oec*. 7.15; cf. Foucault (1990), 161; Pomeroy (1999), 33–42 compares the *Oeconomicus* and the *Advice*, but overly reifying (in my view: see *BMCR* 00.02.22) the differences between the two periods.

[79] Similarly, in his *Consolation to his wife*, Plutarch presents his wife as impressing philosophers with her 'lack of extravagance in bodily adornment and simple lifestyle' (εὐτελείαι . . . τῆι περὶ τὸ σῶμα καὶ ἀθρυψίαι τῆι περὶ δίαιταν), but not as philosophizing herself (*Cons. ad ux.* 609c).

such a way as to reinforce the normative balance of power within the household.

With the loss of *That women too should be educated*, however, it is hard to get the measure of the complexity of the issues raised by Plutarch on the question of female education. As we saw in the case of the issue of class, *paideia* does not simply reinforce social norms: it also contains within it the potential to transform the subject, and to challenge the 'natural' order of things. In order to explore the tensions created by the notion of gendered education, it is necessary to turn to the two essays on the subject (*That women should also philosophize* and *Should daughters be educated alongside sons?*) credited to Musonius Rufus, the Stoic philosopher of the first century CE.[80] The message of these essays is that women, who 'have received from the gods the same reason/language (*logos*) as men' (λόγον . . . τὸν αὐτὸν εἰλήφασι παρὰ θεῶν . . . τοῖς ἀνδράσιν, fr. 3, p. 9 Hense), profit equally from both philosophy and education. Yet it is not that Musonius counters the notion of 'natural' sexual differentiation: while women need virtue as much as men, each sex needs it for 'naturally' different occupations. It would be absurd, he argues, to make men learn weaving and women gymnastics, since 'one should allot the tasks that are most appropriate to the nature (*physei*) of each' (ἑκατέραι φύσει τῶν ἔργων ἀπονεμητέον τὰ προσφορώτατα, fr. 4, p. 17 Hense); 'perhaps it may be that all human tasks exist in common, and are shared by both men and women . . . but some tasks are more fitted to the nature (*physei*) of one, and some to that of the other' (πάντα μὲν γὰρ ἴσως ἐν κοινῶι κεῖται τὰ ἀνθρώπεια ἔργα καὶ ἔστι κοινὰ ἀνδρῶν καὶ γυναικῶν . . . ἔνια δὲ δὴ ἐπιτηδειότερα τὰ μὲν τῆιδε τῆι φύσει, τὰ δὲ τῆιδε, fr. 4, p. 17 Hense). The scope of female 'philosophy' encompasses, predictably enough, no more than the household and childrearing.[81] In Musonius' strongly normative model, then, philosophical virtue motivates men and women alike, but towards different ends: education develops the 'natural' entelechy of both sexes.

Despite the apparent conformity of Musonian education with

[80] Frr. 3–4 Hense. For further discussion of Musonius and the textual problems relating to these works, see Ch. 3, 'Musonius Rufus, the "Roman" "Socrates"'.

[81] These are matters that Musonius treats with great seriousness, though: see e.g. fr. 14, *Is marriage an impediment to the philosopher?* On the widespread importance attributed in the imperial period to conjugality and domesticity in the maintenance of social order, see Foucault (1990), 150–4, Swain (1996), 119–20; (1999).

'nature', however, he cannot avoid insinuating at various points that education transgresses female 'nature', not least because *andreia*, the Greek word for the 'courage' instilled by philosophy, means literally 'manliness'.[82] At one point, he remarks that 'it is appropriate that the educated woman (*pepaideumenēn*) should be more courageous/manly (*andreioteran*) than the uneducated (*apaideutou*), and the philosopheuse more so than the commoneuse' (*καὶ μὴν καὶ ἀνδρειοτέραν εἶναι προσήκει γυναῖκα τῆς ἀπαιδεύτου τὴν πεπαιδευμένην καὶ τὴν φιλόσοφον τῆς ἰδιώτιδος*, fr. 3, p. 11 Hense). In my translation of this passage, I have used two ugly neologisms ('philosopheuse' and 'commoneuse') in order to express the rare linguistic feminizations (*πεπαιδευμένη, ἰδιώτις*) employed by Musonius. These linguistic oddities, however, are as nothing compared with the attribution to educated women of qualities that are *andreios* ('manly'). Although (as we saw in the previous paragraph) Musonius is elsewhere keen to underline the conformity of education with female nature, here he seems to suggest that it masculinizes women. Indeed, as he argues elsewhere, citing the example of the *andreia* of the Amazons (always, of course, paradigms for dangerous female transgression),[83] it is morally necessary for a woman to 'play the man' (*ἀνδρίζεσθαι*).[84] *Paideia* is not always a socially normative principle: as we saw in the case of class hierarchies, its potentially transformative powers can also lead the subject to transgress the boundaries of his or her 'natural' disposition.

As far as the education of males goes, however, *paideia* is always a constitutive phase in the acquisition of virility. As Plutarch puts it, it is philosophy 'alone that can array young men in the manly and truly perfect order that comes from reason' (*ἡ μόνη τὸν ἀνδρεῖον καὶ τέλειον ὡς ἀληθῶς ἐκ λόγου τοῖς νέοις περιτίθησι κόσμον*, *On listening to lectures* 37f). *Paideia* makes the man. Indeed, Plutarch goes further in his virilization of education. As is clearly instanced in the image of the education of the wife as impregnation (*Advice on marriage* 145d–e, discussed above), the matrix of relations that allow for a husband's education of his wife are isomorphous with those that allow for sexual congress. Elsewhere, a man's reason is

[82] On the issues raised in this paragraph, see further Goldhill (1995), 137–43.

[83] See esp. P. duBois (1987), a synchronic/structuralist account of Amazon mythology as paradigms of marital impropriety.

[84] Fr. 4, p. 15 Hense. Goldhill (1995), 137–9 points to Musonius' extremism here.

imaged as an erect phallus. In the arresting comparison that closes his argument that old men should remain active in politics, he explains why certain statues of Hermes are designed the way they are:

That is why those representations of Hermes showing him as an old man are created with no hands and no feet, but with erect member: the intimation is that there is little need for physical vigour in old men, but that they should have, as is fitting, a fertile and productive reason (*logon*).

διὸ καὶ τῶν Ἑρμῶν τοὺς πρεσβυτέρους ἄχειρας καὶ ἄποδας, ἐντεταμένους δὲ τοῖς μορίοις δημιουργοῦσιν, αἰνιττόμενοι τῶν γερόντων ἐλάχιστα δεῖσθαι διὰ τοῦ σώματος ἐνεργούντων, ἐὰν τὸν λόγον ἐνεργόν, ὡς προσήκει, καὶ γόνιμον ἔχωσι. (*An seni* 797f)

The *logos* is correlated with the phallus, on the grounds that both are 'fertile and productive'.[85] In similar vein, Lucian, in a satire directed in part against the second-century polymath Favorinus (who suffered from a congenital incomplete sexation), alludes to the need to have 'the balls [*uel sim.*] for philosophy' (*τὸ αἰδοῖον ἕτοιμον ἐς φιλοσοφίαν*, Luc. *Eun.* 13).[86] As Gleason argues, we are dealing with a period in which the acquisition and display of *paideia* was part of an ongoing process in defining manhood, a central 'form of competitive masculine activity', a surrogate for the military activity that defined the virility of an earlier period.[87] The education of elite males is presented in the literature of the period as the affirmation of the hegemonic power already (and 'naturally') invested in them.

Matters, however, are not quite that simple: the notion of a strict correlation between manhood and *paideia* needs qualification. Although the ethical philosopher Plutarch insists upon the interrelation of manhood and education, in the context of performative display, innovation and surprise are in order. Favorinus, apparently, makes a virtue (*sic*) of his unmanliness: according to Philostratus, one of the celebrated paradoxes espoused by this 'double-natured man-woman' (*διφυὴς . . . καὶ ἀνδρόθηλυς*, *VS* 489)[88] was that 'though a eunuch, he had been convicted of

[85] Imagery of birth and procreation also features heavily in the tract *On the sublime*: see e.g. 13.2; 44.3 (*γονιμωτάτου*); Walsh (1988), 266.

[86] The allusions to Favorinus' biography are noted by Gleason (1995), 132–5. For more on Favorinus, see Ch. 3, 'Favorinus: Exile and Literary Alienation'. On Favorinus' medical condition (Reifenstein's syndrome?), see the speculative arguments of Mason (1979).

[87] Gleason (1995), 159.

[88] Cf. [?Luc.] *Am.* 21, on the 'double nature' (*διπλῆς φύσεως*) of eunuchs.

adultery' (εὐνοῦχος ὢν μοιχείας κρίνεσθαι, *VS* 489). Although eunuchs were often viewed as lusty,[89] Favorinus—at least as Philostratus presents him—deliberately exploits the counter-intuitive mixture of manliness and unmanliness, flamboyantly manipulating his anomalous position within the taxonomy of sex roles. Surprisingly, Gleason's model of *paideia* as 'manly competition' does not explain the success of its prime subject.

Favorinus' gender-duality reflects and underlines the linguistic and generic innovations of his literary production:[90] as so often, self-making and text-making are intertwined. Favorinus was best known in antiquity for the 'Miscellaneous history' (παντοδάπη ἱστορία), a compendium of information that (so far as we can judge from the extant fragments) crossed the boundaries between philosophy, natural history, geography, mathematics, ethnography, and so forth.[91] It is interesting, in this connection, to note Lucian's report of the 'abuse' of the philosophical eunuch Bagoas (a figure modelled partly on Favorinus) as a 'a composite (*syntheton*) thing, mixed (*mikton*), prodigious (*teratōdes*), outside of human nature' (τι σύνθετον καὶ μικτὸν καὶ τερατῶδες, ἔξω τῆς ἀνθρωπείας φύσεως, Luc. *Eun.* 6).[92] These terms make Bagoas sound like a literary product; indeed, *synthetos* ('composite'), 'mixed' (*miktos*), and *teratōdēs* ('prodigious') are all used (or cognate words are) by Lucian in connection with his own generic innovations.[93] In the context of Lucian's own emphasis upon the 'mixing' of innovation and tradition, the reference to Favorinus/Bagoas as 'a composite thing, mixed, prodigious' may not be simply abuse, but also (at a metaliterary level) an allusion to a successful aesthetic mode (indeed, one also espoused by Lucian himself). In certain contexts, then, the demands imposed by paideutic performance for uncompromised virility could be waived in the interests of literary innovation.

Paideia is intrinsically interlinked with manhood, then, but not in an inert or inflexible manner. When one is dealing with the

[89] Pseudetymologically, a *eunoukhos* is sometimes interpreted as the 'possessor' (*-okhos*) of a 'bed' (*eunē*): see Ferrante (1975), 53 for examples.

[90] On Favorinus' linguistic and stylistic innovations, see below, p. 168.

[91] Mensching (1963), 99–142; Barigazzi (1966), frr. 35–90.

[92] Gleason (1995), 132–5 discusses this text, but considers this as unequivocal abuse.

[93] Luc *Bis. acc.* 33 (σύνθετος); *Zeux.* 5, 6 (μίξις); 12 (τεράστιον). See further Ch. 1, 'Art and Artifice'.

education of women, *paideia* can provide the means whereby the subject transcends her 'natural' state, becoming in a sense 'manly' (even if this manliness is only of a limited kind, circumscribed by strategies of male concession and imaged in definitively female terms). In the display culture of competitive oratory, manliness can be forgone in the interests of innovation and display (even if the exception tolerated in the case of Favorinus seems only to have underlined the rule concerning the interlinking of masculinity and *paideia*). *Paideia* is the product of an androcentric culture fixated upon the idea of sustaining masculine dominance; but it also creates the potentiality for unmaking men and for making women men. As we have seen recurrently in this chapter, the consolidatory aspects of *paideia* need to be offset against its transformative aspects.

PAIDEIA AND HELLENISM

Thus far we have considered the construction of *paideia* as a means of consolidating the status of the male, elite subject; we have also considered the tensions and problems in this construction. Let us turn now to a third and final form of social empowering effected by *paideia*, namely the consolidation of Hellenic identity. This aspect is not, as it happens, explicitly broadcast by the Plutarchan texts on paideutic theory; it is, however, implicit at certain junctures. The author of *Education* counsels the use as companions to children of slaves 'who speak clear Greek' (Ἑλληνικὰ καὶ περίτρανα λαλεῖν), 'so as to keep the children from being coloured by (*synanakhrōnnymenoi*) barbarians and people of low character and from assuming some of their baseness' (ἵνα μὴ συναναχρωννύμενοι βαρβάροις καὶ τὸ ἦθος μοχθηροῖς ἀποφέρωνταί τι τῆς ἐκείνων φαυλότητος, *Education* 4a). At the root of the verb *synanakhrōnnysthai* lies the word *khrōma*, 'colour', that can refer either to the 'complexion' of the skin or to a literary or linguistic 'style'. Although the primary reference here must be to the latter meaning (the fear is that the children will assume barbaric inflections in their speaking) the former is metaphorically interwoven. Purity of language is linked to purity of skin: both can be tainted by cultural admixture.

In *Poetry*, one of Plutarch's ethical lessons explains the superiority of Greek over barbarian. He interprets Homer's representations of the differing promises to their superiors of the Trojan Dolon and the Greek Diomedes as a guide to the different behaviour of barbarians and Greeks: Dolon vows to reach Agamemnon's ship, but Diomedes merely asks for a companion in his venture.[94] 'So then,' Plutarch explains, 'foresight is an urbane, Hellenic quality, whilst brashness is a barbaric and base quality: we should emulate the former and despise the latter' (Ἑλληνικὸν οὖν καὶ ἀστεῖον ἡ πρόνοια, βαρβαρικὸν δὲ καὶ φαῦλον ἡ θρασύτης· καὶ δεῖ τὸ μὲν ζηλοῦν τὸ δὲ δυσχεραίνειν, *Poetry* 29f). In this essay as a whole, Plutarch is far from reading *every* hero on the 'Hellenic' (as he calls it, unhomerically) side as a paradigm of virtue;[95] but in this instance he sees a polarization of 'Greek' and 'barbarian' behaviour, and interprets this as an educative protreptic. When Greekness is foregrounded by antithesis with the other, it represents a behavioural ideal towards which the subject must aspire.

In Plutarch's other major corpus of writings, the *Parallel lives*, however, the term *Hellēn* ('Greek') is repeatedly employed to evaluate ethical behaviour (as it is elsewhere in the literature of the period).[96] For Plutarch, to be Greek means to think, and (crucially) to act, in an ethical way. This action is assessed and articulated from a fundamentally intellectual perspective, through the language of the rich moral legacy of the Greek tradition: the key concepts are *philanthrōpia* ('benevolence'), *praiotēs* ('gentleness'), and *epieikeia* ('decency'), terms that recurrently link positively appraised action to education, to social elitism, and to Hellenism.[97] As Simon Swain has demonstrated, Plutarch's ethical

[94] Hom. *Il.* 10.222.

[95] The behaviour of Achilles, for example, is decried (26d, 31a).

[96] Bowie (1991).

[97] Nikolaidis (1986), 239–41. On *philanthrōpia* in Plutarch, and its associations with Hellenism and civilization, see Hirzel (1912), 21–32; H. M. Martin (1961); Nikolaidis (1986), 239–41, and *passim* on Plutarch's connections between Greece and civilization; Humbert (1991), esp. 174–81; Duff (1999), 77–8. The term is Isocratean (e.g. *Ad Nic.* 15, with de Blois and Bons 1992: 171) and Xenophontic (e.g. *Ag.* 1.22, and further, Farber 1979: 509), but also recalls Ptolemaic ideology: see Samuel (1993), 189–91. On the imperial *Nachleben* of the term in the 4th cent., see Downey (1955). On Plutarch's use of *praiotēs*, see H. M. Martin (1960); and on his use of *epieikeia*, and its Aristotelian heritage, see Russell (1963), 27. The association between Hellenism and such qualities is made explicit by Dionysius of Halicarnassus, who writes: 'I count as Hellenic decent (*epieikeis*) and benevolent (*philanthrōpous*) deeds and actions . . .' (τὰς . . . ἐπιεικεῖς καὶ φιλανθρώπους διανοίας τε καὶ πράξεις . . . Ἑλληνικὰς εἶναι λογίζομαι, *AR* 14.6.6). The geographer Strabo goes one step further, explicitly rejecting the (ethical) polarity of Greek and barbarian in favour of that of good and bad (1.4.9). See further Schmitz (1997), 179–80.

Hellenism is also used to evaluate Romans, who are assessed in accordance with their perceived receptivity to the principles and precepts of Greek *paideia*.[98] A particularly impressive instance of this phenomenon arises in the *synkrisis* ('comparison') between the Spartan lawgiver Lycurgus and his Roman counterpart, Numa. According to Plutarch, Lycurgus was characterized by his 'austere' (αὐστηρά, *Lyc.–Num.* 2.6) policy,[99] while Numa is described as having a 'soft, benevolent (*philanthrōpos*) muse' (ἥμερος . . . καὶ φιλάνθρωπος μοῦσα, 1.9); and, strikingly, the latter is pronounced 'by far the Greeker lawgiver' (μακρῶι τινι . . . ἑλληνικώτερον . . . νομοθέτην, *Lyc.–Num.* 1.10)![100] That Romans can be described as 'Greeker' than Greeks in Plutarch's system demonstrates the (broadly Isocratean) presence in these writings of a 'universalist' equation of Hellenism with civilization.[101]

There is a marked paradox in describing a Roman as 'Greeker' than a Greek: Greek ethics cannot completely overwrite Greek ethnics. Plutarch's 'universalizing' concept of Hellenic *paideia* sits in tension with his strong awareness of cultural differences, and of the significance of the term *Hellēn* as a marker of epichoric identity. It cannot be coincidence, however, that the Hellenizing capacities of *paideia* are most clearly visible when they are applied to those who are ethnically non-Greeks. Cultural identity is most heavily contested and policed at its borders, where grey areas are most likely to occur: in Bennington's words, '[f]rontiers are articulations, boundaries are, constitutively, crossed or transgressed'.[102] Cultural boundaries are most clearly asserted at points of transgression,[103] and Plutarch's *Lives* repeatedly test the degree to which Roman history can be appropriated into Greek intellectual theory.

In order to exemplify the broader point, I shall consider briefly

[98] See Swain (1990); also Duff (1999), 287–309.

[99] But cf. *Lyc.* 25.4 for qualification.

[100] Cf. the descriptions of the Thracian Spartacus as 'better and Greeker than his race in intelligence and gentleness (*praiotēs*)' (καὶ συνέσει καὶ πραιότητι τῆς τύχης ἀμείνων καὶ τοῦ γένους Ἑλληνικώτερος, *Crass.* 8.3), and of the Romans as acting 'in a Greek, gentle (*praiōs*) manner' (Ἑλληνικῶς . . . καὶ πράιως, *Marc.* 3.6).

[101] The claims of historiography to interpret 'human nature' in general go back at least to Thucydides' assertion of the utility of his narrative as a guide to *to anthrōpinon* (1.22.4).

[102] Bennington (1990), 121. See also the important discussion of Hartog (1988), 61–111: Herodotus' Scythian boundary serves as a locus for intellectual experimentation with ideas of culture, civilization, and power.

[103] Cf above, p. 24.

two cases, Favorinus (the 'eunuch' whom we have already met in this chapter) and the satirist Lucian. The important point about these figures, for the present purposes, is that each was born a 'barbarian', and each made it his business to 'acquire' Hellenic identity through *paideia*: Favorinus was a Gaul (from Arelate, modern Arles), and Lucian a Syrian (from Samosata in Commagene). I turn first to a well-known passage in Favorinus' *Corinthian oration.*[104] The *Corinthian oration* is one of two speeches preserved in the manuscripts of Dio Chrysostom (no. 37; *On fortune* is no. 64) which are attributed with some certainty to Favorinus. As Maud Gleason argues, this text shows Favorinus representing himself as a paradigmatic example of the transformative effects of *paideia*, the cultural system that allowed him to 'become' Greek.

In it, Favorinus upbraids the Corinthians for removing the statue commemorating him. In part of the speech (22–36), he assumes the voice of the statue as it argues that it should remain in place. This striking prosopopoeia underlines the artificiality of the conceit, as Favorinus' 'voice' is filtered through a mimetic creation. This is doubly striking because of the emphasis which Favorinus gives to the very processes whereby he has mimetically fabricated his own cultural identity: the statue speaks of Favorinus as, although a Roman equestrian, 'having emulated (*ezēlōkōs*) not only the voice but also the mind-set, life and style (*skhēma*) of the Greeks' (*οὐδὲ τὴν φωνὴν μόνον ἀλλὰ καὶ τὴν γνώμην καὶ τὴν δίαιταν καὶ τὸ σχῆμα τῶν Ἑλλήνων ἐζηλωκώς*, 25). *Zēlōsis* ('emulation') can refer either to ethical emulation of behavioural models or to stylistic imitation of literary models.[105] Similarly, *skhēma* ('style') can refer either to personal presentation (clothing and so forth) or to literary style. Favorinus is perfectly self-conscious about the artificial, mimetic aspects of his self-fashioning. As a result, the statue tells us, he is pre-eminent in one quality, in 'both resembling (*dokein*) a Greek and being one' (*Ἕλληνι δοκεῖν τε καὶ εἶναι*, 25). This statement, however, is also a challenge. In what sense can seeming to be Greek and being Greek be said to be a single concept? The use of 'both . . . and' (*τε/καί*) here is ambiguous: the

[104] In what follows, I owe much to the brief but insightful comments of Gleason (1995), 16–17. See further, Bowie (1991), 202–3; Schmitz (1997), 175–7. On the MS tradition of this speech, see Amato (1995), 4–39.

[105] Russell (1979), 9–10; Too (1998), 210.

particles can, in Greek, mean 'not just . . . but in fact also', which would leave the clause meaning 'not only to seem Greek but to be Greek too'.[106] On this interpretation, the clause would refer to a single quality, since 'being Greek' would be a more developed subset of 'seeming Greek'. It goes without saying, however, that this is not the only possible interpretation: indeed, from a traditional perspective, 'being Greek' would be held to be substantively different from (merely) 'seeming Greek'. So Favorinus' expressed aspiration emblematizes a set of problems to do with cultural definition: do those who 'are' Greeks belong to the category of those who 'seem' Greek? Or does 'seeming' imply 'but not *actually* being'? And, more particularly, how has Favorinus crossed over from 'seeming' into 'being'? Presently, he seems to answer the question, commenting that he has displayed to the 'indigenous' (ἐπίχωροι) Greeks how

> having been educated (*to paideuthēnai*) is no different from being so by nature (*to phynai*) in respect of seeming (*to dokein*).
>
> οὐδὲν τὸ παιδευθῆναι τοῦ φῦναι πρὸς τὸ δοκεῖν διαφέρει. (*Cor.* 27)

Favorinus argues not merely that *paideia* provides the resources necessary to transcend 'nature' (the verb *phynai* is at the root of *physis*, 'nature'), a familiar argument,[107] but even that, in respect of seeming at any rate, the 'educated' self and the 'natural' self are indistinguishable. In the performative sphere of display oratory (the context in which Favorinus is currently operating), 'natural' identity is no truer than its constructed, artificial equivalent. The theme of mimetic self-making that runs through the *Corinthian oration* is here explicitly linked to education: *paideia* makes life into as much of an art form as literature. But Favorinus seems to be going further even than this, generalizing his own experience as an instantiation of *all* social identity, a 'universal cultural paradigm' (in Gleason's phrase).[108] After all, the transformative message encoded in the 'example' (παράδειγμα) of Favorinus should be learned, 'the statue' tells us, by all Greeks, Romans, and Celts alike (*Cor.* 27).

[106] The rendering of Crosby (1946), 25. For this use of τε . . . καί, see Denniston (1950), 515.

[107] Cf. e.g. ps.-Plut. *De lib.* 2d: 'that which is contrary to nature (*physis*) overmasters that which is in accordance with nature (*physis*) thanks to toil (*ponos*)' (τὸ παρὰ φύσιν τῶι πόνωι τοῦ κατὰ φύσιν ἐγένετο κρεῖττον); above, '*Paideia* and Social Status'.

[108] Gleason (1995), 16.

In a slightly earlier passage, moreover, the statue explains Favorinus' particular significance for his Corinthian addressees: 'though Roman, he has thoroughly Hellenized, like your own city' (*Ῥωμαῖος ὢν ἀφηλληνίσθη, ὥσπερ ἡ πατρὶς ἡ ὑμετέρα*, 26). The reference here is to Mummius' sack of Corinth in 146 BCE, and the city's subsequent refoundation as a Roman colony by Julius Caesar in 44 BCE.[109] This act of reconstruction makes Corinth a perfect backdrop for Favorinus' mimetic self-making. As Pausanias (writing slightly later) tells us, 'Corinth is inhabited by none of the ancient (*arkhaiōn*) Corinthians any more, only settlers sent by the Romans' (*Κόρινθον δὲ οἰκοῦσι Κορινθίων μὲν οὐδεὶς ἔτι τῶν ἀρχαίων, ἔποικοι δὲ ἀποσταλέντες ὑπὸ Ῥωμαίων*, 2.1.2). The structure of Pausanias' sentence artfully reveals the paradox: Corinth is inhabited by . . . *not* the Corinthians (or, at least, not the *ancient* Corinthians), but Roman settlers. Pausanias deliberately toys with the anomalousness of the situation: indeed, reading the Greek in sequence, the first clause is at first sight completed by the flagrantly counter-intuitive assertion that 'Corinth is inhabited by none of the Corinthians' (*Κόρινθον δὲ οἰκοῦσι Κορινθίων μὲν οὐδείς*). Moreover, the *μέν* . . . *δέ* construction vividly opposes Roman Corinth (non-indigenous, late-coming) with Greek (ancient). It is this paradoxical status of Corinth as a mimetic city that Favorinus exploits.[110] The personified statue reminds its addressees that although their city lays claim to a deeply rooted Hellenism,[111] it depends for its Hellenic credentials upon the 'invention' of antique traditions. In a striking phrase, he refers to Corinth as the 'prow and poop of Greece' (*πρῶιρα καὶ πρύμνα τῆς Ἑλλάδος*, *Cor.* 36): it is both the beginning *and* the end, the earliest and the latest.[112] Corinth is *both* a traditionally Greek *and* a mimetic city. It is appropriate, he implies, that a self-made man should have a statue in a self-made city.

[109] On the city's fluctuation (in time and across social class) between Greek and Roman identities, see Engels (1990), 67–74, though his use of the term 'ethnic' is imprecise and he makes insufficient allowance for creative self-presentation.

[110] Favorinus, then, does not 'stress the Greekness of second-century Corinth' (Swain 1996: 347–8) but explores/contests it.

[111] Cf. 'the walkway of Greece' (*τῶι περιπάτωι τῆς Ἑλλάδος*, 7); also 16, 17, 31, 37 on the Hellenic qualities of Corinth. See further, Schmitz (1997), 176–7.

[112] Though as it happens, Corinth appears only fleetingly in Homer (*Il.* 2.570; 13.664), and this absence motivated an early instance of tradition-inventing by Eumelus in his *Corinthiaca*: see Huxley (1969), 60–79 on Eumelus' identification of Corinth with the better Homerically attested Ephyre.

Lucian of Samosata (in Syrian Commagene) also periodically refers to his 'barbarian' origins,[113] which he offsets against his pride in his linguistic achievements within Hellenic culture, attained through *paideia*.[114] In the short address entitled *On the dream, or Lucian's life*, he narrates the story of how his father wanted him to be a sculptor since he was good at moulding wax, but a dream persuaded him otherwise. In the dream, Sculpture and *Paideia* appear to him in female form, each trying to persuade him to follow her. This text is not, of course, a factual biography, but a clever, metaliterary articulation of Lucian's own aesthetic position, modelled on Prodicus' celebrated 'Choice of Heracles'.[115] As Romm notes, at one level the two figures represent different aesthetic modes within contemporary literary production: both here and elsewhere in Lucian's work, sculpture symbolizes the inflexible, 'monolithic' use of the Greek tradition, as opposed to the dynamic and resourceful manipulation of the heritage symbolized by wax-working.[116] On another level, however, the parable dramatizes a choice between remaining true to the identity with which Lucian was born and transforming himself into a new person. Sculpture claims to be 'a familiar of yours, related to you on your mother's side' (*οἰκεία τέ σοι καὶ συγγενὴς μητρόθεν*, *Somn.* 7),[117] since Lucian's grandfather and uncles were sculptors; and, she promises, if he chooses her, he will achieve fame, but 'you will never go abroad (*epi tēn allodapēn*), leaving behind your fatherland and your family' (*οὔποτε ἄπει ἐπὶ τὴν ἀλλοδαπήν, τὴν πατρίδα καὶ τοὺς οἰκείους καταλιπών*, *Somn.* 7). She spoke these words, Lucian reports, 'with very many slips and barbarisms (*barbarizousa*)' (*διαπταίουσα καὶ βαρβαρίζουσα πάμπολλα*, *Somn.* 8). Sculpture thus represents conformity to the traditions of his barbarian native land: Lucian ironically reverses the perspective of his educated audience, constructing the centres of the empire as (from the viewpoint of 'barbarians') 'abroad' (*tēn allodapēn*, literally 'the foreign place').

Paideia, however, belittles what Sculpture offers him. If he

113 *Bis acc.* 27; *Pisc.* 19; *Pseudolog.* 11; *Scyth.* 9.

114 Swain (1996), 45–9.

115 For the *Choice of Heracles*, see Xen. *Mem.* 2.1.21–34; Prodicus' own model is Hes. *Op.* 288–92. Trapp (1996), 126 n. 1 lists a large number of other imitations of this topos in Roman times.

116 Romm (1990).

117 *μητρόθεν* is Fritzsche's emendation for MS *οἴκοθεν*.

follows Sculpture, she warns, 'you will make yourself less valuable (*atimoteron*) than stone' (ἀτιμότερον ποιῶν σεαυτὸν λίθων, *Somn.* 13), where *atimoteron* puns on the double meaning of *timē*, both 'honour' and 'financial value'. Life, as we have seen throughout this chapter, is a process of self-making, and the construction of the self is analogous to artistic production: if you want to be a stonemason, you will make yourself into a hunk of rock.[118] *Paideia*, on the other hand, offers Lucian the chance to transcend his humble origins:

> You who are now a pauper, the son of a nobody, who had some sort of plan about so ignoble a trade—in a short while, you will inspire envy and jealousy in all, you will be honoured (*timōmenos*) and praised, and held in good repute among the best people, and be regarded by those pre-eminent in birth and wealth, dressed in clothes like this—at this point, she pointed to the extremely effulgent clothing she was wearing—and be deemed worthy of office and promotion.
>
> καὶ ὁ νῦν πένης ὁ τοῦ δεῖνος, ὁ βουλευσάμενός τι περὶ ἀγεννοῦς οὕτω τέχνης, μετ' ὀλίγον ἅπασι ζηλωτὸς καὶ ἐπίφθονος ἔσηι, τιμώμενος καὶ ἐπαινούμενος καὶ ἐπὶ τοῖς ἀρίστοις εὐδοκιμῶν καὶ ὑπὸ τῶν γένει καὶ πλούτωι προὐχόντων ἀποβλεπόμενος, ἐσθῆτα μὲν τοιαύτην ἀμπεχόμενος—δείξασα τὴν ἑαυτῆς· πάνυ δὲ λαμπρὰν ἐφόρει—ἀρχῆς δὲ καὶ προεδρίας ἀξιούμενος. (*Somn.* 11)

The two meanings of *timē*, 'honour' and 'value', are united here: Lucian will be both rich and fêted. It is notable, however, that *Paideia* offers a success premised entirely upon appearance (δόξα): the attraction is that he will be 'in good repute' (εὐδοκιμῶν) and 'regarded' (ἀποβλεπόμενος). The splendid clothing he will wear suggests concealment and deceit. This focus upon appearance is particularly striking in that conventional variations upon the 'Heracles' choice' topos decry the superficially preferable path in favour of the more arduous path of virtue; whereas Lucian reverses the topos, choosing the easy, alluring way.[119] There is more to this than ludic reversal, though: in focusing attention upon the superficial, performative aspects of *paideia*, Lucian (like Favorinus) points to an anti-essentialist vision of education.

[118] Elsewhere, Lucian uses stone as a metaphor for inert literary production: see Romm (1990).

[119] Levine Gera (1995), 239–45. Lucian underlines this point in the *Teacher of rhetoric*, where rhetoric is satirically extolled 'in order that you may ascend to the peak most easily' (ὡς . . . ῥᾶιστα ἐπὶ τὸ ἀκρότατον ἀναβήσηι, 8). Such subversions of traditional moralism are indebted to Cynicism, which had already promised a 'short cut' to virtue (Emeljanow 1965).

Paideia does not simply realize innate destiny: it transforms the subject, crossing sociocultural barriers.

In a passage that recalls the account by the Presocratic philosopher Parmenides of his initiation into philosophy,[120] *Paideia* now invites Lucian into her chariot to survey all the cities 'from the east all the way to the west' (ἀπὸ τῆς ἕω . . . ἄχρι πρὸς τὰ ἑσπέρια, *Somn.* 15). Rather than confining him to his native land, *Paideia* offers him access to the whole world; and, in particular, access to the centre, Rome. Education offers a relocation from the parochial to the universal, from the particular to the general. The transformation wrought upon Lucian is indicated by the fact that when he returns he is wearing different clothes, now 'wearing a purple garment' (εὐπάρυφος, *Somn.* 16), which he shows to his father. *Paideia* has thus delivered on her promise to take him from his native land, and from his inherited identity, and transform him into a new, highly successful, person.[121] Lucian becomes emblematic of transcultural Hellenism, an identity that exceeds geographical barriers.

Yet he never presents the transfigurations of *paideia* as absolute, entirely effacing his barbarian origins: his satirical stance makes a virtue of the culturally junctural position of its author. In the dialogue entitled *Anacharsis*, as Branham shows in a brilliant analysis,[122] athletics are viewed from a bifocal perspective: the Hellenized Scythian Anacharsis[123] finds athletics absurd and risible (*Anach.* 13), while the Athenian Solon, 'the personification of autochthonous Athenian culture',[124] defends the practice resolutely. The satirical effect in this dialogue comes from the incommensurability of the two perspectives, both of which represent aspects of Lucian's own persona. As Branham observes, the dialogic form recalls Platonic precedent; but whereas in Plato one

[120] Fr. 1 DK. See further, Georgiadou and Larmour (1998), 15–16 on the motif of aerial flight in Lucian.

[121] Indeed, the purple garment even seems to hint at a senatorial position (which, as far as we know, the historical Lucian never attained). Cf. *Rhet. praec.* 2, where the orator refers to the large numbers who have become 'wealthy' (πλούσιοι) and 'extremely high-born' (εὐγενέστατοι) thanks to public speaking: the paradox, that *paideia* can even bestow high birth, is pointed.

[122] Branham (1989), 82–104.

[123] The canonical story of Anacharsis' Hellenization comes at Hdt. 4.76; see Kindstrand (1981) on the development of the legend and the apophthegmatic tradition.

[124] Branham (1989), 85.

figure (Socrates) steers the conversation, in Lucian 'neither interlocutor gains control of the conversation'.[125] So far from authorizing the perspective of a single figure, dialogue underlines the relativism inherent in any authoritative claim, and 'the potential incongruity of any single way of seeing a subject'.[126] The humour of the *Anacharsis*, thus, depends upon a relativizing exposure of the blind spots of a certain culture, as Branham concludes; but it also underlines Lucian's own ambivalent self-positioning in relation to Hellenism, *both* fully saturated in Hellenic *paideia and* an outsider.

This discussion of Lucian's ambivalent self-positioning could be extended to include the *Toxaris*, a 'memorable exploitation of cultural relativism in the Roman empire'.[127] In this text the eponymous barbarian sage discusses with a certain Mnesippus the relative merits of Scythian and Greek friendship. Toxaris lays claim, on behalf of barbarians, to superiority over the Greeks, arguing that 'we barbarians have better judgement than you concerning the excellence of men' (*οἱ βάρβαροι εὐγνωμονέστερον ὑμῶν περὶ τῶν ἀγαθῶν ἀνδρῶν κρίνομεν*, *Tox.* 5). This putative superiority is demonstrated by the Scythians' honouring of Orestes and Pylades—who were Greeks—on the grounds of their impressive friendship, whereas the Greeks have not even any notable tomb. According to Toxaris, the Scythians avoid parochial ethnocentrisms in their assessment of Orestes and Pylades:

There is nothing in their foreign origin that prevents the Scythians from having judged them good men, and from their being honoured by Scythian nobles. For we do not scrutinize the provenance of men of noble character, nor do we carp if they are not friends of ours when they have done good deeds, but we consider them familiars (*oikeious*) on the basis of the deeds they do.

κωλύει τε οὐδὲν ὅτι ξένοι ἦσαν ἀλλὰ μὴ Σκύθαι ἀγαθοὺς κεκρίσθαι καὶ ὑπὸ Σκυθῶν τῶν ἀρίστων θεραπεύεσθαι. οὐ γὰρ ἐξετάζομεν ὅθεν οἱ καλοὶ καὶ ἀγαθοί εἰσιν, οὐδὲ φθονοῦμεν εἰ μὴ φίλοι ὄντες ἀγαθὰ εἰργάσαντο, ἐπαινοῦντες δὲ ἃ ἔπραξαν, οἰκείους αὐτοὺς ἀπὸ τῶν ἔργων ποιούμεθα. (*Tox.* 5)

Employing a meritocratic argument (parallelled, as we shall see

125 Branham (1989), 103.

126 Branham (1989), 104.

127 Bowersock (1994), 133. I am not convinced, however, by Bowersock's argument that Lucian is reacting directly to a general weakening of Greek identity in society at large (p. 44: 'It is Lucian to whom we must turn for a reflection of the great change in attitude toward the Hellenic standard').

in the next chapter, by the cosmopolitanism of essays on exile)[128] Toxaris enforces a disjunction between deeds and provenance, culminating with the prima-facie paradox that 'deeds' can make foreigners 'familiar' (*oikeios*, literally 'a member of the household'). This relativism is further underlined in what follows. The two proceed to hold a competition, swapping tales of Greek and Scythian friendship in order to decide which culture is better at friendship (9–11). When they conclude, however, they realize that they have appointed no one to judge between them, and decide instead to become friends (62). This harmonious resolution makes the narrative structure a parable of the thematic content: Greek and barbarian are united. Like the *Anacharsis*, but with a more uplifting message, this dialogue dramatizes the cultural bifocality of Lucian's persona.

In some situations (particularly when referring to linguistic 'barbarisms'), Lucian uses the word 'barbarian' with negative associations, in conformity with regular, Hellenocentric usage.[129] In other circumstances, however, he himself plays the barbarian more proudly. At points, he refers to the 'strangeness' (*to xeinon*) or 'alien quality' (*to allokoton*) of his literary work.[130] He refers to philosophy's eastern origins, an assertion calculated to provoke ardent claimants of philosophy's Hellenic provenance.[131] In the short request for patronage entitled *The Scythian*, Lucian explicitly compares his position to that of Anacharsis, in that 'he too was a barbarian—and you would not say that we Syrians were in any way baser than Scythians' (βάρβαρος μὲν γὰρ κἀκεῖνος καὶ οὐδέν τι φαίης ἂν τοὺς Σύρους ἡμᾶς φαυλοτέρους εἶναι τῶν Σκυθῶν, *Scyth.* 9).[132] The analogy drawn between Lucian's position and

[128] Ch. 3, esp. 'Favorinus: Exile and Literary Alienation'.

[129] e.g. *Bis acc.* 27; *Pisc.* 19; *De merc. cond.* 10; *Pseudolog.* 1; 11. See Swain (1996), 46, 229.

[130] *Zeux.* 1; 3; *Ver. hist.* 1.2; 2 41. Rhetorical purists, on the other hand, use 'strange' (*xenos*) and 'alien' (*allokotos*) as negative terms: see e.g. Phryn. *Ecl.* 330; ps.-Long. *De subl.* 4.1 (but contrast 16.2); and, indeed, Luc. *Lex.* 20, cited above, pp. 6–7 and below.

[131] *Fug.* 6–7. Diog. Laert. 1.1–4 argues vigorously for a Greek origin for philosophy. Spoerri (1959), 53–60 and Gigon (1960) discuss candidates for Diogenes' antagonists here; see Gigante (1986), 45–52 for an interpretation of the proem more sensitive to its role in the structure of Diogenes' text. Precedents for the barbarian origins of philosophy at Pl. *Tim.* 21b; *Epin.* 987d–e; *Alcib.* 122a; [Pl.] *Axioch.* 371a; see further, Momigliano (1974), *passim*, esp. 141–9.

[132] The point is that Scythians are proverbially the limit cases of barbarism: see e.g. *Pseudolog,* 2

that of Anacharsis in this passage is designed to combat the Hellenocentric assumption that only Hellenes can possess wisdom by activating a repertoire of tales concerning barbarian wisdom.[133] This anti-Hellenocentrism, however, only makes sense from within a Hellenocentric context: the figures named by Lucian (Toxaris, Anacharsis) derive from canonical Greek literature, and by assimilating Scythia and Syria on the grounds that both are 'barbarian' states, Lucian recoups the Hellenocentrism that (at one level) he seeks to displace. *Paideia*, as she promised him in his dream, allows Lucian to leave behind his humble origins in Commagene, and takes him to success and fame at the very heart of the Roman empire; yet the question of whether education can fully transform a barbarian into a Greek remains still very much open.

At one level, every word of Greek written by Lucian is a 'performance', an attempt to overlay a Syrian 'self' with a Greek surface. At another level, however, the same may be said of any Atticist who eschews the language of the present for the sake of an artificial, literary *Kunstsprache*. Lucian writes frequently about Atticism, both alluding to his own failures to conform to the strict requirements of the movement and mocking the excesses of others.[134] In a passage we have already seen from the dialogue *Lexiphanes*,[135] he attacks the eponymous speaker for his 'alien' Greek:

> Abandoning us, who converse with him now, he talks to us from a thousand years ago, twisting his tongue, combining these alien elements (*allokota*), and taking himself very seriously in the matter, as if it were a great thing for him to speak a foreign language (*xenizoi*) and debase the established currency of speech.
>
> *καὶ ἡμᾶς τοὺς νῦν προσομιλοῦντας καταλιπὼν πρὸ χιλίων ἐτῶν ἡμῖν διαλέγεται διαστρέφων τὴν γλῶτταν καὶ ταυτὶ τὰ ἀλλόκοτα συντιθεὶς καὶ σπουδὴν ποιούμενος ἐπ' αὐτοῖς, ὡς δή τι μέγα ὄν, εἴ τι ξενίζοι καὶ τὸ καθεστηκὸς νόμισμα τῆς φωνῆς παρακόπτοι.* (*Lex.* 20)

Of course, this is a criticism of *hyper*-Atticism, excessive archaism—but Lucian's satire risks implicating the (Atticizing) reader's own values in his critique. Is *all* Atticism necessarily a departure from demotic, indigenous, 'natural' language for the

[133] Cf. *Pisc.* 19, where 'the Syrian' defends his provenance on the grounds that Aristotle was from Stageira and Clearchus from Soli.

[134] Swain (1996), 45–9. On Atticism, see Introd. n. 23.

[135] Above, pp. 6–7.

sake of something 'alien' (*allokotos*) or 'foreign' (*xenos*)?[136] To the extent that Hellenic *paideia* requires familiarity with the literature of a period separated from the present by an enormous gulf, all *pepaideumenoi* are 'foreigners' to texts they study and seek to replicate. Moreover, the very fact of this gulf is the precondition for Lucian's own success as a *pepaideumenos*, allowing as it does all-comers to compete on equal terms, as 'outsiders'. Lucian's writings (as we shall see further in Chapter 5) do not simply attack inert targets for the satisfaction of a complacent readership; their aggression ramifies, ironizing also Lucian's own persona and discomfiting the reader.

The narratives of Hellenization through education told by both Lucian and Favorinus show just how provisional is *paideia*'s construction of identity. In respect of a world in which the Isocratean ideal of Hellenism as an ethical rather than an ethnic category is widespread, it is instructive to note the persistence of conservative forces that insist upon provenance as a means of defining identity. Both Favorinus and Lucian were forceful characters who turned their origins to their advantage; they were, however, none the less pilloried for their 'barbarisms'.[137] In their (wilfully stylized) autobiographies, both figures dramatize both the power of *paideia* to transfigure cultural identity, to forge the self anew by mimetic processes, and the limits of that power. At the same time, however, both examples expose the frenetic labour that went into *all* attempts to use *paideia* to construct and consolidate Greek identity, and not just those of non-Greeks. In an instructive passage in the essay *On listening to lectures*, addressed to a certain Nicander (who has just come of age and assumed the *toga virilis*), Plutarch compares the process of education in general to taking up citizenship in a foreign city (37e–f). Plutarch's point lies in the contrast between recently arrived outsiders and resident aliens who have spent much of their lives *in situ*: a new experience is less of a discomfiting shock to those who have accustomed themselves. According to this simile, every single person who is educated suffers a form of cultural relocation. Although there is no sugges-

[136] A comparable use of ξενίζειν comes at *Hist. conscr.* 45, referring to the use of poetic language in history.

[137] For criticisms of Favorinus, see Phryn. *Ecl.* 218 Fischer; Swain (1996), 45; see also Swain (1996), 61 for references to and discussion of Galen's criticisms. Lucian's *False critic* tells of an accusation levelled at the author on the grounds of verbal barbarism (*Pseudolog.* 1).

tion here of a policy of parity between citizens and non-citizens in the 'real' world,[138] it is significant that Plutarch metaphorically generalizes the experience of 'becoming other': the implication is that the Hellenization enacted by *paideia*, even in the case of 'ethnic' Greeks, is never simply a consolidation of an anterior identity but the creation of a new, 'foreign' one.

Paideia can never escape from its Hellenocentric orbit: it is fundamentally and incorrigibly bound up with the articulation of Greek superiority. On the other hand, cases like those of Favorinus and Lucian put flesh onto Plutarch's metaphor of education as cultural relocation. In every case, becoming educated is a process of rebirth, the creation of a new self; but in certain cases, it allows for a more radical reorientation, a quite literal (but also symbolically freighted) change of culture.

PEDAGOGY, IDENTITY, POWER

I began this chapter with a quotation from Iamblichus that indicated the power of education to construct social 'difference'. As we have seen throughout, *paideia* is a strategy of self-making, a means of arrogating to the subject a series of empowered identities (articulated, as ever, through marked polarities): particularly masculine, elite, Greek. At the same time, however, the process of *poiēsis* indicated in the term 'self-*making*' should be stressed: the paideutic self lies on a continuum with the literary product, both created by the same techniques and methods. As we saw in the previous chapter, mimetic literary discourse can be conceived of as either a 'natural' or an 'artificial' process, or as somewhere in between the two; similarly, *paideia* can be considered as a natural process of bringing to fruition the entelechy of the subject, or as a creative, innovative, 'unnatural' elaboration upon inert, primal matter. Lucian and Favorinus, 'outsiders' who break into the Greek literary sphere, are prime examples of the latter approach to *paideia*: both forge literary personae that celebrate the transformative, alienating role of literary *paideia*.

It cannot, thus, be claimed that the ideology of education was *simply* a ruse for the legitimation of the power of a select group; or, rather, education did legitimize the power of a select group, but did not do so *simply*. Despite the rhetoric that proclaimed

[138] As observed by T. Morgan (1998), 264–5.

otherwise, *paideia* in Roman Greece was not a self-evident quality 'possessed' by some and not by others, but a site of intense intellectual concern over the distribution of social power. Although education is generally presented, in the literature of the period, as the justification for established social hegemonies—the elite rule because they know best how to do so—it also provides the means for the overturning of such hegemonies by making power and prestige accessible to those who are notionally excluded. Now of course such access was very strictly policed, and the cases where women or non-Greeks have sought to surmount their given conditions are marginalized, belittled, and circumscribed. To a degree, this pluralist accessibility was the very precondition of the enduring success of *paideia* as a means of stabilizing the hierarchies of Greek society, for the very fact of the possibility of transgression of the system's boundaries strategically concealed the permanence of its covert operations. Yet it is important not to reduce *paideia* to a front for stabilizing power: to do so would be to misinterpret its characterization in contemporary thought, which focuses fundamentally upon its positive virtues as a self-making system. At root, *paideia* is the primary means of creating adult identity, and it is the form of precisely that act of creation that is at issue in the writings on the topic. Does it extend, transform, or conceal the 'natural' self? Is it a naturally or artificially mimetic process? If we insist that education was merely a conservative system, we rob these problematic aspects of their force, a force which (to judge by the persistent recurrence of such anxieties) was keenly felt over several centuries.

Part Two
Greece and Rome

3

Rome Uncivilized: Exile and the Kingdom

'[You] do not realize that everything is Greece to a wise man' Philostratus, *Vit. Apoll.* 1.34

'[If] I narrate the course of my exile, men will say, not that I am lamenting, but far rather that I am boasting' Dio Chrysostom (45.1)

The first part of this book focused primarily upon literary culture (*paideia*) as a means of creating Greek identity by exploring the relationship between past and present. The composition and dissemination of texts, and also the construction of the identity of the *pepaideumenos* ('educated man') were not self-evident activities; rather, they provided a matrix wherein identities could be inflected in different ways at different times. The 'secondariness' of Roman Greek literary production conceals a variety of ways of construing the modernity of the present, from decadence through to transformation.

The second part deals more directly with the Roman context. Three chapters deal successively with three paradigmatic modes of engagement between Greek literature and Roman politics. The first deals with a set of narratives of opposition: the recurrent accounts of the exile of Greek philosophers at the hands of Roman emperors. The second considers a more conciliatory model, that of the philosophical adviser of Roman emperors. The final chapter treats Greek satire of Roman power, and in particular the writings of Lucian. In all three, the emphasis will be upon Greekness as a manipulable resource, an identity to be forged and contrived, rather than a self-evidently inner 'essence' that lies anterior to discourse.

EXILE AND THE KINGDOM

Anecdotes telling of principled resistance to corrupt Romans pervade the literature of the principate. In the guise most familiar to modern students, these take the form of Jewish and Christian martyrologies.[1] Yet even before widespread persecution of Christians, there were narratives telling of pagan martyrs who stood up to Roman officials.[2] The Greek novels (apparently the paradigms upon which such Christian martyrologies as *Paul and Thecla* were based)[3] frequently present scenes in which virtuous Greeks stand up to overbearing potentates, who are usually foreigners (though the novels excise all mention of Rome, and these foreigners are often Persian).[4] In particular, there are numerous accounts of first-century pagan philosophers enduring exile at the behest of emperors.[5] This chapter will focus upon Greek narratives (to an extent, the forerunners of and inspiration behind Christian martyrologies)[6] telling of the authors' persecution at the hands of the first-century emperors Nero and Domitian.

Why does this obsession with suffering at the hands of power pervade the Graeco-Roman literature of the period? One answer, the traditional answer, points to the exigencies of establishing the

[1] See Perkins (1995), sparkling on Christianity and the will to suffering; also Bowersock (1995). On martyrology as a counter in the game of self-definition between Christianity and Judaism, see now Boyarin (1999); and Hopkins (1999), 111–23 on martyrology as a performative genre. I have also learned much from Lucy Grig's forthcoming Cambridge Ph.D. thesis.

[2] For the texts, see Musurillo (1954).

[3] Dörrie (1938); Brown (1988), 155–9; Perkins (1995), 26–7; Cooper (1996).

[4] e.g. Char. *C&C* 6.7.8–13; Ach. Tat. *L&C* 6.18–22; Hld. *Aeth.* 8.6.4. The officials in Chariton and Heliodorus are Persians, in Achilles Greek. Persia, however, seems to have been used as a 'front' for covert discussions of Rome: see Swain (1996), 176.

[5] 'The sea was full of exiles' (*plenum exiliis mare*), as Tacitus, writing of 69 CE, puts it (*Hist.* 1.2). Vespasian's ban in 71, intriguingly, exempted the philosopher Musonius Rufus (Cass. Dio 66.13, with B. F. Harris 1977: 109–13); on the date, see Moles (1978), 85 n. 56. Domitian re-enacted the decree: see Suet. *Dom.* 10.3; Tac. *Agr.* 2.1–2; Plin. *Ep.* 3.11.2–3; Philostr. *VA* 7.11. The question of how many expulsions Domitian enacted, and their dating, remains problematic: see B. Jones (1992), 119–20. Clashes between emperors and philosophers in the 1st cent. have been romanticized, sometimes explicitly: see Toynbee (1944) and Braginton (1944), from the perspective of the Second World War; and MacMullen (1992), 46–94 for a post-McCarthyist angle. See also Brunt (1975); Wistrand (1979). For an interpretation from a narrowly political perspective, see Wirszubski (1968), 138–50. On the practical details of Roman exile, see Grasmück (1978).

[6] See e.g. Toynbee (1944), 43–4, 47 on philosophical resistance as 'martyrdom'.

principate. In order to establish sole rule, the argument runs, the emperors had to eradicate all republican sympathies, and did so by brutal means: '[t]he senatorial opposition to the principate was finally crushed by the gradual liquidation of the old families through sentence of death or exile'.[7] Yet this does not explain why Greek literature is so keen to *represent* exile, and less so why Greek writers are keen to flag up their status as exiles. There was, after all, as Dio Chrysostom's epigraph to this chapter makes clear, much prestige and symbolic profit to be derived from portraying oneself as an exile. In Lucian's *Peregrinus*, the eponymous sham philosopher actually contrives his own exile for his persistent nuisance, and turns this to the advantage of his reputation: 'however, even this redounded to his fame and was spoken of everywhere—"the philosopher exiled because of his free speech (*parrhēsian*) and excessive freedom (*eleutherian*)"—and on these grounds, he joined the company of Musonius, Dio, Epictetus, and anyone else who found himself in such a predicament' (*πλὴν ἀλλὰ καὶ τοῦτο κλεινὸν αὐτοῦ καὶ διὰ στόματος ἦν ἅπασιν, ὁ φιλόσοφος διὰ τὴν παρρησίαν καὶ τὴν ἄγαν ἐλευθερίαν ἐξελασθείς, καὶ προσήλαυνε κατὰ τοῦτο τῶι Μουσωνίωι καὶ Δίωνι καὶ Ἐπικτήτωι καὶ εἴ τις ἄλλος ἐν περιστάσει τοιαύτηι ἐγένετο*, 18).[8] Exile was not simply a tool of imperial repression: it was also appropriated by its victims (and, no doubt, by others, too) as a rhetorical resource through which individual agents could articulate their own philosophical status. As Perkins argues (in relation to narratives of both Christian and pagan suffering), there is a powerful strain in the writings of the early empire that connects endurance in the face of oppression with inner personal strength.[9]

Christian martyrology pervasively associates the idea of suffering with the shared identity of the Christian community: in other words, the representation of persecution is a fundamental technique employed by Christian writers to create a sense both of united values and of the potency of the message. With the Greek exilic narratives, matters are rather more complex. It could hardly be said that, for example, Epictetus—a freed slave—represented a status to which all Greeks, or even all Greeks who admired his teachings, might aspire. Philosophical exiles were not in any

[7] Braginton (1944), 392.

[8] This odd use of *προσελαύνω* is not covered by LSJ.

[9] Perkins (1995).

simple sense generalizable paradigms of Greek identity; indeed, to an extent (though this will be qualified presently), exile defined the isolation of the individual from a community and accorded him a uniquely solitary, counter-civic status. Since Socrates (whose example looms large in these texts), the persecuted philosopher had been viewed as an exceptional figure whose integrity it would be impossible to match. Plato's *Phaedo*, which recounts the death of Socrates, closes with the recognition that the philosopher was 'the best, and besides the wisest and most righteous, of those we encountered in those days' (*τῶν τότε ὧν ἐπειράθημεν ἀρίστου καὶ ἄλλως φρονιμωτάτου καὶ δικαιοτάτου*, Pl. *Phaed.* 118a). These superlatives imply both a status of exceptional virtue and an idiosyncrasy beyond the norms of regular society.

Despite the singularity of the persecuted philosopher, however, this chapter will argue that the narratives of philosophical exile that circulated in this period construct a particular vision of the relationship between Greek *paideia* and Roman power. Indeed, certain of the texts to be discussed below do, as we shall see, explicitly arrogate to their subjects the status of paradigm. Although perhaps, when compared with the Christian martyrs, the pagan philosophical exiles appear self-consciously individual, they do represent one particular mode—and a mode that is highly culturally valorized—of engagement between 'Greek' and 'Roman'. I aim in this chapter to explore how the terms 'Greek' and 'Roman'—which I set within quotation marks in order to indicate the partial and provisional nature of this particular construction of Graeco-Roman relations—are knowingly manipulated by sophisticated writers, rather than simply constituting pre-formed identities 'expressed' through language.

In the late republic and early principate, as is well known, a considerable body of Latin writing was devoted to the subject of exile, most notably by Cicero, Ovid, and Seneca.[10] The present chapter considers the Greek counterparts of these writers, who often share similar (predominantly Stoic and Cynic) sources,[11] but present

[10] The bibliography on exile in the Roman writers is immense: in particular, see Doblhofer (1987); G. Williams (1994); C. Edwards (1996), 110–12; Claassen (1996*a*); and esp. (1999).

[11] For records of Cynic discussions of exile and the *polis*, see Diog. Laert. 6.21, 49 on Diogenes; Diog. Laert. 6.93 on Crates. Stilpo's views are preserved, although no doubt in mediated form, in Teles fr. 3 Hense = Stob. *Flor.* 3.40.8. For analysis of the *Quellen* of the exilic writers, see Giesecke (1891).

such ideas from a specifically Greek vantage, and treat specifically of the relationship between Greek *paideia* and Roman power. The focus here is primarily upon a series of philosophical-sophistic tracts composed by those who claim to be the victims of exile,[12] written in Greek, within one hundred years of each other, under the Roman empire: Musonius Rufus' *That exile is not an evil*, Dio Chrysostom's thirteenth oration (together with related texts), and Favorinus' *On exile*.[13] These texts are discussed together[14] because they are united by a common concern to represent the author as the victim of exile. Moreover, the texts show an awareness of the common ground they share: they are united by preoccupations and vocabulary (some scholars have considered this common ground an index of lack of original thought);[15] and the authors, who knew one another,[16] appear to allude to and echo one another.

Although exile has throughout history and across a range of cultures been a powerful literary, theological, and philosophical trope expressing the alienation of the human condition in general,[17] it is crucial to understand the specific dynamics of the

[12] Hence the exclusion from primary consideration of Plutarch's *De exilio*—though Plutarch was also known to Dio (inferred from titles in the 'Lamprias catalogue': 'Speech spoken in reply to Dio at Olympia' (*Ὁ πρὸς Δίωνα ῥηθεὶς ἐν Ὀλυμπίαι*, no. 204); 'Debate with Dio' (*Διάλεξις πρὸς Δίωνα*, no. 227)) and Favorinus (fr. 28 Barigazzi; *Suda* s.v. *Φαβωρîνος*; and further, Bowie 1997).

[13] For a translation of Favorinus *On exile*, see Appendix 1. Also relevant to this chapter are Epictetus' comments on exile (Arr. *Diss. Epict.* 1.1.26–7; 1.11.33; 1.29.6; 3.3.17; 3.22.22; 3.24.29; 4.1.60; 4.1.172; 4.5.29; 4.7.14; 4.7.18; 4.11.23; Epict. fr. 21 Schenkl = Stob. *Flor.* 3.7.16; Epict. *Ench.* 21; 32.3) and Philiscus' speech at Cassius Dio 38.18–29 (see Claassen 1996*b*).

[14] They are discussed as a group e.g. by Grasmück (1978), 141–3.

[15] Grasmück (1978), 142 ('die immer wiederkehrenden Topoi'); Doblhofer (1987), 41 ('einem Arsenal von Trostgründen'); Claassen (1996*b*), 30–1.

[16] Musonius is said to have taught Dio at Fronto p. 135 van den Hout, and the philosopher praised at Dio 31.122 is usually considered to be Musonius: see von Arnim (1898), 216; Lutz (1947), 17 n. 60; C. P. Jones (1978), 12. The report that Dio wrote an essay *Against (?) Musonius* (*πρὸς Μουσώνιον*, attested at Synes. *Dio* 37b) might be taken to contradict this, but, in the baleful words of John Moles, 'it is not unusual for pupils to quarrel with teachers' (1978: 82). Moreover, it is not clear to me that *πρός* necessarily means 'against', and not 'in reply to' (LSJ s.v. *πρός* C4). Dio is said to have taught Favorinus at Philostr. *VS* 490, and Favorinus explicitly mentions Musonius (*De ex.* 2.1; 23.1) and, if Barigazzi's conjecture is correct, Dio (2.1).

[17] e.g. on modernism and exile, see Brennan (1990), 60–4; (with some reservations) S. Martin (1992); on postmodernism and exile, see Robbins (1983), 72; Bevan (1990), 3. Such generalizations of exile, however, can serve to downplay the experiences of genuine refugees: see the comments of Goldman (1995), 127–8; Said (1984), 54–5; Bhabha (1990), 292 = id. (1994), 140–1. The idea of exile as a generalized condition of humanity occurs in the ancient world, too: for the human

culture in question, to site the questions raised by the representation of exile in the context of the issues relevant to the author in question. In the case of the texts discussed here, the fundamental cultural and conceptual context will be Greek culture's self-perception as a tradition reanimating the past as a means of resisting the threat from Rome. As is well known, the Greek literature of the early principate sites itself linguistically, stylistically, and thematically within and against the literary tradition of democratic Athens.[18] This chapter argues that this process of positioning against the Classical past extends from literary fashioning to political revisionism; that the writers under examination strategically reorientate the language of cultural self-definition that was current in that earlier period, reconfiguring (sometimes explicitly) the relationship between self and *polis* in terms more appropriate to the enormous world-empire of the Roman principate.

In the Classical period Aristotle could write that a human is an 'animal that belongs in a *polis*' (πολιτικὸν ζῷον), and that to be 'without a *polis*' (ἄπολις) is to be either greater or lesser than a human (*Pol.* 1253[a]). Social identity, for Aristotle as for all Greeks of his period, was created and articulated through the *polis*, and to lose that was to lose one's self. Exile from the *polis* was, thus, a form of social death, and the horrors of exile are iterated time and again.[19] In the later writings that form the subject of this chapter, however, exile becomes a positive accreditation of philosophical success (as we have already seen in the cases of Dio Chrysostom and Proteus Peregrinus in Lucian). How do we interpret this shift in attitudes to exile from abhorrence to celebration? It is dangerous to assume too quickly that this discursive transformation represents a direct and straightforward response to changes in the identity-defining role of the *polis* in defining Greek identity between the Classical and the Roman periods.[20] Indeed, some of these ideas concerning the tolerability of exile were already current in embryonic form in the late Classical period: the Cynics

or the soul as 'exile' from the divine, see Emped. fr. B 115.13 DK (cited, however, only at Plut. *De ex.* 607c–e); Plotin. 1.6.8; Aug. *Civ. Dei* 1 *praef.*; 18.51; 19 *passim.* On exile as a condition of humanity in Augustine's work, see M. Ferguson (1992); on the medieval development of the idea, see Ladner (1967).

[18] See esp. Reardon (1971); Bowie (1974); Swain (1996), 43–100.

[19] For the sources, see Doblhofer (1987), 21–40.

[20] Foucault's remarks on the need for caution in this respect (1990: 81–4) are well made.

Diogenes, Crates, and Stilpo discussed deracination from the *polis*, and were highly influential upon the exilic writers of the principate.[21] What interests me here, though, is not so much the genealogy of the ideas in question as the self-positioning of Musonius, Dio, and Favorinus against the background of the intellectual and ideological climate of their times, and their *perceived* and *articulated* relationship with earlier Greek tradition. From this perspective, it matters little that some of the ideas expressed have their roots in Classical and Hellenistic philosophy: what counts is the attempt to articulate a new cultural positionality by rewriting the past. It is not necessarily any particular theoretical innovation, but a new intensification and stylization of the discourse of exile that marks these texts' historical site in the Greek culture of the early principate.

Any relationship between past and present is inevitably complex. The texts discussed here do not simply reject the Classical world and its *polis*-based ideology: the very allusive process which accords centrality to the literature of Athens also expresses a perceived *continuity* with the past. We should not imagine the writers on exile under the principate to be simply abnegating the *polis* as a locus of cultural definition: rather, they create and explore a tension between *polis* and *cosmos*, between the traditional parochiality of Greek identity and its new role as the integrative language of the eastern Roman empire. This Janus-like duality is absolutely fundamental to the thought-world of Roman Greece, as we saw in the first chapter: the glorious epoque of democratic Athens is *both* familiar *and* alien, and self-definition in the present involves both the appropriation and the transcendence of the paradigms of the past.

To consider these exilic texts, all 'consolations' for the loss incurred by exile,[22] as explorations of socio-political identity may seem counter-intuitive. Post-Classical Greek philosophy was largely, as Martha Nussbaum has stressed,[23] therapeutic in orientation, and exilic consolation correspondingly seeks to 'cure' exiles

[21] Above, n. 11.

[22] Musonius (fr. 9, p. 41 Hense: παρεμυθήσατο, 'he consoled') and Favorinus (*De ex*. 2.1–2: πα[ρ]ηγορίαν, 'consolation'; 2.14: π̣α̣ρ̣α̣μ̣υ̣ θ̣ίαν, 'exhortation') present their essays specifically as consolations. Dio 13.2 amounts to a 'self-consolation'. For the genre of the consolation, see esp. Kassel (1958); Oehs (1993) is less useful for the present purposes.

[23] See esp. Nussbaum (1994).

of their 'sickness'.[24] These texts can thus be viewed as a continuation of an earlier tradition of private introspection and self-help. As Michel Foucault has most prominently argued, the homiletic literature of the principate manifests a pronounced turn 'inwards', privileging over the explicitly civic ethics of the Classical period 'the care of the self', a cultural code 'wherein the relations of oneself to oneself were intensified and valorized'.[25] Yet these texts do not simply exchange exterior orientation for interior. The distinction between public and private is notoriously difficult to locate: the Greek world did not cease to be 'civic' after the end of the Classical period; and, conversely, it is perfectly possible to see 'inwardness' as a trope of public self-presentation. For Erving Goffman, for example, 'normal' social interaction involves the use of semiotic and rhetorical devices associated with theatre, so that the social 'self' can be said to be an external performance rather than simply an expression of an inner being.[26] It is preferable to consider these consolations as public *dramatizations* of the therapeutic process, packaged 'presentations' of exilic identity, and not simply as aimed at the heart. That is not to deny that exile caused real suffering, and that some of that suffering may have been alleviated by the consolations in question; but it is important also to view the texts as part of an ongoing contest over the public conceptualization and representation of Greek identity. The 'new inwardness' of post-Classical literature, on this interpretation, is a new twist in the tale of Greek culture's ongoing exploration of man's status as a 'political animal'.

In matters exilic, the possibilities of persona-construction were legion. Greek literary history had a long tradition of exiled writers, from the early lyric poets Alcman, Archilochus, and Sappho, through Thucydides and Alcibiades to Diogenes the Cynic.[27] Such well-known exempla clearly contribute to the prestige of an exilic self-fashioning, and the techniques whereby Ovid (and others too) manipulated this exemplary tradition have been well discussed in recent years.[28] The significance of exile, however,

[24] On the 'nosography' of exile, see Doblhofer (1987), 66–72.

[25] Foucault (1990), 43.

[26] Goffman (1969).

[27] On this tradition, see Doblhofer (1987), 21–49; André and Baslez (1993), 283–97. Sappho's exile is not discussed by either: it is recorded on the so-called *Chronicon Parium* (IG^2 12.5, 444.XXXVI).

[28] Not that Ovid necessarily invents his exile (as argued by Fitton Brown 1985),

gained new urgency for philosophers in the early empire: Vespasian and Domitian both banished all philosophers from Rome,[29] and exile became in a sense the hallmark of a free-speaking philosopher. The language of exile thus also bespeaks a polemical engagement with Roman power, and the vaunted transcendence of humiliation and suffering imposed by exile advertises the philosopher's superiority to imperial dominion. Discussions of exile constitute a nodal point where Greek self-representation in cultural-paideutic terms meets Roman power. This chapter seeks to understand exile as a strategy of self-representation, and as a means of constructing and exploring the relationship between *paideia* and the socio-political landscape of the Roman empire.

MUSONIUS RUFUS, THE 'ROMAN' 'SOCRATES'

Musonius Rufus was a Roman citizen of the equestrian order, originally from Etruria (Tuscany) in Italy. He followed Rubellius Plautus after the latter's exile by Nero in 62, we are told by the historians, thus implicating himself in the Pisonian conspiracy against Nero and earning himself his own exile to the desolate island of Gyara in the Greek Aegean.[30] It was this that made his name as an exile.[31] Despite his solid Italian background and his familiarity as a figure in Roman history, however, the words that are transmitted under his name are in Greek,[32] and the Greek

but that his works display a self-conscious manipulation of the literary topology of exile (G. Williams 1994).

[29] Above, n. 5.

[30] For the details, see Lutz (1947), 14. Cassius Dio (in Xiphilinus' epitome) suggests, surprisingly, that Musonius was then *excluded* from Vespasian's subsequent blanket banishment of all philosophers from Rome (66.13.2). The reason for this exemption is unstated, and it is not certain that the text is either secure or accurately epitomized.

[31] Fav. *De ex.* 2.1; 23.1. Luc. *Peregr.* 18; Philostr. *VA* 7.16; [Luc.] *Nero passim*, with Whitmarsh (1999*a*).

[32] Musonius himself, however, may not have composed personally the writings that we have under his name: evidence suggests that a certain disciple named Lucius actually wrote the texts (see van Geytenbeek 1963: ch. 1 *passim*, esp. 9–12). It is impossible to prove the matter conclusively, but the point does not substantially bear upon what follows: it matters little whether Musonius or another is the author of his persona-construction. At any rate, the representation of Musonius as a non-writer serves further to underline his Socratic credentials (see Lutz 1947: 3–4 for his Socratic connection), as is the case with Arrian's ghost-writing of the *Dissertations of Epictetus* (Stadter 1980: 27–8).

literary tradition—in particular, Philostratus—emphasizes his Hellenic qualities.[33] In this respect, Musonius' choice of Greek as a philosophical language (in prominent contrast, for example, to the efforts of Lucretius and Cicero to Latinize Greek philosophy)[34] can be interpreted as a self-conscious (and largely successful) attempt to construct for himself a Greek identity. This turn to Greek at the linguistic level is symbolically matched at the level of (auto)biographical narrative by his exile from Rome to the Greek Aegean.

Commentators often charge Musonius with a want of originality in his arguments.[35] It is undeniable that several of Musonius' arguments do draw upon a traditional repertoire, and indeed at times his language closely shadows that of Teles, his closest extant model.[36] Yet repetition and imitation, as we saw in the first chapter, are not simply tokens of intellectual feebleness: repetition is also a trope, initiating a dynamic process whereby cultural continuity is constructed or contested. Those who point to Musonius' failure to innovate neglect to consider the dramatic and rhetorical framing of the text: what kind of voice is Musonius arrogating for himself? The form of this writing is (as we shall see presently) self-consciously artful, and in particular reminiscent of Xenophon's *Memorabilia of Socrates*; this literary stylization makes a substantial difference to the effect of the arguments. A second fundamental issue of reframing pertains to Musonius' cultural status: what, in the context of the contests for philosophical identity in the first century CE, is the point for a Romano-Etruscan dissident of echoing and reworking traditional Greek philosophical material?

Let us consider first how Musonius evokes and manipulates the political language of democratic Athens. The clearest example of this process comes with his stress upon the importance of *eleutheria* ('freedom') and *parrhēsia* ('free speech') (fr. 9, pp. 48–50 Hense). The notion that the exile lacks these qualities is tradi-

[33] See e.g. [Luc.] *Nero* 1, where Musonius is invoked as an expert upon Greekness; also Philostr. *VA* 7.16, where 'the Greeks' go to visit Musonius in exile.

[34] Lucr. 1.136–9; Cic. *Disp. Tusc.* 1.1–4.

[35] Giesecke (1891), 25 ([*a*]*tque pro certo quidem dici potest, ea quae Stilponi tribuimus in usum suum conuersisse Musonius* . . .); van Geytenbeek 1963: 151 ('[a]s usual, Musonius' argument is not original, but it is attractive and clear'); Doblhofer (1987), 41. For further discussion, see van Geytenbeek (1963), 142–51.

[36] See van Geytenbeek (1963), 147–8 on the arguments; Giesecke (1891), 25–6 on the verbal reminiscences.

tional,[37] but given a new inflection in the first century CE. 'Freedom', as is well known, was a common cry amongst republican dissenters of the first century, prior to Trajan's appropriation of the language for his own propaganda.[38] Musonius' celebration of the 'free speech' of the exile contributes to his own self-representation as a free-speaking philosopher banished by an intolerant tyrant, thus developing the sense that exile reflects more on Nero than on the philosopher. Yet there is a more subtle articulation at work here: Musonius specifically presents his own definition of *parrhēsia* as a reorientation of the Classical definition. Using the rhetorical device known as *anaskeuē* (quotation and refutation),[39] he refutes the famous comment of Euripides' Polynices that it is a slave's lot to lack freedom of speech (*Phoen.* 391–2):[40]

> But, by Zeus, you [i.e. a hypothetical protester] insist, Euripides says that exiles lose their freedom (*eleutherias*) when they are deprived of freedom of speech (*parrhēsias*). For he represents Jocasta asking Polynices, her son, what misfortunes an exile has to bear. He answers,
>
> > One greatest of all, that he does not have freedom of speech (*parrhēsian*).
>
> She replies,
>
> > You name the condition of a slave, not to be able to say what one thinks.
>
> But I should say in rejoinder to Euripides: 'You are right, Euripides, when you say that it is the condition of a slave not to say what one thinks—when one ought to speak, at any rate, for it is not always, nor everywhere, nor before everyone that we should say what we think. But one point, it seems to me, you have not made well, namely that exiles do not have freedom of speech (*parrhēsias*) (if, that is, freedom of speech (*parrhēsia*) means to you not suppressing whatever one happens to think). For it is not exiles who shrink from saying what they think, but men afraid lest from speaking pain or death or punishment or some other such thing befall them. Fear is the cause of this, and not, by Zeus, exile! For many people, nay most who dwell in their native city fear what seem to them the dire consequences of free speech. However, one who is manly (*ho andreios*), in exile no less than at home, is dauntless in the face of all such fears; for that reason also he has the courage to say what he thinks no less when he happens to be in exile than when not.

[37] Eur. *Phoen.* 391–2 (see below); Teles also mentions loss of *parrhēsia* in passing as one loss to which the exile is held to be subject (3.15.16).

[38] Wirszubski (1968), 167–71; Wistrand (1979), 95–6.

[39] Cf. Aphthonius, *Progymnasmata* 5.

[40] Plutarch also discusses this passage, at *De ex.* 605f; cf. 599e.

νὴ Δί' ἀλλ' Εὐριπίδης φησὶν ἐλευθερίας στέρεσθαι τοὺς φυγάδας, ἐπεὶ καὶ παρρησίας. πεποίηκε γὰρ τὴν μὲν Ἰοκάστην πυνθανομένην Πολυνείκους τοῦ υἱέος, τίνα δυσχερῆ τῶι φεύγοντί ἐστιν· ὁ δ' ἀποκρίνεται ὅτι

ἓν μὲν μέγιστον, οὐκ ἔχει παρρησίαν,

ἡ δ' αὖ πρὸς αὐτὸν

δούλου τόδ' εἶπας, μὴ λέγειν ἅ τις φρονεῖ.

ἐγὼ δὲ φαίην ἂν πρὸς τὸν Εὐριπίδην ὅτι, ὦ Εὐριπίδη, τοῦτο μὲν ὀρθῶς ὑπολαμβάνεις, ὡς δούλου ἐστίν, ἃ φρονεῖ μὴ λέγειν, ὅταν γε δεῖ λέγειν· οὐ γὰρ ἀεὶ καὶ πανταχοῦ καὶ πρὸς ὁντινοῦν λεκτέον ἃ φρονοῦμεν. ἐκεῖνο δὲ οὔ μοι δοκεῖς εὖ εἰρηκέναι, τὸ μὴ μετεῖναι τοῖς φεύγουσι παρρησίας, εἴπερ παρρησία σοι δοκεῖ τὸ μὴ σιγᾶν ἃ φρονῶν τυγχάνει τις. οὐ γὰρ οἱ φεύγοντες ὀκνοῦσι λέγειν ἃ φρονοῦσιν, ἀλλ' οἱ δεδιότες μὴ ἐκ τοῦ εἰπεῖν γένηται αὐτοῖς πόνος ἢ θάνατος ἢ ζημία ἤ τι τοιοῦτον ἕτερον. τοῦτο δὲ τὸ δέος μὰ Δία οὐχ ἡ φυγὴ ποιεῖ. πολλοῖς γὰρ ὑπάρχει καὶ τῶν ἐν τῆι πατρίδι ὄντων, μᾶλλον δὲ τοῖς πλείστοις, τὰ δοκοῦντα δεινὰ δεδιέναι. ὁ δὲ ἀνδρεῖος οὐδὲν ἧττον φυγὰς ὢν ἤπερ οἴκοι θαρρεῖ πρὸς ἅπαντα τὰ τοιαῦτα, διὸ καὶ λέγει ἃ φρονεῖ θαρρῶν οὐδὲν ἧττον[41] *ἢ ὅταν ἦι μὴ φυγάς, ὅταν φεύγων τύχηι.* (fr. 9, pp. 48–9 Hense)

As one of the central authors of the Classical period, Euripides becomes representative of democratic ideology in general. In refuting him, Musonius is marking the need to reinvent the political vocabulary inherited from democratic Athens. The word *parrhēsia* was coined in Athens in the fifth century, where it referred to the right to speak in the democratic assembly, one of the centrally enshrined and definitive features of participatory democracy[42] (it is with a certain disruptive irony that Euripides places his words in the mouths of Polynices and Jocasta, a would-be tyrant and a queen). Musonius' response to Euripides, however, redefines *parrhēsia* as a moral imperative to speak what one thinks when one *should* speak. This ethical focus orientates the discussion away from civic rights to philosophical duty, and the (predominantly Stoic) issue of whether and how a philosopher should engage in politics.[43] Whereas Euripides presupposes a context wherein the right to free speech defines the citizen body exclusively, Musonius presupposes an alienated relationship between self and state, where the individual can only display his manhood

[41] I have adopted Gesner's emendation *ἧττον*, recorded in Hense's apparatus, for MS *μᾶλλον* (followed by Hense and Lutz), which gives the wrong sense. Lutz's translation of this passage ('equally at home or in exile') fudges the issue.

[42] Peterson (1929), 283–5; Scarpat (1964), 29–45; Momigliano (1971), 515–23; id. (1973–4), 259; Konstan (1996), 9.

[43] See esp. Mus. Ruf. fr. 8; Plut. *De phil. max. cum princ. diss.*

(note *ho andreios*, 'one who is manly') by resisting the edicts imposed upon him. Free speech is no longer articulated through collective enfranchisement, but through principled resistance and moral integrity. Paradoxically, it is in this self-conscious revision of Classical ideology that Musonius most clearly stakes his claim to an identity as a philosopher in the fashion traditionally enshrined in the Greek paideutic heritage. Like Diogenes, and above all like Socrates, Musonius does not define his identity through society, but in accordance with philosophical truth. Musonius' relationship to the literary-philosophical past is self-consciously selective.

Exile plays a metaphorical role in this connection: Musonius is not merely topographically relocated, but also conceptually isolated from the norms and conventions of regular society. In a literal sense, the emperor banished him from Rome for practising philosophy; at a deeper level, Musonius' decision to philosophize had already condemned him to a kind of exile from society. At an earlier point in the text, Musonius indicates that the philosopher identifies with not the *polis* ('city'), but the *cosmos* ('universe'):

Why should anyone who is not devoid of understanding (*anoētos*) be grieved by exile? It does not deprive us of water, earth, air, or the sun and the other planets, or indeed, even of the society of men, for everywhere and in every way (*hapantakhou . . . kai pantēi*) there is opportunity for association with them. What if we are kept from a certain part of the earth and from association with certain men, what is so dreadful about that? Why, when we were at home, we did not enjoy the whole (*hapasēi*) earth, nor did we have contact with all men.

φυγὴν γάρ, ἔφη, πῶς ἄν τις μὴ ἀνόητος ὢν βαρύνοιτο; ἥτις ὕδατος μὲν καὶ γῆς καὶ ἀέρος, ἔτι δὲ ἡλίου καὶ τῶν ἄλλων ἄστρων οὐκ ἀπείργει ἡμᾶς οὐδαμῶς, ἀλλ' οὐδὲ ἀνθρώπων ὁμιλίας, ἁπανταχοῦ γὰρ καὶ πάντηι τούτων μετουσία ἐστίν. εἰ δὲ μέρους τινὸς τῆς γῆς ἀφαιρούμεθα καὶ τινῶν ἀνθρώπων συνουσίας, τί τοῦτο δεινόν; οὐδὲ γὰρ οἴκοι ὄντες ἁπάσηι τῆι γῆι ἐχρώμεθα, οὐδὲ ἀνθρώποις ἅπασι συνῆμεν. (fr. 9, p. 41 Hense)

This passage draws heavily upon Stoic and Cynic ideas of what scholars call 'cosmopolitanism',[44] the belief that a philosopher is a citizen of the universe. The fundamental opposition for Musonius is between 'part' and 'whole': one 'devoid of understanding'

[44] e.g. Dio Chr. 4.13; Diog. Oen. fr. 30; Arr. *Diss. Epict.* 2.10.3. On cosmopolitanism, see amongst older scholars Baldry (1965) and Stanton (1968), and more recently esp. Schofield (1991), 57–92; Moles (1993). See R. B. Rutherford (1989), 239–40 for further bibliography.

(*anoētos*, literally 'without mind') may feel bound to the part, but philosophers grasp the importance of the 'entirety' (*hapantakhou*, *pantēi*, and *hapasēi* are from the same Greek root, *pas*, meaning 'all' or 'every').[45] The opposition between *polis* and *cosmos* also symbolizes the opposition between a partial and a complete perspective upon the world: the philosopher, divorced by his insight and education from a parochial world-view is, by definition, always already an exile of sorts.[46] Exile—understood here as a relocation from the local to the general, from the specific to the universal—is presented figuratively as a means of constructing philosophical authority. Space and geography serve a powerfully metaphorical role in the articulation of identity.

In the following words, Musonius attributes cosmopolitan doctrine to two Classical writers, Socrates and Euripides. 'Is not the universe (*kosmos*) the common fatherland (*patris*) of all men, as Socrates held?' (*οὐχὶ κοινὴ πατρὶς ἀνθρώπων ἁπάντων ὁ κόσμος ἐστίν, ὥσπερ ἠξίου ὁ Σωκράτης;* fr. 9, p. 42 Hense). 'Euripides too agrees with this when he says, "As all the heavens are open to the eagle's flight | so all the earth is for a noble man his fatherland (*patris*)" '. (*σύμφωνα δὲ τούτοις λέγει καὶ Εὐριπίδης ἐν οἷς φησιν "ἅπας μὲν ἀὴρ ἀετῶι περάσιμος | ἅπασα δὲ χθὼν ἀνδρὶ γενναίωι πατρίς"*, fr. 9, p. 42 Hense; the quotation is Eur. fr. 1047 N^2). At the same time as he distances himself from democratic conceptions of political identity, Musonius also seeks to ground his doctrine in the prestigious literature of the Classical period. The attempt to evoke Classical precedents is doubly striking in that Musonius' is an eminently post-Classical, Stoic vision of the universe: the 'reasonable' man (*epieikēs*), he tells us, should consider himself a 'citizen (*politēs*) of the city (*polis*) of Zeus' (*πολίτης τῆς τοῦ Διὸς πόλεως*, fr. 9, p. 42 Hense), and the *polis* of Zeus (a phrase that recurs in Marcus Aurelius)[47] is glossed in familiar Stoic terminology as a *systēma* ('community'/'compound') of men and gods (*ἣ συνέστηκεν ἐξ ἀνθρώπων καὶ θεῶν* (fr. 9, p. 42 Hense).[48] Having earlier explicitly

[45] The idea that the philosopher can grasp 'everything' (*τὸ πᾶν*) is Stoic: see *SVF* 3.260.5, and *SVF* 2.167.8 for 'the whole' (*τὸ ὅλον*). On the distinction between *τὸ πᾶν* and *τὸ ὅλον*, see LS 44A. Epictetus likewise correlates exile with grasp of *τὸ πᾶν* (Arr. *Diss. Epict.* 3.22.22).

[46] For analogous 'cosmic' representations of philosophical wisdom, see e.g. Lucr. *De rer. nat.* 1.72–4; Philostr. *VA* 3.34–5.

[47] Marc. Aur. *Med.* 4.23.

[48] For the Stoic flavour of this, see esp. *SVF* 2.168.11–14; 169.26–8. In general on the Stoic conception of the cosmic *polis*, see the excellent account in Schofield (1991), esp. ch. 3.

distanced himself from the democratic conception of *parrhēsia*, Musonius here goes out of his way to attribute Stoic cosmological ideas to Classical writers. Democratic Athens provides both the negative exemplum against which the modern view of the world is offset and the source of the prestige in which it must be grounded. Musonius' complex, ambivalent relationship with the literary-philosophical past, an element in the larger grammar of relations between Roman Greece and the Classical past, is clearly foregrounded here.

Exile, in Musonius' writing, is not merely a juridical state, but also a metaphor for philosophical identity. Indeed, to be exiled is to undergo a form of *rite de passage*. The mythical pattern of the *voyage initiatique*, the journey of a young man to a far-off or marginal place and his subsequent return home in a state of maturity, is widespread in Greek literature (the voyages of Jason, Telemachus, Perseus, and Orestes being prominent examples).[49] In pre-Roman periods, it appears that ephebes (young men on the point of initiation to adulthood) were ritually secluded from the *polis*, and sent to its margins to be *peripoloi* ('border-guards').[50] This association between transition and relocation to marginal spaces recurs in narratives telling of the philosophical enlightenment of wise men: the subject travels abroad in a state of ignorance and returns in a state of wisdom. The notion that travel generates wisdom is latent as early as Homer's initial characterization of Odysseus as the man 'who wandered much . . . and saw the cities and attitude of many men' (ὃς μάλα πολλὰ | πλάγχθη . . . | πολλῶν δ' ἀνθρώπων ἴδεν ἄστεα καὶ νόον ἔγνω, Hom. *Od.* 1.1–3). In the post-Homeric tradition, Odysseus is frequently represented as a man of inquiry, a historian or philosopher *avant la lettre*.[51] Following this tradition, Herodotus makes Croesus remark on Solon's fame 'on account of your wisdom and travelling' (σοφίης εἵνεκεν τῆς σῆς καὶ πλάνης, 1.30.2), and comments similarly on the Scythian sage Anacharsis (4.76.1). Stories of travelling philosophers subsequently abound,[52] employing this narrative model of central and peripheral space to articulate initiation into philosophical wisdom.

[49] For more detailed discussion with bibliography, see Whitmarsh (1999*b*), 18–24.

[50] Vidal-Naquet (1986*a*), 106–28; (1986*b*).

[51] Marincola (1996); on his paradigmatic status for the Stoics, see Stanford (1954), 118–27.

[52] See in general André and Baslez (1993), 293–8.

Following this narrative pattern, exile is frequently said to make a philosopher of the man.[53] In the context of a discussion of exile, Cicero lists sixteen philosophers who lived their life abroad.[54] The philosopher who is most identified with exile, however, is Diogenes the Cynic, who, as Musonius himself points out, 'turned from a layman (*idiōtou*) to a philosopher when he had been exiled' (ἐκ . . . ἰδιώτου φιλόσοφος ἐγένετο φυγών, fr. 9, p. 43 Hense),[55] instead of 'sitting' (καθῆσθαι, p. 43 Hense) in his home town of Sinope. Exile is a form of 'training' (ἀσκήσει, pp. 43–4 Hense), turning the inchoate human into a fully-formed philosopher. Musonius uses the example of Diogenes to articulate an exemplary contrast between the health of the exile and the 'sickness' of those who stay at home: the city's sedentary 'softness and luxury' (μαλακίας καὶ τρυφῆς, p. 44 Hense) leads to 'disease' (νοσημάτων, νόσων, νοσηλευόμενος, p. 44 Hense), while the exile is characterized by manliness (ἀνδρικώτερον, p. 44 Hense; cf. ἀνδρίζεσθαι, p. 45 Hense), bodily vigour and health (p. 44 Hense). Exile is a philosophical initiation, a transition to mature manhood.

Musonius' account of Diogenes' 'conversion' during exile implicitly assimilates the celebrated philosophical exile of the past to his own persona. Indeed, at one point, in a breathtaking display of self-dramatization, he explicitly arrogates to himself the same paradigmatic status as that of Diogenes. In order to back up his assertion (discussed earlier) that exiles have *parrhēsia*, Musonius offers two examples of such manliness, Diogenes and himself (pp. 49–50 Hense). The first story tells of Diogenes' imperious behaviour when he came up for auction at the slave-market: he commanded Xeniades the Corinthian to buy him, for the latter's benefit.[56] This *exemplum* is said to illustrate his *parrhēsia* ('freedom of speech', p. 49 Hense) and his *eleutheria* ('freedom', p. 49

[53] André and Baslez (1993), 293–7.

[54] Xenocrates, Crantor, Arcesilas, Lacydes, Aristotle, Theophrastus, Zeno, Cleanthes, Chrysippus, Antipater, Carneades, Clitomachus, Philo, Antiochus, Panaetius, Posidonius (*Tusc. Disp.* 5.108).

[55] See also Diog. Laert. 6.21.

[56] Diog. Laert. 6.29–30; 6.36; 6.74; Höistad (1948), 119–25. On the testimony of Diogenes Laertius (6.29), the story apparently derives from the 3rd-cent. biographer Hermippus 'the Callimachean' (*RE* s.v. Hermippus 6) and Eubulus (probably the sceptical philosopher from Alexandria: *RE* s.v. Eubulus 16), though both these names are problematic: 'Hermippus' is an emendation for MS 'Menippus' (the reading defended by Helm 1906: 249–50), while 'Eubulus' is sometimes emended to 'Eubulides'.

Hense), thus confusing the categories of free and slave: the slave is freer than his master (a fine, Cynic paradox). The second example is that of Musonius himself:

But why should I employ cases of men long ago (*palaia*)? Are you not aware that I am an exile? Well then, have I been deprived of freedom of speech (*parrhēsias*)? Have I been bereft of the power (*exousian*) to say what I think? Have you or anyone else ever seen me cringing before anyone just because I am an exile?

καὶ τί δεῖ τὰ παλαιὰ λέγειν; ἀλλ' ἐγώ σοι οὐ δοκῶ εἶναι φυγάς; ἆρ' οὖν ἐστέρημαι παρρησίας; ἆρα ἀφήιρημαι τὴν ἐξουσίαν τοῦ ἃ φρονῶ λέγειν; ἤδη δέ με εἶδες ἢ σὺ ἢ ἕτερος ὑποπτήσσοντά τωι ὅτι φεύγω; (fr. 9, p. 49 Hense)

Musonius' presentation of himself as a paradigm for imitation links him back with *hoi palaioi*, the men of old, self-consciously constructing a persona for the speaker within, and also in agonistic tension with, the Classical tradition. This strategy informs the essay as a whole: the use of himself as an exemplum of fortitude is only the clearest example of Musonius' creative and selective rereading of the literature of the past for the purposes of self-authorization in the present. In an essay that presents itself as a therapy offered to an addressee, the stylization of the speaker as a paradigm for imitation exposes a new layer of self-advertisement.

The analogy between Diogenes and Musonius also serves to make a more trenchant point about Musonius as a subject of imperial power. Like Diogenes, Musonius has found himself the victim of a hegemonic social relationship: his own treatment at the hands of Nero is implicitly correlated with Diogenes' status as a slave. Yet just as Diogenes inverts his social role, giving commands to his master, so Musonius shows by his actions that he has an authority that the emperor lacks. *Exousia*, rendered as 'power' in the quotation above, is regularly used in the sense of 'political authority'.[57] The deliberately contrived paradox that exile (conventionally viewed as a submission to the power and authority of the emperor) in fact stimulates the (internal, personal) power of the philosopher is implicit throughout the essay. Greeks were fond of punning on the homonyms *rhōmē* ('strength') and *Rhōmē* (Rome),[58] but Musonius deliberately inverts this pun. Exile, we read, *errhōsen* ('strengthened', fr. 9, p. 44 Hense) its victim. It is not Rome that generates power, but distance from it.

[57] LSJ s.v. ἐξουσία II. [58] Introd., n. 91.

Musonius' persona is further cultivated through assimilation to and deviation from the paradigm of Socrates.[59] Socrates' contempt for the punishments inflicted by the Athenian people is the paradigm undergirding most ancient discussions of Musonius' reactions to his exile and mistreatment by Nero. At times this is explicitly mentioned in the sources. Philostratus records such a case, in an anecdote concerning Musonius' imprisonment by Nero. Apollonius secretly asks Musonius if he might help him, and the reply comes by letter: 'Socrates the Athenian, because he refused to be released by his own friends, went before the tribunal and was put to death' (*Σωκράτης ὁ Ἀθηναῖος ὑπὸ τῶν ἑαυτοῦ φίλων λυθῆναι μὴ βουληθεὶς παρῆλθε μὲν ἐς τὸ δικαστήριον, ἀπέθανε δέ*, Philostr. *VA* 4.46 = Musonius, *Epistulae spuriae*, p. 143 Hense). In other cases, such as in *That exile is not an evil*, the relationship with Socrates is more subtle, and involves contrast as well as comparison.

Structurally, the essay, like all the fragments preserved by Stobaeus, resembles an extract from Xenophon's *Memorabilia of Socrates*. It opens with Musonius' response to another's words or actions;[60] this evokes Xenophon's standard means of beginning a Socratic conversation.[61] The Socratic parallels draw an analogy between the two occasions of unjust punishment: Nero's imprisonment of Musonius on Gyara is assimilated to the Athenians' imprisonment of Socrates. As in the accounts of Socrates' trial, punishment becomes implicitly an index of the punisher's intolerance, not of the sufferer's culpability. Musonius suggests as much in his closing lines (fr. 9, p. 51 Hense), where he echoes the celebrated Socratic notion that it is better to suffer wrong than to do it,[62] and specifically claims that in his case ('. . . which is what happened to me . . .') he has suffered rather

[59] He is mentioned at the beginning of *That exile is not an evil* (42.2), and elsewhere in the remains (10.8; 40.7–8; 54.12; 70.14; 102.9). On the subsequent tradition of Musonius as the 'Roman Socrates', see above n. 32. On the importance of Socrates as an exemplum of fortitude elsewhere in the Stoic tradition, see Stanford (1954), 125; Moles (1978), 98.

[60] 'When a certain exile began to lament because he had been exiled, he consoled him somewhat in this manner' (*φυγάδος δέ τινος ὀδυρομένου ὅτι φεύγει, οὕτω πως παρεμυθήσατο αὐτόν*, fr. 9 41.4).

[61] e.g. at *Mem.* 2.5.1–2, Xenophon writes 'I also once heard another speech of his, which seemed to me to exhort (*protrepein*) his listener . . .' (*ἤκουσα δέ ποτε καὶ ἄλλον αὐτοῦ λόγον, ὅς ἐδόκει μοι προτρέπειν τὸν ἀκούοντα*).

[62] Pl. *Cri.* 49c; *Gorg.* 474b; Xen. *Mem.* 4 8.9–10; *Apol.* 26; cf. Thuc. 3.47.5.

than perpetrated injustice. His exile indicates Nero's, rather than his own, culpability.[63]

Yet there is a crucial difference between Socrates, whose devotion to his *polis* leads him to die rather than flee from Athens,[64] and Musonius, whose philosophy is practised in exile. In Plato's works, exile is unceasingly presented with horror.[65] Socrates has only left Athens briefly, to go on military campaign (*Cri.* 53a): he travels intellectually, not physically (*Tht.* 173e). For the 'Roman Socrates', however, matters are very different. 'The city'—now Rome, not Athens—no longer guarantees free speech; indeed, as we have seen, speech is much freer for the exile than for one who remains within striking range of the emperor. Once again, Musonius can be seen to be ransacking the closet of democratic Athenian masks according to a principle of strategic selection. His construction of an exilic persona involves the self-conscious manipulation and appropriation of literary tradition.

As an Etruscan *eques*, Musonius is fully aware that his relationship to the Greek tradition is oblique. He cannot simply style himself a Socrates *redivivus*: though he implicitly shares his philosophical forebear's resilience and principled stance, he cannot claim to be thoroughly Greek. Of course, he is 'Greek' in spirit, and 'Greek' by training; but he is as conscious of his alienation from Classical Athens, the yardstick of Hellenism, as he is of his integration. Moreover, the processes of historical change have meant that the problems he faces are radically different from those of Socrates. The striking fact of Musonius' adoption of the Greek language, and of Greek styles of behaviour, is rarely sufficiently acknowledged,[66] and adds greater depth of resonance to Musonius' complex self-positioning. By Hellenizing in this manner, he constructs a schematic opposition between Greek and Roman in terms of philosophical liberation and oppressive power. Musonius' exile to the Greek Aegean, within the symbolic economy of his autobiography, represents a movement away from the false and domineering world of Rome into the veridical world of Greek philosophy. The point, however, is that he can never be 'at home' in Greece: this self-representation as a Greek philosopher is

[63] A point echoed by Favorinus (*De ex.* 23.1).
[64] For this interpretation of the *Crito*, see Colson (1989), 40–8.
[65] Doblhofer (1987), 39.
[66] See, however, Goldhill (1995), 133.

precisely a representation, the artificial construct of a Roman noble.

It is not simply the case that Greek was the 'natural' language in which a philosopher of this period might choose to write. In the late republic, Cicero and Lucretius had already 'illuminated' Greek philosophy in the Latin language.[67] One only has to contrast Musonius' contemporary, Seneca, and his eminently Roman approach to the exilic consolation in his address *To Helvia, his mother*.[68] Seneca, although not born to a notably more privileged family than Musonius, found himself much more closely integrated into the structures of imperial power. Although the essay *To Helvia* pre-dates his tenure as Nero's friend or tutor (the precise relationship is unclear),[69] he was certainly well connected prior to his exile in 41 CE for alleged adultery: Cassius Dio cites the true reason for his banishment as Claudius' jealousy (59.19.7–8). Seneca returned from exile into the bosom of power. Musonius, on the other hand, permanently relocates from Rome to Greece, linguistically, symbolically, and culturally: his juridical exile is merely a symptom of a more general alienation from Roman power and Roman values.

Musonius' adoption of the persona of the Greek philosopher as a counter-hegemonic self-positioning, and the concomitant ambiguity of his position vis-à-vis Greek culture, is explored in a short dialogue preserved in the manuscripts of Lucian, but probably best ascribed to the Philostratus who composed *The Lives of the sophists* and *The Life of Apollonius*.[70] The scene is apparently Gyara, the site of Musonius' exile: this much is implied by the reference to the place as 'such an unpleasant classroom' (*ἀηδὲς οὕτω φροντιστήριον*, 1). Nero's abandoned attempt to dig through

[67] Above, pp. 12–14.

[68] On the specifically Roman ideas at work in the consolation *To Helvia*, see C. Edwards (1996), 110–11.

[69] Griffin (1976), 67–128, arguing that Seneca was a moral adviser with no direct political role; see, however, Too (1994), who repoliticizes him (albeit on rather different terms).

[70] For brief discussion of textual history, see Macleod (1967), 505–7. On the question of the attribution to a Philostratus (largely on the basis of *Suda Φ* 422, though this is muddled; see however the linguistic parallels cited by Kayser 1838: 123–30; and 1838: 373–5), see Muenscher (1907), 548–52; Solmsen (1940), 569–70; Korver (1950), 319–29; and esp. de Lannoy (1997), 2398–404, who argues plausibly for Philostratean authorship. For a fuller treatment of this text, see Whitmarsh (1999*a*).

the Isthmus of Corinth[71] is discussed by the two interlocutors, a certain Menecrates and the philosopher Musonius Rufus, who is said to have taken part in the digging (1). The discussion broadens out to include Nero's tour of Greece, with a particular focus upon his singing; and it concludes as the news breaks of Nero's death (11).

The discussion revolves around the polarity of Musonius and Nero, the former presented as the embodiment of Hellenic virtue, the latter as a tyrant (as he is styled in the first line of the dialogue). Cutting the Isthmus is a paradigmatically monarchical act: attempts are attested by Periander, Demetrius, Julius Caesar, and Caligula.[72] In the *Lives of the sophists*, Philostratus records the grief of Herodes Atticus—always a 'regal' figure in that text[73]—at not being able to cut the Isthmus himself (*VS* 551). In the *Nero*, the attempted digging is implicitly presented as an affront done by a foreign despot to the nature of the landscape of Greece, through comparison with Darius' bridging of the Bosporus and the 'feats of Xerxes', glossed as the 'grandest of grandiose actions' (μέγιστα τῶν μεγαλουργιῶν, 2).[74] The latter reference is probably to the cutting of Mount Athos and the chaining of the Hellespont, a sequence presented in Herodotus as a tyrannical violence done to the terrain of Greece.[75]

The cutting of the Isthmus is metaphorically linked with Nero's other transgressive actions reported in this text by means of a common focus upon the voice. The Greek word *isthmos* means, literally, 'neck' or 'throat', and the author (as Philostratus does elsewhere)[76] puns upon the idea of the Isthmus as Greece's 'neck'.

[71] Also attested at Jos. *Bell. Jud.* 3.540; Suet. *Ner.* 19.2, 37.3; Plin. *NH* 4.10; Paus. 2.1.5; Philostr. *VA* 4.24; 5.7; 5.19; Cass. Dio 63.16. See further Bradley (1978), 66; Kennell (1989), 240–1; Alcock (1994), 101–3; Arafat (1996), 151–2.

[72] For Periander, see Diog. Laert. 1.7.99; for Demetrius, Plin. *NH* 4.10; for Julius Caesar, Plin. *NH* 4.10; Suet. *Caes.* 44.3; Plut. *Caes.* 58; Cass. Dio 44.5; for Caligula, Plin. *NH* 4.10; Suet. *Calig.* 21.

[73] Ch. 2, nn. 58–60.

[74] Nero's attempt is also a μεγαλουργία (2).

[75] Hdt. 7.22–5, 35–6; see Whitmarsh (1999*a*), 148–9. On the effrontery of Xerxes' 'alteration of the structure of the earth' by isthmus-cutting (Hdt. 7.124), see Romm (1999), 80. Pausanias and Cassius Dio emphasize the violence of Nero's actions: the former comments on the emperor's abandonment of the attempt 'so difficult is it for a man to do violence to divine things' (οὕτω χαλεπὸν ἀνθρώπωι τὰ θεῖα βιάσασθαι, Paus. 2.1.5). Cassius Dio refers to horrific portents prefacing the digging of the Isthmus, including groaning and blood spurting from the earth (63.16.1–2).

[76] In *Apollonius*, the sage predicts Nero's attempt to dig the Isthmus with the

By cutting the Isthmus, Nero is silencing Greece. Musonius also reports an anecdote about Nero's singing, superficially unconnected with the main theme of Isthmus-cutting, but subtly linked through the thematization of voice and silence. An Epirote singer, we hear, refused to cede victory to Nero in the singing contest (established by the emperor, in fact) at the Isthmian games, and competed vigorously (*Ner.* 9). The tyrant was furious, and sent his secretary (his *grammateus*, 'letter-man') on-stage to tell him to yield. The Epirote merely raised his 'voice' (φθέγμα) and continued to compete 'as though it were a democratic event' (δημοτικῶς, 9). Consequently, the emperor sent his actors onto the stage with folded writing-tablets, which they smashed into the singer's 'throat' (φάρυγγα, 9). This brutal act represents more than simply Nero's flouting of the rules of dramatic performance:[77] the collision between the tyrant and the native Greek is thematized as a bloody conflict between writing, emblematized by Nero's servile bureaucrats, and the 'voice' of Greece, which is brilliant, democratic, and free. In referring to Nero's having 'cut out' (ἐκτεμών, 10) the voice of the Epirote, moreover, Musonius recalls the 'cutting' (τομήν; τεμεῖν, 4) of the Isthmus: each is a tyrannical affront to Greece's speech-organs.

Nero's assaults upon the various voices of Greece extended, we read, to silencing the Delphic oracle in anger at its insinuations concerning his matricide. He blocked the Pythian *stomion* ('mouth'), 'with the aim that even Apollo might lose his voice (*phōnē*)' (ὡς μηδὲ τῶι Ἀπόλλωνι φωνὴ εἴη, 10). The reference to mouth-blocking is not merely figurative: according to Cassius Dio, at any rate, Nero literally stuffed the Delphic cleft with the corpses of soldiers.[78] The assault upon Apollo underlines one prominent theme of the dialogue, Nero's inability to recognize his own mortality.[79] What particularly interests me here, though, is the prominent use of the words *stomion* ('mouth') and *phōnē* ('voice'), terms that underline the recurrent emphasis in this dialogue upon

words 'the neck (*aukhēn*) of the land will be cut—or rather it will not' (ὁ αὐχὴν τῆς γῆς τετμήσεται, μᾶλλον δ' οὔ, *VA* 4.24; cf. 5.19).

[77] Bartsch (1994), 56: 'the *dénouement* is represented as a violation of the drama, a symbol of the tyrant's taste for the display of unbridled violence and the flaunting of his immunity'.

[78] Cass. Dio 63.14.2. The question of whether Nero really did silence the Delphic oracle is discussed by Levin (1989), 1605–6, but does not affect the point being made here.

[79] Whitmarsh (1999*a*), 149.

the theme of voice.[80] Nero's desire to possess Greece leads him to attempt to 'gag' its symbolic centre, to silence the very voice of the land.

This nexus of interlocking themes presenting Nero as a violent silencer of Greece's voice implicitly embraces his attempts to silence Musonius, too. Like the Epirote singer, like Pythian Apollo, Musonius speaks out loud and clear, though the cruel emperor represses his speech. Yet there is also a subtly uneasy silence in the text about Musonius' right to emblematize Greece in the same way as Pythian Apollo and the Epirote singer. Musonius is only on Greek territory because he has been exiled there by the emperor. And if the author's choice of the dialogue form is intended to communicate the authentic interaction of spoken speech (as opposed to the 'written' texts favoured by Nero), then we must concede that the genre of the dialogue is a 'fake' substitute for real speech, a form that 'aims for the *effect* of improvisation'.[81] The *Nero* buys its idealization of Musonius as a free-speaking Greek resisting Roman power at the expense of a tacit awareness that he is a late, self-made, and only partially integrated interloper into the tradition of philosophical opponents to power.

To be the 'Roman Socrates', then, is an inherently complex and ambiguous task. The language and rhetoric of exile provide Musonius with a mask, a role, a position, and his audience with a readily assimilable framework within which to understand his actions in relation to the emperor. At the same time, this (constructed, appropriated) identity is neither secure (in the sense that the mask of Socrates could never fit an Etruscan *eques* exactly), nor taken over uncritically. Indeed, as an exile, Musonius to an extent abrogates all sense of geopolitical identity. Although his exile from Rome to the Aegean might be read superficially as a symbolic move eastwards, a severing of ties with Rome and an activation of his status as a Hellenic philosopher, his very status as an exile on Greek soil marks the limits of his integration. As a citizen of the world, Musonius is *neither* exclusively Roman *nor* exclusively Greek, but both and still more. The exile is a problematic, unsettling figure, one who points up the arbitrary and provisional nature of cultural identity.

[80] Although oracular edifices are frequently said to have a *stoma* or *stomion* (see e.g. Paus. 5.14.10; 9.39.11–12; Max. Tyr. 18.2; Σ Ar. *Nub.* 508), this deeply entrenched metaphor is far from banal.

[81] Demetr. *De eloc.* 224.

DIO CHRYSOSTOM: EXILE AND SOPHISTRY

Cocceianus Dio, or Dio 'Chrysostom' ('golden-mouth') as he was later known,[82] was born in around 40 CE into a wealthy family in Prusa (in the province of Bithynia, which covered north-western Asia minor), and he seems to have inherited Roman citizenship from both his father and mother.[83] He was, thus, firmly entrenched in the elite, and the extant orations attributed to him by modern scholars betray the results of an immersive education available only to members of his class.[84] As a public speaker, Dio was well travelled, famous, and successful, moving in the highest echelons of Roman power.[85] Indeed, his self-constructed narrative of his career can be (and has been) viewed as a barometer of the changing temper of the imperial household: prospering under the honest Vespasian, exiled under the tyrannical Domitian, recalled under the noble (but aged) Nerva, embraced by the righteous Trajan, Dio presents his journey through life as having soared and dipped in accordance with the imperial tenor of the time. Yet in respect of this narrative, as with any biography, it is important to remember that this perception of events has been artfully constructed so as to tell a story—and artfully constructed not least by Dio himself.

Modern scholars have been highly suspicious of Dio's claims about his relationships with emperors. His claims to have counselled Flavian emperors are disputed.[86] The following chapter will contest his self-representation as an adviser of Trajan. Most important for the present chapter is his assertion that he accidentally became a philosopher whilst experiencing exile under

[82] For the details of Dio's name, and of its confusion in antiquity with that of the historian Cassius Dio, see Gowing (1990).

[83] For Dio's wealth, see *Or.* 46.3, 5–6; and for brief discussion and further references C. P. Jones (1978), 6; Swain (1996), 190–1. Dio inherited Roman citizenship (*Or.* 41.6), but when did his family gain citizenship? Some think (on the basis of Dio's *cognomen* Cocceianus) under the emperor (Marcus Cocceius) Nerva: this is suggested as a possibility by Momigliano (1969), 257, and elaborated upon by Moles (1978), 86. Sherwin-White (1966), 676–7 suggests a Domitianic date. I prefer a pre-Domitianic date: see Whitmarsh (1998*a*), 199 n. 35, with further details of the debate concerning maternal versus paternal inheritance.

[84] On Dio's aristocratic perspective, see esp. C. P. Jones (1978), 104–14 for the local political background; more generally, Salmeri (1982), 14–45.

[85] On Dio's early successes, see Moles (1978), 82–8.

[86] Dio Chr. 7.66, supported by Philostr. *VA* 5.27–38; disputed by Sidebottom (1996).

Domitian (13.4); this too has been rejected by scholars.[87] Let us briefly recapitulate what Dio says about his dealings with emperors. When Domitian banished all philosophers from Rome,[88] Dio was not apparently included; it was at a later point, apparently, that he was exiled personally from Italy and his native Bithynia.[89] Although Dio (not normally one to miss a trick) tells us in his speech on his exile that the reason for his exile lay in his friendship with an enemy of the emperor (*Or.* 13.1), he elsewhere claims to have been 'railing openly' (ἐρεθίζων ἄντικρυς) against Domitian during his reign, and implies (or does not discourage the implication) that this caused his exile (45.1). (He was perceived in the later tradition to have been exiled for his *parrhēsia*, 'free speech'.)[90] After the death of Domitian, Dio returned from exile under Nerva, whose reign lasted from just 96 to 98 CE.[91] Dio never made it to Rome in time to meet the man he cites, with an unquantifiable degree of justification, as an 'old friend' (πάλαι φίλον, *Or.* 45.2). His major phase of imperial popularity was, he claims, the early part of Trajan's reign, when the *Kingship orations* (the subject of the following chapter) were composed.[92] At this time, Trajan was attempting to regenerate the imperial image, tarnished by the unpopularity of the Flavian emperors, and in particular of Domitian (who had had his memory 'damned' by senatorial decree).[93] The negative image of Domitian was used to construct, by way of contrast, the positive image of Trajan, who laid claim to the foundation of a 'new age'.[94] One means of

[87] Moles (1978). On the degree of fiction in Dio's representation of his travels, see Jouan (1993).

[88] Above, n. 5.

[89] Dio Chr. *Or.* 13.1. A ban from Bithynia and Italy is possible (as C. P. Jones 1978: 45), but it is more likely that the ban was merely from Prusa or Bithynia (so Desideri 1978: 193–4): in *Or.* 13, he seems to go to Rome during his exile (13.29).

[90] Luc. *Peregr.* 18.

[91] Nerva issued a general recall of Domitian's exiles (see C. P. Jones 1978: 52, with p. 176 n. 61 for references).

[92] See Ch. 4, 'Staging the Self: Sophistry in Motion', and Appendix 2.

[93] For the *damnatio memoriae* of Domitian, see Suet. *Dom.* 23.2; Cass. Dio 68.1.1. On the erasure of Domitian's inscriptions in the East, see Grosso (1954), 165–6; on the removal of his images, Pekáry (1985), 138; Stewart (1999), 183.

[94] In his *Panegyricus*, for example, Pliny explicitly articulates the need for a contrast between Trajan's and previous rules (*tantum inter te et illos principes interest*, 91.2), and especially between those of Trajan and of Domitian (*passim*, esp. 53.1); for other such contrasts, see Tac. *Agr.* 3.1; 44.5; *Hist.* 1; Mart. *Epigr.* 10.72. Pliny even tells us that Trajan published a statement contrasting his expenditure with that of Domitian (*Panegyr.* 20.5). Talk of a 'new age' (*nouum saeculum*) under

constructing the new age in opposition to the previous one was to embrace literary and philosophical *paideia*, and to represent the Flavians (and especially Domitian) as having attacked them.[95] It is in the context of this stress upon the representation of renewal, both cultural and political, that Dio's *Kingships* site themselves. These orations (it is often argued) testify to both the affection felt for Trajan after the dark years of Domitian and Trajan's eagerness to project himself as a patron of culture.[96] Dio's autobiography is seductive because it intersects so nicely with the narrative that polarizes the 'evil' Domitian and the 'benevolent' Trajan. But just as revisionist historians have questioned this imperial antithesis,[97] so literary scholarship has paid increased attention to Dio's narrative wiles.

As to Dio's literary production, the major problem faced by modern biographers centres upon the question of his supposed 'conversion' from sophistry to philosophy during his exile. This was first advanced by the fifth-century bishop Synesius of Cyrene.[98] 'Conversion' is, of course, a trope of Christian narrative, and few these days would follow von Arnim in taking Synesius at his word.[99] There is no objective diacritical typology that distin-

Trajan is widespread. Pliny's letters and panegyric to Trajan frequently refer to 'your *saeculum*' (*Ep.* 10.1.2; 10.3.2; 10.37.3; *Panegyr.* 40.5; 46.7; cf. 46.4; 93.2). Florus strikes a similar note when he writes that 'under Trajan's principate, the elderly empire regained its strength, as though youth had been returned to it' (*sub Traiano principe . . . senectus imperii quasi reddita iuuentute reuirescit, Epit. praef.* 8).

[95] The antithesis of Domitian and Trajan in terms of receptiveness to *paideia* (e.g. Plin. *Panegyr.* 47.1–2) was based not so much in fact as in Trajanic rhetoric (B. Jones 1992: 121–2). For Pliny's celebration of the re-emergence of literature under Trajan, see also *Panegyr.* 49.8; *Ep.* 1.10.1; also E. Cizek (1989), 4, and *passim* on Latin literature in the period.

[96] Esp. von Arnim (1898), 324; C. P. Jones (1978), 118–19.

[97] e.g. B. Jones (1992), contra e.g. Levick (1982).

[98] 'Dio converted from a foolish sophist to become a philosopher' (ὁ δὲ Δίων ἐξ ἀγνώμονος σοφιστοῦ φιλόσοφος ἀπετελέσθη, Synes. 13.10–13 = *test.* p. 314.24 von Arnim).

[99] Von Arnim (1898) divides Dio's orations into pre-exilic 'sophistic', exilic 'Cynic', and post-exilic 'philosophical' works. The dangers of over-reliance upon such a crude schema, and of the subjective nature of the judgement of 'sophistry', are clear. Von Arnim is challenged by Desideri (1978), xi, C. P. Jones (1978), 11–12, and, most vigorously, Moles (1978), who sees Synesius' judgement as a development of Dio's own self-representation as having converted to philosophy, which was a 'fraud' (100) designed to cover up his own complicity in Vespasian's philosophical expulsions. Moles is followed broadly by Swain (1996), 188–90. Sidebottom (1990), 1–31 asserts that, on the contrary, Dio *did* convert, but that this conversion should be understood as one of semiotic self-fashioning, not of inner 'belief'.

guishes 'sophists' from 'philosophers':[100] these terms frequently function not simply as descriptive categories but as rhetorical tools to aid self-projection. Thus Dio's interminable attacks upon sophistry in his later compositions[101] need not be seen as evidence of his rejection of the sophistic works of his pre-exilic days, nor indeed as antipathy towards real individuals; nor even as evidence that the man who attacks sophists is not engaging in an eminently 'sophistic' negotiation of rhetorical position.[102] Philostratus, in his third-century biography, presents Dio as one of 'those who philosophize under the guise of sophistry' (τοὺς φιλοσοφήσαντας ἐν δόξῃ τοῦ σοφιστεῦσαι, *Lives of the sophists* 479, 492).[103] 'Philosopher' is not an absolute but a differential category: Dio's self-styling as a philosopher depends for its valency upon a repeated narrative distantiation from sophistry.

Like Musonius, then, he presents his banishment as a definitive moment in his philosophical biography: exile makes the philosopher. Yet with Dio, questions of deception and duplicity come more obviously to the fore. As John Moles has argued vigorously, there are traces of evidence that contradict Dio's claims to have converted.[104] Indeed, Philostratus was not convinced that he was even exiled at all.[105] Yet the question of the historical veracity of the claim is not the only, or indeed necessarily the urgent, question to be asked: certainly, to frame the issue in this way allows us to see more clearly Dio's manipulative side, but to claim that this facet of his self-presentation is evidence of his 'wholly disingenuous' stance or his 'fraud'[106] is to risk under-appreciation of Dio's sophistication, irony, and craft. Dio is not simply attempting to deceive: rather, he is engaged in a subtle negotiation of a literary tradition already overfreighted with exiled philosophers. Moreover, in styling himself in such terms, Dio is following the precedent of his teacher, Musonius.[107] Dio's comments on exile need to be considered in the context of rhetorical praxis, the contest for

[100] See e.g. Stanton (1973), 351–8; Hahn (1989), 46–53; Sidebottom (1990), 4–31.

[101] Moles (1978), 88–9.

[102] Stanton (1973), 354.

[103] See also *VA* 5.40, *Epistula Apollonii* 9.

[104] Moles (1978).

[105] Philostr. *VS* 488.

[106] The quotations are from Moles (1978), 96, 100. They are objected to on different grounds by Russell (1992), 5.

[107] Above, n. 16.

philosophical personae—and not simply as attempts to cloud the truth.

Dio's major account of his exile comes at the beginning of the thirteenth oration, *On exile*. The oration begins with a surprise: he was exiled not, as we might think, for the threat he personally posed to Domitian but 'because of my supposed friendship with a man of no mean station' (φιλίας ἕνεκεν λεγομένης ἀνδρὸς οὐ πονηροῦ, 13.1). Although elsewhere he claims to have abused Domitian openly (45.1: see above), he here downplays any sense that he was exiled on the grounds that he exercised philosophical free speech. According to Dio, he became a philosopher by accident during the period of his banishment, beginning to reason to himself by analogy with clods of earth used by prophetesses (some of which seem to them heavy, and others light):

> 'May not exile then,' I thought, 'and poverty, and old age too and sickness, appear heavy to some and grievous, but to others light and easy? For in the first case perhaps the god lightens the weight according to the importance of the matter in question, and in the second case, I imagine, to suit the strength and the will-power of the afflicted one.'
>
> *μὴ ἄρα καὶ τὸ φεύγειν καὶ τὸ πένεσθαι καὶ γῆρας δὲ καὶ νόσος καὶ πάντα τὰ τοιαῦτα τοῖς μὲν βαρέα φαίνεται καὶ χαλεπά, τοῖς δ' ἐλαφρά τε καὶ εὔκολα· ἐκεῖ μὲν ἴσως κατὰ τὴν τοῦ πράγματος διαφορὰν ἐλαφρύνοντος τοῦ δαιμονίου τὸ βάρος, ἐνταῦθα δὲ οἶμαι πρὸς τὴν τοῦ χρωμένου δύναμιν καὶ γνώμην.* (13.3)

In this way, Dio (we are told) stumbled upon the fundamental truths of exilic consolation. Corresponding to the apparent artlessness of the conversion, the tone is genial and the syntax protean and digressive (there are ninety-seven Greek words before the main verb is reached). There is no formal prologue or introduction to begin the speech: Dio's first words ('When it fell to my lot to be exiled . . .') suggest that his audience have stumbled onto an unscripted conversation (a technique perhaps borrowed from the beginning of Plato's *Symposium* and *Theaetetus*). Elsewhere, he characterizes his prose as 'rambling', just like his travels:[108] here we see a clear instantiation of precisely that errant style. Yet, as Dionysius of Halicarnassus points out in relation to Lysias, there

[108] At 7.1, he forewarns his audience of his *polylogia* ('verbosity'), and that the speech will be *alētikos* ('wandering'); a similar point is made at 7.127 (Moles 1995: 179). See also 12.16: 'erring in my words' (πλανώμενος ἐν τοῖς λόγοις). At 4.37, however, 'erring in their words' (πλανωμένους ἐν τοῖς λόγοις) is used of the sophists from whom Dio wishes to distance himself. For more on Dio's garrulity see Moles (1983), 254 n. 17.

is an art of appearing artless.[109] Dio is a slippery, ironical writer—and never less than when he signals his abandonment of artifice. As we shall see, his writing exploits a tension between its apparently chaotic form and its knowing manipulation of literary models.

Unlike Musonius' exilic consolation, replete as it is with undisguised Cynic and Stoic commonplaces, Dio's self-made (and self-addressed) consolation is presented as not an exercise in philosophical dialectic but the 'natural' consequence of his circumstances. This is an ironically naïve reframing of a central issue of philosophical writing, namely the question 'why do people begin to philosophize?'[110] This affectation of naïveté is further underlined in the philosophical ideas that Dio 'discovers'. The ethical dogma that it is one's character, not the punishment, which determines one's response to exile (cf. Mus. Ruf. pp. 50–1 Hense) is arrived at by means of an inference from popular wisdom, by analogy with prophetesses who are held to lift up clods, some finding them light, others finding them heavy (13.2). His rejection of mass opinion (13.3; 13.7)—a familiar Socratic notion (cf. e.g. Pl. *Crit.* 47c)—is stated as though it were the most obvious thing in the world. Dio's strategy is to present philosophical lore as though it were homespun, and himself (as he puts it in the first *Kingship oration*) as 'self-taught in wisdom' (αὐτουργοὶ τῆς σοφίας, 1.9). Dio's 'wisdom' is not, of course, as naïve as he claims it is: the phrase 'self-taught in wisdom' is borrowed from Xenophon's *Memorabilia of Socrates*, where it is used to describe Socrates' own philosophical enlightenment (1.5).[111] Dio the autodidact is, as he expects his audience to be, well aware of the instructive precedents for autodidacticism.

Let us return to the thirteenth oration. The element of randomness receives further emphasis in a famous passage. Dio presently claims to have visited Delphi, and that the god replied to him with a strange (literally 'out of place', ἄτοπον: a word congenial to this writer's spatial metaphorics)[112] oracle: he should undertake his

[109] Dion. Hal. *Lys.* 8: 'this artless style is artfully devised' (πεποίηται . . . τοῦτο τὸ ἀποίητον); cf. *De imit.* fr. 10 Usener-Rademacher.

[110] Pl. *Tht.* 155d; Arist. *Rhet.* 1371ᵃ; *Met.* 982ᵇ; Arr. *Diss. Epict.* 2.11.

[111] As noted by Moles (1990), 309; the idea, however, goes back to Homer's Phemius, who is *autodidaktos* (*Od.* 23.347; cf. also Pind. *Ol.* 2.86–7).

[112] A favourite word of Dio's: Koolmeister and Tallmeister (1981) list 73 uses, an average of almost one per oration.

exile eagerly, as a fine and fortuitous thing, until he should come to the end of the earth (τὸ ὕστατον . . . τῆς γῆς, 13.9). The dominant theme here is of decentralization, both geographically and semiotically. After a brief self-comparison with Odysseus, the wanderer par excellence, Dio tells us that he took up scruffy clothes (thus rejecting—or disguising?—his former identity as an urban aristocrat), steeled himself, and 'began to wander (*ēlomēn*) everywhere' (ἠλώμην πανταχοῦ, 13.10). Of those who met him, some called him (*alētēs*) 'wanderer', some beggar, and some philosopher (13.11). The idea that Dio is a wanderer (*alētēs*; cf. the etymologically cognate *ēlomēn*) is emphasized here; and Dio recurrently and ironically exploits the notion of wandering for its metaphorical connections with prolixity and deception. In Greek, there is a well-established punning play between 'truth' (*alētheia*) and 'wandering' (*alēteia*), going back to Odysseus' playful hints about his own 'deviations' from the truth.[113] Like his person, his discourse is moving into oblique and marginal territory: a strong hint to the reader that this self-presentation should be treated with great care.

So Dio received his reputation as a philosopher 'by chance' (τυχόν, 13.12). The element of randomness in Dio's story is, however, deliberately ironic. This account parodies the tradition of philosophical enlightenment in exile, as the *faux-naïf* artlessness of Dio the wanderer is mediated through the wiles of Dio the artful narrator. If it was by chance that Dio became a philosopher, it can hardly have been by chance that his account of the process reproduces the patterns of Socrates' enlightenment in the *Apology*: the older philosopher, too, claimed Delphic validation for his role (Pl. *Apol*. 20e–21a).[114] This 'randomness' is carefully scripted: no less than Musonius, Dio is presenting his biography in conspicuously Socratic terms. Yet this Socratic mask is not (as Moles suggests) intended to fool his audience: fraudsters rarely advertise their techniques as prominently as Dio marks his own Socraticism. Rather, Dio is carefully constructing a playful interaction between the randomness and naïveté that he implies with such regularity and the didactic authority of the ancients texts that so prominently inform his account. For a sophisticated reader, the thirteenth

[113] Hom. *Od*. 14.122–7; see Segal (1994), 179–83; Goldhill (1991), 38.

[114] The connection was first spotted by Moles (1978), 99. Note also Xen. *Apol*. 14.

oration's conspicuous focus upon his random discovery of philosophy must be offset against his knowing evocation of a deeply established narrative paradigm. Indeed, it is not just prestige that he has absorbed from Socrates, the philosopher famous for his 'irony'.[115]

Moreover, if we have still not appreciated that Dio is manipulating personae in the thirteenth oration, he proceeds to make it explicit: in chapter 14, the speech turns towards Socrates himself. Dio, we are told, used to direct himself and others towards 'a certain ancient account, spoken by a certain Socrates, that he never stopped saying' (*τινα λόγον ἀρχαῖον, λεγόμενον ὑπό τινος Σωκράτους, ὃν οὐδέποτε ἐκεῖνος ἐπαύσατο λέγων*, 13.14).[116] The repeated indefinite *τις* (here translated as 'a certain') redoubles the ironic play: for whose benefit is ignorance of Socrates' identity being presumed? Is it the wandering philosophical inept who speaks here, or the artful narrator?

The text then proceeds further to complicate the relationship between Dio and Socrates, and also to dissimulate the degree of ingenuity involved. 'I did not pretend that this was my account' (*οὐ . . . προσεποιούμην ἐμὸν εἶναι τὸν λόγον*) Dio tells us (13.15),[117] and anyway he may not be able 'to remember it accurately' (*ἀπομνημονεῦσαι ἀκριβῶς*, 13.15). Whose voice are we to hear, Dio's or Socrates'? For all that he acknowledges his sources, Dio cannot promise to have got the words exactly right. This strategy raises similar issues to those famously adumbrated by Thucydides in his discussion of historiographical speeches (1.22), and also intimated by various Platonic speakers (e.g. *Phaed.* 58d; *Symp.* 172a): if one only presents the gist of what was spoken, then who is to be accredited with authorship? Such questions underlie Dio's coy self-positioning: how much of his philosophical identity is self-taught, natural, the product of chance? How much is conscious, sophisticated, rhetorical imitation? The contemporary imitator deliberately intermingles his persona with that of his prestigious forebear while laying ironic claim to innocence.

Dio then launches into a version of the argument of the

[115] For Socrates' *εἰρωνεία*, see Pl *Symp.* 216e; *Resp.* 337a; Arist. *Eth. Nic.* 1127^{b}.

[116] The phraseology of the final clause evokes Pl. *Apol.* 29d: ('I will not stop philosophizing').

[117] Even this denial of deceit is a rhetorical topos: for the common oratorical phrase 'the story is not mine, but . . .' (*οὐκ ἐμὸς ὁ μῦθος, ἀλλὰ . . .*) see Größlein (1998), 55.

Clitophon, a dialogue the Platonic authorship of which was apparently not doubted in antiquity.[118] The self-consciousness with which Dio changes between his own voice and that of Socrates (as scripted by Plato) is marked. When he switches back into his own voice, we read that he decided to 'imitate' (*μιμούμενος*, 13.29) Socrates' words and 'practise dialectic' (*διαλέγεσθαι*; *διαλέγωμαι*, 13.29) when he visited Rome, and chastised the citizens there for their serious want of good education (*παιδείας*, 13.29; cf. 13.31). The whole speech, then, serves as a self-constructed (and self-deconstructed) aetiology for Dio's reputation as a brave and outspoken purveyor of Greek ideals in the face of Roman authority, a true 'Roman Socrates'. The Musonian pose, the self-dramatization as a Greek philosopher opposing Roman power, is arrived at via a mixture of apparent accident and delightful sophistical ingenuity.

Dio's exilic self-representation, thus, switches between an ironic naïveté, presenting his initiation into philosophical identity as the natural consequence of a series of random accidents, and an extremely arch, knowing manipulation of literary topoi. Whereas Musonius' response to the tradition of exile as a source of philosophical prestige is to seek to inscribe himself into this tradition as another, albeit modern, paradigm of philosophical virtue, Dio (writing in the generation after Musonius, as his pupil) appears much more self-conscious about the overdetermined, even hackneyed nature of the topos of the exiled philosopher, and about the need for reinvention and reinvigoration. The master–pupil relationship between Musonius and Dio has been translated into a contest of the symbolic terrain of literary tropes and allusions, where the pupil is uncomfortably aware of the master's possession of an authoritative identity; he seeks thus to turn his posterity to his own advantage, at once displacing his master's authority by exposing its clichés and claiming it for himself by reconfiguring it and renewing it as a figure of authorial self-representation.[119] Dio's literary-rhetorical-philosophical persona is formed of what Harold Bloom calls 'the psychology of belatedness'.[120]

[118] The most recent editor returns to the view that it is a Platonic text: see Slings (1999), 215–34 (with 94–6 on Dio's version as an embellishment of the original).

[119] This antagonistic master–pupil relationship is speculative, but the report (hard to interpret as it is) that Dio composed a tract *Against* (or *in reply to*?) *Musonius* (see n. 16) may invite such speculations.

[120] Bloom (1975), 35. My formulation in this paragraph owes much to Bloom's work, both there and in Bloom (1997) (1st edn. 1973).

Dio's presentation of his exile, then, is not simply an attempt to deceive his audience into a more positive view of him. The persona of the exiled philosopher is, by this stage, extremely prestigious in terms of the arrogation to oneself of the identity of an authentic Hellenic philosopher. As Dio writes in the third oration, his exile is the 'touchstone' (*βάσανος*, 3.12) of his philosophical credentials: it proves him a habitual free-speaker (although, as we have seen, this assertion is in conflict with the thirteenth oration, where his free-speaking is dated to the period during, not before, his exile). At the same time, however, Dio is fully aware that the persona of the exiled philosopher is hackneyed and overworked. His reinvention of the topoi of exile is both an attempt to reinvigorate the language of exilic resistance to Roman rule and also a knowingly ironic concession that the script is already written by literary tradition.

How do we explain this irony? The majority of Dio's extant orations are post-Domitianic, which is to say, composed subsequent to his recall from exile.[121] His accounts of his opposition to Domitian are inextricably imbricated with an awareness of his subsequent return to a prominent role in relations between Prusa and Rome,[122] and to his tutelage (or, as the next chapter will argue, his *projected* tutelage) of Trajan. This element of retrospection, along with the literary over-determination of the exilic tradition, perhaps partially explains the irony with which he tempers his self-representation as a philosophical exile. Dio's oppositionalism is always narrated safely from a position of re-empowered comfort.

More importantly, his narrative of exile also trades upon the new political rhetoric of the emperor Trajan. Trajan's accession was, as has been noted,[123] marked by a series of explicit attempts to mark the new emperor as the inverse of Domitian. In particular, Trajan is presented as tolerating the free speech that Domitian repressed. To instantiate this phenomenon, let us briefly consider the case of Tacitus, who links the inauguration of his literary career with the advent of the emperor under whom 'you can think what you like and say what you think' (*ubi sentire quae uelis et quae*

[121] There is some disagreement about the dating of Dio's speeches (see e.g. C. P. Jones 1978: 131–14; Brancacci 1980; Moles 1983; Swain 1996: 428–9). By common consensus, however, all the speeches discussed in this chapter are post-Domitianic.

[122] On Dio's role as Prusan ambassador to Rome, see Swain (1996), 226–37.

[123] Above, n. 94.

sentias dicere licet, *Hist*. 1.1). Trajan's reign is presented by Tacitus as a time for bursting into writing, in contrast with that of Domitian, when 'we should have also lost our very memory along with our voice, had it been as much in our power to forget as to be silent' (*memoriam quoque ipsam cum uoce perdidissemus, si tam in nostra potestate esset obliuisci quam tacere*, *Agr*. 2.3).[124] Tacitus (whose very name derives from *tacere*, the word used here to mean 'to be silent') presents Trajan's accession as the necessary condition of his 'voicing' of historiography. Yet there is a rich irony here, for (despite his stated ambition to do so at the beginning of the *Histories*),[125] he never writes of post-Domitianic Rome: his final work, the *Annals*, covered earlier imperial history from Tiberius to Nero. Tacitus' articulation of his views of Trajan under Trajan is, ultimately, as tacit as that of Domitian under Domitian.[126] The reader is left with the sense that to speak freely—or to claim that one is speaking freely—under Trajan is as much a reflection of imperial edict as to remain silent under Domitian.

This hyper-ironization of Trajanic free speech is clearly marked in a passage in Pliny's *Panegyric* (his speech of acclamation to Trajan). 'You order us to be free,' he writes, 'and so we will be! You order us to say publicly what we feel: we shall do so!' (*iubes esse liberos: erimus; iubes quae sentimus promere in medium: proferemus*, *Panegyr*. 66.4). In a brilliantly ironical twist, free-speaking and the execration of tyranny have become themselves the subject of imperial edict (and, simultaneously, Pliny's exposure of Trajan's coercive strategy marks out his own free-speaking effrontery).

The new rhetorical involutions of free-speaking under Trajan provide a suitably coy context for Dio's playful presentation of his exile. 'Freedom' becomes a token of imperial propaganda (Trajan's coins display the legend LIBERTAS, together with representations of the tyrannicide Brutus).[127] In this context, the role of

[124] See *Agr*. 2–3 *passim* on Tacitus' newfound voice. Juvenal presumably parodies this bursting into speech at *Sat*. 1.1.

[125] *Hist*. 1.1: 'I have set aside the principate of the divine Nerva and the *imperium* of Trajan for my old age' (*principatum diui Neruae et imperium Traiani . . . senectuti seposui*).

[126] Similarly, Suetonius (writing under Hadrian) concludes his *Lives of the Caesars* with Domitian.

[127] Toynbee (1944), 45. The imperial reappropriation of the language of *libertas*, so fundamental to the political wrangles of the 1st cent. CE (Wirszubski 1968), had begun as early as the reign of Galba, whose coins also proclaim this term: see MacMullen (1992), 33, and further Hammond (1963).

fearless resister of oppression is scripted not merely by literary tradition, but also (as Pliny testifies) by imperial injunction; and widespread awareness of this renders any claim to free speech liable to the charge of flattery. As Quintilian (an older contemporary of Dio's) puts it, 'flattery often lurks under the guise of free speech' (*frequenter sub hac facie* [*sc. libertatis*] *latet adulatio, Inst. or.* 9.2.28). Dio's equivocal, self-conscious self-presentation as an exile is both conditioned by this hypercritical climate and an attempt to transcend it. In this way, Dio can simultaneously lay claim to the symbolic capital that accrues to the philosophical exile and, using the ironical distancing devices we have observed, construct a buffer against charges of flattery.

FAVORINUS: EXILE AND LITERARY ALIENATION

Favorinus of Arelate (modern Arles) is one of the most prominent figures in the Graeco-Roman literary culture of the second century.[128] In certain respects, he embodies the spirit of eclecticism and innovation that pervades the literature of the period. He is referred to by contemporaries as a philosopher,[129] although he had no allegiance to any single philosophical school.[130] Indeed, Philostratus, who treats him at length in his *Lives of the sophists* (489–92), includes him (along with Dio Chrysostom) amongst those who 'philosophize in the guise of sophistry' (*τοὺς φιλοσοφήσαντας ἐν δόξῃ τοῦ σοφιστεῦσαι*, *VS* 479, 492). The prodigious polymathy of his work is evidenced by his *Miscellaneous history*,[131] an influential work (fundamental for Aelian and Athenaeus, to name only two) of which many fragments survive excerpted elsewhere. As we shall see, his status as a cultural magpie informs the speech on exile to a great degree.

At the socio-linguistic level, also, Favorinus displays his eclecticism. In Aulus Gellius' *Attic nights*, written in Latin, Favorinus is presented as prodigiously skilled in the exegesis of both Roman and Greek culture: 'you are, to be sure, the one man in my memory who is most skilled in both Greek and Roman culture', Caecilius

[128] See also Ch. 2, '*Paideia* and Hellenism'.

[129] Aulus Gellius repeatedly calls him *philosophus*: *NA* 1.3.27; 1.10.1; 3.19.1, 8.2.14, etc.

[130] On Favorinus' philosophical eclecticism, see Holford-Strevens (1997), 203–7

[131] Ch. 2, n. 91.

tells him (*tu es . . . unus profecto in nostra memoria non Graecae modo, sed Romanae quoque rei peritissimus*, 20.1.20).[132] His written Greek is extraordinary, often freighted with numerous linguistic oddities. Despite his evidently sophisticated knowledge of the language,[133] he is at times pilloried by the Atticist Phrynichus for his 'barbaric' solecisms.[134] This no doubt partly represents Phrynichus' snobbishness at the Gaul's 'barbarian' provenance,[135] but it also reflects Favorinus' exploratory, 'outlandish' diction, which does indeed set him at odds with his archaizing contemporaries.[136] As we saw in Chapter 2, his speeches represent him as a cultural hybrid, mimetically fashioned from divergent traditions: his culturally eclectic persona is mirrored by his pluralist approaches to style, genre, and lexis.

The interest of Favorinus for the present project, lies precisely in his self-conscious self-representation as exotic and innovative, and the articulation of that self-representation through the established language of exile. The dialectic between tradition and renewal, as we shall see, is central to the speech *On exile*, to which I now turn.[137] This text, which survives in a fragmentary papyrus discovered in the last century,[138] implies that its author has been exiled to Chios (16.3). If this is true, then Hadrian is the most obvious emperor to have ordered the exile (since Aulus Gellius presents the philosopher as on good terms with Antoninus Pius).[139] This would mean that the date of composition of the speech was some time between 130 and 138.[140] There is, however,

[132] Although he displays a preference for Greek (13.25.4; 14.1 *passim*; 17.10 *passim*), and his sense of the superiority of that tongue is reflected by Gellius himself (12.1.24), the point is to represent him as a syncretist of Greek and Latin.

[133] See Aul. Gell. *NA* 1.15.17; 2.5.1; 5.11.8–14; 12.1.24; 14.1 *passim*, etc. on his superlative knowledge of Greek.

[134] Ch. 2, n. 137.

[135] Phrynicus' severity is well characterized by Swain (1996), 53–5.

[136] For a list of the linguistic experiments in Favorinus' extant works, see Barigazzi (1966), 58–62.

[137] For a translation, see Appendix 1.

[138] The title *On exile* (περὶ φυγῆς) is a guess: the beginning and the end of the papyrus have been lost. The name is given to it by editors on the grounds of the number of otherwise attested Favorinian titles containing περί ('on . . .') (Barigazzi 1966: 349). I cite the text from Barigazzi's edition, using his chapter and paragraph divisions (which make for less unwieldy references) rather than the usual column and line numbers of the papyrus. On the circumstances of the discovery of the papyrus, see Barigazzi (1966), 347. It is securely attributed to Favorinus, since Stobaeus quotes excerpts under his authorship.

[139] See esp. *NA* 20.1.1–3.

[140] Barigazzi (1966), 349.

no external evidence to corroborate the implication in this speech that Favorinus suffered exile unless we interpret the first of his 'paradoxes', namely that he quarrelled with the emperor and 'suffered nothing' (οὐδὲν ἔπαθεν, Philostratus, *Lives of the sophists* 489) to mean that his quarrel with the emperor resulted in nothing more serious than exile (a somewhat forced interpretation).[141] As in the case of Dio, the question of the historicity of Favorinus' exile is mired in uncertainty; and, as with Dio, Philostratus denies that he was exiled. Was he then exiled at all? If so, was he exiled for cleaving to his principles? Or is the speech a rhetorical exercise in a literary form? To an extent, the question of the historical veracity of the phenomenon is not of primary interest here (the *representation* of Favorinus as an exile is itself both a political act and an engagement with literary tradition); yet it remains important to note that as the numbers of philosophical 'exiles' grow, so does the degree of self-consciously fictive invention. This is not to claim that it is impossible that Favorinus was exiled; but, as we shall see, his self-representation in the speech *On exile* is irrevocably bound up with his self-dramatization in accordance with mythical and literary paradigms.

The interrelation between literary models and life is a central theme of *On exile*. In one of the earliest legible passages, Favorinus writes of the benefits to practical life of paradigms from the past. 'The essay', he writes, is 'dedicated as a possession (*ktēma*) for someone else as well' (ἀνακείσεται δὲ ἥ̣δε ἡ̣ γραφὴ κτῆμα καὶ ἄλλωι ποτὲ αὖθις, 2.2); that is, to benefit another who finds himself exiled and incapable of coping. The Thucydidean echo (recalling the historian's famous assertion that his work is intended as a 'possession (*ktēma*) for all time', κτῆμα ἐς αἰεί, Thuc. 1.22.4) underscores Favorinus' claim that the speech, like Thucydides' *Histories* (which provide 'utility' in the place of pleasure, 1.22.4), will have a practical and beneficial effect. How will this work? By showing us, Favorinus writes, which examples not to 'imitate' (μιμεῖσθαι) because they show 'unmanly' (ἀνάνδρως) and 'manic' (μανικῶς) behaviour, and which ones to 'marvel at' (θα̣υ̣μά̣[ζειν, 2.2). The

141 C. P. Jones (1978), 48 interprets this as referring to a denial of exile, but it need not mean this: see most recently Swain (1989*b*), 154 for suspicion. Incidentally, Herodes Atticus is also denied exile by Philostratus (*VS* 562). On the historicity of Favorinus' exile, see Gleason (1995), 147–8; also Swain (1989*b*) and Fein (1994), 244–5, who are both sceptical.

past, for Favorinus, is an active, dynamic resource, interacting profitably with the present.

The question of which paradigms are the right ones occupies Favorinus throughout *On exile*.[142] Later, he writes of the 'many even more ancient paradigms' (παλαίτερα παραδείγματα, 18.1) of friendship in the face of adversity, from amongst which he has selected the case of Adrastus; and talk of paradigms recurs elsewhere (23.2; 25.2 *bis*). In an important passage the author considers his schooling against such troubles as exile comports: '. . . partly by learning about deeds and words of yore (*palaiōn*) that lead one towards virtue, and partly by meeting with (*synousiai*) men of our age (*kath' hēmas*) who are worthy of record . . .' (. . . τοῦτο μὲν παλαιῶν ἔργων τε καὶ λόγων ἐς ἀρετὴν φερόντων μαθήσει, τοῦτο δὲ τῶν καθ' ἡμᾶς ἀξίων λόγου ἀνδρῶν ξυνουσίαι . . . 5.2). The opposition between 'past' (*palai*) and 'our age' (*kath' hēmas*) implies prima facie two different eras, one of literature which can be accessed only through learning, and the other the world of 'being' and reality (the word *synousia*, 'coexistence', is cognate with the verb 'to be').[143] Yet both are equally weighted in terms of their utility: the literature of the past, just as much as moral instruction in the present, provides a crucial resource for remedying the soul. Moreover, the link between theory and practice is not just unidirectional: as the passage just cited shows, 'men of our age' too can be 'worthy of record'; that is, attain paradigmatic status. Practice can itself create new paradigms: near the beginning of the papyrus, he writes that the man who 'aims at virtue' (ἀρετῆς ἐφιέμενος) can not only counsel with 'theory' (λόγωι), but also teach others with 'his own paradigm' (τῶι οἰκείωι παραδείγματι, 2.1). Like Musonius, Favorinus considers that proper action in the present can help one achieve paradigmatic status: it can lead one across the great divide separating 'literature' from 'life', from the transience and uncertainty of existence into the immortal, culturally legitimated realm of literary tradition.

Indeed, as has been stressed, Favorinus approaches the past as though it were not hallowed and untouchable, but a dynamic repertoire of paradigms capable of, indeed requiring, revitalization

[142] The preponderance of paradigms in *On exile* and their central significance to the persuasive strategy are noted by Gleason (1995), 148–58.

[143] This *synousia* may be an index of his familiarity with Plutarch: see above, n. 12 for their acquaintance, and p. 56 on Plutarch's literary *symbiōsis* ('living together').

in the present. The past and the present are not separated by the glass of a museum case. Not for Favorinus the excision of all mention of the Roman present from his works.[144] In the *Corinthian oration* (discussed in Chapter 2) Favorinus shows willing, even in a the context of a Greek *polis*, to style himself a Roman. In *On exile* too he is perfectly willing to use not only Latin literature as a source but even Roman examples of excellence. At several points, Favorinus recalls Seneca's exilic consolation, *To Helvia, his mother*.[145] At one point, he even recalls the example of Aeneas' flight from Troy (26.4), which may well be a reference (the earliest in extant Greek) to Virgil's *Aeneid* (2.705–44). Finally, his 'paradigms' include Musonius (2.1; 23.1), the general Mucius (1; 22.4),[146] and at greatest length, Horatius (22.4). This deployment of Roman paradigms is not arbitrary: it reinforces his claim to have absorbed lessons taught on his travels over 'huge expanses of territory both Greek and barbarian' (*χώρας ἐπὶ πλεῖστον Ἑλλάδος τε καὶ βαρβάρου*, 5.2).[147] It would be misleading to deny that the perspective in *On exile* is predominantly Greek; even so, Favorinus is prepared to display a familiarity, unfashionable in contemporary Greek oratory, with Roman culture. The Roman elements are all the more noticeable in contrast with the absence—or, rather, the palpable suppression—of anything comparable in Musonius and in Dio.

Favorinus' relationship with his literary past is much more intense, but also much more contestatory than those of Musonius and Dio. The level of quotation, reference, and allusion in *On exile* is, as has been stressed by commentators, high.[148] This, however,

[144] The excision of references to Romans from Greek texts of the period is common (Bowie 1974), but in fact by no means as universal as is sometimes held. For example, see the discussion of Pausanias' passages dealing with Roman Greece by Arafat (1996), 36–42, 80–201, contra Elsner (1992); (1995), 132–44.

[145] See (briefly) Barigazzi (1966), 368–9. I see no reason to assume, with Barigazzi, that Favorinus has not read Seneca directly.

[146] The precise reasons for the reference to Mucius Scaevola are somewhat obscure: for textual discussion see Barigazzi (1987), 205–6.

[147] This phrase also recalls Dio Chr. 1.52.

[148] See e.g. Lesky (1957–8), 755: *De ex.* is 'eine Vorstellung von Favorins künstlicher, hier mit Zitaten überladener, Schreibweise'. Homer is cited fourteen times (4.5; 8.1; 8.3; 13.2; 13.3; 15.2 *bis*; 16.4; 21.1; 21.2; 21.3 *bis*; 25.2; 26.5), Euripides twelve times (3.2 *bis*; 7.1; 7.2; 17.1; 17.2; 18.2 *bis*; 18.3; 20.1 *bis*; 20.3), Sophocles four times (11.1; 13.2; 16.4; 19.5), Pindar perhaps three times (5.3—attributed to Pindar, but apparently Bacchylidean; 7.2; 25.2), Menander twice (14.2; 25.3), and Aeschylus (11.4), Chilo (18.2), and Hesiod (26.5) once each. In addition, lines of unknown origin are cited at 8.3, 11.1, and 13.1. References to writers by name (but

is not simply a matter of style, nor does it merely reflect the more general fashion for archaism in the mid-second century CE (though that context must be borne in mind). Favorinus is engaging actively with his sources, at times slipping quotations into his own sentences, at times drawing support from the authority of the classics, but at times also vigorously disputing the *sententiae*. His disputatious procedure is in evidence most clearly in the lengthy refutations of the Polynices of Euripides' *Phoenissae* (7.1–3) and Hesiod (26.3–5). Musonius' refutation of a passage from the *Phoenissae* was discussed above, but Favorinus discusses his (different) passage more systematically and in greater detail. His approach to life, then, is defiantly eclectic, creative, and dynamic. The resources of the past are, for Favorinus, open to appropriation and transfiguration, and not simply inert replication.

This perception of the present as a transfiguration of the past is also troped through the theme of exile, to which I now turn. Exile is read by Favorinus as an enforced relocation from homeland, which represents ancestral values and the past, to another place, which represents the new. Favorinus' consolation is thus directed primarily against those who cling uncritically to their homelands; and this 'consolation' serves the veiled function of figuring a more general critique of nostalgia, of the over-privileging of the canonical past to the detriment of the present. Let us consider first of all his exploration of the notion of the *patris* (fatherland):

And I too love my fatherland (*patrida*); my love is second to no one's, and I should never have left it willingly. On reflection, however, I discover that it is nothing other than the place in which my forebears settled or resided. That a fatherland (*patris*) is not the country in which we ourselves were born is clear from the following: many people, though born elsewhere, regard another land as their fatherland (*patris*). If our fatherland (*patris*) is this, the territory to which our ancestors have become accustomed, why by the same token should we not also love the country in which we currently reside? After all, the land in which one dwells is much closer than that in which one's ancestors dwelled, and my future descendants will have the same reason (or even more just cause) to make my enforced dwelling-place their fatherland (*patrida*).

τὴν δὲ πατρίδα φιλῶ μὲν [καὶ αὐ]τὸς οὐδενὸς δεύτερος καὶ ἑκὼν αὐτῆς οὐκ ἂν

without citation) occur at 4.4 (Homer), 5.3 (Pindar), 7.2 (Euripides and Pindar), 8.2 (Simonides), 9.1 (Plato and Homer), 10.2 (Alcaeus), 13.2 (Sophocles), 19.5 (Sophocles), 25.3 (Homer), and 26.3–5 (Hesiod).

ποτε ἀπελείφθην· λογιζόμενος δὲ εὑρίσκω οὐδὲν ἕτερον οὖσαν ἢ ἐν ἧι οἱ πρόγονοι ἡμῶν κατῴκησαν ἢ διέτριψαν. ὅτι γὰρ οὐκ ἐν ἧι αὐτοὶ ἐγενόμεθα, δῆλον ἐκ τούτου· πολλοὶ γὰρ ἑτέρωθι γεννηθέντες ἑτέραν πατρίδα νομίζουσιν. εἰ δὲ τοῦτό ἐστιν πατρίς, τὸ σύνηθες τοῖς προγόνοις χωρίον, τί δὴ οὐχὶ τῆι αὐτῆι γνώμηι καὶ ταύτην φιλητέον, ἐν [ἧι] τὰ νῦν διατρίβομεν; πολὺ γὰρ ἑκά[στωι ἐγγυτέ]ρω ἐν ἧι αὐτός τις οἰκεῖ ἢ ἐν ἧι οἱ πρόγονοι αὐτοῦ ᾤκ[ησαν, τοῖς δ]ὲ ἐξ ἐμοῦ γενησομένοις ἡ αὐτὴ αἰτία καὶ πολὺ δικα[ιοτέρα τὴν] ἐμὴν ἀναγκαίαν ἐνδιαίτησιν πατρίδα ποιεῖν [. . . lacunose]. (10.1–2)

The first point to make about this passage concerns its relationship to Favorinus' literary identity as a Roman Gaul writing Greek. In emphasizing that the place 'proper' to an individual may be not her or his geographical origin but the place to which he or she subsequently relocates, he is in effect legitimizing his own decision to write in Greek. To this extent, Favorinus, qua Hellenophone writer, is always already an 'exile'. As we saw earlier, Musonius and Dio also accord important figurative roles to exile (in that it is a relocation away from Rome and Roman power); yet Favorinus differs by blurring the lines between metaphorical and literal exile, to the extent that his readers are unsure whether he has been actually banished by the emperor or figuratively 'alienated' by his Hellenization.

Yet this is not merely a literary game: Favorinus' exilic self-representation also interacts in important ways with ideological debates of the time. Central to any construction of Greek cultural identity is the notion of genealogy, either by reference to the provenance of an individual (Dio *of Prusa*) or, by analogy, the 'descent' of a people from a Greek founding father.[149] In 131/2 CE, Hadrian established an institution known as the Panhellenion, centred upon Athens, which would regulate which *poleis* were to be known as Greek and which not, by reference to genealogy.[150] In satirizing the identity-defining role of genealogy, Favorinus is engaging with an issue of immediate political currency.

Elsewhere, Favorinus further underscores the inadequacy of genealogy as a source of identity. Various *poleis* trace their lineages back, we read, but 'if you delve right back (*arkhaiologēis*) to the

[149] 'The importance of descent in Greek self-definition can be illustrated in numerous ways: by rituals celebrating heroic founders; by appeals to such myths in inter-state diplomacy; and by the long academic researches conducted into the origins of various Greek and non-Greek peoples' (Woolf 1994: 129). See also Swain (1996), 68–79; Schmitz (1997), 184–93.

[150] Introd., n. 101.

earliest times (*to palaitaton*), you will find that all people everywhere are foreigners and exiles' (ἐὰν [τὰ] τοιαῦτα εἰς τὸ παλαίτατον ἀρχαιολογῇς, ἅπαντας ἁπαντα[χο]ῦ ξένους τε καὶ φυγάδας εὑρήσε[ι]ς, 10.3). There is no such thing as an 'original' land: using a proto-Derridean argument,[151] he insists that, while the myth of the 'origin' is necessary in order to substantiate identity (as traditionally defined), when we look critically at the point of origin we only find displacement. The idea of a point of foundation by exiles is relatively unfamiliar in the Greek tradition (although Herodotus does talk of population moves prior to the inauguration of the Greek tribes),[152] and may demonstrate something of the range of Favorinus' cultural experience: it is Rome that is best known as a city founded by exiles (as Seneca observes in his own exilic consolation),[153] and Aeneas was of course himself an exile (*profugus*, Virg. *Aen.* 1.2).

Also significant in the passage just quoted is Favorinus' emphasis upon the role of language (*logos*) in the construction of cultural identity through 'delving' or 'tracing history back' (*arkhaiologia*). Narrative is fundamental to identity. Later, Favorinus advances a similar argument in relation, not this time to civic, but to personal genealogy. Supplementing the words of Euripides' Jocasta to Eteocles concerning the pernicious nature of ambition (*philotimia*),[154] he extends the discussion to the worthlessness of genealogy: 'Do you not know that if you trace back all those ancient (*palaias*) noble ancestries (*eugeneias*), you will trace them back to Promethean mud or the stones of Deucalion?' (ἦ οὐκ οἶσθ[α ὅτι ἐ]ς πάσα[ς] τ[ὰς] παλαιὰς ἐκείνας εὐγενείας ἀναφέρων ἀνοίσεις ἢ εἰς τὸν Προμηθέως πηλὸν ἢ εἰς τοὺς Δευκαλίωνος λίθους; 20.5). The primary point here is that all humans have a common, primeval

[151] I refer to Derrida's theory of the linguistic sign (or 'trace'), that signifies (so he argues) by necessary reference to an original signified, but in fact gains its significance by means of its position within a system of signifiers. As he puts it, with characteristic ellipsis: 'to wrench the concept of the trace from the classical scheme, which would derive it from a presence or from an originary nontrace and make it an empirical mark, one must speak of an originary trace or arche-trace. Yet we know that that concept destroys its name and that, if it all begins with the trace, there is above all no originary trace' (Derrida 1976: 61).

[152] Hdt. 1.56–8.

[153] Sen. *Ad. Helv. matr.* 6–7. The notion that Rome is a 'city of exiles' recurs elsewhere in imperial Latin literature: see C. Edwards (1996), 110–33.

[154] Eur. *Phoen.* 531–5. Jocasta's words are addressed not (as Favorinus asserts) to Polyneices but to Eteocles. Dio Chrysostom also cites these lines with approval (Dio Chr. 17.8).

origin; but there is also a suggestion that the search for origins can only ever reveal mythical narrative (hence the references to Prometheus and Deucalion). Genealogies are at root mythical stories.

Let us turn now to Favorinus' challenge to the myth of cultural origins par excellence, autochthony. For democratic Athens, autochthony, the belief that the founders of Athens were born from the soil, provided an 'official narcissism',[155] a mythical legitimation of the exclusivity of Athenian political identity. This idea of the biological relationship between the Athenians and the soil of Attica was advanced with a particular intensity after Pericles' reform of the citizenship laws in 451/450 BCE, which made it necessary for an Athenian citizen to have both parents of Athenian origin (a measure clearly designed to protect the supposed purity of Athenian blood from contamination by non-autochthonous 'outsiders').[156] Favorinus makes great sport of this notion:

If some small number of people think that they are autochthonous (*autokhthones*), and give themselves airs for this reason, then these truly are empty boasts: for sure, mice and other more insignificant animals are born in the earth, but it is right for humans to be born from no other source than a human. What is more, if these people affiliate themselves more closely to the earth than all others for this reason—well, one should not deal with one's own portion (*meros*) of the earth alone (like someone who has emerged from a pothole), but inhabit the whole earth (*pasan tēn gēn*), as it is the same mother and nourisher of all.

ϵ[ἰ] δὲ [τι]νϵς ὀλίγοι αὐτόχθονϵς ϵἶ̣ν[αι ἡγούμϵ]νοι ἐπὶ τούτωι μ̣[έγα φρον]οῦσ̣ι̣ν, οὗτοι ὄντ̣[ω]ς ἀλαζον[ϵύονται· ἦ]ν γάρ τοι καὶ μυῶ̣ν̣ κα̣ὶ̣ ἄ̣[λλων ϵ]ὐτϵλϵστέρ[ων] ζώιων [χθονογέ]νϵια, ἀνθρώπωι δὲ ὄντι οὐ κα̣λ̣ὸ̣ν̣ μὴ ἐξ ἀ̣ν̣θρώπο[υ γϵνέσθαι]. ϵἰ δ' αὖ διὰ τοῦτο π̣ρ̣ὸ̣ς τὴν γῆ̣ν̣ ο̣ἰ̣κϵιότϵρον ἑτέρων [ἁπά]ντ[ων ὁμο]ιοῦνται, ἀλλ' οὐχ ὥσπϵρ ἐκ τρυμαλιᾶς ἐξαναδύντα χρὴ [. . . ἐκ]ϵῖνο τὸ καθ' αὑτὸν μέρος μόνον πϵριέπϵιν, ἀλλὰ πᾶσαν τὴν γῆν οἰκϵῖν ὡς πάντων μητέρα καὶ τροφὸν τὴν αὐτὴν οὖσαν. (10.4)

Favorinus reverses the implications of birth from the soil by ironically assimilating autochthons to mice: to be born from the soil implies not cultural prestige but bestiality. Furthermore, in a neat twist, the notion of cosmopolitanism (so central to Musonius'

[155] Loraux (1993), 37. On the mythical narratives of autochthony, see Rosivach (1987); R. Parker (1988), 193–5; on their symbolic and ideological values, see Ober (1989), 261–6; Loraux (1993), 3–71.

[156] Davies (1977).

essay, as we saw) is introduced here: if one wishes to associate oneself with the earth, one should do so not with the part (*meros*) but with the whole (*pasan tēn gēn*). The language of part and whole recalls very strongly that used by Musonius in his essay.[157] The central reason for citing this passage here, though, is to show how once again Favorinus is interrogating the ideological structures of his literary predecessors. In contesting the definitive significance of autochthony for identity, *On exile* inverts the topology and ideology of a famous body of precedents in the genre of epideictic oratory, the Athenian funeral speeches.[158] Let us contrast, for the sake of example, what Demosthenes says about autochthony in his funeral speech:

For it is possible for each of them [i.e. the dead citizens] to trace his ancestry not only to his father (*patēra*), and the fathers of his remote ancestors, man by man, but also to the entire fatherland (*patrida*), which they have in common, from which they are agreed to be autochthonous (*autokhthones*). For alone (*monoi*) of all men, these inhabited the fatherland from which they were born, and passed it on to those born from them, so that one might justly consider those interlopers who enter cities and are called citizens of them to be similar to suppositious children, while considering our citizens the children of the fatherland (*patridos*) by legitimate birth.

οὐ γὰρ μόνον εἰς πατέρ' αὐτοῖς καὶ τῶν ἄνω προγόνων κατ' ἄνδρα ἀνενεγκεῖν ἑκάστωι τὴν φύσιν ἔστιν, ἀλλ' εἰς ὅλην κοινῆι τὴν ὑπαρχουσαν πατρίδα, ἧς αὐτόχθονες ὁμολογοῦνται εἶναι. μόνοι γὰρ πάντων ἀνθρώπων, ἐξ ἧσπερ ἔφυσαν, ταύτην ᾤκησαν καὶ τοῖς ἐξ αὐτῶν παρέδωκαν, ὥστε δικαίως ἄν τις ὑπολάβοι τοὺς μὲν ἐπήλυδας ἐλθόντας εἰς τὰς πόλεις καὶ τούτων πολίτας προσαγορευομένους ὁμοίους εἶναι τοῖς εἰσποιητοῖς τῶν παίδων, τούτους δὲ γνησίους γόνωι τῆς πατρίδος πολίτας εἶναι. (Dem. *Or*. 60.4)

Demosthenes' strategy here depends upon an elision of the distinction between father (*patēr*) and fatherland (*patris*): the myth of autochthony allows him to present citizens as bound by a genetic ancestral relationship to the soil of the fatherland itself, and interlopers into the city's space as 'suppositious' (*εἰσποιητοῖς*) bastards. Favorinus' response (not specifically to this passage, but to the ideology that it encapsulates) is to expose mockingly the ludicrous corollary of assimilating *patris* and *patēr*: this makes human beings into animals. His rejection of autochthony as a myth of identity,

[157] Cf. Mus. Ruf. fr. 9, p. 41, discussed above, pp. 145–6.

[158] The classic account of ideology in the funeral oration is Loraux (1986).

moreover, accompanies an overhaul of the entire democratic ideology of citizenship. Where Demosthenes substantiates citizen identity by reference to a biological connection with the *patris*, Favorinus argues that the *patris* is merely a name given to the place to which one has become accustomed, settled there by chance;[159] where Demosthenes specifically rejects the claims to citizen identity of interlopers, Favorinus considers all inhabitants of a place to have been interlopers at one point; and where Demosthenes focuses upon the exclusive, distinctive qualities possessed by one group alone (*monoi*), Favorinus' scope deliberately encompasses different cultures. The rewriting of the political ideology of Classical Athens, which we have identified throughout as a feature of the writers on exile of the early principate, can be seen at its clearest here. What is more, this very process of appropriating and recreating the literary and ideological structures of the past itself underlines the point Favorinus makes here, that the past does not determine the present, that the present writes the past, that one's identity is created, rhetorically and strategically, in the here and now.

The distinction between the perspectives of Demosthenes and Favorinus is best summed up in terms of the opposition, current in cultural studies, between 'tradition' and 'translation'. In Stuart Hall's terms, the former consists in 'powerful attempts to reconstruct purified identities . . . in the face of hybridity and diversity'; while the latter marks 'those identity formations which cut across and intersect natural [*leg.* national?] frontiers'.[160] Both are responses to diversification, but the one attempts to arrest the process by centralizing identities, while the other celebrates the position of marginality. Favorinus, the man of paradoxes, makes exile an emblem of his own alienated state.

Exile thus serves as a trope through which Favorinus, like Musonius and Dio, fashions his identity. An outsider, a latecomer, an exotic paradox, the Gallic Roman presents himself as a literary refugee in a terrain littered with native traditions. He is not content, however, with his marginal position; or, rather, the notion

[159] The Greek *tykhē* means both 'chance' and 'fate'. Favorinus refers to its role in siting individuals at 8.1; 12.1; 21.1; at other times, he ascribes this role to 'the god' (2.3 *tris*; 5.3; 13.4; 14.1; 21.1; 21.2; 21.3; 22.1 *bis*; 22.3). The term seems to have some connotations of bastardy: at any rate, when Oedipus discovers he was not the son of the parents he thought his, he refers to himself as 'the son of *tykhē*' (Soph. *Oed. tyr.* 1080).

[160] S. Hall (1992), 310–11.

of cultural centrality is for Favorinus irredeemably bankrupt. What is it to 'belong'? What is it to be 'indigenous'? These concepts, we are told, rest upon a deluded narrative fiction with no solidity. For Favorinus, literary and social identity is and was ever a state of exile, a fact carefully and strategically concealed by the absurd state mythology of exclusivist systems such as that of democratic Athens. Although his self-representation is that of an exiled interloper, then, Favorinus ultimately makes himself a generalizable emblem of all literary and social identity. To 'Hellenize', to 'be Greek', is to *seem* Greek: all identities are fictions narrated and performed in the present.

This is not to claim that Favorinus is a pluralist or a multiculturalist. As much as he challenges received definitions, he also constructs new ones. His claims to 'be Greek' are premised upon his prodigious *paideia*,[161] a signal of elite status. 'Greekness' is still to be an exclusivist system, but now differently orientated in terms of the requirements of a vast network of Hellenizing elites throughout the empire. Favorinus' response to identity-creating mechanisms is not simply nihilistic, seeking a position of neutrality beyond the circuits of power. Rather, he aims to open new routes of access to the prestigious symbolic capital associated with Hellenism, and, ultimately, to authorize and empower himself as a writer and orator in the present.

CONCLUSION

This chapter has sought to show how the trope of exile was used to construct identity in the Greek literature of the early principate. As we have seen, the essays discussed here should not be considered simply as trite repetitions of Hellenistic philosophical *données*: rather, they need to be read in the context both of Roman Greek literary culture (with its reinvention of the literature and values of Classical Athens) and of the strategies of self-presentation of the authors in question. Both these contexts are interrelated: as we have seen, the process of negotiating a relationship with the Athenian past was the central means, for these authors, of constructing literary identity and cultural authority.

Exile, especially in the light of the expulsions of philosophers by Vespasian and Domitian, inevitably implied an antagonism

[161] See Fav. *Cor.* (= ps.-Dio Chr. 37) 27.

towards imperial power and movement away from Rome (as well as all that Rome represented: oppression, luxury, excess) into a world of introspection, ascesis, philosophical self-discovery, and autotherapy through meditation upon the paradigms of the past. Yet this was not simply a case of crossing the barrier between Roman power and Greek philosophy, between oppressive control and self-control, between present and past: the language of exile, as we have seen, encouraged a continual interweaving of the two, so that the Greek philosophical tradition was renewed and revitalized as an active, dynamic system for self-presentation in the here and now. Exile was presented not as an enforced seclusion from the 'reality' of the Roman present but as an intense (if stylized) engagement with highly topical issues of power and identity.

Exile, then, implied a combative relationship to Roman power. What also emerges from these texts, however, is the sense that exile simultaneously figures an alienation from *Greek* culture. As much as Rome represents the space moved away from, Greece is an alien territory where (in the cases of Musonius and Favorinus, at least) one resides as an interloper. In terms of the construction of literary identity through the language of exile, this is highly significant: it implies that the writers in question saw themselves as outsiders and latecomers to Greek language and culture. This observation provides a crucial corrective to the dominant view of Greek literature under the principate, that it displayed a self-satisfied confidence in its possession of its cultural heritage: what we have seen, on the contrary, is that its engagement with the past was much more ambivalent and problematic. To write in Greek necessarily involved breaking into a closed, centripetal tradition from outside (and the problem was redoubled in the case of an Etruscan, a Prusan, and a Gaul). It involved a painstaking process of education and imitation of cultural paradigms, but also (crucially) a transformation and reconfiguration of these paradigms into something new. It also involved the construction of a literary persona, the negotiation for oneself of a place in the tradition and the justification of innovation. To write *in* the Greek tradition necessitated, for the 'strong' writer,[162] an agonistic self-positioning *against* that tradition. The language of exile expressed the writer's alienation from the tradition and values of the Classical

[162] I refer here to Bloom's theory of 'strong' poets (see esp. Bloom 1975: 63–80).

world; it also underlined his manly strength, as he struggled with the adversity of his condition of belatedness.

'Greek' and 'Roman', for these writers, do not describe an inner state motivating action and language; they are, rather, *products* of action and language, clusters of symbolic attributes available for the manipulation of the writers in question. This does not mean that these texts are simply ludic and contrived (exile and punishment are matters of immense gravity), but that narratives of exile are also explorations of cultural identity. And, as we have seen, that identity is not (to be) taken for granted: Greekness is not the explanation for writing, but part of the issue under interrogation; a subtly nuanced question, not an answer.

4

Civilizing Rome: Greek Pedagogy and the Roman Emperor

> They, the Romans, admire our arts and crafts but hold us, ourselves, in contempt. It is a paradox, and never ceases to annoy me.
>
> Golding, *The double tongue*[1]

The previous chapter considered the representation of inter-cultural stand-off, a scenario in which the emperor is negatively assessed on the grounds of his rejection of pedagogical advice, while the philosopher is positively appraised for his manly, serene triumph over adversity. This chapter considers the more constructive counterpart of the exilic paradigm, namely the harmonious coexistence of philosophy and the principate. What sort of issues are raised when an educated Greek advises a god among men,[2] the man from whom (symbolically, at any rate) all political power in the Roman empire derives? How does he authorize his persona as a truth-telling one? How does he negotiate accusations of flattery and subservience that inevitably surface when a Greek addresses a social superior? And, most importantly, what are the implications for the cultural definition of 'Greekness' and 'Romanness'?

This chapter considers the pedagogical relationship between Greek wisdom and Roman imperial power, especially as refracted through the genre of speeches *On kingship* (περὶ βασιλείας), distillations of Greek literary, philosophical, and anecdotal advice on sole rule.[3] Or, rather, it considers the dramatic framing of the delivery

[1] Golding (1995), 65.

[2] The cult of the living emperor was in general localized in the Greek East: see Price (1984) on ruler-cult in Asia Minor, emphasizing the degree to which ruler-cult grew out of (and into) Greek civic life. As will become clear below, I consider that (for Dio at least) the relationship between gods and men was a site for contest, and not just accommodation.

[3] On the tradition of philosophical advice on kingship, see esp. Murray (1971), unfortunately never published. There is a large bibliography of works on kingship

of such advice: rather than discussing the texts in question in terms of their therapeutic power and manipulation of philosophical ideas, this chapter addresses the paradigmatic status of the dyad of emperor and pedagogue, and the use of these paradigms as a mode of constructing and exploring identity. The central figure here will be Dio Chrysostom, a figure who became, for later antiquity, the regular example of a *symboulos*, or philosophical guide to a Roman emperor. Dio not only exploited the literary past (the works of Homer,[4] Demosthenes,[5] and Plato[6] in particular) for his own self-representation, but also himself invented a whole new idiom: this 'pedagogical paradigm' became, with Dio, a means of constructing an idealized relationship between Greek and Roman. Dio thus was in turn himself an

themes in earlier authors: on wise advisers such as Solon (and the post-lapsarian Croesus) in Herodotus, see Lattimore (1939); on Xenophon's *Hiero*, see Gray (1986); on the *Cyropaedia* as kingship theory, see Farber (1979); Mueller-Goldingen (1995), 25–49; and on its philosophical *Nachleben* esp. Rawson (1975), 154; Tatum (1989), 3–35. On Plato's *Politicus*—subtitled 'on kingship' (*περὶ βασιλείας*) in some manuscripts—see Lane (1997), and on kingship in the *Republic*, see C. D. C. Reeve (1988), 191–5 for summary discussion and further bibliography. The extent of Aristotle's influence on the tradition is hard to gauge owing to the loss of his *De regno* (frr. 646–7 Rose). The discussion of kingship at *Pol.* 1310^b–15^b concerns the coming and passing of monarchies, and is not especially relevant to the present discussion. For Aristotle on kingship, see Murray (1971), 56–100. Isocrates is crucially influential on the tradition, too: esp. *Evagoras*, an encomium of the king designed to teach other monarchs (76–7); *To Nicocles* is an epistle on the art of kingship; *Nicocles* is a tract on the art of being ruled (!); *To Philip* and *Archidamus* are long essays to the kings Philip and Archidamus. On Hellenistic kingship theory, see Goodenough (1928), now superseded by Murray (1971); also Aalders (1975); Chesnut (1978); Walbank (1984), 75–81; Bringman (1993); Hahm (2000), 458–64. See also, on individual texts, Murray (1965; 1967; 1987). There is a useful though schematic survey of the topoi of Hellenistic kingship theory, as well as further bibliographical orientation, at Cairns (1989), 12–24. On Epicurus, see Gigante and Dorandi (1980); on Philodemus, see the edition of Dorandi ed. (1982), with Murray (1965); Gigante (1984). To Hermippus 'the Callimachean' is attributed an intriguing title, 'On those who converted from philosophy to power' (*περὶ τῶν ἀπὸ φιλοσοφίας εἰς δυναστείας μεταστάντων*): see Philodem. *Ind. Stoic.* col. 16. On the *Letter to Philocrates* (*c.*100 BCE) of ps.-Aristeas, a synthesis of Jewish thought with kingship theory, see Murray (1967; 1987); Mendels (1979). On Stoic kingship theory (*SVF* 3.694–700; cf. 611–24), see Devine (1970); Murray (1971), 211–44. On similar themes in middle Platonism, see Dillon (1977), 153–5, 198 and esp. Centrone (2000). On the kingship fragments by Diotogenes, Ecphantus, and Sthenidas (Thesleff ed. 1965: 33, 71–5, 79–84), see Goodenough (1928), Chesnut (1978); Centrone (2000).

[4] Kindstrand (1973), 13–44.

[5] On Dio's role as a *symboulos* of cities in the Demosthenic mould, see C. P. Jones (1978), 65–114.

[6] Trapp (1990), 141–55.

exemplar to be imitated by later writers: not just by the more obvious examples of Themistius and Julian (who subsequently of course became emperor himself), and in the medieval tradition of the 'mirror of princes',[7] but, also, as we shall see, by Marcus Aurelius and Philostratus.[8] These two figures represent very different approaches to the Dionic paradigm of emperor and philosopher, and from very different angles, the former being an emperor himself (161–77 CE) and the latter a third-century Greek sophisticate with an ironical perspective upon the Roman empire.

STAGING PHILOSOPHY: THE DIONIC MAN

As the previous chapter showed, Dio's autobiography is intimately interrelated with an ethical assessment of the emperor of the time. Domitian, who exiled him, was bad; Nerva, who recalled him, was his 'old friend'; Trajan, who (supposedly) harkened to his philosophical disquisitions, was an excellent paradigm of imperial virtue. The dating of Dio's speeches is always a problem, but it is most probable that the *Kingship orations*[9] were composed in the Trajanic period.[10] Indeed, the previous chapter suggested that the 'exile' speeches too are post-Domitianic; and, furthermore, circumscribed by an ironic awareness of Trajan's propaganda of the 'new age' of imperial benevolence.[11] As in the previous chapter, then, I shall not be concerned with the vexed questions of change, continuity, and development in Dio's writing: in my view

[7] Hadot (1972).

[8] On Themistius' use of Dio (to whom he alludes explicitly: see *Orr.* 5.63d; 11.145b; 13.173c) as a paradigm in the 4th cent., see Vanderspoel (1995), 7–9; C. P. Jones (1997), 149; on Julian's relationship to Dio, see Praechter (1892); Asmus (1895), 1–31; François (1915); Bouffartigue (1992), 293–4; on that of Synesius, see Asmus (1900); Brancacci (1986), 137–97. On Dio and the pseudo-Aristidean speech *To the emperor,* see Librale (1994), 1285, 1301 (I am unconvinced, however, that similarities suggest that the latter is Trajanic: why not conscious imitation of Dio?). The fact that the epithet 'Chrysostom' is shared by St John Chrysostom also suggests Dio's paradigmatic status. See Brancacci (1986) generally on the ancient *Rezeptionsgeschichte* of Dio.

[9] The *Kingships* will be treated for the purposes of this chapter as a unity in terms of subject-matter (although there are striking differences, e.g. in the representation of Alexander between *Orr.* 2 and 4). It is granted, however, that the collocation of these four texts is neither necessary nor exclusive: see Appendix 2.

[10] I am unpersuaded by Desideri (1978) that the third *Kingship* is Nervan (p. 297) and that the fourth is Domitianic (p. 283; see also Höistad 1948. 219–20). For effective rebuttals of these views, see, respectively, Moles (1984; 1983).

[11] Ch. 3, 'Dio Chrysostom. Exile and Sophistry'.

(which is in this respect only a modification of Moles's assessment of Dio's 'fraudulent' self-representation), the narration of Dio's life in terms of stages and conversions is a retrospective, *post factum* construction. Moreover, the focus here (as will become clear) will be upon the paradigmatic implications of the *Kingships* for cultural definition, rather than upon the personality of the author: although the neglect of the 'conversion' issue here is not intended to suggest that such analyses are fruitless, the reorientation away from the 'individual' Dio and his 'personality' onto the wider cultural framing of the *Kingships* is deliberate and strategic.

Trajan's proclamation of a 'new age' and its aftermath inspired a surge of interest in what might be called 'kingship theory', renewing and refashioning Classical and Hellenistic wisdom on sole rule. In Latin literature, Tacitus and Suetonius both show a considerable amount of interest in the ethical evaluation of emperors using categories drawn from Hellenistic kingship theory.[12] In Greek, in addition to Dio's works, Plutarch (an acquaintance of Dio's)[13] wrote a pair of moral essays on the relationship between kingship and *paideia*: *That a philosopher should especially converse with emperors* (*Philosopher* = *Mor.* 776a–779c), *To an uneducated ruler* (*Ruler* = *Mor.* 779d–782f); two other of his moral essays, *Should an old man take part in politics?* (*Old man* = *Mor.* 783b–797f) and *Advice on statecraft* (*Statecraft* = *Mor.* 798a–827c) also have some relevant passages. Like Dio in the *Kingships*, Plutarch in these essays combines Isocratean ideas with Platonism[14] (this assimilation of the two constituting a strategic 'misreading', since Plato and Isocrates were in the fourth century ideological opponents). All four essays bear the heavy imprint of the Platonic *Republic*, *Laws*, and *Epistles*, grafted onto the Isocratean conception of the philosopher's relationship to the empowered.[15] As in Plato (esp.

[12] See e.g. Hammond (1963); Claassen (1988) on Tacitus; Wallace-Hadrill (1983), 146 on Suetonius. Wallace-Hadrill (1981) points to the widespread representation of Roman emperors according to standard 'virtues' derived from Hellenistic theory.

[13] Ch. 3, n. 12.

[14] On Plutarch's philosophical allegiances, see Ch. 1, n. 45.

[15] On Platonic and Isocratean influence in these, see esp. Aalders (1982*a*), 41–4; Aalders and de Blois (1992), 3389–97; de Blois and Bons (1992; 1995); Hershbell (1995). Ziegler (1949), 823 alludes to Stoic elements in *Max. cum princ.* (played down by Babut 1969: 355–62); Masaracchia (1995) discusses Aristotelian aspects in *An seni* and *Praec. ger.* More generally on these texts, see Carrière (1977); Quet (1978); Pavis d'Escurac (1981); Desideri (1986); Squilloni (1989); all treating approximately the same subject, Plutarch's distillation of traditional political

Resp. 520b), the primary message is that philosophy is not an abstract, rarefied activity, but politically engaged.[16]

The two more important essays for our purposes are *Philosopher*, which encourages a philosopher to cultivate a friendship with a potentate named Sorcanus (776a, if the otherwise unattested name is not corrupt), and *Ruler*, a text influenced by Musonius Rufus[17] which makes the same point from the opposite perspective: the ruler should listen to philosophy.[18] In this diptych of essays, Plutarch stresses that philosophy deserves to achieve maximal impact, and can only do so 'if it attaches itself to a man of power, politics and public life, and fills him with nobility' (ἂν . . . ἄρχοντος ἀνδρὸς καὶ πολιτικοῦ καὶ πρακτικοῦ καθάψηται καὶ τούτον ἀναπλήσηι καλοκαγαθίας, *Philosopher* 777a). The ruler is not absolute, but must himself be 'ruled' by philosophy: most rulers, Plutarch tells us, fear to accept 'rationality (*logos*) as a ruler' (τὸν . . . λόγον ὥσπερ ἄρχοντα), fearing that it will 'enslave' (δουλωσάμενος) them (*Ruler* 779d–e); most rulers, 'misguided as they are' (κακῶς φρονοῦντες), consider that the good aspect of 'rule' (τῶι ἄρχειν) lies in 'not being ruled' (τὸ μὴ ἄρχεσθαι, 780b).[19] The

theory into a pragmatic response to the new realities of Roman rule. See also Tirelli (1995); (on *Max. cum princ.*) Meriani (1991); (on *Praec. ger.*) Renoirte (1951); Desideri (1991*a*); Swain (1996), 161–86. Barigazzi (1982; 1984) provides philological notes on the political writings. I accept the Plutarchan attribution of the *De unius*, following Caiazza (1995) contra Aalders (1982*b*). The loss of his other political writings is keenly felt: the Lamprias catalogue mentions *Benefits to cities, in 3 books* (πόλεων εὐεργεσίαι βιβλία γ', 51), *Should everyone speak publicly?* (εἰ πᾶσι συνηγορητέον, 156), *Should the citizen give advice that he knows will not be accepted?* (εἰ δώσει γνώμην ὁ πολίτης προειδὼς ὅτι οὐ πείσει, 164, corrected from MSS . . . οὐ πονήσει), *On public speakers* (περὶ τῶν συνηγορούντων, 198); the consecutive entries printed by Ziegler in the Teubner edition as *On politics, in 3 books* (πολιτικῶν βιβλία γ', 52) and *On Theophrastus' 'Timely Politics'* (περὶ Θεοφράστου ⟨πολιτικῶν⟩ πρὸς τοὺς καιρούς, 53), may in fact refer to a single work: Sandbach (1969), 12 prints *On Theophrastus' 'Timely Politics', in 2 books* (περὶ Θεοφράστου πρὸς τοὺς καιροὺς πολιτικῶν βιβλία β'). On Plutarch's use of this Theophrastean work, see Mirhady (1995).

[16] See Muccioli (1995) on Plutarch as an interpreter of Plato's ideas about political involvement. Massaro (1995) discusses the combination in the *Statecraft* of philosophy with political 'realism', even 'Machiavellianism' (242; the same comparison is made by Tirelli 1995: 442; the influence of *Statecraft* on Machiavelli is discussed by Desideri 1995*b*).

[17] See Mus. Ruf. fr. 8 Hense, *That kings too should engage in philosophy* (ὅτι φιλοσοφήτεον καὶ τοῖς βασιλεῦσιν), and further van Geytenbeek (1963), 124–9.

[18] Some have argued that Trajan is the addressee of *Ruler*, most recently Moles (1990), 367 n. 18. The theory is (rightly, to my mind) rejected by Rawson (1989), 250–1.

[19] The idea that the king needs ruling is also found in passing in *Philosopher*:

problem is condensed into an apophthegm: 'Who then will rule the ruler?' (*τίς οὖν ἄρξει τὸν ἄρχοντα;* 780c). The ideal ruler is metaphorically 'ruled' by philosophy, a message that implies an intercultural drama of power and authority. Rome may rule Greece politically, but to do so well necessitates submission to Greek learning.

Old man also stresses the pragmatic importance of philosophy: old men can take part in politics, for 'politics are identical to philosophy' (*ὅμοιον . . . ἐστὶ τῶι φιλοσοφεῖν τὸ πολιτεύεσθαι*, 796d). The old man excels as an 'adviser' (*σύμβουλος*, 784d; 796b), one whose authority comes from intellectual rather than physical acumen. The idea that age represents symbouleutic authority is first made in Homer's representation of Nestor (*Il.* 1.247–9 etc.),[20] but also importantly inflected by Isocrates.[21] The citation of Nestor as an example (795b), however, may deliberately evoke Dio's fifty-seventh oration, which (as we shall see presently) probably stood as an introductory preamble to the *Kingships*. Moreover, in terms of broader cultural paradigmatics, the old man is figured as the site of distillation of Greek wisdom, the emblem of an ancient people aware of the art that lies beneath the surface of political power.

THE *KINGSHIP ORATIONS*: PERFORMANCE AND/OF POWER

Let us turn to consider the *Kingships*. The initial problem for consideration concerns the performance space in which they were enacted. The traditional assumption has been that they were delivered before Trajan; but, as I show in Appendix 2, the evidence for this is fragile. The only evidence we have concerning the performance of a Dionic speech on kingship clearly envisages a Greek audience. This comes in Dio's fifty-seventh oration, *Nestor*. In this short piece, Dio defends Nestor against the charge of being an *alazōn* ('charlatan', 57.2; cf. also 57.3; 10) when he extols

'Certainly, if the words of philosophers are inscribed onto and govern the souls of rulers and men of civic office, they take on the power of law' (*καὶ μὴν οἱ λόγοι τῶν φιλοσόφων, ἐὰν ψυχαῖς ἡγεμονικῶν καὶ πολιτικῶν ἀνδρῶν ἐγγραφῶσι βεβαίως καὶ κρατήσωσι, νόμων δύναμιν λαμβάνουσιν*, 779b; cf. Dio Chr. 62.1). For similar ideas in the Classical period, see Xen. *Cyr.* 1.6.20 with Tatum (1989), 81–2; Pl. *Leg.* 643e–644a.

[20] On the importance of counsel in the *Iliad*, see Schofield (1986).

[21] Too (1995), 43–5.

the deeds of his youth (Hom. *Il.* 1.260–8; 273–4), on the grounds that he was 'advising' (*συμβουλευσάσθαι*, 57.4) Achilles and Agamemnon. Dio then proceeds, analogously, to defend himself against the same charge of being an *alazōn* (57.10) as he turns to report 'the words I spoke to the emperor' (*τοὺς ῥηθέντας πρὸς τὸν αὐτοκράτορα* [sc. *λόγους*], 57.11). As von Arnim noted, this speech is probably a preamble (or *prolalia*) to a performance in the Greek East of one or more of the *Kingships*.[22]

Given Dio's propensity towards fiction in his accounts of his dealings with Romans, it is preferable to take his assertion that he has spoken before the emperor not as self-evident truth but as another instance of rhetorical self-dramatization. One might note, moreover, that the fifty-seventh oration betrays a degree of self-consciousness about this process of persona-construction. Dio's awareness of the possible charge of *alazoneia* implies the agonistic atmosphere of public sophistic performances. *Alazōn* means more than simply 'braggart', as it is sometimes translated. The first point to note is that its literal meaning is 'wanderer': Dio's use of this term thus implicitly and ironically subverts his own self-representation as *alētēs* (the usual, etymologically linked, term for 'wanderer').[23] Secondly (and more importantly for the present purposes), *alazōn* implies *untruthful* self-vaunting,[24] and is a term elsewhere explicitly connected with sophistry by Dio (e.g. 4.33: see below). The fifty-seventh oration is a knowing defence against the charge that his self-representation as an imperial adviser is a fiction. Dio is attempting (with a certain ludic swagger) to counter the awareness among a certain proportion of the audience that his self-dramatizations are not always to be believed.

There is no secure evidence to suggest a performance of the *Kingships* before Trajan, whilst there *is* evidence that they were (?re)performed dramatically elsewhere. Although we cannot tell for sure whether Trajan heard them or not, we should at any rate explore the more solid proposition that a (if not the only) correct context in which to interpret the *Kingships* is one or more of the highly sophisticated rhetorical centres of the urban East, probably in a theatre or civic assembly-space.[25] This public, performative

[22] Von Arnim (1898), 410–14; Mras (1949), 74–5. For *prolaliai*, see Ch. 1, n. 137.

[23] Above, p. 162.

[24] MacDowell (1990), 291.

[25] On the spaces appropriate to sophistic performance, see Russell (1983), 76, and esp. Korenjak (2000), 27–33. Korenjak emphasizes the diversity of

frame will be fundamental to my analysis. From this perspective, Trajan is not so much 'the addressee' of the *Kingships* (since the process of addressing is probably fictional), but (to purloin a narratological term) 'the narratee'.[26] I propose to read the *Kingships* as a *performance* of identity, not as an expression of inner personality. In this context, the key question is no longer whether these texts are 'sincere'.[27] As we have seen, the 'narrative' persona of the *Kingships* cannot automatically be identified with the 'real' Dio. Greek declamatory rhetoric was fundamentally a role-playing activity: it often involved the impersonation of celebrated figures from the past, or the assumption of a 'stock' persona (the tyrannicide, or the father whose son has squandered his inheritance and so forth).[28] Indeed, *ēthopoeia*—the art of characterization—had been central to rhetorical theory from its earliest days.[29] Greek audiences were thoroughly habituated to fictive presentation, and fictive self-presentation, in rhetorical contexts.

In order to contextualize such ideas of self-presentation and competition within competitive space, let us consider briefly Philostratus' *Lives of the sophists*, a text composed in the early third century CE, but incorporating Dio (486–8) and his contemporaries within its purview.[30] Philostratus' work is devoted primarily to what he calls the 'Second Sophistic', a style of oratory in which the speaker assumes a fictitious persona.[31] Rhetorical presentations are conducted in a highly energized, agonistic context.[32] The sophists are quasi-heroes: their manliness is repeatedly stressed (the subject is often referred to simply as 'the man', e.g. *VS* 537,

performative spaces, different contexts being appropriate to different performances. There is no internal evidence suggesting what kind of (Greek) performance space Dio envisages in the *Kingships*.

26 See Prince (1980).

27 e.g. Moles (1990), 364: 'a sincere effort to teach Trajan true philosophy', contra e.g. Desideri (1978), 303: 'squallida adulazione'. The 'sincerity' question dogs much modern criticism of encomium, panegyric, and kingship speech: see e.g. Petit (1955), 185; Bowersock (1978), 37; Athanassidi-Fowden (1981), 61; Pernot (1997), 51. See the objections of Bartsch (1994), 148–68; and, more generally on the problems of 'sincerity', Goffman (1969), 61–6; Elliott (1982), 35–62.

28 Russell (1983), 87–8.

29 Arist. *Rhet.* 1377^{b} (also Quint. *Inst. or.* 9.2.58; Hermog. *Prog.* 9 = 2.15 Spengel); see Carey (1994), 34–43 for discussion, and examples of ἦθος in action; and Volkmann (1885), 273–4 on the Roman reception.

30 On this text, see also below, 'Dio and Philostratus'.

31 Ch. 1, 'A Secondary Society'.

32 See the excellent discussions of Gleason (1995) and Schmitz (1997), 97–135.

564, 586), and it is a mark of praise that there is 'nothing feminine or ignoble' (οὐδὲν θῆλυ οὐδὲ ἀγεννές, *VS* 596) about one of them. Rhetoric is metaphorically linked with physical competition: sophists are compared to athletes (*VS* 525–6), and reference is made to 'stripping for the contest (*agōn*)' (*VS* 601; rhetorical contests are also called *agōnes*, e.g. at *VS* 526, 580). Sophistry is also linked with warfare: Scopelian claims, through his rhetoric, to 'beat on the shield of Ajax' (*VS* 520); Polemo cites the Homeric passage in which Patroclus asks for Achilles' armour (Hom. *Il.* 16.40) when he prays for Scopelian's persuasiveness (*VS* 521).

The most striking example of this connection between sophistic display and Homeric *aristeia* ('striving for excellence') comes with Hermocrates at 611–12.[33] Philostratus comments that he partly inherits his *kleos* ('fame') from his grandfather, just as an Olympic victor is *eukleesteros* ('more famous') if he is from a family of Olympic victors, and a soldier *gennaioteros* ('nobler') if he is from military stock (*VS* 612).[34] This suggestion of ennoblement through war or athletics is integrated into the story, as the life of the 'ephebically' (*VS* 612) beautiful Hermocrates is cut short. The echoes of the Archaic and Classical ideologies of the 'beautiful death' in war[35] are compounded by Philostratus' final comment that 'the land and tombs of his fathers received him' (ἐδέξατο αὐτὸν ἡ πατρῴα γῆ καὶ αἱ πατρῷαι θῆκαι, 612), hinting at the notion of public burial merited through death in public service.[36] Hermocrates is presented as a warrior-sophist, whose exploits within the competitive space of sophistry have earned him glory. Finally, we should note the importance to Philostratean sophistry of the 'zero-sum game', the process whereby one bolsters one's own authority by impugning that of others.[37] Philostratus' sophists are

[33] Fant (1981), 242 points out a similar example with Nicetes at *VS* 512.

[34] This contrasts oddly with the assertion elsewhere (*VS* 480, 521–2) that achievements are more important than genealogy.

[35] See Vernant (1991), 84–91.

[36] e.g. Hdt. 1.30.5; Thuc. 2.34; see also Eur. *Tro.* 386–90 for 'the most beautiful fame' (τὸ κάλλιστον κλέος) of death on behalf of one's country and burial in one's ancestral land. On the centrality of the funeral speech to Athenian democratic ideology, see Loraux (1986).

[37] The idea of a 'zero-sum game' is that '[t]he cultural understanding of competition was not simply that winners gained rewards and honor, but that losers were stigmatized with shame and penalties in proportionate amounts, or, to put it another way, winners won at the direct expense of losers' (Winkler 1990: 47). For Roman Greek sophistry, see Gleason 1995: xxiii: 'For one man to triumph, the members of his audience had to allow themselves to be swept away—and this in a

commonly found trading insults and put-downs, often of the witty type that redound to the credit of the speaker.[38]

The highly energized world of sophistic competition evoked by Philostratus, as we shall see, suits the *Kingships*. Dio repeatedly engages in the ferocious competition for manhood and cultural authority, and he does so by attacking and denigrating rivals in *paideia*.

STAGING THE SELF: SOPHISTRY IN MOTION

Studies of Classical rhetoric have undergone something of a sea change in recent years.[39] The traditional (and, fundamentally, Platonic) view of rhetoric is that it presents a view of reality maliciously distorted by a self-seeking speaker before an audience too fickle and foolish to realize what is going on. Recent critics, however, have countered that no representation of reality can be absolutely 'true', since all representation is necessarily selective and partial (though, of course, some representations may be 'truer' than others). If one follows this approach, rhetoric is freed from the accusation of misrepresenting reality: instead, it can be viewed as contributing to a larger social matrix of social power, in competing to define and control certain views of the way the world works. Rhetoric does not distort reality, it *creates* it; or, rather, by intervening in a larger system of competing 'realities', it seeks to naturalize certain (necessarily partisan) perspectives. In particular, this approach facilitates the understanding of the role of rhetoric in the construction of personal, civic, and cultural identity. The conceptual categories that organize the world—self and other, male and female, Greek and Roman, past and present, and so forth—are thus not linked immutably to a single, foundational act of definition, rather they are continually being undermined and rebuilt in an ongoing *process*.

The most important identity in any rhetorical delivery is that of the speaker, and for two main reasons. First, it is upon his or her performance that the success or otherwise of the oration depends: an unattractive, implausible, or unauthoritative enuncia-

society where an intensely competitive ethos made it difficult to grant another man success. The relationship between performers was definitely a zero-sum game.'

[38] e.g. *VS* 541, 563, 578–9; Gleason (1995), 21–54; Schmitz (1997), 125–7.

[39] See esp. Perkins (1992); Gleason (1995); Too (1995).

tive persona will wreck the chances of the content being accepted by the audience. Secondly (and relatedly), rhetoric is inherently egotistical: by arrogating to oneself the right to command attention, the speaker makes certain claims about his or her exceptional status. Let us turn, then, to consider how Dio constructs his persona in the course of the *Kingship orations*.

The primary facet is his identity as a philosopher. As the previous chapter emphasized, the status of philosopher is for Dio a differential rather than an absolute state: it is arrogated by opposition to sophistry.[40] In the fourth oration, modelled on the celebrated (and assuredly fictitious) encounter of Diogenes and Alexander found in the historians,[41] Diogenes is distinguished from 'the sophists' on the grounds that he does not retain an entourage (4.14). This characterization links Diogenes to Dio, renowned as a solitary wanderer. Diogenes is here, as elsewhere in the corpus of Dio's work,[42] a persona adopted by and adapted by his near-namesake. Later, Diogenes speaks of a 'twofold *paideia*' (διττὴ . . . παιδεία), distinguishing between 'divine' (δαιμόνιος) and 'human' (ἀνθρωπίνη) *paideia* (4.29).[43] Human *paideia*, Diogenes says, is what the many mean by the term: knowledge of writing (Persian, Greek, Syrian, or Phoenician), and the type of learning practised by sophists (4.33–6). It is mere *paidia* ('play', 4.30, a well-known pun).[44] The other kind of *paideia* is sometimes called 'manliness and high-mindedness' (ἀνδρείαν καὶ μεγαλοφροσύνην, 4.30), and is 'instilled naturally' (πεφυκώς, 4.31) at birth; its possessor requires little other instruction (4.31; just as, at 1.61, the paradigmatic simplicity of Heracles' education is stressed). The principles of kingship are so deeply entrenched in its possessor that fire would not burn them out (4.32); and he does not have to learn, only to recall.[45]

[40] Ch. 3, 'Dio Chrystostom: Exile and Sophistry'.

[41] Plut. *Alex* 14.2–5, with Hamilton (1969), ad loc.

[42] Moles (1978), 99.

[43] This distinction evokes the two Aphroditae of Pausanias' speech in Plato's *Symposium* (180d–182a), the 'heavenly' (οὐρανία) and the 'vulgar' (πάνδημος). Its more direct heritage, however, is Cynic, probably originating with Antisthenes: see Diog. Laert. 6.70–1 for Diogenes' 'twofold training' (διττὴ ἄσκησις), and Antisth. fr. 27 Caizzi. See further Höistad (1948), 56–7 on the Cynic origin of Dio's pedagogics here, rejected by Desideri (1978), 340–1 n. 28 but upheld (rightly, I think) by Moles (1983), 270

[44] Also at Pl. *Leg*. 656c; Plut. *Quomodo quis suos in uirt*. 80c.

[45] οὐ . . . μαθεῖν, ἀλλ' ὑπομνησθῆναι δεῖται (*Or* 4.33), recalling the 'recollection' (*anamnēsis*) effected by the slave boy in Plato's *Meno* (82b–84a). This reference to

How are we to interpret this distinction into two kinds of *paideia*? One answer, premised upon the assumption that the fourth oration was delivered to Trajan, takes this as a sop to the emperor whose tolerance of literature and philosophy was limited: Trajan can, Dio is claimed to be suggesting, be a true king without having to work too hard on the theory ('mortal' *paideia* being of limited value).[46] If, however, we consider the *Kingships* as a performance enacted in a Greek sophistic context, we reach a different interpretation. The contrast between the two modes of *paideia* is not necessarily a polite apologetic for Greek culture, but a programmatic distinction between two kinds of *paideia within* Greek culture. The divine *paideia*, in fact, seems most appropriate to Diogenes, the Cynic whose extreme philosophy leads him to reject 'luxurious' approaches to learning in favour of the life 'according to nature' (κατὰ φύσιν). Given the close interrelations between Diogenes and the persona of Dio, this divine *paideia* represents a means of bolstering Dio's own manly, philosophical identity. Indeed, it is also consistent with what he says elsewhere in the *Kingships*: in the first oration he characterizes himself as educated by experience rather than schooling ('self-taught in wisdom', αὐτουργοὶ τῆς σοφίας, 1.9; cf. 13.10–13).[47]

In the fourth *Kingship*, the true, manly, 'strong', ascetic *paideia* of Diogenes is structurally opposed to puny, castrated *paideia*—just as Dio elsewhere in his works vaunts his own 'labours' (πόνοι) and decries 'softness' (μαλακία).[48] The most striking condemnation of sophistry comes in Diogenes' own words, during the description of how the king travels from potential to fulfilment:

> And, furthermore, if [the king seeking guidance] comes upon a man who, as it were, knows the road, this man easily displays (*epedeixen*) it to him, and on learning (*mathōn*) this, the king at once goes on his way. If, however, he falls in with some ignorant and charlatan (*alazoni*) sophist, this fellow will wear him out by leading him hither and thither, dragging him now to the East and now to the West and now to the South, not knowing anything himself but merely guessing, after having been led far afield himself long before by impostors (*alazonōn*) like himself.

the doctrine of recollection is deleted as un-Cynic by von Arnim, followed by Desideri (1978), 341 n. 29; see contra (and again rightly, in my view) Moles (1983), 271 n. 74.

46 Cohoon (1938), 183 n. 1; Moles (1983), 270.

47 See Ch. 3, n. 111, on this phrase.

48 Brunt (1973), 9–19.

προσέτι δέ, ἐὰν μὲν ἀνδρὶ περιπέσηι ὥσπερ ὁδὸν ἐπισταμένωι, ῥαιδίως ἐκεῖνος ἐπέδειξεν αὐτῶι, καὶ μαθὼν εὐθὺς ἄπεισιν· ἐὰν δὲ ἀγνοοῦντι καὶ ἀλαζόνι σοφιστῆι,[49] κατατρίψει περιάγων αὐτόν, ὁτὲ μὲν πρὸς ἀνατολάς, ὁτὲ δὲ πρὸς δύσιν, ὁτὲ δὲ πρὸς μεσημβρίαν ἕλκων, οὐδὲν αὐτὸς εἰδώς, ἀλλὰ εἰκάζων, καὶ πολὺ πρότερον αὐτὸς ὑπὸ τοιούτων ἀλαζόνων πεπλανημένος. (4.33)

Dio stages a contrast here between two types of education, and indeed two types of performer (the true educator 'displays' the way to the king, the verb *epideiknunai* suggesting a rhetorical *epideixis* or performance). The contrast between the 'man who knows' and the *alazōn* recalls the fifth-seventh oration, *Nestor* (plausibly interpreted, as discussed earlier, as a preamble to a performance of one or more of the *Kingships* in the Greek East). There, we recall, Dio defends himself against an imagined charge of *alazoneia* on the grounds that he is presuming to recount the words he spoke to the emperor (57.11). Dio's denial of fictionalizing self-promotion is best taken not at face value, but as a gambit in the fierce competition of self-representation that occurs on the rhetorical stage (and thus, from one perspective at any rate, it *constitutes* a prime example of *alazoneia*). In the passage quoted above from the fourth *Kingship*, Dio shows the same awareness of the need to combat accusations of lying and self-promotion, but in this instance he invokes the central principle of agonistic persona-construction, the zero-sum game.

The theme of masculinity, foregrounded by the association of 'divine' *paideia* with *andreia* ('manliness'), also serves to legitimize Dio's persona. As Gleason has emphasized, rhetorical self-presentation in this period focused heavily upon the theme of competition for manhood, the masculinity of the speaker being constructed often through impugning that of the opponent.[50] Indeed, the unmanliness of Dio's sophists is reconfirmed in the following section, where he compares the sophist to a 'licentious eunuch' (εὐνούχου ἀκολάστου, 4.35). Glossing this comparison, Diogenes explains that wanton eunuchs lie with women, but 'nothing more comes of it' (γίγνεται . . . οὐδὲν πλέον, 4.36),[51]

[49] Von Arnim's proposed deletion of σοφιστῆι (presumably qua gloss on ἀλαζόνι) is unnecessary. For the adjectival use of ἀλαζών, see LSJ s.v. II. 3.

[50] Gleason (1995). The model of competitive manhood is taken from Herzfeld (1995); see also Winkler (1990), 45–70.

[51] The phraseology recalls (as Richard Hunter observes to me) the double entendre at Pl. *Symp.* 222d (cf. 222e): 'let nothing come of it for him' (μηδὲν πλέον αὐτῶι γένηται).

while sophists grow old in ignorance, 'wandering in their words' (πλανωμένους ἐν τοῖς λόγοις, 4.37). This is a strikingly literal example of the 'phallocentrism' of philosophy: philosophical education is perceived in terms of male reproductive power.[52] Combining the theme of unmanliness with the important motif of wandering (which runs through all of his corpus),[53] Dio impugns his sophistic straw men for their errant, castrated *logos*. This stands in strong contrast with the *andreia* ('manliness') attributed to the heavenly *paideia* (4.30), and thus (implicitly, I have argued) to Dio himself: whereas sophistry is presented as sterile and unproductive, philosophy is generative and procreative.[54] On a similar theme, but this time granting the sophists a little more genital potency, Dio(genes) recounts late on in the fourth *Kingship* the story of Ixion. The latter, we are told, made love to a cloud thinking it was Hera (4.130), and thereby begat the 'varied (*poikilos*) and eclectic race of the Centaurs' (τὸ τῶν Κενταύρων γένος ποικίλον καὶ συμπεφορημένον, 4.130). The terminology of *poikilia* ('variation') suggests a literary mode practised by sophists;[55] and, indeed, the Centaurs are then compared to 'the political acts of certain demagogues and the treatises of the sophists' (δημαγωγῶν τινων πολιτεύματα καὶ ξυγγράμματα σοφιστῶν, 4.131). Once again, sophistry is linked with inability to perform 'proper' sexual union. Dio, who elsewhere shows himself a fierce proponent of exclusively marital, reproductive sex,[56] here heavily stigmatizes what he presents as sexual deviance, which he links thematically with his paideutic opponents.

In the third oration (3.12–24), Dio mobilizes the polarity of friendship and flattery, once again constructing a positive persona by means of rhetorical opposition.[57] Flatterers are castigated for

[52] There are several parallels in the literature of this period for the association of philosophy with the male genitalia: see above, pp. 113–14.

[53] Ch. 3, 'Dio Chrysostom: Exile and Sophistry'.

[54] A Platonic idea: see *Tht.* 149b–151d; cf. *Symp.* 209a–c; Ar. *Nub.* 135–7.

[55] At least in later literature: cf. e.g. Aelian's *Varied history* (ποικίλη ἱστορία), and the programmatic use of the term *poikilos* in Athenaeus (Lukinovich 1990: 267–8; G. Anderson 1997: 2182–3).

[56] Dio Chr. 4.102; 7.149; 33 *passim*; 36.8; 77/78.36; Swain (1994), 170–1; (1996), 126–7, 214–16. In praising only marital sexuality, Dio reflects the moral thinking of his age: see Foucault (1990), 150–232; Swain (1996), 118–31; Pomeroy (1999), 36.

[57] For the polarity of free speech and flattery, see Philodem. *De lib.*, with Glad (1996); Plut. *Quomodo adulat.*; Max. Tyr. 14; Konstan (1996); (1997), 98–105. Trajan's accession, with his paraded liberation of speech (above, pp. 165–7) and association with Zeus Philios (there was a temple to Trajan and Zeus Philios in

betraying precisely the causes and effects that Dio seeks to deny to his own *logos*: self-interest, including desire for pecuniary reward (3.14–16), pleasure-seeking (3.16), perversion of the truth, and corruption of the meaning of words (3.18–24). This is a magnificent display of ingenuity: Dio seeks simultaneously to defuse potential charges against him of rhetorical investment, and to construct a positive persona by eminently rhetorical means. In particular, Dio uses the narrative of his exile (discussed in the previous chapter) under Domitian as a guarantee of his identity: there is no fear that he will appear to be speaking 'in flattery', since he has formerly presented a 'touchstone (*basanos*) of my free-mindedness' (*βάσανον τῆς ἐλευθερίας*, 3.12). The metaphor of the 'touchstone' pre-empts the later comparison of the flatterer to the debaser of coinage (3.18).[58] It also, however implies a form of initiation into philosophical identity: the *basanos* implies not only a proof that the reader may apply to Dio to test his 'value', but also an ordeal which he has already undergone so as to prove himself a free-speaking philosopher. The metaphor of the touchstone thus serves to construct Dio's identity as a genuine, initiated philosopher.

Dio perseveres with this self-dramatization, constructing (typically) a polarity between himself and everyone else: in the time of Domitian, when 'everyone, out of fear, thought it compulsory to lie, I alone dared to tell the truth—and when it endangered my life, at that' (*ὅτε πᾶσιν ἀναγκαῖον ἐδόκει ψεύδεσθαι διὰ φόβον, μόνος ἀληθεύειν ἐτόλμων, καὶ ταῦτα κινδυνεύων ὑπὲρ τῆς ψυχῆς*, 3.13). The immediate rhetorical point of this sentence is to create an argument from plausibility: given this, is it likely that he should lie now, when there is no danger present (3.13)? At the same time, however, Dio underlines his own hardiness and uncompromising integrity, this time contrasting his behaviour not just with a select group but with the weakness of *all* others. As the 'only' man willing to stand up to Domitian,[59] Dio arrogates to

Pergamum: see Price 1984: 156, 182, 252) intensifies the discourse of flattery and friendship.

[58] The use of the language of coinage to mark 'genuine' and 'counterfeit' friends is conventional: see Theogn. 116–17, 417–18, 449–53, 956–6. On the range of meanings of the term *basanos*, see Leo (1966), 114; P. duBois (1991), 9–33. For the 'touchstone' of philosophical identity, see also Philostr. *VA* 2.30 (*ἐκβασανίζεσθαι*); 4.37 (*βάσανος*).

[59] It is instructive, in this connection, to compare the eightieth oration, where

himself the status of a paradigm, as though this alienated figure somehow essentialized the true values of the Greek philosophical heritage, values that have elsewhere been diluted or dissipated.

Dio's self-dramatization as an outsider (exile, loner, Cynic) characterized by manliness and fortitude is designed, I suggest, to win over an audience in a sophistic centre in a Greek city. If we hypothesize, as I have done, that the *Kingships* were presented in an urban centre of learning in the Greek East, then it transpires that Dio is implicitly presenting himself, the 'anti-urban' man who has come in from outside, as a rival to various claimants to the title of embodiment of the values of Greek *paideia*.[60] This geographical opposition between the culturally central and the culturally marginal enacts a semiotic distinction between others (sophists, flatterers, sexual deviants, sedentary soft men) and himself (the true-speaking, manly, travelling philosopher)—although it does so, it must be said, in an eminently 'rhetorical' manner. This interpretation implies an agonistic context, one in which self-definition (and self-defence against accusations of flattery and charlatanry) need to be fought for.

It is important, also, to emphasize the degree to which Dio is *self-conscious* in his manipulation of this splendid, chimerical array of rhetorical masks. I want to return now to the passage disavowing flattery, touched upon briefly above, and particularly to its conclusion:

So that I may avoid furnishing those who are out to slander with an accusation of flattery against me, and an accusation of wishing to be praised to your face against you, I shall turn to speak on behalf of the ideal king.

ἵνα δὲ μήτε ἐγὼ κολακείας αἰτίαν ἔχω τοῖς θέλουσι διαβάλλειν μήτε σὺ τοῦ κατ' ὀφθαλμοὺς ἐθέλειν ἐπαινεῖσθαι, ποιήσομαι τοὺς λόγους ὑπὲρ τοῦ χρηστοῦ βασιλέως . . . (3.25)

The reference to 'those who are out to slander' is best interpreted as an ingeniously rhetorical attempt to defuse hostile reaction on the part of his audience by stigmatizing any negative

Dio describes himself as 'standing apart from all the things about which most people concern themselves' (*ἀποστὰς περὶ ἃ οἱ πολλοὶ σπουδάζουσι*, 80.1), wandering about at random and even 'holding an assembly' on his own (*ἐκκλησιάζων . . . μόνος αὐτός*, 80.2)! Here, too, Dio constructs his persona as solitary, distanced from the many and inverting the regular patterns of civic existence.

[60] For the contrast between sophist and philosopher as between conventional and marginal see Hahn (1989), 47–8; Sidebottom (1990), 29; Schmitz (1997), 86.

responses as 'slander'. My major point, however, concerns the strategy of declining to speak *ad hominem*. There is a striking paradox at work here: in a gesture designed to underline his avoidance of flattery and his commitment to frankness, Dio turns away from discussing the narratee. This leaves the reader with a question: to what extent is Dio equating Trajan with the ideal king? And is he really turning away from flattery to frankness? This ironic concern to mask identities recurs elsewhere in the *Kingships*. Each of the orations begins with an anecdote, in which we are invited to pair up the subjects with Dio and 'Trajan'.[61] Scholars have been keen to try to 'see through' these anecdotes, to decode their supposedly encrypted allegories,[62] and we are surely invited to do so; but it is important to note that the very process of encrypting veils, rather than rendering pellucid, the identities of the figures. In the first *Kingship*, Dio draws attention to the similarities between his position and that of Timotheus—but then, crucially, alerts the reader to *differences* between the two (1.4–8). All of which begs the question: *how*, precisely, do the subjects of the anecdote match up with Dio and the narratee?

The most marked example of this technique of deferral of identity comes at 1.48 and following, where Dio introduces what he calls (tellingly) a 'sacred, pure narrative disguised with the *skhēma* ("style") of a myth' (ἱερὸν καὶ ὑγιῆ λόγον σχήματι μύθου, 1.49). The word *skhēma* can refer to both clothing and a rhetorical 'figure' that dissimulates the intended sentiment. In this context, both meanings are activated. Dio comments a couple of sentences later that he was wandering in exile 'clothed in the style (*skhēma*) of a beggar' (ἐν ἀγύρτου σχήματι καὶ στολῆι, 1.50). Like Odysseus, the precedent for beggarly concealment here evoked,[63] Dio knows that disguise can apply both to clothing and to language. The *skhēma* is doubly dissimulated, however: in intertextually evoking Odysseus, he impersonates the impersonator (and, in the post-Homeric tradition, the sophist)[64] par excellence.

[61] The anecdotal style is signalled by the phrases 'they say that once . . .' (φασί ποτε, 1.1; 4.1) and 'it is said that once . . .' (λέγεται ποτε, 2.1).

[62] See e.g. below, n. 88 for Desideri's 'decoding' of the second oration.

[63] Dio's ἀγύρτου picks up ἀγυρτάζειν at *Od.* 19.284, used by the disguised Odysseus in one of his false narrations to Penelope, describing her husband's current status (ironically, of course, this aspect of his story is truthful). Odysseus was often portrayed as the archetypal long-suffering exile: see Stanford (1954), 175.

[64] *Sophismata* are attributed to Odysseus at Soph. *Phil.* 14; Eur. *Hec.* 238.

The story in question further underlines Dio's ironic narrative strategy. It details a meeting with an old woman of Elis or Arcadia, the prophecy she uttered, and the fable she told him (1.49–84). Dio's role-playing is particularly intense here: the literary models include, most obviously, Prodicus' myth of Heracles' choice,[65] but also several Platonic passages: the classic topographic description in the *Phaedrus*,[66] the myths that conclude the *Phaedo*, *Republic*, and *Politicus*, and the story of Socrates' encounter with Diotima in the *Symposium*. In addition, Hesiod's ambiguous 'riddle' (αἶνος) of the hawk and the nightingale, specifically addressed to 'the kings' (βασιλῆες), is distantly evoked.[67] The multiple allusions to literary precedents serve to underline the sense of disguise at work here: the literary persona, as well as the *logos*, is concealed beneath multiple 'styles'.

Dio puts off speaking of Zeus and his government of the universe as being a subject 'too big for the present occasion' (πλείων . . . τοῦ καιροῦ τοῦ παρόντος, 1.48):[68] as in the case of the third oration's refusal to discuss the narratee directly, this deferral underlines the sense that Dio's omissions are motivated by rhetorical strategy, that he is not being completely straight with us. Indeed, so far from being straight, this *logos* seems as crooked as the path of the errant Dio. The anecdote is dominated by images of wandering and randomness. In the narrative time of the myth, he 'happened (*etykhon*) to be wandering (*alōmenos*) in exile' (ἔτυχον ἐν τῆι φυγῆι ποτε ἀλώμενος, 1.50) from Heraea (in Arcadia) to Pisa, when he 'fell upon' (ἐπετύγχανον, 1.52) a road which led into the woods and some rough country, whereupon he 'lost his way and began to roam (*eplanōmēn*)' (διαμαρτάνω τε καὶ ἐπλανώμην, 1.52). Dio's errant imagery now takes a metaphorical turn. He then met, he tells us, with an old woman wearing rustic clothes who prophesied, using the Doric dialect, that 'there would not be much more time for my wandering (*alē*), and misery—"neither for you, nor for humanity"' (οὐ πολὺς χρόνος ἔσοιτό μοι τῆς ἄλης καὶ τῆς

Antisthenes' version of the debate over the arms of Achilles, moreover, clearly casts Odysseus in the role of glib sophist (frr. 2–3 Giannantoni; cf. Ov. *Met.* 13.1–381). See also Philostr. *Her.* 33.24.

65 Xen. *Mem.* 2.1.21–34; Ch. 2, n. 115.

66 Trapp (1990), 141–4 for full discussion.

67 Hes. *Op.* 202–11.

68 Deferral of discussion is a characteristically Dionic technique: see 3.12; 36.27–8.

ταλαιπωρίας, οὔτε σοί, εἶπεν, οὔτε τοῖς ἄλλοις ἀνθρώποις, 1.55).[69] The topographical markers and the reference to the Doric dialect serve to mark Dio's disquisition as an eccentric, 'off-the-beaten-track', effort: just as he strayed when travelling, so he is now straying thematically. The Doric dialect was traditionally viewed as 'broad' (πλατύς) and uncultured.[70] Yet there is a knowing wink in all of this: the primitivist 'authenticity' of the old woman is framed and apostrophized by self-conscious play. One conspicuous index of this is the fact that the woman's words have been reproduced by Dio not in the Doric dialect but in the Attic Koine.[71] Another is that the whole scene evokes Plato's memorable scene-setting in the *Phaedrus*.[72] It is no fluke that we have ended up here. The theme of digressive wandering (ἀλώμενος, ἐπλανώμην, ἄλης) and chance (ἔτυχον, ἐπετύγχανον) barely masks—indeed subtly draws attention to—an artfully constructed (and protreptically directed) narrative. The following words, however, underline with masterfully bathetic irony the deeply embedded association in Greek culture between spatial wandering and errors of judgement:

> You will meet one day a powerful man, the ruler of most of the world and most people. You must not hesitate to tell him this myth, even if some people will inevitably despise you as a chatterbox and a rambler (*planēs*).
>
> *συμβαλεῖς δέ, ἔφη, ποτὲ ἀνδρὶ καρτερῶι, πλείστης ἄρχοντι χώρας καὶ ἀνθρώπων· τούτωι μήποτε ὀκνήσῃς εἰπεῖν τόνδε τὸν μῦθον, εἰ καί σου καταφρονεῖν τινες μέλλοιεν ὡς ἀδολέσχου καὶ πλάνητος.* (1.56)

The 'some people' alluded to here are, once again, potential miscreants in Dio's (Greek) audience. Interestingly, the accusation anticipated is that he is a 'rambler' (*planēs*): but does this refer to his mendicant existence or his verbal rambling? This ambiguity allows Dio both to reinforce the wandering, disguised, Odyssean persona adopted by the speaker here and to engage in a playful undermining of the authority of his rhetorical persona. Are we to

[69] As Moles (1990), 321 points out, Dio here makes his own wandering allegorical of the wider 'wandering' of the human race under Domitian (and forthcoming 'restitution' under Trajan). I do not, however, understand why Moles reads Dio as admitting to a 'moral error' here.

[70] Theocr. 15.87–95; esp. Demetr. *De eloc.* 177 for the opposition between Attic and Doric. Very few Doric forms are found in inscriptions under the empire, and usually (as here) subsumed into a larger framework of Attic Koine: see Schmitz (1997), 70–1.

[71] Just like the speech of the Euboean peasants in the seventh oration: see above, p. 104. Dio, though, is only a moderate Atticist. see Schmid (1887–96), 1.72–191.

[72] Pl. *Phaedr.* 229a ff · see Trapp (1990), 141–4.

expect truth or (as it were) *error* from a wanderer? As in the speech on exile, so here Dio plays on the verbal similarity between *alētheia* ('truth') and *alēteia* ('wandering').[73]

Dio's self-presentation as a wanderer, however, also serves as a source of cultural authority, to construct a more positive identity for him, that of the travelling *sophos* or wise man. The woman of the first oration tells him that he has met her 'not without divine fate' (οὐκ ἄνευ θείας τύχης, 1.55): his wandering is not meaningless, but part of a divine plan. As was discussed in the previous chapter, Dio often employs the persona of the celebrated wanderers Odysseus, Diogenes, and Homer,[74] and this should be linked to his narrativization of his life in terms of philosophical initiation. Yet this culturally authoritative aspect of his wandering does not exclude the ironic aspect: the two converge on the central figure of Odysseus, who is *both* the prototype wandering wise man *and* the manipulator par excellence of lies, fictions, and personae.

GREEK PEDAGOGY AND ROMAN RULE

If this interpretation is correct, and Dio is staking a claim to emblematize a certain kind of *paideia* within an agonistic context, what then is the role of the emperor in the (fictitious) drama of the *Kingships*? What are the cultural implications of the pedagogical narrative that sets Greek *pepaideumenos* in a symbouleutic role in relation to the ruler of 'most of the world and most people' (πλείστης ἄρχοντι χώρας καὶ ἀνθρώπων, 1.56)? This section will propose that the *Kingships* enact, for the benefit of their Greek audience, a drama of cultural hegemony between Roman power and Greek *paideia*.[75]

Dio's self-representation as an expert in *paideia* plays a fundamental role in the *Kingships*. Although elsewhere Dio defines Hellenism in terms of both *paideia* and genealogy,[76] the emphasis here, as we shall see, is restricted to the former. For a start, these texts (as one might expect) contain much material drawn from the

[73] Ch. 3, 'Dio Chrysostrom: Exile and Sophistry'.

[74] Moles (1978), 96–100, who, however, omits discussion of Dio's presentation of Homer as a wanderer (on which see Kindstrand 1973: 114).

[75] This is to disagree with Palm (1959), 29–30, who argues that Dio is projecting the notion of a de-romanized, cosmopolitan empire: the Greek–Roman dynamic, as we shall see, is fundamental to the staging of Dio's self-representation.

[76] Bowie (1991), 196–8.

canonical works of Greek literature. Homer is accorded a central place in Dio's exposition of kingship, not only in the framing preamble (the fifty-seventh oration), but also in the *Kingships* themselves (1.11–15, 38, 47; 2 *passim*; 3.9; 4.27, 39–45).[77] In addition, Dio places great store by the prose stylists of the fourth century, especially Plato; and his historical examples are drawn entirely from the period down to and including the accession of Alexander, the historical juncture that generally marked the cut-off point for interest in the past in the Greek literature of the Roman principate.[78] The figures he uses for analogy are 'old' Greek (i.e. Alexander, Timotheus, and Heracles in the first *Kingship*, Alexander and Philip in the second, Socrates in the third, Diogenes and Alexander in the fourth), or non-Greeks extracted from a classical paradigm of barbarian 'otherness' (Sardanapallus in the first *Kingship*; the Persian king in the third). I am not so interested here, however, in cataloguing literary allusions and references, although Dio elsewhere (e.g. *Orr.* 11, 18) explicitly presents himself as a learned and recherché reader of the Hellenic classics. Nor shall I consider the conventional praise of the emperor's own education, although it is important to bear in mind that this appears to have been a topos of imperial encomium.[79] My interest here is in Dio's representation of *himself* as a paideutic specialist,[80] an educator of Trajan, and thus as a paradigm of Greek culture as defined against the unlearned but empowered Roman.

In order to explore the pedagogical relationship between Greek philosopher and Roman emperor, let us turn to the second oration, the account of a conversation on kingship that supposedly took place between Alexander the Great and Philip. As is well known, the public imagery of the emperor Trajan connected him with Alexander,[81] and although there is no evidence specifically for the early phase of his reign (to which the *Kingships* are generally dated) it is fair to assume that Alexander would have provided a

[77] Desideri (1978), 350 n. 3.

[78] On Dio's narrow historical focus, see Bowie (1974), 170; Sidebottom (1990), 168.

[79] See e.g. Plin. *Panegyr.* 47.1–2; [Ael. Ar.] *Ad princ.* 11–12; Jul. *Or.* 1.14b–c; 2.50c; 75b.

[80] In the preamble, for example, Dio refers allusively to himself as 'imitating Nestor's teaching' (*μιμούμενος τὴν τοῦ Νέστορος διδασκαλίαν*, 57.10).

[81] On Trajan's *Alexandri imitatio*, see Moles (1990), 299–300; Sidebottom (1990), 204–20.

readily identifiable paradigm of imperial power (especially for a Greek audience). Alexander is thus a 'figure' for Trajan in the second oration. Dio begins the oration *sua voce*, with a characterization of Alexander that, as Moles notes, 'sets the interpretative framework for the whole speech'.[82] The Macedonian prince is described as a *meirakion* ('youth') conversing with his father (2.1). The term is particularly appropriate to a boy on the threshold of adulthood, in the dangerous and liminal period between childhood and full socialization. This youthful double-sidedness is underlined in the comparison of Alexander to 'noble puppies':

[Alexander] was unable to restrain himself, like those well-born puppies that cannot put up with being left behind by the others as they rush towards the prey; instead, they often break their bonds and follow along with them. Now, sometimes they cause havoc to the job, making a noise before the proper time because of their youth (*neotēs*) and enthusiasm (*epithymia*) and startling the quarry; but on other occasions they bound ahead and catch it themselves.

ὁ δὲ οὐχ οἷός τ' ἦν κατέχειν αὑτόν, ὥσπερ οἱ γενναῖοι σκύλακες οὐχ ὑπομένουσιν ἀπολείπεσθαι τῶν ἐπὶ θήραν ἐξιόντων, ἀλλὰ ξυνέπονται πολλάκις ἀπορρήξαντες τὰ δεσμά. ἐνίοτε μὲν οὖν ταράττουσιν ἐν τῶι ἔργωι, διὰ τὴν νεότητα καὶ τὴν ἐπιθυμίαν φθεγγόμενοι πρὸ τοῦ καιροῦ καὶ τὸ θηρίον ἀνιστάντες· ἐνίοτέ ⟨γε⟩ μὴν εἷλον αὐτοὶ προπηδήσαντες. (2.1–2)

At first blush, this seems a description of a reasonably straightforward amphibole: it is in the nature of youth either to succeed spectacularly or to cause chaos. Yet there is, in fact, not much that is flattering in this comparison. The comparison with an animal is not a comforting one, given Greek culture's association of bestiality with the untrammelled forces of primal nature.[83] That it is a '*well-born* puppy' does suggest that there are good features about the puppy (especially since the phrase looks back to Plato's description of the guardians of his ideal state),[84] but these features are apparently discarded in the thrill of the moment. The bonds that are broken by the puppy suggest the civilizing reins of acculturation, and the coupling of *neotēs* ('youth') with *epithymia* ('enthusiasm' or 'appetite') suggests that Alexander is in the grip of dangerous emotions. In particular, the simile has a Platonic ring

[82] Moles (1990), 338.

[83] On such 'estranging images' in Plato, see Burnyeat (1992), 184; cf. Lane (1998), 44–5.

[84] Pl. *Resp*. 375a; noted by Moles (1990), 338.

to it: it evokes the famous chariot simile of the *Phaedrus*, a familiar reference point for writers of the period, where the horse representing the lust of untrained youthfulness strains at the reins of self-control.[85] What is more, *neotēs* ('youth') is commonly associated in Greek literature with social disorder. Tyrants are traditionally represented as recent incumbents of a position of unstable power.[86] *Neōterismos* (literally 'renewing' or 'going over to the young') is the standard euphemism for 'revolution'. In Plutarch's *Should an old man take part in politics?*, there is a recurrent opposition between the sagacity of the old and the impulsiveness of the young: 'elderly prudence, when mixed in the assembly with boiling youth (driven mad as it is by glory and competitiveness), takes away the manic and excessively intemperate part' (εὐλάβεια γεροντικὴ κεραννυμένη πρὸς ζέουσαν ἐν δήμωι νεότητα, βακχεύουσαν ὑπὸ δόξης καὶ φιλοτιμίας, ἀφαιρῆι τὸ μανικὸν καὶ λίαν ἄκρατον, *Old man* 791c).[87]

The social bonds that partially restrain Alexander are, implicitly, those of *paideia*: he has received 'no mean education' (οὐδὲ παιδείας φαυλοτέρας, 2.15) from Aristotle, and knows certain principles of 'the kingly education and precept of self-controlled kings' (παίδευμα καὶ δίδαγμα βασιλικὸν τῶν σωφρόνων βασιλέων, 2.70). By framing the second oration with such images of bestial nature barely controlled by a paideutic superstructure, Dio not only creates a framework of narrative anticipation for what will follow (will Alexander offend Philip?), but also represents a very strong cultural paradigm. Understood within the framework of a Greek cultural system, the new ruler is incomplete and requires the admixture of more philosophy. For his Hellenic audience, this passage of Dio's articulates the overarching importance of *paideia*, its necessary priority to good kingship. As Philip the father is to Alexander the 'youth', so Dio is to Trajan, so Greek culture is to Roman *imperium*: old, authoritative, and (ideally, if not always) in control.[88]

[85] Pl. *Phaedr.* 246a–249d. Dio also evokes the *Phaedrus* at 1.52–8; 36.39–57: see Trapp (1990), 141–4, 148–55, and *passim* on the influence of the *Phaedrus* in the Roman period. For a recent discussion of the chariot simile, with bibliography, see Ferrari (1987), 185–203.

[86] Griffith (1983) ad Aesch. *PV* 35; Pl. *Ep.* 3.316c.

[87] Cf. *An seni* 793f-794a; 796b–c; cf. 788e; Cuvigny (1984), 66–9.

[88] 'Philip' is sometimes identified with Nerva (Desideri 1978: 317–18; Moles 1990: 338), an identification largely premised upon the assumption that the *Kingships* were performed at the imperial court. Greece's relationship to Rome is

The oration as a whole consists of a series of questions put by Philip to Alexander, and a series of responses. As the puppy simile might have suggested, these responses are sometimes ludicrous and naïve, sometimes laudable: the double-sidedness of youth is a theme of the dialogue as a whole. Philip's reactions to Alexander express this clearly. On the one hand, he laughs at (*γελάσας*, 2.13, 17) and teases (*παίζων*, 2.19) his son;[89] on the other hand, he betrays awe (*ἠγάσθη*, 2.7), something close to anger (*μικροῦ παροξυνθείς*, 2.16), and delight (*ἡσθείς*, 2.79) at his son's precocity. The Greek audience is encouraged to identify affectively with this condescending superiority, this sense of knowingness which allows for an evaluation of the success of the young; at the same time, they must share in the father's admiration of the son, and his acknowledgement that the son must supplant him. The tensions in this father–son relationship come to the fore at 2.16, where Philip becomes almost angry (*μικροῦ παροξυνθείς*) when Alexander claims that he could not stand having someone king over him; the son continues that he obeys him as a father, not as a king. Alexander's submission is one of respect, rather than political inferiority. On the other hand, Alexander recognizes the king's need for symbouleutic advice, referring to the important role in the *Iliad* played by the rhetorical prowess of Nestor, Diomedes, and Odysseus (2.19–24). This has implications for the paradigmatics of Graeco-Roman cultural relations: Romans may respect Greeks and value their contributions to political life, but they respect them as sons rather than submitting to them as subjects. Yet the very spikiness of Philip's reactions and the ambivalent characterization of Alexander show that this interpretation is not uncontested, at least at the verbal and conceptual levels; and that any complementarity of Greek and Roman along the political lines of power and *paideia* is not a comfortable accommodation but an uneasy, and at times fractious, alliance.

The fourth oration, focusing upon the relationship between Diogenes and Alexander, is widely held to be the spikiest of the four. In this oration, discussed briefly in the previous section,

also characterized as one of paternity, e.g. at Ael. Ar. *Ad Rom*. 96.1: this marks not just the seniority of Greek culture, but also its self-arrogated status of paternal authority.

[89] For other instances of humour and irony in the *Kingships*, see Sidebottom (1990), 108–9.

Diogenes abuses the king roundly, and the latter is frequently upset by his rebukes.[90] The greater competitiveness in this oration is accompanied by a greater attention to characterization, and to the possibilities of a character clash.[91] Alexander is described by the narrator as 'the biggest glory-hunter and lover of repute of all men' (ἀνθρώπων φιλοτιμότατος καὶ μάλιστα δόξης ἐραστής, 4.4), and as taken by a great desire to rule the world and make his name (4.4–5). His response to stories of Diogenes is ambiguous, but always marks his moral inferiority: he 'contemns' (κατεφρόνει) his poverty (4.6), but also 'admires and envies' (ἐθαύμαζε καὶ ἐζηλοτύπει) his courage, endurance, and fame (4.7), while he is also described as bitten by envy for his reputation before the two have met (4.11). Although this Alexander has the odd redeeming feature (4.1; 4.15), he is up against a much less tolerant figure here than the Philip of the second oration. In particular, Diogenes—for all that he knows how to sweeten the king for strategic purposes (4.19; 4.79)—is an exponent of Cynic *parrhēsia* or 'free speech' (4.15; see also 4.10). Indeed, at one point, the narrator tells us, Diogenes 'released all the cables [i.e. the ropes that tighten the sails] and began the final part of his speech in a particularly lofty and fearless manner' (πάντα ἀνεὶς κάλων μάλα ὑψηλῶς καὶ ἀδεῶς τὸν ἑξῆς διεπέραινε λόγον, 4.81).

So negative is the presentation of Alexander (and, conversely, so aggressive that of Diogenes) that some scholars have seen continuities with the anti-tyrannical tirades of the sixth oration, and dated both orations to Domitian's reign, when Dio is supposed to have criticized the emperor openly.[92] Such interpretations both smooth out the ambivalence of the presentation of Alexander (who is not altogether bad) and neglect the specifically *pedagogic* aspect of the relationship between Diogenes and Alexander, which better fits the paradigm Dio constructs for his relationship with Trajan. The educational aspect is suggested by the narrator's explanation for Alexander's contumelious behaviour, namely his youth and the way in which he was 'brought up' (τραφείς, 4.6). The abusive

[90] 'He flushed and grew angry' (ἠρυθρίασε . . . καὶ ὠργίσθη, Dio Chr. 4.18); 'in fear' (φοβηθείς, 4.26); 'he became upset and aggrieved' (ἐλυπεῖτο καὶ ἤχθετο, 4.49).

[91] Moles (1983), 264–7.

[92] Höistad (1948), 213–20; Desideri (1978), 283, 287–97. See Dio Chr. 45.1 for his claim to have criticized Domitian openly (a claim which might, of course, be taken more lightly than it often is).

aspect of the fourth oration should not taken simply as disdain: it is also a philosophical quality, underlining the Cynic flavour of the oration,[93] and the abuse is specifically said to be conducted 'in an attempt to improve' Alexander (προτρέπων αὐτὸν, 4.65; see also 4.77–8). The fourth oration figures itself not as denigration of Domitian but as pedagogic exhortation of Trajan, the spirited but ethically incomplete ruler. Dio, conversely, is implicitly constructed (as we saw in the previous section) as an embodiment of a divine *paideia*. The dramatized relationship between Dio and the emperor is fundamentally pedagogical. The role of educator is characterized as paternal and manly, and also as paradigmatic of an ideal relationship between Greek and Roman.

As the previous section showed, Dio's persona is constructed differentially, by means of a series of polarities: free-speaking versus flattery, manliness versus softness, and so forth. The ethical status of the monarch is likewise explored by polarity. On the structural map of the *Kingships*, legitimate monarchy is marked out as 'kingship' (βασιλεία), as opposed to 'tyranny' (τυραννίς). This opposition constitutes a major theme of these texts: the first, third, and fourth orations, in particular, present a strict set of opposing qualities that are ascribed to the tyrant and the king respectively.[94] The tyrant–king dyad has its origin in the Classical period.[95] The criticism of institutional monarchy emerged in Athens of the fifth century, on the tragic stage (especially in the pseudo-Aeschylean *Prometheus Bound*), and in Otanes' speech in the *Histories* of Herodotus (3.80, where the canonical definition of kingship as 'unaccountable rule' first appears).[96] The antithesis of tyrant and king is not attested until the fourth century:[97] it is first found in Xenophon (*Mem.* 4.6.12), but developed most substantially and

[93] See generally Moles (1983) on the Cynic elements of the fourth oration.

[94] Höistad (1948), 184–90 presents the oppositions in tabular form.

[95] On the emergence of the language of tyranny, see esp. de Romilly (1959); Cerri (1975), 15–22, 40–3; Lanza (1977); Bushnell (1990), 1–36; McGlew (1993).

[96] '. . . monarchy, which may do what it likes without accountability' (μουναρχίη, τῇι ἔξεστι ἀνευθύνωι ποιέειν τὰ βούλεται, 3.80.3). See further on this passage Lasserre (1976); Bushnell (1990), 11–13; McGlew (1993), 33. Waters (1971) is less helpful. For the subsequent canonicity of the definition, see Pl. *Leg.* 761e; [Pl.] *Def.* 415b; Arist. *Pol.* 1295ᵃ; Diod. Sic. 1.70.1; Dio Chr. 3.5; 56.5; 56.11 (in this last passage, as Murray 1971: 502–3 points out, Dio is overturning the accepted definition by pointing out that Agamemnon *is* accountable—to Nestor). 'Unaccountable rule' is '[t]he accepted definition of kingship by Hellenistic times' (Murray 1971: 300; see also Schofield 1991: 138–9 n. 4).

[97] It may be latent in Herodotus, however (Ferrill 1978, contra Waters 1971).

influentially by Plato in the *Republic* (576d–577e).[98] Tyranny is, for Plato, of the four types of polity the extreme state of constitutional 'sickness' (*Resp.* 544c). Yet it is not simply the city that is corrupted by tyranny. Politics, for Plato, are analogous with psychology:[99] the tyrant is like his city, wretched (576c); his soul is enslaved to desire, as much as his city is enslaved to his own lusts (577d ff.).

As scholars have traditionally interpreted the *Kingships* in the context of Trajan's court, they have been quick to associate representations of tyranny with the emperor Domitian, and of kingship with Trajan:[100] an interesting enactment of the principle (normally confined to the post-structuralist tradition) that literary meaning is not embedded in texts but a function of interpretative context. Yet as we have seen, the imperial frame should not be assumed too hastily. Once the *Kingships* are relocated into the Greek East, Dio's discourse of tyranny and kingship becomes more indeterminate. Neither Domitian nor Trajan is anywhere named in the *Kingships*, and the refusal to nail down the references to kingship and tyranny onto specific people suggests that the opposition between tyranny and kingship is strategically withheld. For sure, ancient sources dealing with Domitian's reign do ascribe to him many of the characteristics of the philosophers' tyrant,[101] and any reference under Trajan to 'the tyrant' would no doubt invite association with him. Dio's procedure when discussing kings and tyrants, however, deliberately resists overt correlations, and it is important to understand the dynamic relationship between the two.

[98] For a clear, if analytically naïve, description of Plato's presentation of tyrants, see Heintzeler (1927).

[99] Andersson (1971), 188–92; see further B. Williams (1973). The correspondence is not entirely new with Plato: see Rusten (1990), 99. Neu (1971) argues against the notion that Plato held an 'organic' view of state, but without explaining what in that case the 'organic' metaphors are doing.

[100] C. P. Jones (1978), 118–19; Moles (1990), 305, 329. Similarly, the Great King of the sixth oration is repeatedly identified with Domitian: von Arnim (1898), 261–3; Desideri (1978), 201–2, 288; Brancacci (1980), 92–3. Cf. Starr (1949), 20, who argues that Epictetus' tyrant 'is, in brief, Domitian'.

[101] On Domitian's disguises, see Tac. *Agr.* 39.1 (cf. Plin. *Panegyr.* 16.3); 42.2; 43.3–4, with R. H. Martin and Woodman (1989), 29 on this as a characteristic of the Tacitean tyrant. Suetonius calls him 'savage' (*saevus*, 10.1; 10.5–11.1); cf. 'the bestial and wild quality' (τὸ . . . θηριῶδές τε καὶ ἄγριον) of Plato's tyrant (Pl. *Resp.* 571c). Cassius Dio's account of his reign thematically recurs to blackness, ghostliness, and night (67.5.6; 67.8.4; 67.9).

The distinction between tyrant and king, I argue, is a matter of degree, not of essence: there is no necessarily *substantive* difference between (for example) Domitian and Trajan. Trajan's ethical superiority, rather, lies in his exposure to philosophical *paideia*—which, in the economy of the speech, is represented by Dio. In order to clarify this point, let us consider how Dio resists conceiving of the 'nature' of the king as an innate, unchangeable essence, refocusing his audience's attention onto the acculturating role of pedagogy. Let us consider in particular the complex, Heraclitean theory of personal *daimones* ('geniuses'), that, according to the fourth oration, inspire human behaviour (4.75–139).[102] This might appear at first sight to be a profoundly 'essentialist' position, negating (or, at least, minimizing) the role of education in the formation of behavioural patterns. If each ruler has his own *daimōn* determining the type of his rule, what is the point of *paideia*? But Dio (or, rather, Diogenes) is specifically not saying this:

So, wishing to please him, and at the same time to show him that he was not incapable of raising his oration whenever he wanted to, like a well-trained, obedient horse, he spoke as follows about *daimones*: people's bad and good *daimones* (who bring disasters and good fortunes), he said, do not come upon them from outside, but each man's mind (*nous*) constitutes the *daimōn* of its possessor.

βουλόμενος οὖν χαρίσασθαι αὐτῶι, ἅμα τε ἐπιδεῖξαι ὅτι οὐκ ἀδύνατός ἐστιν ὥσπερ ἵππον εὐμαθῆ καὶ πειθόμενον, ὅταν αὐτῶι δοκῆι, τὸν λόγον ἐπᾶραι, λέγει πρὸς αὐτὸν οὕτως περὶ δαιμόνων, ὅτι οὐκ εἰσὶν ἔξωθεν τῶν ἀνθρώπων οἱ πονηροὶ καὶ ἀγαθοὶ δαίμονες, οἱ τὰς συμφορὰς καὶ τὰς εὐτυχίας φέροντες αὐτοῖς, ὁ δὲ ἴδιος ἑκάστου νοῦς, οὗτός ἐστι δαίμων τοῦ ἔχοντος ἀνδρός. (4.79–80)

The *daimōn* is, then, not an external force impelling the behaviour of each individual, but coextensive with the mind (*nous*) of each. Recalling a Heraclitean aphorism,[103] Dio/genes proposes that *daimones* are not external, supernatural forces, but identifiable with character.[104] Dio/genes, moreover, is absolutely clear that the

[102] See further Moles (1983), 256–8, whose interpretation I follow with minor modifications.

[103] 'Character is a person's *daimōn*' (ἦθος ἀνθρώπωι δαίμων, Heraclit. fr. 119 DK). This statement is (presumably, deliberately) ambiguous: does it mean that one's destiny (*daimōn*) is all down to one's character, or that one's character is constituted by divine force (*daimōn*)?

[104] Noted by Moles (1983), 256: see n. 27 for other parallels, adding Plut. *Sert.* 10.6.

'quality' of an individual is to be gauged by ethical behaviour: the extended elucidation, closing the fourth oration, of the various *daimones* is presented as a description of the 'behaviours' (*τρόπους*, 4.87) they inspire, and their 'cast' (*χαρακτῆρα*) and 'shape' (*μορφήν*) as they can be gleaned 'from the characters (*ēthea*) and deeds (*erga*)' (*ἀπὸ τῶν ἠθῶν καὶ τῶν ἔργων*) of various rulers (4.88). The discussion of the *daimones*, then, is focused closely upon the ethical and behavioural characteristics of different monarchs.

How does *paideia* affect ethical behaviour? At the conclusion of the fourth oration, and of the discussion of *daimones*, Dio/genes offers to hymn the 'good, self-controlled *daimōn* and god' (*ἀγαθὸν καὶ σώφρονα . . . δαίμονα καὶ θεόν*, 4.139). The oration breaks off before this 'hymn', but not before reporting how we might access this *daimōn*, we 'to whom the good Fates have decreed it that we should receive that *daimōn*, if we share in the pure *paideia* and *logos*' (*οἷς ποτε ἐκείνου* [sc. *τοῦ δαίμονος*] *τυχεῖν ἐπέκλωσαν ἀγαθαὶ Μοῖραι παιδείας ὑγιοῦς καὶ λόγου μεταλαβοῦσι*, 4.139).[105] The good *daimōn*, leading to good kingship, is accessible through *paideia* and philosophy: the choice and agency of the king are implicitly stressed through the conditional clause at the end (the participle *μεταλαβοῦσι* is best interpreted as conditional). The route to good kingship can be voluntarily chosen and accessed through Greek literary-philosophical acculturation.

In the first oration Dio advances the notion, also found in his contemporary and acquaintance Plutarch,[106] that ethical behaviour is dependent upon the conjunction of *paideia* and a good *physis*:

> Solely the doctrine (*logos*) of the clever and wise (as were many of those of the previous age) is a sufficient and complete leader (*hēgemōn*) and helper of a compliant and good nature (*physis*), cajoling it towards all kinds of virtue and leading it expertly.
>
> *μόνος δὲ ὁ τῶν φρονίμων τε καὶ σοφῶν λόγος, οἷοι γεγόνασιν* [*οἱ*] *πολλοὶ τῶν πρότερον, ἀνενδεὴς καὶ τέλειος ἡγεμὼν καὶ βοηθὸς εὐπειθοῦς καὶ ἀγαθῆς φύσεως, πρὸς πᾶσαν ἀρετὴν παραμυθούμενός τε καὶ ἄγων ἐμμελῶς.* (1.8)

Dio here appropriates the language of political power to describe the Greek philosophical tradition, which is now the

[105] I accept here the deletion (proposed by Emperius and followed by subsequent editors) of MSS *καὶ δὴ πεπρωμένον αὐτοῖς ἐκ θεῶν ἐγένετο* (apparently interpolated from Synesius).

[106] Plut. *Sert.* 10.6; *Mor.* 243b–d; Brenk (1977), 178–9. On Plutarch's acquaintance with Dio, see Ch. 3, n. 12.

hēgemōn ('leader') of the emperor. This focus upon the 'sole' (μόνος) route to monarchic felicity, namely the conjunction of innate *physis* with acculturated *paideia* based upon traditional Greek lore, resurfaces at several points in the *Kingships*. At the end of the first oration Dio tells of the allegory presented by the old woman, based upon Prodicus' 'Choice of Heracles':[107] Heracles is taken, on Zeus' orders, by Hermes to visit the twin peaks Mount Royalty and Mount Tyranny, and asked to choose between them. At 1.65, the old woman explains Zeus' reasons for this: he recognized his noble nature (φύσιν), but also that there was a 'mortal' (θνητόν) element in him. This element made him susceptible to false teaching: 'many distract the man who is good by nature, against his will, from his own nature and opinion' (πολλοὶ παρατρέπουσιν ἄκοντα τὸν πεφυκότα ὀρθῶς ἔξω τῆς αὑτοῦ φύσεώς τε καὶ γνώμης, 1.65). Like the fourth oration, with its implicit opposition between the sophists who drag the king around and Dio/genes the steadfast educator (4.33),[108] this passage underlines the opposition between the solitary exponent of true *paideia* (implicitly, Dio) and the many fraudulent claimants (implicitly, his competitors for cultural prestige).

The distinction between tyrant and king, then, is not simply one of substance or essence. Although 'nature' is a necessary cause of good kingship, it is far from a sufficient cause: Dio goes to great lengths to demonstrate that the ethical evaluation of a monarch is based upon not simply an internal 'being', but upon the degree to which the individual is cultivated, and in particular led by himself (agonistic self-promotion being the primary aim of these texts). The imperial addressee is required to partake actively of Greek *paideia* in order to receive praise, and so pedagogy plays a more dynamic role in the *Kingships*. There are several instances where Dio's praise of Trajan is explicitly stated to be conditional upon his submission to the canons of Greek philosophical instruction. At 1.36 Dio employs the traditional performative formula known as a *makarismos* (or 'formal blessing')[109] in relation to his addressee—*if* the words apply to him:

[107] Ch. 2, n. 115.

[108] Above, pp. 192–3.

[109] A traditional feature of the Greek language from earliest times: e.g. Hom. *Od.* 5.306; 6.154–9; Hes. fr. 211.7 Merkelbach–West; and for examples of the conditional or indefinite-temporal *makarismos*, e.g. Eur. *Rhes.* 196; Bion fr. 12.1 Gow; Hardie (1994), 134 (on Virgil's fondness for the unreal conditional construction).

If any of these qualities [i.e. the attributes of the good king] seems to apply to you, then you yourself are blessed (*makarios*) in your intelligence and good nature, and we are blessed (*makarios*) in that we share in them with you.

τούτων δὲ εἴ τι φαίνεται προσήκειν σοι, μακάριος μὲν αὐτὸς τῆς εὐγνώμονος καὶ ἀγαθῆς φύσεως, μακάριοι δὲ ἡμεῖς οἱ συμμετέχοντες. (1.36)

The 'conditionality' (to use John Moles's word)[110] of Dio's praise is a marked feature of the *Kingships*. In the third oration Dio repeats his conditional *makarismos*, making Trajan's fitness to rule dependent upon his openness to Greek philosophy:

When I see you encountering those men of old, emperor, and understanding their thoughtful and truthful words, I pronounce you a blessed (*makarios*) man, in that you both possess the greatest authority (after the gods) and use the power invested in you in the best way.

ἐπειδὴ ὁρῶ σε, αὐτοκράτορ, ἐντυγχάνοντα τοῖς παλαιοῖς ἀνδράσι καὶ συνιέντα φρονίμων καὶ ἀκριβῶν λόγων, φημὶ δὴ σαφῶς ἄνδρα εἶναι μακάριον, τὸν μεγίστην μὲν ἔχοντα δύναμιν μετὰ τοὺς θεούς, κάλλιστα δὲ τῶι δύνασθαι χρώμενον. (3.3)

The temporal clause here is almost conditional in meaning: there is a direct causal relationship expressed between Trajan's heed to the doctrines of 'the men of old' and the likelihood of Dio pronouncing his *makarismos*. At one level, this sentence constitutes an exquisite rhetorical implicature: Dio's addressee is coerced into a position wherein he must pay heed to Greek *paideia*—and, crucially, to its representative, Dio—in order for the praise to work. Of course, if we accept that the *Kingships* are performed in a Greek civic context, then the point of including this rhetorical implicature becomes to display, before a knowing audience appreciative of technical virtuosity, the speaker's mastery of this skill. Equally importantly, however, it also illustrates a general principle that the *Kingships* seek to establish: *paideia* is the sine qua non of good rule, and Greek wisdom must guide Roman power.

For the Greek audience, the implication is comforting, that Greek wisdom has an active importance in the government of the

[110] Moles (1990), 313, an important discussion. The construction after *εἰ*, and especially after *εἴπερ*, can mean 'if [which is obviously the case]. . .', but, of course, does not do so of necessity. *γε* would have clarified the 'positive' meaning (Dawe 1982: 130).

world, even a controlling influence. The evaluation of Roman emperors is conducted entirely within terms which would have been culturally familiar to an educated Greek audience. Homer is repeatedly cited.[111] Homer, of course, is generally presented as the fount of Greek culture (Dio himself uses him in this role elsewhere).[112] To make Homer the arbiter of good and bad kingship is to imply that the Greeks invented kingship, and that the Greek cultural tradition provides the key to its mastery (contrary, for example, to the assertion of Aelius Aristides in his speech *To Rome* that, prior to the advent of Rome, 'there was no knowledge of how to rule', οὔπω ἦν . . . τὸ ἄρχειν εἰδέναι, *Ad Rom*. 51). The Greek philosophical heritage also constitutes a major source of monarchical wisdom.[113] The process of evaluating the Roman emperor in Greek cultural terms constitutes an act of cultural translation. There is not a single allusion to Roman history in the *Kingships*, and no concession to specifically Roman means of conceptualizing monarchy: nothing, particularly, to correspond to the fundamental polarity in Roman thought between the 'king' (*rex*) and the 'emperor' (*princeps*). Indeed, Dio even seems deliberately to flout that convention: although the only explicit vocative styles his (supposed) addressee *autokratōr* (3.3, a regular Greek translation of *princeps*), the term he uses in general to express good monarchical rule is *basileus* (a term that risks offence in that it

[111] Dio Chr. 1.11–15; 1.38; 1.47; 1.50; 2 *passim*; 3.9; 3.46; 4.39–45. In this devotion to Homer as the fount of kingship theory, Dio follows the precedent of Hellenistic theory, and in particular of Philodemus' *On the good king according to Homer* (Desideri 1978: 350 n. 3; Milazzo 1978 argues plausibly that Dio in the second *Kingship* knows and uses Philodemus).

[112] Especially in the thirty-sixth oration, where the Borysthenites' devotion to Homer is an index of their (embattled) Hellenism. See Kindstrand (1973), 13–44 on Dio's presentation of Homer in general.

[113] Cf. e.g. Dio's description of the the disturbances in the tyrant's soul (1.13) with Pl. *Resp*. 571a–c. Several images are drawn from Plato: the king as sun (1.24; 3.11, 57, 73–81), whilst building on an association encouraged by Hellenistic monarchs (Palm 1959: 27 n. 2; see Koenen 1993: 60 on Alexander as Amun-Re; and Bunge 1975 on the Helios coins of Antiochus IV), also evokes the pure light of knowledge expressed in Plato's famous simile of the cave and the sun (*Resp*. 514a–518b). The comparison between the tyrant and Phaethon, the 'insufficient charioteer' (οὐχ ἱκανὸς ὢν ἡνίοχος, 1.46) evokes the famous chariot simile of the *Phaedrus* (Pl. *Phaedr*. 246a–249d; the allusion is apparently not accepted by Trapp 1990). Stoic wisdom plays a prominent part in the idealization of the king, especially in the more cosmological aspects (1.33–47; 3.51–4): see Höistad (1948), 190–3; Sidebottom (1990), 230–5. On Cynicism in the *Kingships*, see Höistad (1948), 150–222; Moles (1983). On the difficulty of identifying Cynic doctrine in these orations, see Moles (1990), 303.

corresponds most closely to the Latin *rex*).[114] Roman politics and power are, for Dio, evaluated entirely according to Greek categories and terminology.

This process of appropriation, whereby Roman power is subsumed within the terms and framework of the Greek heritage, serves a twofold purpose. First, it consolidates Dio's persona as an ambassador of Hellenism: having emphasized throughout his own singularity as a true exponent of *paideia* (in opposition to the 'many' fraudulent sophists), he becomes a Greek, paideutic antitype of the emperor himself. Indeed, there is an extent to which the *Kingships* seem to suggest that the best ruler *is*, precisely, the ideal Greek *pepaideumenos*. This has been argued most forcibly by Höistad, who claims that Dio reflects accurately earlier Cynic views concerning the nature of power: in Dio, just as in Antisthenes (as reported in Xenophon's *Symposium*, at least), '[t]he terminology of ὁ πεπαιδευμένος [the *pepaideumenos*] is the same as that applied to the *basileus* [king]'.[115] Höistad places particular emphasis upon the role of suffering (*ponos*) in Dio's presentation of the ideal king:[116] *ponos* is also a key element in the definition of the Cynic philosopher,[117] and Dio's own self-presentation as a suffering, wandering exile is engaged by such language.[118] Other subtle analogies occur between Dio and the ideal king: both, for example, speak 'simply' (ἁπλότητα/ἁπλῶς, 1.26, 36); Dio travels 'most of the earth' (πλείστην γῆν, 1.50), while Trajan rules 'most of the world' (πλείστης . . . χώρας, 1.56).[119] In such extreme situations, Dio is not merely represented as the Hellenized doppelgänger of the Roman emperor, but even assumes the Herculean attributes of the emperor himself.

Concomitant with this act of symbolic appropriation comes an

[114] *Basileus* is not used as an official term for 'emperor' before the Byzantine period, and not in inscriptions before the time of Hadrian. Although the term is used of the *princeps* in verse from the time of Augustus (*AP* 10.25), and derivatives are found in Plutarch in this sense, Dio's is apparently the first prose use of the term for the emperor: see Mason (1974), 120–1 (who, however, omits discussion of Dio). See Sidebottom (1990), 65 on Dio's risky strategy in using *basileus* in the *Kingships*.

[115] Höistad (1948), 194.

[116] φιλόπονος ('toil-enduring') or similar is found regularly in the *Kingships*: see e.g. 1.21; 3.83, 123, 137. See further Höistad (1948), 195–222.

[117] Goulet-Cazé (1986), 42–71.

[118] e.g. at 1.9, Dio refers to his own experiences as 'toils (*ponoi*) and labours' (πόνοις τε καὶ ἔργοις).

[119] For further parallels, see Sidebottom (1990), 229; Moles (1990), 315.

implicit challenge to the power of Rome—or, at least, an insistent recognition that it is necessarily circumscribed. In the last major passage cited, for example, Dio describes his addressee as possessing 'the greatest power *after the gods*'. The question of how the emperor relates to divinity is fundamental to any interpretation of the *Kingships*, and indeed of many other products of this society in which the primary means of engagement with the emperor was through cult.[120] Dio uses 'images and paradigms' (*εἰκόνες . . . καὶ παραδείγματα*, 3.50)[121] drawn from the divine sphere to express monarchical power, but this mode of description (which is Platonic in origin)[122] does not entail the corollary that Trajan is actually divine (any more than the images of bees and bulls at 3.50 imply that he is a beast). The notion of the king as god*like*, after all, is as old as Archaic Greece.[123] In certain passages of the *Kingships*, the divine represents an unattainable limit of power, and a warning to the emperor not to overreach mortal boundaries:[124] the king needs to 'cultivate' (*θεραπεύσει, θεραπεύειν*, 3.51–2) and 'propitiate' (*ἱλάσκεται*, 3.52) the gods. Divinity (particularly in the case of the figures of Zeus and Helios) in the *Kingships* functions as a transcendent signifier of kingship, in a dual role: it provides *both* a divine paradigm validating kingship as an institution *and* a warning that human kingship will always, in some measure, fall short of the plenitude of divinity.

The *Kingships* are not, however, in any sense 'anti-Roman': in that they use the symbolic potency of the emperor strategically, so as to bolster Dio's own paideutic persona, they underscore the former's enormous charisma and power (even as they seek to appropriate them). Across the full range of Dio's works, however, the degree of approbation of Roman rule varies enormously.[125] The best-known example of apparent disapproval comes with the

[120] This formulation—i.e. suggesting that the impetus to worship the emperor came from the *πόλεις* as a means of understanding and assimilating imperial power—follows Price (1984): see esp. 239–48.

[121] For such imagery, see 1.24; 1.58 ff.; 3.11, 57, 73–81.

[122] See Lane (1998), 40–75 on the use of paradigms to represent the king in Plato's *Politicus*. Schofield (1991), 88 notes the conventional (and pre-Hellenistic: see Isoc. *Nic.* 25–6) representation of kingship through the language of divinity.

[123] Hom. *Il.* 8.540; 9.155; 12.312; 16.605; 22 434; Hes. *Th.* 91; cf. Theocr. 17.16.

[124] Similar points are made apropos of *Or.* 12 by Moles (1995), 181–3 and Swain (1996), 203–6. I cannot agree with Bowersock (1973), 191–5 that Dio's 'views . . . in respect to the emperor's relation to the gods are . . . entirely in accord with the ideology of the central government' (p. 194).

[125] Swain (1996), 208–25.

tale of the short-haired Borysthenite who is pilloried by his fellow citizens as a 'flatterer of the Romans' (κολακεύων τοὺς Ῥωμαίους, 36.17). This is not so unambiguously anti-Roman as is sometimes argued[126] (why should a sophisticated Greek audience side unequivocally with the uncultured, primitivist Borysthenites against this figure?), but even this ambiguity poses the question of affiliations and sympathies for the audience. Again, the second part of the thirteenth oration, *On exile*, concludes with an attack upon decadence at Rome, an attack which (or so we are told) was actually delivered at Rome.[127] On the other hand, elsewhere, Dio expresses apparent pride in his Roman citizenship (41.6, in strong contrast to his contemporary Plutarch, who never mentions his own citizenship).[128]

How to reconcile these two sets of beliefs, the 'pro-Roman' and the 'anti-Roman'? More profitable than trying to decide which set is genuine and which merely rhetorically expedient—the 'expressive-realist' approach, seeking to reconstruct the plenitude of Dio's internal beliefs—is an interpretation in terms of rhetorical self-representation. Dio does not write 'from the heart'. Even leaving aside the philosophical debate as to whether *any* author's true intention can be gauged from literary works, it is (I hope) clear that Dio operates in a sophistical context in which the primary motivation is to trump antagonist claimants to paideutic authority. As an accomplished rhetorician, accustomed to the wiles of oratorical self-presentation, Dio knows how to manipulate strategically the symbolic values attached to Rome: at times, he plays the outspoken parrhesiast, the harsh critic of Roman decadence; at other times, he presents himself as the philosophical pillar of the entire empire. The gap between Roman *imperium* and Greek philosophy can be strategically opened and closed at will. What matters to Dio is the construction and dramatization of a philosophical persona for himself, for (on the present interpretation) he is not so much attempting to communicate dogma as competing for public validation in the highly charged, highly agonistic space of sophistic performance. Dio is ever the man of masks. For

[126] See further Moles (1995), 186 (contra Russell 1992: 220) on the apparent 'direct hostility to the encroachment of Roman imperialism and culture'; also Palm (1959), 18; Swain (1996), 215–16.

[127] Dio Chr. 13.29–37. See Swain (1996), 211–14 for Dio's remarks on Roman luxury.

[128] For Dio's pro-Roman comments, see Swain (1996), 206–11.

Dio, Rome (and, most emblematically, the emperor) represents absolute power and non-traditional modernity. These phenomena are not definitively 'good' or 'bad'; but they offer fundamental resources for the stylization of the *pepaideumenos*, whether as oppositionalist (the pose he adopts in his writings on exile) or as adviser (the pose he adopts in the *Kingships*).

There is a certain risk involved in playing the chameleon when the stakes are so high. Over the centuries, reactions to Dio's perceived fraudulence have been at times intensely hostile. For Dio, however, elusiveness and tricksiness are the central components of the Hellenic tradition he affects to emblematize; and literary subtlety, as well as the paradigmatic relationship between emperor and philosopher, is one of the keynotes of later responses to Dionic narrative.

MARCUS AURELIUS: INTERNALIZED PEDAGOGY

One of the earliest signs of the immediate and widespread impact that Dio had on constructions of Graeco-imperial relations comes in the writings of an actual emperor, Marcus Aurelius' *Meditations*.[129] The first book of this text, sometimes considered to be a separate work,[130] consists of a series of assertions that indicate the origins of various of his own qualities. These take the form 'from *x*, the qualities *y* etc.', where *x* is a source of inspiration. The fourteenth chapter begins as follows:

From my brother, Severus: love of family, love of truth, and love of justice. To have got by his help to know Thrasea, Helvidius, Cato, Dio, Brutus, and to have conceived of the idea of a commonwealth wherein all are equal under the law (*politeias isonomou*), managed according to equality and free speech for all (*isēgorian*), and of a monarchy cherishing above all the liberty (*eleutherian*) of the subject.

[129] The title of this text is a matter of some uncertainty. The earliest explicit reference is to the 'exhortations' (*παραγγέλματα*, Them. *Or.* 6.81c). The Byzantine lexicon known as the *Suda* refers to Marcus' 'education of his own life' (*τοῦ ἰδίου βίου ἀγωγή*, s.v. *Μάρκος* 1). The title 'To himself' (*τὰ εἰς ἑαυτόν*), used in the Palatine MS on which Xylander based the *editio princeps*, goes back at least to the tenth century, when Arethas composed the scholia to Lucian (*τὰ εἰς ἑαυτὸν ἠθικά*, *Σ* Luc. *Pro imag.* 3 (= p. 207 Rabe); cf. *ἠθικά* at *Σ De salt.* 63 (= p. 189 Rabe)). If, as is conventionally thought (see below), Marcus did not envisage a readership wider than himself, the text may have been untitled. For more discussion of the title, see R. B. Rutherford (1989), 9–10; Asmis (1989), 2228 n. 1.

[130] See R. B. Rutherford (1989), 90–125, arguing (in my view rightly: see below) for thematic continuity between book 1 and books 2–12.

παρὰ Σεουήρου τὸ φιλοίκειον καὶ φιλάληθες καὶ φιλοδίκαιον· καὶ τὸ δι' αὐτὸν γνῶναι Θρασέαν, Ἑλβίδιον, Κάτωνα, Δίωνα, Βροῦτον· καὶ φαντασίαν λαβεῖν πολιτείας ἰσονόμου, κατ' ἰσότητα καὶ ἰσηγορίαν διοικουμένης, καὶ βασιλείας τιμώσης πάντων μάλιστα τὴν ἐλευθερίαν τῶν ἀρχομένων. (1.14.1)

Among the list of names he has learned from Severus[131] comes that of Dio. There is some debate as to which Dio is being referred to here, and the consensus shows a slight inclination towards Dio of Syracuse, the friend of Plato who (at least according to later accounts) sought to implement a philosophical kingship in Syracuse.[132] Yet this Dio would seem anomalous in a list of Roman Stoics who opposed autocracy (Thrasea and Helvidius are the most prominent members of the so-called 'Stoic opposition' to the Flavians;[133] Brutus and Cato are the celebrated opponents of Julius Caesar);[134] a much better case could be made for Dio Chrysostom, in his role as Domitian's opponent (see esp. Dio Chr. 45.1).[135] That this Dio is reported subsequently to have found imperial favour under Trajan does not disqualify him from candidature here:[136] rather, Marcus is precisely continuing the process that began with Trajan and Dio, namely the co-option of oppositional rhetoric into the machinery of imperial representation. Just as Trajan puts Brutus' head and the crypto-republican legend *libertas* ('liberty') on his coins,[137] so Marcus celebrates Brutus and the *eleutheria* he has learned from Severus; and just as Trajan is (at

[131] A problematic name. The MSS transmit the phrase 'my brother' (*τοῦ ἀδελφοῦ μου*), but no brother is known with that name. Recent editors delete the name. Some, moreover, emend 'Severus' to 'Verus' (Marcus' co-ruler in the initial years of his reign). Farquharson (1944), 458 argues for Gnaeus Claudius Severus Arabianus, cos. 146 CE, father of the Severus who married Marcus' youngest daughter.

[132] Particularly in Plutarch's *Dio*, a fascinating text illustrating its author's preoccupation with philosophy in practice (Pelling 1989: 224). Prominent adherents of the view that Marcus refers to Dio of Syracuse are Farquharson (1944), 459; R. B. Rutherford (1989), 64 n. 51. For the contrary view, see Desideri (1978), 16–19.

[133] For Thrasea, see Tac. *Ann.* 16.22–8; Toynbee (1944), 49–51; Brunt (1975): 26–8; MacMullen (1992), 21–3; for Helvidius, Tac. *Hist.* 2.91; 4.6; 4.8; Juv. 5.36–7; Suet. *Vesp.* 15; Plin. *Ep.* 9.13.2; Tac. *Agr.* 45; Epict. *Diss.* 1.2.19–24; Cass. Dio 65.12.2; 65.7; 66.12; Toynbee (1944), 51–2, 54; Brunt (1975), 28–31; MacMullen (1992), index s.v. 'Helvidius Priscus the elder'.

[134] See MacMullen (1992), 18–45 on the idealization of Brutus and Cato by neo-republicans under the principate.

[135] See also Luc. *Peregr.* 18, a text composed in Marcus' reign, where Dio Chrysostom appears in a list of principled opponents of tyranny.

[136] So R. B. Rutherford (1989), 64 n. 51.

[137] Ch. 3, n. 127.

least) represented as heeding Dio's philosophical advice, so Marcus represents himself as acquainted with the example of Dio. By means of an implicit self-distancing from the tyrannies of Nero and the Flavians, as much as by the language obviously appropriated from democratic Athens (*isēgoria*, 'free speech for all'; *isonomia*, 'equality before the law'),[138] Marcus constructs himself as the ideal ruler. Marcus' appropriation of this quasi-republican positionality from his primary influence, Epictetus,[139] is something of a paradox: whereas Epictetus was a victim of tyrannical oppression, Marcus was 'himself, in potentiality, the tyrant'.[140] Yet this aspect of Marcus' writing is not simply paradoxical: it also marks a strong continuity with all post-Domitianic imperial rhetoric, a discourse that repackages oppositional language in terms of imperial virtues.

This mention of Dio is fleeting and, in itself, insubstantial: Dio's name does not appear again in the text. Even so, the Dionic paradigm informs much of the structure of the *Meditations* as a whole. The text casts itself in the form of Greek philosophical advice given by the emperor to himself, often in the imperative mood, or in the form of strongly protreptic assertions and conditionals. Although self-scrutiny, verbal self-castigation, and interior dialogue are intrinsic parts of the post-Classical philosophical tradition as a whole,[141] the *Meditations* demand contextualizing in terms of the specifically second-century paradigmatics that associate Greek wisdom and Roman rule. Marcus, I argue, transfigures an external, publicly represented relationship between pedagogy and principate into an interior dialogue. This recomposition of an external mode into an inward one is characteristic of a writer who repeatedly advises himself to retreat not to physical hideaways (an echo of Tiberius' retreat to Capri?)[142] but into himself.[143]

Such a pedagogical interpretation also provides a structure that overarches the entire work, linking the apparently anomalous first

[138] For this feature of Antonine ideology, cf. Ael. Ar. *Ad Rom.* 90, and see further Farquharson (1944), 459–61; Oliver (1953), 942; Asmis (1989), 2235. In general on the principate as a democracy, see Cass. Dio 52.14.3–5; Philostr. *VA* 5.35; Starr (1952), 13–14.

[139] On the influence of Epictetus, see esp. *Med.* 1.7.3, and (most recently) Hadot (1998), 59–72.

[140] R. B. Rutherford (1989), 65.

[141] Misch (1950), 445–52; R. B. Rutherford (1989), 8–21.

[142] See e.g. Tac. *Ann.* 4.67.

[143] 4.3; 6.11–12; 7.28; Brunt (1974), 3–4.

book to the remainder. On this interpretation, the first book constitutes a *rite de passage*, marks out the teaching he has learned from others, whereas the rest of the text presents him as having assumed the responsibility of self-teaching. Indeed, the first book focuses closely upon the theme of Marcus' education. In strikingly stark and predominantly verbless sentences, he details what he received 'from' (παρά) certain figures. This technique makes for more than 'a list of the examples Marcus had received':[144] it also humbly and submissively acknowledges the forces that created Marcus' self. Teaching is a recurrent theme. From his mother's grandfather, he learned 'not to attend public schools but to enjoy good teachers (*didaskalois*) at home' (τὸ μὴ εἰς δημοσίας διατριβὰς φοιτῆσαι καὶ τὸ ἀγαθοῖς διδασκάλοις κατ' οἶκον χρήσασθαι, 1.4). From his 'tutor' (τοῦ τροφέως) he learned to avoid the races and to enjoy labour (1.5). A number of the figures cited are pedagogues: Diognetus (1.6, his painting instructor); Junius Rusticus (1.7, a Stoic mentor who introduced him to Epictetus' writings, 1.7.3); Apollonius of Chalcedon (1.8, a Stoic philosopher mandated by Antoninus to instruct the young Marcus); Sextus of Chaeronea (1.9, a philosopher who taught Marcus after he assumed power); Alexander Cotiaensis (1.10, a noted grammarian); Cornelius Fronto (1.11, Marcus' rhetorical instructor, a large amount of whose correspondence with Marcus survives, fortuitously);[145] Alexander (1.12, a rhetorician known as 'the clay-Plato'); Cinna Catulus (1.13, a Stoic philosopher); Claudius Severus (1.14, an Aristotelian); Claudius Maximus (1.15, a Stoic).[146] Although not all of these figures are well documented to us, it is clear that their overriding unifying aspect is their pedagogical role. Of the remaining chapters, five deal with family members (including the lengthy, idealized portrait of Antoninus at 1.17), and the last is 'the gods'. Marcus makes it clear that his receipt of good qualities from his kin is due not to an accidental genetic acquisition, but to the sustained acculturating (which is to say, pedagogical) role of these various exemplary figures. In the chapter on the gods, he writes that he has 'the sort of disposition (*diathesis*) that would lead him, in certain circumstances' (διάθεσιν ἔχων τοιαύτην ἀφ' ἧς, εἰ

[144] Hadot (1998), 28; cf. Bompaire (1993), 205.

[145] Champlin (1980).

[146] See Farquharson (1944), 272–5 on the known details concerning these figures.

ἔτυχε . . .) into transgression (1.17.1). The gods are praised primarily for producing the conditions wherein his faults might be minimized and his virtues nourished: 'it was the goodness of the gods that no conjunction of events came about that was likely to expose my weakness' (*τῶν θεῶν δὲ εὐποιία τὸ μηδεμίαν συνδρομὴν πραγμάτων γενέσθαι, ἥτις ἔμελλέ με ἐλέγξειν*, 1.17.1).

All these pedagogical features in the first book, however, are presented in the past tense. Marcus' education from others is now over, and the only place where he implies a current relationship with tutors is in view of the education of his sons (1.17.8). Book one finishes with the expression of Marcus' particular gratitude to the gods that he did not 'meet with any sophist or retire to unpick texts or syllogisms or busy myself with abstract ponderings' (*μὴ ἐμπεσεῖν εἴς τινα σοφιστὴν μηδὲ ἀποκαθίσαι ἐπὶ τοῦ συγγραφὰς ἢ συλλογισμοὺς ἀναλύειν ἢ περὶ τὰ μετεωρολογικὰ καταγίνεσθαι*, 1.18.9). A too intense obsession with being tutored by others would, it is implied, hinder his ability to assume the adult responsibilities of empire. In the later books, both metaphorical references to the figure of the *paidagōgos* ('schoolteacher') represent him as someone one would wish to flee (5.9; 11.36). On this interpretation, book one of the *Meditations* is thoroughly integral to the project of the whole: it marks his transition from the adolescent state wherein he was educated by others to the the mature state wherein he educates himself. At a later stage in the *Meditations*, he writes: 'in writing and reading, you are not master before you have been mastered; this is much truer of living' (*ἐν τῶι γράφειν καὶ ἀναγινώσκειν οὐ πρότερον ἄρξεις πρὶν ἀρχθῇς. τοῦτο πολλῶι μᾶλλον ἐν τῶι βίωι*, 11.29). Book one represents the stage of 'being mastered' through which Marcus must pass in order to master the empire, and master himself.

Ruling the world is a lonely task, and the overwhelming sense of solitude that emerges from the *Meditations* is a function of the unremitting insistence that the emperor must guide himself, rather than being guided by others. 'Who will rule the ruler?' (*τίς οὖν ἄρξει τὸν ἄρχοντα; To an uneducated ruler* 780c) asks Plutarch, rhetorically: for Marcus, the answer would be 'he will'. There are, for sure, limits and nuances to his isolation: as a mere constituent part of the whole, he is bound by his commonality with others (*τὸ κοινωνικόν*),[147] and he guards against the arrogant belief that he is

[147] 3.4.2; 5.6.2; 5.30; 6.14; 7.19. See further Rist (1982), 39–40

beyond correction by others.[148] In general, the impingement of others represents a threat: he warns himself periodically against the influence of acolytes, which manifests itself in its worst form as praise and flattery.[149] What holds at the political level also holds at the psychological level. The central dogma of this heautocentric philosophy is the notion that the 'ruling principle' (τὸ ἡγεμονικόν)[150]—which refers, technically, to the part of the soul that rules the lower parts, but also implies Marcus' own political rule—should be purged of all exterior influences. A soul that is dominated by impulses and desires is, according to a striking and recurrent metaphor, 'puppeted' by them.[151] Just as Marcus must rule alone, assuming power without submission to any other, so must his soul's 'ruling principle' be free from any emotive guidance.

One consequence of this emphasis upon autopedagogy is a psychic schism, an internal distribution of the roles of teacher and student within Marcus' own self. At the level of form, this manifests itself in the very presentation of the *Meditations*: addressed by self to self, they enact a marked fissure within Marcus' being. This is a crucial point to emphasize, since this text is often interpreted as a crucial staging-post in teleological histories of 'the discovery of the self': according to this interpretation, the *Meditations* present, for the first time, the 'inner unity of the person',[152] by means of a 'new form of self-presentation . . . [that] disengaged itself from the relation to the public implied in [earlier literature's] rhetorical character'.[153] If the argument I have made is correct, this sort of assertion is misguided: the *Meditations* do not reveal a new, unified inner self, rather they stage an internalization of a dyad of roles sanctioned by literary tradition, those of emperor and Greek pedagogue. As Edwards observes in connection with Seneca's *Letters*, the process of interiorization is only partial and provisional, and the sense that the self is isolated from society is a (rhetorical) *effet du réel* rather than the result of Marcus' 'perfect

[148] See the discussion of Brunt (1974), 13–14.

[149] 2.17.1; 4.3.3; 4.19; 7.3; 7.6; 9.30.

[150] τὸ ἡγεμονικόν occurs *passim*, e.g. 2.2; 5.26; 6.8; 7.16; 8.3; 10.24; 11.19; 12.2; 12.53; etc. On the centrality of this traditional Stoic term to Marcus' thought, see Farquharson (1944), 497–8; Rist (1982), 31; Asmis (1989), 2243.

[151] νευροσπαστεῖσθαι at 2.2; 3.16; 6.28; 7.3; 7.29; 10.38; 12.19.

[152] Misch (1950), 457.

[153] Misch (1950), 443.

candour'.[154] The emperor's inner being is not a preformed entity that is 'expressed' in writing; rather it is the site of an unresolved tension between Marcus' philosophy and his resistant mundanity. The self is not whole and self-sufficient, but schismatic and processual: hence the recurrent emphasis upon Marcus' failures, despite his repeated efforts, to become truly philosophical.[155]

To write of the *Meditations* in such terms is to invite the charge of gross churlishness that levels itself against any attempt to open up the sacral 'inner citadel' of Marcus' mind to the glare of public self-representation. The *Meditations* are a deeply personal, at times embarrassingly personal,[156] set of reflections. They constitute a doubly enfolded autobiography, a text about the self that speaks to the self, constructing the reader from 'outside' as a prying interloper. What John Sturrock says of autobiography in general, then, is all the truer of the *Meditations*: 'Autobiography is the certificate of a unique human passage through life and the theorist who comes to it full of sceptical questions about its rhetorical nature knows that he is playing an unkind game.'[157] Still, this feeling of discomfort should not deter the critic from seeking to expose the strategies employed by a writer in order to foster a text's sense of the personal. Scholars who read Marcus 'with the grain' pursue an 'expressive-realist' agenda,[158] assuming that he gives a candid account of his own inner torments. Yet as Sturrock notes, it is crucial to distinguish 'the dance from the dancer, or the self as impersonal performance from the self as unique and transcendent originator of the text'.[159] Marcus the author, the controlling consciousness that brought forth these words, is lost to us; what we do have is 'Marcus' the textual construct, the being engendered by the words on the page. The pages of the *Meditation* are not an unproblematic map of Marcus' psyche: to conclude as much is to be lulled by the text's narrative effects.

[154] C. Edwards (1997), 27–8; also Riggsby (1998), 92–3 on Pliny the younger. I take the phrase 'perfect candour' from Brunt (1974), 2.

[155] See the passages discussed at Brunt (1974), 3.

[156] Brunt (1974), 5 cites 1.17.2 (late loss of his virginity) and 1.17.7 (abstaining from 'Benedicta and Theodotus') as embarassments. In a culture less fixated on the privacy of sexuality, however, these 'confessions' are better read as advertisements of self-control.

[157] Sturrock (1993), 3.

[158] For expressive-realism, see Introd., 'The Politics of Imitation'.

[159] Sturrock (1993), 9.

This brings us to the central crux of scholarship on the *Meditations*: was this text composed solely for the purposes of self-edification, or is it orientated towards a larger audience? Recent writers have been unanimous in their assertion of the former.[160] There is, of course, no way of determining the issue either way for sure: any argument to the effect that Marcus implies that he is the only reader can be turned around by a sceptic claiming that that is precisely the rhetorical effect of the text. (And Marcus himself is far from naïve about affectations of simplicity and candour: 'How rotten and counterfeit is the man who says: "I have chosen to treat you with simplicity" ', ὡς σαπρὸς καὶ κίβδηλος ὁ λέγων· ἐγὼ προῄρημαι ἁπλῶς σοι προσφέρεσθαι, 11.15.) To oppose the two positions in such stark terms, however, may be misguided. If Marcus *did* write only for his own eyes, that process of self-orientation can never have been complete: as anyone who has kept a diary will know, private writing is always conditioned by an awareness of the threat of exposure. One only has to consider the sources of the imperial biographer Suetonius to realize that an emperor's private papers can readily become public property.[161] Conversely, we do not need to assume that, if Marcus envisaged a broader audience, he was simply attempting to hoodwink them into believing that he was a philosopher-king (indeed, at thirteen books of complex and at times technical prose, the *Meditations* would make for a rather excessive form of confidence trick). The question of whether the *Meditations* were intended for private or public consumption is too crude: this is a text in which the public repeatedly leaks into the private, and vice versa. The *Meditations* depend for their power upon inhabiting precisely the junction between the two.

Marcus' self-arrogated position at the point of confluence of public role and private study undoubtedly influenced his reception among Greek-speakers in the empire. There is no certain reference to the *Meditations* before Themistius in the fourth century,[162] but it is clear that earlier Greek writers understand the centrality of

160 Esp. Brunt (1974), a sustained argument for this position; see also e.g. Rist (1982), 23–4, 43–4; R. B. Rutherford (1989), 9–10; Asmis (1989), 2228–9; Bompaire (1993), 204–6; Hadot (1998), 21.

161 On Suetonius' use of Augustus' private letters, see Wallace-Hadrill (1983), 91–5.

162 Them. *Or.* 6.81c. There is, however, a reference to Marcus' writings (γραφέντα) by Herodian in the 3rd cent. (1.2.3), though this may refer to the emperor's other writings (cf. *Med.* 1 6).

pedagogics to Marcus' stylization of sole rule.[163] Writing in the third century, Cassius Dio is full of praise for Marcus' reign, not only in his explicit praise of the emperor's vigour, benevolence, clemency, and constancy (71.34.2–4), but also implicitly in his references to his patronage of Greek *paideia* at Athens (71.31.3). It is to his education (at the hands of Fronto, Herodes, Junius Rusticus, and Apollonius: see 71.35.1) that Dio attributes his excellence: 'he was naturally good anyway, but was aided to the greatest degree by his education (*paideia*)' (ἄλλως τε καλῶς ἐπεφύκει καὶ ἐκ τῆς παιδείας ἐπὶ πλεῖστον ὠφελήθη, 71.35.6). For this reason, Marcus' reign is famously styled by Dio a 'golden age of kingship' (χρυσῆς . . . βασιλείας, 71.36.4). Writing in a tradition that evaluates Romans in accordance with their degree of receptivity towards Greek culture,[164] Dio perceptibly links Marcus' paideutic qualities to his fitness to rule (as, indeed, does the emperor himself).

A similar pattern emerges from the histories of another third-century Greek writer, Herodian. Marcus' reign stands at the head of Herodian's *History of the empire after Marcus*, representing a pinnacle of excellent kingship from which his successors can only decline.[165] Herodian, a writer thoroughly at home in the tradition of evaluating Roman institutions from a Greek perspective,[166] extols Marcus' *paideia* in a twofold manner. Like Cassius Dio, he praises the emperor's sensitivity towards Greek culture (he was a 'lover of ancient writings', λόγων . . . ἀρχαιότητος . . . ἐραστής, 1.2.3); but he focuses particularly upon the emperor's concern for the education of his children. Marcus chooses the best husbands, not the richest, for his daughters (1.2.1–2), and fears for the future of his son, Commodus, if he is allowed to relax his studies (1.3.1). Whether Herodian has had access to the *Meditations* or not, this concern with the need for constant paideutic vigilance chimes with Marcus' assessment of his own situation. Unfortunately, in the case of Commodus, certain courtiers prey upon him and undo the good work done by his father's tutors, diverting him instead towards the pleasures of Rome.[167] The old Marcus, saturated in

[163] In the later empire, of course, Marcus is even more conspicuously idealized: see Stertz (1976–7).

[164] Particularly conspicuous in the case of Plutarch: see Pelling (1989); Swain (1990).

[165] Hdn. 1.1–4; Widmer (1967), 20, 22; cf. Sidebottom (1998), 2804–5; Marasco (1998), 2840–57.

[166] Sidebottom (1998), 2822–6.

[167] Hdn. 1.6.1; see Sidebottom (1998), 2805–7.

the wisdom of ancient texts, is thematically opposed to the 'youthful' Commodus: 'for', Herodian writes, 'the souls of the young slip with extreme ease into pleasure, and are diverted away from the excellent qualities of education' (*ῥᾷστα γὰρ αἱ τῶν νέων ψυχαὶ ἐς ἡδονὰς ἐξολισθαίνουσαι ἀπὸ τῶν παιδείας καλῶν μετοχετεύονται*, 1.3.1). Standing at the beginning of this history, Marcus plays a crucial narrative role, embodying the age-old values of tradition and culturally sanctioned authority from which the younger succession will decline into tyranny and perversity.[168] Throughout, he remains a paradigm against which the reader is implicitly (and, in the case of Pertinax, the 'imitator' of Marcus, all but explicitly)[169] invited to measure later emperors.

Marcus' *Meditations*, then, are not simply an exercise in private reflection: they also engage with the emperor's own public self-image as a cultured ruler in the post-Domitianic mould, representing an attempt to negotiate the 'pedagogical paradigm' whereby the emperor accedes to wise advice. Marcus' innovation is to internalize the pedagogical relationship, so that he becomes both master and pupil. This play between public duty and inner contemplation is the dominant theme of the *Meditations*. It is testament to the power of this self-representation that writers such as Cassius Dio and Herodian underline his paradigmatic status and represent him as the apogee of philosophical kingship.

DIO AND PHILOSTRATUS

Dio's pedagogical relationship to the Roman empire is also brought out in the course of Philostratus' *In honour of Apollonius of Tyana* (*Apollonius*)[170] and *Lives of the sophists* (*Sophists*), and it is to these texts that I now turn. Both texts were composed in the first half of the third century. Although the question of the attribution of the numerous extant Philostratean texts is complicated (since there were at least two, and possibly four, Philostrati writing around about this period),[171] it is certain that both these texts were

[168] On the traditional association of tyranny with youth, see this chapter, n. 86.

[169] Hdn 2.4.2; see Sidebottom (1998), 2807; Marasco (1998), 2850.

[170] i.e. *τὰ ἐς τὸν Τυανέα Ἀπολλώνιον*. The title *Lives of the sophists* (*βίοι σοφιστῶν*) may owe its currency to Eunapius (*VS* 454), rather than to Philostratus himself: see C. P. Jones (1974), 11.

[171] See Muenscher (1907); Solmsen (1940); G. Anderson (1986), 291–6; Flinterman (1995), 5–14; and esp. de Lannoy (1997).

composed by the same author, as the latter text cites the former (referring to an anecdote which 'was told in my composition in honour of Apollonius', εἴρηται . . . ἐν τοῖς ἐς Ἀπολλώνιον, *VS* 570).[172] This author's full name was, most likely, Lucius Flavius Philostratus, as recorded on an inscription commemorating the 'hoplite general' in Athens of that name, a reference to an important (non-military) position that involved the control of trade and the supervising of ephebes.[173] His works manifest a keenness to parade contacts with the imperial household: the *Apollonius* tells us that the text was commissioned by Julia Domna, wife of the emperor Septimius Severus (1.3);[174] *Letter* 73 (probably also composed by this Philostratus) is addressed to the same empress, and while one should not necessarily assume that the addressee is genuine in a letter that refers to Plutarch as if he were still alive (a literary conceit modelled on Pl. *Phaedr.* 269a–e; 278b–d),[175] it is unsurprising that an author who claims to have belonged to the 'circle' (κύκλος) of the empress (*VA* 1.3) should wish to present himself as on epistolary terms with her.[176] A further instance of Philostratus' parading of connections comes in the dedication of the *Lives of the sophists* to a certain consul called Gordian; the most likely candidate is the future emperor Gordian I.[177] Philostratus thus was, or wanted his readers to think that he was, very closely linked with imperial power. In his literary works, the figure of

[172] Even so, the order of composition of the two texts remains debated: Bowie (1978), 1669 suggests an overlapping period of composition.

[173] *IG*^{2} 2.1803; Traill (1971), 321–6 (no. 13). Follet (1976), 101–2 argues as forcibly as the evidence permits, against Traill, for the identification with our Philostratus. For the non-military nature of the post of hoplite general, see *VS* 526, and further Sarikakis (1976), 11–25.

[174] The lack of a formal dedication is not evidence that Julia was dead by the time of publication: see Bowie (1978), 1670 n. 71.

[175] As observed by G. Anderson (1977); see also Penella (1979*a*).

[176] See Bowersock (1969), 101–7 for critical discussion of Julia's 'circle'.

[177] As argued for by Bowersock (1969), 7–8; Nutton (1970); Avotins (1978); G. Anderson (1986), 297–8; Flinterman (1995), 26–7. Whether, as Avotins and Flinterman claim, the *Lives of the sophists* can therefore be dated to 237–8, when Gordian's proconsulate of Africa is attested, remains unclear in the light of the paucity of evidence concerning Gordian's life. The central problem with the identification with Gordian I lies with Philostratus' reference to him as 'in a line of descent from Herodes' (ἐς Ἡρώδην τὸν σοφιστὴν ἀναφέροντι, *VS* 479): the genealogies of Gordian I and Gordian II are unclear, but a descent from Herodes seems more probable in the case of the latter, and so Barnes (1968) argues he is Philostratus' honorand. Nutton, however, followed by Anderson, argues that Philostratus is referring to literary, not filial, succession. It is not clear how the debate could move beyond speculation.

Dio Chrysostom allows him the opportunity to explore many of the issues pertinent to the relationship of a Greek *pepaideumenos* to imperial power.[178] Philostratus' representations of Dio constitute an important stage in the latter's 'mythicization', a process that became increasingly intense in the later Roman and early Byzantine empires[179]—although it began, of course, with Dio himself, always his own most artful biographer. Philostratus, however, provides us with the fullest early response to Dio's self-dramatization.

Let us consider first the earlier work, *Apollonius*. In the course of this laudatory biography of the first-century holy man, Dio appears at one crucial moment: together with Euphrates, the three philosophers meet with the emperor Vespasian and consider the ideal constitution (5.27–40). Dio's *Kingships* are a resonant intertext for this venture into political theory, although (as we shall see) he has some surprising twists in store for the reader who is familiar with those texts. In addition, Philostratus emphasizes the aspect of Dio's orations that we have observed above, namely their rhetorical qualities and the author's ingenious facility with self-dramatization: 'Dio's philosophy seemed too rhetorical to Apollonius' (*ἡ δὲ τοῦ Δίωνος φιλοσοφία ῥητορικωτέρα τῷ Ἀπολλωνίῳ ἐφαίνετο*, 5.40; see also *Letters of Apollonius* 9). Although Apollonius counts Dio as his closest friend,[180] the latter represents an antitype of slippery sophistry to which Apollonius, the true philosopher possessed of divine wisdom, is opposed.

At times, however, Apollonius appears to be constructed more in the likeness of the principles Dio narrativized by his own orations. The drama of *Apollonius* is staged against the first-century backdrop of varying degrees of warmth and hostility in emperors' treatment of philosophers, a backdrop that (as we saw above) is crucial to Dio's own self-dramatization.[181] Like Dio, Apollonius is prosecuted by Domitian (8.1–10); and, again like Dio, he delivers a laudatory oration upon kingship, although to Vespasian and not to Trajan (5.35). The difference between the two lies in Apollonius' superhuman qualities: as a *theios anēr* ('divine man'),[182] Apollonius outstrips his mortal counterpart,

[178] On Philostratus' Hellenism, see further Follet (1991).

[179] Brancacci (1986).

[180] Philostr. *VA* 8.7, section (ii) in the Loeb edition's helpful subdivisions.

[181] On Apollonius' relationship with emperors, see Flinterman (1995), ch. 4.

[182] Apollonius' divinity is alluded to at 2.40; 5.36; 7.38; 8.15. Bieler (1935–6) is

both bamboozling Domitian in the trial and contradicting Dio during the course of the debate.

So Apollonius outphilosophizes his prototype. On occasion, he even seems to excel in Dionic sophistry. Several scholars have noted the programmatic importance of the comparison at the outset between Apollonius and the tricky Egyptian Proteus, described as 'variable (*poikilos*), taking different forms at different times' and 'too elusive to be captured' (ποικίλος . . . ἄλλοτε ἄλλος . . . κρείττων τοῦ ἁλῶναι, 1.4).[183] Since Plato, Proteus has been a common *comparandus* for sophists.[184] Although a major theme of the text, and particularly of the trial scene that concludes it, is taken up with establishing that Apollonius is a philosopher rather than a *goēs* ('wizard', a term often associated with sophistry),[185] the text at one point seems to contradict its own denial. Apollonius asks Domitian how he thinks he can imprison him, if he is a *goēs*, in which case he would be able to escape (7.34); shortly afterwards, however, he miraculously slips his leg out of its fetter (7.38)![186] As we have seen in our discussions of Dio, the term 'philosopher' can mark a differential positioning rather than an absolute state. To style someone a philosopher is not to engage in a foundational act of

fundamental on the typology of the θεῖος ἀνήρ (in which category he includes Apollonius: see esp. 25, 28, 58, 94, 119). On the transgressive nature of such men, between 'godlike' and 'divine', see Cox (1983), 19–23. The argument of Belloni (1980), contrasting Apollonius' divinely inspired σοφία with that of earlier 'empirical' philosophers is, however, overly crude: as Reitzenstein (1906), 51 already saw, Philostratus underplays the revelatory aspects of his subject's wisdom.

[183] See G. Anderson (1986), 138, 144, 227; Flinterman (1995), 52.

[184] Pl. *Euthyphr.* 15d; *Euthyd.* 288b; *Ion* 541e; see also Athen. *Deipn.* 258a; Hld. *Aeth.* 2.24.4; Nonn. *Dion.* 1.14. The 'sophist' Peregrinus was nicknamed Proteus: see *VS* 563–4; Luc. *Peregr.* 1; *Demon.* 21; *Adu. indoct.* 14. According to the *Suda*, Philostratus 'the Lemnian' (i.e. the author of *VA*) 'wrote a *Proteus the dog, or the Sophist*' (ἔγραψε . . . Πρωτέα κύνα ἢ σοφιστήν, *Suda* Φ 422), probably dealing with Peregrinus (Korver 1950: 326; Bowersock 1969: 3). It is possible (but unlikely: de Lannoy 1997: 2398), however, that two separate works are alluded to here (i.e. Πρωτεύς and κύων ἢ σοφιστής). On the 'sophistry' of the *VA*, see G. Anderson (1986), 121–53; (1994), 71–2. On the origins of the Proteus legend, see O'Nolan (1960).

[185] Also an intertextual assertion on Philostratus' part, denying earlier accusations of Apollonian *goēteia*: see Luc. *Alex.* 5; Cass. Dio 77.18. 4; Orig. *Contr. Cels.* 6.41. For *goēteia* and sophistry, see e.g. Pl. *Symp.* 203d: 'a cunning *goēs*, a sorcerer, and a sophist' (δεινὸς γόης καὶ φαρμακεὺς καὶ σοφιστής); Dem. *De coron.* 276. In Philostratus' sophisticizing account, the associated qualities of cunning and trickery are expropriated into a more positive context; but even so, I have been unable to find a laudatory usage of the term. The speculation of Burkert (1962) that *goēs* once meant 'shaman' seems overly speculative.

[186] See Koskenniemi (1991), 13 n. 51.

definition, but to initiate an ongoing process whereby the 'other' ('sophist', *goēs*) is excluded. The pleasure of reading Apollonius lies in Philostratus' teasing his reader with the possibility of the return of the other: in the final analysis, there is a marked ambiguity as to whether Apollonius is a practitioner of sophistry and *goēteia*.

A similar equivocation is attached to the status of the text itself. Is it a pious biography or a playful exercise in sophistry? Modern scholars have often vainly sought in *Apollonius* the 'truth' about the 'real' Apollonius (attested in various other sources);[187] but, as less credulous commentators have observed, Philostratus' primary concern does not lie in accurate historical record.[188] Indeed, he even seems actively to play with the boundary between truth and fiction. At first sight, Philostratus appears keen to stress the truthfulness of his text, through his invention of the Damis-memoirs as a *Beglaubigungsapparat* or 'plausibility-enhancing device' (1.3)[189] and his agonistic rejection of the account of Moeragenes, 'who was extremely ignorant about the man's life' (πολλὰ . . . τῶν περὶ τὸν ἄνδρα ἀγνοήσαντι, 1.3).[190] Yet as recent scholars have emphasized, the *Apollonius* presents itself as a generic admixture, a combination of fictionality and 'factuality'.[191] The text constructs a

[187] Luc. *Alex.* 5; Cass. Dio 77.18.1–4; see also the letters attributed to Apollonius (most readily available in the edition of Penella 1979*b*). Apollonius is often cited in later antiquity as a pagan counterpart (and antitype) to Christ: for brief discussion and references, see Francis (1995), 83–4 n. 1; Swain (1996), 382–3.

[188] Bowie (1978), building on Meyer (1917). Bowie (pp. 1663–7) argues that the *VA* plays on its generic affinity to the novel: see also Swain (1991), 150; Bowie (1994*b*); G. Anderson (1996); also Reardon (1971), 189–90; Hägg (1983), 115–17; Reardon (1991), 147–8; Billault (1991). Other scholars, however, consider it to be, at least partially, historically accurate, e.g. Jackson (1984); Dzielska (1986); Bowersock (1989), 97; Puskás (1991); André (1992). None of these attempts to prove the veracity of the text ultimately convinces, and Bowie's conclusions should be upheld: for crucial objections to the use of Eastern literary traditions to support the *VA*, see G. Anderson (1986), 173 n. 106; Koskenniemi (1991), 10 n. 34. Koskenniemi (1991), 83–4 pertinently objects to the alternative theory of G. Anderson (1986), 135–73, who uses the Persian tradition.

[189] Speyer (1971), 78–9, and esp. Bowie (1978), 1663–7. For more on the 'Damis question', see M. J. Edwards (1991).

[190] On Moeragenes, see Raynor (1984). The title of Moeragenes' work, *Memorabilia of Apollonius of Tyana, magician and philosopher* (τὰ Ἀπολλωνίου τοῦ Τυανέως μάγου καὶ φιλοσόφου ἀπομνημονευμάτα), is recorded at Orig. *Contr Cels.* 6.41. On Maximus of Aegeae, also cited by Philostratus as a source (1.3), see Graf (1984–5). Most recently on the sources, see Flinterman (1995), 67–88 (though over-credulous).

[191] Bowie (1994*b*), 194. Philostratus himself hints that not everything he writes is true: at one point in the Indian episode, he comments 'it would be profitable

hierarchy of truth over fiction, integrity over manipulation, and then playfully undermines its own claims to primacy in these terms. The *Apollonius* is as tricky and elusive as its subject. We should never be lured into treating this as historical biography, any more than 'straight' hagiography. Like its subject, the text itself partakes of a characteristically Dionic ambivalence, oscillating between principled, philosophical integrity and ludic, rhetorical mask-making. Yet it is not simply a matter of Dio's exerting an inert 'influence' upon Philostratus: as we shall see, *Apollonius* seeks actively and dynamically to 'trump' its literary model, constructing its place in literary history agonistically by supplanting its celebrated forebear. Dio's *Kingships* represent both a privileged 'model' for Philostratus' Apollonius and a counter-paradigm proving how weak is a mere mortal's attempt to confront Roman power.

Philostratus' 'king-making' scene in Alexandria involving Apollonius, Vespasian, Dio, and Euphrates (5.27–38) is, in historical terms, fictitious.[192] The tripartite constitutional discussion is, in fact, modelled closely upon a literary source, Herodotus' 'Persian debate', where the three speakers argue strongly for the primacy of monarchy, aristocracy, and democracy (3.80–2).[193] The debate in the *Life of Apollonius*, however, pays little attention to oligarchy (although it is not omitted: Dio rates it highest of all, 5.34), focusing largely on the dyad of monarchy (Apollonius) and democracy (Euphrates), with Dio suggesting a plebiscite to decide between the two. Apollonius' expression of preference for monarchy (suggesting the egregious, 'regal' nature of his philosophical persona), strongly evokes the topoi of the kingship

neither to believe nor disbelieve everything' (*κέρδος ⟨ἂν⟩ εἴη μήτε πιστεύειν, μήτε ἀπιστεῖν πᾶσιν* (3.45; cf. Hdt. 4.96.1). Again, he comments of the *account* of the pearl-divers that 'it is a most pleasant fabrication' (*πλάττεται ἥδιστος*, 3.57). At 5.14 Apollonius argues for the edifying value of 'mythology' (*μυθολογία*) such as is composed by Aesop.

[192] Bowie (1978), 1660–2; Brancacci (1986), 71–2; Flinterman (1995), 137 n. 42. For the historical details of Vespasian's visit to Alexandria, see Heinrichs (1968). The assertion of Derchain and Hubaux (1953), that Philostratus preserves traces of a genuine, Serapist acclamation of Vespasian, is rightly dismissed by Bowie (1978), 1660–2 and Levi (1981), 292.

[193] Flinterman (1995), 194–5; Swain (1996), 389. On Hdt. 3.80–2, see Lasserre (1976); Bushnell (1990), 11–13; McGlew (1993), 33. Constitutional debates, however, were also composed in the intervening period: see Polyb. 6; Plut. *De unius*; Max. Tyr. 14.7.

tradition (the titular phrase *peri basileias*, 'on kingship', is actually used at *VA* 5.36). Apollonius urges Vespasian to use Euphrates and Dio as *xymbouloi* ('philosophical advisers', *VA* 5.28; Vespasian later offers to make the latter two *xymbouloi*, 5.32), and Vespasian replies with an apophthegm that resonates with the pieties of the kingship tradition: 'May I rule over wise men, and wise men over me' (σοφῶν μὲν ἐγὼ ἄρχοιμι, σοφοὶ δὲ ἐμοῦ, 5.28).

The 'king-making' scene, then, serves a literary purpose (rather than simply recording a real event). The whole text constructs and explores the sophic persona of Apollonius in a variety of contexts, and this particular episode serves to show that, despite the otherworldly nature of his wisdom ('I have no interest in politics', he says at one point, 'for I live under the gods': ἐμοὶ πολιτείας μὲν οὐδεμιᾶς μέλει, ζῶ γὰρ ὑπὸ τοῖς θεοῖς, 5.35),[194] he can deliver an effective kingship speech. Throughout this sequence of events, Philostratus underlines his subject's philosophical qualities by opposing his behaviour to that of inferior philosophers, or emphasizing Vespasian's submissiveness to his suggestions. Thus when Vespasian arrives in Alexandria to the acclamation of the people, Apollonius, unlike all the other philosophers, does not present himself, and shows no eagerness to be involved (5.27).[195] The usual situation is reversed: the emperor is required to ask for an interview with Apollonius, and Dio (who acts as a kind of attendant) avers that the sage has consented. Later, after Apollonius has made initial pronouncements on kingship, the emperor replies: 'I am your follower, for I consider everything that issues from you to be divine: teach me all that a good king should do' (ἕπομαι δή σοι, θεῖον γὰρ ἡγοῦμαι τὸ ἐκ σοῦ πᾶν, καὶ ὁπόσα χρὴ τὸν ἀγαθὸν βασιλέα πράττειν δίδασκε, 5.36). Although imperial submissiveness ('I am your follower') should never be read as a simple abrogation of power (since the surprise generated by this staged abasement subtly reinforces the idea of the emperor's exceptional position), the hierarchical dynamics of authority are conspicuously marked here. Philostratus is less interested in developing any idealization

[194] This does not mean that Apollonius is an apolitical philosopher, as argued by Billault (1990): coming as it does within a knowing political oration, it constitutes a rhetorical disavowal ('unaccustomed as I am . . .'), rather than a factual statement.

[195] This reluctance to involve himself in politics recalls that of the good philosopher in Plato's ideal city, who is initially unwilling to assume the kingship (*Resp.* 521b).

of Vespasian[196] than in constructing Apollonius' identity, in emphasizing his pedagogical role and its 'divine'[197] aspect.

The function of the scene is to demonstrate that, among the many facets of Apollonius' philosophy, he is an excellent pedagogical adviser of kings. When asked for counsel, Apollonius replies that he cannot teach kingship (οὐ διδακτά με . . . ἐρωτᾷς, 5.36), for it is 'the greatest thing among mortals, and unteachable' (μέγιστον μὲν τῶν κατ' ἀνθρώπους, ἀδίδακτον δέ, 5.36). The point is not that Apollonius does not know—he proceeds to offer advice concerning 'how it seems to me you would do best by acting' (ὁπόσα . . . μοι δοκεῖς πράττων ὑγιῶς ἂν πρᾶξαι, 5.36), in the standard kingship mode—but that the adviser cannot ensure proper *reception* of the advice.[198] There is a strong echo here of Dio's theories about ideal kingship as a happy combination of *paideia* and (crucially) a suitably receptive nature.[199] The note of caution sounded here turns out to be provident, since Vespasian does turn out to be, to an extent, deaf to Apollonius' advice: his repeal of the freedom of Greece is the reason for Apollonius' refusal subsequently to meet the emperor (5.41).[200] Despite the text's very marked proclamation that Vespasian is a 'good' emperor, he does not ultimately conform either exactly or consistently to the absolute paradigm of the philosopher-monarch. The Alexandrian episode of the *Apollonius* is not simply Apollonius', or indeed Philostratus', proclamation of a political ideology that supports Vespasian's (or, indeed, any other) monarchy,

[196] This is not to deny that Vespasian is presented as a good ruler: his reign is implicitly contrasted with the previous 'tyrannies' (5.27; Vitellius is singled out: 5.29, 32, 33), and approved by both Apollonius (5.28, 31, 32, 35) and, albeit to a limited extent the narrator (5.27: Vespasian converses 'nobly and gently', γενναῖά τε καὶ ἥμερα). On the other hand, he is criticized for removing Greece's liberty: see the following paragraph.

[197] This use of ἐκ to mark the action of an agent may also convey a suggestion of divinity, recalling some famous uses of the phrase ἐκ Διός: Hom. *Il.* 1.63; 2.70; etc. and esp. Hes. *Th.* 96 (= *Hom. Hymn.* 25.4; Call. *Hymn.* 1.78); Arat. *Phaen.* 1.

[198] In an erotic context, compare Ach. Tat. *L&C* 1.10.2, where Clinias, the *erōtodidaskalos* ('teacher of desire') declines to teach Clitophon the method of seduction on the grounds that it is impossible, but agrees to elucidate 'as much as is common to all situations and not dependent upon a lucky break' (ὅσα . . . ἐστι κοινὰ καὶ μὴ τῆς εὐκαίρου τύχης).

[199] Dio Chr. 1.8; above, 'Greek Pedagogy and Roman Rule'.

[200] Vespasian's judgement is also called into question when he refers to Claudius as 'excellent' (χρηστός, *VA* 5.32): at 5.27 we are specifically told by the narrator that Claudius was not an 'excellent' (χρηστός) ruler.

but part of an ongoing attempt to characterize Apollonius as a vehicle of divine wisdom.

A central device in Philostratus' extolling of Apollonius consists in the 'zero-sum game' whereby he is praised to the detriment of other philosophers, notably, in this episode, Dio and Euphrates.[201] Philostratus carefully sets up the debate on kingship as a form of competition for status between the three philosophers. After Apollonius' initial meeting with Vespasian behind closed doors, Dio and Euphrates ask him *philotimōs* ('zealously', 'competitively', 'aggressively') about the *xynousia* ('meeting'). There are echoes here of the beginning of Plato's *Symposium*, where Apollodorus reports the enquiries of Glaucon concerning the *synousia* ('meeting') of Socrates and Agathon (172b–c); yet by using the adverb *philotimōs*, Philostratus strikes a different note, placing this particular discussion under the sign of agonistic jealousy.[202] Apollonius has gained admission to Vespasian, and Dio and Euphrates feel their status impugned by their failure to do so.

The distinction between Apollonius and the other two philosophers is further underlined by the spatial dynamics that separate the exterior from the interior, both literal (the inner room where the emperor remains) and metaphorical (his trust and confidence). In a text that constructs Rome as the centre of the world, the emphasis upon centres and margins of power plays a fundamental symbolic role.[203] When Apollonius meets Dio and Euphrates, they are waiting 'at the door' (ἐπὶ θύραις), but the former is 'summoned in first' (ἐσκληθεὶς . . . πρῶτος, 5.31). Apollonius asks Vespasian to allow them in too, to which he responds 'I keep my doors unlocked to wise men, but to you I have decided to open my breast as well' (ἀκλείστους . . . θύρας παρέχω σοφοῖς ἀνδράσι, σοὶ δὲ καὶ τὰ στέρνα ἀνεῴχθαι δοκεῖ τἀμά, 5.31). This sense that Apollonius enters not only the emperor's house but also his heart is confirmed later on, where Vespasian responds to Apollonius' speech with the words 'if you dwelled in my heart, you could not more clearly announce my thoughts' (εἰ τὴν ψυχὴν . . . τὴν ἐμὴν ᾤκεις, οὐκ ἂν οὕτω σαφῶς ἃ ἐνεθυμήθην ἀπήγγειλας, 5.36). Whatever access Euphrates and Dio have to Vespasian, Apollonius always has more.

[201] Brancacci (1986), 74.

[202] On *philotimia*, see Introd., n. 20.

[203] Elsner (1997*b*), 32–4 on Rome as the centre of the world in *Apollonius*; see Geertz (1993) on 'symbolic centres', with Ch. 5, 'The Wrongs of Passage: *On salaried posts*'.

The dialectics of power, quadrangulated between the emperor and the three philosophers, are also articulated through the theme of visuality. The text repeatedly marks philosophical status in terms of concealment and visibility. In this instance, however, it also articulates different statuses within Greek *paideia*. When Apollonius meets Dio and Euphrates at the door, he reports what Vespasian said at their private interview, but 'kept quiet about his own opinions' (*τὰς δὲ αὑτοῦ δόξας ἀπεσιώπησεν*, 5.31). This is in marked contrast with the behaviour of Euphrates and Dio. The former at first, during Apollonius' exchange with Vespasian, 'was invisibly jealous of Apollonius, observing how the king paid more attention to him than consultants do to oracles; presently, however, he welled up beyond what was moderate, and raised his voice higher than it usually was' (*ὁ δ' Εὐφράτης ἀφανῶς μὲν ἤδη ἐβάσκαινε τῶι Ἀπολλωνίωι προσκείμενον αὐτῶι τὸν βασιλέα ὁρῶν μᾶλλον ἢ τοῖς χρηστηρίοις τοὺς ἐς αὐτὰ ἥκοντας, ἀνοιδήσας δὲ ὑπὲρ τὸ μέτρον τότε καὶ τὴν φωνὴν ἐπάρας παρ' ὃ εἰώθει* . . . 5.33). Euphrates can only repress his feelings 'invisibly' for a while, before he goes beyond 'what is moderate' (*τὸ μέτρον*): in Greek psychics, the brewing of a storm standardly images a dominance of passion over reason.[204] Moderation is here associated with the ability to control not only one's internal emotions but also the external symptoms of those emotions. In this theatrical competition for philosophical authority, traces of loss of control, such as raising one's voice above its normal pitch, lose one vital prestige. Philostratus' narrative strategy here reinforces this sense of theatrical agonistics. Although the episode is recounted by an 'external narrator' (i.e. not one of the participants), it is 'focalized' through their eyes.[205] Euphrates 'observes' (*ὁρῶν*) Vespasian's affection for Apollonius, but he also becomes an object of visibility: he moves from 'invisible' (*ἀφανῶς*) jealousy to betraying himself. By pointing out the index that gives away his inner feelings (namely the raising of his voice above its usual pitch), Philostratus re-enacts for the reader the intense atmosphere of scrutiny that surrounds this contest for sophic prestige.

Similarly, 'during Euphrates' speech Apollonius saw that Dio was agreeing with this opinion, since he revealed (*epedēlou*) as much by nodding in approval of his words' (*τοσαῦτα τοῦ Εὐφράτου*

[204] Gill (1983), 481.

[205] For these terms, see most conveniently Bal (1997), 16–31, 142–61.

εἰπόντος ὁρῶν ὁ Ἀπολλώνιος τὸν Δίωνα προστιθέμενον τῆι γνώμηι, τουτὶ γὰρ καὶ τῶι νεύματι ἐπεδήλου καὶ οἷς ἐπήινει λέγοντα, 5.34). The narrative is here focalized through Apollonius, who 'reads' Dio's sentiments from an external index (nodding). Apollonius is the watcher, not the watched. Possession of the gaze implicitly empowers Apollonius (a technique also used, as we shall see in the following chapter, by Lucian in his satire *On salaried posts*). Indeed, in this instance, even Vespasian, whom we would expect to be in ultimate control, is watched by Apollonius: 'his face revealed (*epedēlou*) the conflict of his opinion' (τὸ πρόσωπον τοῦ βασιλέως ἀγῶνα ἐπεδήλου τῆς γνώμης, 5.35). (That it is again Apollonius through whom this realization is focalized is indicated by the following sentence, where his next speech is presented as motivated by this observation.) The same word, 'revealed' (*epedēlou*), is used (in the same form), of *Vespasian's* exposure of his feelings: Apollonius is the primary observer of all of the participants, including the emperor. Apollonius has usurped the position that 'should' belong to Vespasian, a technique for constructing sophic authority that we have already seen. Presently, the emperor assumes his 'proper' role in this paideutic contest, that of acute observer: when Euphrates, seeking to impugn Apollonius, makes a barbed comment, the emperor 'realizes' (ξυνῆκεν) and changes the subject (5.37). In contrast to the emperor's perceptiveness, Euphrates 'failed to notice that he was slandering himself' (ἔλαθε διαβαλὼν ἑαυτόν, 5.37). Even so, the emperor 'did not reveal (*epedēlou*) any anger towards these events' (οὐδὲ ἐπεδήλου τι ὀργῆς πρὸς ταῦτα, 5.37). Once again this word *epedēlou*, although this time it is used in the negative: Vespasian has assumed the position of guardian of the gaze, and will not betray himself to the view of others. Power is closely allied to the ability to perceive the feelings of others, and to conceal one's own.

Vespasian has now shifted roles. The surprise in the earlier part of the dialogue on power, set up at first sight as a contest between three *pepaideumenoi* for the emperor's ear, lay in the exchange of positions between Apollonius and Vespasian, so that the former became the arbiter and the latter subject to scrutiny. Now, however, the emperor has become a judge of the three philosophers, and we move to his verdict: Euphrates he suspects but treats with respect, Dio he likes and appreciates as an orator, but Apollonius he 'submits to' (ὑπέκειτο, 5.37). By allowing both Apollonius and Vespasian in turn to assume the position of controlling viewer, Philostratus ingeniously implies simultaneously that (i) Apollonius, as observer par excellence, occupies the position of ultimate authority in this scene, and (ii) in the eyes of Vespasian, Apollonius is adjudged the victor in the competition for paideutic status with Dio and Euphrates. Apollonius both wins the contest and transcends its terms.

As regards the content of Apollonius' speech, most modern scholars have found themselves disappointed. Flinterman, for example, notes that much (though not all) of it is hackneyed, explaining that 'speeches to monarchs on how to exercise their power were not expected to display originality'.[206] In particular, the speech appears to owe much to Dio's *Kingships*: the analogy between the king and a shepherd (5.35) is strongly reminiscent of that of Dio,[207] as is the stress upon the need to observe the law (5.36),[208] and the idea of the unteachability of kingship (5.36),[209] and the need for the king, who has been granted his rule by the gods, to cultivate the gods (5.36).[210] The point, however, is not that Apollonius' speech is unremarkable and assimilable to any other kingship speech, but that it is carefully situated at a point in time substantially earlier than Dio's *Kingships*, with Dio himself listening in. By 'pre-empting' Dio, Philostratus simultaneously appropriates for Apollonius the dramatic power of Dio's composition and implicitly divests the latter—now 'exposed' as a mere imitator—of all originary power. On behalf of his subject, Philostratus undertakes a negotiation of literary posterity that Harold Bloom styles 'kenosis': 'his stance *appears* to be that of his precursor . . . but the meaning of the stance is undone; the stance is *emptied* of its priority, which is a kind of godhood'.[211] There are, however, risks in this process: in order to mark the (supposedly) derivative nature of Dio's texts, Philostratus is constrained to reduce Apollonius' own speech to a parade of banal clichés. In

[206] Flinterman (1995), 208–16; quotation from p. 208. Flinterman also notes certain non-conventional features, which he attributes either to the specificities of the historical situation under Vespasian or to Philostratus' 3rd-cent. perspective.

[207] Dio 3.41; cf. Pl. *Polit.* 261d–262a, both building upon the Homeric notion of the 'shepherd of the people' (ποιμὴν λαῶν). On the history of this comparison, see Schofield (1991), 104, 107–8.

[208] Dio Chr. 1.43; 3.10, 39, 43; Flinterman (1995), 211.

[209] Dio Chr. 4.26–35; Desideri (1978), 340 n. 25.

[210] Dio Chr. 1.11–14; 3.51; Flinterman (1995), 212.

[211] Bloom (1997), 90.

Bloom's idiolect, this 'kenosis' is 'a self-emptying that seeks to defend against the father [Dio], yet radically undoes the son [Philostratus/Apollonius]'.[212]

Philostratus' 'kenosis' of Dio's *Kingships* has another twist. Like Apollonius and Euphrates, Dio himself delivers an oration upon the theme of the best political set-up at Rome. Surprisingly, for any of Philostratus' readers aware of the *Kingships* (as most, presumably, would have been), Dio presents himself as a partisan not of monarchy but of aristocracy: in the circumstances of the current political crisis he proposes a free vote for the people of Rome (5.34).[213] The discrepancy between this oligarchic Dio and the monarchist of the *Kingships* has caused some puzzlement among scholars. Brancacci, for example, considers whether or not Dio's views evolved between Vespasian's accession and that of Trajan.[214] Although ultimately he rejects that explanation (arguing instead that Philostratus has distorted his source material), it contains an important insight. If we accept the principle that Philostratus expects his readers to know Dio's *Kingships*, then it follows that he is *deliberately* positing a discontinuity of expressed beliefs between the two stages of Dio's career. Without stating as much—and without having to do so—he implies both that Dio is a fickle philosopher and that he has cribbed his opinions on kingship from Apollonius. What more would we expect from the figure whose 'philosophy seemed too rhetorical to Apollonius' (ἡ . . . φιλοσοφία ῥητορικωτέρα τῷ Ἀπολλωνίῳ ἐφαίνετο, 5.40)?

Philostratus' intertextual (ab)use of Dio's *Kingships* is ingenious. On the one hand, as 'source' texts for his literary project, they represent an important repertory of ideas and drama. The representation of Apollonius as an adviser of kings depends for much of its power upon the scenarios constructed by Dio. On the other hand, Philostratus strategically sets about emptying Dio's self-representation by literary kenosis, ironically suggesting that, so far from Philostratus modelling his subject on Dio, Dio appropriated his own dramatic role as imperial *symboulos* ('adviser') from Apollonius. Dio, Philostratus makes it clear, is cunningly rhetorical, and the self-projection we read in the *Kingships* is implicitly subverted. In this respect, Philostratus amplifies one feature that

212 Bloom (1997), 90.

213 For the political-philosophical roots of Dio's position, see Flinterman (1995), 197–9.

214 Brancacci (1986), 72–3.

we have already located in our discussion of the *Kingships* themselves, namely the pleasure in mask-wearing and mask-shifting; but whereas Dio emphasizes the transferability of his identities in a game of ironic self-subversion, Philostratus does so in order to impugn his literary model to the benefit of his own subject.

Dio's ability to manipulate personae is also highlighted in the *Lives of the sophists*, albeit in a rather different way, as befits the differing aims of the two texts. Where *Apollonius* focuses monophthalmically upon its central figure (the singular focus marking the exceptional status of the 'divine man', as in the Gospels and Lucian's satirical *Alexander the false prophet*), the *Lives of the sophists* presents a diverse array of colourful characters, who represent a plurality of (sometimes conflicting) paradigms of sophistic performance.[215] Although included within a group that is in a sense marginalized by Philostratus, namely 'those who philosophize in the guise of sophistry' (*τοὺς φιλοσοφήσαντας ἐν δόξῃ τοῦ σοφιστεῦσαι* *VS* 479, 492) rather than acting as sophists *tout court*, the account of Dio in the *Lives of the sophists* is the first of major length in the text.[216] After a brief opening discussion of his style of speaking (*VS* 486–7), Philostratus focuses upon the aspects of Dio's life that we have considered above, namely his relationships with emperors. The reader expects to hear of Dio's celebrated quarrels with emperors, and, sure enough, Philostratus alludes to his avoidance of Rome, 'for fear of tyrannies in the capital, by which all philosophy was being driven out' (*δέει τῶν κατὰ τὴν πόλιν τυραννίδων, ὑφ' ὧν ἠλαύνετο φιλοσοφία πᾶσα*, 488). This is familiar Dionic territory: the philosopher makes a principled stand against tyranny. Or is it? In fact, in the key sentence in which Philostratus introduces the theme of philosophy and kingship, he specifically *denies* that Dio was exiled:

[215] The bibliography on the *VS* is small and usually unappreciative (e.g. Papalas 1979–80: 95: 'lack of a sense of balance . . . lop-sided'; Bowersock 1989: 95: 'inadequate, even injudicious'; Wardy 1996: 6: 'second- (or third-) rate . . . mediocrity'). Even G. Anderson (1986), who is largely sympathetic, does not go beyond e.g. 'journalistic aplomb' (38) and 'sophistic sweep . . . marred by the very nature of his eclectic sketches' (115). On the sources, see C. P. Jones (1974); Swain (1991). On individual episodes, see Pack (1947); Norman (1953); Papalas (1978; 1979–80); Schmitz (1996); Whitmarsh (1998*a*); Campanile (1999). Rothe (1989) provides commentary on selected lives.

[216] Philostr. *VS* 486–8, 57 lines of Teubner text, more than the total devoted to all the previous biographies (54 lines); it is also the first biography to take place in identifiably Roman times. Of the 57 lines, 31 are concerned with Dio's imperial sojourn abroad and his return.

The man's exit (*parodos*) towards the Getic peoples I cannot call exile, since he was not commanded into exile, nor a mere sojourn, since he disappeared from view, stealing himself away from the eyes and ears of men, doing various things in various lands for fear of the tyrannies in the capital, by which all philosophy was being driven out.

τὴν δὲ ἐς τὰ Γετικὰ ἔθνη πάροδον τοῦ ἀνδρὸς φυγὴν μὲν οὐκ ἀξιῶ ὀνομάζειν, ἐπεὶ μὴ προσετάχθη αὐτῶι φυγεῖν, οὐδὲ ἀποδημίαν, ἐπειδὴ τοῦ φανεροῦ ἐξέστη κλέπτων ἑαυτὸν ὀφθαλμῶν τε καὶ ὤτων καὶ ἄλλα ἐν ἄλληι γῆι πράττων δέει τῶν κατὰ τὴν πόλιν τυραννίδων, ὑφ' ὧν ἠλαύνετο φιλοσοφία πᾶσα. (488)

Scholars have speculated as to why Philostratus denies that his subject was exiled,[217] but it is important to read these comments in the light of Dio's own self-projection in his orations as a fearless, manly exile. Philostratus is cleverly subverting Dio's own role-playing: he was (in his biographer's eyes) not punished for his outspoken criticism of the regime, rather he timidly stole himself from view. Dio is presented as a showman who performs before the 'eyes and ears of men', but who, during Domitian's principate, makes a crafty 'exit' (the *parodos* is the passageway on- and off-stage on either side of the Greek theatre). As in the *Apollonius*, Philostratus underlines Dio's rhetorical trickiness and subtly subverts his own self-mythicizing account. Moreover, this passage (not for the last time in Philostratus' account of Dio) suggests affinities between the philosophical sophist who did 'various things in various lands' (*ἄλλα ἐν ἄλληι γῆι*) and the arch-trickster Odysseus, another man who disappeared from view 'and saw the cities and learned the thought of many men' (*πολλῶν δ' ἀνθρώπων ἴδεν ἄστεα καὶ νόον ἔγνω*, Hom. *Od.* 1.3). In other words, Philostratus is slyly suggesting what John Moles has argued influentially,[218] namely that Dio's own version of his exile is ingeniously manipulative, employing the techniques of disguise and impersonation in order to perpetuate a heavily loaded perception of himself.

Indeed, Philostratus' account of Dio's exile and return places a heavy emphasis upon his role-playing. Describing his travels, Philostratus tells us that he took two books with him, Plato's

[217] C. P. Jones (1978), 48 suggests that Philostratus conceals this 'blemish' in Dio's biography. Dio's exile under Domitian was not, however, a blemish, but (as the previous chapter sought to show) a mark of particular pride. Von Arnim (1898), 225–6 and Desideri (1978), 36 suggest that Philostratus denies exile to Dio in order to reserve all the kudos of confrontation with Domitian for his hero, Apollonius of Tyana. This is unsatisfactory, not least because Apollonius does not appear directly in the *Lives of the sophists*.

[218] Moles (1978).

Phaedo and Demosthenes' *On the false embassy*. These texts are not simply sustaining reading-matter for the journey:[219] rather, Philostratus is indicating the subtexts that Dio manipulates during his exile. The *Phaedo* tells of the death of Socrates, the greatest philosopher: it focuses upon his calm acceptance of his unjust fate, and provides a clearly positive paradigm for Stoic philosophical resistance. *On the false embassy*, on the other hand, tells of Demosthenes' opposition to a collusion with a tyrant aiming to subdue Greece. These texts are scripts for Dio's performance of the role of martyred champion of free Greece.

When news of Domitian's death reaches the military camp in which Philostratus' Dio happens to be, his performance reaches its peak:

> Dio leaped naked on to a high altar (*bōmos*), and began his harangue with the verse:
>
> Then Odysseus of many counsels stripped himself of his rags
>
> and having said this and thus revealed that he was no beggar, nor what they believed him to be, but Dio the wise (*sophos*), he delivered a spirited and energetic indictment of the tyrant, teaching the soldiers to have better thoughts and do what the Romans wanted.
>
> *ἀλλὰ γυμνὸς ἀναπηδήσας ἐπὶ βωμὸν ὑψηλὸν ἤρξατο τοῦ λόγου ὧδε· "αὐτὰρ ὁ γυμνώθη ῥακέων πολύμητις Ὀδυσσεύς," καὶ εἰπὼν ταῦτα καὶ δηλώσας ἑαυτόν, ὅτι μὴ πτωχός, μηδὲ ὃν ᾤοντο, Δίων δὲ εἴη ὁ σοφός, ἐπὶ μὲν τὴν κατηγορίαν τοῦ τυράννου πολὺς ἔπνευσεν, τοὺς δὲ στρατιώτας ἐδίδαξεν ἀμείνω φρονεῖν τὰ δοκοῦντα Ῥωμαίοις πράττοντας.* (488)

Dio leaps up onto a 'high altar' (*bōmos*)—recalling perhaps the *bōmos* that forms the point of maximal dramatic intensity in a Greek theatre—and delivers a performance. But is it really true to say that Dio had 'revealed himself' (*δηλώσας ἑαυτόν*) here? Is he really 'naked' (*γυμνὸς*)? As Philostratus recounts it, it is precisely at the moment when Dio claims to be revealing himself that he is most masked, that the parallel with Odysseus comes to the fore. As we have earlier had cause to note, an emulation of Odysseus, the arch-emulator, is doubly ironic.[220] Philostratus is again drawing attention to Dio's rhetorical manipulations. Indeed, it is not simply 'Dio' whom the soldiers see, but Dio 'the *sophos*': does the word *sophos* here mean 'wise', 'clever', or 'crafty'?

The Odyssean comparison can be taken further by considering

[219] C. P. Jones (1978), 48. [220] Above, p. 197.

the precise context in which Dio's Homeric citation originally appears. The line is from the beginning of *Odyssey* 22, where Odysseus leaps onto the 'great threshold' (compare Philostratus' 'high altar') and shoots Antinous, the leader of the suitors. So in Dio's script, as directed by Philostratus, Domitian is playing Antinous, a corrupt usurper of another's property. Dio's indictment of tyranny is a shaft aimed by Greece at the neck of the Roman oppressors. But Odysseus then proceeds to slaughter the remaining suitors, and re-establish his place as rightful ruler; Dio, by way of contrast, quells the mutiny and goes on to take his place beside Trajan on the emperor's chariot. Once again, Dio's 'hard-line' philosophical credentials are stripped away to reveal a manipulator of masks.

But does he really side unequivocally with the Romans? Philostratus apparently tells us that Dio taught the soldiers 'to have better thoughts and do what the Romans wanted'; but the Greek is ambiguous, and could equally well mean 'taught the soldiers, who were doing what the Romans wanted, to think better of it' (*τοὺς δὲ στρατιώτας ἐδίδαξεν ἀμείνω φρονεῖν τὰ δοκοῦντα Ῥωμαίοις πράττοντας*, 488). On this latter interpretation, Dio's actions would encourage not acquiescence to 'the Romans', but resistance. This Dio seems to follow the script of the *Odyssey* much more closely: the soldiers represent not the suitors whom he must slaughter, but Philoetius and Eumaeus, his rustic allies in the battle against those who step in to take the place of the dead Antinous. Yet the Philostratean ambiguity should not be resolved either way: as an undecidable ambiguity, it typifies Dio's own equivocation in the face of Roman power. We never know Dio's true feelings towards Rome, since he only ever presents us with performances.

Continuing the theme of emperors and philosophers, Dio proceeds to the celebrated account of Dio's presence on Trajan's chariot:

> For in fact the persuasion of the man was such as to charm even those who do not accurately understand Greek matters. For example, the Emperor Trajan set him in front of all Rome, by his side on the golden chariot in which the emperors ride in procession when they celebrate their triumphs in war, and often he would turn to Dio and say: 'I do not know what you are saying, but I love you as I love myself.'

καὶ γὰρ ἡ πειθὼ τοῦ ἀνδρὸς οἵα καταθέλξαι καὶ τοὺς μὴ τὰ Ἑλλήνων ἀκριβοῦντας· Τραιανὸς γοῦν ὁ αὐτοκράτωρ ἀναθέμενος αὐτὸν ἐπὶ τῆς Ῥώμης ἐς τὴν χρυσῆν ἅμαξαν, ἐφ' ἧς οἱ βασιλεῖς τὰς ἐκ τῶν πολέμων πομπὰς πομπεύουσιν, ἔλεγε θαμὰ ἐπιστρεφόμενος ἐς τὸν Δίωνα "τί μὲν λέγεις, οὐκ οἶδα, φιλῶ δέ σε ὡς ἐμαυτόν". (488)

Once again, Dio is performing, this time 'in front of all Rome' (as *ἐπὶ τῆς Ῥώμης* should be translated: Wright's 'in Rome' in the Loeb is too weak). Moreover, his rhetorical side is stressed, his persuasion (*peitho*) and ability to charm (*thelgein*), words which have been associated with rhetorical language since Gorgias,[221] and may even remind the reader of Odysseus: as well as the avenging father returned from exile, Odysseus is also the master of duplicity and advantageous manipulation.[222]

The most striking (and famous) aspect of this passage, however, is its emphasis upon Trajan's non-comprehension of Dio's words.[223] There are two points to make here. First, it was traditional for a *triumphator* to procession with a slave belonging to the state beside him in his chariot, reminding him, 'look behind you, remember that you are mortal' (*respice post te, hominem te esse memento*).[224] For Dio to take the place of this slave is an intriguing twist to the power play in Philostratus' anecdote. Does Dio's assumption of the submissive role of the slave represent his passive role in the circuits of power? Yet the slave represents the voice of state duty: Trajan's non-comprehension, then, reflects his failure to recognize the limits of his power, his dangerous excess. Like Pentheus in Euripides' *Bacchae*, Philostratus' Trajan may be seen as a ruler dangerously close to ignorance of the boundaries of monarchical prerogative. Who is in control here? Does the Greek author (Philostratus) control the representation of the Roman emperor, or does the Roman emperor co-opt the Greek philosopher (Dio) to his cause?

[221] e.g. Gorgias fr. 11.10 DK: 'when the power of the spell combined with the soul's perception, it bewitched (*ethelxe*) her and persuaded (*epeise*) her and changed her mind with its wizardry', *συγγινομένη γὰρ τῇ δόξῃ τῆς ψυχῆς ἡ δύναμις τῆς ἐπῳδῆς ἔθελξε καὶ ἔπεισε καὶ μετέστησεν αὐτὴν γοητείαι*. Philostratus also emphasizes Dio's speaking abilities at *VA* 5.37.

[222] On the importance of *thelgein* to the *Odyssey*'s poetics, see Walsh (1984), 14–15. On Odysseus' deceptive faculties, the bibliography is large: see Goldhill (1991), 34, with the references cited there.

[223] The usual point of consideration is the question of whether Trajan would, in fact, have been able to understand Dio: see e.g. Moles (1990), 300; Swain (1996), 194 n. 32, 397.

[224] Versnel (1970), 57.

My second point concerns Trajan's failure to understand 'Greek matters'. It is notoriously difficult to specify exactly what Philostratus means here: scholars usually assume that Philostratus means 'the Greek language', and are content to note that Trajan did in fact receive a Greek education.[225] Yet in this context which stresses Dio's slipperiness and rhetorical manipulation, it is tempting to interpret Philostratus as referring not to Trajan's ignorance of the Greek language, or even of Greek culture, but to his ignorance of the *paideia*, the complex and elaborate behavioural etiquette and linguistic coding assumed to be proper to Greeks.[226] Is Philostratus suggesting that Trajan could not (or, perhaps, would not) comprehend the implications of a Roman *princeps* having a Greek philosopher with him? If this is correct, then Trajan is cast in the role of inexpert reader, a role constructed by Philostratus to emblematize overhasty reading of ingenious, elusive rhetoric (such as, of course, that of the *Lives of the sophists*). Trajan is incapable or unwilling to see behind the superficies, to unpack the sophisticated implications that undermine the prima-facie appearance of support for the principate. Just as Dio's 'opposition' to Domitian is exposed by Philostratus as stage-managed and untruthful, so his 'support' for Trajan is presented as partial and equivocal. There is nothing straight in Dio's relationship with Roman power. At the same time, however, it may be that Philostratus' Trajan is not so naïve: understanding that power consists in spectacle, and that the spectacle of the submission of the *pepaideumenos* is a crucial constituent of the symbolics of Roman power, Trajan may be attempting to frame Dio as a 'sophiste-ornement-du-pouvoir . . . dont les paroles importent moins que leur éclat ou leur chant'.[227] For the theatre of imperial propaganda to be successful, Dio's rhetoric, with all its complexities and ruses, must be systematically misinterpreted as simple, unequivocal support for the establishment.

The presentation of Dio in the *Lives of the sophists*, then, needs to be considered in the light of the recurrent concerns of the *Kingships* themselves with role-playing and impersonation in the creation of the pedagogical relationship between emperor and pedagogue. As Philostratus presents it, Dio cannot be read simply

[225] Moles (1990), 300, with references; Desideri (1991*b*), 3885 n. 9; Swain (1996), 194 n. 32.

[226] See also Schmitz (1996).

[227] Charles-Saget (1986), 112.

as one who 'resisted' Domitian and 'supported' Trajan. As we have seen, Dio's relationship with emperors is characterized by Philostratus as fundamentally 'rhetorical' (tricky and theatrical, as well as eloquent), and little of the image which he presents can be said to be certain. *Paideia*, in this instance, is the locus not for an uncontested display of imperial power, but for a confluence of competing modes of power, some consolidatory, some resistive. This is not to argue that Philostratus presents Dio as directly 'opposing' Roman power, but that the construction of this pedagogical relationship is an uneasy process of negotiation, rather than a simple expression of monarchical power. This negotiation involves threats of violence and coercion (on the emperor's side) and of tyrannicide (on the philosopher's side), which intermittently puncture the veil of intercultural harmony. The pedagogical instruction of the potentate, Philostratus tells us, is a complex business in which multiple positions are staked out and multiple roles are played.

To a degree, Philostratus' own text is necessarily complicit in this equivocation before Roman rule. This is not to say that Dio represents a typical or central paradigm in the *Lives of the sophists*: there are other figures (Polemo, Herodes Atticus) to whom a larger section of the text is devoted, and who embody different modalities of relationship between *paideia* and power; moreover, as noted above, Philostratus marginalizes the group of 'rhetorical philosophers' to which Dio belongs. Nevertheless, by virtue of its length and proximity to the start, the biography of Dio assumes a programmatic role for the reader, inviting attentive interpretation: the focus upon language and understanding necessarily gestures self-referentially towards wider issues in the reading of the *Lives of the sophists* itself. To this extent, the narrative of Dio's life emblematizes the figuring of Philostratus' own writing, one particular (though by no means the exclusive) cipher through which the author explores his own problematical relationship with Roman *imperium*.

CONCLUSION: ON KINGSHIP

The Greek tradition provided an extensive and multifarious set of resources for conceptualizing kingship. To an extent, there is a palpably conservative feel to the kingship tradition: the same commonplaces and analogies are drawn from Homer, the same philosophical definitions pillaged from Aristotle and the anecdotal accounts of Herodotus and Xenophon. What is missed by any analysis that focuses upon continuity, however, is a sense of the dynamism and intellectual vigour of later writers, as they strategically select and rework the tradition in order to serve their own objectives within the specific confines of their immediate situations. In particular, a figure like Dio Chrysostom—who looms heavily over kingship theory in the Roman principate—is no slavish imitator, but a conscious, indeed *self*-conscious, manipulator. Dio's writings show how ideas that appear firmly grounded in the centuries-old thought of Greek culture can be reappropriated for the purposes of addressing a non-Greek monarch. Dio's *Kingships*, as we have seen, explore the role of the Greek *pepaideumenos* in relation to Roman power, seeking to establish the critical role of *paideia* in the positive or negative evaluation of the monarch in question.

At the same time, however, *paideia* provides the author with an array of sophisticated devices for masking identities and deferring commitment. The *pepaideumenos*, as Dio presents him, is ideally suited to the intense scrutiny of the Roman court (even if, ultimately, it is unlikely that the *Kingships* were written for that context), precisely because he can slip ironically between roles. Dio is *both* the resister of imperial tyranny *and* the advocate of imperial beneficence, and it is his knowing sophistication that provides for this elusiveness. Education not only authorizes the subject to speak, but also allows him to walk the delicate line between giving away too much and withholding one's feelings.

Marcus Aurelius' *Meditations* represent a very different approach to the dyad of emperor and philosopher, constructed this time from the perception of the Roman monarch himself. Marcus appropriates the role of Greek adviser, internalizing it as an admonitory voice inside his own dualist psyche. Although the emperor's approach to the role of Greek philosophical educator is less obviously ludic than that of Dio, it is none the less bound up (as we have seen) with questions of public representation. The categories of public and private leak into one another in the *Meditations*, a text that sites itself upon the cusp between the two.

With Philostratus' portraits of Dio, we return to the more playfully self-conscious manipulator of masks. On the one hand,

Philostratus inflates the slipperiness and rhetorical charm of Dio to the extent that it becomes his defining feature: Philostratus' Dio is a sophistic self-promoter, inconsistent and unoriginal but persuasive and bewitching in his proclamations. On the other hand, Dio is used as a model both for Apollonius and for his own literary persona in the *Lives of the sophists*. Apollonius' sophic identity is constructed (in general) agonistically, by negative contrast with Dio; in the *Lives of the sophists*, on the other hand, the cruces concerning intercultural comprehension and the compatibility of Greek *paideia* with Roman imperial power become emblematic of a certain set of problems shared by all Greek literati, including Philostratus himself.

All three writers under consideration in this chapter exploit the paradigmatic nature of a relationship between Greek pedagogue and Roman empire for their own purposes. In each of these cases, the roles of pedagogue and potentate are labile, open to manipulation and appropriation in accordance with the will of and exigencies faced by the author in the contest for cultural authority. The utterances of the pedagogue are privileged and legitimized—but also contested and challenged. To represent oneself as the teacher of an emperor involves entering a world in which recrimination and suspicion fly fast and thick (this goes even for Marcus' self-representation). All these issues cluster around the figure of Dio Chrysostom, the *pepaideumenos* who most famously declaims before an emperor. Of course, we are not considering what it was 'really' like to address Trajan: the scenario presented by Dio was probably fictitious, and by the time of Marcus and Philostratus, it is certainly 'mythicized'. The crucial question concerns the *representation* of the interaction between Greek and Roman, for it is here that we can perceive how Greek writers conceptualize the problematic. And, as we have seen, for Dio Chrysostom, the problematic focuses upon the relationship between Greek identity, activated through retrospection over centuries of literary and philosophical production, and the spectacularized, scrutinizing society of the Roman empire.

5

Satirizing Rome: Lucian

> The Roman, like the Englishman who follows in his footsteps, brought to every new shore on which he set his foot (on our shore he never set it) only his cloacal obsession. He gazed around in his toga and he said: *It is meet to be here. Let us construct a watercloset.*
>
> Joyce, *Ulysses*[1]

In the last two chapters we have seen how the polarization of 'Greece' and 'Rome'—as though the two entities were discrete—is fraught with an ironic awareness of the mutual implication of the two. The texts on exile articulate an alienated distancing from Rome into the canonical past of free-speaking Greek autonomy, but in a self-conscious manner that knowingly bespeaks the Romanness of their authors. The tradition of imperial pedagogy is similarly playful: the roles of emperor and adviser are manipulable, even (in the cases of Marcus Aurelius and Apollonius of Tyana) partially reversible. What is demonstrated by these narrative attempts to construct paradigmatic subject-positions for 'Greece' (literature, intellect, 'culture') and 'Rome' (authority, power) is the degree of slippage involved in the construction of identity. The two are defined and constituted by an ongoing process of differentiation from one another through discourse, but this process is subject to ironic play, contestation, and subversion.

In this chapter I want to address another literary means of constructing (and hence probing) the distinction between Greece and Rome: satire (the term will be discussed below). This chapter will focus primarily upon the ways in which Rome is attacked (reified, objectified)—particularly by the exemplary satirist Lucian, whom we have already met periodically.[2] This most irrepressibly

[1] Joyce (1993), 126 (spoken by Professor MacHugh).

[2] On the details of Lucian's life and career, see Schwartz (1965), and more reliably Baldwin (1973), 7–20; Strohmaier (1976) on the evidence from the Arabic Galen; J. Hall (1981), 1–63; C. P. Jones (1986), 6–23; Swain (1996), 298–308. Such

brilliant of writers, however, does not simply reflect an already inscribed relationship between Greek literature and the Roman empire (a coherent set of opinions or views), but rather he *performs* the construction of such a relationship—while simultaneously displacing that very act of construction. The argument of this chapter, then, is contiguous to that of the previous two: the sociopolitics of satire, as with exilic and pedagogic writings, are performative not descriptive. In Bogel's words, 'satire is not a response to a prior difference but an effort to *make* a difference, to create distance, between figures whom the satirist—who is one of those figures—perceives to be insufficiently distanced'.[3]

SATIRE AND SATIRICAL IDENTITY

The English word 'satire' comes from the Latin word *satira* or *satura,* of debated etymology even in antiquity.[4] The fact that the word is rooted in Latin is significant. Roman literary culture generally narrativized itself as secondary to that of the originary Greeks,[5] but Quintilian (in a discussion of models to be emulated by students) famously stakes a claim for the Roman invention of satire: *satira quidem tota nostra est* ('satire, however, is totally ours', *Inst. or.* 10.1.93). The word *quidem* ('however'), often omitted in citations of this famous phrase, plays a crucial role in the articulation of cultural difference, marking satire as the exception that proves the general rule about the filial relationship of Roman literature to Greek. Indeed, in choosing filthy, 'realist' *satire* to exempt from Greek influence, Quintilian only underscores the idea that 'idealist' art comes from abroad. The specifically Roman temper of satire is also emphasized by the Latin satirists themselves, with their emphasis upon the concrete and

studies, though, can be vitiated by literalism: the wiles of self-representation and self-disguise are precisely what Lucian's autobiographies thematize. See also Goldhill (forthcoming), excellent both on Lucian's elusiveness and scholars' ideological attempts to pin him down.

[3] Bogel (1995), 45.

[4] Diomedes, *Grammatici Latini* 1.485 Keil offers three options: (i) from *satyrus*, 'satire'; (ii) from *lanx satura*, a 'full dish', or a type of stuffing; (iii) from the *lex per saturam*, a political bill with many subsections. The best modern discussion is Gowers (1993), 110–17, who favours the second etymology. The term was probably first used in a narrowly generic sense by Horace: see *Serm.* 2.1.1, with Hendrickson (1911).

[5] Introd., 'Greek Literature and the Roman Empire'.

transient mundanities of Rome, and their mockery of high-minded cultural ambitions (indeed the poems of Juvenal, in particular, contain some notoriously anti-Greek utterances).[6]

Generic definitions, however, are of necessity strategic: they are both polemical in their exclusions and provisional in their demarcations. Quintilian's attempt to describe the genre as exclusively Roman is not per se authoritative: it has a clear agenda, performing a cultural-political double bind (a bid for freedom from 'the tyranny of Greek' that simultaneously reinforces it). Greek culture itself had a strong tradition of offensive, 'low' poetry (including, notably, Archilochus, Hipponax, Aristophanes, and Callimachus), and this was immensely influential upon Lucilius, Horace, and the other Roman satirists.[7] To style the Greek texts 'iambographic' and their Roman inheritors 'satirical' is not to describe any essential differences between the two but to enact and perpetuate the cultural stereotypes that associate Romans with earthy (or, to use James Joyce's term cited in my epigraph, 'cloacal') functionality and the Greeks with literary panache. My point is not that there are no differences between Greek and Roman in this respect, but that the boundaries of genre are policed—in criticism as much as in literature—by identity politics.

This discussion is designed to foreground the point that caution is required when considering matters of literary genre. Lucian is not simply a 'satirist': there is, in fact, no general name for Lucianic texts (either in his own works or those of his contemporaries, who apparently ignored him). As has been discussed in earlier chapters,[8] he presents his work as a prodigious mixture of different traditions, just as he presents himself as a mixture of cultural traditions. Promiscuity is the keynote of the Lucianic text: just as 'satire' can style itself as distinctively Roman, so Lucian's writing styles itself as (generically and culturally) hybrid. In the course of this chapter I do refer (and have already referred) to Lucianic 'satire', but only to avoid cumbersome periphrasis: it is crucial to bear in mind the point that Lucian's writing, just like his literary persona, is avowedly anti-generic and parasitical.

The matter is important, since this chapter deals primarily with

[6] 3.76–8, 114–15; 6.184–99; 8.224–6; Petrochilos (1974), 52–3.

[7] Hendrickson (1927); Freudenburg (1993), esp. 96–103 for the Greek influence on Horace.

[8] Ch. 1, 'Art and Artifice'; Ch. 2, '*Paideia* and Hellenism'.

identity-construction. When we consider Lucian on 'Greece versus Rome' (as several recent scholars have done),[9] it is crucial to recognize that his complicity in Greekness is only ever partial and provisional: he grew up on the banks of the Euphrates, probably speaking Aramaic. How can we identify Lucian's stake in Greekness and Romanness? Swain's solution, most recently, is to invoke Greek 'cultural-cognitive' identity:[10] Lucian may not have been 'ethnically' Greek, but he felt 'culturally' Greek. Lucian's texts criticizing Rome and Roman values can (according to Swain) be used as evidence for how Greeks—the category defined not by blood but by 'feel'—thought of Rome. Swain, searching for the 'opinions' and 'attitudes' of the authors he studies, seeks a baseline of sincere expression in Lucianic writing. But for Lucian (always exploiting his marginal position vis-à-vis the Graeco-Roman mainstream), identity is, as we shall see, not the motivating force for composing, but part of the literary game that he plays: it is a ludic construct, not an inspirational force. Lucian dons and doffs the masks of identity with disturbing (to an 'expressive-realist' critic) regularity.

The attempt to identify Lucian's feelings towards Rome has been one of the major features of scholarship upon this author over the last century. There are certain Lucianic texts (*How to write history*, *Portraits*, and *In defence of portraits*, arguably *On the dance* and *Alexander*)[11] that present Roman power in a seemingly acceptable guise;[12] there are others (*Nigrinus* and *On salaried posts*, to be discussed below)[13] that are much more polemical. Which is the true Lucian? In response to the overwrought assertions of older

[9] Palm (1959), 44–66; Forte (1972), 371–90; Dubuisson (1984–6); C. P. Jones (1986), 78–89; Swain (1996), 312–29.

[10] Swain (1996), 306.

[11] Too much weight has been placed upon Lucian's use of the first person plural (τοῖς ἡμετέροις) in connection with the Roman army at *Alex*. 48 (cf. *Hist. conscr*. 5, 17, 29, 31): see Palm (1959), 54; J. Hall (1981), 250–1; C. P. Jones (1986), 89: in the *Alexander*, Lucian plays the interloper on the margins between inclusion and exclusion, scandalizing Rome and the Greek literary circle alike (see *Alex* 2, where he promises a rotten tale) The first-person pronoun is thus provocative and tendentious. (I owe this interpretation to an unpublished paper by Julie Lewis.) On the other hand, the supposed earlier parallels at Polyb. 1.3.9; Strab. 1.2.32; 2.5.6; 4.4.5 (Dubuisson 1984–6: 198; Swain 1996: 312–13) are unconvincing: in these instances, it is not Rome that is 'we' but a generalized Mediterranean culture.

[12] C. P. Jones (1986), 66–77; Swain (1996), 312–14.

[13] *Demon*. 40, sometimes discussed in this connection, is in fact not 'anti-Roman' as such.

scholars that the satirist was 'anti-Roman',[14] scholars have tended to be conservative in their estimation of the degree of Lucian's criticism of Roman values.[15] Bompaire argues that Lucian's criticisms of Rome are hackneyed repetitions of literary topoi, while proposing that 'c'est dans la mésure où l'œuvre de Lucien témoigne, dans un petit nombre de passages, d'une attitude de parfaite soumission à Rome, qu'elle porte la marque d'une expérience personelle et actuelle'.[16] Jones even goes so far as to say that he displays a 'casual acceptance of Roman power', and that he was beginning to cease to recognize the distinction between Greece and Rome.[17]

Swain's more nuanced discussion, on the other hand, allows for a 'complex' Lucian, who was generally accepting of Rome, but critical in cases when 'Greek culture was abused by Roman power'.[18] Yet here again there is a desire to grade the intensity of Lucian's true feelings. Implicit in Swain's account is the proposition that the 'pro-Roman' texts manifest insincere 'flattery' of Lucius Verus, and others convey his 'real' view.[19] Yet there is a problem with all these approaches. What they share is a belief that Lucian aims—in some texts at least—to articulate his 'opinions' sincerely. Whether insincerity is held to lie (as Bompaire and Jones consider) with the 'anti-Roman' texts (qua unreflective regurgitations of literary *données*) or with the 'pro-Roman' ones (on the grounds that they are mere blandishments), the drive is always to reconstruct an integrated and internally consistent set of authorial beliefs. This is a classic case of the so-called 'expressive-realist' fallacy. In fact, the very multiplicity of constructions of Lucian's 'view' betrays the degree to which the intentionality of the author is irrecoverable, except as an interpretative projection.[20]

[14] Peretti (1946); Baldwin (1961), an interpretation later disowned by its author (Baldwin 1973: 107).

[15] Palm (1959), 94–6; J. Hall (1981), 221–51; Dubuisson (1984–6); C. P. Jones (1986), 78–89.

[16] Bompaire (1958), 512.

[17] C. P. Jones (1986), 89.

[18] Swain (1996), 298–329 (quotations from p. 329).

[19] Esp. Swain (1996), 314–15 ('seeking good will . . . flattery').

[20] Apparent flattery can be recouped as parody; apparent oppositionalism can be dismissed as posturing. Cf. e.g. D. F. Kennedy (1992), 41: 'The degree to which a voice is heard as conflicting or supportive is a function of the audience's—or critic's—ideology, therefore, of *reception*.' Bartsch (1994) is a sophisticated study of this phenomenon in early imperial Rome.

Lucianic satire, as we shall see, specifically undermines any belief in true opinions: his is a world of masks and illusions.

The concept of the persona has been central to all modern theorizing of Roman and Augustan English satire over the last forty years.[21] In Clark's words, 'satire over the ages has regularly tended to turn fictional and create "voices" that are, among other things, self-exposing'.[22] On this interpretation, satire does not simply reflect the views of its authors, rather it constructs a multiplicity of voices—including, crucially, that of the narrator—that swagger absurdly (and thus themselves invite the reader's laughter and/or censure). There are merits and demerits in any general theory of a literary form, and particularly in the case of satire: it is clearly dangerous to generalize about the essential form, abiding 'over the ages', of a such a protean genre (and, in any case, attempts by critics to classify Lucian's works unilaterally risk attenuating his ludic parasitism). Nevertheless, this aspect of satire criticism presents the opportunity for a helpful advance from 'expressive-realist' studies of Lucian on Rome.

Let us be clear, though, that persona-theory will not allow for interpretative closure via the back-door readmission of intentionalism: there is no question that by identifying Lucian's masks we can reconstruct the face underneath.[23] Rather, as we shall see, the proliferation and infinite regress of personae is precisely the abiding preoccupation of his writing. These texts thematize the recurrent failure of any search for authoritative, 'true' utterances. This is a comedy of nihilism: as Lucian famously (and Socratically) puts it at the beginning of the *True stories*, the only truth is that all is lies.[24] The palimpsestic evanescence of the author's voice as a guarantee of truth and narrative guidance is part of the delirious pleasure of reading these texts.

[21] On the persona in English satire, see esp. Ehrenpreis (1963); Elliott (1982); Clark (1995). On Roman satire, see esp. Highet (1974); on Horace, Henderson (1993), 76; Freudenburg (1993), 14–16; on Juvenal, W. Anderson (1964), ineffectively critiqued by Highet (1974), 329–37; Braund (1988), *passim* esp. 178–96; Henderson (1995), 103 ('self-satirising absurdist'); (1997), vii. On the possibility (which is all it can be) that Lucian has read Juvenal, see Mesk (1912–13); Bompaire (1958), 504–8.

[22] Clark (1995), 22.

[23] The approach suggested by Ehrenpreis (1963), 37.

[24] *VH* 1.4: 'I shall speak this one truth, namely that I am lying' (*ἓν . . . τοῦτο ἀληθεύσω λέγων ὅτι ψεύδομαι*). Modelled on Pl. *Apol.* 21d (see Rütten 1997: 30–1; Georgiadou and Larmour 1998: 57–8). There is also an echo of Epimenides' Cretan liar paradox (fr. B1 DK; cf. Bowersock 1994: 5).

The self-subversive aspect of this writing is fundamental. Lucian the author employs a range of devices to mark his distance from his narratorial persona, particularly the dialogic form and the technique of employing names other than his own for the satirical persona: 'Lycinus', 'The Syrian', 'Parrhesiades' ('Free-speaker'), 'Tychiades' ('Man of fortune'), 'Momus' ('Blame').[25] These names are tantalizingly close to the figure of Lucian, but distant enough to frustrate attempts to identify the two: they are instances of what Ehrenpreis calls the 'ironic persona', 'a mask that the reader at first supposes to be genuine but at last sees removed'.[26] As Dubel puts it, 'Lucien est un auteur qui se dérobe en se multipliant'.[27] This is not to deny that there is a an identifiably coherent Lucianic manner at the levels of genre and style; but the authorial unity of his oeuvre is a function of textuality, not of self-disclosure. These texts are best read not as sincere expressions, but as open-ended and self-undermining explorations of the conflicts between different claims for cultural authority.

The search for Lucian's 'views of Rome', then, is doubly limited. First, the reconstruction of an internally coherent set of opinions is hermeneutically naïve: it necessitates problematical judgements concerning the relative sincerity and insincerity of different utterances. Secondly, it assumes a unified subjective consciousness inspiring the texts; whereas Lucian's deracinated writing specifically manipulates the identities of his narrating personae.

[25] The name 'Lucian' appears only rarely in his works, at *Nigr.* 1; *VH* 2.28; *Pseudosoph. passim* (not in the substance of the text, only to mark a change of interlocutor); *Somn.* (in the alternative title: 'The dream, or Lucian's life'); *Alex.* 55; *Peregr.* 1; *Epigr.* 1 Macleod. Of these instances, the *Nigrinus* and *Peregrinus* passages are epistolary formulae; the *Pseudosophistēs* and epigram may be spurious (and, in the case of the former, the original text may well have not indicated the dramatis personae: see Wilson 1970 on dialogic conventions in extant papyri). Only the *True stories* and the *Alexander* present uncontested cases of esodiegetic self-disclosure (neither of these is a dramatic dialogue); and the *True stories* at any rate is explicitly marked as an unadulterated lie (1.4)! On Lucian's polyonomy, see also Goldhill (forthcoming).

[26] Ehrenpreis (1963), 34.

[27] Dubel (1993), 26. I am not convinced, however, that Lucian's masking 'empêche sans doute que la satire ne se retourne contre le satiriste' (ibid.); indeed, precisely the opposite, it is a means of self-ironization.

ROME, CITY OF SPECTACLES

One of Lucian's favourite images is of the world—and particularly Rome—as a theatre (*theatron*, literally 'viewing-place').[28] This chapter will make significant use of the concept of Rome (and its dependent territories) as a 'spectacular society', a quasi-theatrical space in which display and performance count for more than inner being. The phrase deliberately recalls Debord's vision of *la société du spectacle*,[29] the phase of late twentieth-century consumerism that (he argues) privileges style over content. Of course, there are fundamental (and obvious) differences between postmodern capitalism and the culture of the Roman principate; but, conversely, it is a form of twenty-first-century vanity to claim that ours has been the first period in human history to have expressed and explored its own ideological and epistemological crises through the spectacular. Fifth-century Athens exploited the theatre as a means of exploring its own ideological and political relationship to the past, and thereby created and disseminated an 'epistemological' distinction between inner life (represented by the inscrutable set-building at the back of the stage) and public proclamation.[30] The word 'tragedy' came to signify *both* unimpeachable didactic authority *and* an untrustworthy mismatch between inner feelings and outward display. In Hellenistic Alexandria, too, the Ptolemies exploited the fascination of the spectacle to serve a very different ideological agenda. As we can see from Theocritus' fifteenth idyll, which portrays two women chatting on the way to the festival of Adonis at the palace, the lure of the spectacular was both keenly felt and knowingly patronized by the court. Indeed, Alexandria itself was a monument to the power of visuality. Cleitophon, the narrator of Achilles Tatius' erotic novel, *Leucippe and Cleitophon*, wanders the streets of the city awestruck, an 'insatiable spectator' (*θεατὴς ἀκόρεστος*, *L&C* 5.1.4), before concluding that 'we are defeated, my eyes' (*ὀφθαλμοί, νενικήμεθα*, 5.1.5).[31]

[28] *Nec.* 16; *Nigr.* 20; *Nav.* 46; *Gall.* 26; *Rhet. praec.* 12; *Pisc.* 31; *Icar.* 29; *Apol.* 5. This is a Cynic motif: see e.g. Teles fr. 2, p. 3; fr. 2, p. 11; fr. 6, p. 40 Hense; Dio Chr. 13.20; 64.22; Fav. *De ex.* 3.3–4. It is also attributed to other philosophers: see e.g. Ael. *VH* 2.11 (Socrates); Diog. Laert. 7.160 (Aristo).

[29] Debord (1996), 1st pub. in French in 1967. The title of the English edition, *The society of the spectacle*, is translationese.

[30] Padel (1990).

[31] On the theme of visuality in this text, with particular emphasis upon predatory sexuality, see Morales (1994).

It is in imperial Rome and its dependent territories, however, that the spectacular reached unparalleled heights (as generations of film directors have realized). The buildings of Rome were amazing: the splendid golden temple of Jupiter Capitolinus,[32] the Augustan mausoleum, the palaces of emperors, the Circus Maximus, the Flavian amphitheatre; while the Roman calendar was filled with triumphs, processions, funerals, gladiatorial shows, games, executions, races, at which individual nobles (and, after 31 BCE, the *princeps*) could manifest their power and status.[33] Imperial Latin literature parades the spectacular as a means of reflecting upon Roman power and identity.[34] Rome was one great spectacle, an aggregate of all the visual marvels of the empire: only an 'all-seeing Argos' could view all of the city.[35] Many of these cultural forms were exported to the empire as a whole.[36] In the words of the most recent commentator on this phenomenon, '[t]he spectacular and the theatrical became pervasively embedded in every aspect of public life under the emperors'.[37] Such *spectacula*, as scholars have emphasized, were means of distributing, articulating, and competing for social power: with the inescapable ubiquity of the gaze, the convenors of such events were as much 'on show' as were the performers themselves;[38] while claqueurs and spies at times observed the audience themselves, monitoring and prompting audience responses.[39]

This disciplinary *panopticisme*, to use Michel Foucault's word, centred upon and emanated from the figure of the emperor, without ever being subject to his absolute control.[40] We have already encountered this phenomenon in the previous chapter: Apollonius

[32] See C. Edwards (1996), 70 on the metaphorical values of this temple's 'goldenness'.

[33] Beacham (1999) provides a useful distillation of the sociological issues surrounding Roman spectacular entertainment.

[34] See Leigh (1997) on Lucan; Feldherr (1998) on Livy; Walters (1998) on Juvenal. See also Goldhill (2001) on the gaze in Roman Greek literature.

[35] Ael. Ar. *Ad Rom.* 6.2; 11.2–3.

[36] For the Greek East, see Woolf (1994), 125–30.

[37] Beacham (1999), xi.

[38] Hopkins (1983), 14–20 on gladiatorial games as 'political theatre'. Cf. Coleman (1990), 72, on gladiatorial mimes: '[t]he survival of an autocracy depends upon the visible exercise of power by the autocrat himself'; also ead. (1993), on aquatic display; Bartsch (1994), *passim*, C. Edwards (1994) on theatre; and on the arena, esp. Gunderson (1996), an effective Althusserian analysis. Veyne (1990), 398–403 is surprisingly nugatory.

[39] Bartsch (1994), 7–9.

[40] Foucault (1979).

and Vespasian, we recall, monitor the participants in the contest for civic authority at Alexandria. The subversion and dissemination of the imperial gaze, however, is widespread. Ovid, ever one to appropriate hegemonic social conventions, advises his readers to go to the Circus for a different kind of viewing, namely to eye women: 'Venus' son has often been the fighter in that sand, and the spectator of wounds has been himself wounded . . . he himself has become part of the spectacle' (*illa saepe puer Veneris pugnauit harena | et, qui spectauit uulnera, uulnus habet . . . et pars spectati muneris ipse fuit*, *Ars am.* 1.165–6, 170). In the context of such a proliferation of gazes, whether conforming to or contesting the agendas of political authorities, it is no surprise that moralists (and especially Christians) disapproved of the seductions of spectacles.[41] The gaze is a potent, but ultimately dangerously uncontrollable, means of creating and articulating social authority.[42]

Greek literature in the Roman empire was often publicly performed.[43] This will be readily accepted in the case of the grand sophists who toured the theatres and odeons of Rome and the Greek East. Indeed, even the very medium, the sophistic declamation *in persona*, was a form of theatrical role-playing.[44] This chapter, however, will argue that the theatricalization of Greek literature was not confined to such high-profile instances of public self-display. My point is not simply that a surprising range of events were performed in theatrical space (including philosophical discourses and even medical operations),[45] but also that the 'theatricalization' of literary culture extended into dining rooms, courts, and other notionally 'private' spaces. Greek *paideia*, as we shall see, was constantly threatened with subsumption into Roman strategies of domination through display of power.

In the competitive, hierarchical structure of elite Rome, the display of literary 'taste' was a disguised transvaluation of socio-

[41] e.g. Sen. *Ep.* 80; Tert. *De spect.* (with Goldhill 2001); Clem. *Prot.* 2 (24); Gunderson (1996), 114; James (1999), 75–6.

[42] See the discussion of Bartsch (1994), 63–97 on the potential for subversion at the theatre.

[43] Generally, see Korenjak (2000), 20–40.

[44] Schouler (1987), 275–7.

[45] See e.g. Cass. Dio 65.15.3–5; Hdn. 1.9.3–5 for impromptu philosophical performances in the theatre. On the theatrical aspects of medicine, see Barton (1994), 147–9. See in general Korenjak (2000), 21 n. 5 on the evidence for public performance of all kinds of cultural activity.

political power and economic status. As was discussed in the Introduction to this book, Rome placed a high capital premium on Greek culture: ever since the second century BCE, when the Hellenization of Rome began apace, Greek culture (whether artworks, books, or teachers) had been appropriated, recontextualized, and marketed at a high value.[46] By the time that the East was finally (largely) subdued, in 31 BCE, Rome had effectively usurped the place of Alexandria as the cultural capital of the world. Greek authors begin to refer recurrently to the immense resources available for *pepaideumenoi* at Rome, and to the generosity of Roman patronage.[47]

It is against this backdrop that Lucian's satire is staged. The theatricalization of Greek *paideia*—the requirement that it be subsumed into the competitive and patronal structures of display required by Rome's power-pyramid—is one of the most enduring objects of his vituperation. Yet, as the previous section suggested, this is not simply a matter of a subject (Lucian) expressing negative opinions about an object (Rome). The critique of the spectacularization of *paideia* encompasses Lucian (or, better, his satirical persona) too: at any level beyond the superficial, Lucian's writing (replete as it is with masks and other signs of dramatic performativity) is a symptom of, rather than an antidote to, the general insincerity, deviousness, moral bankruptcy, and trickery of Roman Greek *paideia*. It is impossible to prevent accusations of superficiality and disingenuousness from rebounding against their authors.

THE SATIRICAL SHOW

Lucian's writing repeatedly recurs to the conflicts between the high-minded idealism of Greek *pepaideumenoi* and the shallow, sordid, mercantile preoccupations of the contemporary world (dominated by Rome).[48] Two texts, *Demonax* and *Nigrinus* (the latter to be discussed below), are laudatory portraits of individual philosophers, while *Peregrinus* is a witty satire upon the

[46] Introd., 'Greek Literature and the Roman Empire', with nn. 51–4.

[47] Diod. Sic. 1.4.2–3; cf. Athen. *Deipn*. 2b–3d.

[48] See G. Anderson (1976), 113–34; J. Hall (1981), 151–93; Alexiou (1990), arguing that Lucian systematically equivocates as to whether his work is philosophical or mocking of philosophy.

eponymous cynic.[49] The *Hermotimus* mocks the gullible who fall for the lofty pronouncements of philosophers.[50] *Zeus refuted* stages the clash between philosophy and Olympian theology in the form of a dialogue between Zeus and a certain Cyniscus.[51] *Icaromenippus* presents Menippus flying to the moon, and thence gaining a better perspective on the world than the philosophers (a theme echoed in the *True stories*).[52] The *Symposium* recounts, in a form reminiscent of Plato's *Symposium*, the drunkenness and fighting that occurred at a symposium attended by a number of philosophers.[53] In certain texts, to be discussed in this chapter, Lucian specifically explores the paradigmatic relationship(s) between Greek *paideia* and Roman socio-economic domination. This is not to revert to the interpretation of Lucian as a proto-Marxist: there are plenty of instances in which he appears delighted with the money he has personally earned.[54] His texts are not straightforward political pamphlets, but playful mockeries of contemporary literary culture. Contemporary materialism and Roman economic patronage constitute Lucian's explanation for the parlously vapid state of contemporary *paideia*; but that criticism, of course, also implicates his own writing, the most (designedly) superficial of all. . . .

It is in his dialogue entitled the *Sale of lives* that Lucian most graphically mocks the commodification of *paideia*. Zeus and Hermes (the god of, amongst other things, mercantile transaction) hold a slave auction, selling off a series of 'philosophical lives' (the Cynic, the Academic, the Stoic, and so forth), each personified as the founder of the sect in question. Lucian's dialogue parodies the well-known story of the sale of Diogenes the Cynic.[55] Yet whereas the tale of Diogenes exemplifies the Cynic's ethical *eleutheria* ('freedom'), paradoxically even when society marks him as most enslaved, Lucian's representation of philosophers as slaves parading before buyers emphasizes their demeaned state.[56] So far

[49] For Peregrinus Proteus, see Ch. 4, n. 184.

[50] M. J. Edwards (1993), and now von Möllendorff (2000).

[51] Größlein (1998): good on philosophical sources but otherwise somewhat unhelpful.

[52] Georgiadou and Larmour (1998), 15–16 (the interpretation of the passage as a metaphor for philosophical initiation is, however, tendentious).

[53] Jeanneret (1991), 150–2.

[54] *Bis acc.* 27; *Apol.* 15; Swain (1996), 310.

[55] Ch. 3, n. 56.

[56] In the companion piece to this dialogue, the *Fisherman* (to be discussed

from transcending their situation by displaying their indifference to social and economic conventions, these philosophers show themselves to be thoroughly mired in them.

Whilst there is no mention of Rome in this dialogue, the dramatic time is the current one.[57] Lucian's satire is directed against the practitioners of philosophical education, but also against the buyer and the commercial/patronal system that treats *paideia* as a form of commercial exchange. Wealth demands and creates the spectacular:[58] the slave-auction reduces the philosophical life to a series of superficial visual signs. At the outset, Zeus tells the attendant to beautify the philosophers, 'so that they will appear attractive and allure as many people as possible' (ὡς εὐπρόσωποι φανοῦνται καὶ ὅτι πλείστους ἐπάξονται, *Sale* 1); they are then 'brought on' one by one, the word used for this being *paragein*, 'introduce into public view', 'bring on-stage'.[59] In such a context, profound reflections count for little against saleable indices. Diogenes, for example, is 'dirty' (αὐχμῶντα, 7), carries a 'wallet' (πήραν) and single-folded cloak (ἐξωμίας), has a grumpy (σκυθρωπόν), supercilious (κατηφές) expression (7), carries a stick (ξύλον, 7–8) and wears a short tunic (τριβώνιον, 8).[60] Philosophy is here reduced to the level of instantly recognizable external semiotics.[61]

If the *Sale of lives* dramatizes the effects of commercialization upon philosophical *paideia*, then its companion piece, the *Fisherman*, provides a further self-referential twist. Employing a device he uses elsewhere, Lucian in this text presents a reply to criticism of the first dialogue in the form of an *apologia* ('apology'; cf. *Pisc.* 8).[62] He thus represents the contest for cultural authority begun in

shortly), the philosophers complain of the 'insulting behaviour' (ὕβρις, *Pisc.* 4, 5, 6, 23, 27) levelled at them in the *Sale of lives*.

[57] Emphasized particularly in the companion piece, the *Fisherman*, where the contrast is drawn between the founders of the philosophical sects and their contemporary acolytes.

[58] Cf. *Tim.* 27, where Wealth is said to go masked, though he is considered to be unmasked (αὐτοπρόσωπον).

[59] παραγαγών (*Vit. auct.* 1); παραγάγωμεν (2); παράγωμεν (7); παράγε (13). For this meaning, see LSJ s.v. παράγω III.

[60] Lucian frequently presents external markers as definitive of philosophical identity: see Baldwin (1973), 71–2; R. B. Rutherford (1989), 82, 183 (with refs.); also Alexiou (1990), 37–9, emphasizing the comic origins of this topos, and Hahn (1989), 33–6 on the phenomenon in general.

[61] J. Hall (1981), 188–9.

[62] Cf. *Imagines* & *Pro imaginibus*, and *De mercede conductis* & *Apologia* (see below on the latter pair).

the *Sale of lives* as an ongoing process, a process indeed that directly engages the satirist himself. The satirical persona is subjected to critical scrutiny, and not simply allowed to snipe from outside. In this dialogue, set on the Athenian acropolis, the dead philosophers satirized in the *Sale of lives* return from Hades to avenge themselves upon Lucian, or rather upon his intratextual surrogate, 'Parrhesiades'. In a characteristically Lucianic narrative sequence, the satirical biter is bitten: the authority of the satirist (or, at least, his persona) is threatened with undermining.

The personified Philosophy, surprised to see the revenants,[63] prevents them from harming Parrhesiades and insists on a fair trial, during the course of which the latter is acquitted (on the grounds that he satirized false philosophers, and not the august founders of the sects), and mandated to continue his career as a debunker of pretension by trying the philosophers in the city. The latter are then summoned to the Acropolis with two proclamations, the second (sweetened with a promise of two minas per person) being necessitated by the failure of the first; but when the philosophers hear that they are to be tried, they flee. The dialogue concludes with Parrhesiades casting a fishing line, baited with figs and gold, into the city, and pulling in numerous false philosophers, whom he has the remit to brand. The dialogue as a whole has an Aristophanic air, with the initial confrontation recalling the clash between Dicaeopolis and the traditionalists in *Acharnians*, and the anti-philosophical conclusion echoing the destruction of Socrates' *phrontistērion* ('thinking-shop') at the end of the *Clouds*.[64]

As in the *Sale of lives*, the declining standards in philosophical ethics are interlinked with the commercialization of *paideia*. The fake philosophers *say*,[65] Parrhesiades tells us, that they despise wealth and so forth, 'but even such things they teach at a salary, and they fawn before the rich and fall agape before money' (οἱ δὲ καὶ αὐτὰ ταῦτα ἐπὶ μισθῶι διδάσκουσιν καὶ τοὺς πλουσίους τεθήπασιν

[63] Philosophy's expression of surprise (*Pisc.* 14) is modelled on Anticleia's astonishment at seeing the living Odysseus in the underworld (Hom. *Od.* 11.155–6).

[64] Diogenes himself points to Aristophanes and Eupolis as precedents for Parrhesiades' behaviour (*Pisc.* 25; cf. *Bis acc.* 33). See further Branham (1989), 14–15, 32–3.

[65] Reading φασίν, with Jacobitz (Teubner) and Macleod (Oxford), contra the radical variant in the β MS followed by Harmon (Loeb).

καὶ πρὸς τὸ ἀργύριον κεχήνασιν; *Pisc.* 34, cf. 12). This behaviour stands in implicit contrast with that of Socrates, the philosopher par excellence who famously refused to accept money for teaching (Pl. *Apol.* 19d). When others have money, Parrhesiades continues, these philosophers encourage them to share it by arguing that it is worthless; but when others ask them for money, they recant their doctrines (35–6). It is this desire for wealth and power, the goals of social activity, that motivates the philosophers to act; and philosophy has become a means of arrogating to oneself the superficial trifles of conventional society that it once sought to displace. This text enacts a disjunction between canonical past and decadent present in terms of the reduction of philosophy to spectacle and display.

The central thematic opposition in the dialogue is between truth and disguise, Parrhesiades' argument being that most current practitioners of philosophy employ the external markers of philosophy without making their lives (βίοι) conform to their words (λόγοι, 34). His ire was raised by his observation that most have gained the status of philosophy by mere *mimēsis*, by external self-presentation:

Seeing that many were not captivated by desire for philosophy but were aiming merely at a reputation (*doxa*) for this thing, and that they properly resembled good men in respect of the obvious, common signs that are easy for anyone to imitate (*mimeisthai*), I mean the beard and the walk and the clothing, but that in their lives (*bios*) and actions they were contradicting their style (*skhēma*), and their practices were the opposite of yours, and that they destroyed the standing of the principles they proclaimed, I grew angry . . .

ὁρῶν δὲ πολλοὺς οὐκ ἔρωτι φιλοσοφίας ἐχομένους ἀλλὰ δόξης μόνον τῆς ἀπὸ τοῦ πράγματος ἐφιεμένους, καὶ τὰ μὲν πρόχειρα ταῦτα καὶ δημόσια καὶ ὁπόσα παντὶ μιμήσασθαι ῥάιδιον εὖ μάλα ἐοικότας ἀγαθοῖς ἀνδράσι, τὸ γένειον λέγω καὶ τὸ βάδισμα καὶ τὴν ἀναβολήν, ἐπὶ δὲ τοῦ βίου καὶ τῶν πραγμάτων ἀντιφθεγγομένους τῶι σχήματι καὶ τὰ ἐναντία ὑμῖν ἐπιτηδεύοντας καὶ διαφθείροντας τὸ ἀξίωμα τῆς ὑποσχέσεως, ἠγανάκτουν . . . (*Pisc.* 31)

As in the *Sale of lives*, the focus here is upon the superficial social performance of philosophers, their *skhēma* (a personal or linguistic 'style' that masks the true self). The word *skhēma* (which recurs elsewhere in this dialogue)[66] marks the philosophers' self-

[66] Cf. 12: 'all grumpy (*skythrōpoi*), with unadorned styles of clothes (*skhēmata*) and thoughtful expressions' (ἁπάντων σκυθρωπῶν καὶ τὰ σχήματα εὐσταλῶν καὶ

presentation as an artificial creation that works at the level of mere appearance (*doxa*), the product of knowing *mimēsis*.[67] Philosophy, here, is all surface: beard, walk, and clothing. The gap between the idealized classical past, when philosophers acted like philosophers, and the present, in which philosophers *act* like philosophers, is articulated in terms of the self-conscious process of imitative, stylistic self-creation discussed in my first and second chapters.

The process of mimetic assimilation to classical precedents, so fundamental to Greek *paideia*'s perception of its role as creator of cultural continuity, is evaluated in negative terms: these imitative philosophers are superficially convincing, but they do not fool Parrhesiades' trained eye. When the philosophers flock up to the Acropolis in response to the second proclamation (with the added promise of two minas), they are at first blush intermingled with the few genuine philosophers who responded to the first:

the few that came up in response to the first proclamation are unremarkable and indistinguishable, mixed in as they are with the masses of others, and they have disappeared thanks to the similarity of the styles (*skhēmatōn*) of the others.

οἱ ὀλίγοι δέ, ὁπόσοι πρὸς τὸ πρῶτον κήρυγμα ἐκεῖνο ἀνήιεσαν, ἀφανεῖς καὶ ἄσημοι, ἀναμιχθέντες τῶι πλήθει τῶν ἄλλων, καὶ λελήθασιν ἐν τῆι ὁμοιότητι τῶν[68] ἄλλων σχημάτων. (*Pisc*. 42)

As a result of this highly effective, duplicitous *mimēsis*, the *goētes* ('quacks', 'wizards') are often 'more plausible' (πιθανώτεροι) than the true philosophers (42). The angle and position of viewing is, however, crucial here: Philosophy and Parrhesiades are looking from a distance at a massive spectacle. When one looks from afar, it is difficult to distinguish accurately. Parrhesiades' specifically visual acuity, on the other hand, allows him subsequently to distinguish true from false: 'I could not stand seeing this, but started exposing them and distinguishing them from you' (οὐκ ἤνεγκα ὁρῶν

φροντιστικῶν τὴν πρόσοψιν); 13: 'I can see many who are similar in their style (*skhēma*), their walk and their clothing' (πολλὰς ὁμοίας ὁρῶ τό γε σχῆμα καὶ τὸ βάδισμα καὶ τὴν ἀναβολήν).

[67] Very similar phraseology at *Fug*. 13 (Philosophy speaking): 'they stylize and adorn themselves to look very much like me' (σχηματίζουσιν καὶ μετακοσμοῦσιν αὑτοὺς εὖ μάλα εἰκότως καὶ πρὸς ἐμέ, 13); 'the external signs' (τὰ προφανῆ) of the philosopher are 'readily imitable' (ἐς μίμησιν πρόχειρα, 14).

[68] It seems to me probable that a haplography has caused a second τῶν to drop out before ἄλλων, and I have translated accordingly.

ἔγωγε, ἀλλ' ἤλεγχον αὐτοὺς καὶ διέκρινον ἀφ' ὑμῶν, *Pisc.* 33).[69] Parrhesiades sees and reveals the mismatch between appearance and reality, and for him the false philosophers are definitely *not* 'plausible' (πιθανοί, 37). Parrhesiades is the possessor of a penetrating insight that is superior to the superficial gaze of society as a whole.

Philosophy has become a spectacle, and different viewers respond with differing degrees of visual penetration. Lucian's dominant image for this process is theatrical (cf. e.g. 46).[70] The false philosophers, Parrhesiades tells us, are like a 'soft, womanly' (μαλθακὸς . . . καὶ γυναικίας) tragic actor playing the part of Achilles, Theseus, or Heracles—when he is not even appropriate for Helen or Polyxena; if Heracles saw such a performance, he would smash both man and mask (31). They are like monkeys wearing masks, we hear, or the ass at Cumae that wore a lion's skin (32);[71] Parrhesiades also tells a story of a certain pharaoh who trained monkeys to behave like humans (36).[72] Manliness and humanity are implicitly linked with undeceptive simplicity: a real, male human would not need to play a role. The philosophy of the age is symptomatic of a general decline: lesser (effeminate, bestial) beings attempt to pass themselves off as the objects of their ineffectual imitation.

Yet, as ever with Lucian, there is a self-ironizing twist. Is there not also something theatrical about Lucian's role in all this? After all, he has concealed his own identity behind the mask of Parrhesiades ('Free-speaker'), a game of self-concealment that he operates analogously throughout his oeuvre.[73] The philosophers warn that Parrhesiades is a clever, manipulative speaker (7, 9, 18), and his claim at the beginning of his speech that he has converted from rhetoric to philosophy (23), yet another instance of philosophical status being constructed 'differentially' by opposition to rhetoric, invites interpretation as an eminently rhetorical disavowal of rhetoric.[74] The *locus classicus* for such recusation comes

[69] The participle 'seeing' (ὁρῶν) is also used of Parrhesiades' observation of the false philosophers at *Pisc.* 31, 33; cf. also ἰδών at 33.

[70] A common idea in Lucian: see G. Anderson (1976), 10, adding *Peregr.* 3; *Nigr.* 29–30.

[71] For the ass at Cumae, see also *Pisc.* 37; *Philops.* 5.

[72] The same story is told at *Apol.* 5.

[73] Above, n. 25.

[74] The 'rhetoric of anti-rhetoric', in Jonathan Hesk's phrase (Hesk 1999). For other instances of this topos, see Lys. 19.1–2; Isae. 10.1.

in Plato's *Apology of Socrates* (Pl. *Apol.* 17a–b), an important intertextual reference point for Parrhesiades' own apology.[75] At the very point at which Lucian, in the guise of Parrhesiades, claims to reject rhetorical duplicity, he appropriates a celebrated rhetorical topos. . . .

Indeed, one of the charges levelled against Parrhesiades is precisely his theatrical hypocrisy. According to Diogenes in his prosecution, Lucian's writing is a performance: the *Sale of lives* was written, using Dialogue as a 'fellow competitor and actor' (συναγωνιστῆι καὶ ὑποκριτῆι, *Pisc.* 26), because its author wanted 'to be clapped and applauded by the spectators' (κροτεῖσθαι καὶ ἐπαινεῖσθαι πρὸς τῶν θεατῶν, *Pisc.* 25). This does not mean that Lucian's dialogues were necessarily performed before live audiences: the theatricality is figurative rather than literal.[76] Diogenes is (perhaps surprisingly!) appropriating the familiar Platonic contempt for showmanship, public display, and playing to the gallery.[77] 'For the majority of the populace', Diogenes continues, 'are naturally like that, enjoying those who indulge in mockery and abuse' (φύσει γάρ τι τοιοῦτόν ἐστιν ὁ πολὺς λεώς, χαίρουσι τοῖς ἀποσκώπτουσιν καὶ λοιδορουμένοις, *Pisc.* 25). Lucian's work, according to the prosecution, makes a spectacle of itself. Although he proceeds to assert the social utility of satirical writing, Parrhesiades pointedly does not countermand Diogenes' accusations of spectacular theatricality. Indeed, with the quasi-dramatic dialogic form, Parrhesiades' vivid description of the false philosophers 'as though in a painting' (καθάπερ ἐπί τινος γραφῆς, 38),[78] his announcement 'in the tragic style' (τραγικώτερον, 39), and (as noted) the Aristophanic tenor of the mockery of philosophical quacks, this text seems to draw attention to its own spectacular, theatrical qualities.

Lucian, then, does not exonerate himself from the general spectacularization of literary culture: in the *Fisherman*, as in other texts we shall consider in this chapter, Lucian ironically advertises

[75] Cf. *Pisc.* 10 for explicit allusion; cf. also *Pisc.* 11 and Pl. *Apol.* 21b–d (with Macleod 1991: 261); *Pisc.* 33 and Pl. *Apol.* 36d.

[76] E. Rohde (1914), 328 n. 1 (recently supported by Korenjak 2000: 24) argues for oral performance of Lucian's dialogues; but the *Sale of lives* at any rate was composed to be read, as is confirmed by *Pisc.* 26, where Diogenes states that Parrhesiades' malicious remarks 'filled a thick book' (εἰς παχὺ βιβλίον).

[77] Pl. *Leg.* 817a–d.

[78] For other 'word-paintings', see *Alex.* 3; *Imag.* 3.

his own complicity in the mimetic identity-crisis of his age. All sophic authority—*including Lucian's own*—is subject to the accusation of display, repetition, and mimicry. Indeed, even Lucian's literary strategy might be understood in the context of this self-ironization, this exposure of the author's own superficial mimeticism: his dialogues borrow themes and structures eclectically from literary tradition (and particularly from Plato and Aristophanes). Rudolf Helm, the right-wing German philologist, even accused him of arrant plagiarism in the *Sale of lives* and the *Fisherman*.[79] 'Plagiarism' is too crude and insensitive a term to describe Lucian's subtle appropriations and reconfigurations, a dynamic engagement with literary tradition rather than a fraudulent theft. Helm stumbled across one important point, though he misinterpreted it: Lucian's literary form is *self-consciously* imitative, a (deliberately constructed) symptom of a paideutic culture that focuses more on appearance than substance.

NIGRINUS: YEARNING FOR PHILOSOPHY

In two texts, *Nigrinus* and *On salaried posts*, Lucian explicitly links the spectacularization of Greek *paideia* with Roman socio-economic power. Much has been made of both these essays: the idea of the idealizing Hellene inveighing passionately against Roman materialism is now unfashionable,[80] but they remain nevertheless prime quarries for Lucian's 'views' of Rome.[81] As we shall see, however, just as much as the *Fisherman* and the *Sale of lives*, these texts enact an unresolved, self-ironizing, theatrical contest for an authoritative voice. Lucian constructs a scenario in which there is no secure position from which to 'comment' upon Rome: in the society of the spectacle, all positionality is open to the charge of superficiality.

Interpretative problems with *Nigrinus* have long been recognized.[82] The centrepiece of the text (12–35) consists of a binary

[79] Helm (1906), 227–53 (*Vit. auct.*); 292–306 (*Pisc.*). Helm's arguments are ludicrously overstated (for easy rebuttals, see McCarthy 1934; Neef 1940), but it is clear that Lucian's writing here is self-consciously mimetic.

[80] Peretti (1946), 41, 121–2; Baldwin (1961), 207.

[81] Bompaire (1958), 512–13; Palm (1959), 45–52; Baldwin (1973), 114–15 (a palinode); J. Hall (1981), 242–8; C. P. Jones (1986), 78–89; Swain (1996), 315–21.

[82] See esp. Caster (1935); Bompaire (1958), 502–11; G. Anderson (1978); J. Hall (1981), 157–64.

comparison between Athens and Rome.[83] The philosopher Nigrinus[84] is said to have praised the one for its philosophical simplicity, 'purity' (τὸ καθαρόν, 12) and resistance to 'luxury' (τρυφήν, 12), and accused the other of superficiality and decadence. So far, so good: a straightforward juxtaposition of rhetorical 'praise' (ἔπαινος) and 'blame' (ψόγος),[85] a paired structure paralleled elsewhere in Lucian.[86] But this central report of Nigrinus' words is surrounded by two frames, which subvert any 'easy' reading of the text. The text opens with a letter from Lucian to Nigrinus, in which he politely apologizes for sending a book to the philosopher, as though he were in need of learning (*praef.*). We then enter the text proper, only to encounter another frame, a dialogue between two unnamed interlocutors, one of whom persuades the other to tell of his recent encounter with the philosopher Nigrinus, who has completely won him over (2–11, 35–8). What is Lucian's aim here? Is this an earnest statement of the author's 'conversion' to a philosophical doctrine? Or an anti-Roman polemic? Or merely an ironic game?[87] And, ultimately, how committed is Lucian to Nigrinus' viewpoint?

[83] 'The city' (ἡ πόλις, 2, 29) *tout court* is Rome: see 30 for 'the Romans' (οἱ Ῥωμαίων παῖδες).

[84] Otherwise unknown, and hardly sufficiently individuated to invite identification. C. P. Jones (1986), 25 n. 7 offers some unconvincing speculations. See most recently Tarrant (1985) for the argument that Nigrinus is a (Latin) pun on the name of the philosopher Albinus.

[85] *Synkrisis* ('comparison') is often used in encomia: Xen. *Ag.* 9.1–5; Isoc. *Evag.* 37–9; *Panath.* 39–41 (a comparison between Athens and Sparta); Focke (1923), 332–9. It is treated by the rhetorical handbooks tentatively as a form of 'preliminary exercise' (προγύμνασμα): see Nicol. *Progymn.* 10 (3.485–8 Spengel); Hermog. *Progymn.* 8 (2.14–15 Spengel); Aphth. *Progymn.* 10 (2.42–4 Spengel); Theon *Progymn.* 9 (2.112–15 Spengel); Focke (1923), 331.

[86] Notably in *Amores* (which I am not convinced is un-Lucianic), where the merits of heterosexuality and pederasty are argued in turn (although the use of different speakers is a slightly different technique). G. Anderson (1978), 368 notes anxiously that much more space is devoted to the ψόγος than the ἔπαινος, but this is only a problem if we imagine that symmetry is necessary for a contrast.

[87] Caster (1935) argues for the 'conversion' reading, against 'irony'; Peretti (1946) agrees, but considers also that Lucian is 'converted' to a polemically anti-Roman point of view; Bompaire (1958), 511 notes the 'bizarreries' of the text, but offers no explanation; G. Anderson (1978) interprets the oddities by observing that *Nigrinus* follows patterns visible in other Lucianic texts. Anderson's suggestion that structural parallels fully explain apparent anomalies is unconvincing, dependent as it is on the palpably misguided assertion that 'Lucian is a facile writer, who tends to fall back on . . . a basic structure that can be adapted to fit as many situations as possible' (p. 371). I cannot, moreover, comprehend the inference from the premise that structural patterns exist in Lucian's work that Lucian is therefore

Such issues exercise critics only when they assume that Lucian must have been aiming to communicate a single, coherent message, and not presenting an ingenious interpretative challenge to the reader. There are a multitude of signals in this text that suggest that the author is, so far from ineptly conflating two different motifs, fully in control of the material. The double-embedding device is an elegant reworking of the opening of Plato's *Symposium*, a canonical dramatization of the lust for narration, in which '[e]ach framing narrative recedes to disclose another nested inside it, one containing the other like a set of lacquered Chinese boxes'.[88] As we shall see presently, these frames, so far from enclosing and demarcating the sense of the text, encourage a proliferation of unstable and self-subverting interpretations that engulf Lucian himself, and the reader too. As Goldhill comments (in a different context), 'the frame, as the source and site of difference, is the figure which always already undermines the rigid determination of the boundaries of sense, the sense of boundaries'.[89]

Let us begin by considering how Lucian and Nigrinus construct Rome as a 'city of spectacles'. Nigrinus' criticism of Rome (19–34), the city he inhabits, focuses primarily upon its false and theatrical qualities and the resulting moral decay. The seductive city is compared to the song of the Sirens, and represented by synecdoche as 'so many appetites, so many sights, so many sounds' (τοσαύταις μὲν ἐπιθυμίαις, τοσούτοις δὲ θεάμασι τε καὶ ἀκούσμασι, 19). The changeability of individuals' fortunes in the city is compared by Nigrinus to a 'play with many parts in it' (πολυπροσώπωι δράματι, 20), in which each periodically changes role—but despite 'seeing' (βλέποντες, 20) this lesson, no one learns from it.[90] The display of *imagines* at a funeral is also referred to as a 'drama' (δρᾶμα,

solely interested in literary form, and not in critiquing contemporary society (p. 374). Schäublin (1985), 126–7 also interprets the text in formal terms, as a (?)parody of the *logos protreptikos* ('conversion-dialogue') form.

[88] Halperin (1992), 97–8; see this article *passim* for an excellent discussion of the narrative complexities of the *Symposium* and their relationship to the central themes of that text. The many echoes of Plato in the *Nigrinus* are discussed by Neef (1940), 23–4.

[89] Goldhill (1988), 96.

[90] One of several echoes of the story of Croesus in Herodotus 1 (1.32.4–9; 1.86.6; cf. 1.5.4). The rich man's anticipation of envy amongst the Athenians (*Nigr.* 13) recalls Hdt. 1.30.3, as does the observation that all the rich wish to be marvelled at (23).

30). Rich men at Rome 'display' (προφαίνοντες) the external signals of their wealth (purple clothing and rings, 21). The city is full of 'harassings and shovings and theatres and the hippodrome and statues of charioteers and the names of horses and conversations down alleyways about those things' (τὰς . . . ταραχὰς . . . καὶ τὸν ὠθισμὸν καὶ τὰ θέατρα καὶ τὸν ἱππόδρομον καὶ τὰς τῶν ἡνιόχων εἰκόνας καὶ τὰ τῶν ἵππων ὀνόματα καὶ τοὺς ἐν τοῖς στενωποῖς περὶ τούτων διαλόγους, 29): the polysyndeton conveys the limitless variety of spectacular Rome.

Why is Rome so spectacular? According to Nigrinus, there is a specific answer, economic power:

I, however, consider that the flatterers are much more destructive than their patrons, and that they are all but responsible for the arrogance of the latter: for whenever they marvel at (*thaumasōsin*) their wealth and laud their gold and fill their porches from dawn and approach them addressing them as 'master', what thoughts are likely to be running through their patrons' minds? But if by common agreement they held back from this willing slavery (*ethelodouleias*) even for a short while, do you not think that the opposite would happen—that the rich would themselves go to the doors of the beggars, and ask them not to leave their wealth unobserved (*atheaton*) and unattested, the splendour of their tables and the grandeur of their houses worthless and unused? For they do not desire wealth so much as to be exalted for their wealth. That is how it is: the inhabitant has no need for a beautiful house, or gold, or ivory if no one marvels at (*thaumazoi*) it.

ἐγὼ μέντοι γε πολὺ τῶν κολακευομένων ἐξωλεστέρους τοὺς κόλακας ὑπείληφα, καὶ σχεδὸν αὐτοὺς ἐκείνοις καθίστασθαι τῆς ὑπερηφανίας αἰτίους· ὅταν γὰρ αὐτῶν τὴν περιουσίαν θαυμάσωσιν καὶ τὸν χρυσὸν ἐπαινέσωσιν καὶ τοὺς πυλῶνας ἕωθεν ἐμπλήσωσιν καὶ προσελθόντες ὥσπερ δεσπότας προσείπωσιν, τί καὶ φρονήσειν ἐκείνους εἰκός ἐστιν; εἰ δέ γε κοινῶι δόγματι κἂν πρὸς ὀλίγον ἀπέσχοντο τῆσδε τῆς ἐθελοδουλείας, οὐκ ἂν οἴει τοὐναντίον αὐτοὺς ἐλθεῖν ἐπὶ τὰς θύρας τῶν πτωχῶν δεομένους τοὺς πλουσίους, μὴ ἀθέατον αὐτῶν μηδ' ἀμάρτυρον τὴν εὐδαιμονίαν καταλιπεῖν μηδ' ἀνόνητόν τε καὶ ἄχρηστον τῶν τραπεζῶν τὸ κάλλος καὶ τῶν οἴκων τὸ μέγεθος; οὐ γὰρ οὕτω τοῦ πλουτεῖν ἔρωσιν ὡς τοῦ διὰ τὸ πλουτεῖν εὐδαιμονίζεσθαι. καὶ οὕτω δὲ ἔχει, μηδὲν ὄφελος εἶναι περικαλλοῦς οἰκίας τῶι οἰκοῦντι μηδὲ χρυσοῦ καὶ ἐλέφαντος, εἰ μή τις αὐτὰ θαυμάζοι. (*Nigr.* 23)

The morning salutation is a familiar topic of satire, especially in Lucian's writing, where it is a common emblem of societal corruption.[91] By an amusing but pointed inversion, the clients—or

[91] *De merc. cond.* 10; *Nav.* 22.

'flatterers'—are presented as more powerful than their patrons. It is they who are 'responsible' (αἰτίους) for this state of affairs, and the patrons who are presented as 'needier' (the verb δεῖσθαι, here translated 'ask', also means 'need') than them. This inversion points up the vacuity of the conventional perception of power. Both sides are equally bankrupt in terms of the (ethical) values that Nigrinus cherishes, but the rich 'need' the poor because material possessions (again listed in polysyndeton) require an arbitrary desirability in order that their bogus value may be maintained. This desirability is imaged by Lucian in terms of the gaze: wealth needs to be 'marvelled at' (*thaumasōsin, thaumazoi*); and to be 'unobserved' (*atheatos*) spells its evanescence. Economic power exists primarily at the symbolic level: it is only substantial to the degree that it is coveted by others.

Whereas the philosophers in the *Sale of lives* were presented as slaves, the 'flatterers' of *Nigrinus* indulge in *ethelodouleia* ('willing slavery'), a word coined by Plato in the *Symposium* (the model, as we have seen, for *Nigrinus*' embedded dialogic form).[92] Although it is self-willed, this slavery contrasts heavily with the 'freedom' at Athens (ἐλευθερία, 14, 15), a freedom that is primarily 'Epicurean' (i.e. freedom from disturbing appetites)[93] but none the less resonates with socio-economic implications. The freedom–slavery polarity is also articulated through different modes of relationship between *paideia* and power. In Athens, a rich visitor is shorn of his pretensions and love of wealth when he is 'educated' (πεπαιδευμένος, 13) by the citizens: Athens is a 'teacher of such great virtues' (τοσούτων διδάσκαλον ἀγαθῶν, 16).[94] In Rome, by way of contrast, *paideia* becomes a marketable commodity. It would be a more moderate problem, Nigrinus asserts, if the flattery and fawning were only performed by 'commoners who openly admit their lack of education (*apaideusia*)' (ἄνδρας ἰδιώτας καὶ ἀναφανδὸν τὴν ἀπαιδευσίαν ὁμολογοῦντας, 24); but as it is, the latter are joined by 'fake philosophers' (τῶν φιλοσοφεῖν προσποιουμένων, 24) who dress themselves in finery but 'in other respects play their role in the drama precisely' (τὰ ἄλλα γε ὁμοίως ὑποκρινόμενοι τοῦ δράματος,

92 Pl. *Symp.* 184c; also at *De merc. cond.* 5.

93 See esp. *Nigr.* 14: 'the freedom there' (τὴν ἐλευθερίαν τὴν ἐκεῖ) is linked with/glossed by 'satisfaction with a moderate lifestyle, peace and calm' (τῆς διαίτης τὸ ἀνεπίφθονον, ἡσυχίαν τε καὶ ἀπραγμοσύνην).

94 An echo of Pericles' famous words concerning Athens: 'an education (*paideusis*) for Greece' (τῆς Ἑλλάδος παίδευσιν, Thuc. 2.41.1).

24). Nigrinus proceeds to recall mockingly 'those who philosophize for a salary and set out their virtue for sale, as if it could be bought from a market-place' (*τῶν ἐπὶ μισθῶι φιλοσοφούντων καὶ τὴν ἀρετὴν ὤνιον ὥσπερ ἐξ ἀγορᾶς προτιθέντων*, 25). In Rome, *paideia* is shorn of its true values and sucked into the spectacular system of commerce and financial exchange.

In his critique of Rome's spectacular qualities, Nigrinus recurs to familiar Lucianic themes. This is not an accident: the text elaborates upon the association between the two figures, teasing the reader with the proposal that Nigrinus might be a 'cover' for the author. First, Nigrinus' example inspires typically Lucianic clear-sightedness (compare Parrhesiades' visual acuity in the *Fisherman*): the central interlocutor in the framing dialogue claims to have gone to Rome in search of a cure for a disease of the eyes (2), but on meeting Nigrinus ends up forgetting his ophthalmic problems because he 'gradually became more sharp-sighted in the soul' (*τὴν . . . ψυχὴν ὀξυδερκέστερος κατὰ μικρὸν ἐγιγνόμην*, 4). The keenness of the philosopher's vision leads him to laughter at the absurdity of the various practices at Rome (*γελᾶν*, *γελοῖοι*, 21; *γελοιότεροι*, 22; *γελοιότερα*, 24; *γελοῖα*, 25), a laughter that knowingly evokes the oblique, probing humour of Lucian's other works. When the interlocutor notes that Nigrinus 'imitates Momus' speech' (*τοῦ Μώμου τὸν λόγον μιμησάμενος*, 32), we recall that Lucian himself has used the figure of Momus ('the reproacher') in his own works.[95] Nigrinus is an 'imitator' of Momus in more than one sense: at a metaliterary level, his voice is convergent with (i.e. constructed by *mimēsis* of) the Lucianic satirical persona. At one particularly Lucianic moment, Nigrinus states that

> having seated myself as though somewhere very high up in an extremely populous theatre, I look down upon events, events that can both provide much entertainment and laughter and also yield the proof of whether a man has any true integrity.
>
> *καθίσας ἐμαυτὸν ὥσπερ ἐν θεάτρωι μυριάνδρωι σφόδρα που μετέωρος ἐπισκοπῶ τὰ γιγνόμενα, τοῦτο μὲν πολλὴν ψυχαγωγίαν καὶ γέλωτα παρέχειν δυνάμενα, τοῦτο δὲ καὶ πεῖραν ἀνδρὸς ὡς ἀληθῶς βεβαίου λαβεῖν.* (18)

[95] 'A personification of mockery and criticism, notorious for his fault-finding' (Georgiadou and Larmour 1998: 179, citing *Jup. trag.* 19–31; *Icar.* 31; *Hist. conscr.* 33). Momus is the 'Lucianic' persona in the *Assembly of the gods*; cf. *Dion.* 8: Lucian acts 'in the fashion of Momus' (*κατὰ Μῶμον*, 8). Other references to Momus at *VH* 2.3; *Dear. iudic.* 2; *Herm.* 20.

Not only does this condense neatly the serio-comic combination of humour and philosophical purpose that is definitive of Lucianism,[96] but it also employs the motifs of viewing from above, used as we have seen in the *Fisherman* (but in fact common in Lucian's works),[97] and of the contemporary world as a theatrical spectacle. This series of overlaps would suggest that Nigrinus is a fictitious character created (like 'Lycinus', 'Tychiades', 'Parrhesiades', and so forth) in order to articulate Lucianic preoccupations; or, at the very least, a 'real' figure whose voice has been co-opted into the Lucianic echo chamber.

Yet there is a problem with this interpretation, since the framing epistle is addressed 'from Lucian to Nigrinus' (*Λουκιανὸς Νιγρίνωι εὖ πράττειν*, *praef.* 1). This extremely rare intrusion of the author's *nomen proprium* into a Lucianic text seems to foreclose the possibility that Nigrinus is *simply* a Lucianic alter ego. Roles and identities appear to be artfully dissimulated in this complex text. In order to explore these issues further, I wish to take a detour into the literary dynamics of the text, its exploration of the role of narrative and its construction of the reading experience. This detour, however, is not irrelevant. As we shall discover presently, Lucian's own theatrical artfulness is fundamentally interlinked with his relationship to Rome, the city of spectacles.

Let us return to the matter of the relationship between the frames (the introductory epistle and the dialogue between anonymous interlocutors) and the substance of the text (Nigrinus' reported speech). The employment of recessive frames itself (as in Plato's *Symposium*) already problematizes the articulation of authorial perspective. Although in the introductory epistle, Lucian (or perhaps in this textual hall of mirrors we should properly call him 'Lucian', the authorial persona) claims that he wishes 'to reveal his opinion' (*δηλῶσαι τὴν ἐμὴν γνώμην*), the choice of narrative presentation does quite the opposite: it masks the authorial 'I' behind layers of reported speech. Dialogue is, as ancient literary criticism knew well, a deceptive imitation: it employs textual form to replicate spoken language.[98] Like drama, it is a form of what Plato's Socrates would call 'complex narration', a literary form in which the author's utterances *in propria persona*

96 See esp. Branham (1989), 26–8; 67–123.

97 e.g. *Icar.*; *Astrol.* 13–19; *Somn.* 13.

98 Demetr. *De eloc.* 223–5.

are limited or non-existent (and that perceived disingenuousness is the reason for Socrates' disapproval).[99] The literary form of the *Nigrinus*, and particularly the marked turn to the dialogue mode, reinforces the (self-consciously introduced) problems with locating the author's voice in this text.

In this connection, it is important to note the rich vein of theatrical imagery that is used right from the start of the dialogic sequence of the text. In the first section, the principal interlocutor cites a phrase, 'thrice-blessed' (τρισόλβιος), 'from the stage' (ἀπὸ τῆς σκηνῆς, 1).[100] The principal interlocutor intensifies the association at chapter 8, where he expresses modesty about his ability to do justice to Nigrinus (a modesty that his companion rightly spots as a rhetorical device, 10). The speaker claims to fear comparison with 'bad tragic or comic actors' (τραγικοὺς ἢ . . . κωμικοὺς φαύλους . . . ὑποκριτάς) who spoil excellent plays with bad performances. This initiates an extended series of metaphors, all underlining the central point that the interlocutor (like an actor) is not reproducing his own words: 'drama' (δράματος, 8), 'plot' (ὑπόθεσις, 8), 'poet' (ποιητής, 9), 'set' (σκηνῆς, 9), 'theatre' (θεάτρωι, 9), 'actor' (ὑποκρίτης, 9), 'tragic messenger' (ἀγγέλου . . . τραγικοῦ, 9). In this way, Lucian draws explicit attention to both the problems involved in representing the voice of another, and to the theatrical, mimetic aspects of that process.

The issues are revisited in chapter 11. Here the principal interlocutor states his decision to use indirect speech to report Nigrinus' words, lest he resemble 'actors' (ὑποκρίταις) who wear the masks and dress of great kings or heroes but then 'emit a tiny, weak, effeminate voice' (μικρὸν φθέγγονται καὶ ἰσχνὸν καὶ γυναικῶδες, 11). The following sentence is brilliant:

So, in order that I may not be convicted of wearing a mask (*prosōpeion*) much too grand for my own head and of disgracing my costume, I wish to speak to you with my own face bare (*apo gymnou . . . prosōpou*), so that I do not drag down with me when I fall the hero whose part I am acting.

[99] Pl. *Resp*. 394b distinguishes between 'simple narration' (ἁπλῆ διήγησις), its 'opposite' (ἐναντία, i.e. complex narration), and a mixture between the two. The paradox that Socrates effects this distinction within a literary dialogue (i.e. a form of complex narration) is well known: see e.g. Prendergast (1986), 10–12; Lyotard (1988), 25, and further Whitmarsh (1999*a*), 155–6. On Plato's choice of the dialogue form, see esp. Desjardins (1988); Mittelstrauss (1988); Griswold (1988); Frede (1992); Halperin (1992); Sayre (1995), 1–32.

[100] Cf. Soph. fr. 837 *TGF*; Ar. *Eccl*. 1129. Another allusion, 'after the style of the comic' (κατὰ τὸν κωμικόν), comes at ch. 7.

ἵν' οὖν μὴ καὶ αὐτὸς ἐλέγχωμαι πάνυ μεῖζον τῆς ἐμαυτοῦ κεφαλῆς προσωπεῖον περικείμενος καὶ τὴν σκευὴν καταισχύνων, ἀπὸ γυμνοῦ σοι βούλομαι τοὐμοῦ προσώπου προσλαλεῖν, ἵνα μὴ συγκατασπάσω που πεσὼν τὸν ἥρωα ὃν ὑποκρίνομαι. (11)

This passage explains and emphasizes the idiosyncratic form of Nigrinus' speech, which is entirely reported either in indirect speech or interspersed with periodic reminders that 'he said' (*ἔφη*), 'he recalled' (*ἐμέμνητο*), and the like.[101] In its disavowal of theatricality, however, it only draws attention to the complex masking of the author's voice in this text. If the interlocutor claims to be speaking 'with my own face bare', then Lucian is certainly not doing so: locating the author's voice in this the text is a (deliberately) frustrating exercise. Nigrinus' speech—which, as we have noted, looks suspiciously Lucianic—is reported by a supposedly 'unmasked', but none the less unnamed, interlocutor, whose appearance in the text is framed (and therefore authorially distanced) by the initial epistle.

The passage just quoted signals this feline narrative involution by using the closely related terms *prosōpon* and *prosōpeion* in distinct ways. The former means both 'face' and 'mask', while the latter only means 'mask'. At first blush, Lucian's interlocutor seems to construct a firm opposition between speaking with a mask (*prosōpeion*)—which would mean assuming the voice of Nigrinus—and speaking 'with my own face (*prosōpou*) bare ' (*ἀπὸ γυμνοῦ . . . τοὐμοῦ προσώπου*)—which means indirect reporting.[102] But by emphasizing '*my own* face (*prosōpon*)' (<u>*τοὐμοῦ*</u> *προσώπου*), the speaker exploits the ambiguity inherent in the word *prosōpon*: the choice is not so much between mask and no mask, as between his own *prosōpon* and that of Nigrinus. A face is a mask, a mask is a face. Indeed, even after this disavowal, his companion subsequently ticks him off for continuing to theatricalize: 'Come off it! Are you not going to stop using against me all this mass of theatricality and tragedy all day?' (*οὗτος ἀνὴρ οὐ παύσεται τήμερον πρός με πολλῆι τῆι σκηνῆι καὶ τῆι τραγωιδίαι χρώμενος;* 12). In the context of a work in which roles and identities are already dissembled, even (especially?) a professed attempt to denude oneself looks like an act

[101] A device modelled on Pl. *Phaedr.* 228d, as noted by G. Anderson (1978), 368.

[102] Cf. the opposition at *Tim.* 27 between 'wearing a mask (*prosōpeion*)' (*προσωπεῖον . . . περιθέμενος*) and 'with one's own face (*autoprosōpon*)' (*αὐτοπρόσωπον*).

of dissimulation. *Qui parle?* Where is Lucian in all this? *Who* is Lucian in all this?

Lucian's narrative of imbricated voices and concealed personae teases and taunts the reader with flashes of the face beneath the mask. For the reader, the pleasures of this text lie in testing the simultaneous embodiment and evanescence of the author's ego: in Barthes's words, 'it is [the] flash itself which seduces, or rather: the staging of an appearance-as-disappearance'.[103] The pleasurability that accrues from rebuffed searches for the author's *ipsissima uerba* is, in fact, specifically played out in the dialogic portion of the text, where (as in Plato's *Symposium*, such a fundamental intertext for the *Nigrinus*) the conversation is motivated by the fact that the principal interlocutor has heard the words of Nigrinus, while the other has not. The conversation begins with the latter noting that the former looks 'very haughty and lofty (*meteōros*)' (σεμνὸς . . . σφόδρα καὶ μετέωρος, 1), and demands to know why. The reason, of course, lies in his exposure to Nigrinus: 'I am aflutter and high (*meteōros*) because of his speech (*logos*)' (γαῦρός τε . . . ὑπὸ τοῦ λόγου καὶ μετέωρος, 5), he comments (subtly reappropriating the word *meteōros* in a more positive sense). The scenario generally evokes Socrates' response to hearing a reading of a work by Lysias in Plato's *Phaedrus* (234d).

It is Nigrinus' language, the direct experience of his voice, that has created this effect. He proceeds to image this experience in terms of transports of delight, using two images. First, he compares the intoxicating effects of wine upon the Indians on their first encounter with it: 'they were completely bacchicized, and went doubly mad' (ἐξεβακχεύθησαν καὶ διπλασίως . . . ἐξεμάνησαν, 5).[104] His interlocutor corrects him, saying that he has been rendered, not drunk, but sober by this speech, but still comments that 'I should like, if possible, to hear the very words' (ἐγὼ δὲ βουλοίμην ἄν, εἰ οἷόν τε, αὐτῶν ἀκοῦσαι τῶν λόγων, 6).[105] The premium placed upon the *ipsissima uerba* is re-emphasized in the principal interlocutor's response, where he introduces the second

[103] Barthes (1975), 10.

[104] Specifically echoing Socrates' 'bacchic' response to the speech of Lysias (συνεβάκχευσα, Pl. *Phaedr.* 234d), but also a fairly common metaphor in responses to rhetoric (Korenjak 2000: 99–100).

[105] Lucianic scepticism is linked to sobriety also at *Herm.* 47, where the tag 'sober up and remember to mistrust' (νῆφε καὶ μέμνησο ἀπιστεῖν, Epicharm. fr. 250 Kaibel) is cited.

image. He repeats 'the words spoken' (*τὰ εἰρημένα*) in his head two or three times a day, he says (6), before comparing himself to a lover imagining his boyfriend's words and deeds in his absence (7). This besotted eroticism is predicated on absences, on the gap interposed between lover and beloved: Lucian's reader is forcibly reminded via this simile that her or his literary pleasures consist in traversing and re-traversing the gap between direct experience of the philosopher and his second-order representation in a literary text. The *Nigrinus* enacts an excellent example of what Halperin calls 'the erotics of narrativity':

> Narrative . . . is erotic insofar as the illusion of dramatic immediacy it provides typically serves to collapse the distance between the occurring and the recounting of an event, or between the characters in a tale and its audience, while the very fact of narrative serves to consolidate that distance, to institutionalize and perpetuate it.[106]

Beginning with a breathless 115 words, a concatenation of clauses and subclauses, the principal interlocutor evokes the languorous eroticism of calling to mind the words of the absent Nigrinus:

> Just as the lovers of boys who are not present recall any deeds of theirs, and the words they have spoken, and deceptively assuage the illness by passing the time in such pursuits, as though their beloveds were present to them—some, for example, think they are even speaking to them, and take pleasure in things they once heard as though they were only just spoken to them, and they fixate their souls onto the memory of things past, and have no time for inconveniences that lie to hand—just so, I myself gather up and unfurl to myself the words I once heard of philosophy that is no longer present, and it gives me no small consolation, and it is just as though I were being tossed around at sea in the dead of night, and this were a beacon that I saw: I think that that man is present at all the things I do, and that I am always as it were listening to him saying the same things to me; sometimes, especially whenever I focus my soul upon him, his face even appears to me, and the sound of his voice remains in my ears; for he truly has, in the words of the comic, 'left something of his sting in his audience'.
>
> *καὶ ὥσπερ οἱ ἐρασταὶ τῶν παιδικῶν οὐ παρόντων ἔργ' ἄττα καὶ λόγους εἰρημένους αὐτοῖς διαμνημονεύουσι καὶ τούτοις ἐνδιατρίβοντες ἐξαπατῶσι τὴν νόσον, ὡς παρόντων σφίσι τῶν ἀγαπωμένων—ἔνιοι γοῦν αὐτοῖς καὶ προσλαλεῖν οἴονται καὶ ὡς ἄρτι λεγομένων πρὸς αὐτοὺς ὧν τότε ἤκουσαν ἥδονται καὶ προσάψοντες*

106 Halperin (1992), 106.

τὴν ψυχὴν τῆι μνήμηι τῶν παρεληλυθότων σχολὴν οὐκ ἄγουσιν [ἐν] τοῖς ἐν ποσὶν ἀνιᾶσθαι—οὕτω δὴ καὶ αὐτὸς φιλοσοφίας οὐ παρούσης τοὺς λόγους οὓς τότε ἤκουσα συναγείρων καὶ πρὸς ἐμαυτὸν ἀνατυλίττων οὐ μικρὰν ἔχω παραμυθίαν, καὶ ὅλως καθάπερ ἐν πελάγει καὶ νυκτὶ πολλῆι φερόμενος, ἐς πυρσόν τινα τοῦτον ἀποβλέπω, πᾶσι μὲν παρεῖναι τοῖς ὑπ' ἐμοῦ πραττομένοις τὸν ἄνδρα ἐκεῖνον οἰόμενος, ἀεὶ δὲ ὥσπερ ἀκούων αὐτοῦ τὰ αὐτὰ πρός με λέγοντος· ἐνίοτε δέ, καὶ μάλιστα ὅταν ἐνερείσω τὴν ψυχήν, καὶ τὸ πρόσωπον αὐτοῦ μοι φαίνεται καὶ τῆς φωνῆς ὁ ἦχος ἐν ταῖς ἀκοαῖς παραμένει· καὶ γάρ τοι κατὰ τὸν κωμικὸν ὡς ἀληθῶς ἐγκατέλιπέν τι κέντρον τοῖς ἀκούουσιν. (7; quotation = Eupol. fr. 102.7 KA)

The dominant theme of this passage is the polarity of absence and presence, on both the temporal and the spatial axis. As regards space, the Greek verb *pareinai* ('to be present'), recurs (whether negated or not) four times in this extract; and as regards time, the speaker represents memory as a link to 'things past' (τῶν παρεληλυθότων), a temporality marked by a brutally vague 'then' (τότε, *bis*), the word indicating nothing more specific than 'not-now'. Lucian's 'erotics of narrativity' are tied to a lingering sensuality and physicality: to report the words of Nigrinus is to imagine the 'sound of his voice' (τῆς φωνῆς ὁ ἦχος) and 'his face' (τὸ πρόσωπον), just as the lover takes consolation in imagining the words and 'acts' (ἔργα)[107] of intimacy with his beloved. The concrete immediacy of presence, though, is contrasted with the abstraction of 'the memory of things past' (τῆι μνήμηι τῶν παρεληλυθότων), at constant risk of evanescence if it is not assiduously reactivated. Only memorialization can keep memory alive. Yet paradoxically, memorialization also marks death (it is not the living who are commemorated), or at least an attempt to compensate for death with a surrogate posterity: 'the investiture of an emptiness, a veil of illusion cast over a nonbeing'.[108] Lucian's interlocutor is under no illusions as to the ontologically 'unreal' state of memory: lovers 'deceptively assuage the illness' (ἐξαπατῶσι τὴν νόσον) of desire. Remembering is a form of deceit, a false presence.

[107] For ἔργον as 'sexual act', see Strato, *Anth. Pal.* 12.209.3; Ach. Tat. 1.9.4–5; 1.10.2; 1.10.4, etc. (with O'Sullivan 1980: 158); and cf. Adams (1982), 156–7 on the Latin *opus*.

[108] Vernant (1991), 189. Vernant refers here to the Homeric *psykhē* ('ghost'), but his remarks concerning the substantiality of the *mnēma* (memorial-stone) and the insubstantiality of the ghostly presence that appears in dreams or in the underworld are germane to the present discussion.

The effects of this alluring philosophical *logos* are profoundly ambiguous, encompassing both pleasure and pain, joy and mourning. When Nigrinus finished speaking, the principal interlocutor, he reports, 'underwent what happened to the Phaeacians' (*τοῦτο . . . τὸ τῶν Φαιάκων πάθος ἐπεπόνθειν*), being at first 'enchanted' (*κεκηλημένος*) in silence (35).[109] He then experienced a multiple reaction, fissured by contradictions: 'seized by a great confusion (*synkhysei*) and giddiness (*ilingōi*), I poured with sweat, and though I wanted to speak, I failed and was knocked back, my voice left me and my tongue erred, and finally in exasperation (*aporoumenos*) I burst into tears' (*πολλῆι συγχύσει καὶ ἰλίγγωι κατειλημμένος τοῦτο μὲν ἱδρῶτι κατερρεόμην, τοῦτο δὲ φθέγξασθαι βουλόμενος ἐξέπιπτόν τε καὶ ἀνεκοπτόμην, καὶ ἥ τε φωνὴ ἐξέλειπε καὶ ἡ γλῶττα διημάρτανε, καὶ τέλος ἐδάκρυον ἀπορούμενος*, 35). In literary terms, this owes as much to Sapphic as to Platonic precedent: the *aporia* ('exasperation') and 'giddiness' (*ilingos*) allude to the responses of Socratic interlocutors,[110] while the emphasis upon sweat, bodily liquefaction (even the word *synkhysis*, 'confusion', implies flux) and speechlessness strongly recalls the celebrated symptomatology of desire in Sappho, fragment 31. The emphasis upon ambiguous response continues in what follows, where Nigrinus is compared to an archer, shooting the soul with an arrow dipped with a poison that is 'both gently biting and sweet' (*ἠρέμα δηκτικῶι τε καὶ γλυκεῖ*, 37): as a result, his listeners 'feel pleasure and cry' (*ἥδονται καὶ δακρύουσι*, 37).

This conflation of different affective responses, of course, has a long tradition in erotic literature.[111] The specific interest of this particular passage lies in its metaliterary application. Nigrinus' words, even at the point of their reception, inspire a mixed reaction that (when placed alongside the passage discussed previously) seems to construct the process of reading narrative as engendering simultaneously the joy of immediate presence and the pain of fleeting insubstantiality. The other interlocutor, on hearing this report, describes how this ambiguous response was also transmitted to him, like the madness of a rabid dog-bite:[112] he is filled

[109] Cf. *κηληθμός* at Hom. *Od.* 11.333–4; 13.1–2; Walsh (1984), 14.

[110] e.g. Pl. *Lys.* 216c, *εἰλιγγιῶ ὑπὸ τῆς τοῦ λόγου ἀπορίας* (I am giddy because of my exasperation at your words); cf. Philostr. *VA.* 8.5; 8.9.

[111] See Fusillo (1999) on the Greek novels, and further Ch. 1, n. 147.

[112] The dog-bite is a Cynic motif: cf. Diog. Laert. 6.60, and esp. Luc. *Herm.* 86 and *Alex.* 55, where Lucian (another rare appearance of the *nomen proprium*) bites

with 'ambrosia and lotus' (τῆς ἀμβροσίας καὶ τοῦ λωτοῦ, 38), but 'pains' when his friend 'stops' (παυσαμένου ἄχθομαι, 38). The soporific, lethargic effects of the lotus fill him with pleasure, but the moment of separation is grievous. This interpretative chain-reaction cues the reader to assess his or her response in like manner.

The dialogic frame for the text, then, constructs the reader as enforcedly secluded from the voice or *logos* of the text, glimpsing its power through seductive veils of secondary representation. Listening to or reading narrative is a profoundly ambiguous experience: seductive and alluring, but also mournful in that it reminds the reader of the insubstantiality of his or her experience. The initial epistle, we might add, confirms this sense of seclusion: as eavesdroppers on the correspondence between recipient and addressee, we are necessarily constructed as outsiders and interlopers. The pleasures and sadnesses of reading Lucian's *Nigrinus* are self-consciously thematized in the text itself: the text's evasiveness about the location of the authorial ego, its theatrical masking of Lucian's identity, its rhetorical ingenuity, and its literary dexterity combine to create a highly sophisticated meditation upon the absence and the presence of literary voice, upon the veiling and revelation of the author's views.

How do these teasing games with the concealment of the authorial voice relate to the the critique of the spectacular society? It is characteristic of Lucianic satire, as we have seen, to advertise the author's own complicity in his criticisms of mimetic superficiality. Paradoxically, Lucian's own theatricality and self-concealment in this text implicate him in precisely Nigrinus' criticisms of Rome: who is more theatrical, more masked, than Lucian? Is not Rome, with all its duplicities, the ideal context for Lucian? And, we might add, for Nigrinus: after all, we might ask, if he so despises Rome, why does he remain there? No straight answer to this question is given, except that he settled into enjoying the 'entertainment and laughter' (ψυχαγωγίαν καὶ γέλωτα, 18) to be had observing life at Rome. Sceptical mockery—that most Lucianic of phenomena—is localized at Rome. Finally, then, Rome

Alexander's hand. The comparison here is modelled on Alcibiades' 'snake-bitten' reaction to Socrates at *Symp* 215e. Branham (1989), 266–7 n. 34 has a good discussion of this topos. G. Anderson (1978), 372–3 n. 18 notes 'complimentary' references to aesthetic effects as 'biting'.

is the proper place for Lucianism, and Lucian in this dialogue subtly hints at his own implication in Rome's pleasures.

The *Nigrinus* constructs the image of a truth-telling, free-speaking, philosophical voice that might speak out against the vanity and superficiality of Rome, only to expose the hologrammatic nature of the image, construed fictively from within Lucian's hall of mirrors. This text does not take a morally superior view of Rome, so much as force the reader to confront his or her own secondary, imitative, theatrical, and ultimately *Romanized* position in relation to the inherited discourse of philosophical freedom and self-control. Rome is the new Athens, the centre of philosophical patronage: to imagine that we could disimplicate ourselves from that condition and return to a liberated, free-speaking Greece is an impossible dream.

THE WRONGS OF PASSAGE: *ON SALARIED POSTS*

The Lucianic text that most explicitly interconnects the themes we have traced so far (philosophy, commerce, spectacle, slavery, Roman power) is *On salaried posts*. This text, composed in the Plutarchan style of an advisory epistle addressed to a friend named Timocles,[113] warns against the trend for educated Greeks to accept the patronage of wealthy Romans. (Other Greeks are patronized by Romans, Lucian tells us, but it is explicitly only in the *pepaideumenoi* that he is interested: 4.) This sort of lifestyle is repeatedly referred to as 'slavery' (1, 5, 8, 17, 22, 23, 24, 26), a humiliatingly sycophantic existence made doubly embarrassing for that it was voluntarily entered into (5, 24) by a philosopher who professes 'freedom' and outspokenness (24). There are echoes throughout of Plato's *Symposium*: but whereas Socrates describes the *scala amoris* that elevates the philosopher to the elevated heights of philosophical knowledge, Lucian drags his abused academic through an Aristophanic mire of rotting food, sagging bellies, gout, vomiting, dog-piss, shit, and chamber-pots.

Peretti's argument that the text indicates Lucian's 'opposizione a Roma' is overstated and simplistic,[114] but so are many of the

[113] No doubt a fictitious *nomen loquens* ('famous-for-honour', suggesting covetousness towards glory): see C. P. Jones (1986), 78.

[114] Peretti (1946), 121–31. For easy rebuttals, see C. P. Jones (1986), 81–2; Swain (1996), 317.

counter-arguments that seek to neutralize the force of the critique. The fact that the criticism of wealth and exploitation can be paralleled in Juvenal[115] does not show that Lucian's humour is directed solely 'at the patron's wealth, not at his nationality'.[116] The parallels are hardly decisive, and anyway Juvenal's criticism, in Latin, of his adoptive city is necessarily different from Lucian's self-consciously external perspective upon Rome and its treatment of Greek *paideia*. Furthermore, a satire on wealth need not exclude a satire on Rome:[117] as we have seen, Lucian associates the one closely with the other. Wealth is an important theme in *On salaried posts*, and in particular the role played by wealth *within the coercive structure of Roman domination*.

Let us begin with the geographical mapping of the house, a spatial system that (as we shall see) emblematizes the symbolic structures of Roman power. *On salaried posts* traces the *pepaideumenos*' gradual journey from the outside of the house towards the interior.[118] The importance of this linear diagram is underlined at the conclusion of the text, where Lucian adapts to his own use the *Picture* (*Tabula*) of pseudo-Cebes, an exegetical account of an allegorical cipher (consisting of concentric circles) representing the difficulty of accessing true *paideia*.[119] Lucian satirically reverses his model: his own topography marks the progress of the *pepaideumenos* towards dissolution, ruin, and moral bankruptcy. Yet there is more to *On salaried posts* than simply literary parody: the model of centre and periphery also describes the machinations

[115] Esp. Juv. *Sat.* 3; 5. See Helm (1906), 44–55; Mesk (1912–13); Palm (1959), 52; J. Hall (1981), 246–8; C. P. Jones (1986), 80–1. Not all the parallels are convincing, but the following are at least suggestive (listed with the Juvenal reference before the slash): 5.19/24; 22 (clients have to rise in the middle of the night); 5.84–5/26 (size of portions served); 5.59–60/26 (not getting served); 5.166/7 (initial hopes of success); 5.12/22 (ironic reference to *merces/γέρας* for one's troubles). I am not convinced, however, that this shows anything other than that there was a well-known set of complaints about the life of a *cliens*. These were no doubt common property and needed no literary source (like the complaints of junior doctors or teachers nowadays).

[116] C. P. Jones (1986), 82. Cf. contra Swain (1996), 319: Lucian's 'depiction here of the Roman rich of the city of Rome cannot be considered as anything but hostile'.

[117] Cf. Swain (1996), 321, suggesting that Lucian is criticizing Rome *and not* wealth.

[118] The in/out opposition is most clearly emphasized at *De merc. cond.* 21 (quoted and discussed subsequently; see also 23), but, as will become clear, runs throughout.

[119] One of the earliest mentions of the *Tabula*: see J. T. Fitzgerald and White (1983), 5.

of Roman power. As Geertz has emphasized,[120] the symbolics of power (what he calls, following Weber, 'charisma') depend fundamentally upon the symbolic relations between centre and periphery. For the excluded onlooker, power is simultaneously legitimized and mystified by theatrical effects that magnify while obscuring the centre of society.

From the outside, Lucian tells us, life within looks extremely alluring:

Men on the outside afterwards envy you, seeing that you spend your time within the protected circle, you enter unhindered, and you have become one of those thoroughly on the inside.

οἱ μὲν δὴ ἔξω ἄνθρωποι τὸ μετὰ τοῦτο ζηλοῦσί σε ὁρῶντες ἐντὸς τῆς κιγκλίδος διατρίβοντα καὶ ἀκωλύτως εἰσιόντα καὶ τῶν πάνυ τινὰ ἔνδον γεγενημένον. (21)

The idea of the protected centre within the *κιγκλίς* (literally the wicker gates that fence off the area accessible only to dicasts in a court or councillors in a council-chamber)[121] has a crucial symbolic value in this text, as it does in the original *Tabula*.[122] Those wishing to cross the various boundaries are led on by 'hope' (*ἐλπίς*, 7, 21–2, 42) to covet 'initiation' into the inner circle of power, prestige, and influence. *On salaried posts* hurls a chaotic hailstorm of mixed metaphors at the reader, but the teletic imagery of mystery religion recurs throughout in a particularly significant way. It is highlighted from the start, where Lucian refers to 'those who . . . had completed the entire initiation (*teletēs*), from neophytes to the highest grade (*epopteusantes*)' (*τῆς τελετῆς διεξεληλυθότες καὶ πάντα ἐξ ἀρχῆς εἰς τέλος ἐποπτεύσαντες*, 1). An *epoptēs* is one who has accessed the highest grade of initiation into the Eleusinian mysteries and is permitted to behold the epiphany of the goddess Demeter.[123] When combined with the evocation of the allegorical *Tabula*, this imagery serves to create an air of ironic mysticism about the *pepaideumenos*' progress towards

[120] Geertz (1993), esp. 143: 'No matter how peripheral, ephemeral or free-floating the charismatic figure we may be concerned with—the wildest prophet, the most deviant revolutionary—we must begin with the center and with the symbols and preoccupations that prevail there if we are to understand him and what he means.'

[121] Rhodes (1972), 33–4.

[122] See the excellent remarks of Elsner (1995), 40–6.

[123] J. E. Harrison (1991), 515, 546.

the centre. As well as engaging in Geertzian anthropology, this model serves to structure the text into a series of initiatory 'stages'.

Unlike initiations into the cult of Demeter at Eleusis, however, this one is never completed. Changing the metaphorical register to the erotic, Lucian recounts how the desire of the *pepaideumenos* is ever frustrated and the consummation systematically deferred:

Therefore, like unlucky, unsuccessful lovers, they fall into the hands of artful (*entekhnoi*), knowing (*tribōnes*) boys who treat them contemptuously, flattering them so as to make sure that they will always desire them, but not allowing them in return to enjoy even so much of their boyish charms as a brushed kiss—for they know that in success lies the dissolution of desire. For that reason, they keep that locked away, and guard it jealously; but in other respects, they keep their lover always in hope, fearful that despair might divert him from his passionate desire, and that he might fall out of love.

τοιγαροῦν ὥσπερ δυσέρωτας αὐτοὺς καὶ κακοδαίμονας ἐραστὰς ἔντεχνοί τινες καὶ τρίβωνες ἐρώμενοι παραλαβόντες ὑπεροπτικῶς περιέπουσιν, ὅπως ἀεὶ ἐρασθήσονται αὐτῶν θεραπεύοντες, ἀπολαῦσαι δὲ τῶν παιδικῶν ἀλλ' οὐδὲ μέχρι φιλήματος ἄκρου μεταδιδόντες· ἴσασι γὰρ ἐν τῶι τυχεῖν τὴν διάλυσιν τοῦ ἔρωτος γενησομένην. ταύτην οὖν ἀποκλείουσιν καὶ ζηλοτύπως φυλάττουσιν· τὰ δὲ ἄλλα ἐπ' ἐλπίδος ἀεὶ τὸν ἐραστὴν ἔχουσιν. δεδίασι γὰρ μὴ αὐτὸν ἡ ἀπόγνωσις ἀπαγάγηι τῆς ἀγὰν ἐπιθυμίας καὶ ἀνέραστος αὐτοῖς γένηται. (7)

The sophistication (*entekhoi . . . tribōnes*) of the Roman masters, like that of boys giving the come-on, lies in their coy, tantalizing teasing of the appetites of the *pepaideumenoi*. The temporal framework is significant: the pleasures of pederastic desire are conventionally linked to its intense but transitory appeal,[124] whereas these artful boys attempt to make it last forever (the word *aei*, 'always', occurs twice in this passage). 'Then', Lucian continues, 'before they know it, both have aged, the one too old to desire and the other too old to reciprocate' (*εἶτ' ἔλαθον ἄμφω γηράσαντες, ἔξωροι γενόμενοι καὶ οὗτος τοῦ ἐρᾶν κἀκεῖνος τοῦ μεταδιδόναι*, 7). This erotic metaphor interlinks with the initiatory metaphor that runs throughout *On salaried posts*, both focusing upon the idea that a period of struggle should be—but in this case is not—followed swiftly by access to the object sought. Indeed, the notion of the deferred centre is also subtly introduced in this passage: the observation that the boys keep the satisfaction of the lover's desire 'locked away, and guard it jealously' implies an innermost recess,

[124] Cf. e.g. Ach. Tat. 2.36.1.

both the bodily interior that the lover longs to penetrate and the interior of the house that the *pepaideumenos* longs to access.

The Roman patron, then, strategically fosters the misperception that entry into the households will yield access to the wealth and authority he oversees, seeking both to lure *pepaideumenoi* to him and to maintain his own position at the symbolic centre of the power-system. The attractive view from outside the house, however, is (so Lucian reports) false: stories of what goes on inside are no more reliable than travellers' tales (1–2). The life of a *pepaideumenos* employed in such a capacity is shown throughout to be extremely unpleasant. It is not just the owners, however, who perpetrate this deception: the *pepaideumenoi* themselves advance disingenuous pretexts (e.g. penury, old age, illness) for their actions, pretexts that are nothing but a 'veil' (*προκάλυμμα*, 5) for their true motive, greed. To combat this disinformation, Lucian promises to reveal what 'truly' (*ὡς ἀληθῶς*, 5; cf. *ἀληθέστατον*, 7) goes on in the houses. This is a familiar Lucianic gambit: the satirist represents himself as exposing to the public certain negative qualities that are strategically concealed from view by the superficial appearance of positive qualities. What is specific to this essay, however, is the focus upon the relationship between Greek *paideia* and Roman power, and upon the strategic attempts on the part of the wealthy to perpetrate and manipulate this dissimulation.

This text is of particular importance to the present chapter, however, because of the stress Lucian places upon the complex visual fields that surround the *pepaideumenos* as he enters into the heart of the house. *On salaried posts* is dominated by images of looking, staring, scrutinizing, and seeing. The theatrical metaphors that we saw in the *Fisherman* and the *Nigrinus* do find their way into *On salaried posts*,[125] but the dominant spectacular metaphors in this text are drawn from the competitive contests of civic life: the courts, the games, and the public examination (*δοκιμασία*). These images recur with particular intensity during the primary stages of the *pepaideumenos*' initiation. Like all *rites de passage*,[126] this one begins with a boundary: the first step involves

[125] See *De merc. cond.* 10 (*ἡ καταστροφὴ τοῦ δράματος*); 11 (*τραγικοῦ . . . θεοῦ*); 19 (*ἀτραγῴδητα*); 27 (*ὑποκρίνασθαι*); 28 (*κορυφαῖος*); 41 (*δρᾶμα* etc.).

[126] See Schmitz (1997), 132 on Lucian's meal as *rite de passage*; van Gennep (1960), 15–25 on *rites de passage* and boundaries.

camping on the threshold (*θυραυλίας*, 10), being locked out, and pandering to a doorkeeper (*θυρωρῶι*, 10); then, after crossing this boundary, come the processes of scrutiny and testing that Lucian emphasizes so heavily. The owner does not even look at (*προσβλέπει*) the aspirant for several days (11). Then, if he does see (*ἴδηι*) him and ask him a question, the *pepaideumenos* sweats profusely (*πολὺς . . . ὁ ἱδρώς*), and suffers from trembling (*τρόμος*) and giddiness (*ἴλιγγος*)—precisely the responses that a philosopher normally *elicits*, as we saw above[127]—and his nervous terror causes him to blurt out the wrong answer (11). This draws laughter from *hoi parontes* ('those present', 11). This group of onlookers, the *parontes*, as we shall see, are a recurrent feature in the description of the house, reinforcing the idea that the initiation of the aspirant is an entry into a discrete but diverse community—and also, crucially, a civic spectacle. Like the *corona* of spectators so frequently mentioned in ancient accounts of the lawcourts,[128] these bystanders help to sustain the air of ubiquitous scrutiny and suspicion. Indeed, Lucian implicitly compares the scenario here with a court, referring to the *pepaideumenos* as having 'convicted' (*καταδικάσας*) himself with his error (11).

If one is successful at this stage, the next obstacle is an 'examination' (*ἐξέτασις*, *ἀντεξεταζομένοις*, 11; cf. *ἐξεταζόμενον*, 12). This word implies an official or institutional inspection, and further underlines the sense that the house is an autonomous political state. The owner enjoys the event, Lucian tells us, but the *pepaideumenos* perceives it as a 'contest (*agōn*) for his soul and entire life' (*ὁ ὑπὲρ τῆς ψυχῆς ἀγὼν καὶ ὑπὲρ ἅπαντος τοῦ βίου*, 11). The agonistic nature of the process is attributed to two features, the *pepaideumenos*' sense of the gains and losses at stake if he is *adokimos* ('tested and found wanting', 11), and the presence of 'many others' who are opposed to him, 'of whom each one secretly, as it were, has shot at you from a hiding-place' (*ὧν ἕκαστος ὥσπερ ἐκ λόχου τοξεύων λέληθεν*, 12). The word *adokimos* evokes the Athenian *dokimasia*, a quasi-juridical site for the scrutiny of potential citizens by others, 'a repository of innuendo, rumor, hearsay, and gossip'.[129] Like the bystanders discussed in the previous paragraph, the 'others' confronted by the *pepaideu-*

[127] See n. 110.
[128] Lanni (1997).
[129] V. Hunter (1994), 108; see more generally 106–11.

menos reinforce the atmosphere of innumerable, suspicious eyes. Meanwhile, he is also looking, straining intently at the face of the master (as the latter observes his triallist), hoping to catch a glimpse of his reaction (11). Unlike the all-powerful gaze of the master, however, and unlike the authoritarian gaze of public suspicion (resentful of change and intimidating as it is), the peering of the *pepaideumenos* is disempowered and fragile, merely responding passively to the hints it perceives on the master's face. In this empire of the senses, visual hierarchies are rigorously structured.

There then follows a stage in which one's whole life is pried into (12). This section is built around a series of metaphors implying public ordeals. Grudge-bearing fellow citizens and former neighbours are brought forward to bear false witness (the word μάρτυς, 'witness', underlines the quasi-juridical atmosphere), whilst all who offer compliments are rejected as 'suspicious' (ὑπόπτοι, 12: another word that has visual connotations in Greek). Success at this stage is also presented as an (unlikely) agonistic triumph: you will only 'win' (εὐτυχῆσαι) if you are lucky, and you have 'absolutely no opposition' (μηδὲν ὅλως ἐναντιωθῆναι, 12). If the *pepaideumenos* does happen to 'win', the result is like an Olympic victory or the capture of a great city (13). Unlike in an epinician context, however, the fruits of victory are not awarded immediately. This victory should in theory, Lucian proposes, mark the completion of the *pepaideumenos*' initiation, and the beginning of his access to the wealth and power he naïvely craves: 'indeed, you *should* receive the very greatest benefits in return for such great ordeals (*ponoi*)' (δεῖ δή σοι ἀντὶ τῶν τοσούτων πόνων μέγιστα ἡλίκα γενέσθαι τἀγαθά, 13). The insistent message of *On salaried posts*, however, is that ordeals are never over and the process of initiation is never complete: in the terms of the striking metaphor of chapter 7, discussed above, the *pepaideumenos*' desire is never consummated. The mechanism of exploitation is concealed and perpetuated by the promise of advancement to the symbolic centre of the house, the locus of power and prestige, but that moment is always deferred.

Indeed, the next step is also a false peak, another ordeal: a dinner party (δεῖπνον) that serves (as Lucian puts it) as 'a preliminary initiation (*proteleia*) into your future companionship' (τὰ προτέλεια τῆς μελλούσης συνουσίας, 14). The initiatory imagery (*proteleia*) promises progress towards the centre, but the knowing irony is heavy.[130] In the Greek tradition, a meal or symposium constitutes an idealized paradigm of harmony, equality, and friendship, especially in the wake of Plato's and Xenophon's *Symposia*.[131] To Lucian's eye, however, idealized paradigms are there to be debunked: his own *Symposium*, for example, presents drunken philosophers fighting. The dinner thrown by the house-owner in *On salaried posts*, though not disordered, is far from being a model of equality and sodality. The dinner proves to be a site of agonistic conflict, and the *pepaideumenos* finds himself the object of the aggressive, scrutinizing gaze of his rivals and patrons.[132]

The complex network of gazes that greets the *pepaideumenos* serves systematically to disempower him. Like Trimalchio, the dinner host in Petronius' *Satyricon*,[133] the owner wants to make the meal into a visual panorama: 'spectacles arrive on top of spectacles, for he wishes to display to you all his possessions' (*θεαμάτων ἐπὶ θεάμασι παριόντων—ἅπαντα γὰρ ἐπιδείξασθαί σοι τὰ αὑτοῦ βούλεται*, 18). Yet the effect of all this display upon its intended viewer is not welcoming: when the *pepaideumenos* arrives at the meal, he finds everything 'foreign and unknown' (*ξένα . . . καὶ ἄγνωστα*, 15), and gazes at everything 'as though it were the house of Zeus' (*ὥσπερ ⟨εἰς⟩ τοῦ Διὸς τὸν οἶκον*, 15).[134] His awe-filled staring marks him out as a newcomer; and, conversely, it is observed by others: 'the servants stare at you, and each one of those present (*hoi parontes*) watches out to see what you will do' (*ἥ τε οἰκετεία εἰς σὲ ἀποβλέπει καὶ τῶν παρόντων ἕκαστος ὅ τι πράξεις ἐπιτήρουσιν*, 15). As in the earlier 'competition', the *parontes* constitute an additional spectatorship, creating extra disciplinary

[130] Schmitz (1997), 132, although he underplays Lucian's irony: 'Das Gastmahl wird hier zur Prüfung, zu einem *rite de passage*, der darüber entscheidet, ob ein Außenstehender in die Grüppe kooptiert werden kann oder nicht.'

[131] Plutarch writes of 'the table's capacity to make friendship' (*τὸ φιλοποιοῦν . . . τῆς τραπέζης*, *Quaest. conu.* 612d; cf. *Cat. maj.* 25.4). An unidentifiable character in the first book of Athenaeus' *Sophists at dinner* derives *dais* ('feast'), with only slight etymological elasticity, from *dateisthai* ('to divide'), before quoting Zenodotus on Homer: 'an equal feast means a goodly feast' (*δαῖτα ἐίσην τὴν ἀγαθήν*, 12c). See further Jeanneret (1991), 62–70.

[132] See Schmitz (1997), 127–33 for an excellent discussion of intellectual competition at mealtimes.

[133] See esp. Rosati (1983). There is a body of evidence for actual theatrical performances at dinner-times: see C. P. Jones (1991).

[134] An allusion to Telemachus' comments concerning Menelaus' house at Hom. *Od.* 4.74–5.

pressure upon the *pepaideumenos* to conform, even as he himself stares. This process of reciprocal viewing is redoubled: the owner has mandated some of his servants to watch over (ἐπισκοπεῖν) how he looks at (ἀποβλέψεις, 15) his sons, wife, or courtesans.[135] The servants of his fellow diners mock him when they observe (ὁρῶντες, 15) his inexperience. He is terrified to eat or drink in case he seems overly appetitive, and needs to sneak a glance at (ὑποβλέπειν) his neighbour so as to know what to do (15). This process of ubiquitous observation, whether it is the *pepaideumenos* doing the looking or being looked at, recurrently serves to emphasize his powerlessness.

To an extent, the prominent position of the *pepaideumenos* at this feast grants him social superiority. On this occasion—'that first and sweetest dinner' (τὸ πρῶτον . . . καὶ ἥδιστον ἐκεῖνο δεῖπνον, 19)—he is greeted 'with great honour' (πάνυ ἐντίμως, 14) by his host, prestigiously seated,[136] and vouched much honour. Of course, this is merely a seductive ruse, designed to keep up his hopes (16). What is more, this conspicuousness also works to his disadvantage. His exalted position is observed by the other guests, and occasions much jealousy on the part of those who have endured 'many years of slavery' (πολυετῆ δουλείαν, 17): they comment upon the iniquity of the situation, complain that Greeks are prized above others, discuss his drinking, and predict that he will be in their position in five days' time (17). Their 'slanders' (διαβολάς, 17) serve to restore the social balance to a mathematical equilibrium: this malicious gossip subtracts from the honour (τίμη) that the owner had added to his stock.[137] Even when the *pepaideumenos* is viewed as in a position of power, negative social forces seek to rob him of that power and return him to a lowly state.

Lucian now passes to the next stage, the consideration of the *pepaideumenos*' fee. The owner summons his new charge into his

[135] Some have identified a widespread concern with the moral character of tutors in this period: see esp. Bonner (1977), 104–10; further references at R. B. Rutherford (1989), 98 n. 19. It is more likely that the idea of the lecherous tutor has its roots in satirical readings of Classical pederasty, particularly in Plato's dialogues.

[136] On seating plans at Roman meals see D'Arms (1990).

[137] Cf. V. Hunter (1994), 117, on gossip. The various contests for *timē* within the household constitute a recurrent theme: cf. *De merc. cond.* 19, 26, 27. Lucian's own *Slander* refers to the prevalence of slander in situations where one person's honour outweighs that of his rivals: Luc. *Calumn.* 12; cf. 2.

presence—although as usual there are other *parontes* standing by (19). The owner's speech is a masterpiece of ironic deception:

You have already seen (*heōrakas*) what sort of place my household is: there is not a drop of pretension in it, and everything is untheatrical (*atragōidētos*), prosaic and democratic. You must act as if we have everything in common.

τὰ μὲν ἡμέτερα ὁποῖά ἐστιν ἑώρακας ἤδη, καὶ ὡς τῦφος ἐν αὐτοῖς οὐδὲ εἷς, ἀτραγῴδητα δὲ καὶ πεζὰ πάντα καὶ δημοτικά, χρὴ δὲ σε οὕτως ἔχειν ὡς ἁπάντων ἡμῖν κοινῶν ἐσομένων. (19)

The *pepaideumenos* certainly has 'seen' (and, indeed, been seen by) much in the household, but the master's words are of course heavily ironic: his new charge's experience of the household has been of, so far from 'untheatrical', a spectacular, duplicitous scenario. The suggestion that they should have everything 'in common' (*κοινῶν*) recalls the widespread connection of 'sharing' with the egalitarian ethics of aristocratic friendship.[138] Yet this particular 'friendship' is far from the communal sodality celebrated by the Greek sympotic tradition. Manipulating this rhetoric of friendship, the owner proceeds, subtly, to coerce the *pepaideumenos* into a position of weakness:

I see (*horō*) that your character is moderate and self-sufficient, and I know you did not come to my house in the hope of a salary, but for the sake of other things: my goodwill and the universal honour in which you will be held.

ὁρῶ μὲν τὸ μέτριον καὶ αὔταρκες τοῦ σοῦ τρόπου καὶ συνίημι ὡς οὐχὶ μισθοῦ ἐλπίδι προσελήλυθας ἡμῶν τῆι οἰκίαι, τῶν δὲ ἄλλων ἕνεκα, τῆς εὐνοίας τῆς παρ' ἡμῶν καὶ τιμῆς, ην παρὰ πᾶσιν ἕξεις. (19)

Despite the earlier disavowal of pretension, such statements are precisely theatrical, in that the owner conceals his oppression of his charge behind an unblinking adherence to the 'script': the philosopher is a virtuous and ungrasping man, unmotivated by the 'hope of a salary' (*μισθοῦ ἐλπίδι*, 19), and the owner is immediately receptive to the philosophical ideals of equality and sharing between men. Cunning rhetoric: if the *pepaideumenos* were to challenge the owner's statement, he would risk thereby unmasking himself and losing his own stake in the matter. The owner then asks his new employee to suggest a salary for himself, thus rendering him complicit in his own exploitation (and disguising the

[138] Above, n. 131.

coercion as voluntary choice). The *pepaideumenos*, Lucian tells us, is thereby rendered 'tame' (τιθασόν, 20), and out of embarassment entrusts the decision to his master (20). ('Too right, Lucian,' comments a mournful scholiast at this point, 'this has often happened to me, too.')[139] This is, Lucian hints, exploitation theatrically disguised as friendship and sharing.

The Roman household, then, constitutes another locus for the economic exploitation and 'spectacularization' of the *pepaideumenos*. The idea that the philosopher exerts some authority in the household and the language of self-restraint and equality are all for show, dissimulating the workings of hierarchical power: the Roman system of economic patronage creates the desire in the Greek *pepaideumenos* for the mysterious power located (significantly) in the centre of the house, but always postpones any satisfaction of that desire. To an extent, this teaches us a more general lesson about the nature of power: the owner needs to create a system wherein there are coveters, in order to convince himself and others that he has something. Power is a primarily symbolic attribute, always concealing its tracks and mystifying itself: it can only be manifested in symptoms (such as others' lust for it), and cannot be itself displayed. To reveal the secret would make it a secret no more, and power depends upon secrecy:[140] the rich fear, Lucian tells us near the end, that old *pepaideumenoi* who have finally been expelled might expose the 'mysteries of their nature' (τῆς φύσεως ἀπόρρητα, 41), since they have 'seen the epiphany of (*epōpteukotes*) their nakedness' (γυμνοὺς αὐτοὺς ἐπωπτευκότες, 41). The final revelation—to complete the metaphorical cycle of initiation into a mystery religion—is not of an enlightenment, but of a depressing secret: that power consists in its own masking. Socio-economic power cannot exist independently of the theatre that mystifies it: once one has realized that, one risks exposing '[t]he very thing that the elaborate mystique of . . . ceremonial is supposed to conceal—that majesty is made, not born . . .'.[141]

Desire for public display is the motivation that drives the house.

[139] παναληθῆ ταῦτα, ὦ Λουκιανέ· πέπονθα γὰρ κἀγὼ τὰ ὅμοια . . . (Σ *De merc. cond.* 20 Rabe).

[140] 'The emperor is never naked . . . only an innocently idealist conception of the intrinsic force of justice, founded on the implicit dissociation of force from the legitimacy which it necessarily engenders, could lead one to speak . . . of "naked power"' (Bourdieu and Passeron 1990: 36).

[141] Geertz (1993), 124.

There is much in *On salaried posts* about the cravings of *pepaideumenoi* for the 'reputation' (δόξα) that supposedly comes with such positions (9, 19); but it is interesting to note that the owner also craves the attention of *pepaideumenoi* primarily as a theatrical prop:

He does not want you at all for that purpose [i.e. instruction]; but because you have a long beard and a serious appearance and you are dressed modestly in a Greek cloak and everyone knows that you are a grammarian, rhetorician or philosopher, it seems good to him for such a man to be mixed in with his retinue and escort. For this will make him seem a lover of Greek knowledge and altogether a man of taste when it comes to education (*paideia*). As a result, my friend, there is a danger that you have hired out your beard and cloak, rather than your splendid speeches.

δεῖται δή σου ἐπ' ἐκεῖνα μὲν οὐδαμῶς, ἐπεὶ δὲ πώγωνα ἔχεις βαθὺν καὶ σεμνός τις εἶ τὴν πρόσοψιν καὶ ἱμάτιον Ἑλληνικὸν εὐσταλῶς περιβέβλησαι καὶ πάντες ἴσασί σε γραμματικὸν ἢ ῥήτορα ἢ φιλόσοφον, καλὸν αὐτῶι δοκεῖ ἀναμεμῖχθαι καὶ τοιοῦτόν τινα τοῖς προϊοῦσι καὶ προπομπεύουσιν αὐτοῦ· δόξει γὰρ ἐκ τούτου καὶ φιλομαθὴς τῶν Ἑλληνικῶν μαθημάτων καὶ ὅλως περὶ παιδείαν φιλόκαλος. ὥστε κινδυνεύεις, ὦ γενναῖε, ἀντὶ τῶν θαυμαστῶν λόγων τὸν πώγωνα καὶ τὸν τρίβωνα μεμισθωκέναι. (25)

The *pepaideumenos* is displayed as part of the spectacle of Roman power: the main attributes being hired are his superficial semiotics, the beard and cloak. What matters to the Roman is what he will 'seem': for that reason, the *pepaideumenos* must 'always be seen' (ἀεὶ . . . ὁρᾶσθαι, 25) with him, he must present himself early at his house 'to be seen' (ὀφθησόμενον, 25) in his retinue, so that the owner can 'make a display' (ἐπιδεικνύμενος, 25) of his culture to those he meets. Although it is clear that the Roman is in control here, there is an interesting reciprocal arrangement: the presence of the Greek *pepaideumenos* is an expression of his power, a power that (as we have seen) is primarily articulated in the field of display and performance. The same could be said of the Greek pedagogues in this context as is argued by feminist psychoanalysts apropos of women in films and romances: they 'serve as a sign, as something unreal which can be passed around in the place of the intangible real—wealth, the phallus, or power'.[142] Power signifies only through theatrical spectacle, doomed to be devalorized if it is demystified.

The empire of the senses atrophies the power of all individuals

[142] Elsom (1992), 213.

bar the man at the top: it is an effective means of disseminating and policing hierarchies under the guise of civilized values and free will. Yet this disciplinary *panoptisme* is not *all*-controlling: there is one *pepaideumenos* who stakes a claim for freedom from Roman control. That person is, of course, the satirist himself, whose quasi-Plutarchan pose of moralism and free-speaking, insightful scepticism arrogate to him a privileged vantage. In a world of irony, masking, and theatrical deceit, what claim can the satirist press to speak 'truly' (ὡς ἀληθῶς, 5; cf. ἀληθέστατον, 7; ἐκ ἀληθείας, 8)? Is there any position exterior to the circuits of power? Or is the Lucianic voice subject to its own critique? Do we have here a Lucianic instance of satire's general tendency (to revisit Clark's quotation) to 'create "voices" that are, amongst other things, self-exposing'?[143]

Like the *Sale of lives*, the *On salaried posts* has a sequel, the *Apology*. In this text, composed as a letter to a certain Sabinus, Lucian observes that, since he wrote the former text, he himself has benefited from preferment to a post in the Roman administration of Egypt:[144] he is thus open to the charge that there is a 'great dissonance between my present life and what I wrote' (πολλὴ . . . ἡ διαφωνία τοῦ νῦν βίου πρὸς τὸ σύγγραμμα, *Apol.* 1). The authoritative, knowing voice of the *On salaried posts* is here placed at risk: is Lucian himself just as hypocritical as those he earlier criticized?[145] Such is the seemingly inevitable 'accusation' (κατηγορία, 5; cf. 3, 4, 6, 8, 11); and, as in the *Fisherman*, the Lucianic persona finds itself in need of a 'defence-speech' (ἀπολογία, 3, 4, 8, 11, 15). Conventionally, scholars have taken the *Apology* at face value, as a response, written later in Lucian's life, to real criticism consequent upon his promotion.[146] There are good reasons, however, to read it less in biographical than in literary terms. In particular, the device of using a second text to defend the first is characteristically Lucianic. There are three such instances of self-defence in his oeuvre, and each represents itself in legal terms as an 'apology'.[147]

[143] Clark (1995), 22.

[144] Apparently, Lucian attained the post of *eisagōgeus* (legal clerk) in Egypt (cf. *Apol.* 12). See van der Leest (1985); C. P. Jones (1986), 21; Swain (1996), 322.

[145] A similar strategy to that employed by Horace in *Satires* 2.7, where his slave Davus (taking advantage of the licence offered by the *Saturnalia*) satirizes Horace's own performance. See most recently W. Fitzgerald (2000), 18–24.

[146] e.g. Peretti (1946), 141–6; Swain (1996), 321.

[147] The *Apology* (κατηγορία, *Apol.* 5; cf. 3, 4, 6, 8, 11; ἀπολογία, 3, 4, 8, 11, 15);

By evoking the agonistic, antiphonal structures of the lawcourts, Lucian introduces a contrapuntal, dissonant voice that challenges the narratorial persona of the initial piece; and, at the same time, he encourages his audience to take a more active role in judging the case, in assessing the validity of his position. In what follows, I propose to take the *Apology* as an integral part of the dialectic struggle for cultural authority begun in *On salaried posts*, not simply as a later epilogue: it is a deliberate subversion of the narratorial voice of the earlier text.

The central strategy of the *Apology* involves Lucian imagining Sabinus turning his own words in *On salaried posts* against him. In misaligning his self-presentation and his true self, Sabinus is imagined to presume, he acts like 'tragic actors, on stage each an Agamemnon, Creon or even Heracles, but off it, when they have taken their masks off, a Polus or Aristodemus, playing the part for money' (τοῖς τραγικοῖς ὑποκριταῖς . . . οἳ ἐπὶ μὲν τῆς σκηνῆς Ἀγαμέμνων ἕκαστος αὐτῶν ἢ Κρέων ἢ αὐτὸς Ἡρακλῆς εἰσιν, ἔξω δὲ Πῶλος ἢ Ἀριστόδημος ἀποθέμενοι τὰ πρόσωπα γίγνονται ὑπόμισθοι τραγωιδοῦντες, 5).[148] The theatrical imagery of *On salaried posts* and (in particular) of the *Fisherman* is here turned against its author.[149] At another point, Lucian imagines a Homeric line used in the earlier text ('it wet the lips, but not the palate', χείλεα μέν τε δίην', ὑπερώιην δ' οὐκ ἐδίηνε)[150] used now as an accusation against him (*Apol.* 6; cf. *De merc. cond.* 20). The suggested (but ultimately rejected) defences of Lucian's undertaking imperial service on the grounds that he was seeking to escape poverty and mitigate old age (*Apol.* 10) recall the false pretexts used by the *pepaideumenoi* in *On salaried posts* (*De merc. cond.* 5–6). The metaphor of the 'bait' also occurs in both texts (*De merc. cond.* 3; *Apol.* 9). In numerous ways, the *Apology* proposes, at least in the first instance, to subvert the authority of the voice in *On salaried posts* by turning back its own rhetoric.

To these charges Lucian replies vigorously, arguing that he had not enslaved himself to the will of any individual, but entered

the *Fisherman* (ἀπολογία, *Pisc.* 8); the *Defence of portraits* (κατηγορία, κατήγοροι, ἀπολογία, 15).

148 Polus and Aristodemus were well-known actors of the 4th cent. (cf. e.g. Aul. Gell. *NA* 6.5; 11.9.2; the names are also conjoined at *Jup. trag.* 3).

149 Also reminiscent of the *Fisherman* is the story of Cleopatra's monkey (*Apol.* 5; cf. *Pisc.* 36).

150 Hom. *Il.* 22.495.

public service for the good of society as a whole (11); it is not payment itself that is objectionable, but payment in private households under the pretext of education (12). Yet not all readers have been convinced by this self-defence (as Lucian himself foresees at the conclusion of the text, ch. 15): Simon Swain, notably, has pointed out that the *Apology* conveniently overlooks the anti-Roman strain in *On salaried posts*, strategically under-representing the bite of the earlier text's satire.[151] The Lucian of this later date is now complicit in the networks of Roman power, and this change of perspective is mirrored in the change of addressee, from the unnamed Greek of *On salaried posts* to the Roman Sabinus of the *Apology*. Yet this deliberate refocusing of attention is not an attempt simply to delude the reader or convince him or her that Lucian is a man of integrity; rather, it is part of an ongoing process of subversion and re-establishment of the authority of Lucian's own literary voice. Indeed, this very text draws attention to its author's characteristically elusive facility with role-playing and persona-shifting. By casting his text in the form of an apology, Lucian necessarily recalls the precedents of the canonical *Apologies of Socrates* of Plato and Xenophon. This intertextual allusiveness reminds the reader that Lucian's articulation is invariably refracted through the prism of literary history. Moreover, the central conceit of the text, namely Lucian's self-accusation in the name of his addressee, is itself an act of impersonation: it would be good, he states near the start, 'if I put on your mask and start acting' (*ἢν . . . ὑποδὺς τὸ σὸν πρόσωπον ὑποκρίνωμαι*, 2). This is a wink to the alert reader: the Lucianic voice, for all that it speaks of exposure and *parrhēsia* ('freedom of speech'), ever seeks (provisional) rhetorical authority through persona-construction rather than absolute truth.

CONCLUSION

Life, as we are frequently reminded by Lucian, is like a play: social identities have no more stability than dramatic roles and costumes. For Lucian, the society he inhabits is distinguished from earlier Greece by its intensification of this theatrical element, its conversion of (particularly philosophical) *paideia* into a commercial spectacle. The rhetorical contrast found in the *Sale of lives* and

[151] Swain (1996), 322.

(especially) the *Fisherman* between 'then' (the times when the philosophical schools were founded) and 'now' is carried on into the texts that deal more obviously with the impact of Roman rule upon Greek philosophy: *Nigrinus* (where the opposition is between Athens and Rome) and *On salaried posts* and the *Apology* (where the opposition is between Roman patronage and freedom from it). Philosophy, and Greek *paideia* generally, are now reduced to a matter of show and performance.

Such polarizations of Greece and Rome seem at first sight to evoke a securely Greek subjectivity for the author and the reader, a complicity of values reinforced by abhorrence of Rome's appropriation and commercialization of Greek literature. Yet the distance that Lucian opens up between Greece and Rome—'the difference satire makes'[152]—constantly threatens to disappear. Lucian's texts point the finger at others for their pretence and hypocrisy, but his own, highly cultivated writing is as culpable as anyone's: the succession of personae adopted in the dialogues is only the most visible sign of this author's preoccupation with the theatricalization of his own literary identity. The Greekness of this Hellenized Syrian is another pose.

Lucian's Rome is the spectacular society par excellence: its structures of patronage necessitate a ludicrous string of perfomances and display. Greek *paideia* debases itself and renders itself risible when it submits to the demands of the Roman socio-economic hierarchy. What this chapter has sought to show, though, is that Lucian also ironizes any attempt to assume a high-mindedly Hellenic position of exteriority to this system. Although Lucian's value-system privileges the integrity, truth, and honesty extolled by the Greek philosophical tradition, any claim to have attained such a position is subject to radical scepticism. His works offer no securely authoritative moral position, only a recurrently frustrated process of challenge and counter-challenge. This makes his works also a satire upon 'expressive-realism', the desire to access secure and sincere opinions. Lucian's deeply held views are a chimaera: what his writings dramatize is the elusiveness of the heartfelt voice, the evanescence of 'Greek views of Rome'.

[152] Bogel (1995).

Conclusion

Cultural identity is not innate, but constructed and vied for in social space. In Stuart Hall's terms, it is 'not an essence but a *positioning*'.[1] Assumptions that Greek identity in any period stemmed organically from a single, integral radical risk complicity with nineteenth-century racial theory: the explicitly biological metaphors ('blood', 'vitality', 'reinvigoration') may have gone, but the familiar talk of a renaissance or 'flourishing'[2] of Hellenism in Roman Greece implies similar assumptions about the natural unity of a people and their articulation of their *Geist* in a coherent cultural aesthetic. What this book has sought to show is that Greek cultural identity in the early Roman period (the period often called 'the Second Sophistic') was an intense concern, but it was never taken for granted: identities were made, contested, masked, ironized, dissimulated, or disavowed, but not received as self-evident. Literature was not the medium of expression for the coherent and self-identical 'voice' of Greece, but both a site of conflict between different interest-groups and an opportunity for resourceful play on the part of some brilliantly imaginative writers.

Identity is never self-evident, but it can be experienced or constructed as such. Paradigms of identity-construction may be more or less unified in some cultures than in others. It is important to be precise on this point, because I am categorically not stating that harmonious socio-political conditions lead axiomatically to a sense of security amongst the people in relation to patterns of identity. Notwithstanding that it is empirically untrue, this is also a flawed means of describing historical change: there is a danger of imposing a seductively trite historiographical narrative that describes a movement from order to fragmentation (such is sometimes employed in relation to the emergence of 'the postmodern condition': a peculiar narcissism, to imagine that there were no

[1] S. Hall (1990), 226. [2] G. Anderson (1994), 2–3.

identity conflicts in the nineteenth century). No society is 'stable', in the sense of being free from the tensions and currents that make the future an object of struggle. 'Continuity' is only visible in retrospect: as such, it is a historiographical fiction rather than a necessarily accurate characterization of contemporary experience in the society in question. Victor Turner makes the point eloquently:

> The social world is a world in becoming, not a world in being (except insofar as 'being' is a description of the static, atemporal models men have in their heads), and for this reason studies of social structure *as such* are irrelevant.[3]

Stability does not inhere in societies: it is a function of perception, of interpretation, of what men (*sic*) have in their heads. It follows from this that what in some societies encourages a sense of confidence in the self-sufficient truth and permanence of their identity-paradigms is not a social, economic, or political order, but a brutally efficient technology of *representation*. Rallies, parades, festivals: all aim to consolidate the symbolic unity of a people and their subservience to a dominant set of objectives. It is in not the socio-political register but the *mimetic* (one might almost say 'aesthetic') that identities are forged.

Identities do not 'exist', except in so far as fictions have real and indelible effects upon people's lives.[4] They have no essential or natural being: they are created and contested discursively, in the field of representation. In the field of representation, as structuralists assert, no sign is free-standing: a signifier acquires its meaning from its position in the systemic code of representation, rather than from any self-evident relationship to 'reality'. Thus it is with identity: the concepts of 'femininity' and 'homosexuality', for example, do not simply 'refer' to something in the nature of people, as much as mark a site of *difference* ('not-masculine', 'not-heterosexual'), and of clusters of socially constructed stereotypes. The correct procedure to understand femininity or homosexuality would not be to conduct psychological tests upon petite women or gay people (as though these qualities were latent in them), but to seek to interpret the construction of axes of difference, and the ideological reasons that underlie them, in social representation as a whole.

[3] V. Turner (1974), 24.

[4] Good introduction to the ideas in this paragraph in S. Hall (1992).

In fifth-century Athens, the source of most of the literature canonized by later Greek society, technologies of cultural representation were extraordinarily powerful. Athens invented two means of identity-construction, one to construct 'Greekness' and one for 'Athenianness'. 'Greeks' were defined by antithesis to 'barbarians', a process that began apace when the Athenians began to mythologize their victories over the Persians at Marathon and Salamis, partly in order to justify their imperial strategy in the Aegean sea (purportedly a defence force against Persia).[5] Athens had much at stake in representing Greece as a unified territory, since it was attempting to engineer for itself a position as Panhellenic leader. As Edith Hall has emphasized, it is primarily (though not exclusively) in tragedy—a public art-form performed before (notionally) the entire citizen body—that the polarity of Greeks and barbarians was constructed and explored.[6] Tragedy provided a means of representing (and of exploring and contesting) the fundamental technique of identity-construction by difference underpinning Athenian notions of Greekness.

'Athenianness', meanwhile, was constructed by means of a different trope, the rhetoric of genetic traditions. 'Autochthony'—the myth that the first Athenian, Erechtheus or Erichthonius, was born from the soil of Athens—began circulating around the time of Pericles' citizenship law of 451–450, which stipulated that an Athenian citizen had to be born of two Athenian parents.[7] The myth and the law are interrelated: both serve to foster the illusion of the Athenians as a pure race, descended unproblematically from a single parent. This identity-construction was also the subject of widescale public representation: not only was the horror of adultery repeatedly articulated in tragedy (and in particular in the dramas telling of the house of Atreus), but also public funeral speeches repeatedly recurred to the theme of autochthony.[8] Those who died in war defending the fatherland were buried with pomp and ceremony at state expense in the same place (in the Kerameikos) that the first Athenian had been born, a cycle of symbolic renewal that celebrated the permanence of the city as against the transience of the individual.[9]

[5] E. Hall (1989), esp. 16–17, 59–60.

[6] E. Hall (1989); cf. also on Herodotus Hartog (1988) and Cartledge (1993), 55–62.

[7] For bibliography on autochthony, see Ch. 3, n. 155.

[8] Loraux (1986).

[9] Loraux (1993), 42.

Athens's representative strategies were logically indissociable from political, military, and ideological imperatives: it is impossible to say whether identity-construction was so heavily resourced through a knowing attempt to shore up an imperialist policy, or whether that policy was inspired by a deeply entrenched belief in the supremacy of Athens. The fundamental point, however, is that representation is not a second-order phenomenon, a mere symptom of an underlying politics: it is, on the contrary, the very means of enactment of politics. Athens's attempts to control representation (by arrogating enormous prestige to its drama and public architecture) constituted an eminently political process.

In the larger context of Greece, fifth-century Athenian identity-construction embodied a paradox. On the one hand, Greece was (to be) united through cultural, linguistic, and religious practices, in opposition to the barbarian 'other'. On the other hand, it was radically differentiated internally, partly upon precisely the same grounds (different cities have different dialects, practices, and characteristics: one of the messages of Aristophanes' *Lysistrata*), but partly because of Athens's innate superiority. The Athenians were not the only autochthonous people (though this fact could be forgotten: see e.g. Dem. 60.4), but Thebes's autochthony was represented (by the Athenians, of course) not as a positive benefit but as spiralling inwards into fratricide and incest.[10] The Panhellenic message that substantiated the Athenian empire was balanced against authochthonic narratives that vaunted the exceptional status of the Athenian people.

I have taken up a certain amount of space in recapping the techniques of identity-making current in democratic Athens because that culture generated much of the intellectual currency circulating in Roman Greece. (Not, of course, on the grounds that Athens provided a model of 'stability' that might offset the 'fragmentation' of the later period.) If identity is primarily a matter of representation, then intertextuality with the literary canon allows for a certain self-conscious inflection in the later culture. As I have emphasized throughout, Roman Greece also constructed identity through representation, and primarily (though not exclusively) through what I have called 'literary' (but perhaps more properly 'paideutic') writing. Part One explored the trope of *mimēsis* as tradition-making, a negotiation of relationships

[10] Zeitlin (1990*b*), 139–42.

between past and present. The cultural values attached to literary *mimēsis*, however, are manifold and contested (Chapter 1): while a Plutarch (or, in a more deliberately ambiguous way, a Longinus) could construct the relationship between past and present in terms of natural continuity, others chose to emphasize the disruption effected by modernist *mimēsis*. The *Nachleben* (in Lucian and the Greek novels) of Dionysius' images of imitation as a combination of limbs from different models, or a combination between 'natural' birth and the imprint of an 'artificial' artwork, demonstrates an abiding focus upon the transformative, innovative effects of writing within a literary tradition. This process is not confined to literary texts: the personal identity of the *pepaideumenos* is also created and explored through literary *mimēsis*, and there too (as Chapter 2 sought to show) there is a radical uncertainty concerning the extent to which *paideia* reproduces and the extent to which it marks a break with traditional Greek values. Does education replicate and revivify Greekness? Or does it provide others with the resources to fake their way into the tradition?

Next to Athens's 'tradition'-orientated economy of identity, Roman Greece presents (albeit not without contestation) a paradigm of 'translative' identity.[11] Greekness is now not simply a question of ethnicity, but can be acquired: it can provide a medium for cultural and linguistic unity across geopolitical frontiers. There are two important qualifications to be made here. First, this is not, let us be clear, an ancient 'multiculturalism': it was exclusive to (indeed, to an extent, definitive of) the elite; and, moreover, it did not constitute a form of cultural pluralism (we know of, for example, no celebration of Gallic custom on Favorinus' part; and Lucian's only self-diagnosed Syrianism, the essay *On the Syrian goddess*, is heavily mediated through the Hellenocentric tradition). Secondly, this 'inclusivist' paradigm is not altogether new: indeed, it is already found in the fourth-century writings of Isocrates.[12] The crucial point, however, is not whether the idea was new or old, but that it is employed self-consciously to articulate a clash between new values and old: indigenous tradition is contrasted with exotic innovation. The representation of literary ingenuity is knowingly coupled with

[11] For these terms, see Ch. 3, 'Favorinus: Exile and Literary Alienation', with n 160.

[12] Isocr. *Panegyr.* 50.

self-stylization as culturally 'other'. In this respect, writing literature becomes a form of self-making: the person is an artefact, an object of craft.

Set against this 'translative' paradigm of identity, however, must be assertions of tradition and continuity in the face of a repellent hybridity. The prime example here is the case of Agathion, as reported by Philostratus in his *Lives of the sophists* (552–4).[13] Agathion—who, like the Classical Athenians, is reported by some to have been born from the earth (553)—inveighs heavily against the deterioration of Greek-speaking in Athens under the influence of the 'barbarians' (βαρβάρων), preferring instead to frequent the rural interior (μεσογεία) of Attica, which is 'untainted by barbarians' (ἄμικτος βαρβάροις). In reinvoking the Greek–barbarian contrast and insisting upon purism, Agathion represents a very different, and more 'tradition-orientated', form of Hellenism.

Part Two considered the construction of Greece by 'differentiation' from Rome. Polarity is fundamental to signification, but Rome posed a particular problem to Greek self-definition. The Classical Greek–barbarian antithesis had been if not intellectually simple then at least elegantly precise in practice, but Rome was a new *tertium quid* that recused simple polarization: not only was the *urbs* now a centre of culture itself, but also many Greeks (indeed, as far as one can tell, all those studied in this book) were Roman citizens themselves. For all that definitional dichotomies were advanced (Roman is to Greek as power is to culture, exploitation is to integrity, the spectacular is to the contemplative), they continually risked collapsing. Constructing Greece as a category opposed to and exclusive of Rome required a substantial labour, a labour the futility of which the best writers exploit with wit and ingenuity. Dio Chrysostom and Lucian, in particular, expose (while manipulating) the self-conscious masking that underpins the pose of principled Hellene standing before Rome. In other cases—notably those of Musonius Rufus and Marcus Aurelius—the adoption of a Greek literary voice constitutes a radical attempt by men who were native Latin-speakers to disavow the distasteful aspects of Roman hegemony (Musonius by confrontation with the emperor, Marcus by enfolding pedagogy into the heart of empire). The texts studied in this book do not simply reflect the 'views' of Rome held by an alienated group of Greeks, as though 'Greece'

[13] Ch. 2, '*Paideia* and Social Status'.

and 'Rome' were discrete phenomena occupying static and independent positions; rather, they *perform* the very processes of aggregation and disaggregation.

Cultural identity, as manifested in literature, is hermeneutically inseparable from literary strategy. This is not to suggest that it serves a purely aesthetic (though 'pure' aesthetics are a chimaera anyway), disengaged, non-political function: literary self-presentation, in Roman Greece, was (as has been repeatedly emphasized) a crucial aspect of the competitive structure of elite society. Nor do I mean that studies of cultural identity (in the broader sense) should be subordinated to literary studies. My point is, rather, that we should not expect these sophisticated, highly self-conscious texts simply to 'reflect' an ontologically anterior essence, a core of inner expression that bespeaks an author's experience qua Greek. Identity, in these texts, is constructed and explored *within* the work itself, and its subtle and nuanced inflections require interpretation within the dense and often complex weft of literary texture.

APPENDIX 1

Translation of Favorinus, *On Exile* (*P.Vat.* 11)

TEXT

The text translated is that of Barigazzi (1966).

SYMBOLS

[. . .] lacuna
⟨. . .⟩ suggested lacuna
[] probable sense of lacuna
⟨⟩ probable sense of suggested lacuna

NOTES ON THE TRANSLATION

- I have used the chapter system of Barigazzi, rather than the unwieldy papyrus column numbers.
- I have not bracketed all the supplements to the papyrus in the translation (which would have made for an unreadable text), only those where I think that Barigazzi's supplements are especially contentious, or that the papyrus permits no confidence at all. In some places where no whole words can be read for several lines, I offer no translation at all, since to translate would be to extrapolate too far.
- I have only recorded the sources of explicit quotations. Other echoes and allusions are fully documented by Barigazzi.

From the proem? (unattributed fragment preserved in Stobaeus)

A man raised in true loftiness of spirit and philosophy has, in the face of adversity, reserves of equanimity in his mind; but the need for consolation from another when confronting disasters goes beyond the appropriate time for magnanimity.

From the papyrus

1–6 Proem

1.[1] [. . .] even if someone were to suspect [the veracity] of this essay, thinking that it is composed out of imposture [and a desire for glory] in some inopportune circumstance. For if I am addressing [certain] exhortations to myself, nevertheless *I* shall be the one to obey them and act in this way, it is I who am in a position to bear my situation [with dignity. But] this essay [has been composed in view of] the possibility that someone, perhaps even [an educated person], might require [help, so that] his will [might become] surer [in the face of his circumstances.] For I think [that by using] myself [as an example] I can prove that [every man might rein in] his emotions and disdain [every misfortune, thanks to this very essay. Moreover,] granted [some people have become] very brash [because they trusted] in rhetoric [rather than bodily strength], or, rather, their attitude [makes them such]; but those whom [you observe to be stiffened by the exercise] of virtue [can more easily attain] such [manliness as allows them to preserve constantly their equanimity, and sometimes even to become famous. For we receive no small alleviation of our woes] from [the sharing of our fates, even when it is a question of a different kind of] grievance. Or was it not in a state of misfortune that Empedocles, Heracles and Mucius, the Roman general, [were praised] (Empedocles was praised for his virtue, Heracles for his immortality and Mucius for his manliness)?

2. (1) Different people may show contempt for exile for different reasons, but Diogenes of Sinope, Crates of Thebes, [Chrysippus of Soli], [Dio of Prusa], and the Etruscan Musonius showed contempt for it out of neither hatred of their fatherlands nor enmity towards their fellow citizens, but because they accepted as part of the human condition all the circumstances that befell them. So as to avoid spending too long comparing dissimilar reasons for similar sentiments, let us say that the distinction between equanimity and an unschooled approach is made with a minor difference of vocabulary but with a major difference in actuality. The man who shows equanimity and aims at virtue in such a situation is capable of dealing with matters himself, and also most suitable for advising someone else too, not just verbally but also exhorting him with his own example: he treats his words as teachers of his deeds, and displays deeds that are keen students of his words. (2) This essay will be dedicated as a possession for someone else as well, who might not be capable of furnishing himself with such resources when he encounters a similar situation—so long as he does not, like the most foolish of the common folk, take the trials of men of the

[1] This chapter consists largely of a translation of Barigazzi's reconstruction of the lacunose beginning of the papyrus.

past or present as a consolation for his own troubles, and lighten the burden of what belongs to the human condition because others have tripped up, but rather quite the opposite: so that by observing these examples he may turn to his own use the reflections and actions in these situations of those praiseworthy men of old who suffered similar fates; and so that, if Alcibiades, Themistocles, and Coriolanus plotted against their fatherlands in their grief, he should neither approve nor imitate them, nor indeed anyone who has borne exile or death less than manfully, or again less than sanely; but so that he should admire, and count as consolation, the words and deeds of Socrates [of Athens] in prison. (3) When it was open to him to [escape] with his friends' aid and to reprove those who had condemned him, he considered that the god was the ruler of the city, and that nothing was unjust that the god approved; and so he did not reprove his jury one bit, and made a clear choice not to escape but to endure death with equanimity, since the god must be obeyed.

3. (1) The same Socrates always [. . .] used to think that tragic actors obey the poet when they are dispatched down whatever path he chooses: now they act king Agamemnon, now Telephus the beggar, now Tydeus the exile, now the limping Philoctetes, now [. . .] (2) Formerly, for example, they were [. . .] but now [. . .] with a view to what is appropriate to the play as regards their costume and voice, and not awestruck because, while they lately dwelled in Mycenaean royal palaces, accepted the sceptre of Pelops handed down from their ancestors, acquired the golden fleece and lorded it over the entire Peloponnese, in the same theatre, on the same day, they gird themselves with rags and beg in another's court, with no care, it seems, that 'Oedipus was at first a fortunate man; but then he became the most miserable of mortals.'[2] For they understand, I imagine, that none of these things is intrinsic to themselves, neither the kingdoms nor the wealth nor the 'halls of wealthy Aleus',[3] nor indeed descent from Tantalus or Labdacus, nor poverty and exile. They belong, rather, to the myth, and to the poet, and they themselves must play different roles at different times until they have completed the play. (3) What of us? Is it obedience to the poet of the whole cosmos if, in life's drama, we complain when he bids us play now rulers, now exiles, now wealthy men and now paupers again? Do actors consider themselves egregious and blessed when they are in their kingdoms and tyrannies, judging their present circumstances secure? Do they consider themselves forlorn of everything when they are in the midst of disasters and exiles? Do they not consider, rather, that they have changed the style of their clothing and their mask, that their true selves reside within, like little bodies? That they have promoted themselves from the children they are inside to Caesars and rulers simply by alternating between all kinds of costume in accordance with the narratives?

[2] Eur. *Ant.* fr. 157/158 N^2. [3] A new fragment, probably of Euripides.

(4) For in theatrical competitions it is not those who play Oenomauses and Pandions who actually win; in fact, even those who play beggars and exiles, if they portray the suffering better than the actors who portray the successful, so that [. . .] are praised [. . .] because of the [. . .]

4. (1) [. . .] if you bear the misfortunes that befall you with no more difficulty than the good fortunes, looking to the wisest of the men of old, who acquired no less renown from disasters than from successes. (2) Consider Diogenes, whom I recalled a little earlier: at home he did not even have the reputation of being a good assayer, but as an exile and in new quarters he became more famous not only than those in Sinope [. . .], but even the whole wide world, in a state of penury, exile and utter destitution. (3) Consider also Heracles: at home he was counted as a human and the son of Amphitryon, but when harried by Eurystheus, contending with all kinds of beasts, encountering all kinds of humans and reaching the limits of bodily endurance, then it was that he was counted as the son of Zeus and immortal was the renown he acquired. (4) Or take Odysseus, on whose subject so great a poet as Homer composed half his oeuvre, on the grounds that he became a wise man: when he ruled over Ithaca, Cephallenia and the neighbouring islands, with Penelope as his wife and his household entirely under his tutelage, he seemed no greater than any of the islanders—indeed, he even acquired a reputation among the Achaeans for cowardice, shrink as he did from marching with them towards Troy; and, what is more, when in those battle-ranks he was considered a poor soldier. Later, however, he revealed himself to be a man of exceptional virtue, when he endured shipwrecks, was racked with hunger, lost his companions, slept in filthy, shameful rags, and—the ultimate ordeal—all this out of trust in the habits of one woman. (5) What Phoenician or Phaeacian sailor has such strength of will, when his ship is running surely, as Odysseus had when shipwrecked? What Sybarite, Ionian or Sicilian shows as much equanimity at his table when it is crammed with all kinds of dishes, as he did in his hunger? Who had so much power thanks to his mass of friends and his authority as that man did when he had lost all his comrades? What mighty potentate gained such mastery over his enemies as he did whilst begging in his own house? What sort of man would be so fine a counsellor of another as he was of himself, with these words (amongst others): '"Bear up, my heart," he said, "you once endured even greater brutality.'"[4] [. . .]

5. (1) Now I do not want to give up, or grow weary of, exhorting myself, neither in good circumstances alone nor, like some, in other situations; rather, even in this state, I would rather be wise and display my learning. (2) Consider what happens when athletes enter the stadium. Their friends and colleagues, amongst other things, call out exhortations: 'these games

[4] Hom. *Od.* 20.18.

in Pisa', they say, 'because of which they have used up so much effort, time and sweat, bear the name of Zeus'; and they should keep these things in mind whilst they contend, in case they should be used up to no avail. Well this, as I see it, is how I exhort and remind myself in my present situation, as if it were one man to another: 'these accidents and changes of fortune that attend you are the same as those against which you have been chastising and schooling your soul since childhood, partly by learning about deeds and words of yore that lead one towards virtue, and partly by meeting with the men of our age who are worthy of record; and, what is more, by travelling over huge expanses of territory both Greek and barbarian, and by seeing, hearing and memorizing the things that happened in and concerning each territory, and contributed towards this schooling in virtue. (3) Look, then, the sanctioned day is here, not 'the eleventh day of fifty months' (in the words of Pindar),[5] in the presence of all, by decree of Pelops or some Dactylus of Ida, nor indeed by man at all, but by the god and by time. On the ordained hour, you must strip, stand alone and contend without shirking, if that is at all possible; and your many famous competitors will [confront] you, vaunting, with the support of the toils of yore. You must not despise them: quite the opposite, you must try to overcome them with your will, as if to pay them back for all the mortal illusions, desires, [. . .], emotions and appetites that burden all other occasions and now wish to render exile itself more difficult.

6. (1) It is not inopportune, in the present circumstances, to list and (as it were) herald them by name. First, then, is [. . . love of one's fatherland . . .] Second is strong affection for one's kin and familiar companionship. Third would no doubt be, what is apparently not granted to most people, enjoyment of wealth, property and private possessions. Along with this comes what the majority affect to despise, but in truth lust after: an appetite for honours and reputation in one's own land, and, related to it, a horror of ill-repute and a bad name amongst the people. In addition to all these, and (as it were) waiting on the byline, is the mightiest and most alluring figure: liberty, much coveted, consisting of freedom of action and in the use of property. (2) All these figures confront the single soul of the sufferer, wanting to humble it, to knock it down, to trip it up, binding it to the point of painful suffocation, seizing it both individually and as a unit (for they are unwilling to follow the rules of the competitions by dividing up amongst themselves: all together they confront the single soul, plotting against it). (3) Most of the crowd of spectators there also side with them, clapping and urging them on from the stands, as if they were the kin and familiars of the competitors. You, though, must not be overawed at their zeal and clamour: you must not give in, for the contest is not held on the stage, nor in the theatre of Dionysus at all (where the man achieves

[5] Actually Bacchylides (*Epinic.* 7.2).

victory who can manipulate the zeal of the crowd to make the largest number of them cry or laugh when he steps on stage), but in the temple of Heracles, in the stadium of virtue. The contest is one of deeds, and not of words. (4) You must despise the clapping, the whistling, the cheers, the jeers, and all that kind of racket: standing alone with your hopes, your soul stripped bare, under the bright sun, in the arid dust, you must endure manfully. For the prize that lies before us, if we avoid suffering in this event, is great: it is that of happiness.

7–14. The first adversary, desire for the fatherland

7. (1) First of all, I summon desire for one's fatherland. She dresses herself, well I know it, with many, most attractive, devices: she brandished the soil of our fatherland and our country (where our ancestors since ancient times have flooded in accordance with convention, and by familiarizing themselves have finally become indigenous), 'and the altars of the gods, | and the gymnasia where I was trained, and the water of the Dirce; | unjustly driven from these, I dwell in a foreign city, | streaming floods of tears from my eyes'.[6] Such are the words of Euripides' Polynices to his mother. (2) But listen now, Polynices, I shall address *you*. The man to whom it is granted to love his fatherland and stay in it without harm should stay, defend it and never willingly leave it. But if he is driven and harried from it, 'whether justly or no' (to use the phrase of your compatriot, Pindar),[7] he should not weep in his mother's skirts like a child, nor be within the walls, hiding out of fear, 'so as to bear sword in his hand through the city',[8] nor march with an army against his fatherland, which you yourself claim to be the dearest thing to mortals, nor engage his brother in single combat for the sake of those altars, that water and those gymnasia; he should endure his necessity manfully, and accept his circumstances. (3) There are 'altars of the gods' in Argos too, and also, the most sacred element in those altars, the gods themselves: divine nature, providence and Heracles himself (who is traditionally worshipped by the Argives). The gymnasia there are beautiful. So too is the water of the Lerna: if you drink it in a manner worthy of a free man, nothing will seem more paltry than the water of Thebes, but if you drink it in grief, if will seem bitter to you (as if not even a stream following you from the Choaspes would be enough for you if you were in exile). And even if Argos has been called 'thirsty',[9] how can you really think that there has been up until now enough to water those thirsty Argives, but there is not enough for one Theban exile?

6 Eur. *Phoen.* 367–70.
7 Pind. *Ol.* 2.16.
8 Eur. *Phoen.* 363.
9 Hom. *Il.* 4.171; *Thebaid* fr. 1 Allen; cf. Hes. fr. 128 Merkelbach–West.

8. (1) Generally as regards the gods, you should consider that they are likely to heed a wretched, unjust man nowhere, whether he pray to them in his fatherland, whether as close as one can get to heaven, or whether in Troy, where, as Homer says, gods mixed with men. It was here that Athena turned back Ajax, and (in Homer's words) 'Pallas Athena refused' the prayers of the Trojan women;[10] and he says elsewhere that 'Phoebus Apollo left him'.[11] And fate betrayed Polycrates of Samos. (2) But the gods will pay heed everywhere to a good and pious man, whether he call upon them on the Athenian Areopagus (where Apollo conversed with Orestes), or on beautiful [Scheria] (where Pallas conversed with Odysseus), or in the symposium of the Scopades like the poet Simonides, or whether he pray from Hades, where (so they say) Protesilaus called up to the heavenly ones to heed him, or whether sailing at sea 'on a mat'[12] (as the saying goes), like Odysseus on his raft or Arion of Methymnos when he was carried on the dolphin. (3) And whereas a single fish saved Arion, not even the rock was a safe vehicle for Ajax. If we were to commune with Athena only in Athens, Hera only in Argos, Zeus only in Elis and so forth, 'many cities' (in Homer's words) 'would lack', not 'a butler', but a divinity.[13] Given that not even a symposium could be organized without a butler, how could a city, a territory or any race survive without a divinity? This, I suggest, is what Ammon especially wanted to reveal: when the Aphytaeans came to consult him from Thrace, he ordained that they should no longer send people to Libya to consult him, but should learn his responses there in Thrace, since he would heed them there too; and he did indeed begin to heed them, 'for he travels on the swell of the sea | and the land and the meadows | leafy, through the [. . .] limitless water, does Zeus the all-seeing'.[14]

9. (1) If anyone thinks that the dead have ceased to exist, he should consider that they follow him nowhere. But if, in accordance with the words of Plato and Homer, he considers that souls are immortal, it is right that he should believe Homer in the following passage too: when Odysseus dug a trough (and not a deep one at that) in the land of the Cimmerii, and sacrificed the sheep into it, all the dead responded to him in that very spot, as if they had all been buried beside that very ditch: his mother, who died in Ithaca; Achilles, buried at Troy; Elpenor, as yet unburied; Ajax, related to him neither in intelligence nor by kin; and, in addition, Tyro the daughter of Salmoneus, Chloris the daughter of Amphion, and many other women of whose death we know neither the place nor the circumstances. (2) The Athenians, however, placed great value upon burial at home: witness the common burial-ground, and the fact that, although they drove out Theseus while he was alive, they brought back his corpse

[10] Hom. *Il.* 6.311. [11] Hom. *Il.* 22.213. [12] Proverbial for a feeble vessel.
[13] Hom. *Il.* 2.128. [14] *TGF* adesp. fr. 167a.

from Scyros four hundred years later. And, again, whereas they used to purify graves on Delos (since it was sacrilegious either to bury or to die on the island), they themselves buried Cecrops on the acropolis, and the daughters of Erechtheus hard by the very temple of Athena Polias. I for one find the Egyptian bird, the phoenix, ludicrous: it lives abroad for many generations, but returns, for the sake of a single day, to die in Egypt, as if every other land were insignificant for the burial of one bird. A small part of Sicily was enough for Enceladus and Typho!

10. (1) And I too love my fatherland: my love is second to no one's, and I should never have left it willingly. On reflection, however, I discover that it is nothing other than the land in which my forebears settled or resided. That a fatherland is not the country in which we ourselves were born is clear from the following: many people, though born elsewhere, regard another land as their fatherland. (2) If our fatherland is this, the territory to which our ancestors have become accustomed, why by the same token should we not also love the country in which we currently reside? After all, the land in which one dwells is much closer than that in which one's ancestors dwelled, and my future descendants will have the same reason (or even more just cause) to make my enforced dwelling-place their fatherland [because they] received me [hospitably] as an exile. Such are the words of Alcaeus of Lesbos,[15] a man most devoted to his fatherland. (3) And yet, if you were to trace your own stock and that of your entire fatherland back to the ancients, you would find that they were either colonists from another land, like the Aeginetans who went to Thyraea, or that they had settled from elsewhere, like the Ionians, the Aeoleans and the entire Dorian race; and you would find men driven from their own land by exile, Greeks driven to barbarian lands (like the Argives amongst the Amphilochi, the Arcadians who went to Phrygia with Dardanus, and the Eretrians from Euboea in Persian Sousa) and barbarians driven to Greek lands (like the Thracians who went to Attica with Eumolpus, and the Phoenicians and Arabs who settled in Boeotian Thebes with Cadmus). If you delve right back to the most distant time, you will find that all people everywhere are foreigners and exiles (the primary reason for the foundation of cities was, I imagine, the strife and faction of that period). (4) If some small number of people think that they are autochthonous, and give themselves airs for this reason, then these truly are empty boasts: for sure, mice and other more insignificant animals are born in the earth, but it is right for humans to be born from no other source than a human. What is more, if these people affiliate themselves more closely to the earth than all others for this reason—well, one should not deal with one's own portion of the earth alone (like someone who has emerged from a pothole), but inhabit the whole earth, as it is the common mother and nourisher of all.

[15] No obvious parallel in the extant fragments of Alcaeus.

11. (1) 'One is the race of mortals, one day | brought us from our father and mother'.[16] 'One god alone established for humans | this common allotment of the sun',[17] preventing anyone from altering the language with which he was reared. (2) What is more, I tell you, the god made the sea a single fatherland for marine creatures, and heaven a single fatherland for winged creatures, and apportioned to those creatures that walk on the ground the earth, placing a secure foundation underneath, roofing it over with heaven and walling it in with the ocean. (3) Now birds and fish preserve the allotment that they inherited from Zeus, as do all the other animals that go on the ground; but humans have divided up the earth out of greed, chopping up the god's gift. They separate Asia, Europe, and Libya from one another with rivers; neighbouring peoples with mountains; local inhabitants with city walls; fellow citizens with houses; co-habitants with doors; and even those who share the same ceiling with coffers and boxes. (4) This is the reason for the wars, sieges, 'destructions of palaces',[18] and ravagings: people march against a neighbouring land, often in the same territory, as if it were a foreign land. Some march with Erechtheus, some with Eumolpus; sometimes they are even divided into three groups, with those from the coast following Megacles the Alcmaeonid, those from the plain Lycurgus the son of Aristolaides, and those from the uplands Peisistratus the son of Hippias. (5) And then there are cases of strife between those of the same city, when those from within the walls and those from Phyle fight, and the other cases in which the entire Ionic, Dorian, and Pelasgian races have divided up and poured together their lands, the disputes of Polynices and Eteocles, and of the children of Heracles, and (by Zeus!) other siblings who have divided up not a tyranny but a single household.

12. (1) Cranes have loftier spirits than us: when they leave Thrace for Egypt they consider neither Thrace their fatherland nor Egypt their land of exile, but that these are simply migrations in respect of place, and winter and summer residences. The story about the Pygmies was, perhaps, a literary fiction; but the winter drove the cranes from Thrace, just as fate drives us, each from a different land. There is no dispute between a bird and the Pygmies (or, indeed, any other bird) over a part of the air, nor does one fish plot against another for the sake of the coast or a rock, but, in whatever part of the sea he happens to be residing, he considers that he is living in his own fatherland. (2) And yet I shall not deprive of virtue those humans who imitated such a creature. The Athenians left not only Attica, but even dry land, and climbed aboard ships, valuing their liberty more than walls and stones, and reckoning that they had all the tribes there, if they fought with valour. (3) When the Phocaeans failed to appease the world, they threw their anvils into the sea,

[16] Soph. fr. 591 *TGF*. [17] *TGF* adesp. fr. 167b. [18] Aesch. *Cho*. 50.

and swore that they would not return home before the anvils swam back; and even to this day the Phocaeans inhabit Massalia, since they have settled far from their own land, near the Etruscan sea. (4) The Amazons were counted as the daughters of Ares, since they left the river of Thermodon and travelled every land in search of a home. Well, then, if the Amazons (women, Scythians and Sauromatae as they are are) do not desire a single city for the purposes of piracy and pillage, will we not, for the purpose of a life free of misfortune and grief, consider it right, not (by Zeus!) to despise our fatherland (for that could not be called pious), but to avoid bringing foolish anxieties to our soul through inopportune yearnings, and consider the memory of our fatherland to be a cause more of joy than of grief?

13. (1) There are some who, out of love for their land, consider not only exile but even foreign travel to be the limit case of misery: it is in their minds that they exile themselves in respect of their fatherlands, voluntarily, with no necessity imposed on them. 'Foolish is he who hopes that the god alone | favours with blessings that city of men' in which he resides, 'for there are, there are indeed others worthily endowed | and they are a care to some god, Zeus or grey Athena'.[19] (2) As for me, however, my life even before my compulsory exile was mostly spent roaming around many parts of the earth and the sea, and in meetings abroad with foreign men. 'I liked not labour | nor care of the house, which rears glorious children, | but I always liked oared ships | and wars, polished spears and arrows';[20] and so it is not appropriate that I should bewail my current travel abroad, as if I were suffering from an excessive desire for my fatherland, 'since I know that I myself was reared as a foreigner', like Sophocles' Theseus, 'and that as a single man abroad | I underwent a great number of dangers to my life'.[21] (3) Even at the time when my parents were alive, and my sister, dearer to me than all, lived still, I considered my home-life less dear, because my journey occurred when I was young, and because it was on the pretext of magnifying my station. 'Now that I am grown, and my learning comes through hearing | report of others',[22] my parents and sister are dead and I am living abroad with my remaining household and what was forced upon me has become dominant, shall I display less equanimity? Shall I pride myself more on my past, because I held a position of power over others, than on my present, if I can show power over myself (which is the greatest form of power), and master my sufferings? (4) The god has often given positions of power and mortal honours, even to worthless men (thinking that he was giving away nothing significant), and to others even such honours as can be taken

[19] *TGF* adesp. fr. 167c.

[20] Hom. *Od.* 14.222–5.

[21] Soph. *Oed. Col.* 563–4, reading εἷς for (Barigazzi's supplement) τις.

[22] Hom. *Od.* 2.314–15.

away, money for example; but a will capable of not exalting itself when in positions of power, and of not being crushed by misfortunes, he has given to few, and once he has given he has not yet taken it away.

14. (1) If some of the locals will consider me a foreigner and a stranger, well, I shall treat them as my fellow citizens, and this land as my fatherland, both in what I say and in what I do. The god, who has repatriated me wherever and in whichever way he has chosen, is a mightier founder of cities, much mightier, than Capys, Ilus, Alexander, and anyone else who gave his name to a tiny part of the world by circumscribing it with walls. I consider a benevolent man much closer, in both the political and the private senses, than someone who exalts in the name of a clan, phratry and family but proves himself a stranger with his actions: for it is not laws, nor the metic tax, that make men foreigners, but will. (2) Emboldening myself with my will, I enrol myself into this city not with a public inscription but with my benevolence: I consider Zeus of ancestors to be the same god as Zeus of hospitality and Zeus of friendship; I acknowledge Hestia as common mother of gods and men, and that each man's table of hospitality is much more pious than a private table, if one handles it with reverence. Or was it not the very table of hospitality that made Priam a guest of Achilles, while it was the supposedly *ancestral* table of Atreus that proved his brother to be his greatest enemy, and filled him with such a banquet before sending him on his way? Personally, I would not have any old 'necklaces and tokens'[23] to help me recognize my companions. I would acquire many more things, and much better: (3) for the progress of time, mark you, makes all people better acquainted, and up until then we must meet a familiar with benevolence and a guest with warmth. We are human, after all, whereas the nature of dogs is as follows: before they know whether it is some excellent dog or a wretched one that they have met, they react angrily at first encounter with the unfamiliar. This is why the Greeks have been portrayed by Homer as, in the first instance, inviting in for hospitality those whom they meet, and inquiring who they are and where they are from after the meal, so that questions that are in some way hostile might not interfere with the generosity of the reception.

15–18. The second adversary, attachment to friends and kin

15. (1) Longing for friends and relatives at home, which is linked to love for one's fatherland, has appeared before us as a second contest, in addition to that previous one: it reminds one of one's birth, and of one's common upbringing since childhood, assailing one with trips together to school, time shared together in gymnasia and pleasurable meetings with contemporaries and those who were enrolled at the same time, drugs and lures (as it were) for the soul. I think we shall need less exhortation and

[23] Men. *Epitr.* 303 Sandbach.

sweat against this opponent. (2) For my fatherland (composed as it is of immobile and lifeless elements) was incapable of filling in the gaps between the periods I spent there (for those were solely dependent upon my absence or presence). It was altogether necessary that my fatherland should be where it is set by nature, and the force of convention kept me there (it is hard to confront two necessities, that of nature and that of convention, with the strength of one will!). But the god gave man a mobile nature, and he traverses 'on dry land and the wave',[24] now walking on foot, now travelling on every kind of territorial and marine vehicle, exchanging one country, one sea, for another, for the sake of profit, merchandise or marriage with foreigners; he 'assembles stout companions, | mixes with foreigners', seduces 'a handsome woman'[25] if necessary. He crosses from West to East, from East to West, extending his course to equal the sun's; he crosses from South to West, and then runs the course backwards, refusing neither to climb mountains nor to take difficult roads, neither intensity of heat nor chill of winter; even if his ship is wrecked and he swims free of it, he boards another vessel, and will consider everywhere accessible and traversible, thanks to his own daring. (3) Whoever wishes to be his friend is his friend; and if he truly is a friend, and understands the secret of friendship, and remains his partner, sharing in every kind of reputation, enterprise and fate, will he hesitate, when he has travelled abroad for a few days, to provide himself with the sight which is the fairest of pageants and spectacles, that of a friend? Will he hesitate, on his part, to lighten the misfortune for his friend?

16. (1) That certainly was not the attitude of Jason's friends; rather, they rejoiced to follow him from their various homes to Colchis as he journeyed abroad. They knew neither where he was sailing, nor indeed how to sail at all, for the sea was still without ships. They did not inquire into the reason for the voyage, but recognized Jason's fate as a sufficient pretext for their voyage abroad. That ship, which was the first to be rigged out among mortals, was filled with friends (and not with hired men), the majority of them kings, and some even the sons of gods, and they felt no shame in volunteering to sail. (2) 'But,' you object, 'that was a single ship.' What of it? Were not a thousand Achaean ships, weighed down with freight, dispatched against Troy when the best men in Greece followed a single friend who had been wronged? They stood by him, not only praying for themselves and their own food, but also turning their backs upon what they held dearest both at home and in the army: Protesilaus and Odysseus their wives, Nestor his sons, Teucer his brother, Achilles his boyfriend, and finally even himself (for, although his mother had predicted that he would be immortal if he remained at home, but would die very young if he sailed to Troy, he chose to stand by Agamemnon, and

[24] Hom. *Il.* 14.308; *Od.* 20.98; *Hom. hymn. Cer.* 43.

[25] Hom. *Il.* 3.47–8.

when he was hardly his best friend, at that). (3) What, did not Pylades follow his friend, though he was harried and driven mad by the Furies? Did not Theseus travel abroad with Pirithous, though he was departing for Hades? The former put before his friend neither caution towards divine wrath nor pollution among humans, but was willing to share a hearth and a roof with a matricide; and as for Theseus, do you think he would have hesitated to traverse the paltry sea between Mimas and Chios, given that he willingly sailed with his friend to Acheron, and sat with him on the rock of Lethe, and was uprooted thence against his will, thanks to Heracles' aggression? (4) *These* men, and men such as they, were friends. Will a friend of mine think that a life of grief on one's own is such a woeful and miserable existence in my case (just as, I suppose, another figure bereft of friends 'wept, pouring out tears to the barren sea'),[26] but for himself willingly forgo my company when both nature and law allow it to him, and then pity me as if he himself were not more pitiable? Why should I be any more the exile in his eyes than he to me, for that he does not see me? The only distinction is that I lack the opportunity, and he the will. So if he desires, he will come, and I shall not grieve ⟨. . .⟩. 'Go! | Let us live our lives here! For we should not | live badly, even thus, if we were content.'[27] (5) How could we consider a friend such a man as is outdone by swallows and plovers? When these birds have once compacted a friendship, swallows with humans, and plovers with crocodiles, though the species are different, they would never desert their friends: wherever a human lives, you will find there also a swallow, and wherever there is a crocodile you will find there also a plover. Therefore I do not care whereabouts I am on land or on sea.

17. (1) 'Of such a kind is human misfortune. | May he who is even moderately well-disposed towards me | not meet with that, the surest test of friendship.'[28] Fire is naturally good for assaying gold and silver, storms the running of ships, and changes of fortune friends. (2) Everyone wants to be a friend of the man who seems to be successful: they pour out from every corner, and neither can doors shut them out nor shame inhibit their flattery. So long as the wind follows his course, as the saying goes, all the sailors are loyal, all is equal and there are no differences or distinctions. The machinations of flattery, you see, are most wicked in that they set about imitating true friendship. When fate's squall hits them, however, it blasts the insubstantial and artificial from among his apparent friends and disperses them, like wind blowing chaff from a heap; few are the true friends who, like wheat, remain. 'It is now that you are in need of friends. | So long as the gods give us honour, we have no need of friends; | it is

[26] Odysseus: see Hom. *Od.* 5.84, 158.

[27] Soph. *Oed. Col.* 797–9.

[28] Eur. *Herc. fur.* 57–9.

enough when the god aids who he wills.'[29] (3) Do you not think that Pirithous had plenty of apparent friends in Thessaly, and Orestes even more in Mycenae? When they encountered fortune of this kind, however, alone of their companions an Athenian was left for the Thessalian and a Phocaean for the Mycenaean: adverse fortune dispersed the other Thessalians and Mycenaeans. (4) This, they say, was the reproach levelled by Momus against Prometheus: that, while the other parts of a human were arranged properly, he had been wrong to conceal the heart beneath the breast; he should have inserted a gap through which we might observe the intention of the man who approaches, before sharing any of his company. In the following respect, however, I think that Momus was wrong: misfortune provides a gap sufficient to reveal what man someone is, and the intention held by those who approach. The surest friend and companion is he who accompanies one who is down on his luck; for obviously he will not desert him when his luck improves.

18. (1) The man who was previously no friend, but has begun his friendship when one is down on one's luck, is even surer than one's former friends: he considers not his own need but virtue a pretext for friendship. I could cite many examples of such men from my own lifetime, and many more from long ago, but I shall mention only the house of Adrastus. Did not he not receive and purify Thyestes, a man who did not even deserve to be allowed into one's house on account of the gravity of his crimes, when he was being harried by his brother? Did he not also on one day make not only guests but even in-laws of two exiles, one from Argos and the other from Thebes, and on the next march out to war in their defence? (2) Does not such a man seem to you to have rewritten the words that Euripides composed to be spoken to a friend, 'Farewell! Friends disappear if one is down on one's luck!'?[30] It would be better, in the case of Adrastus, to say, 'Farewell! True friends are doughty, if one is down on one's luck'—true friends whom the same poet somewhere calls 'friends and ever friends'.[31] (3) And again, we hear in the proverb that 'the man who has nothing has no friend', and in the saying of Chilo of Sparta, 'you should befriend thus a man expecting him to hate you'.[32] I would rewrite these more accurately, the former as 'the man who has nothing has sure friends', the latter as 'you should befriend a man expecting his luck to change for the worse'. If one approaches friendship on these terms, exile will not repel one from one's friend, nor bond hold him back, nor indeed death, mightiest of all, end one's friendship. Quite the opposite: these and such circumstances protract and augment friendship, providing a spur for the friend's benevolence towards him in the period when he is prospering,

[29] Eur. *Herc. fur.* 1337–9.
[30] Eur. *Phoen.* 403.
[31] Eur. *Phoen.* 536.
[32] Variously attributed to Chilo and Bias of Priene: see Barigazzi's note ad loc.

and revealing to him a steadiness of will in the face of necessity when he is down on his luck.

19–27. The third adversary, wealth and station

19. (1) A good man takes even less notice of the value of wealth, human honours, ancestry, rank, and public opinion. For those things mentioned earlier are extrinsic: a fatherland, children, kinship, friends, and all the rest are not mine to the extent that they are not under my control. I certainly do, however, lay claim to and call my own the ability not to crave these things (for that *is* under my control). Since everything that is not under our control is extrinsic, all this business about honours, opinions, and wealth is the most extrinsic of all. (2) Here is the evidence: even animals can somehow acquire some natural disposition towards children, places, and friends (they enjoy familiar places and animals that share their customs, and most of all their children and parents); but no animal other than a human being bothers about wealth and honour, thinking instead that a good supply of food (which is essential for life) is wealth enough. No animal nature could become impoverished in this respect. Positions of power are assumed in accordance not with the opinion of the other animals, but with superior virtue in the respect in which that animal excels. (3) No horse, for example, ever paid attention to his honour or dishonour in the eyes of other animals: he thinks, rather, that since he outdoes other animals in speed he has a certain natural form of power in respect of the racetrack. Nor does the lion value highly what the other animals think or say about him; rather, he thinks that, since he excels in strength, this constitutes for him the truest form of power and honour amongst the weaker beasts. (4) Human beings, on the other hand, as if they had acquired their rationality not through contempt of these features but through these features themselves, ⟨. . .⟩. They place wealth above the nourishment that is essential for life, and consider anything beyond that to be unlimited and unbounded. For example, there is no one so rich that he does not have less than he wants; and even if he reaches that state, he pushes the horizon of his desire still further back. (5) Honours are apportioned to one in respect of the capacity not of mastering virtue, but of controlling public opinion: sometimes the people judges the good man worthless but the bad man worthy of honour, if that is how you come across; and they attribute qualities worthy of repute not to the soul but to the crown, the purple, and the tiara, considering it contemptible to take them away again, and a source of shame for those who have had them removed. For me suffices, in the words of Sophocles' Electra, 'nourishment alone, so long as it grieves me not; | I do not lust after your honours'.[33]

[33] Soph. *El.* 363–4.

20. (1) And yet, even though this is the case, they feel no shame in preening themselves at these things, whether the masses rise from their seats or they make way for them. If someone refuses to do this, they call out such things as Euripides' Laius did: 'Stranger, cede from the path of tyrants!',[34] unaware that the stranger will himself turn out to usurp his kingdom and wife a little later on, and that after this usurpation he will become 'the most wretched of mortals',[35] and his children more wretched still. (2) It is said that the king of the Eastern Ethiopians removes one of his cloths (that is the Ethiopians' dress) and gives it to anyone among the natives who wishes to be honoured. As long as he marches around girt in this way, all who meet him prostrate themselves and respect him; but when the king decides that he should remove the cloth, none of the Ethiopians who meets him thinks to address even a very common greeting to him. (3) To those puffed up in this way, one might speak Jocasta's words of reproach to Polynices: 'Why, my son, do you pursue the vilest of divinities, | ambition? Do not! That goddess is unjust: | she visits many wealthy houses and cities, | ⟨and leaves⟩ with ruinous results for those who cultivate her. | She is the one whom you are craving madly.'[36] (4) I would supplement the words of Jocasta as follows: why are you boasting, you wretched man, and why do you exalt in your station? Watch out in case the masses before you change their minds, in case they adorn you with purple today but, if some other person, much inferior to you, takes over this position, alter the objects of their praise [. . .] for they will fawn upon that man, and others too. By the gods, do you feel no shame in strutting around in robes coloured with foreign dyes, with an enormous, handsome bronze portrait of your body in the town hall, but carrying around inside yourself a disgraceful and paltry portrait of your soul, exalting in the names of your ancestors, as though you had no name yourself, and bragging absurdly about your ancestry? (5) Do you not know that if you trace back all those ancient, noble ancestries, you will trace them back to Promethean mud or the stones of Deucalion? Why do you not set aside and strip off those symbols, and present yourself to us naked, as you really are? Or, rather, not even naked, but girt in poverty instead of purple, crowned with lack of offices, instead of your office and your headband? And if then some good man marvels at you or your honours, *then* go and publicly inscribe your ancestry, starting from yourself. You should never think over-highly of yourself, nor should you despise yourself; you should reckon instead that true honour is immortal and cannot be taken away.

21. (1) Do you not see what sort of a man Odysseus was, when he had filthy rags around his body, so that the suitors marvelled at (amongst other things) 'what a thigh the old man reveals from underneath the

[34] Eur. *Phoen.* 40. [35] Eur. fr. 158 N^2. [36] Eur. *Phoen.* 531–5.

rags!'[37] The suitors marvel at his thigh, but I marvel at something else, what strength of will and bravery he shows from underneath his rags—and, what is more, a wanderer, more destitute than Irus, at that! He does not reproach the god for his misfortunes, nor does he grow angry with fate when things are going badly, but greets cheerfully and with decency all that the god marshalls against him. (2) It seems to me that, when beset by these changes of fate, he constantly says to the god: 'If you want me to be king of Ithaca, O Zeus, I too wish it, and I shall not rule like Echetus, Sardanapallus or Arbaces. You wish me to be shipwrecked? I too wish it, and I shall be a more pious shipwreck than Ajax. Do you wish me to endure hunger? I shall endure this too, but with more self-control than my companions. Do you wish me to play the beggar? I do not refuse, but I shall beg with more moderation than Irus. Though beaten most viciously and pelted by my enemies, I shall endure it with decency, if you wish it. Then I shall rule again, if you bid me, and I shall sail again, if you wish it, "until I come upon the men | who do not know the sea, nor eat their food with salt in it".'[38] (3) So spoke the Ithacan, for he understood, I think, though he had been raised on an island, what is intrinsic to the self and what is not, and that one must obey Zeus, god that he is, without complaint and on the terms on which one entered life. How can it be that we, the 'leaders and commanders'[39] of the islanders, could think that all other animals should yield to us, and live in the way that we choose and that suits us (some in luxury, some fighting with each other, some competing in the games, some sacrificed: now we compel them to plough, tomorrow we yoke them 'under a wagon'[40] and once again sacrifice them—and, by Zeus, we sometimes adorn a horse for a parade, and at other times send the same horse to compete in the Olympics, and sometimes compel him to bear loads over mountains and wander who knows where)—while we will not gladly follow the god who expounds what is good for the entire universe? (4) Shall we obey Solon, Draco, Charondas, and Lycurgus, and if someone orders us to be whipped, submit to being whipped on an altar in full view of the Greeks, thinking that there is nothing abominable in this, thinking that the lawgiver established these floggings with a view to the common good and advantage (the most noble of the Persians submit to eating cardamom in their food and lying on the ground; the Arimaspoi obey the law by losing one of their eyes immediately on leaving childhood, the Amazons one of their breasts), but not trust that the gods command us with a view to what is right? (5) And yet we are not so different from the other animals as the gods are from us. Nor are we responsible for as many benefits to animals as the gods are to us. To some species we do not even grant food, instead we let them draw it out of

[37] Hom. *Od.* 18.74.

[38] Hom. *Od.* 11.122–3 = 23.269–70.

[39] e.g. Hom. *Il.* 2.79; *Od.* 7.136.

[40] Hom. *Il.* 24.782.

the earth for themselves; but, seeing that we have received the greatest boons from the gods as a gift—mind, intelligence, speech, reason, the virtues that cannot be removed, and correct use of sense-impressions—do we show no gratitude to them for these gifts?

22. (1) If they make us certain loans, such as honours, reputations, offices, wealth, and civic rights, giving them in season but recalling them when our time is up, shall we grow angry and grudging towards our creditor, because he has allowed us to enjoy his possessions for such time as was fated, and wants instead to loan them to someone else? Or, quite the opposite, shall we prove ourselves courteous and trustworthy debtors, differing from bad ones in that, whereas the latter repay unwillingly, moaning, under no less coercion than if they had involuntarily vomited up something inedible, we do so gladly and with pleasure, thinking that we are liberating ourselves from debt? For, we think, if we lay aside offices, honours, and wealth, it is an act of moderation; but if we also give up to the god our civic rights and life, then we are free in every respect, since we have paid off everything extrinsic to ourselves. (2) Indeed, we should consider that the gods themselves condemn those who show a bad and grudging temper when they repay, holding such opinions concerning them as creditors hold concerning ungracious debtors. For when they needed them, they went straight away to the temple doors, and filled the altars with sacrifices and the festivals with prayers, pouring splendid libations, performing rites in the holy months, holding vigils, taking part in the choruses together with their children, publicly proclaiming thanks to them with their words and chants; but when they are required to repay, they become indignant and reproach the very gods who bestowed these things upon them, because it is not open to them to take away the property of others. (3) If one human should deny that he had received a deposit from another human, the man would be a criminal; and if he failed to abide by a contract, a perjurer. Consider, however, those who have been admitted on these terms, namely that they should undergo and perform whatever the god who made us decides: if we do not abide by this contract, shall we not think (just as we would think of others in the matter of legal oaths) that we have committed the greatest injustice, against the very gods, that we have at once broken faith, committed a crime and perjured ourselves? And, on the other hand, if they repay cheerfully and gladly, abiding by their contract, are they not just, pious, and worthy of trust? If they were ever to need something from their creditor again, would they not quickly be granted it? (4) Such were the thoughts of Mucius when he sacrificed his office, Cynegirus when he sacrificed his hand, Philip his eye, Polyzelus both eyes, Heracles when, sloughing off his body as if it were a tunic and no part of him, he surrendered it with no moaning or grief, Pericles when he willingly paid to the gods the

penalty imposed upon him, Crates when he sacrificed his possessions, Themistocles control of the sea, Aristides his fatherland; Xenophon gave up his son, Demosthenes his daughter, and Horatius the Roman surrendered three kin (two sons and [. . .] a daughter, who were killed by each other), losing that which is most precious to a man, and nevertheless conducted sacrifices and entertained his friends with victory celebrations, wearing a wreath.

23. (1) One might well think that the disasters of these and such men were more fortunate than the apparent success of others. For how could a good man not choose to lose his eyes like Polyzelus rather than see as Athamas saw, the man who shot his own children, thinking that he was looking at deer? Who would not wish to have cut off his hands like Cynegirus, rather than to own the sort of hands that Autolycus owned? Who would not pray to die like Socrates, rather than to live as Anytus and Meletus did? Or to be punished like Pericles rather than to hold power like Cleon? To be poor like Aristides rather than rich like Callias, to be stripped of one's position like Thrasybulus rather than to rule like Critias, to be an exile like Musonius rather than to rule like Nero? Laius and Jocasta, I think, would have much preferred to cast out their child, as Xenophon did, than to have had the experience that they did of the living Oedipus. (2) Moreover, entire cities would provide examples of such behaviour: how could a right-thinking populace not wish to leave behind its fatherland, like the Athenians, indeed even to destroy it with their own hands, rather than betray the common liberty of Greece for the sake of the preservation of its own walls, like the Thebans? Those who feel shame at the name of dishonour must not appear more dishonourable in their actions: neither are those who remain altogether good nor are exiles altogether bad, since neither does virtue lie within city-walls nor evil beyond territorial boundaries, and such things are not decided in the assembly or lawcourt.

24. (1) The legal process would be worth a good deal indeed, if jurors could decide between evil and virtue with their pierced and unpierced pebbles. Perhaps Rhadamanthys in Hades can uncover these qualities, but the jurors on the Areopagus cannot, nor can the Spartan ephors [. . .] those lawcourts that are reputedly the most accurate in Greece. (2) After all, these are they who unanimously put to death the generals who won victory at Arginusae, and many other excellent men, though a little later they came to despise the accuser of these men as an informer; they set the penalty for Pericles, releasing Cleon and Lysander; they acquitted Pausanias of wrongdoing, but killed the same man a little later by starving him in the temple of Athena of the brazen house. What is more, Alcibiades, whom they exiled on the grounds of impiety to the gods and outrage to humans, they later crowned and elected general; and a little while afterwards they exiled him once again, from his camp. Anyone look-

ing at the legal decisions taken by these men would come to conflicting opinions on the subject of Alcibiades. It is impossible to say that he was an excellent man when he was a general, and a bad man when he was in exile, for the same nature does not metamorphose alternately in accordance with the decrees of jurors. (3) So one should not consider that there is anything appalling about all these judgements, for this reason: it is not the judgement that makes the man on whom it is passed just or unjust, but he makes the judgement unjust if he proves himself excellent, and just if he proves himself bad. Here is the proof: the jurors did not render Socrates a bad, unjust man with their vote, but Socrates rendered them unjust and criminal; nor, again, did the Athenians render Aristides unjust, but those who exiled him [. . .] they called it just. Apollo addressed Lampo of Megara, when he was in exile, as follows: 'a famous man has come in search of his family and abode'; and, indeed, he revealed that Socrates was 'the wisest of all' when the latter was away from home.[41] If such a witness was even for the Athenians insufficient to counter the trumped-up charges of Anytus and Meletus, is there anyone of high intelligence who still feels shame to be called a convict, when the god has revealed that the man punished with death was the wisest of all, and the man punished with exile the most famous, and those who condemned Aristides bore witness that he was the most just? (4) So it is not exile and remaining at home, nor loss of honour and honour, nor injustice and ⟨justice, nor liberty and⟩ slavery, nor wealth and poverty that are good and bad, but the proper handling of these things is good and the improper bad; and, on the other hand, a cheerful ⟨. . .⟩ is shameful and grievous.

25. (1) We should not learn for the first time when some change of fortune befalls us that we are human, and that we have been raised largely for these disasters, for then we shall be late acquirers of self-knowledge. When we are successful, too, we must foresee from afar and anticipate troubles, and prepare a plan for them, just as good pilots make preparations before the storm, and the [. . .] justice [. . .] I [. . .] before [. . .] when the ship is enjoying a following wind, a mighty swell suddenly hits it, dashing the prow or even striking its broadside and capsizing it. (2) Instead, if you see someone else who has encountered disaster, as though you were beholding from afar another ship in a storm, expect that the storm over there will reach you; and if you see that the ship has sunk, then, indeed, it has allowed you to see your own fate in a comparable example. For your ship too is destructible, and 'may be borne by the waves, and the gusts of all kinds of winds',[42] and composed of planks (although human differs from human in respect of foresight, solidity, and strength). If, however, you see a ship on its return journey, you have an example of solidity; and if you see it docking safely, imitate this too. If you

[41] Pl. *Apol.* 21a. [42] Pind. fr. 33d 1–2 Snell–Maehler, slightly adapted.

see it sailing smoothly, its sails full, 'rejoicing in Zeus' breeze',[43] [. . .] do not underestimate fortune's plans for you, so long as you happen to be on the sea of life, for they can shift and alter their form. (3) Sometimes those who are running along with a following wind are sunk along with the boat, when it becomes waterlogged; sometimes, when they are using the sails unsparingly, a violent wind attacks from behind, and, in Menander's words, 'dashes out and throws overboard all the men at once'.[44] It is then that great and incurable errors occur. In the panic inspired by a storm, a sailor cuts off the sail or throws overboard most of the cargo to lighten the vessel, or he even directs his boat towards the shallows and runs it aground, or, as a last resort, he thinks of some plank or jar, and plunges into the sea clinging on to this. In times of success and good fortune, on the other hand, unmanned by lack of due care, men are often uprooted, like large trees.

26. (1) The man who wishes to show equanimity must look to those less well off when he is doing well, and to those whose luck is even worse when he is doing badly. If, on the other hand, you look to acquiring more when you are doing well, and to your greater need when you are doing badly, you will always be subject to grief and envy (grief is sorrow at one's own misfortunes, and envy is pain felt at others' blessings). (2) I am not saying that one should take pleasure in others' misfortunes (that would be churlish), but that one should lighten one's load by appreciating parallels between the two circumstances, and by considering that humans share common fates. No one could become so misfortunate that he could not, if he searched among people, find someone even less fortunate, since *every* excess of troubles, even if one thinks that one's own problems are the absolute, in the long term [. . .] made [. . .] a man who had not only gone blind, but even defiled his mother's bed. Tereus might be said to be even more pitiable, in that he ⟨ate his child, and Thyestes, who not only⟩ ate his children, but even besmirched his one remaining, beloved daughter. How much better it would have been for him to set her before himself at the same table, along with her brothers, and eat her, than to produce children from such a marriage in the same way that he successfully brought up his first children. (3) Why, even if we did not have the tragedians, who is so inexperienced of the changes in human fortune that he has not encountered many such events? Not even someone who was born in the way described in Hesiod. For it is not only, as you say, O Hesiod, the iron race that is full of disasters, but also the fourth, third, second, and even the first: their fates too were quick to change (so you need not weep alone). (4) And these men whom I recently mentioned were sons of gods and their descendants: that man Tantalus (you may have heard of him somewhere, or even seen him in Hades, thirsting) shared the table of the gods, as did

[43] Hom. *Od.* 5.176; *Hom. hymn. Ap.* 427

[44] Men. fr. 701 Koerte.

Tityus and Sisyphus. Peleus was of the third generation of descendants of Zeus, and the wife he took was one of the sea-deities, and yet he lost his son before his due season, and was driven from his fatherland by his enemies, old and grieving; and, moreover, his grandson was unable to defend him, since he too was in exile. Do you wish me to recount to you the second and third races? Sarpedon was Zeus' son, and he died young, whilst others grew to old age. Aeneas, that man who wandered without home or city, was a son of Aphrodite, and he went into exile with his father, Aphrodite's beloved, on his shoulders, and his son in tow. (5) Do you—you, a citizen of Ascra, a town that you call 'bad in winter, harsh in summer, never good',[45] a son of Dius and Pycimede, of whom no one knows whether they were freeborn—do you, Hesiod, make these laments and complaints, and denounce the gods because they made you a poet instead of a shepherd, and gave you eternal fame instead of obscurity? None of the poets of the golden race is remembered, mark you; but, born in that race during which the Muses taught you, but 'stopped the song of Thracian Thamyris',[46] do you lack reputation? They may have taught you the generations of the gods, but they did not think you worthy to be a student of divine intention—even though according to you Zeus governs everything with a view to what you find pleasant or think just.

27. (1) But in reality he also concentrates on what is truly just and in the interest of the cosmos, just as a good pilot concentrates on the safety of his ship and all his passengers [. . .] deviation from the course [. . .] and hurling these things outside the ship down to the depths of Tartarus, as if for the common safety [. . .] (2) If you consent and show equanimity, you will complete the course of life well and without mishap, thanks to your foreknowledge of it, and will arrive at the sheltered harbour of happiness, where you will disembark, and see the long-renowned benefits of the Elysian plains. You will remain there, with no fear that the boat [. . .] from the greatest pilot; [. . .] it will travel in safety, and pick up other passengers from other places.

28– The fourth adversary, liberty

28. (1) The remaining part of this contest for the crown of magnanimity, the greatest, remains as if on the byline: liberty. She challenges me plausibly with the claim that the matter of my exile is neither under my control nor of my willing, and claims that I [spend] my whole time shut up on one island, bereft of a share of liberty, just like the beasts raised in a Persian park, which Cyrus claims to be thin, mangy, and devoid of strength (whilst those raised on the plains are sleek, wide-ranging, and free). (2) Now these words are fine for Cyrus—a Persian, whose arrogance led him to desire to chase animals that flee, the sleeker kind—and they are

[45] Hes. *Op.* 640. [46] Hom. *Il.* 2.595.

appropriate to his style of speaking. One who is inquiring into the liberty of a man (whose liberty of conduct lies not in the name, but in his will), however, should know that a good man's soul is restrained by neither sea nor jail, nor the bonds of Ares, nor the bronze chamber of Acrisius, nor the iron of Hephaestus, nor Ocean who encircles everything; wherever you bind and fence in the soul, it is unwilling to leave (for it is not right that it should flee, or transgress the laws, be they the words of the god or those laws that stood guard over Socrates), but in that very place, ever indestructible, unconstrained, unchained, it has its share in liberty. (3) The man who wishes to quit life [. . .] thus he will wish [. . .] the law [. . .] these things.

29. (1) For the practice of nomads does not suit [. . .] but matters of true liberty. If you prevent [. . .] this is your liberty; but if you constantly lust after [impossible things], that is your slavery: you will always fail in this. (2) Shall we look to the mainland from our island and feel pain because we cannot leave it, but feel no pain when we look from earth to heaven because a human cannot rise up to it? And yet that is much less likely. Things that are possible we [. . .] from it, even in [. . .]; but we expend neither energy nor vain effort on impossible things, as Otus and Ephialtes did, who attempted to pile mountains upon mountains so that they might rise up to heaven [. . .]

[*Papyrus becomes hopelessly ragged.*]

APPENDIX 2

The performative context of Dio's *Kingship orations*

The internal evidence of the *Kingships* suggests that at least two of them were performed before an emperor: the first oration addresses a 'leader' (ἡγεμόνα, 1.5), a 'powerful man who rules over most of the earth and most people' (ἀνδρὶ καρτερῶι πλείστης ἄρχοντι χώρας καὶ ἀνθρώπων, 1.56); the third addresses an 'emperor' (αὐτοκράτορ, 3.2; 3.3). The second and fourth have no explicit addressees, but given the narrative situations—Philip and Diogenes respectively addressing Alexander—it is not difficult to assume that Trajan (who revived the imperial practice of imitating Alexander) is envisaged.[1] As a result, scholars have generally concurred that the *Kingships* were performed before Trajan.[2] But Dio's self-representations are not to be taken at face value: his autobiographies display a marked inclination towards deceptive self-dramatization.[3] This appendix briefly reviews the evidence for Trajanic performance, concluding that the performative scenario is likely to have been a fiction.

There is no external evidence that the *Kingships* were performed before Trajan. Philostratus' famous account of Dio addressing Trajan while standing on his triumphal chariot[4] does not allude specifically to the *Kingships*; nor even is it necessarily a trustworthy record, since Philostratus may well be following Dio's own (fictionalizing) account. The proposition of an imperial audience for these texts becomes even less plausible once we consider that the four *Kingships* are not a self-evidently unified collection. First, the fourth *Kingship* could be bracketed, along with 6 and 8–10, as a 'Diogenes oration'; and secondly, and more

[1] On Trajan's *Alexandri imitatio*, see Moles (1990), 299–300; Sidebottom (1990), 204–20.

[2] But cf. Waters (1974), 237: '[t]he "dramatic framework" of the [*Kingship*] orations is . . . totally fictitious; they may, in substance, have been orally delivered, but the presence of the emperor need not be anything but a convenient device'. The assertion is, however, unsubstantiated: hence the equivocation between certainty ('totally fictitious') and caution ('need not'). Swain (1996), 193–4 is also sceptical about the Trajanic audience of the orations (and particularly the fourth, with its aggressive tone).

[3] Ch. 3, nn. 86–7.

[4] Philostr. *VS* 488: see Schmitz (1996); Whitmarsh (1998*a*), and Ch. 4, 'Dio and Philostratus'.

importantly for our purposes, there are other orations of Dio that pertain to the theme of kingship (notably *Orr.* 6, 12, 56, 57, 62). *Oration* 5, meanwhile, constitutes an alternative ending for the fourth *Kingship* (as Photius already notes).[5] The idea that the four speeches *On kingship* form a self-sufficient and exclusive unity goes back at least to Photius in the ninth century (assuming that the 'four speeches' to which he refers are those we call *Orr.* 1–4) and plausibly to Synesius in the fifth;[6] but to attribute this collocation to Dio himself rather than an early editor would be (I think) a leap too far. If we remove the certainty about which of Dio's texts are 'on kingship', then it falls to proponents of a Trajanic performance to enumerate how many of these orations we are to imagine the emperor as having endured. Did he listen, for example, to both versions of the fourth *Kingship*? As Sidebottom (who nevertheless adheres to the idea of an imperial context) notes, 'while it is hard to imagine Trajan sitting through orations one to four, it is impossible to imagine him sitting through oration four twice, each time with a different ending'.[7] Questions of plausibility notwithstanding, the fifth oration in any case refers to 'younger' listeners (5.24), another indication that a broader audience than simply Trajan is envisaged.

It is as well here to dispose of two possible objections to the thesis that the *Kingships* make sense outside of an imperial context. (i) It is sometimes held that the existence of the 'alternative' ending to the fourth oration (i.e. the fifth oration) points to there having been two versions, one bowdlerized for imperial consumption.[8] This is entirely conjectural.[9] (ii) Christopher Jones argues that the *Kingships* are specifically appropriate to Trajan's personality: he was a military man, fond of hunting, and so forth.[10] This does not prove anything: if *we* know about aspects of Trajan's likes and dislikes, the information would no doubt have been widely available—and easily manipulable—in antiquity. Moreover, these images of hunting and so forth, even if they are tailored to Trajan, are part of the traditional repertoire of kingship speeches.[11]

The one piece of reasonably secure information about the performance of the *Kingships* is *Oration* 57, apparently a *prolalia* introducing 'the words I spoke to the emperor' (*τοὺς ῥηθέντας πρὸς τὸν αὐτοκράτορα* [sc.

[5] Phot. *Bibl.* cod. 209 = Dio, *test.* 2.414 Budé/2.321 von Arnim.

[6] Phot. *Bibl.* cod. 209 = Dio, *test.* 2.414 Budé/2.321 von Arnim: 'his four speeches on kingship' (*τῶν . . λόγων αὐτοῦ δ' περὶ βασιλείας*); Synes. *Dio* 39 = Dio, *test.* 2.409 Budé refers to 'the last speech on kingship' (*τὸν ἔσχατον περὶ βασιλείας*), the subsequent description clarifying that he is referring to *Or.* 4.

[7] Sidebottom (1990), 78.

[8] Von Arnim (1898), 402–4, 412–14.

[9] Moles (1983), 276–7.

[10] C. P. Jones (1978), 115–23, followed by Moles (1990).

[11] Sidebottom (1990), 142–66.

λόγους], 57.11).[12] What is secure about this, however, is not (given what we know about Dio's proclivity towards fictionalizing self-representation) the assertion that the speeches were delivered in an imperial context, but the evidence that Dio performed some material on kingship in a civic context *on the pretext that* it had been delivered before the emperor. I conclude, then, that the civic context is the appropriate one in which to discuss these texts.

[12] Von Arnim (1898), 410–14; Mras (1949), 74–5. For *prolaliai*, see Ch. 1, n. 137.

References

Greek and Latin works are cited from the most recent Oxford Classical Text (or, where none exists, from the most recent Teubner edition), excepting the following:

Achilles Tatius J.-P. Garnaud, *Achille Tatius d'Alexandrie,* Le roman de Leucippé et Clitophon (Paris, 1991).

Aelius Aristides H. Keil, *Aelii Aristidis, Omnia quae supersunt*, vol. 2 (Berlin, 1898).

Dio Chrysostom J. von Arnim, *Dionis Prusaensis quae exstant*, 2 vols. (Berlin, 1893–6; repr. 1962).

Heliodorus R. M. Rattenbury and T. W. Lumb, *Héliodore,* Les Ethiopiques, 3 vols., 2nd edn. (Paris, 1960).

Marcus Aurelius A. S. L. Farquharson, *The* Meditations *of the Emperor Marcus Antoninus*, 2 vols. (Oxford, 1944).

Scholarly works

Periodicals are indexed according to the abbreviations used in *Année philologique*, with some obvious Anglicizations (*CP* for *CPh* etc.).

Aalders, G. J. D. (1975) *Political thought in Hellenistic times* (Amsterdam).

——(1982*a*) *Plutarch's political thought* (Amsterdam).

——(1982*b*) 'Plutarch or pseudo-Plutarch? The authorship of *De unius in re publica dominatione*' (*Mnemosyne*, 35: 72–83).

——and de Blois, L. (1992) 'Plutarch und die politische Philosophie der Griechen' (*ANRW* 2.36.5: 3384–404).

Adams, J. N. (1982) *The Latin sexual vocabulary* (London).

Ahl, F. (1984) 'The art of safe criticism in Greece and Rome' (*AJP* 105: 174–208).

Albini, F. (1997) 'Family and the formation of character: aspects of Plutarch's thought', in Mossman ed. (1997), 59–71.

Alcock, S. E. (1993) *Graecia capta: the landscapes of Roman Greece* (Cambridge).

——(1994) 'Nero at play: the emperor's Grecian odyssey', in Elsner and Masters eds. (1994), 98–111.

——ed. (1997) *The early Roman empire in the East* (Oxford).

Alexiou, A. S. (1990) 'Philosophers in Lucian', Ph.D. thesis (Fordham).

Amato, E. (1995) *Studi su Favorino: le orazioni pseudo-crisostomiche* (Salerno).

Ameling, W. (1983) *Herodes Atticus*, 2 vols. (Hildesheim).

——(1984) 'L. Flavius Arrianus neos Xenophon' (*EA* 4: 119–22).

——(1986) 'Tyrannen und schwangere Frauen' (*Historia*, 35: 507–8).

Amirault, C. (1995) 'The good teacher, the good student', in Gallop ed. (1995), 64–78.

Anderson, B. (1983) *Imagined communities: reflections on the origin and spread of nationalism* (London).

Anderson, G. (1976) *Lucian: theme and variation in the Second Sophistic* (Leiden).

——(1977) 'Putting pressure on Plutarch: Philostratus *Epistle* 73' (*CP* 72: 43–5).

——(1978) 'Lucian's *Nigrinus*: the problem of form' (*GRBS* 19: 367–74).

——(1986) *Philostratus: biography and belles-lettres in the third century A.D.* (Beckenham).

——(1990) 'The second sophistic: some problems of perspective', in Russell ed. (1990), 91–110.

——(1993) *The second sophistic: a cultural phenomenon in the Roman empire* (London).

——(1994) *Sage, saint and sophist: holy men and their associates in the early Roman empire* (London).

——(1996) 'Philostratus on Apollonius of Tyana: the unpredictable on the unfathomable', in Schmeling ed. (1996), 613–18.

——(1997) 'Athenaeus: the sophistic environment (*ANRW* 2.34.3: 2173–85).

Anderson, W. (1964) *Anger in Juvenal and Seneca*, California Studies in Classical Philology 19.3 (Berkeley).

Andersson, T. J. (1971) *Polis and psyche: a motif in Plato's Republic* (Göteborg).

André, J.-M. (1987) 'Les écoles philosophiques aux deux premiers siècles de l'Empire' (*ANRW* 2.36.1: 5–77).

——(1992) 'Apollonios et le Rome de Néron', in Baslez *et al*. eds. (1992), 113–24.

——and Baslez, M.-F. (1993) *Voyager dans l'antiquité* (Paris).

Arafat, K. (1996) *Pausanias' Greece: ancient artists and Roman rulers* (Cambridge).

Arnim, H. von (1898) *Leben und Werke des Dion von Prusa* (Berlin).

Ash, R. (1997) 'Severed heads: individual portraits and irrational forces in Plutarch's *Galba* and *Otho*', in Mossman ed. (1997), 189–214.

Ashfield, A., and de Bolla, P., eds. (1996) *The sublime: a reader in British eighteenth-century aesthetic theory* (Cambridge).

Asmis, E. (1989) 'The Stoicism of Marcus Aurelius' (*ANRW* 2.36.3: 2228–52).
Asmus, J. R. (1895) *Julian und Dio Chrysostomus* (Tauferbischofsheim).
——(1900) 'Synesius und Dio Chrysostomus' (*ByzZ* 9: 85–151).
Athanassidi-Fowden, P. (1981) *Julian and hellenism: an intellectual biography* (Oxford).
Aujac, G. (1992), *Dénys d'Halicarnasse: opuscules rhétoriques*, vol. 5 (Paris).
Avotins, I. (1975) 'The holders of the chairs of rhetoric at Athens' (*HSCP* 79: 313–24).
——(1978) 'The date and recipient of the *Vitae sophistarum* of Philostratus' (*Hermes*, 106: 242–7).
Babut, D. (1969) *Plutarque et le stoïcisme* (Paris).
——(1975) 'ἱστορία οἷον ὕλη φιλοσοφίας: histoire et réflexion morale dans l'œuvre de Plutarque' (*REG* 88: 206–19).
Bal, M. (1997) *Narratology: introduction to the theory of narrative*, 2nd edn. (Toronto).
Baldry, H. C. (1965) *The unity of mankind in Greek thought* (London).
Baldwin, B. (1961) 'Lucian as a social satirist' (*CQ* 11: 199–208).
——(1973) *Studies in Lucian* (Toronto).
——(1982) 'The date of Alciphron' (*Hermes*, 110: 253–4).
Bargheer, R. (1999) *Die Gottesvorstellung Heliodors in den Aithopika* (Berne).
Barigazzi, A., ed. (1966) *Favorino di Arelate, Opere: introduzione, testo critico e commento* (Florence).
——(1982) 'Note critiche ed esegetiche agli scritti politici di Plutarco, II [*sic*]' (*Prometheus*, 8: 61–79); rev. and corr. in Barigazzi (1994), 263–85.
——(1984) 'Note critiche ed esegetiche agli scritti politici di Plutarco I' (*Prometheus*, 10: 37–64); rev. and corr. in Barigazzi (1994), 235–61.
——(1987) 'Per il testo del *De exilio* di Favorino' (*Prometheus*, 12: 204–8).
——(1994) *Studi su Plutarco* (Florence).
Barnes, T. D. (1968) 'Philostratus and Gordian' (*Latomus*, 27: 581–97).
Barthes, R. (1975) *The pleasure of the text*, trans. R. Miller (New York).
——(1977) *Image music text*, ed. S. Heath (London).
——(1986) *The rustle of language*, trans. R. Howard (Oxford).
——(1990) *S/Z*, trans. R. Miller (Oxford).
Barton, T. S. (1994) *Power and knowledge: astrology, physiognomics, and medicine under the Roman Empire* (Ann Arbor).
Bartsch, S. (1989) *Decoding the ancient novel: the reader and the role of description in Heliodorus and Achilles Tatius* (Princeton).
——(1994) *Actors in the audience: theatricality and double-speak from Nero to Hadrian* (Cambridge, Mass.).
Baslez, M.-F., Hoffmann, P., and Trédé, M., eds. (1992) *Le monde du*

roman grec. Actes du colloque international tenu à l'Ecole Normale Supérieure (Paris).

—— —— and PERNOT, L., eds. (1993) *L'Invention de l'autobiographie d'Hésiode à Saint Augustin* (Paris).

BEACHAM, R. C. (1999) *Spectacle entertainments of early imperial Rome* (New Haven).

BEARD, M., and CRAWFORD, M. (1985) *Rome in the late Republic: problems and interpretations* (London).

BELLONI, L. (1980) 'Aspetti dell'antica σοφία in Apollonio di Tiana' (*Aevum*, 54: 140–9).

BELSEY, C. (1980) *Critical practice* (London).

BENJAMIN, A., ed. (1988) *Post-structuralist classics* (London).

BENNINGTON, G. (1990) 'Postal politics and the institution of the nation', in Bhabha ed. (1990), 121–37.

BERRY, E. G. (1958) 'The *De liberis educandis* of pseudo-Plutarch' (*HSCP* 63: 387–99).

BEVAN, D., ed. (1990) *Literature and exile* (Amsterdam).

BHABHA, H. K., ed. (1990) *Nation and narration* (London).

—— (1994) *The location of culture* (London).

BIELER, L. (1935–6) *ΘΕΙΟΣ ΑΝΗΡ: das Bild des 'göttlichen Menschen' in Spätantike und Frühchristentum*, 2 vols., 2nd edn. (Vienna; repr. Darmstadt, 1967).

BILLAULT, A. (1990) 'Un sage en politique: Apollonios de Tyane et les empereurs romains', in F. Jouan and A. Motte, eds., *Mythe et politique: actes du colloque de Liège, 14–16 sept. 1989* (Geneva), 23–32.

—— (1991) 'Les formes romanesques de l'héroisation dans la *Vie d'Apollonios de Tyane*' (*BAGB* 1991: 267–74).

—— (1996) 'La nature dans *Daphnis et Chloë*' (*REG* 109: 506–26).

BING, P. (1988) *The well-read muse: present and past in Callimachus and the Hellenistic poets* (Göttingen).

BLOIS, L. DE (1984) 'The third century crisis and the Greek élite in the Roman empire' (*Historia*, 33: 358–77).

—— and BONS, J. A. E. (1992) 'Platonic philosophy and Isocratean virtues in Plutarch's *Numa*' (*AncSoc* 23: 159–88).

—— —— (1995) 'Platonic and Isocratean concepts in Plutarch's *Lycurgus*', in Gallo and Scardigli eds. (1995), 99–106.

BLOMQVIST, K. (1997) 'From Olympias to Aretaphila: women in politics in Plutarch', in Mossman ed. (1997), 73–97.

BLOOM, H. (1975) *A map of misreading* (New York).

—— (1994) *The Western canon: the books and schools of the ages* (New York).

—— (1997) *The anxiety of influence: a theory of poetry*, 2nd edn. (New York).

BLUM, R. (1991) *Kallimachos: the Alexandrian Library and the origins of bibliography*, trans. H. Wellisch (Madison).

BOGEL, F. V. (1995) 'The difference satire makes: reading Swift's poems', in Connery and Combe eds. (1995), 43–53.

BOMPAIRE, J. (1958) *Lucien écrivain: imitation et création* (Paris).

——(1993) 'Quatre styles de l'autobiographie au IIe siècle après J.-C.: Aelius Aristide, Lucien, Marc-Aurèle, Galien', in Baslez *et al.* eds. (1993), 199–209.

BONNER, S. F. (1977) *Education in ancient Rome* (London).

BOSWORTH, A. B. (1972) 'Arrian's literary development' (*CQ* 22: 163–85).

——(1993) 'Arrian and Rome: the minor works' (*ANRW* 2.34.1: 226–75).

BOUFFARTIGUE, J. (1992) *L'Empereur Julien et la culture de son temps* (Paris).

BOULANGER, A. (1923) *Aelius Aristide et la sophistique dans la province d'Asie au IIe siècle de notre ère* (Paris).

BOULOGNE, J. (1994) *Plutarque: un aristocrate grec sous l'occupation romaine* (Lille).

BOURDIEU, P., and PASSERON, J. C. (1990) *Reproduction in education, society and culture*, 2nd edn. (London).

BOWERSOCK, G. W. (1965) *Augustus and the Greek world* (Oxford).

——(1969) *Greek sophists in the Roman empire* (Oxford).

——(1973) 'Greek intellectuals and the imperial cult' (*FHE* 19: 179–206).

——ed. (1974) *Approaches to the second sophistic* (Pennsylvania).

——(1978) *Julian the apostate* (London).

——(1986) 'Subversion in the Roman provinces' (*FHE* 33: 291–316).

——(1989) 'Philostratus and the second sophistic' (in *CHCL* 1.4: 95–8).

——(1994) *Fiction as history: Nero to Julian* (Berkeley).

——(1995) *Martyrdom and Rome* (Cambridge).

——and JONES, C.P. (1974) 'Appendix II: a guide to the sophists in Philostratus' *Vitae sophistarum*', in Bowersock ed. (1974), 35–40.

BOWIE, E. L. (1974) 'Greeks and their past in the second sophistic', in M. I. Finley, ed., *Studies in ancient society* (London), 166–209; minimally revised from *P&P* 46 (1970), 3–41.

——(1978) 'Apollonius of Tyana: tradition and reality' (*ANRW* 2.16.2: 1652–99).

——(1982) 'The importance of sophists' (*YCS* 27: 29–59).

——(1985) 'Theocritus' seventh *Idyll*, Philetas and Longus' (*CQ* 35: 67–91).

——(1989) 'Greek sophists and Greek poetry' (*ANRW* 2.33.1: 209–58).

——(1990) 'Greek poetry in the Antonine age', in Russell ed. (1990), 53–90.

——(1991) 'Hellenes and Hellenism in writers of the early Second Sophistic', in Saïd ed. (1991), 183–204.

——(1994*a*) 'The readership of Greek novels in the ancient world', in Tatum ed. (1994), 435–59.

——(1994*b*) 'Philostratus: writer of fiction', in Morgan and Stoneman eds. (1994), 181–99.

——(1997) 'Hadrian, Favorinus, and Plutarch', in Mossman ed. (1997), 1–15.

——and HARRISON, S. J. (1993) 'The romance of the novel' (*JRS* 83: 159–78).

BOYARIN, D. (1999) *Dying for God: martyrdom and the making of Christianity and Judaism* (Stanford).

BRADLEY, K. R. (1978) 'The chronology of Nero's visit to Greece AD 66/7' (*Latomus*, 37: 61–72).

BRAGINTON, M. V. (1944) 'Exile under the emperors' (*CJ* 39: 391–407).

BRANCACCI, A. (1980) 'Tradizione cinica e problemi di datazione nelle orazioni diogeniane di Dione di Prusa' (*Elenchos*, 1: 92–122).

——(1986) *Rhetorike philosophousa: Dione Crisostomo nella cultura antica e bizantina* (Naples).

BRANHAM, R. B. (1985) 'Introducing the sophist: Lucian's prologues' (*TAPA* 115: 237–43).

——(1989) *Unruly eloquence: Lucian and the comedy of traditions* (Cambridge, Mass.).

——(1993) 'Diogenes' rhetoric and the invention of cynicism', in Goulet-Cazé and Goulet eds. (1993), 445–73; repr. as 'Defacing the currency: Diogenes' rhetoric and the invention of cynicism' (*Arethusa*, 27: 329–59); repr. in Branham and Goulet-Cazé eds. (1996), 81–104.

——and GOULET-CAZÉ, M.-O., eds. (1996) *The cynics: the cynic movement in antiquity and its legacy* (Berkeley).

BRAUND, S. H. (1988) *Beyond anger: a study of Juvenal's third book of Satires* (Cambridge).

BRENK, F. (1977) *In mist apparelled: religious themes in Plutarch's* Moralia *and* Lives (Leiden).

BRENNAN, T. (1990) 'The national longing for form', in Bhabha ed. (1990), 44–70.

BRINGMAN, K. (1993) 'The king as benefactor: some remarks on ideal kingship in the age of Hellenism', in Bulloch *et al.* eds. (1993), 7–24.

BRINK, C. O. (1971) *Horace on poetry*, vol. 2: *The* Ars Poetica (Cambridge).

——(1982) *Horace on poetry*, vol. 3: Epistles *book II* (Cambridge).

BROWN, P. (1978) *The making of late antiquity* (Cambridge, Mass.).

——(1988) *The body and society* (London).

BRUNT, P. (1973) 'Aspects of the social thought of Dio Chrysostom' (*PCPS* 19: 9–34); repr. in id., *Studies in Greek history and thought* (Oxford, 1993), 210–44.

BRUNT, P. (1974) 'Marcus Aurelius in his *Meditations*', *JRS* 64: 1–20.

——(1975) 'Stoicism and the principate' (*PBSR* 30: 7–35).

——(1994) 'The bubble of the Second Sophistic' (*BICS* 39: 25–52).

——and MOORE, J., eds. (1967) *Res gestae diui Augusti* (Oxford).

BULLOCH, A. W., GRUEN, E. S., LONG, A. A, and STEWART, A. F., eds. (1993) *Images and ideologies: Self-definition in the Hellenistic world* (Berkeley).

BUNGE, J. G. (1975) 'Antiochus-Helios: Methoden und Ergebnisse der Reichspolitik Antiochus IV Epiphanes Syrien im Spiegel seines Münzen' (*Historia*, 24: 164–88).

BURKE, P. (1997) *Varieties of cultural history* (Cambridge).

BURKERT, W. (1962) '*ΓΟΗΣ*: zum griechische "Schamanismus"' (*RhM* 105: 36–58).

——(1987) *Ancient mystery cults* (Cambridge, Mass.).

BURNET, J. (1924) *Plato,* Euthyphro, Apology of Socrates, Crito (Oxford).

BURNYEAT, M. F. (1992) 'Utopia and fantasy: the practicability of Plato's ideally just city', in J. Hopkins and A. Savile, eds., *Psychoanalysis, mind and art: perspectives on Richard Wollheim* (Oxford), 175–87.

BUSHNELL, R. W. (1990) *Tragedies of tyrants: political thought and theater in the English renaissance* (Ithaca).

BUTLER, J. (1993) *Bodies that matter: on the discursive limits of 'sex'* (New York).

CAIAZZA, A. (1995) 'A proposito della paternità plutarchea del *De unius*' (*Prometheus*, 21: 131–40).

CAIRNS, F. (1989) *Virgil's Augustan epic* (Cambridge).

CAMERON, A. (1969) 'Petronius and Plato' (*CQ* 19: 367–70).

CAMPANILE, D. (1999) 'La costruzione del sofista: note sul *βίος* di Polemone', in B. Virgilio, ed., *Studi Ellenistici* (Pisa), 269–315.

CAREY, C. (1994) 'Rhetorical means of persuasion', in I. Worthington, ed., *Persuasion: Greek rhetoric in action* (London), 26–45.

CARNEY, E. D. (1981) 'The death of Clitus' (*GRBS* 22: 149–60).

CARRIÈRE, J. C. (1977) 'A propos de la politique de Plutarque' (*DHA* 3: 237–51).

CARTLEDGE, P. (1993) *The Greeks: a study of self and others* (Oxford).

CASTER, M. (1935) 'La composition du *Nigrinos* et les intentions ironiques attribuées à Lucien', in *Mélanges M. Octave Navarre* (Toulouse), 471–85.

CAVE, T. (1988) *Recognitions: a study in poetics* (Oxford).

CENTRONE, B. (2000) 'Platonism and pythagoreanism in the early empire', in Rowe and Schofield eds. (2000), 559–84.

CERRI, G. (1975) *Il linguaggio politico nel Prometeo di Eschilo: saggio di semantica* (Rome).

Certeau, M. de (1984) *The practice of everyday life*, trans. S. Rendall (Berkeley).

Chalk, H. H. O. (1960) 'Eros and the Lesbian pastorals of Longus' (*JHS* 80: 32–51); repr. in H. Gärtner, ed., *Beiträge zum griechischen Liebesroman* (Hildesheim, 1984), 388–407; and in B. Effe, ed., *Theokrit und die griechische Bukolik* (Darmstadt, 1986), 402–38.

Champlin, E. H. (1980) *Fronto and Antonine Rome* (Cambridge, Mass.).

Charles-Saget, A. (1986) 'Un miroir-du-prince au 1er siècle après J.C. (Dion Chrysostome *Sur la royauté* 1)', in B. Cassin, ed., *Le plaisir du parler: études de sophistique comparée* (Paris), 111–29.

Chesnut, G. F. (1978) 'The ruler and the *logos* in Neopythagorean, middle Platonic, and late Stoic political philosophy' (*ANRW* 2.16.2: 1310–32).

Cizek, A. N. (1994) Imitatio et tractatio*: die literarisch-rhetorischen Grundlagen der Nachahmung in Antike und Mittelalter* (Tübingen).

Cizek, E. (1989) 'La littérature et les cercles culturels et politiques à l'époque de Trajan' (*ANRW* 2.33.1: 3–35).

Claassen, J. (1988) 'Tacitus: historian between republic and principate' (*Mnemosyne*, 41: 93–116).

——(1996*a*) 'Exile, death and immortality: voices from the grave' (*Latomus*, 55: 571–90).

——(1996*b*) 'Dio's Cicero and the consolatory tradition' (*Papers of the Leeds Latin Seminar*, 9: 29–45).

——(1999) *Displaced persons: the literature of exile from Cicero to Boethius* (London).

Clark, J. R. (1995) 'Vapid voices and sleazy styles', in Connery and Combe eds. (1995), 19–42.

Cohoon, J. W., ed. (1938) *Dio Chrysostom, Orations*, vol.1: *Discourses 1–12* (Cambridge, Mass.).

Coleman, K. (1990) 'Fatal charades: Roman executions staged as mythological charades' (*JRS* 80: 44–73).

——(1993) 'Launching into history: aquatic displays in the early empire' (*JRS* 83: 48–74).

Colson, A. (1989) 'Crito 51a–c: to what does Socrates owe obedience?' (*Phronesis* 34: 27–55).

Connery, B. A., and Combe, K., eds. (1995) *Theorizing satire: essays in literary criticism* (New York).

Cooper, K. (1996) *The virgin and the bride: idealized womanhood in late antiquity* (Cambridge, Mass.).

Coulter, J. A. (1964) '*περὶ ὕψους* 3.3–4 and Aristotle's theory of the mean' (*GRBS* 5: 197–213).

Court, F. E. (1992) *Institutionalizing English literature: the culture and politics of literary study, 1750–1900* (Stanford).

COX, P. (1983) *Biography in late antiquity: the search for the holy man* (Berkeley).

CRAWFORD, R., ed. (1988) *The Scottish invention of English literature* (Oxford).

——(1992) *Devolving English literature* (Oxford).

CRESCI, L. (1999) 'Longus the sophist and the pastoral tradition', in Swain ed. (1999), 210–42.

CRONJE, J. V. (1993) 'The principle of concealment (*TO ΛΑΘΕΙΝ*) in Greek literary theory' (*AClass* 36: 55–64).

CROSBY, H. L. (1946) *Dio Chrysostom IV:* Discourses *xxxvii–lx*, Loeb Classical Library (Cambridge, Mass.).

CURTY, O. (1995) *Les parentés légendaires entre cités grecques. Catalogue raisonné des inscriptions contenant le terme syngeneia et analyse critique* (Geneva).

CUVIGNY, M. (1984) *Plutarque:* Œuvres morales *tome XI—première partie* (Paris).

D'ARMS, J. (1990) 'The Roman *convivium* and the idea of equality', in Murray ed. (1990), 308–20.

DAUDE, C. (1991) 'Le roman de Daphnis et Chloé, ou comment ne pas être un "animal politique" ', in N. Fick and J. Carrière, eds., *Mélanges Etienne Bernard* (Paris), 203–25.

DAVIES, J. K. (1977) 'Athenian citizenship: the descent group and the alternatives' (*CJ* 73.2: 105–21).

DAWE, R. D. (1982) *Sophocles,* Oedipus Rex (Cambridge).

DAWSON, D. (1992) *Cities of the gods: communist utopias in Greek thought* (New York).

DAY, J. M. (1980) *The glory of Athens: the popular tradition as reflected in the* Panathenaicus *of Aelius Aristides* (Chicago).

DE STE CROIX, G. (1954–5) 'The character of the Athenian empire' (*Historia*, 3: 1–41).

DEBORD, G. (1996) *The society of the spectacle*, 3rd edn., trans. D. Nicholson-Smith (New York).

DELCORNO, C. (1989) *Exemplum e letteratura, tra medioevo e renascimento* (Bologna).

DENNISTON, J. (1950) *The Greek particles*, 2nd edn. (Oxford; repr. London, 1996).

DERCHAIN, P., and HUBAUX, J. (1953) 'Vespasien au Sérapéum' (*Latomus*, 12: 38–52).

DERRIDA, J. (1976) *Of Grammatology*, trans. G. Spivak (Baltimore).

——(1982) 'Signature, event, context', in id. *The margins of philosophy,* trans. A. Bass (Brighton), 309–30.

DESIDERI, P. (1978) *Dione di Prusa: un intellettuale greco nell'impero Romano* (Messina).

——(1986) 'La vita politica cittadina nell'impero: lettura dei *Praecepta gerendae rei publicae* e dell'*An seni res publica gerenda sit*' (*Athenaeum*, 64: 371–81).

——(1989) 'Teori e prassi storiografia di Plutarco: una proposta di lettura della coppia Emilio Paulo—Timoleonte' (*Maia* 41: 199–215).

——(1991*a*) 'Citazione letteraria e referimento storico nei "*Precetti politici*" di Plutarco', in D'Ippolito and Gallo eds. (1991), 225–33.

——(1991*b*), 'Dione di Prusa fra ellenismo e romanità' (*ANRW* 2.33.5: 3882–902).

——(1995*a*) ' "Non scriviamo storie, ma vite" (Plut. *Alex.* 1.2): la formula biografica di Plutarco' (*Arachnion*, 1.3: no pages).

——(1995*b*) 'Plutarco e Machiavelli', in Gallo and Scardigli eds. (1995), 107–22.

DESJARDINS, R. (1988) 'Why dialogue? Plato's serious play', in Griswold ed. (1988), 110–25.

DEVINE, F. C. (1970) 'Stoicism on the best régime' (*JHI* 31: 323–36).

DIHLE, A. (1956) *Studien zur griechischen Biographie* (Göttingen).

DILKE, O. A. W. (1980) 'Heliodorus and the colour problem' (*PP* 35: 264–71).

DILLON, J. (1977) *The middle Platonists: a study of Platonism from 80 BC to AD 220* (London).

DIMUNDO, R. (1983) 'Da Socrate a Eumolpo: degradazione dei personaggi e delle funzioni nella novella del fanciullo di Pergamo' (*MD* 10–11: 255–65).

D'IPPOLITO, G., and GALLO, I., eds. (1991) *Strutture formali dei* Moralia *di Plutarco* (Naples).

DOBLHOFER, E. (1987) *Exil und Emigration: zum Erlebnis der Heimatferne in der römischen Literatur* (Darmstadt).

DORANDI, T., ed. (1982) *Filodemo, Il buon re secondo Omero: edizione, traduzione e commento* (Naples).

DÖRRIE, H. (1938) 'Die griechischen Romane und das Christentum' (*Philologus*, 93: 273–6).

——(1971) 'Die Stellung Plutarchs im Platonismus seiner Zeit', in R. B. Palmer and R. Hamerton-Kelly, eds., *Philomathes: studies in honour of Ph. Merlan* (The Hague), 35–56.

DOWNEY, G. (1955) 'Philanthropia in religion and statecraft in the fourth century after Christ' (*Historia*, 4: 199–208).

——(1956) 'Education and public problems as seen by Themistius' (*TAPA* 86: 291–307).

DOYLE, B. (1989) *English and Englishness* (London).

DUBEL, S. (1994) 'Dialogue et autoportrait: les masques de Lucien', in A. Billault, ed., *Lucien de Samosate* (Lyon), 19–26.

DUBOIS, J. (1978) *L'Institution de la littérature: introduction à une sociologie* (Brussels).

DUBOIS, P. (1987) *Centaurs and amazons: women and the pre-history of the great chain of being* (Ann Arbor).

——(1991) *Torture and truth* (New York).

DUBUISSON, M. (1984–6) 'Lucien et Rome' (*AncSoc* 15–17: 185–207).

DUFF, T. (1999) *Plutarch's Lives: exploring virtue and vice* (Oxford).

DUNCAN, I. (1988) 'Adam Smith, Samuel Johnson and the institutions of English', in Crawford ed. (1988), 37–54.

DUQUESNAY, I. (1979) 'From Polyphemus to Corydon: Virgil, *Eclogues* 2 and the *Idylls* of Theocritus', in West and Woodman eds. (1979), 35–69.

DZIELSKA, M. (1986) *Apollonius of Tyana in legend and history*, trans. P. Pienkowski (Rome).

EAGLETON, T. (1983) *Literary theory: an introduction* (Oxford).

EDWARDS, C. (1994) 'Beware of imitations: theatre and the subversion of imperial identity', in Elsner and Masters eds. (1994), 83–97.

——(1996) *Writing Rome: textual approaches to the city* (Cambridge).

——(1997) 'Self-scrutiny and self-transformation in Seneca's *Letters*' (*G&R* 44: 23–38).

EDWARDS, M. J. (1991) 'Damis the epicurean' (*CQ* 41: 563–6).

——(1993) 'Lucian and the rhetoric of philosophy: the *Hermotimus*' (*AC* 62: 195–202).

EGGER, B. (1999) 'The role of women in the Greek novel: woman as heroine and reader', in Swain ed. (1999), 108–36.

EHRENPREIS, I. (1963) '*Personae*', in C. Camden, ed., *Restoration and eighteenth-century literature: studies in honor of H. D. McKillop* (Chicago), 25–37.

ELLIOTT, R. C. (1982) *The literary persona* (Chicago).

ELSNER, J. (1992) 'Pausanias: a Greek pilgrim in the Roman world' (*P&P* 135: 3–29).

——(1995) *Art and the Roman viewer: the transformation of art from Augustus to Justinian* (Cambridge).

——(1997*a*) 'The origins of the icon: pilgrimage, religion and visual culture in the Roman East as "resistance" to the centre', in Alcock ed. (1997), 178–99.

——(1997*b*) 'Hagiographic geography: travel and allegory in the *Life of Apollonius of Tyana*' (*JHS* 117: 22–37).

——and MASTERS, J., eds. (1994) *Reflections of Nero: culture, history and representation* (London).

ELSOM, H. E. (1992) 'Callirhoe: displaying the phallic woman', in Richlin ed. (1992), 212–30.

EMELJANOW, V. (1965) 'A note on the Cynic "short cut to happiness"' (*Mnemosyne*, NS 18: 182–4).

Engels, D. W. (1990) *Roman Corinth: an alternative model for the classical city* (Chicago).

Erskine, A. (1995) 'Rome in the Greek world: the significance of a name', in A. Powell, ed., *The Greek world* (London), 368–79.

Fant, J. C. (1981) 'The choleric official of Philostratus *Vitae sophistarum* p.512: L. Verginius Rufus' (*Historia*, 31: 240–3).

Fantham, E. (1996) *Roman literary culture: from Cicero to Apuleius* (Baltimore).

Farber, J. J. (1979) 'The *Cyropaedia* and Hellenistic kingship' (*AJP* 100: 497–514).

Farenga, V. (1981) 'The paradigmatic tyrant: Greek tyranny and the ideology of the proper' (*Helios*, 8: 1–31).

Farquharson, A. S. L. (1944) *The* Meditations *of the Emperor Marcus Antoninus*, 2 vols. (Oxford).

Feeney, D. (1998) *Literature and religion at Rome: cultures, contexts, and beliefs* (Cambridge).

Fein, S. (1994) *Die Beziehungen der Kaiser Trajan und Hadrian zu den litterati* (Stuttgart).

Feldherr, A. (1998) *Spectacle and society in Livy's History* (Berkeley).

Ferguson, M. (1992) 'Saint Augustine's region of unlikeness: the crossing of exile and language', in Hexter and Selden eds. (1992), 69–94.

Ferrante, D. (1975) *Dione Crisostomo ΠΕΡΙ ΒΑΣΙΛΕΙΑΣ (Or. IV), introduzione, testo, traduzione e commentario* (Naples).

Ferrari, G. R. F. (1987) *Listening to the cicadas: a study of Plato's* Phaedrus (Cambridge).

——(1989) 'Plato and poetry', in G. A. Kennedy ed. (1989), 92–148.

Ferrary, J.-L. (1988) *Philhellénisme et impérialisme: aspects idéologiques de la conquête romaine du monde hellénistique, de la seconde guerre de Macédoine à la guerre contre Mithridate* (Rome).

Ferrill, A. (1978) 'Herodotus on tyranny' (*Historia*, 27: 385–98).

Fitton Brown, A. D (1985) 'The unreality of Ovid's Tomitian exile' (*LCM* 10.2: 18–22).

Fitzgerald, J. T., ed. (1996) *Friendship, flattery, and frankness of speech: studies on friendship in the New Testament world* (Leiden).

——and White, L. M. (1983) *The* Tabula *of Cebes* (Chico).

Fitzgerald, W. (2000) *Slavery and the Roman literary imagination* (Cambridge).

Flashar, H. (1978) 'Die klassizistische Theorie der *Mimesis*' (*FHE* 25: 79–96).

Flinterman, J.-J. (1995) *Power, paideia & Pythagoreanism: Greek identity, conceptions of the relationship between philosophers and monarchs and political ideas in Philostratus' Life of Apollonius* (Amsterdam).

Focke, F. (1923) '*Synkrisis*' (*Hermes*, 58: 327–68).

FOLLET, S. (1976) *Athènes au IIe et IIIe siècle. Études chronologiques et prosopographiques* (Paris).

——(1991) 'Divers aspects de l'Hellénisme chez Philostrate', in Saïd ed. (1991), 205–16.

FORD, A. (1992) *Homer: the poetry of the past* (Ithaca).

FORTE, B. (1972) *Rome and the Romans as the Greeks saw them* (Rome).

FOUCAULT, M. (1979) *Discipline and punish: the birth of the prison*, trans. A. Sheridan (London).

——(1981) *The history of sexuality*, vol. 1: *an introduction*, trans. R. Hurley (Harmondsworth).

——(1987) *The history of sexuality*, vol. 2: *the use of pleasure*, trans. R. Hurley (London).

——(1990) *The history of sexuality*, vol. 3: *the care of the self*, trans. R. Hurley (London).

FOWLER, R. (1998) 'Genealogical thinking, Hesiod's *Catalogue*, and the creation of the Hellenes' (*PCPS* 44: 1–19).

FRANCIS, J. (1995) *Subversive virtue: asceticism and authority in the second-century pagan world* (Pennsylvania).

FRANÇOIS, L. (1915) 'Julien et Dion Chrysostome' (*REG* 28: 417–39).

FRASER, P. M. (1972) *Ptolemaic Alexandria*, 2 vols. (Oxford).

FRAZIER, F. (1988) 'A propos de la "philotimia" dans les "Vies": quelques jalons dans l'histoire d'une notion' (*RPh* 62: 109–27).

——(1992) 'Contribution à l'étude de la composition des *Vies* de Plutarque: l'élaboration des grandes scènes' (*ANRW* 2.33.6: 4487–535).

FREDE, M. (1992) 'Plato's arguments and the dialogue form', in J. C. Klagge and N. D. Smith, eds., *Oxford studies in ancient philosophy* (suppl. vol.) (Oxford), 201–19.

FREUDENBURG, K. (1993) *The walking muse: Horace on the theory of satire* (Princeton)

FUSILLO, M. (1989) *Il romanzo greco: polifonia ed eros* (Venice).

——(1999) 'The conflict of emotions in the Greek erotic novel', in Swain ed. (1999), 60–82.

GALINSKY, G. K. (1972) *The Heracles theme: the adaptations of the hero in literature from Homer to the twentieth century* (Oxford)

GALLO, I., and SCARDIGLI, B., eds. (1995) *Teoria e prassi politica nelle opere di Plutarco. Atti del V convegno plutarcheo (Certosa di Pontignano 7–9 giugno 1993)* (Naples).

GALLOP, J., ed. (1995) *Pedagogy: the question of impersonation* (Bloomington).

GEERTZ, C. (1973) *The interpretation of cultures* (New York).

——(1979–80) 'Blurred senses: the refiguration of social thought' (*American scholar*, 49: 165–79).

——(1993) 'Centers, kings, and charisma: reflections on the symbolics of power', in id., *Local knowledge* (London), 121–46.

GELLNER, E. (1987) *Nations and nationalism* (Oxford).

GENNEP, A. VAN (1960) *The rites of passage*, trans. M. B. Vizedom and G. L. Caffee (London).

GEORGIADOU, A., and LARMOUR, D. H. J. (1998) *Lucian's science fiction novel* True Histories*: interpretation and commentary* (Leiden).

GEYTENBEEK, A. VAN (1963) *Musonius Rufus and Greek diatribe*, trans. B. L. Hijmans (Assen).

GIESECKE, A. (1891) *De philosophorum ueterum quae ad exilium spectant sententiis* (Leipzig).

GIGANTE, M. (1984) 'Per l'interpretazione del libro di Filodemo *Del buon re secondo Omero*' (*PP* 39: 285–98).

——(1986) 'Biografia e dossografia in Diogene Laerzio' (*Elenchos,* 7: 7–102).

——and DORANDI, T. (1980) 'Anassarco e Epicuro "Sul Regno"', in F. Romano, ed., *Democrito e l'atomismo antico* (Catania), 479–97.

GIGON, O. (1960) 'Das Prooemium des Diogenes Laertius: Struktur und Probleme', in G. Luck, ed., *Horizonte der Humanitas: Freundesgabe für Walter Wili zu seinen 60. Geburtstag* (Bonn), 37–64.

GILL, C. (1983) 'The question of character development: Plutarch and Tacitus' (*CQ* 33: 469–87).

GLAD, C. E. (1996) 'Frank speech, flattery and friendship in Philodemus', in J. T. Fitzgerald ed. (1996), 21–59.

GLEASON, M. W. (1995) *Making men: sophists and self-presentation in ancient Rome* (Princeton).

GOFFMAN, E. (1969) *The presentation of self in everyday life* (London).

GOLDHILL, S. (1986) *Reading Greek tragedy* (Cambridge).

——(1988) 'Desire and the figure of fun', in Benjamin ed. (1988), 79–105.

——(1991) *The poet's voice: essays on poetics and Greek literature* (Cambridge).

——(1994) 'The failure of exemplarity', in I. F. de Jong and J. P. Sullivan, ed., *Modern critical theory and classical literature* (Leiden), 51–73.

——(1995) *Foucault's virginity: ancient erotic fiction and the history of sexuality* (Cambridge).

——(2001) 'The erotic eye: visual stimulation and cultural conflict', in Goldhill ed. (2001).

——ed. (2001) *Being Greek under Rome: the Second Sophistic, cultural conflict and the development of the Roman empire* (Cambridge).

——(forthcoming) *Who needs Greek?*.

——and OSBORNE, R., eds. (1999) *Performance culture and Athenian democracy* (Cambridge).

GOLDING, W. (1995) *The double tongue* (London).

GOLDMAN, A. H. (1995) 'Comparative identities: exile in the writings of Frantz Fanon and W. E. B. Dubois', in M. G. Henderson, ed., *Borders, boundaries and frames: essays in cultural criticism and cultural studies* (New York), 107–32.

GOODENOUGH, E. R. (1928) 'The political philosophy of Hellenistic kingship' (*YCS* 1: 55–104).

GOODY, J. (1997) *Representations and contradictions: ambivalence towards images, theatre, fiction, relics and sexuality* (Oxford).

GOULET-CAZÉ, M.-O. (1986) *L'Ascèse cynique: un commentaire de Diogène Laërce VI 70–71* (Paris).

——and GOULET, R., eds., (1993) *Le cynisme ancien et ses prolongements* (Paris).

GOW, A. S. F., (1952) *Theocritus, edited with a translation and commentary*, 2 vols. (Cambridge).

GOWERS, E. (1993) *The loaded table: representations of food in Roman literature* (Oxford).

GOWING, A. M. (1990) 'Dio's name' (*CP* 85: 49–54).

GRAF, F. (1984–5) 'Maximos von Aigai: ein Beitrag zur Überlieferung über Apollonios von Tyana' (*JbAC* 27–8: 65–73).

GRAFF, G. (1987) *Professing literature: an institutional survey* (Chicago).

GRAHAME, M. (1998) 'Material culture and Roman identity: the spatial layout of Pompeian houses and the problem of ethnicity', in Laurence and Berry eds. (1998), 156–78.

GRAINDOR, P. (1930) *Un milliardaire antique: Hérode Atticus et sa famille* (Cairo).

GRASMÜCK, E. L. (1978) *Exilium: Untersuchungen zur Verbannung in der Antike* (Paderborn).

GRAY, V. J. (1986) 'Xenophon's *Hiero* and the memory of the wise man and the tyrant in Greek literature' (*CQ* 36: 115–23).

GREEN, P., ed. (1993) *Hellenistic history and culture* (Berkeley).

GREENBLATT, S. (1990) 'Culture', in F. Lentricchia and T. McLaughlin, eds., *Critical terms for literary study* (Chicago), 225–32.

GRIFFIN, M. (1976) *Seneca: a philosopher in politics* (Oxford).

——and BARNES, J., eds. (1989) *Philosophia togata: essays on philosophy and Roman society* (Oxford).

GRIFFITH, M. (1983) *Aeschylus, Prometheus Bound* (Cambridge).

GRISWOLD, C. L., jr. (1988) 'Plato's metaphilosophy: why Plato wrote dialogues', in Griswold ed. (1988), 143–67.

——ed. (1988) *Platonic writings, Platonic readings* (New York).

GRONINGEN, B. A. VAN (1965) 'General literary tendencies in the second century A.D.' (*Mnemosyne*, 18: 41–56).

GRÖßLEIN, P. (1998) *Untersuchungen zum* Juppiter Confutatus *Lukians*

(Frankfurt am Main).

GROSSO, F. (1954) 'Aspetti della politica orientale di Domiziano' (*Epigraphica*, 16: 117–79).

GRUEN, E. S. (1984) *The Hellenistic world and the coming of Rome*, vol. 1 (Berkeley).

——(1990) *Studies in Greek culture and Roman policy* (Leiden).

——(1992) *Culture and national identity in republican Rome* (Ithaca).

GRUMET, M. (1995) '*Scholae personae*: masks for meaning', in Gallop ed. (1995), 36–45.

GUAL, C. (1992) 'L'initiation de Daphnis et Chloé', in A. Moreau, ed., *L'Initiation: l'acquisition d'un savoir ou d'un pouvoir; le lieu initiatique; parodies et perspectives*, 2 vols. (Montpellier), i. 157–66.

GUERLAC, S. (1985) 'Longinus and the subject of the sublime' (*New Literary History* 16: 275–87).

GUNDERSON, E. (1996) 'The ideology of the arena' (*CA* 15: 113–49).

HABINEK, T. (1998) *The politics of Latin literature: writing, identity, and empire in ancient Rome* (Princeton).

——and SCHIESARO, A. (1997) 'Introduction', in Habinek and Schiesaro eds. (1997), xv–xxi.

————eds. (1997) *The Roman cultural revolution* (Cambridge).

HADOT, P. (1972) 'Fürstenspiegel' (*RAC* 8: 555–632).

——(1998) *The inner citadel: the* Meditations *of Marcus Aurelius*, trans. M. Chase (Cambridge, Mass.).

HÄGG, T. (1983) *The novel in antiquity* (Oxford).

HAHM, D. E. (2000) 'Kings and constitutions: Hellenistic theories', in Rowe and Schofield eds. (2000), 457–75.

HAHN, J. (1989) *Der Philosoph und die Gesellschaft: Selbstverständnis, öffentliches Auftreten und populäre Erwartungen in der hohen Kaiserzeit* (Stuttgart).

HALFMANN, H. (1979) *Die Senatoren aus dem östlichen Teil des Imperium romanum bis zum Ende des 2 Jh. n. Chr.* (Göttingen).

HALL, E. (1989) *Inventing the barbarian: Greek self-definition through tragedy* (Oxford).

HALL, J. (1981) *Lucian's satire* (New York).

HALL, J. M. (1995) 'The role of language in Greek ethnicities' (*PCPS* 41: 83–100).

——(1997) *Ethnic identity in Greek antiquity* (Cambridge).

HALL, S. (1990) 'Cultural identity and diaspora', in J. Rutherford ed. (1990), 222–37.

——(1992) 'The question of cultural identity', in id. *et al.*, eds., *Modernity and its futures* (Cambridge), 273–316.

——and DU GAY, P., eds. (1996) *Questions of cultural identity* (London).

HALLIWELL, S. (1989) 'Aristotle's *Poetics*', in G. A. Kennedy ed. (1989),

149–83.
HALPERIN, D. M. (1992) 'Plato and the erotics of narrativity', in Hexter and Selden eds. (1992), 95–126.
HAMILTON, J. R. (1969) *Plutarch, Alexander: a commentary* (Oxford).
HAMMOND, M. (1963) 'Res olim dissociabiles: principatus ac libertas' (*HSCP* 67: 93–113).
HARDIE, P. R. (1994) *Virgil, Aeneid book IX*, Cambridge Greek and Latin Classics (Cambridge).
HARRIS, B. F. (1977) 'Stoic and Cynic under Vespasian' (*Prudentia*, 9: 105–14).
HARRIS, W. V. (1989) *Ancient literacy* (Cambridge, Mass.).
HARRISON, J. E. (1991) *Prolegomena to the study of Greek religion*, 3rd edn. (Princeton; 1st pub. 1922).
HARRISON, S. J. (1999) 'Introduction: twentieth century scholarship on the Roman novel', in S. J. Harrison ed. (1999), xi-xxxix.
——ed. (1999) *Oxford readings in the Roman novel* (Oxford).
HARTOG, F. (1988) *The mirror of Herodotus: the representation of the other in the writing of history*, trans. J. Lloyd (Paris).
HÄUSLER, R. (1995) 'Zur Datierung der Schrift vom Erhabenen', in B. Kühnert *et al.*, eds., *Prinzipät und Kultur in 1. und 2. Jahrhundert: wissenschaftliche Tagung der Friedrich-Schiller-Universität Jena und der Iwane-Dshawachischwili Universität Tblissi, 27–30 Oktober 1992 in Jena* (Bonn), 141–63.
HEATH, M. (1999) 'Longinus, *On sublimity*' (*PCPS* 45: 43–74).
HEINRICHS, A. (1968) 'Vespasian's visit to Alexandria' (*ZPE* 3: 51–80).
HEINTZELER, G. (1927) *Das Bild des Tyrannen bei Platon: ein Beitrag zur Geschichte der griechischen Staatsethick* (Stuttgart).
HEISERMAN, A. (1977) *The novel before the novel: essays and discussions about the beginnings of prose fiction in the west* (Chicago).
HEITSCH, E., ed. (1963–4) *Die griechische Dichterfragmente der römischen Kaiserzeit*, 2 vols. (Göttingen).
HELM, R. (1906) *Lukian und Menipp* (Leipzig).
HEMELRIJK, E. A. (1999) *Matrona docta: educated women in the Roman elite from Cornelia to Julia Domna* (London).
HENDERSON, J. (1988) 'Entertaining arguments: Terence *Adelphoe*', in Benjamin ed. (1988), 192–222.
——(1993) 'Be alert (your country needs lerts): Horace, *Satires* 1. 9' (*PCPS* 39: 67–93).
——(1995) 'Pump up the volume: Juvenal, *Satires* 1. 1–21' (*PCPS* 41: 101–37.
——(1997) *Figuring out Roman nobility: Juvenal's eighth Satire* (Exeter).
HENDRICKSON, G. L. (1911) '*Satura*, the genesis of a literary form' (*CP* 6: 129–43).

——(1927) '*Satura tota nostra est*' (*CP* 22: 46–60).

Hershbell, J. P. (1995) '*Paideia* and *politeia* in Plutarch: the influence of Plato's *Republic* and *Laws*', in Gallo and Scardigli eds. (1995), 209–19.

Hertz, N. (1983) 'A reading of Longinus' (*Critical inquiry*, 9: 579–96).

Herzfeld, M. (1985) *The poetics of manhood: contest and identity in a Cretan mountain village* (Princeton).

Hesk, J. (1999) 'The rhetoric of anti-rhetoric in Athenian oratory', in Goldhill and Osborne eds. (1999), 201–30.

Hexter, R., and Selden, D., eds. (1992) *Innovations of antiquity* (New York).

Hidber, T. (1996) *Das klassizistische Manifest des Dionys von Halikarnass: die praefatio zu De oratoribus ueteribus* (Stuttgart).

Highet, G. (1974) 'Masks and faces in satire' (*Hermes*, 102: 321–37).

Hillyard, B. P. (1981) *Plutarch,* De audiendo*, a text and commentary* (New York).

Hinds, S. (1998) *Allusion and intertext: dynamics of appropriation in Roman poetry* (Cambridge).

Hirzel, R. (1912) *Plutarch* (Leipzig).

Hobsbawm, E. J. (1992) *Nations and nationalism since 1780: programme, myth, reality*, 2nd edn. (Cambridge).

Höistad, R. (1948) *Cynic hero and cynic king: studies in the cynic conception of man* (Uppsala).

Holford-Strevens, L. (1997) 'Favorinus: the man of paradoxes', in J. Barnes and M. Griffin, eds., *Philosophia togata II: Plato and Aristotle at Rome* (Oxford), 188–217.

Holzberg, N. (1988) 'Lucian and the Germans', in A. C. Dionisotti *et al.*, eds., *The uses of Greek and Latin: historical essays* (London), 199–209.

Hope, V. M. (1998) 'Negotiating identity and status', in Laurence and Berry eds. (1998), 179–95.

Hopkins, K. (1983) *Death and renewal: sociological studies in Roman history* (Cambridge).

——(1999) *A world full of gods: pagans, Jews and Christians in the Roman empire* (London).

Hopkinson, N. (1994*a*) *Greek poetry of the imperial period: an anthology* (Cambridge).

——(1994*b*) 'Nonnus and Homer', in Hopkinson ed. (1994), 9–42.

——ed. (1994) *Studies in the Dionysiaca of Nonnus* (Cambridge).

Horrocks, G. (1997) *Greek: a history of the language and its speakers* (London).

Householder, F. (1941) *Literary quotation and allusion in Lucian* (New York).

Humbert, S. (1991) 'Plutarque, Alexandre et l'hellénisme', in Saïd ed. (1991), 169–82.

HUNT, L. (1989) 'History, culture, and text', in ead., ed., *The new cultural history* (Berkeley), 1–22.

HUNTER, R. (1983) *A Study of* Daphnis and Chloë (Cambridge).

——(1993) *The* Argonautica *of Apollonius: literary studies* (Cambridge).

——(1996) *Theocritus and the archaeology of Greek poetry* (Cambridge)

——(1997) 'Response to Morgan', in Sommerstein and Atherton eds. (1997), 191–205.

——ed. (1998) *Studies in Heliodorus* (Cambridge).

HUNTER, V. (1994) *Policing Athens: social control in the Attic lawsuits, 420–320 B.C.* (Princeton).

HUSKINSON, J. (1999) 'Women and learning: gender and identity in scenes of intellectual life on late Roman sarcophagi', in Miles ed. (1999), 190–213.

HUXLEY, G. L. (1969) *Greek epic poetry: from Eumelos to Panyassis* (London).

INNES, D. (1995) 'Longinus, sublimity, and low emotions', in Innes *et al.*, eds. (1995), 323–33.

——HINE, H., and PELLING, C., eds. (1995) *Ethics and rhetoric: classical essays for Donald Russell on his seventy-fifth birthday* (Oxford).

JACKSON, S. (1984) 'Apollonius and the emperors' (*Hermathena*, 127: 25–32).

JAEGER, M. (1997) *Livy's written Rome* (Ann Arbor).

JAMES, P. (1999) 'Prudentius' *Psychomachia*: the Christian arena and the politics of display', in Miles ed. (1999), 70–94.

JAX, K. (1936) *τόποι* (*WS* 54: 43–51).

JEANNERET, M. (1991) *A feast of words: banquets and table-talk in the Renaissance*, trans. J. Whiteley and E. Hughes (Cambridge).

JENKS, C. (1993) *Culture* (London and New York).

JOHNSTON, J. (1990) *Carnival of repetition: Gaddis'* The Recognitions *and postmodern theory* (Philadelphia).

JONES, B. (1992) *The emperor Domitian* (London).

JONES, C. P. (1966) 'Towards a chronology of Plutarch's works' (*JRS* 61: 61–74).

——(1970) 'Sura and Senecio' (*JRS* 60: 98–104).

——(1971) *Plutarch and Rome* (Oxford).

——(1974) 'The reliability of Philostratus', in Bowersock ed. (1974), 11–16.

——(1978) *The Roman world of Dio Chrysostom* (Cambridge, Mass.).

——(1986) *Culture and society in Lucian* (Cambridge, Mass.).

——(1991) 'Dinner theater', in W. J. Slater, ed., *Dining in a classical context* (Ann Arbor), 139–55.

——(1996) 'The Panhellenion' (*Chiron*, 26: 29–56).

——(1997) 'Themistius and the speech *To the king*' (*CP* 92: 149–52).

JONES, R. M. (1916) *The Platonism of Plutarch* (Menasha).

JOUAN, F. (1993) 'Les récits de voyage de Dion Chrysostome', in Baslez *et al.* eds. (1993), 189–98.

JOYCE, J. (1993) *Ulysses: the 1922 text* (Oxford; 1st pub. 1922).

KAIBEL, G. (1885) 'Dionysius von Halikarnass und die Sophistik' (*Hermes*, 20: 497–513).

KASSEL, R. (1958) *Untersuchungen zur griechischen und römischen Konsolationsliteratur* (Munich).

KASTER, R. A. (1988) *Guardians of language: the grammarian and society in late antiquity* (Berkeley).

KAYSER, C. L. (1838), *Philostrati* Vitae sophistarum (Heidelberg).

——(1870–1) *Philostratus, Opera* (Leipzig).

KENNEDY, D. F. (1992) '"Augustan" and "anti-Augustan": reflections on terms of reference', in A. Powell, ed., *Roman poetry and propaganda in the age of Augustus* (Bristol), 26–58

KENNEDY, G. A. ed. (1989) *The Cambridge history of literary criticism*, vol. 1: *Classical criticism* (Cambridge).

——(1994) *A new history of Classical rhetoric* (Princeton).

KENNELL, N. M. (1989) '*ΝΕΡΩΝ ΠΕΡΙΟΔΟΝΙΚΗΣ*' (*AJP* 109: 239–51).

KINDSTRAND, J. F. (1973) *Homer in der zweiten Sophistik* (Uppsala).

——(1981) *Anacharsis: the legend and the apophthegmata* (Uppsala).

KOENEN, L. (1993) 'The Ptolemaic king as a religious figure', in Bulloch *et al.*, eds. (1993), 25–115.

KÖNIG, J. (2000) 'Athletic training in the Greek literature of the Roman empire', Ph.D. thesis (Cambridge).

KONSTAN, D. (1994) *Sexual symmetry: love in the ancient novel and related genres* (Princeton).

——(1996) 'Friendship, frankness and flattery', in J. T. Fitzgerald ed. (1996), 7–19.

——(1997) *Friendship in the classical world* (Cambridge).

KOOLMEISTER, R., and TALLMEISTER, T. (1981) *An index to Dio Chrysostomus* (Uppsala).

KORENJAK, M. (2000) *Redner und Publikum: ihre Interaktion in der sophistischen Rhetorik der Kaiserzeit* (Munich).

KORUS, K. (1981) 'The motif of Panthea in Lucian's encomium' (*Eos*, 69: 47–56).

KORVER, J. (1950) 'Néron et Musonius: à propos du dialogue du pseudo-Lucien *Néron ou Sur le percement de l'isthme de Corinth*' (*Mnemosyne*, 3: 319–29).

KOSKENNIEMI, E. (1991) *Der philostrateische Apollonios* (Helsinki).

KRAUS, C. (1994) 'No second Troy: topoi and refoundation in Livy book 5' (*TAPA* 124: 267–89).

LADNER, G. B. (1967) 'Homo viator: mediaeval ideas on alienation and order' (*Speculum*, 42: 233–59).

LAMBERTON, R. (1986) *Homer the theologian: neoplatonist allegorical reading and the growth of the epic tradition* (Berkeley).

LAMBROPOULOS, V. (1988), *Literature as national institution: studies in the politics of modern Greek criticism* (Princeton).

LANE, M. S. (1997) *Method and politics in Plato's Statesman* (Cambridge).

LANNI, A. M. (1997) 'Spectator sport or serious politics? οἱ περιεστηκότες and the Athenian lawcourts' (*JHS* 117: 183–9).

LANNOY, L. DE (1997) 'Le problème des Philostrate (état de la question)' (*ANRW* 2.34.3: 2362–449).

LANZA, D. (1977) *Il tiranno e il suo pubblico* (Turin).

LASSERRE, F. (1976) 'Hérodote et Protagoras: le début sur les constitutions' (*MH* 33: 65–84).

LATTIMORE, R. (1939) 'The wise adviser in Herodotus' (*CP* 34: 24–35).

LAURENCE, R., and BERRY, J., eds. (1998) *Cultural identity in the Roman empire* (London).

LAURENTI, R. (1987) 'Introduzione ad una lettura del *Peri hypsous*', in L. Russo, ed., *Da Longino a Longino: i luoghi del sublime* (Palermo), 17–31.

LEEST, J. VAN DER (1985) 'Lucian in Egypt' (*GRBS* 26: 75–82).

LEIGH, M. (1997) *Lucan: spectacle and engagement* (Oxford).

LEO, F. (1901) *Die griechisch-römische Biographie nach ihrer litterarischen Form* (Leipzig).

——(1966) *Plautinische Forschungen* (Darmstadt).

LESKY, A. (1957–8) *Geschichte der griechischen Literatur* (Berne).

LÉTOUBLON, F. (1993) *Les lieux communs du roman: stéréotypes grecs d'aventure et d'amour* (Leiden).

LEVI, M. A. (1981) 'Il *ΒΑΣΙΛΙΚΟΣ ΛΟΓΟΣ* di Apollonio di Tiana', in L. Gasperini ed., *Scritti sul mondo antico in memoria di Fulvio Grosso* (Rome), 289–93.

LEVICK, B. (1982) 'Domitian and the provinces' (*Latomus*, 41: 50–73).

LEVIN, S. (1989) 'The old Greek oracles in decline' (*ANRW* 2.18.2: 1599–649).

LEVINE GERA, D. (1995) 'Lucian's choice: *Somnium* 6–16', in Innes *et al.* eds. (1995), 237–50.

LÉVY, E. (1991) 'Apparition des notions de Grèce et les grecs', in Saïd ed. (1991), 49–69.

LEWIS, N. (1981) 'Literati in the service of Roman emperors: politics before culture', in L. Casson and M. Price, eds., *Coins, culture and history in the ancient world: numismatic and other studies in honor of Bluma L. Trell* (Detroit), 149–66; repr. in N. Lewis, *On government and law in Roman Egypt* (Atlanta, 1995), 257–74.

LIBRALE, D. (1994) 'L'εἰς βασιλέα dello pseudo-Aristide e l'ideologia traianea' (*ANRW* 2.34.2: 1271–313).

LIVINGSTONE, N. (1998) 'The voice of Isocrates and the dissemination of cultural power', in Too and Livingstone eds. (1998), 263–81.

LLOYD, G. E. R. (1966) *Polarity and analogy: two types of argumentation in early Greek thought* (London).

——(1987) *The revolutions of wisdom: studies in the claims and practice of ancient Greek science* (Berkeley).

LONGO, O. (1989) 'Codici alimentari, rovesciamento regressione—Gnatone nel romanzo di Longo Sofista', in id. and P. Scarpi, eds., *Homo edens: regimi, miti e practiche dell'alimentazione nella civilità del Mediterraneo* (Milan), 295–8.

LORAUX, N. (1986) *The invention of Athens: the funeral oration in the classical city*, trans. A. Sheridan (London).

——(1993) *The children of Athena: Athenian ideas about citizenship and division between the sexes*, trans. C. Levine (Princeton).

LOVEJOY, A. O., and BOAS, G. (1965) *Primitivism and related ideas in antiquity* (New York).

LUKINOVICH, A. (1990) 'The play of reflections between literary form and the sympotic theme in the *Deipnosophistae* of Athenaeus', in Murray ed. (1990), 263–71.

LUTZ, C. E. (1947) 'Musonius Rufus, the Roman Socrates' (*YCS* 10: 3–147).

LYOTARD, J.-F. (1988) *The differend: phrases in dispute*, trans. G. van den Abbeele (Manchester).

MCCARTHY, B. (1934) 'Lucian and Menippus' (*YCS* 4: 3–55).

MACDOWELL, D. (1990) 'The meaning of ἀλαζών', in E. Craik, ed., *'Owls to Athens': Essays on classical subjects presented to Sir Kenneth Dover* (Oxford), 287–92.

MCGLEW, J. F. (1993) *Tyranny and political culture in ancient Greece* (Ithaca and London).

MACLEOD, M. D. (1967) *Lucian, vol. 8*, Loeb Classical Library (Cambridge, Mass.).

——(1991) *Lucian: a selection* (Warminster).

MACMULLEN, R. (1992) *Enemies of the Roman order: treason, alienation and unrest in the Roman empire*, new edn. (London).

MCNAMARA, J. A. (1999) 'Gendering virtue', in Pomeroy ed. (1999), 151–61.

MAFFEI, S. (1986) 'Le *Imagines* di Luciano: un "patchwork" di capolavori antichi: il problema di un metodo combinatorio' (*SCO* 36: 147–64).

MANTERO, T. (1966) *Ricerche sull'*Heroikos *di Filostrato* (Genoa).

MARASCO, G. (1998) 'Erodiano e la crisi dell'impero' (*ANRW* 2.34.4: 2837–927).

MARINCOLA, J. (1996) 'Odysseus and the historians' (*Histos*, 1: no pages).

MARROU, H. (1956) *A history of education in antiquity*, trans. G. Lamb (London).

MARTIN, H. M. (1960) 'The concept of *praotes* in Plutarch's *Lives*' (*GRBS* 3: 65–73).

——(1961) 'The concept of *philanthropia* in Plutarch's *Lives*' (*AJP* 82: 164–75).

MARTIN, R. H., and WOODMAN, A. J. (1989) *Tacitus, Annals book IV*, Cambridge Greek and Latin Classics (Cambridge).

MARTIN, S. (1992) *The great expatriate writers* (Basingstoke).

MASON, H. (1974) *Greek terms for Roman institutions* (Toronto).

——(1979) 'Favorinus' disorder: Reifenstein's syndrom in antiquity?' (*Janus*, 66: 1–13).

MASARACCHIA, A. (1995) 'Tracche aristoteliche nell'*An seni respublica gerenda sit* e nei *Praecepta gerendae reipublicae*', in Gallo and Scardigli eds. (1995), 227–34.

MASSARO, D. (1995) 'I *Praecepta gerendae reipublicae* e il realismo politico di Plutarco', in Gallo and Scardigli eds. (1995), 235–44.

MATTINGLEY, H. (1993) 'L. Porcius Licinus and the beginning of Latin poetry', in H. D. Jocelyn and H. Hurt, eds., *Tria lustra: essays presented to John Pinsent* (Liverpool), 163–8.

MAZZUCHI, C. M. (1990) 'Come finiva il περὶ ὕψους?' (*Aevum antiquum*, 3: 143–62).

MENDELS, D. (1979) '"On Kingship" in "The temple scroll" and the ideological *Vorlage* of the seven banquets in the *Letter of Aristeas to Philocrates*' (*Aegyptus*, 59: 127–36).

MENSCHING, E. (1963) *Favorin von Arelate, der erste Teil der Fragmente,* Memorabilien *und* Omnigena Historia (Berlin).

MERIANI, A. (1991) 'Citazioni e strategia argomentiva nel "*Maxime cum principibus philosopho esse disserendum*"', in D'Ippolito and Gallo eds. (1991), 235–45.

MESK, J. (1912–13) 'Lucians *Nigrinus* und Juvenal' (*WS* 34–5: 373–82, 1–33).

MEYER, E. (1917) 'Apollonios von Tyana und die Biographie des Philostratos' (*Hermes*, 52: 371–424); repr. in id. *Kleine Schriften* (Halle, 1924), 2.131–91.

MILAZZO, A. (1978) 'Il discorso περὶ βασιλείας di Dione di Prusa e l'opusculo περὶ τοῦ καθ' Ὅμηρον ἀγαθοῦ βασιλέως di Filodemo' (*Sileno*, 4: 73–107).

MILES, R. (1999) 'Introduction: constructing identities', in Miles ed. (1999), 1–15.

——ed. (1999) *Constructing identities in late antiquity* (London).

MILLAR, F. (1964) *A study of Cassius Dio* (Oxford).

——(1977) *The emperor in the Roman world* (London).

MIRHADY, D. C. (1995) 'Plutarch's use of Theophrastus' πρὸς τοὺς καιρούς', in Gallo and Scardigli eds. (1995), 269–73.

MISCH, G. (1950) *A history of autobiography in antiquity*, 2 vols., trans. E. W. Dickes (London).

MITTELSTRAUSS, J. (1988) 'On Socratic dialogue', in Griswold ed. (1988), 126–42.

MOLES J. L. (1978) 'The career and conversion of Dio Chrysostom' (*JHS* 98: 79–100).

——(1983) 'The date and purpose of the fourth *Kingship Oration* of Dio Chrysostom' (*ClAnt* 2: 251–78).

——(1984) 'The addressee of the third *Kingship Oration* of Dio Chrysostom' (*Prometheus*, 10: 65–9).

——(1990) 'The *Kingship Orations* of Dio Chrysostom' (*Papers of the Leeds Latin Seminar*, 6: 297–375).

——(1993) 'Le cosmopolitisme cynique', in Goulet-Cazé and Goulet eds. (1993), 259–80; trans. and repr. in Branham and Goulet-Cazé eds. (1996), 105–20.

——(1995) 'Dio Chrysostom, Greece, and Rome', in Innes *et al*. eds. (1995), 177–92.

MÖLLENDORFF, P. VON (2000) *Lukian:* Hermotimos oder Lohnt es sich, Philosophie zu studieren? *Herausgegeben, übersetzt und kommentiert* (Darmstadt).

MOMIGLIANO, A. (1969) 'Dio Chrysostomus', in id. *Quarto contributo alla storia degli studi classici e del mondo antico* (Rome), 256–69.

——(1971) 'La libertà di parola nel mondo antico' (*RSI* 83: 499–524).

——(1973–4) 'Freedom of speech in antiquity', in P. P. Wiener, ed., *Dictionary of the history of ideas: studies of selected pivotal ideas* (New York), 2.252–63.

——(1974) *Alien wisdom: the limits of hellenization* (Cambridge).

——(1993) *The development of Greek biography*, expanded edn. (Cambridge, Mass.).

MONTROSE, L. (1989) 'Professing the renaissance: the poetics and politics of culture', in Veeser ed. (1989), 15–36.

MORALES, H. L. (1994) 'A scopophiliac's paradise: vision and narrative in Achilles Tatius' *Leucippe and Clitophon*', Ph.D. thesis (Cambridge).

MORGAN, J. R. (1989*a*) 'A sense of the ending: the conclusion of Heliodorus' *Aithiopika*' (*TAPA* 119: 299–320).

——(1989*b*) 'The story of Knemon in Heliodorus' *Aithiopika*, (*JHS* 109: 92–113).

——(1994) 'The *Aithiopika* of Heliodorus: narrative as riddle', in Morgan and Stoneman eds. (1994), 97–113.

——(1997) '*Erotika mathemata*: Greek romance as sentimental education', in Sommerstein and Atherton eds. (1997), 163–89.

MORGAN, J. R. and STONEMAN, R., eds. (1994) *Greek fiction: the Greek novel in context* (London).

MORGAN, T. (1998) *Literate education in the Hellenistic and Roman worlds* (Cambridge).

——(1999) 'Literate education in classical Athens' (*CQ* 49: 46–61).

MORRIS, I. (1996) 'Periodization and the heroes: inventing a dark age', in M. Golden and P. Toohey, eds., *Inventing ancient culture: historicism, periodization and the ancient world* (London), 96–131.

MOSSMAN, J. M., ed. (1997) *Plutarch and his intellectual world* (Swansea).

MOST, G. (1992) '*Disiecti membra poetae*: the rhetoric of dismemberment in Neronian poetry', in Hexter and Selden eds. (1992), 391–419.

MRAS, K. (1949) 'Die προλαλιά bei den griechischen Schriftstellern' (*WS* 64: 71–81).

MUCCIOLI, F. (1995) 'I livelli della politica in Platone secondo Plutarco', in Gallo and Scardigli eds. (1995), 275–85.

MUELLER-GOLDINGEN, C. (1995) *Untersuchungen zu Xenophons Kyrupädie* (Stuttgart and Leipzig).

MUENSCHER, K. (1907) *Die Philostrate* (*Philologus* suppl. 10: 469–558).

MURRAY, O. (1965) 'Philodemus *On the Good King According to Homer*' (*JRS* 55: 161–82).

——(1967) 'Aristeas and Ptolemaic kingship' (*JTS* 18: 337–71).

——(1971) '*περὶ βασιλείας*. Studies in the justification of monarchic power in the Hellenistic world', D.Phil. thesis (Oxford).

——(1987) 'The letter of Aristeas', in B. Virgilio, ed., *Studi Ellenistici II* (Pisa), 15–29.

——ed. (1990) *Sympotica: a symposium on the symposium* (Oxford).

MUSURILLO, H., ed. (1954) *The acts of the pagan martyrs* (Oxford).

NEEF, E. (1940) *Lukians Verhältnis zu den Philosophenschulen und seine μίμησις literarischer Vorbilder* (Greifswald).

NESSELRATH, H.-G. (1985) *Lukians Parasitendialog* (Berlin).

——(1990) 'Lucian's introductions', in Russell ed. (1990), 111–40.

NEU, J. (1971) 'Plato's analogy of state and individual: the *Republic* and the organic theory of the state' (*Philosophy*, 46: 238–54).

NIJF, O. VAN (1997) *The civic world of professional associations in the Roman East* (Amsterdam).

——(1999) 'Athletics, festivals and Greek identity in the Roman east' (*PCPS* 45: 176–200).

NIKOLAIDIS, A. G. (1986) '*Ἑλληνικός—βαρβαρικός*: Plutarch on Greek and barbarian characteristics' (*WS* 20: 229–44).

NORDEN, E. (1898) *Die antike Kunstprosa vom 6en Jahrhundert vor Christus bis in die Zeit der Renaissance* (Leipzig).

NORMAN, A. F. (1953) 'Philostratus and Libanius' (*CP* 48: 20–3).

NUSSBAUM, M. (1994) *The therapy of desire: theory and practice in*

Hellenistic ethics (Princeton).

NUTTON, V. (1970) 'Herodes and Gordian' (*Latomus*, 29: 719–28).

OBER, J. (1989) *Mass and elite in democratic Athens: rhetoric, ideology, and the power of the people* (Princeton).

OCHS, D. J. (1993) *Consolatory rhetoric: grief, symbol, and ritual in the Greco-Roman era* (Columbia).

OLIVER, J. H. (1953) *The ruling power: a study of the Roman empire in the second century after Christ through the* Roman oration *of Aelius Aristides* (Philadelphia).

——(1972) 'Herm at Athens with portraits of Xenophon and Arrian' (*AJA* 76: 327–8).

O'NOLAN, K. (1960) 'The Proteus legend' (*Hermes*, 88: 1–19).

O'SULLIVAN, J. N. (1980) *A lexicon to Achilles Tatius* (Berlin).

PACK, R. A. (1947) 'Two sophists and two emperors' (*CP* 42: 17–20).

PADEL, R. (1990) 'Making space speak', in Winkler and Zeitlin eds. (1990), 336–65.

PALM, J. (1959) *Rom, Römertum und Imperium in der griechischen Literatur der Kaiserzeit* (Lund).

PANDIRI, T. A. (1985)'*Daphnis and Chloë*: the art of pastoral play' (*Ramus*, 14: 116–41).

PAPALAS, A. J. (1978) 'Lucius Verus and the hospitality of Herodes Atticus' (*Athenaeum*, 56: 182–5).

——(1979–80) 'Herodes Atticus and the wrath of Philagrus' (*RCCM* 21/2: 93–104).

PARKER, H. (1992) 'Love's body anatomised: ancient erotic handbooks and the rhetoric of sexuality', in Richlin ed. (1992), 90–107.

PARKER, R. (1988) 'Myths of early Athens', in J. Bremmer, ed., *Interpretations of Greek mythology* (London), 187–214.

PAVIS D'ESCURAC, H. (1981) 'Périls et chances du régime civique selon Plutarque' (*Ktema*, 6: 287–300).

PEKÁRY, T. (1985) *Das römische Kaiserbildnis in Staat, Kult und Gesellschaft. Dargestellt Anhand der Schriftquellen* (Berlin).

PELLING, C. B. R. (1988) 'Aspects of Plutarch's characterisation' (*ICS* 13: 257–64).

——(1989) 'Plutarch: Roman heroes and Greek culture', in Griffin and Barnes eds. (1989), 199–232.

——(1990) 'Truth and fiction in Plutarch's *Lives*', in Russell ed. (1990), 19–52.

——(1995) 'Il moralismo delle *Vite* di Plutarco', in Gallo and Scardigli eds. (1995), 343–61.

PENELLA, R. J. (1979*a*) 'Philostratus' letter to Julia Domna' (*Hermes*, 107: 161–8).

——(1979*b*) *The Letters of Apollonius of Tyana: a critical text with*

prolegomena, translation and a commentary (Leiden).
Peretti, A. (1946) *Luciano: un intellettuale greco contro Roma* (Florence).
Pérez Jiménez, A. (1995) '*Proairesis*: las formas de acceso a la vida pública y el pensiamento politico de Plutarco', in Gallo and Scardigli eds. (1995), 363–81.
Perkins, J. (1992) 'The "self" as sufferer' (*HTR* 85: 245–72).
——(1995) *The suffering self: pain and narrative representation in the early Christian era* (London).
——(1999) 'An ancient "passing novel": Heliodorus' *Aithiopika*' (*Arethusa*, 32: 97–214).
Pernot, L. (1993) *La rhétorique de l'éloge*, 2 vols. (Paris).
——(1997) *Éloges grecs de Rome* (Paris).
Peterson, E. (1929) 'Zur Bedeutungsgeschichte von παρρησία', in W. Koepp, ed., *Festschrift Reinhold Seeberg* (Leipzig), i. 283–97.
Petit, P. (1955) *Libanius et la vie municipale à Antioche au IVe siècle après J.-C.* (Paris).
Petrochilos, N. K. (1974) *Roman attitudes to the Greeks* (Athens).
Petts, D. (1988) 'Landscape and cultural identity in Roman Britain', in Laurence and Berry eds. (1998), 79–94.
Pfeiffer, R. (1968) *A history of classical scholarship from the beginnings to the end of the Hellenistic age* (Oxford).
Pomeroy, S. (1999) 'Reflections on Plutarch, *Advice to the bride and groom*: something old, something new, something borrowed', in Pomeroy ed. (1999), 33–42.
——ed. (1999) *Plutarch's* Advice to the bride and groom *and* A consolation to his wife*: English translations, commentary interpretative essays, and bibliography* (Oxford).
Praechter, K. (1892) 'Dio Chrysostomus als Quelle Julians' (*AGP* 5: 42–51).
Pratt, M. L. (1992) *Imperial eyes: travel and transculturation* (London).
Prendergast, C. (1986) *The order of mimesis: Balzac, Stendhal, Nerval, Flaubert* (Cambridge).
Price, S. R. F. (1984) *Rituals and power: the Roman imperial cult in Asia Minor* (Cambridge).
Prince, G. (1980) 'Introduction to the study of the narratee', in J. Tompkins, ed., *Reader-response criticism: from formalism to post-structuralism* (Baltimore), 7–25.
Puech, B. (1992) 'Prosopographie des amis de Plutarque' (*ANRW* 2.33.6: 4831–93).
Puskás, I. (1991) 'Myth or reality? Apollonius of Tyana in India' (*ACD* 27: 115–23).
Quet, M.-O. (1978) 'Rhétorique, culture et politique: le fonctionnement du discours idéologique chez Dion de Pruse et dans les *Moralia* de

Plutarque' (*DHA* 4: 51–118).

Quint, D. (1989) 'Repetition and ideology in the *Aeneid*' (*MD* 23: 9–54); repr. and cited from P. Hardie, ed., *Virgil: critical assessments* (London, 1999), 117–57.

Rawson, E. (1975) 'Caesar's heritage: Hellenistic kings and their Roman equals' (*JRS* 65: 148–59).

——(1985) *Intellectual life in the the late Roman republic* (Baltimore).

——(1989) 'Roman rulers and the philosophic adviser', in Griffin and Barnes eds. (1989), 233–57.

Raynor, D. H. (1984) 'Moeragenes and Philostratus: two views of Apollonius of Tyana' (*CQ* 34: 222–6).

Reardon, B. P. (1971) *Courants littéraires grecs des IIe et IIIe siècles après J.-C.* (Paris).

——(1991) *The form of Greek romance* (Princeton).

Reeve, C. D. C. (1988) *Philosopher-kings: the argument of Plato's* Republic (Princeton).

Reeve, M. D. (1989) 'Conceptions' (*PCPS* 215: 81–112).

Reitzenstein, R. (1906) *Hellenistische Wundererzählungen* (Leipzig).

Renoirte, T. (1951) *Les conseils politiques de Plutarque: une lettre ouverte aux grecs à l'époque de Trajan* (Louvrain).

Rhodes, P. J. (1972) *The Athenian boule* (Oxford).

Richlin, A., ed. (1992) *Pornography and representation in ancient Greece and Rome* (Oxford).

Riggsby, A. M. (1998) 'Self and community in the younger Pliny' (*Arethusa*, 31: 75–97).

Rist, J. M. (1982) 'Are you a Stoic? The case of Marcus Aurelius', in B. F. Meyer and E. P. Saunders, eds., *Jewish and Christian self-definition*, iii: *Self-definition in the Greek and Roman world* (London), 23–45.

Rizakis, A. (1997) 'Roman colonies in the province of Achaia: territory, land and population', in Alcock ed. (1997), 15–36.

Robbins, B. (1983) 'Homelessness and worldiness' (*Diacritics*, 13.3: 69–77).

Robert, L. (1969) 'Théophane de Mytilène à Constantinople' (*CRAI* 1969: 42–64).

Robins, K. (1996) 'Interrupting identities: Turkey/Europe', in S. Hall and du Gay eds. (1996), 61–86.

Rogers, G. (1991) *The sacred identity of Ephesos: foundation myths of a Roman city* (London).

Rohde, E. (1886) 'Die asianische Rhetorik und die zweite Sophistik' (*RhM* 41: 170–90); repr. in id., *Kleine Schriften*, 2 (Tübingen, 1901), 75–97.

——(1914) *Der griechische Roman und seine Vorläufer*, 3rd edn. (rev.

W. Schmid, Berlin; repr. Hildesheim, 1960).

Rohde, G. (1937) 'Longus und die Bukolik' (*RhM* 68: 23–49).

Romilly, J. de (1959) 'Le classement de constitutions d'Hérodote à Aristote' (*REG* 72: 81–99).

Romm, J. (1990) 'Wax, stone and Promethean clay: Lucian as plastic artist' (*ClAnt* 9: 74–98).

——(1992) *The edges of the earth in ancient thought: geography, exploration, and fiction* (Princeton).

——(1999) *Herodotus* (New Haven).

Rommel, H. (1923) *Die naturwissenschaftlich-paradoxographischen Exkurse bei Philostratos, Heliodoros und Achilleus Tatios* (Stuttgart).

Rosati, G. (1983) 'Trimalchio on stage', trans. B. Graziosi, in Harrison ed. (1999), 85–104.

Rosivach, V. J. (1987) 'Autochthony and the Athenians' (*CQ* 81: 294–306).

Rothe, S. (1989) *Kommentar zu ausgewählten Sophistenvitae des Philostratos: die Lehrstuhlinhaber in Athen und Rom* (Heidelberg).

Rouveret, A. (1989) *Histoire et imaginaire de la peinture ancienne (Ve siècle av. J.-C.–1er siècle ap. J.-C.)* (Paris).

Rowe, C., and Schofield, M., eds. (2000) *The Cambridge history of Greek and Roman political thought* (Cambridge).

Russell, D. A. (1963) 'Plutarch's *Life of Coriolanus*' (*JRS* 53: 21–8); repr. in Scardigli ed. (1995), 357–72.

——(1964) *'Longinus'* On the Sublime, *edited with introduction and commentary* (Oxford).

——(1966) 'On reading Plutarch's *Lives*' (*G&R*, ns 13: 139–54); repr. in Scardigli ed. (1995), 75–94.

——(1972) *Plutarch* (London).

——(1979) 'De Imitatione', in West and Woodman eds. (1979), 1–16.

——(1981) *Criticism in antiquity* (London).

——(1983) *Greek declamation* (Cambridge).

——(1989) 'Greek criticism of the empire', in G. A. Kennedy ed. (1989), 297–329.

——ed. (1990) *Antonine literature* (Oxford).

——(1992) *Dio Chrysostom, Orations 7, 12, 36* (Cambridge).

——and Wilson, N. G. (1981) *Menander Rhetor, edited with translation and commentary* (Oxford).

Rusten, J. S. (1990) *Thucydides,* The Peloponnesian War *book II* (Cambridge).

Rutherford, I. (1998) *Canons of style in the Antonine age:* idea *theory in its literary context* (Oxford).

Rutherford, J. (1990) 'A place called home: identity and the cultural politics of difference', in J. Rutherford ed. (1990), 9–27.

——ed. (1990) *Identity* (London).

RUTHERFORD, R. B. (1989) *The Meditations of Marcus Aurelius: a study* (Oxford).

RÜTTEN, U. (1997) *Phantasie und Lachkultur: Lukians* Wahre Geschichten (Tübingen).

SAID, E. W. (1978) *Orientalism* (London).

——(1984) 'The mind of winter: reflections on life in exile' (*Harpers Magazine*, Sept. 1984: 49–55).

SAÏD, S., ed. (1991) *ΈΛΛΗΝΙΣΜΟΣ: quelques jalons pour une histoire de l'identité grec* (Leiden).

——(1999) 'Rural society in the Greek novel, or the country seen from the town', in Swain ed. (1999), 83–107.

SALAMONE, S. (1993) 'Sublime paradossale—paradosso sublime', in S. Feraboli, ed., *Mosaico: studi in onore di Umberto Albini* (Genoa), 185–95.

SALMERI, G. (1982) *La politica e il potere: saggio su Dione di Prusa* (Catania).

SAMUEL, A. E. (1993) 'The ptolemies and the ideology of kingship', in Green ed. (1993), 168–92.

SANDBACH, F. H. ed., *Plutarch, Moralia XV*, Loeb Classical Library (Cambridge, Mass.).

SARIKAKIS, T. (1976) *The hoplite general in ancient Athens and the generals in the Hellenistic age* (Chicago).

SAYRE, K. M. (1995) *Plato's literary garden* (Notre Dame).

SCARDIGLI, B., ed. (1995) *Essays in Plutarch's* Lives (Oxford).

SCARPAT, G. (1964) *Parrhesia: storia del termine e delle sue traduzione in latino* (Brescia).

SCHÄUBLIN, C. (1985) 'Konversionen in antiken Dialogen?', in id., ed. *Catalepton: Festschrift für Bernhard Wyss zum 80. Geburtstag* (Basel), 117–131.

SCHECHNER, R. (1988) *Performance theory*, rev. edn. (London).

——(1993) *The future of ritual: writings on culture and performance* (New York).

SCHEMAN, N. (1995) 'On waking up one morning and discovering that we are them', in Gallop ed. (1995), 106–16.

SCHIEFFELIN, E. L. (1985) 'Performance and the cultural construction of reality' (*American ethnologist*, 12: 707–24).

——(1998) 'Problematizing performance', in F. Hughes-Freeland, ed., *Ritual, performance, media* (London), 194–207.

SCHMELING, G., ed. (1996) *The novel in the ancient world* (Leiden).

SCHMID, W. (1887–96) *Der Atticismus in seinen Hauptvertretern von Dionysius von Halikarnass bis auf den zweiten Philostratus*, 4 vols. (Stuttgart).

SCHMITZ, T. (1996) 'Trajan und Dion von Prusa: zu Philostrat, *Vit. Soph.* 1.7 (488)' (*RhM* 139: 315–19).

——(1997) *Bildung und Macht: zur sozialen unde politischen Funktion der zweiten Sophistik in der griechischen Welt der Kaiserzeit* (Munich).

SCHOFIELD, M. (1986) '*Euboulia* in the *Iliad*' (*CQ* 36: 6–31); repr. in id., *Saving the city: philosopher-kings and other classical paradigms* (London, 1999), 3–30.

——(1991) *The Stoic idea of the city* (Cambridge).

SCHOULER, B. (1987) 'Les sophistes et le théâtre au temps des empereurs', in P. Ghiron-Bistagne and B. Schouler, eds., *Anthropologie et théâtre antique: actes du colloque international Montpellier 6–8 mars 1986* (Montpellier), 273–94.

SCHWARTZ, J. (1965) *Biographie de Lucien de Samosate* (Brussels).

SEGAL, C. P. (1959) '"Ὕψος and the problem of cultural decline in the *De sublimitate*' (*HSCP* 64: 121–48).

——(1994) *Singers, heroes and gods in the* Odyssey (Ithaca).

SELDEN, D. (1998) '*Aithiopika* and Ethiopianism', in R. Hunter ed. (1998), 182–217.

SHATZMAN, I. (1974) 'Tacitean rumours' (*Latomus*, 33: 549–78).

SHEAR, T. L. (1981) 'Athens: from city-state to provincial town' (*Hesperia* 50: 356–77).

SHERWIN-WHITE, A. N. (1966) *The letters of Pliny: a historical and social commentary* (Oxford).

—— (1973) *The Roman citizenship*, 2nd edn. (Oxford).

SIDEBOTTOM, H. (1990) 'Studies in Dio Chrysostom *On Kingship*', D.Phil. thesis (Oxford).

——(1996) 'Dio of Prusa and the Flavian dynasty' (*CQ* 46: 447–56).

——(1998) 'Herodian's historical methods and his understanding of history' (*ANRW* 2.34.4: 2775–836).

SIMON, R. I. (1995) 'Face-to-face with alterity', in Gallop ed. (1995), 95–105.

SIRAGO, V. A. (1989) 'La seconda sofistica come espressione della classe dirigente del II sec.' (*ANRW* 2.33.1: 36–78).

SKUTSCH, O. (1970) 'On three fragments of Porcius Licinus and the Tutiline gate' (*BICS* 17: 120–3).

SLINGS, S. R. (1999) *Plato,* Clitophon*: edited with introduction, translation, and commentary* (Cambridge).

SOLMSEN, F. (1940) 'Some works of Philostratus the elder' (*TAPA* 71: 556–72).

SOMMERSTEIN, A. H., and ATHERTON, C., eds. (1997) *Education in Greek fiction* (Bari).

SÖRBOM, G. (1966) *Mimesis and art: studies in the origin and early development of an aesthetic vocabulary* (Uppsala).

SPAWFORTH, A. (1989) 'Agonistic festivals in Roman Greece', in Walker and Cameron eds. (1989), 193–7.

—— and WALKER, S. (1985) 'The world of the Panhellenion. I: Athens and Eleusis' (*JRS* 75: 78–104).

—— —— (1986) 'The world of the Panhellenion. II: three Dorian cities' (*JRS* 76: 88–105).

SPEYER, W. (1971) *Die literarische Fälschung im heidnischen und christlichen Altertum: ein Versuch ihrer Deutung* (Munich).

SPIVAK, G. C. (1988) *In other worlds: essays in cultural politics* (London).

SPOERRI, W. (1959) *Späthellenistische Berichte über Welt, Kultur und Götter* (Basel).

SQUILLONI, A. (1989) 'L'Ideale de buon governante nel pensiero politico di Plutarco' (*CCC* 10: 225–43).

STADTER, P. A. (1965) *Plutarch's historical methods: the* Mulierum Virtutes (Cambridge, Mass.).

—— (1967) 'Flavianus Arrianus: the new Xenophon?' (*GRBS* 8: 155–61).

—— (1980) *Arrian of Nicomedia* (Chapel Hill).

—— (1999) '*Philosophos kai philandros*: Plutarch's view of women in the *Moralia* and *Lives*', in Pomeroy ed. (1999), 173–81.

STANFORD, W. B. (1954) *The Ulysses theme: a study in the adaptability of a traditional hero* (Oxford).

STANTON, G. R. (1968) 'The cosmopolitan ideas of Epictetus and Marcus Aurelius' (*Phronesis*, 13: 183–95).

—— (1969) 'Marcus Aurelius, emperor and philosopher' (*Historia*, 18: 570–87).

—— (1973) 'Sophists and philosophers: problems of classification' (*AJP* 94: 350–64).

STARR, C. P. (1949) 'Epictetus and the tyrant' (*CP* 44: 20–9).

—— (1952) 'The perfect democracy of the Roman empire' (*American Historical Review*, 58: 1–16).

STEMPLINGER, E. (1913) '*Mimesis* im philosophischen und rhetorischen Sinne' (*Neue Jahrbücher für das klassischen Altertum*, 31: 20–36).

STEPHENS, S. A., and WINKLER, J. J. (1995) *Ancient Greek novels, the fragments. Introduction, text, translation, and commentary* (Cambridge, Mass.).

STERTZ, S. A. (1976–7) 'Marcus Aurelius as ideal emperor in late-antique Greek thought' (*CW* 70: 433–9).

STEWART, P. C. N. (1999) 'The destruction of statues in late antiquity', in Miles ed. (1999), 159–89.

STIERLE, K. (1972) 'L'histoire comme exemple, l'exemple comme histoire: contributions à la pragmatique et à la poétique des textes narratifs' (*Poétique*, 3: 176–98).

Strohmaier, G. (1976) 'Übersehenes zur Biographie Lukians' (*Philologus*, 120: 117–22).

Sturrock, J. (1993) *The language of autobiography: studies in the first person singular* (Cambridge).

Swain, S. (1989*a*) 'Character change in Plutarch' (*Phoenix*, 43: 62–8).

——(1989*b*) 'Favorinus and Hadrian' (*ZPE* 79: 150–8).

——(1990) 'Hellenic culture and the Roman heroes of Plutarch' (*JHS* 110: 126–45); repr. in Scardigli ed. (1995), 229–64.

——(1991) 'The reliability of Philostratus' *Lives of the sophists*' (*ClAnt* 10: 148–63).

——(1994) 'Dio and Lucian', in Morgan and Stoneman eds. (1994), 166–80.

——(1996) *Hellenism and empire: language, classicism, and power in the Greek world, AD 50–250* (Oxford).

——(1999) 'Plutarch's moral program', in Pomeroy ed. (1999), 85–96.

——ed. (1999) *Oxford readings in the Greek novel* (Oxford).

Syme, R. (1982) *Greeks invading the Roman government* (Brookline); repr. in A. Birley, ed., *Roman papers*, iv (Oxford, 1988), 1–20.

Tarrant, H. A. S. (1985) 'Alcinous, Albinus, Nigrinus' (*Antichthon*, 19: 87–95).

Tatum, J. (1989) *Xenophon's imperial fiction: on the* Education of Cyrus (Princeton).

——ed. (1994) *The search for the ancient novel* (Baltimore).

Teske, D. (1991) *Der Roman des Longos als Werk der Kunst* (Münster).

Thesleff, H., ed. (1965) *The Pythagorean texts of the Hellenistic period* (Åbo).

Tirelli, A. (1995) 'L'intellettuale e il potere: pedagogia e politica in Plutarco', in Gallo and Scardigli eds. (1995), 439–55.

Tobin, J. (1997) *Herodes Atticus and the city of Athens: patronage and conflict under the Antonines* (Amsterdam).

Tonnet, H. (1988) *Recherches sur Arrien, sa personnalité et ses écrits atticistes*, 2 vols. (Amsterdam).

Too, Y. L. (1994) 'Educating Nero: a reading of Seneca's *Moral Epistles*', in Elsner and Masters eds. (1994), 211–24.

——(1995) *The rhetoric of identity in Isocrates: text, power, pedagogy* (Cambridge).

——(1998) *The idea of literary criticism* (Oxford).

—— and Livingstone, N., eds. (1998) *Pedagogy and power: rhetorics of Classical learning* (Cambridge).

Toynbee, J. M. C. (1944) 'Dictators and philosophers in the first century AD' (*G&R* 13: 43–58).

Traill, J. S. (1971) 'Greek inscriptions honouring *prytaneis*' (*Hesperia*, 40: 308–29).

Trapp, M. B. (1990) 'Plato's *Phaedrus* in the second century', in Russell ed. (1990), 141–73.

——(1995) 'Sense of place in the orations of Dio Chrysostom', in Innes *et al.* eds. (1995), 163–75.

——(1996) *The* Philosophical Orations *of Maximus of Tyre, translated with an introduction and notes* (Oxford).

Trédé, M. (1991) 'Quelques définitions de l'Hellénisme au IVe siècle avant J.-C. et leurs implications politiques', in Saïd ed. (1991), 71–80.

Turner, P. (1960) '*Daphnis and Chloe*: an interpretation' (*G&R* 7: 117–23).

Turner, V. (1957) *Schism and continuity in an African society* (Manchester).

——(1974) *Dramas, fields, and metaphors: symbolic action in human society* (Ithaca).

——(1982) 'Dramatic ritual/ritual drama', in id., *From ritual to theatre. The human seriousness of play* (New York), 89–102.

Usher, S. (1993) 'Isocrates: *paideia*, kingship and the barbarians', in H. A. Khan, ed., *The birth of the European identity: the Europe–Asia contrast in Greek thought* (Nottingham), 131–45.

Vanderspoel, J. (1995) *Themistius and the imperial court: oratory, civic duty, and* paideia *from Constantius to Theodosius* (Ann Arbor).

Veeser, H. A., ed. (1989) *The new historicism* (New York).

Vernant, J.-P. (1991) *Mortals and immortals: collected essays*, ed. F. I. Zeitlin (Princeton).

Versnel, H. S. (1970) *Triumphus: an inquiry into the origin, development and meaning of the Roman triumph* (Leiden).

Veyne, P. (1990) *Bread and circuses: historical sociology and political pluralism*, trans. B. Pearce (London).

Vidal-Naquet, P. (1986*a*) *The black hunter: forms of thought and forms of society in the Greek world*, trans. A. Szegedy-Maszak (Baltimore).

——(1986*b*) 'The black hunter revisited' (*PCPS* 32: 126–44).

Villari, E. (1988) 'Il *chalinos* come *sphragis* del tiranno' (*CCC* 9: 111–21).

Viswanathan, G. (1990) *Masks of conquest: literary study and British rule in India* (London).

Vitanza, V. (1997) *Negation, subjectivity and the history of rhetoric* (Albany).

Volkmann, R. (1885) *Die Rhetorik der Griechen und Römer in systematischer Übersicht*, 2nd edn. (Leipzig; repr. Hildesheim, 1963).

Walbank, F. W. (1972) *Polybius* (Berkeley).

——(1984) 'Monarchies and monarchic ideals' (*CAH*[3] 7.1: 62–100).

Walker, S., and Cameron, A., eds. (1989) *The Greek renaissance in the Roman empire*, *BICS* suppl. 55 (London).

WALLACE-HADRILL, A. (1981) 'The emperor and his virtues' (*Historia*, 30: 298–323).

——(1983) *Suetonius: the scholar and his Caesars* (London).

——(1988) 'Greek knowledge, Roman power', review of Rawson (1985) (*CP* 83: 224–33).

——(1997) '*Mutatio morum*: the idea of a cultural revolution', in Habinek and Schiesaro eds. (1997), 3–22.

WALSH, G. B. (1984) *The varieties of enchantment: early Greek views of the nature and function of poetry* (Chapel Hill).

——(1988) 'Sublime method: Longinus on language and imitation' (*ClAnt* 7: 252–69).

WALTERS, J. (1998) 'Juvenal, *Satire* 2: putting male sexual deviance on show', in L. Foxhall and J. Salmon, eds., *Thinking men: masculinity and its self-representation in the Classical tradition* (London), 148–54.

WARDMAN, A. (1974) *Plutarch's Lives* (London).

WARDY, R. (1996) *The birth of rhetoric: Gorgias, Plato and their successors* (London).

WATERS, K. H. (1971) *Herodotus on tyrants and despots: a study in objectivity* (Wiesbaden).

——(1974) 'Trajan's character in the literary tradition', in J. A. S. Evans, ed., *Polis and imperium: studies in honour of E. T. Salmon* (Toronto), 233–52.

WEBER, G. (1991) *Dichtung und höfische Gesellschaft: die Rezeption von Zeitgeschichte am Hof der ersten drei Ptolemäer* (Stuttgart).

WEST, D., and WOODMAN, A., eds. (1979) *Creative imitation in Latin literature* (Cambridge).

WEST, M. L. (1995) ' "Longinus" and the grandeur of God', in Innes *et al.* eds. (1995), 335–42.

WHITE, P. (1993) *Promised verse: poets in the society of Augustan Rome* (Cambridge, Mass.).

WHITMARSH, T. (1998*a*) 'Reading power in Roman Greece: the *paideia* of Dio Chrysostom', in Too and Livingstone eds. (1998), 192–213.

——(1998*b*) 'The birth of a prodigy: Heliodorus and the genealogy of Hellenism', in R. Hunter ed. (1998), 93–124.

——(1999*a*) 'Greek and Roman in dialogue: the pseudo-Lucianic *Nero*' (*JHS* 119: 142–60).

——(1999*b*) 'The writes of passage: cultural initiation in Heliodorus', in Miles ed. (1999), 16–40.

——(2001) 'Exile and identity in the second sophistic', in Goldhill ed. (2001), 269–305.

WHITTAKER, J. (1987) 'Platonic philosophy in the early centuries of the Roman empire' (*ANRW* 2.36.1: 81–123).

WIDMER, W. (1967) *Kaisertum, Rom und Welt in Herodians META*

ΜΑΡΚΟΝ ΒΑΣΙΛΕΙΑΣ ΙΣΤΟΡΙΑ (Zurich).

WILAMOWITZ (1900) (WILAMOWITZ-MÖLLENDORFF, U. VON) 'Asianismus und Atticismus' (*Hermes*, 35: 1–52).

——(1925) (WILAMOWITZ-MÖLLENDORFF, U. VON) review of Boulanger (1923) (*Litteris*, 2: 125–30).

WILLIAMS, B. (1973) 'The analogy of city and soul in Plato's *Republic*', in E. N. Lee *et al.*, eds., *Exegesis and argument: studies in Greek philosophy presented to Gregory Vlastos* (Assen), 196–206.

WILLIAMS, G. (1994) *Banished voices: readings in Ovid's exile poetry* (Cambridge).

WILLIAMS, R. (1958) *Culture and society* (London).

——(1976) *Keywords* (London).

——(1986) *Culture* (London).

WILSON, N. G. (1970) 'Indications of speaker in Greek dialogue texts' (*CQ* 20: 305).

WINKLER, J. J. (1982) 'The mendacity of Kalasiris and the narrative strategy of Heliodoros' *Aithiopika*' (*YCS* 27: 93–158); repr. in Swain ed. (1999), 286–350.

——(1985) *Auctor & actor: a narratological reading of Apuleius'* The Golden Ass (Berkeley).

——(1990) *The constraints of desire: the anthropology of sex and gender in ancient Greece* (New York).

——and ZEITLIN, F. I., eds. (1990) *Nothing to do with Dionysus? Athenian drama in its social context* (Princeton).

WIRSZUBSKI, C. (1968) *Libertas as a political idea at Rome during the late republic and early principate* (Cambridge)

WISTRAND, E. (1979) 'The Stoic opposition to the principate' (*StudClas* 18: 93–101).

WOOLF, G. (1994) 'Becoming Roman, staying Greek: culture, identity and the civilizing process in the Roman East' (*PCPS* 40: 116–43).

——(1997) 'The Roman urbanisation of the East', in Alcock ed. (1997), 1–14.

WRIGHT, W. C. (1921) *Philostratus and Eunapius: Lives of the Sophists*, Loeb Classical Library (Cambridge, Mass.).

YOUNG, R. (1990) *White mythologies: writing history and the West* (London).

ZANKER, P. (1995) *The mask of Socrates: the image of the intellectual in antiquity*, trans. A. Shapiro (Berkeley).

ZEITLIN, F. I. (1990*a*) 'The poetics of *eros*: nature, art and imitation in Longus' *Daphnis and Chloe*', in D. M. Halperin *et al.*, eds., *Before sexuality: the construction of erotic experience in the ancient Greek world* (Princeton), 417–64.

ZEITLIN, F. I. (1990*b*) 'Thebes: theater of self and society in Athenian drama', in Winkler and Zeitlin eds. (1990), 130–67; repr. and rev. from J. P. Euben, ed., *Greek tragedy and political theory* (Berkeley, 1986), 101–41.

ZIEGLER, K. (1949) 'Ploutarchos' (Stuttgart; repr. 1963); also repr. in *RE* 21.1: 636–962.

Index Locorum

Note: this index refers to passages with pendant discussions; see also the general index for discussions of texts in their entireties.

ACHILLES TATIUS 1.10.2 232 n. 198
2.37.7, 2.38.5 81
4.14.7–8 79
5.1.4–5 254
7.6.2 80

AELIUS ARISTIDES
Hymn to Sarapis 4–8 27 n. 122
To Rome 8 21 n. 91
51 212
63 25

ANDRON *FGH* 246 F 1 8

APOLLONIUS OF TYANA *Epistle* 9 227

ARISTEAS *Letter of Aristeas* 9 8

ARISTOTLE
Poetics 1406b 56 n. 66
1448b 51–2
Rhetoric 1370a 51

ARRIAN
Arrangement against the Alani 10, 22 27 n. 120
On hunting 16.6 27 n. 120

AULUS GELLIUS 20.1.20 167–8

CAECILIUS fr. 50 Ofenloch 64 n. 94

CASSIUS DIO 59.19.7–8 152
71.31.3, 71.34.2–4, 71.35.6, 71.36.4 224

CICERO
Against Verres 2.1.49–61 14 n. 56
Brutus 254 11 n. 45
Letters to Atticus 1.8.2 14 n. 56
7.2.1 26
Tusculan disputations 1.1–4 142
1.1–6 12–14
5.108 148

DEMETRIUS *On style* 224 155

DEMOSTHENES *Oration* 60.4 176–7, 298

DIO CHRYSOSTOM
Oration 1.8 209–10
1.4–8 197
1.36 211
1.48 198
1.49 197
1.50 197–8
1.52 198
1.55 198–9, 200
1.56 199, 200, 325
1.65 210
2.1–2 202–3
2.15 203
2.16 204
2.19–24 204
2.70 203
3.3 211
3.12 165, 195
3.13, 3.18 195
3.50 214
4.4, 4.6, 4.7, 4.11 205
4.29–32 191
4.33 192–3
4.35, 4.36 193
4.37 193–4
4.65 206
4.79–80 208
4.81 205
4.87–8 209

DIO CHRYSOSTOM (*cont.*)
4.130, 4.131 194
4.139 209
13.29 164
13.29–37 215
36.17 214–15
41.6 215
57.2 186
57.4, 57.10 187
57.11 187, 326–7
80.1–2 195–6 n. 59

DIOGENES LAERTIUS 1.1–4 126 n. 131

DIONYSIUS OF HALICARNASSUS
Lysias 8 160–1
On the ancient orators 1 43 n. 13
1.2 67 n. 108
On imitation fr. 1 97
fr. 2 72
fr. 6.1 72–4
fr. 6.5 75
On syntax 4.14 26
Roman antiquities 1.2.3 67 n. 108
14.6.6 117 n. 97

EUPOLIS fr. 102.7 KA 276

EURIPIDES
fr. 1047 N² 146
Phoenician women 391–2 143–4
531–5 174

FAVORINUS
Corinthian oration 25 119
25–7 24
27 120
36 121
On exile 2.1 170
2.2 169
5.2 170, 171
7.1–3 172
10.1–2 172–3
10.3 173–4
10.4 175–6
18.1 170
20.5 174–5
see also Appendix 1

GENESIS 1: 3–9 66

GORGIAS *Encomium of Helen* 11.21 102 n. 42

HELIODORUS *Ethiopian story* 2.21.4–6 84 n. 168
2.33.5 93
2.34.1 84 n. 168
2.35.5 84
3.14.2–4 84 n. 168
4.8.3–5 86
7.14.5–6, 9.24.8 85
10.14.4 84 n. 166
10.14.7, 10.15.1 86
10.16.2 85
10.16.7 85 n. 172
10.27.1–4, 10.29.1 87

HERACLITUS (allegorist) *Homeric questions*
1 52 n. 53

HERACLITUS (philosopher) fr. 119 DK 208

HERODIAN 1.1–4 224–5

HERODOTUS 1.30.2 147
3.80 206
3.80–2 230
4.76.1 147
8.144.2 22 n. 98

HESIOD
Works and days 24 60
202–11 198

HOMER
Iliad 1.5 53
1.260–8, 273–4 187
10.222 117
16.40 189
22.495 292
Σ Iliad 16.574, 24.257 26
Odyssey 1.1–3 147
1.3 239
14.122–7 162
19.284 197 n. 63
22.1 240–1

HORACE
Art of poetry 1–23 74 n. 130
Epistle 2.1.156–60 11–12

IAMBLICHUS, *Life of Pythagoras* 44 90–1

ISOCRATES
Antidosis 293–5 8 n. 28
Panegyric 50 8

JULIAN, *Oration* 1 4d 54 n 60

LIVY 34.4.3 11 n. 45

'LONGINUS' *On the sublime* 1.1 61 n. 83, 62
2.1–2 63
5.1 65 n. 97
9.7–8 52 n. 53
9.9, 12.3–5 66
12.4–5 68
13.2 58, 66
13.4 60
15 9, 17.1 60 n. 80
22.4 65
30.1, 33.2, 36 2 61
36.3 86 n. 175
44 47 n. 32, 66–8

LONGUS *praef.* 1 102
praef. 3 50 n. 47, 101
1.8.1 83
1.20–2 102
1.22.4 81–2
3.14.5, 3.15.1, 3.18.4, 3.19.1 82
4.2.5 83
4.7–8 102
4.17.3 102 n. 45
4.40.3 101–2

LUCIAN
Alexander 2 97 n. 22
Anacharsis 13 124
Apology 1 291
2 293
5, 6 292
Demonax 1 106
The dream 7–8 122–3
11 123
15–16 124
Eunuch 13 114
Fisherman 25–6 264
31 260
34 259–60
38–9 264
42 262
How to write history 8 27 n. 122
Icaromenippus 5 5
Judgement of the vowels 7 7 n. 24
Lexiphanes 20 6–7, 127
The mistaken critic 1 128 n. 137
Nigrinus praef. 271
1 274
4 270
5, 6 274
7 275–6
11 272–3
12 273–4
18 270–1
19, 20 267
23 268–9
24 269–70
25 270
29 268
32 270
35, 37 277
On the hall 2 80, 97
On salaried posts 1 281
7 282
11, 12 284
12, 13 285
14 285, 287
15 286, 287
17 287
18 286
19 287, 288
20 289
21 281
25 290
41 289
Peregrinus 18 134
Sale of lives 1 259
Scythian 9 126
The teacher of rhetoric 2 124 n. 121
Toxaris 5 125
9–11 126
True stories 1.4 252
Twice accused 33 76
You are a Prometheus in words 4–5 77
Zeuxis 1–3 77–8
6–7, 12 78

PS.-LUCIAN *Dialogue on love* 21 114 n. 88
Nero see under Philostratus

LUCRETIUS 1.136–9 10 n. 39, 142

MARCUS AURELIUS 1.4 219
1.14.1 216–17
1.17.1 219–20
11.15 223

MENANDER RHETOR 372.5 Russell and Wilson 54 n. 60

MUSONIUS RUFUS fr. 3 p. 11 Hense 113
fr. 4 p. 17 Hense 112
fr. 9 p. 41 Hense 145
fr. 9 p. 42 Hense 146–7
fr. 9 pp. 43–4 Hense 148
fr. 9 p. 49 Hense 149
fr. 9 p. 51 Hense 150
Epistles p. 143 Hense 150

OVID
Art of love 1.165–6, 1.170 256
Fasti 3.103–4 15 n. 58

PAUSANIAS 2.1.2 121
2.1.5 153 n. 75

PETRONIUS *Satyricon* 87 93–4

PHILOSTRATUS
Dialexis II p. 260.3 Kayser 75 n. 131
Epistle 73 109 n. 70, 226
Heroic tale 1.1–2, 1.7, 4.2, 4.5, 4.6, 4.9 104
4.10 105
In honour of Apollonius of Tyana 1.3 109 n. 70, 229
1.4 228
3.43 24
3.45, 3.57 229–30 n. 191
4.46 150
5.14 229–30 n. 191
5.31–41 230–7
5.40 227
7.34, 7.38 228
8.1–10 227
Lives of the sophists 479 159, 167, 238
481 42
488 42 n. 12, 238–44
489 114–15, 169
492 159, 167, 238
507 42
511 42, 67 n. 108
520, 521, 525–6 189
551 153
552–4 105–8, 300
564 47 n. 32
568–70 25
570 226
596, 601, 612 189
624–5 108
625 21
Nero 1 152
2 153
9, 10 154

PLATO
Apology 17a–b 264
19d 261
20e–21a 162
Crito 53a 151
Phaedo 118a 136
Phaedrus 234d 274
264c 74
Republic 337e–78a 52
394b 271–2
398a 50
491d–2a 63 n. 91
521b 231 n. 195
576d–77e 207
603a, 605a–c, 607b 50
Symposium 172b–c 233
Theaetetus 173e 151

PLUTARCH
Advice on marriage 145d–e 111, 113
145e–6a 111
Consolation to his wife 609c 111 n. 79
How a young man should listen to poetry
14f, 15a 95
15d 51, 96
15e–f 95
15f 51
16e 95
18a–d 51
18d 95
18f, 19a 52
19e–f 53
20c–22a 52 n. 52
23a 64 n. 94
23a–24c, 25b 53
25d 95
26a 52
26b 96
28d, 28e 95
29f 117
31c 96
33b 53
35f 95
Life of Aemilius Paulus 1.1–2 56
1.2–4 55
Life of Alexander 1.2–3 54
Life of Crassus 8.3 118 n. 100

Life of Marcellus 3.6 118 n. 100
Life of Romulus 1.1 21 n. 91
Lycurgus-Numa synkrisis 1.9, 1.10, 2.6 118
On listening to lectures 37e–f 128–9
37f 113
38c 72 n. 122
On moral virtue 441d 51, 95
443b–c 95
443b–d 51
452c–d 51
On the Pythian oracle 403a–9d 27 n. 123
Should an old man take part in politics?
784d 186
791c 203
795b, 796b, 796d, 797f 186
That a philosopher should especially converse with emperors
776a, 777a, 779d–e, 780b, 780c 185
To an uneducated ruler 780c 220
Virtues of women 242f, 243d 110

PS.-PLUTARCH *On the education of children*
1b–c, 2a, 2b 98
2d 72 n. 122, 120 n. 107
4a 116
5d, 7c–8d, 8c 98
8f 98–9
14b 110

POLEMO *Oration* 1.11, 1.36, 2.11 79 n. 144

POLLUX 2.139 100 n. 31

PORCIUS LICINUS fr. 1 *FPL* 9

QUINTILIAN
Education of the orator 9.2.28 167
10.1.93 248

SAPPHO fr. 31 277

*SIG*³ 829a 22

STRABO 1.4.9 117 n. 97
13.4.17 25

THUCYDIDES 1.22 163
1.22 4 169
2.8.4 7 n. 26
2.41.4 7
2.63.2 7 n. 26

VIRGIL *Aeneid* 1.2 174
2.705–44 171
6.847–53 15
8.347–8 10

XENOPHON *Memorabilia* 1.5 161
4.6.12 206

Index of Greek Words

ἀλαζών 186–7
αὐτοκράτωρ 212–13
βασιλεύς 212–13
γόης 228–9
δαιμόνιον 59 n. 75
ἐκ (with names of deities) 232 n. 197
ἐλευθερία, *see* General Index, *eleutheria/ libertas*
ἐπιείκεια 117
ἐξουσία 149
ἔμφασις 52
ἔργον (sexual innuendo) 276
ζήλωσις 119
ἡγεμονικόν, τό 221
θαῦμα 86–7
ἰσθμός 153
κοινωνικόν, τό 221
μακαρισμός, *see* General Index, *makarismos*
μίμησις, *see* General Index, *mimēsis*
νεότης/νεωτερισμός 77 n. 138, 203
νεώτεροι 26
ὁμοιότης 51, 73, 86
παράγειν 259
παρρησία, *see* General Index, *parrhēsia*
πραιότης 117
προλαλιά 77
σχῆμα 64 n. 94, 119, 197, 261–2
σχολαστικός/σχολικός 61
συγγένεια 25–6
σύγκρισις, *see* General Index, *synkrisis*
σύστημα 146
τροπή 64 n. 94
φιλανθρωπία 117
φιλοτιμία, *see* General Index, *philotimia*
χρῶμα 116

General Index

Achaea (Roman province) 21, 33
Achilles Tatius 79–81, 254; *see also* Index Locorum
Adrastus 170
Aegeae 25, 36
Aelian (Claudius Aelianus) 21, 100, 108
ps.-Aeschylus, *Prometheus Bound* 206
Agathion 105–8, 300
Alcibiades 140
Alcidamas 56 n. 66
Alciphron 100
Alcman 140
Alexander 'the clay-Plato' 219
Alexander Cotiaensis 219
Alexander the Great 191–3, 201–6
Alexandria 8–9, 26, 32, 254
Anacharsis 124–5, 126–7, 147
anaskeuē (refutation) 143
Antiochus, P. Antius 25, 36
Antisthenes of Athens 197–8 n. 64, 213
Antoninus Pius, emperor 168, 219
Apollonius of Chalcedon 219
Apollonius of Tyana 24, 225–38
Archilochus 140, 249
Aristarchus of Samothrace 26
Aristides, Aelius 25, 212; *see also* Index Locorum
ps.-Aristides, *To the emperor* 183 n. 8
Aristophanes 249
  works:
  Acharnians 279
  Clouds 279
  Lysistrata 298
Aristotle 46–7, 51–2, 138
  on the education of women 109 n. 71
  on kingship 182 n. 3
  on the mean 65
  on *mimēsis* 46, 51–2
  see also Index Locorum
Arnim, H. von 187
Arrian (Flavius Arrianus) 6 n. 21, 21, 27, 97 n. 22, 141 n. 32
  On hunting with dogs 47 n. 32
  see also Index Locorum
Athens 254, 266, 269, 297–8
athletics 6
Atticism 1, 6–7, 104, 106–8, 127–8, 199
Augustus, C. Octavius, emperor 9–10, 23
autochthony 106, 108, 175–7, 297–8

Barthes, R. 30, 74 n. 127, 274
Beacham, R. 255
belatedness 44–5
Belsey, C. 30
Bennington, G. 118
Billault, A. 83 n. 161
Bloom, H. 41, 59, 89, 164, 179, 236–7
Bogel, J. 248
Bompaire, J. 251
Bourdieu, P. 19, 94
Bowersock, G. 1, 2, 43
Brancacci, A. 237
Branham, B. 124–5
Brink, C. 11
Brutus, M. Iunius 217
Butler, J. 31

Caecilius of Caleacte 61 n. 83
Caesar, C. Julius 121
Callimachus 8, 25, 249
Cassius Dio Cocceianus 224
Cato 'the younger' (M. Porcius Cato Uticensis) 217
ps.-Cebes, *Picture* 280–1
Certeau, M. de 34
Chariton 79 n. 143, 81 n. 151; *see also* Index Locorum
Christ, Jesus 229 n. 187
Christianity 5, 134, 256
Chrysippus 50 n. 44
Cibyra 24–5
Cicero, M. Tullius 12–14, 68, 136, 142, 148, 152; *see also* Index Locorum
Cinna Catulus 219

Clark, J. R. 252, 291
Claudius (Tiberius Claudius Nero Germanicus), emperor 232 n. 200
Claudius Maximus 219
Cleanthes 53
colour of skin 84, 116
comedy:
  middle 100 n. 35
  new 93
  old 75–6
  see also Aristophanes
Commodus, L. Aelius Aurelius, emperor 224–5
consolations 139–40
Corinth 121
cosmopolitanism 145–6, 175–6
Croesus 147
'culture' 16, 17–20, 35–7
cynicism 103 n. 47, 123 n. 119, 136, 192
  on exile 138–9
  on freedom of speech 205

Damis 24, 229
Debord, G. 254
Delphi, oracle of 27, 58–9, 154–5, 161–2
Demosthenes 68, 70, 176–7, 182, 239–40
Derrida, J. 47 n. 31, 90, 174
dialogue (literary form) 76, 124–5, 271–2
Dio Cassius, *see* Cassius Dio
Dio Chrysostom (Cocceianus Dio) 33, 119, 135
  'conversion' to philosophy 158–61
  exile 138–9, 156–67
  on freedom of speech 205
  life 156–7
  on kingship 181–216, 325–7
  Marcus Aurelius and 217–18
  Musonius Rufus and Favorinus, acquaintance with? 137 n. 16
  Philostratus and 225–44
  Plutarch, acquaintance with? 137 n. 12
  and verbosity 160
  works:
  Against (?) Musonius 137 n. 16
  Oration 1 (*On kingship*) 197–200, 210–11
  Oration 2 (*On kingship*) 201–4
  Oration 3 (*On kingship*) 194–7
  Oration 4 (*On kingship*) 191–4, 204–9
  Oration 5 (*Libyan oration*) 326
  Oration 7 (*Euboean oration*) 103–4
  Orations 6, 8–10 (Diogenes orations) 325
  Oration 13 (*On exile*) 160–4
  Oration 36 (*Borysthenite oration*) 214–15
  Oration 57 (*Nestor*) 186–7, 326–7
  see also Index Locorum
Dio of Syracuse 217
Diogenes of Sinope 140, 145, 148–9, 191–3, 204–6, 258, 264, 325
Dionysius of Halicarnassus 72–5, 86, 92–3, 97; *see also* Index Locorum
Domitian (T. Flavius Domitianus), emperor 15, 34, 134, 141, 156–8, 165–7, 207–8, 217, 227–9, 239–40
Doric (dialect) 198–9
Dubel, S. 253
DuQuesnay, I. 46

Edwards, C. 221
Eleusis, mysteries of 281–2
eleutheria / libertas 142–3, 148–9, 166–7, 217–18, 258
Elsner, J. 23, 88–9
emperor cult 181, 214
Epictetus 6 n. 21, 135, 137 n. 13, 141 n. 32, 218
Epicureans 269
Erechtheus / Erichthonius 297
ēthopoeia (oratory *in persona*) 42 n. 12, 188
Eumelus of Corinth 121 n. 112
eunuchs 114–15, 193–4
Euphrates, philosopher 227, 230–7
Euripides 143–4, 146, 172, 174, 242; *see also* Index Locorum
exile 134–80
'expressive-realism' 30, 68, 215, 222, 250–2

Favorinus 24, 108 n. 66
  acquaintance with Dio Chrysostom? 137 n. 16
  acquaintance with Plutarch? 137 n. 12
  on cultural identity 119–21
  eclecticism 167
  on exile 168–78
  sexual dimorphism 114–15

style and diction 167–8
see also Index Locorum
flattery 194–7
Flinterman, J.-J. 236
focalization 234–5
food, and social harmony 285–7
Forte, B. 2
Foucault, M. 18–19, 140, 255
freedom, see *eleutheria/libertas*
freedom of speech, see *parrhēsia*
Freud, S. 88
Fronto, M. Cornelius 219

Gallop, J. 94
Geertz, C. 19, 30, 281
Gellius, Aulus 167–8
genealogy, as trope 24–5, 35–6, 59–61, 85–6, 173–5
Gleason, M. 23, 114, 119
Goffman, E. 140
Goldhill, S. 82, 267
Goody, J. 30 n. 132
Gordian I (M. Antonius Gordianus), emperor 226
Gorgias of Leontini 95, 242
gospels 238
Groningen, B. van 41–2, 44, 48, 89
Gyara 141

Hadrian (P. Aelius Hadrianus), emperor 16, 23, 24, 49 n. 40, 168
Hall, E. 297
Hall, S. 36, 77, 295
Halperin, D. 267, 275
Heath, M. 66–7
Heliodorus of Emesa 83–7, 93
dating of 83 n. 164
see also Index Locorum
Helios, cult of 84–5, 212 n. 113, 214
Hellenistic period 8–9, 22
Helm, R. 265
Helvidius Priscus 217
Henderson, J. 93
Heraclitus of Ephesus 208
Hermocrates of Phocaea 189
Herodes Atticus 47 n. 32, 105–6, 153, 169 n. 141, 244
Herodian of Syria 224–5
Herodotus 230; *see also* Index Locorum
Hesiod 172, 198; *see also* Index Locorum
Hesk, J. 263 n. 74
Hinds, S. 9 n. 35, 28
Hipponax 249
Höistad, R. 213
Homer 33, 58, 116–17, 182, 201, 212
allegories of 53–4
on Corinth 121 n. 112
'father Homer' 59 n. 77
on the gods 52–3
Plato's emulation of 60–1
scholiasts on 26
see also Index Locorum
Horace (Q. Horatius Flaccus) 11–12, 101; *see also* Index Locorum
Hunter, R. 81 n. 154
hyperbaton, 'Longinus' on 62, 64

Iamblichus 90–1
identity 31, 35–7, 94, 295
and boundaries 24, 118
imitation, see *mimēsis*
inscriptions 22, 37
Isocrates 92, 118, 128
on Hellenism 8, 299
on kingship 182 n.3
Plutarch and 184
see also Index Locorum

Jones, C. P. 251, 280, 326
Joyce, J. 249
Judaism 5, 66
Julia Domna, empress 109 n. 70, 226
Julian (Flavius Claudius Julianus), emperor 183
Juvenal (Decius Iunius Iuuenalis) 107, 249, 280

Kennedy, D. F. 3
kenosis 236–7
kingship, theories of 181–2
terms for 212–13

Lewis, J. 250 n. 11
libertas, see *eleutheria/libertas*
'literature' 4–5
Livius Andronicus 14
'Longinus' 47 n. 30, 57–71, 114 n. 85; *see also* Index Locorum
Longus 44, 81–3, 100–3
Lucian 5, 24, 33, 249–94
as 'barbarian' 76, 115
on education and cultural identity 122–8
on literary innovation 75–8

Lucian (*cont.*)
works:
Alexander or the false prophet 250
Anacharsis 124
Apology 291–3
Defence of portraits 250
Demonax 257
Fisherman 259–65
Hermotimus 258
Nigrinus 265–79
Peregrinus 135, 257–8
Portraits 73 n. 126, 250
On salaried posts 279–91
Sale of lives 258–60
Symposium 258, 271
On the Syrian goddess 299
Toxaris 125
True stories 252
Zeus refuted 258
ps.-Lucian *Nero*; *see under* Philostratus
see also Index Locorum
Lucretius (T. Lucretius Carus) 142, 152; *see also* Index Locorum
Lycurgus 118

McNamara, J. 110
makarismos (blessing) 210–11
Marathon, battle of 297
Marcellus, M. Claudius 14
Marcus Aurelius, emperor 16, 21, 42, 146
intended readership 223
Meditations 216–25
reception of 224–5, 245
title 216 n. 129
see also Index Locorum
martyrs 134, 136
Maximus of Aegeae 229 n. 190
memory 276
Menander 100 n. 35
Miles, R. 36
mimēsis 26–9, 46–89, 92–3, 261–3
Moeragenes 229
Moles, J. 159, 184, 199 n. 69, 202, 234
Montrose, L. 31
Morgan, J. R. 81 n. 152, 84 n. 169
multiculturalism 299
Mummius (L. Mummius Achaicus) 14
music 6
Musonius Rufus, C. 135, 159, 164, 170, 171
life 141–2
taught Dio Chrysostom? 137 n. 16
works:
Should daughters be educated alongside sons? 112–13
That exile is not an evil 141–52
Is marriage an impediment to the philosopher?
That women should also philosophize 112–13
see also Index Locorum

narratee 188
'nationality' 21–2, 24
nature and culture 51, 59, 73, 98–9, 112
neoterics 26
Nero Claudius Caesar, emperor 34, 134, 141, 149, 152–5, 218
Nerva, M. Cocceius, emperor 15, 156–7, 203–4 n. 88
Nestor 186–7
Nicetes of Smyrna 42
novels, Greek 27 n. 122, 78–87
and martyrology 134
paradoxes in 78–81
and Philostratus, *In honour of Apollonius* 229 n. 188
Scheintod in 80
see also Achilles Tatius; Chariton; Heliodorus; Longus; Xenophon of Ephesus; *also* Petronius
Numa Pompilius 118

Odysseus 147, 162, 197, 239, 240–2
as sophist 197–8 n. 64
Ovid (P. Ovidius Naso) 82, 136, 140, 256; *see also* Index Locorum

paideia 5–9, 13, 17, 37, 161, 182, 235, 243
Dio Chrysostom and 200–1
and gender 109–16
and Hellenism 116–29
Marcus Aurelius and 218–20
and social status 96–108
Panhellenion, the 23–5, 35–6, 173
Panhellenism 22, 297
Parmenides 124
parrhēsia ('freedom of speech') 67, 142–4, 148–9, 205, 293
Peregrinus 135, 138, 228 n. 184
Peretti, A. 279
performativity 22, 30–1, 127, 215
Pericles 7–8, 110, 175, 297

Perkins, J. 135
Persia 22, 134
persona, in satire 252–3
Pertinax, P. Helvius, emperor 225
Petronius Arbiter 93–4, 286
phallus 113–14, 194, 290
Philetas of Cos 82
Philip of Macedon 201–4
Philodemus of Gadara 182 n. 3, 212 n. 111
philosophy 5–6, 10, 158–9, 161, 191, 228–9, 230–7, 258–63
  and phallocentrism 113–14, 194
Philostratus, L. Flavius 21, 33, 225–44
  problems of attribution 152, 225–6
  works:
  Heroic tale 103–5
  In honour of Apollonius of Tyana 226–38
  Lives of the sophists 188–90, 238–44
  Nero 152–5
  see also Index Locorum
philotimia ('competition for status') 6, 233
Photius, patriarch of Constantinople 326
Phrynichus Arabius 24, 168
Pindar 24
Plato 5, 46–8, 69, 70, 201, 202–3, 264, 277
  dialogue form 124–5, 271–2
  on the education of women 109
  emulation of Homer 61–2
  on exile 151
  on inspiration 58–9
  on kingship 182 n. 3, 212 n. 113
  on *mimēsis* 50
  myths 198
  on narrative 271–2
  on recollection (*anamnēsis*) 101
  on rhetoric 63 n. 90
  works:
  Apology 264, 293
  Clitophon 163–4
  Epistles 184
  Laws 184
  Phaedo 136, 239–40
  Phaedrus 96, 199, 203, 274
  Symposium 94, 233, 258, 267, 274, 279, 286
  see also Index Locorum
Pliny (G. Plinius Caecilius Secundus), *Panegyric* 166
Plutarch (L. Mestrius Plutarchus) 22, 27, 33
  acquaintance with Dio Chrysostom and Favorinus 137 n. 12
  on character 54 n. 60
  on education 95–7
  ethics and Platonism of 49–51
  on kingship 184–6
  life 48–9
  works:
  Advice on marriage 110–12
  How a young man should listen to poetry 49–54, 95–6, 116–17
  On listening to lectures 113
  On moral virtue 96
  Parallel lives 54–6, 116–17
  On the sign of Socrates 59 n. 75
  Should an old man take part in politics? 114, 186, 203
  That a philosopher should especially converse with emperors 185–6
  That women too should be educated 109
  To an uneducated ruler 185–6
  Virtues of women 110
  see also Index Locorum; ps.-Plutarch
ps.-Plutarch, *On the education of children* 98–100, 109–10, 116; *see also* Index Locorum
polarity, and socio-cultural definition 91
Polemo, M. Antonius 79, 189, 244
Porcius Licinus 9
pornography 74 n. 127
postmodernism 31, 45, 254, 295–6
'power' 17–20, 37, 289
Price, S. 18
Prodicus of Ceos, *Choice of Heracles* 122, 198, 210
prolalia (introductory speech) 77, 187, 326
prose 27
prosimetry 77
Protesilaus/Protesileus 103–5
Proteus Peregrinus, *see* Peregrinus
Proteus, as sophistic emblem 228

Quintilian (M. Fabius Quintilianus) 167, 248–9

'race' 35; *see also* colour of skin
rhetoric 72, 97, 188, 196
  chairs of rhetoric in Athens 97 n. 26

rhetoric (*cont.*)
  current theories of 190–1
  see also sophistry
rites of passage 147–8
Robins, K. 26
Rohde, E. 43
Rome:
  Dio Chrysostom on 213–16
  Hellenization of 9–15
  Lucian on 249–52
  puns on *Rhōmē* 21, 149
  Roman citizenship 18, 22, 68, 156 n. 83
  Romans as 'we' in Greek texts 68–9, 250 n. 11
  as 'spectacular society' 254–7
Romm, J. 122
Rubellius Plautus 141
Russell, D. 48
rusticity, *see* urban and rural
Rusticus, Junius 210

Sappho 101, 140, 277
Sardis 24
satire, definition of 248–9
Schmitz, T. 19
Scopelian of Clazomenae 189
'Second Sophistic' 1, 42–5
Segal, C. P. 67–8
Seneca, L. Annaeus 136
  To his mother Helvia 152, 171, 174
  Letters 221
Senecio, Q. Sosius 68–9 n. 115
Severus, Claudius 219
sex, and the 'natural' 73
  between teacher and student 94
  and pedagogical power 111, 113–14
  sexual imagery in Lucian 275–6, 282–3
Sextus of Chaeronea 219
Sidebottom, H. 326
Smith, M. E. 41
Socrates 59 n. 75, 107, 136, 145–6, 150–1, 162–4, 201, 240, 252
Solon 124–5, 147
sophistry 5–6, 33, 43, 79, 158–9, 188–90, 228–9; *see also* rhetoric
Sostratus 106
speech and writing 154–5
Stoicism 50 n. 44, 63
  on the education of women 109 n. 71
  on exile 136
  on kingship 182 n. 3
  'Longinus' and 65 n. 100
  Plutarch and 50 n. 45
  on politics 146
Strabo 24
structuralism 296
Sturrock, J. 222
sublimity, *see* 'Longinus'
Suetonius (C. Suetonius Tranquillus) and kingship theory 184
  sources of 223
Sulla (L. Cornelius Sulla Felix) 14
Swain, S. 3, 19, 22, 102–3 n. 46, 117–18, 250, 251, 293
Synesius of Cyrene 326
syngeneia 35–6; *see also* genealogy
synkrisis ('comparison') 266
Synnada 24

Tacitus, Cornelius 67
  on free speech and oppression 165–6
  and kingship theory 184
Teles of (?) Megara 142
Thebes 298
Themistius 183
Theocritus 101, 254
Theophanes of Mytilene 96 n. 22
'third sophistic' 45
Thrasea Paetus, P. Clodius 217
Thucydides 6, 7, 110, 140; *see also* Index Locorum
Tiberius (Tiberius Julius Caesar Augustus), emperor 218
Too, Y. L. 61
traditions 26, 37
Trajan (M. Ulpius Traianus), emperor 15–16, 143, 156–8, 165–7, 186–7, 203, 207–8, 217–18, 227, 241–3, 325–7
  imitation of Alexander the Great 201, 325
triumphs, Roman 242
Turkey, post-Kemalist 26
Turner, V. 30, 32, 296
tyranny 206–8

urban and rural 100–8

Vernant, J.-P. 276
Verus, Lucius, emperor 251
Vespasian (Titus Flavius Vespasianus), emperor 34, 141, 156
Virgil (P. Vergilius Maro) 10, 15, 46, 171, 174; *see also* Index Locorum